THE VICTORIA HISTORY
OF THE
COUNTIES OF ENGLAND

A HISTORY OF
WILTSHIRE

VOLUME XII

THE VICTORIA HISTORY
OF THE
COUNTIES OF ENGLAND

EDITED BY C. R. ELRINGTON

THE UNIVERSITY OF LONDON
INSTITUTE OF
HISTORICAL RESEARCH

Oxford University Press, Walton Street, Oxford OX2 6DP
London Glasgow New York Toronto
Delhi Bombay Calcutta Madras Karachi
Kuala Lumpur Singapore Hong Kong Tokyo
Nairobi Dar es Salaam Cape Town
Melbourne Auckland

and associated companies in
Beirut Berlin Ibadan Mexico City Nicosia

Oxford is a trade mark of Oxford University Press

Published in the United States by
Oxford University Press, New York

© University of London 1983

ISBN 0 19 722759 7

Printed in Great Britain
at the University Press, Oxford

INSCRIBED TO THE
MEMORY OF HER LATE MAJESTY
QUEEN VICTORIA
WHO GRACIOUSLY GAVE THE TITLE TO
AND ACCEPTED THE DEDICATION
OF THIS HISTORY

MILDENHALL

The church of St. John the Baptist

A HISTORY OF

WILTSHIRE

EDITED BY D. A. CROWLEY

VOLUME XII

RAMSBURY HUNDRED

SELKLEY HUNDRED

THE BOROUGH OF MARLBOROUGH

PUBLISHED FOR

THE INSTITUTE OF HISTORICAL RESEARCH

BY

OXFORD UNIVERSITY PRESS

1983

Distributed by Oxford University Press until 1 January 1986
thereafter by Dawsons of Pall Mall

CONTENTS OF VOLUME TWELVE

LIST OF ILLUSTRATIONS

Thanks are rendered to the following for permission to reproduce material: Mr. and Mrs. John Atwater, the Bodleian Library, Oxford, the Trustees of the British Museum, the Cambridge University Committee for Aerial Photography, *Country Life*, the Courtauld Institute of Art (for photographs of the Buckler paintings), the Master of Marlborough College, Marlborough Town Council, the National Monuments Record of the Royal Commission on Historical Monuments (England), the Public Record Office, Mr. D. S. Wills, Wiltshire Archaeological and Natural History Society, Wiltshire Library and Museum Service, and Wiltshire Record Office. Photographs dated 1979 and 1982 are by A. P. Baggs.

LIST OF ILLUSTRATIONS

LIST OF MAPS AND PLANS

All the maps were drawn by K. J. Wass, of the Department of Geography, University College, London, from drafts prepared by D. A. Crowley, Jane Freeman, and Janet H. Stevenson. The plan of Littlecote House was drawn by A. P. Baggs. The parish, tithing, and township boundaries on the hundred and parish maps are, with the exception of the tithing boundaries on the map of Ramsbury hundred, taken from inclosure and tithe maps of the later 18th century and earlier 19th, and from Ordnance Survey maps of the later 19th.

EDITORIAL NOTE

L IKE its predecessors, the present volume, which is the thirteenth to be published of the *Victoria History of Wiltshire*, has been prepared under the superintendence of the Wiltshire Victoria County History Committee. The Editorial Note to Volume VII, the first to be published, described the origin and early constitution of the Committee; new arrangements were introduced in 1975, as mentioned in the Editorial Note to Volume XI, the Committee providing the funds with which the Institute of Historical Research of the University of London meets the cost of employing the editorial staff and of other necessary expenses. The University has pleasure once again in thanking the Local Authorities which contribute to the funds and send representatives to the Committee, thus enabling the continued publication of the Wiltshire *History*.

Since the publication of Volume XI two men whose efforts and abilities were invaluable to the Wiltshire *History* have died. Group Captain F. A. Willan, C.B.E., D.F.C., D.L., died in November 1981 shortly after being succeeded as Chairman of the Wiltshire Victoria County History Committee by Mr. N. J. M. Anderson, M.C., D.L., who had earlier succeeded him as Chairman of the County Council. Group Captain Willan's unflagging support for the Wiltshire *History* had made it possible for the enterprise to continue without diminution or deceleration in a period of financial difficulty. Professor R. B. Pugh, D.Lit., died in December 1982. He had been General Editor of the Victoria County History from 1949 to 1977 and had particularly strong associations with the Wiltshire *History*, being closely involved with its initiation in 1946, serving as its honorary editor from 1949 to 1955 (jointly with G. M. Young until 1953), and writing substantial parts of six of the volumes.

Thanks are offered to the many people who have helped in the compilation of the volume by granting access to documents and buildings in their care or ownership, by providing information, or by giving advice. Most of them are named in the footnotes to the articles with which they helped and a few in the preamble to the List of Illustrations. Special mention must be made of the assistance given in many ways by the County Archivist (Mr. K. H. Rogers) and his staff. It is a pleasure also to thank the Town Clerk of Marlborough (Mr. N. A. Cluer) and the Bursar of Marlborough College (Captain J. Asbury, C.B.E., R.N.).

The *General Introduction* to the *Victoria History*, published in 1970, gives an outline of the structure and aims of the series, with an account of its origins and progress.

WILTSHIRE
VICTORIA COUNTY HISTORY COMMITTEE

As at 1 January 1983

Councillor N. J. M. Anderson, m.c., d.l., *Chairman* } Councillor J. O. T. Underwood	*Representing the Wiltshire County Council*
Councillor A. J. Masters } Councillor L. M. Smith	*Representing the Thamesdown Borough Council*
Councillor Mrs. M. J. Hunt-Grubbe	*Representing the Kennet District Council*
Councillor the Hon. Mrs. J. I. Morrison	*Representing the Salisbury District Council*
Councillor M. B. Moore	*Representing the North Wiltshire District Council*
Councillor A. J. C. Pearce	*Representing the West Wiltshire District Council*
Mr. C. R. Elrington	*Representing the Central Committee of the Victoria County History*
Mr. B. Sykes	*Representing the Wiltshire Archaeological and Natural History Society*

Co-opted Members

Dr. R. F. Hunnisett
Mr. M. J. Lansdown
Dr. G. D. Ramsay

Miss Susan Reynolds
Dr. C. F. Slade

Mr. D. M. Kent, *Hon. Secretary*
Mr. E. J. P. Thornton, *Hon. Treasurer*

LIST OF CLASSES OF DOCUMENTS
IN THE PUBLIC RECORD OFFICE
USED IN THIS VOLUME
WITH THEIR CLASS NUMBERS

Exchequer and Audit Department
AO 3   Accounts, various

Chancery
            Proceedings
C   1   Early
C   2   Series I
C   3   Series II
C   5   Six Clerks Series, Bridges
C   6   Collins
C 12   1758–1800
C 33   Decrees and Orders, Entry Books
C 52   Cartae Antiquae Rolls
C 53   Charter Rolls
C 54   Close Rolls
C 60   Fine Rolls
C 66   Patent Rolls
C 78   Decree Rolls
            Inquisitions post mortem
C 136   Series I, Ric. II
C 137   Hen. IV
C 139   Hen. VI
C 140   Edw. IV and V
C 141   Ric. III
C 142   Series II
            Ancient Deeds
C 146   Series C
C 148   Series CS
C 219   Writs and Returns of Members to Parliament

Court of Common Pleas
            Feet of Fines
CP 25 (1)   Series I
CP 25 (2)   Series II
CP 40   Plea Rolls
CP 43   Recovery Rolls

Duchy of Lancaster
DL 1   Equity Proceedings, Pleadings Depositions and Examinations
DL 3   Series I
DL 4   Series II
DL 5   Decrees and Orders, Entry Books
DL 25   Deeds, Series L
DL 28   Accounts (Various)
DL 29   Ministers' Accounts
DL 30   Court Rolls
DL 31   Maps
DL 36   Cartae Miscellaneae
DL 42   Miscellaneous Books
DL 43   Rentals and Surveys
DL 44   Special Commissions and Returns

Exchequer, Treasury of the Receipt
E 36   Books
            Ancient Deeds
E 40   Series A
E 42   Series AS

Exchequer, King's Remembrancer
E 106   Extents of Alien Priories etc.
E 112   Bills, Answers, etc.
E 126   Decrees and Orders, Entry Books, Series IV
E 134   Depositions taken by Commission
E 135   Ecclesiastical Documents
E 142   Ancient Extents
E 150   Inquisitions post mortem, Series II
E 154   Inventories of Goods and Chattels
E 159   Memoranda Rolls
E 178   Special Commissions of Inquiry
E 179   Subsidy Rolls etc.
E 210   Ancient Deeds, Series DD

Exchequer, Augmentation Office
E 301   Certificates of Colleges and Chantries
E 310   Particulars for Leases
E 315   Miscellaneous Books
E 317   Parliamentary Surveys
E 318   Particulars for Grants of Crown Lands
            Ancient Deeds
E 326   Series B
E 328   Series BB

Exchequer, Lord Treasurer's Remembrancer's and Pipe Offices
E 364   Rolls of Foreign Accounts (Pipe Office)
E 372   Pipe Rolls

Ministry of Education
ED 7   Public Elementary Schools, Preliminary Statements
ED 21   Public Elementary School Files
ED 49   Endowment Files

Home Office
HO 40   Correspondence etc., Disturbances
HO 52   Counties: Correspondence
            Census Papers
HO 107   Population Returns
HO 129   Ecclesiastical Returns

LIST OF CLASSES OF DOCUMENTS

Inland Revenue
    IR 29   Tithe Apportionments
    IR 30   Tithe Maps

Justices Itinerant, Assize and Gaol Delivery Justices, etc.
    JUST 1   Eyre Rolls, Assize Rolls, etc.

Court of King's Bench (Crown Side)
    KB 27   Coram Rege Rolls

Maps and Plans
    MPC, MR   Maps, plans, or pictures taken from various classes

Probate
    PROB 11   Registered Copies of Wills proved in the Prerogative Court of Canterbury

Court of Requests
    REQ 2   Proceedings

General Register Office
    RG 4   Non-parochial Registers
    RG 31   Registers of Places of Worship

Special Collections
    SC 2   Court Rolls
    SC 6   Ministers' and Receivers' Accounts
    SC 8   Ancient Petitions
    SC 12   Rentals and Surveys, Portfolios

State Paper Office
    SP 46   State Papers Domestic, Supplementary

Court of Star Chamber
                Proceedings
    STAC 2   Hen. VIII
    STAC 8   Jas. I

Court of Wards and Liveries
    WARD 2   Deeds and Evidences

NOTE ON ABBREVIATIONS

Among the abbreviations and short titles used are the following, in addition to those listed in the Victoria History's *Handbook for Editors and Authors*.

Acct. of Wilts. Schs.	*An Account of Schools for the Children of the Labouring Classes in the County of Wiltshire*, H.C. 27 (1859 Sess. 1), xxi (2)
Aubrey, *Nat. Hist. Wilts.* ed. Britton	John Aubrey, *Natural History of Wiltshire*, ed. John Britton (London, 1847)
Aubrey, *Topog. Coll.* ed. Jackson	*The Topographical Collections of John Aubrey*, ed. J. E. Jackson (Devizes, 1862)
Ch. Com.	Church Commissioners
Char. Com.	Charity Commission
Colvin, *Brit. Architects*	H. M. Colvin, *Biographical Dictionary of British Architects, 1600–1840* (London, 1978)
D. & C. Sar.	Dean and Chapter of Salisbury
D. & C. Windsor	Dean and Canons of St. George's chapel, Windsor
D. & C. Winton.	Dean and Chapter of Winchester
Dors. R.O.	Dorset Record Office
Educ. Enquiry Abstract	*Abstract of Returns relative to the State of Education in England*, H.C. 62 (1835), xliii
Educ. of Poor Digest	*Digest of Returns to the Select Committee on the Education of the Poor*, H.C. 224 (1819), ix (2)
Endowed Char. Wilts.	*Endowed Charities of Wiltshire*, H.C. 273 (1908), lxxx (northern division); H.C. 273–i (1908), lxxxi (southern division)
Finberg, *Early Wessex Chart.*	H. P. R. Finberg, *Early Charters of Wessex* (Leicester, 1964)
Glos. R.O.	Gloucestershire Record Office
Herts. R.O.	Hertfordshire Record Office
Hist. of Parl. Trust	History of Parliament Trust
Hoare, *Mod. Wilts.*	Sir Richard Colt Hoare and others, *History of Modern Wiltshire* (London, 1822–43)
N.M.R.	National Monuments Record
N.R.A.	National Register of Archives
Nightingale, *Wilts. Plate*	J. E. Nightingale, *Church Plate of Wiltshire* (Salisbury, 1891)
P.N. Wilts. (E.P.N.S.)	J. E. B. Gover, Allen Mawer, and F. M. Stenton, *Place-Names of Wiltshire* (English Place-Name Society, xvi)
P.R.O.	Public Record Office
Pevsner, *Wilts.* (2nd edn.)	Nikolaus Pevsner, *Buildings of England: Wiltshire*, revised by Bridget Cherry (London, 1975)
Phillipps, *Wilts. Inst.*	*Institutiones Clericorum in Comitatu Wiltoniae*, ed. Sir Thomas Phillipps (priv. print. 1825)
Poor Law Abstract, 1804	*Abstract of Returns relative to the Expense and Maintenance of the Poor* (printed by order of the House of Commons, 1804)
Poor Law Abstract, 1818	*Abstract of Returns to the House of Commons relative to Assessments for the Relief of the Poor*, H.C. 82 (1818), xix
Poor Law Com. 1st Rep.	*First Annual Report of the Poor Law Commissioners for England and Wales*, H.C. 500 (1835), xxv
Poor Law Com. 2nd Rep.	*Second Annual Report of the Poor Law Commissioners for England and Wales*, H.C. 595 (1836), xxix (1)
Poor Rate Returns, 1816–21	*Poor Rate Returns, 1816–21*, H.C. 556 App. (1822), v
Princ. Regy. Fam. Div.	Principal Registry of the Family Division, Somerset House
Rep. Com. Eccl. Revenues	*Report of the Commissioners appointed to Inquire into the Ecclesiastical Revenues of England and Wales* [67], H.C. (1835), xxii
2nd Rep. Nat. Soc.	*Second Annual Report of the National Society for Promoting the Education of the Poor in the Principles of the Established Church* (London, 1814)

NOTE ON ABBREVIATIONS

Return of Non-Provided Schs.	*Return of Schools Recognised as Voluntary Public Elementary Schools,* H.C. 178–xxxi (1906), lxxxviii
Returns relating to Elem. Educ.	*Returns relating to Elementary Education,* H.C. 201 (1871), lv
S.R.O.	Somerset Record Office
Swindon corp. rec.	Swindon corporation records held by the borough of Thamesdown, Civic Offices, Swindon
W.A.M.	*Wiltshire Archaeological and Natural History Magazine*
W.A.S.	Wiltshire Archaeological and Natural History Society
W.A.S. Libr.	Library of W.A.S. in the Museum, Long Street, Devizes
W.N. & Q.	*Wiltshire Notes and Queries* (8 vols. 1893–1916)
W.R.O.	Wiltshire Record Office
W.R.S.	Wiltshire Record Society (*formerly* Records Branch of W.A.S.)
W.S.R.O.	West Sussex Record Office
Walters, *Wilts. Bells*	H. B. Walters, *Church Bells of Wiltshire* (Devizes, 1927–9)
Wilts. Cuttings	Volumes of newspaper and other cuttings in W.A.S. Libr.
Wilts. Inq. p.m. 1242–1326 (Index Libr.)	*Abstracts of Wiltshire Inquisitiones post mortem in the reigns of Henry III, Edward I, and Edward II, 1242–1326,* ed. E. A. Fry (Index Library, xxxvii)
Wilts. Inq. p.m. 1327–77 (Index Libr.)	*Abstracts of Wiltshire Inquisitiones post mortem in the reign of Edward III, 1327–77,* ed. Ethel Stokes (Index Library, xlviii)
Wilts. Inq. p.m. 1625–49 (Index Libr.)	*Abstracts of Wiltshire Inquisitiones post mortem in the reign of Charles I, 1625–49,* ed. G. S. and E. A. Fry (Index Library, xxiii)
Wilts. Tracts	Collections of tracts in W.A.S. Libr.

RAMSBURY HUNDRED

IN THE late 11th century Ramsbury hundred contained only a 90-hide estate of the bishop of Salisbury.[1] The pre-Conquest history of the estate and hundred is not documented: it is likely that the estate included Bishopstone,[2] and that the hundred was created because the bishops of Ramsbury, predecessors of the bishops of Salisbury, had in respect of the estate immunities, which may have been as old as the estate itself.[3] The bishop of Salisbury's liberties in his manors were defined by grant in the 13th century,[4] but liberties of some kind almost certainly existed earlier in the private hundred of Ramsbury.

Ramsbury and Bishopstone were the only two pre-Reformation parishes in the hundred. East and north-east of Marlborough they lie in the Kennet and Cole valleys and across the chalk downs of the watershed: they adjoin Berkshire and, since 1974, Oxfordshire. The chapelry and tithing of Baydon in Ramsbury parish established itself in the late 18th century as a third parish and separated the other two.[5] The very large parish of Ramsbury contained eight tithings in the 16th century and six, including Baydon, in the 18th.[6]

In the later Middle Ages the bishop of Salisbury exercised liberties in a biannual court called a law hundred which the men of Bishopstone may have attended.[7] The right to hold a view of frankpledge at Ramsbury passed to a layman in 1545 and afterwards with Ramsbury manor.[8] The bishop kept his right to hold a view of frankpledge for Bishopstone.[9] The lords of Ramsbury manor still claimed to hold a hundred court and their view of frankpledge, attended by several tithingmen, was like that of a hundred,[10] but in 1545 Ramsbury hundred ceased to exist as a liberty. It survived, however, as a division of the county for fiscal and other administrative purposes.

---

[1] *V.C.H. Wilts.* ii, pp. 121, 183.
[2] Ibid. pp. 84, 183 where it is wrongly stated that Little Hinton was in the hund.
[3] Ibid. v. 45.
[4] *Cal. Chart. R.* 1226–57, 24–5.
[5] Below, Baydon, introduction.
[6] Below, Ramsbury, local govt.
[7] Ibid.
[8] *L. & P. Hen. VIII*, xx (2), p. 411; below, Ramsbury, manors.
[9] Below, Bishopstone, local govt.
[10] Below, Ramsbury, local govt.

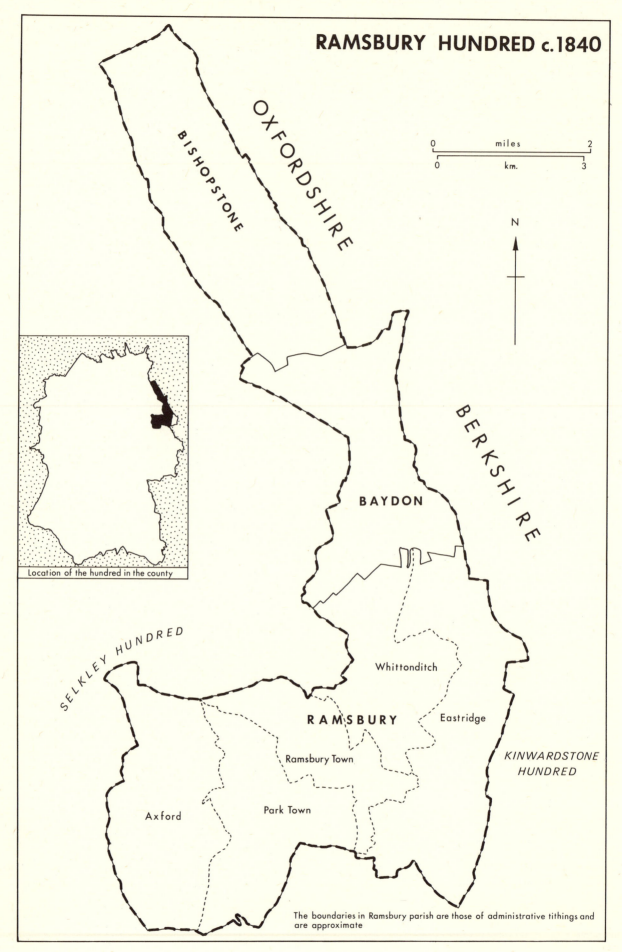

RAMSBURY HUNDRED c.1840

OXFORDSHIRE

BISHOPSTONE

0   miles   2
0   km.   3

N

BERKSHIRE

Location of the hundred in the county

BAYDON

SELKLEY HUNDRED

Whittonditch

RAMSBURY

Eastridge

Ramsbury Town

KINWARDSTONE HUNDRED

Axford

Park Town

The boundaries in Ramsbury parish are those of administrative tithings and are approximate

2

BISHOPSTONE

BISHOPSTONE is 10 km. east of Swindon on Wiltshire's border with that part of Oxfordshire which was formerly part of Berkshire.[1] The parish, 3,520 a. (1,424 ha.), was increased to 2,299 ha. (5,681 a.) in 1934 when its neighbour Little Hinton was added to it.[2] It was long and narrow, 7 km. by 2 km., one of several such parishes running north-west and south-east across the flat clay land of the Cole valley up the chalk of the Marlborough and Berkshire Downs, and, with roughly equal amounts of each kind of land, it conformed to the type. The village is on a narrow band of Upper Greensand which out-crops across the middle of the parish at the bottom of the north facing scarp of the downs, at c. 122 m. The escarpment is cut by two deep coombs; south of it the land is higher with Lammy Down over 244 m. and two summits over 229 m., but the relief is gentler with a large area of flat land at the eastern edge of the parish. The chalk is covered by clay-with-flints on Lammy Down. In the north part of the parish, where the land falls northwards to 97 m. no more than 1 in 150, Gault, Lower Greensand, and small areas of Kimmeridge Clay outcrop.[3] The distribution of arable, meadow, and pasture land normal in such parishes was made at Bishop-stone. Furthest from the village the northern lowland and southern upland were permanent pasture, and arable land lay across the centre of the parish where, south of the village, only Lammy Down and the coombs were not ploughed. In historical times there has not been more than a few acres of woodland in the parish. A small circular wood, Bishopstone Folly, was growing above the west coomb in the 18th century.[4]

Bishopstone is in some aspects of its history strikingly similar to its namesake near Salisbury.[5] Not named in Domesday Book, both were out-lying parts of episcopal and hundredal manors, the northern Bishopstone of the bishop of Salis-bury's manor of Ramsbury, with which it marched only along a short downland boundary at its south end. Neither is known to have been a parish before the 13th century, and their names, identical and of similar origin, do not appear earlier.[6] Bishopstone near Ramsbury was so called in 1208.[7]

The nicety of the rectangle formed by the parish and the fact that the village is in its centre suggest that compactness and symmetry were sought after more than natural boundaries when Bishopstone's lands were defined. Its western boundary was related in pre-Conquest charters of Little Hinton and Wanborough. To plot the ancient boundary would be difficult if the modern was not known, but plausible attempts have been made to correlate the two.[8] Only by a headstream of the Cole and by the bottom of a dry valley in the northern part of that boundary was Bishop-stone delimited by natural features.

Four possibly ancient roads crossed the parish from east to west. The Ridge Way is at the top of the scarp. Below and north of it the parallel Icknield Way follows the contours and links the villages on the Upper Greensand. At the north end of the parish the Rogues Way followed the parish boundary, and a Thieves Way crossed the southern downs.[9] None was turnpiked. Neither the Thieves Way nor the Rogues Way was marked on a map of 1758,[10] and there was nothing to be seen of them in 1980: the Ridge Way has never been made up. The Icknield Way, the road from Swindon to Wantage (Berks., later Oxon.), was in places a field path in 1758. It was a road in 1773 and has become the main line of communication for the parish. In the 18th century a path branched from it west of the village and led northwards to Shrivenham (Berks., later Oxon.), and other paths led across the lowland from near the church and from Golds Green. The westernmost was established as a road at inclosure in 1813, when a new road from Golds Green was made to join it. The other two have gone out of use.[11] None of the roads leading south from the Swindon-Wantage road leaves the parish, and in 1980 Russley Park on the downs could be approached by road only from the south.

Evidence of an early Iron-Age settlement has been found near Russley Park and part of a Roman tessellated pavement on the downs east of Lammy Down. Other artefacts, barrows, ditches, and a 50-a. field system also attest prehistoric activity on the downs.[12] On the steep north facing slope below the Ridge Way near the western boundary of the parish is a broad flight of well preserved strip lynchets which was excavated in the 1950s. It was then suggested that the lynchets had been made for cultivation.[13]

Bishopstone grew up north of the Swindon-Wantage road where the two coombs converge. A stream, called Westbrook in 1773,[14] rises in the

---

[1] This article was written in 1980. Maps used include O.S. Maps 1″, sheet 34 (1828 edn.), sheet 157 (1968 edn.); 1/50,000, sheet 174 (1974 edn.); 1/25,000, SU 27 (1960 edn.), SU 28 (1960 edn.); 6″, Wilts. XVI (1887 edn.).
[2] V.C.H. Wilts. iv. 341 n.; xi. 159; Census, 1931, 1971.
[3] Geol. Surv. Maps 1″, solid and drift, sheet 252 (1974 edn.), solid, sheet 253 (1971 edn.), drift, sheet 253 (1971 edn.), drift, sheet 267 (1947 edn.).
[4] W.R.O., Ch. Com., map 4 (1758).
[5] Cf. V.C.H. Wilts. xi. 3, 6, 16.
[6] The earliest refs. in P.N. Wilts. (E.P.N.S.), 392 are

probably to Bushton in Clyffe Pypard, rather than to this Bishopstone as suggested in V.C.H. Wilts. xi. 3 n.
[7] Mem. R. 1208 (Pipe R. Soc. N.S. xxxi), 66.
[8] Arch. Jnl. lxxvi. 172-80; W.A.M. lvii. 201-11.
[9] W.A.M. lvii, map facing p. 210.
[10] W.R.O., Ch. Com., map 4.
[11] Ibid.; ibid. inclosure award; Andrews and Dury, Map (W.R.S. viii), pl. 15.
[12] V.C.H. Wilts. i (1), 42, 159, 252, 273.
[13] W.A.M. lvi. 12-16; lvii. 18-23.
[14] Andrews and Dury, Map (W.R.S. viii), pl. 15.

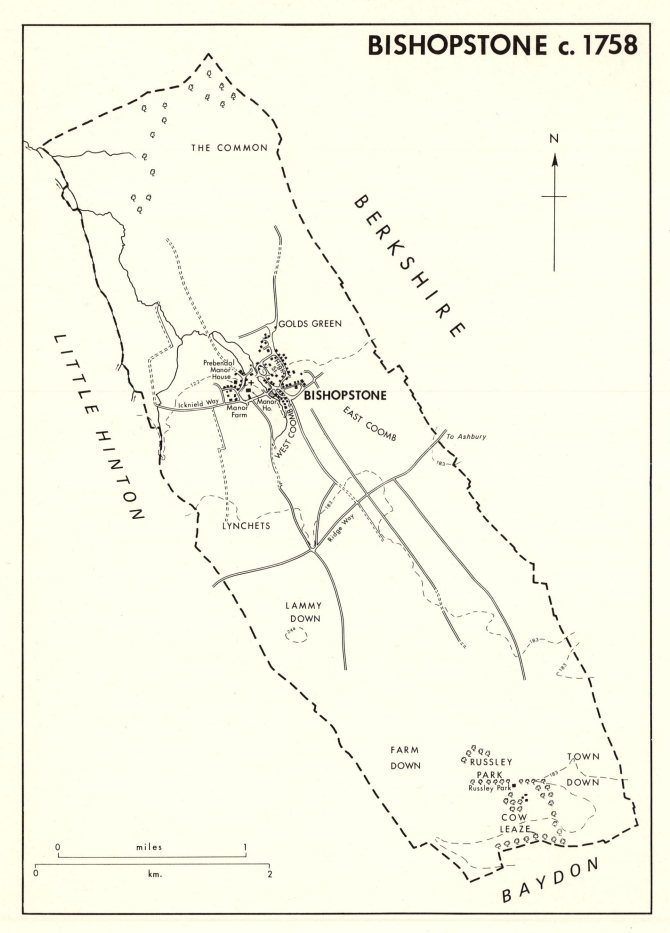

BISHOPSTONE c. 1758

west coomb and flows northwards across the lowland to the Cole: it is joined from the west by another springing north of the Swindon–Wantage road. Between the two the church, manor house, and demesne farmstead of Bishopstone manor were built, and the mill was built north of the road on the eastern stream with its pond south of the road where it remains a prominent feature. The village developed in an arc around that nucleus. It was a community of many small farmsteads, closely grouped, and linked with the Swindon–Wantage road by a network of lanes.[15] The copyholders held more land on the east side of the parish than the west, and their farmsteads were more numerous in the east part of the village, especially beside the lane, leading north to the lowland, which was called High Street in 1758. The open space near the mill in the centre of the village was then called Hocker Bench.[16] The village was apparently wealthy in the Middle Ages: the assessment for taxation in 1334 was above average and in 1377 the number of poll-tax payers, 169, was very high.[17] Taxation assessments in the 16th century were also high.[18] Apparently in the 18th century the village spilled over to the south side of the Swindon–Wantage road. East of the mill pond a line of cottages was then built on the waste in an arc in the west coomb, and along a short path west of the pond a few more cottages were built.[19] In the 19th century several more cottages and houses were built in those areas, and the school was also built beside the mill pond. In the 20th century several houses, including the present vicarage house and in 1977 a village hall,[20] have also been erected south of the road. As the number of farms in the parish decreased the population fell by a third between 1881 and 1901.[21] Not many farmhouses and cottages in the northern and eastern parts of the village were demolished, but the balance of the village was then being shifted by the demolition of the old manor house and by the building of two large red-brick houses, Forest House and Eastbrook Farm,[22] and most new houses and cottages beside the Swindon–Wantage road and at the east end of the village. In 1801 the population was 530. By 1851 it had risen to a peak of 755 and by 1901 had declined to 404. It was 449 in 1911 and 371 in 1934 when figures for Bishopstone alone are last available.[23] More than half of the 569 inhabitants of the enlarged parish lived in Bishopstone in 1971.[24]

In 1980 the older buildings were scattered about the lanes north of the Swindon–Wantage road and concentrated in the west coomb. The predominant building materials before the 20th century were chalk, often used with red-brick quoins and window surrounds, and thatch. Manor Farm beside the Swindon–Wantage road at the west end of the village has a long 17th-century range and a later wing to the east, and there is another 17th-century farmhouse behind it. Another 17th-century farmhouse survives north-east of the church and there are some 15–20 cottages and small houses apparently of 17th- and 18th-century origin in High Street and the parallel lane west of it. The True Heart in High Street was open in the earlier 19th century and rebuilt c. 1900: the Royal Oak in the lane west of High Street was built in 1907 on the front of an 18th-century building.[25] South of the Swindon–Wantage road some 18th-century cottages and a variety of 19th-century houses and cottages survive. In the mid 20th century the balance of the village has shifted back to its northern and eastern parts, where there are few 19th-century dwellings, with the building of various private houses and some 30 council houses. There has been little settlement in the parish outside the village. Russley Park was built on the downs c. 1700[26] and several houses stood there in 1980. Starveall Farm, a pair of cottages and farm buildings of chalk with brick dressings erected in the early 19th century, and Ridgeway Farm, buildings and a pair of cottages of the late 19th century, are also on the downs, and two farmsteads have been built on the lowland in the 19th and 20th centuries.

MANORS AND OTHER ESTATE. It has been plausibly suggested that in 1086 the bishop of Salisbury's Ramsbury estate included Bishopstone, not itself named in Domesday Book,[27] and early ownership by the bishops is implied by the place name:[28] the earliest express record of an episcopal estate there was in 1208.[29] In 1294 the bishop was granted free warren in his demesne lands.[30] The manor of BISHOPSTONE passed with the see of Salisbury until the Civil War. In 1647 it was sold to John Oldfield and Matthew Kendrick, apparently trustees or agents of the lessee Gilbert Keate.[31] The manor was returned to the see at the Restoration.[32] It passed in 1869 to the Ecclesiastical Commissioners, later the Church Commissioners, owners in 1980.[33]

In the early 16th century the bishops leased their demesne lands to members of the Precy family and in 1542 Bishop Salcot granted a lease of them until 1605 to John Precy.[34] In 1548 the bishop leased the whole manor, subject to the Precys' interest, to John Knight for 99 years.[35]

[15] e.g. W.R.O., Ch. Com., map 4. An air view of most of the village in 1949 is in M. W. Beresford and J. K. S. St. Joseph, *Medieval Eng.: Aerial Survey* (1979 edn.), p. 83.
[16] W.R.O., Ch. Com., maps 4–5.
[17] *V.C.H. Wilts.* iv. 301, 310.
[18] *Taxation Lists* (W.R.S. x), 26, 94.
[19] e.g. W.R.O., Ch. Com., maps 4–7.
[20] Char. Com. file; inf. from the vicar, the Revd. J. T. Walker.
[21] *V.C.H. Wilts.* iv. 341; below, econ. hist.
[22] Below, manors, econ. hist.
[23] *V.C.H. Wilts.* iv. 341.
[24] *Census*, 1971.
[25] *Kelly's Dir. Wilts.* (1848); W.R.O. 1451/40.

[26] Below, manors.
[27] *V.C.H. Wilts.* ii, p. 84.
[28] *P.N. Wilts.* (E.P.N.S.), 286, where the earliest ref. may be to Bushton in Clyffe Pypard.
[29] *Mem. R. 1208* (Pipe R. Soc. n.s. xxxi), 66; *Civil Pleas, 1249* (W.R.S. xxvi), pp. 77–8.
[30] *Cal. Chart. R. 1257–1300*, 454.
[31] P.R.O., C 54/3371, no. 12; W.R.O., Ch. Com., bpric. 8/1, ct. held 18 Oct. 1646.
[32] W.R.O., Ch. Com., bpric. 7/2.
[33] Wilts. Cuttings, xvii. 185; inf. from Mr. D. J. Harvey, Estates Dept., Ch. Com.
[34] W.R.O., Ch. Com., bpric. 460, ff. 35 and v., 107v.–108.
[35] Ibid. f. 172.

Knight was possibly a trustee of the Precys. Charles Precy held the manor from 1600 or earlier until his death in 1626.[36] It passed to Thomas Precy and Henry Shelley, possibly his executors. In 1626–7 they sold the lease to Gilbert Keate (d. 1657–8) to whom new leases were granted in 1629 and 1636.[37] Gilbert was succeeded by his son Jonathan (created a baronet in 1660) to whom a new lease was granted in 1661.[38] Keate assigned his lease in 1663–4 to Christopher Willoughby (d. 1681) and it passed to Christopher's cousin George Willoughby (knighted in 1686, d. 1695).[39] In 1692–3 Willoughby settled his leaseholds of the manor and prebend of Bishopstone and new leases were granted to his trustees.[40] They passed together to his son Christopher (d. 1715), to Christopher's son George (d. 1751), and to George's son Henry.[41] In 1757 the lease of Bishopstone manor was sold after proceedings in Chancery to a trustee of the paymaster-general, Henry Fox (created Baron Holland in 1763, d. 1774),[42] and was apparently settled on Fox's son Stephen (d. 1774).[43] The lease passed with the Holland title to Stephen's son Henry Richard (from 1800 Henry Richard Vassall) Fox (d. 1840) and grandson Henry Edward Fox (d. 1859),[44] whose relict Mary sold it to the Ecclesiastical Commissioners in 1862.[45]

In 1647 there was on the manor a ten-room house, built of and roofed with stone, with thatched outbuildings.[46] It stood south-west of the church, between the church and the Swindon–Wantage road, and was lived in by the Willoughbys.[47] In 1757 it was settled for life on Jane, relict of George Willoughby (d. 1751).[48] From 1803 it was held by James Puzey (d. 1837) who kept a school in it.[49] In 1840 the house was said to be large, dilapidated, and only partly occupied. Drawings of it made in 1845 show it to have been in a mixture of styles. Wings were taken down in 1852. In 1862 the house was taken into the prebendal estate by the Ecclesiastical Commissioners in exchange for land, and was demolished.[50]

The manor of *BISHOPSTONE PREBEND* was presumably taken from Bishopstone manor by a bishop of Salisbury to endow the prebend of Bishopstone,[51] and, consisting of tithes and demesne and customary land, it belonged to the prebendaries until the Civil War. In 1651 the lands were sold to Gilbert Keate.[52] They presumably passed to Sir Jonathan Keate but at the Restoration were given back to the prebendary.[53] Land was allotted to replace the tithes in 1813.[54] The last prebendary died in 1838. The income from the manor was paid to Queen Anne's Bounty until in 1840 the manor and the profits from 1838 were vested in the Ecclesiastical Commissioners.[55] The land was part of the Church Commissioners' Bishopstone estate in 1980.[56]

In 1538 and 1573 prebendaries leased their manor to Thomas Davy.[57] In 1584 a new lease was granted to a trustee of the Davy family, members of which took the profits until at least 1620.[58] In 1633 John Barnstone, the prebendary, leased the prebend to William Barnstone for lives which possibly survived the Interregnum.[59] In 1672 the prebend was leased to Christopher Willoughby, and new leases were granted to the lessees of Bishopstone manor until in 1751 and 1755 they were granted to Jane, relict of George Willoughby (d. 1751).[60] By 1780 Henry Richard Fox, Lord Holland, had become lessee.[61] In 1784 the prebendal manor was leased to John Hepworth, rector of Grafham (Hunts., later Cambs.),[62] and in 1813 a lease was held by the executors of William Church of Upper Upham in Aldbourne.[63] From 1820 to 1855 Richard Webb (d. 1837) and his executors were lessees.[64]

There was a house on the manor in 1341 and 1631.[65] In 1758 the house stood north-west of the church.[66] In 1862–3 the Ecclesiastical Commissioners built on the estate a new red-brick house, Forest House, later Prebendal Farm, between the site of the demolished Bishopstone manor house and the Swindon–Wantage road. The house north-west of the church was demolished between 1884 and 1922.[67]

A sporting estate was established on Russley down as part of Bishopstone manor, possibly by the Willoughbys in the late 17th century or the early 18th. In 1758 there was a house with a main block of five bays and a symmetrical front of two storeys with attics and a basement. It lay near the centre of a partly hedged and partly paled park

[36] P.R.O., E 179/198/334; W.R.O., Ch. Com., bpric. 8/1; W.R.O. 1364/1.

[37] W.R.O., Ch. Com., bpric. 8/1; bpric. 461, ff. 203–205v.

[38] Burke, *Ext. & Dorm. Baronetcies* (1838), 286; W.R.O., Ch. Com., bpric. 7/2.

[39] W.R.O., Ch. Com., bpric. 8/1; W.R.O. 1364/2; P.R.O., PROB 11/365 (P.C.C. 18 North, will of Chris. Willoughby).

[40] P.R.O., CP 25(2)/888/4 Wm. & Mary Mich.; CP 25(2)/888/4 & 5 Wm. & Mary Hil.; D. & C. Sar. Mun., lease bk. VIII, pp. 146–9; W.R.O., Ch. Com., bpric. 7/3; below.

[41] W.R.O., Ch. Com., bpric. 7/3; bpric. 7/34; bpric. 8/2.

[42] Ibid. Ch. Com., bpric. 7/6; bpric. 470, p. 50; *Complete Peerage*.

[43] W.R.O. 212A/27/22/3, lease, Fox to Craven.

[44] Ibid. Ch. Com., bpric. 7/7–26; *Complete Peerage*.

[45] W.R.O., Ch. Com., bpric. 7/28; Ch. Com. file 24868.

[46] W.R.O., Ch. Com., bpric. 468.

[47] Ibid. Ch. Com., map 4; ibid. Ch. Com., bpric. 10/1. The Willoughbys were said to be 'of Bishopstone': e.g. *W.N. & Q.* vi. 31.

[48] W.R.O., Ch. Com., bpric. 7/6; bpric. 7/34.

[49] Ibid. Ch. Com., bpric. 13/1; bpric. 23/1; bpric. 472.

[50] Ibid. Ch. Com., bpric. 472; bpric. 7/27; Wilts. Cuttings, xvii. 185.

[51] Below, church.

[52] P.R.O., C 54/3606, no. 33.

[53] D. & C. Sar. Mun., press I, box 30, bdle. 1, augmentation of vicarage (1672).

[54] W.R.O., inclosure award.

[55] *Lond. Gaz.* 17 Jan. 1871, pp. 156–7; 5 & 6 Wm. IV, c. 30; Cathedrals Act, 3 & 4 Vic. c. 113, s. 49.

[56] Inf. from Mr. Harvey.

[57] W.R.O., Ch. Com., bpric. 460, ff. 73v.–74; D. & C. Sar. Mun., lease bk. II, pp. 137–9.

[58] D. & C. Sar. Mun., lease bk. II, pp. 272–3; P.R.O., C 2/Jas. I/M 10/50; C 2/Jas. I/P 10/70; C 2/Jas. I/D 14/21.

[59] D. & C. Sar. Mun., lease bk. III, pp. 379–82; P.R.O., C 54/3606, no. 33.

[60] D. & C. Sar. Mun., press I, box 30, bdle. 1, augmentation of vicarage; lease bks. VIII, pp. 146–9; X, pp. 175–81, 338–41; XI, ff. 39v.–41, 110–12, 157–158v.; XII, ff. 23v.–26, 165–166v.; XIII, ff. 15–17v., 90–92v.

[61] W.R.O., land tax.

[62] Ibid. 1043/1.

[63] Ibid. inclosure award.

[64] Ibid. Ch. Com., prebends 37/3–7; Ch. Com., survey bk. Z 1, p. 803.

[65] *Inq. Non.* (Rec. Com.), 175; W.R.O., dean, glebe terrier.

[66] W.R.O., Ch. Com., map 4.

[67] Above; Wilts. Cuttings, xvii. 185; O.S. Maps 6″, Wilts. XVI (1887 edn.), XVI. NE. (1925 edn.).

of 119 a. in which avenues ran south, east, and west.[68] The house was lived in by Henry Willoughby and passed with the lease of Bishopstone manor to the Foxes.[69] Russely park was sublet with sporting rights over the whole parish, from 1771 to William Craven, Lord Craven (d. 1791), who owned the neighbouring Ashdown Park in Ashbury (Berks., later Oxon.). It was held until his death in 1825 by Lord Craven's son William, Lord Craven, who from *c.* 1803 further sublet it.[70] In 1826 Lord Holland sublet the Russley estate to Thomas Hedges of Highworth and in 1864 the sublessee was J. Challoner Smith.[71] In 1870 the Ecclesiastical Commissioners sold the estate to Thomas Challoner Smith, and in 1899 it seems to have belonged to Henry Challoner Smith.[72] About then the old house was demolished and a new one built on its site. The estate belonged to racehorse trainers. In 1907 W. T. Robinson of Foxhill in Wanborough sold it to W. Hall Walker who sold it in 1916 to the Secretary of State for War as agent for the Board of Agriculture.[73] A large farm and stable complex was erected south-east of the house, initially for use as a stud farm.[74] In 1931 the War Department sold it to Thomas Oakley.[75]

ECONOMIC HISTORY. From the 13th century or earlier Bishopstone was divided between the bishop of Salisbury's and the prebendary's manors,[76] and from the later Middle Ages two areas of cultivation, Eastbrook and Westbrook, were distinguished.[77] Each manor included land in each area of cultivation. There are references to Eastbrook and Westbrook in 1425, and in the early 17th century the words were used freely to locate holdings.[78] The division may have originated in the position of farmsteads on either side of the stream rising in the west coomb. The pastures at each end of the parish were outside them and by the later 18th century the origins of, and the line between, the Eastbrook and Westbrook divisions had become obscure.[79]

Although the number and extent of the arable fields in the Middle Ages is not clear, the existence of a biennially sown south field in 1425 suggests a simple two-field system.[80] A much more fragmented arrangement in the mid 17th century is evident but the practice of leaving half fallow again suggests a two-field origin.[81] The bishop's manor was larger than the prebendary's and in 1291 three times as valuable.[82] The bishop's demesne farm was apparently in hand in

the 13th century and was not leased until after 1438.[83] The manor was independent of the bishop's manor of Ramsbury, but exchanges of stock and produce were made among the demesnes of Bishopstone, Ramsbury, and Baydon.[84] The fact that in 1286 it was recorded that 43 oxen customarily passed from bishop to bishop indicates much arable cultivation at some time.[85] There were 201 a., 603 selions, of demesne land sown in 1425; 82 a. of meadow land were mown; and at Michaelmas there were flocks of 379 wethers and 311 ewes.[86] In 1438 there were 171 a. sown and 652 sheep kept.[87] The customary works owed by the tenants may have been sufficient to cultivate the demesne, but by the earlier 15th century they had been commuted and the demesne was largely cultivated by wage labour. In 1425 the customary holdings, for which rents totalled £17 5s., seem to have been small and numerous: they included 35 of 1 yardland and 19 of ½ yardland.[88] In 1508 the rent for the demesne lands was £18; in 1535 customary rents were £22.[89] A demesne warren was referred to in 1542.[90] The most valuable part of the prebendary's manor was presumably the tithes of grain, hay, and sheep which in the Middle Ages were due from the whole parish.[91] In 1341 the demesne land included an arable carucate, meadow land, and several pasture for 100 sheep and 14 cattle.[92] Rents amounting to £1 12s. were paid by the customary tenants, of whom there were eight holding a total of 8 yardlands in 1405. The prebendal estate was then held by lease.[93] It was valued at £19 9s. in 1535.[94] There were 41 a. of demesne in 1631.[95]

About 1647–9 there were *c.* 50 farmsteads with small areas of pasture in the village and 1,750 a. of arable land in the centre of the parish. North of that all the meadows and pasture on the lowland seem to have been used in common for part, if not all, of the year. South of it most of the upland pastures, including Russley, 250 a., for cattle, were likewise common. The demesne farm of Bishopstone manor, 750–800 a., was in the west half of the parish. The copyholders of the manor held 70 yardlands, 1,450 a., of which more than 50 were in Eastbrook. There were 42 tenants and only one holding clearly over 100 a.: nine holdings exceeded 50 a. Each yardland had feeding rights for 30 sheep, 2 horses, and 3 beasts. The copyholds included 125 a. of 'lanes', pastures of some 1–10 a. scattered among the arable furlongs. Lammy Down, 42 a. north of the Ridge Way, was later a several part of the episcopal demesne.

[68] W.R.O., Ch. Com., maps 4–5; see plate facing p. 192.
[69] W.R.O. 1364/38; ibid. Ch. Com., bpric. 7/34.
[70] Ibid. 212a/27/22/3, lease, Fox to Craven; ibid. land tax; *V.C.H. Berks.* iv. 504, 506; *Complete Peerage.*
[71] Ch. Com., survey bk. Z 4, pp. 239, 331–5.
[72] Ibid. pp. 331–5; file 43294; *Kelly's Dir. Wilts.* (1899).
[73] Ch. Com. file 79592; inf. from Property Services Agency, Tolworth Tower, Surbiton, Surr.
[74] See plate facing p. 145.
[75] W.R.O. 1008/37; inf. from Property Services Agency.
[76] Above, manor; below, church.
[77] D. & C. Sar. Mun., press I, box 4, no. 52.
[78] Ibid.; W.R.O., Ch. Com., bpric. 8/1, ct. held 8 Oct. 1616.
[79] W.R.O., Ch. Com., map 4; ibid. Ch. Com., bpric. 10/1.
[80] D. & C. Sar. Mun., press I, box 4, no. 52.

[81] W.R.O., dean, glebe terrier, 1631; ibid. Ch. Com., bpric. 468.
[82] *Tax. Eccl.* (Rec. Com.), 193–4.
[83] *Sar. Chart. and Doc.* (Rolls Ser.), 364; D. & C. Sar. Mun., press I, box 31, no. 18.
[84] D. & C. Sar. Mun., press I, box 4, no. 52.
[85] *Sar. Chart. and Doc.* (Rolls Ser.), 364.
[86] D. & C. Sar. Mun., press I, box 4, no. 52.
[87] Ibid. box 31, no. 18.   [88] Ibid. box 4, no. 52.
[89] W.R.O., Ch. Com., bpric. 460, ff. 35 and v.; *Valor Eccl.* (Rec. Com.), ii. 70.
[90] W.R.O., Ch. Com., bpric. 460, ff. 107v.–108.
[91] Ibid. dean, Chaundler's reg. f. 60.
[92] *Inq. Non.* (Rec. Com.), 175.
[93] Ibid.; W.R.O., dean, Chaundler's reg. f. 60.
[94] *Valor Eccl.* (Rec. Com.), ii. 75.
[95] W.R.O., dean, glebe terrier.

The prebendal tithes were worth £140 in 1649. The demesne of the prebendal manor measured 33 a. and the ten prebendal copyholders held 8 yardlands in Eastbrook and 1 yardland in Westbrook with feeding rights similar to those of the episcopal copyholders.[96]

Common husbandry in Bishopstone was in general altered little in the 18th century although it was constantly being refined and amended in detail.[97] Before 1758, however, 120 a. of Russley down was inclosed and made into a sporting estate.[98] The remaining downs were divided between Farm down, 400 a., and Town down, 240 a. for the episcopal and prebendal copyholders. Bishopstone common, 350 a., at the north-east corner of the parish was only for the episcopal copyholders. The meadows and pastures at the north-west corner, 200 a., were apparently a several part of the demesne farm of Bishopstone manor, Bishopstone farm. Between the upland and lowland pasture the arable land was in 1758 in 163 furlongs, characteristically divided into ½-a. strips, totalling some 2,000 a. The Bishopstone farm arable land, 430 a., was in complete furlongs in Westbrook but apparently commonable. The farm, with buildings west of the manor house in the village, had been sublet by the Willoughbys until taken in hand, and badly managed, by Henry Willoughby after 1751. There were 40 other farmsteads in the village and only a downland barn outside it. The prebend was sublet for £145 a year and at least some of the tithes further sublet to the occupiers of the land.[99]

In 1784, when the parish measured 3,520 a., there were 1,725 a. of arable land, over 700 a. of meadow and lowland pasture, and over 800 a. of upland pasture and down. Of the arable land 441 a. were sown with wheat, 254 a. with barley, 125 a. with oats, 344 a. with peas, beans, and vetches, and 49 a. with clover and ryegrass; 512 a. were fallow. Bishopstone farm measured 955 a., Russley park 120 a., the prebendal demesne 42 a., and the vicar's glebe 16 a. The 69½ copyhold yardlands of Bishopstone manor amounted to 1,401 a., the 9 of the prebendal manor 145 a. There were 600 a. in Bishopstone common and Town down. The 78½ copyhold yardlands were held by a total of 45 tenants and there were no more than 22 occupiers of the land, some of them, including William Phillips who occupied over 330 a., holding entirely as undertenants. There were several farms over 100 a., the majority were 30–100 a., and a few were under 30 a.[1]

It seems likely that in the 18th century the number of farms fell and that their sizes increased,[2] but the amount of subletting makes

that impossible to prove. In the 19th century, however, the concentration of the land into a few large farms can be clearly seen. The commonable lands, all the arable land and Town down and Bishopstone common, were inclosed and allotted in 1813 under an Act. At the same time all the prebendal and vicarial tithes were exchanged for land and there were various exchanges of land.[3] Bishopstone (later Manor) farm remained a long narrow strip on the west side of the parish, 840 a. in 1840.[4] From 1813 to 1901 members of the Dore family occupied it.[5] In 1840 it had additional buildings on the lowland and in 1864 more on Farm down.[6] The prebendary was allotted 640 a. in narrow strips north and south of the village immediately east of Bishopstone farm. Prebendal farm was worked from the prebendal manor house and buildings beside the Ridge Way until 1862–3 when new buildings were erected on the site of Bishopstone manor house.[7] The vicar's glebe was worked as a farm, 133 a., in the late 19th century and early 20th.[8] The eastern side of the parish was occupied by 17 inclosed copyhold farms over 20 a., including one over 200 a. and four over 100 a., and by 33 smallholdings, but the number of separately worked farms is uncertain.[9] In 1864 over 1,000 a. of the 1,600 a. of copyhold land was in four holdings. Between 1865 and 1880 the Ecclesiastical Commissioners took in hand most of the copyholds and by 1883 had merged much of them into Eastbrook farm, 981 a., with a newly erected house and enlarged farm buildings at the east end of the village. Over 200 a. of Bishopstone common were leased to a farmer in another parish and some 233 a. remained copyhold.[10] In the 19th century and early 20th Starveall and Ridgeway were smaller upland farms,[11] but since the Second World War there have been only three principal farms in the parish, Manor, Prebendal, and Eastbrook, of which Manor and Prebendal have sometimes been held together.[12] In 1980, when the farming in the parish was mixed, they measured respectively 836 a., 961 a., and 1,338 a.[13] Watercress was cultivated in beds north and south of Bishopstone mill from 1878 or earlier until the 1930s or later.[14] There have been occasional references to clothworking in Bishopstone and in 1927 hemp was said to be produced commercially.[15]

Russley park was enlarged to 245 a. in 1882 when its owner acquired the southernmost part of Town down.[16] In 1895 its owner was training racehorses on Bishopstone downs by arrangement with the farmers, and stables were established at Russley. In 1904 gallops on the downs for a maximum of 80 horses were leased to the

[96] W.R.O., Ch. Com., bpric. 468; bpric. 10/1; ibid. Ch. Com., maps 4–5; D. & C. Sar. Mun., press I, box 1, no. 22.
[97] W.R.O., Ch. Com., bpric. 8/1–4.
[98] Ibid. Ch. Com., map 4.
[99] Ibid. Ch. Com., bpric. 7/34; bpric. 10/1; ibid. Ch. Com., maps 4–5.
[1] Ibid. Ch. Com., bpric. 7/34.
[2] Cf. ibid.; bpric. 468.
[3] Ibid. inclosure award.
[4] Ibid.; ibid. Ch. Com., bpric. 472.
[5] Ibid. land tax; ibid. 838/27–8; ibid. Ch. Com., bpric. 12/1–4; Ch. Com., survey bk. Z 4, p. 235; survey bk. Z 7, p. 433.
[6] W.R.O., Ch. Com., bpric. 472; Ch. Com., survey bk. Z 4, p. 263.

[7] W.R.O., inclosure award; Ch. Com., survey bk. Z 1, p. 812.
[8] W.R.O., inclosure award; below, church.
[9] W.R.O., inclosure award.
[10] Ch. Com., survey bk. Z 4, pp. 241–9; survey bk. Z 7, p. 433; map 16806.
[11] O.S. Maps 1″, sheet 34 (1828 edn.); 6″, Wilts. XVI (1887 edn.); Ch. Com. file 79592.
[12] Ch. Com. file 79592.
[13] Inf. from Mr. D. J. Harvey, Estates Dept., Ch. Com.
[14] Owen, Dir. (1878); Kelly's Dir. Wilts. (1931, 1939); Ch. Com., survey bk. Z 7, p. 441; map 16806.
[15] Sess. Mins. (W.R.S. iv), 95 (1584); W.N. & Q. vi. 223 (1673); W.A.M. xliv. 287.
[16] Ch. Com., survey bk. Z 1, p. 811.

owners of the stables at Foxhill. The gallops continued to be used from Foxhill until *c.* 1950. Because they prevented inclosure and thus anything but inconvenient sheep grazing they were then abandoned in order to improve the farms.[17]

MILLS. There was a mill at Bishopstone in the mid 13th century, apparently four in the mid 14th, and two on the demesne of Bishopstone manor in the early 15th.[18] A mill remained part of that manor.[19] The mill buildings near the centre of the village were said in 1788 to house two water grist mills.[20] The mill was rebuilt by the lessee Peter Knight in 1818.[21] In 1864 it was said to house three pairs of stones and in 1886 was a flour mill.[22] Milling was apparently stopped between 1903 and 1907.[23]

LOCAL GOVERNMENT. The bishops of Salisbury's right to exercise royal jurisdiction in Bishopstone came from their rights in Ramsbury hundred,[24] and it is not clear whether separate views of frankpledge were held for Bishopstone in the Middle Ages. The right to hold courts was leased with Bishopstone manor from 1548 and it was later made clear that public jurisdiction was over the whole parish.[25] In the 17th century the lessees held an annual view of frankpledge but, especially from the 1620s, it dealt with little more than the election of constables and tithingmen. The court baron of Bishopstone manor was held in autumn on the day of the view, and additional courts were sometimes held. Much copyhold and agrarian business was done: overseers of the commons, 'leazelookers', and other officers were appointed.[26] Since common husbandry and copyhold tenure lasted long at Bishopstone those matters remained the main business of the courts in the 18th century.[27] The court baron of the prebendal manor was held occasionally in the late 17th century and the 18th. The proceedings of fifteen courts held between 1663 and 1753 were separately recorded and those of others were recorded with those of Bishopstone manor courts. The courts dealt only with copyhold business.[28] In the mid 18th century the lessee of the two manors merged the courts, but they were again separate in the late 18th century. Both were held for copyhold business and little else in the 19th century.[29]

Annual expenditure on the poor was £153 in 1775–6 and £240 in 1802–3 when 14 adults were relieved regularly and 55 occasionally.[30] The parish, which had no workhouse, spent an average of £520 a year on the poor 1833–5, a figure not abnormal for the size of parish. Bishopstone joined Highworth and Swindon poor-law union in 1835.[31] In the early 19th century there were two surveyors of highways who, for their purposes, divided the parish into east and west tithings.[32]

CHURCH. Bishopstone church was standing in the 12th century.[33] By analogy with Bishopstone in Downton hundred it may first have been served from Ramsbury, but was later a parish church.[34] The church's revenues were assigned to endow a prebend in Salisbury cathedral, possibly before 1226 and certainly before 1291.[35] The parish became a prebendal peculiar: prebendaries held visitation courts and administered the ecclesiastical affairs of the parish until the death of the last prebendary in 1838.[36] A vicarage had been ordained by 1305.[37] The parish was transferred to Gloucester and Bristol diocese in 1837 and has been in Bristol diocese since 1897.[38] In 1946 the benefices and ecclesiastical parishes of Little Hinton and Bishopstone were united.[39]

The advowson of the vicarage belonged to the prebendary.[40] For reasons that are not clear the bishop of Winchester presented in 1348 and the queen in 1582. In 1667 Christopher Willoughby presented by grant of a turn.[41] In 1840 the advowson was transferred by Act to the bishop of Gloucester and Bristol and in 1897 to the bishop of Bristol, the patron in 1980.[42]

The vicar's income in 1535 included an annuity of 4 marks from the prebendary, said to have been long paid.[43] The living was valued at only £20 *c.* 1620 when the prebendary's lessee was accused of failing to pay the annuity.[44] The poverty of the living led to an augmentation of tithes by John Barnstone, prebendary 1601–43, but in 1649 the vicarage was still said to be worth no more than £30.[45] A state augmentation of £15 13s. 4d. was given and taken away before 1655.[46] After the Restoration Barnstone's augmentation

[17] Ibid. file 79592.
[18] *Crown Pleas, 1249* (W.R.S. xvi), p. 173; *Inq. Non.* (Rec. Com.), 175; D. & C. Sar. Mun., press I, box 4, no. 52.
[19] e.g. W.R.O., Ch. Com., bpric. 468 (1647).
[20] Ibid. Ch. Com., map 4; ibid. Ch. Com., bpric. 14/1.
[21] Ibid. Ch. Com., bpric. 14/3; bpric. 472; tablet on bldg.
[22] Ch. Com., survey bk. Z 4, p. 315; W.R.O., Ch. Com., bpric. 14/9.
[23] *Kelly's Dir. Wilts.* (1903, 1907).
[24] Below, Ramsbury, local govt.
[25] W.R.O., Ch. Com., bpric. 460, f. 172; bpric. 468.
[26] Ibid. Ch. Com., bpric. 8/1.
[27] Ibid. Ch. Com., bpric. 8/2–3; above, econ. hist.
[28] W.R.O., Ch. Com., prebends 44A; ibid. Ch. Com., bpric. 8/2.
[29] Ibid. Ch. Com., bpric. 8/3–8.
[30] *Poor Law Abstract, 1804,* 568–9.
[31] *Poor Law Com. 2nd Rep.* 559.
[32] W.R.O. 1364/32.
[33] Below.
[34] *V.C.H. Wilts.* xi. 16; W.R.O., dean, Chaundler's reg. f. 60.

[35] *Reg. St. Osmund* (Rolls Ser.), ii. 74; *Tax. Eccl.* (Rec. Com.), 190.
[36] e.g. W.R.O., prebend, ct. and vis. papers; *Lond. Gaz.* 17 Jan. 1871, p. 156.
[37] *Reg. Ghent* (Cant. & York Soc.), i. 166.
[38] *Rec. Dioc. Bristol,* ed. I. M. Kirby, pp. xvi, xviii.
[39] *V.C.H. Wilts.* xi. 163; *Lond. Gaz.* 27 Feb. 1940, pp. 1164–5.
[40] Phillipps, *Wilts. Inst.* i. 15, 30, 46, 49, 52, 81–2, 179, 188; ii. 13; W.R.O., dean, reg. inst. ff. 3, 5, 6v., 7v., 9v., 14v., 21–2, 28a, 82v., 95, 110, 114v., 142, 165 and v., 174v., 177.
[41] Phillipps, *Wilts. Inst.* i. 43; W.R.O., dean, reg. inst. ff. 14, 63.
[42] Cathedrals Act, 3 & 4 Vic. c. 113, s. 41; *Crockford* (1896 and later edns.).
[43] *Valor Eccl.* (Rec. Com.), ii. 75; W.R.O., Ch. Com., bpric. 460, ff. 73v.–74.
[44] P.R.O., C 2/Jas. I/M 10/50.
[45] W.R.O., dean, glebe terrier, 1670; Phillipps, *Wilts. Inst.* ii. 2; *D.N.B.*; D. & C. Sar. Mun., press I, box 1, no. 22.
[46] *Cal. S.P. Dom.* 1655, 142.

was continued and Henry Kinnimond, prebendary 1660–78, gave a further £12 a year from the prebend.[47] In 1716 Thomas Coker, prebendary 1696–1741, increased the pensions from the prebend to the vicars by £15 6s. 8d. to £30,[48] and that sum was paid until the lease of the prebend was surrendered to the Ecclesiastical Commissioners in 1855.[49] The vicar's annual income of £208 in the period 1829–31 was nevertheless still below average.[50]

The vicar had all lesser tithes in 1405.[51] Barnstone assigned to the vicars tithes of corn, hay, wool, and lambs from the 9 copyhold yardlands of the prebendal manor.[52] In the 1780s the vicar was also said to have the tithes of Bishopstone common.[53] In 1631 the vicar's glebe was a yardland of 21 a. without common feeding rights on Town down.[54] In 1813 the vicar was allotted 136 a. to replace his tithes and glebe.[55] In the 1880s and 1890s the vicar tried unsuccessfully to sell the land to the Ecclesiastical Commissioners and in 1904 was himself forced to buy the buildings necessary for it to be worked as a farm. The Ecclesiastical Commissioners bought those buildings as an endowment for the vicarage in 1917, but in 1920 bought the whole glebe.[56] There was a glebe house in 1582.[57] A new house with four rooms on each floor was built a little north of the churchyard in 1721.[58] Part of it was rebuilt in 1873.[59] In 1880 the Ecclesiastical Commissioners gave to the vicar by exchange land between the vicarage house and the churchyard, and on the enlarged site a new vicarage house was built.[60] That house was sold in 1969 when the vicar moved to a house built c. 1947 on the south side of the Swindon–Wantage road near the east end of the village.[61]

As might be expected from the poverty of the living there were few notable vicars. John Wilson, vicar from 1626, was deprived before 1650.[62] The living was held by a succession of ministers 1649–59 until Wilson (d. c. 1667) was restored in 1660.[63] In 1737 Thomas Coker was prebendary, a younger Thomas Coker was vicar, and Henry Coker was curate.[64] In 1783 Nowes Lloyd was incumbent of both Little Hinton and Bishopstone: his assistant curate lived at Bishopstone and held services alternately in the two parishes.[65] Whittington Landon, dean of Exeter, became vicar in 1817, prebendary in 1822. He presented his son J. W. R. Landon to succeed him as vicar

in 1825, and the son remained non-resident vicar until his death in 1880.[66] On Census Sunday in 1851 there were congregations of 90 at the morning and 130 at the afternoon services, above average for Bishopstone but small for a parish as populous.[67] In 1680 Christopher Willoughby gave £2 a year to the vicars for preaching two sermons and 10s. a year for keeping a register for his other charities. In 1896 the sermon charity was separated from the other Willoughby charities.[68] It was still being paid in 1980.[69]

The church of ST. MARY, so called by 1405,[70] is of coursed sarsen and has a chancel, an aisled nave with incorporated north porch, and a west tower. A fragment of an 11th- or 12th-century string course set high on the west wall of the chancel is probably in situ: other remains of the 12th-century church are the reset north doorway of the chancel,[71] carved fragments above the south doorway of the nave, and the font.[72] The outer arch of the porch is of the later 12th century and was apparently reset when the porch was built in the early 14th century. The east window of the south aisle and some of its painted glass are also of the 14th century. The tower was built in the 15th century, by which time the church seems to have reached its full extent. The arcades and most of the outer walls of the aisles and chancel were rebuilt in the late 15th century or the early 16th. The church was restored in 1882, when the west gallery was removed, under the direction of Ewan Christian, and again restored in 1891 after a serious fire in the tower.[73] In 1680 Christopher Willoughby gave £1 a year for bell ringing.[74] By will proved 1796 Thomas Goddard gave £300 in trust for ringing and preserving the bells, or for beautifying or repairing the church. In the 19th century the charity provided substantial sums to maintain and improve the church fabric. By 1867–9, however, £466 had been accumulated. The income of £14, from which the ringers received £2, was spent.[75] In 1980 at least part of the income was still used for bell ringing.[76]

The church had a chalice and paten in 1405.[77] A chalice of 6 oz. was left for the parish in 1553 when 2 oz. of silver were taken for the king. It was replaced by a chalice dated 1627, a flagon hallmarked 1634 given in 1719, a paten hallmarked 1719, and an almsbowl hallmarked 1761.[78] In 1553 there were three bells and a sanctus bell.[79]

[47] W.R.O., dean, glebe terrier, 1670; Phillipps, *Wilts. Inst.* ii. 22, 35.
[48] Phillipps, *Wilts. Inst.* ii. 44, 69; D. & C. Sar. Mun., lease bk. X, pp. 175–81.
[49] W.R.O., Ch. Com., prebends 37/3–7; Ch. Com., survey bk. Z 1, p. 803.
[50] *Rep. Com. Eccl. Revenues*, 824–5.
[51] W.R.O., dean, Chaundler's reg. f. 60.
[52] Ibid. dean, glebe terrier, 1672.
[53] Ibid. Ch. Com., bpric. 7/34.
[54] Ibid.; ibid. dean, glebe terrier.
[55] Ibid. inclosure award.
[56] Ch. Com. file 26876; Bristol R.O., registrar's bdles., folder 93A.
[57] W.R.O., dean, chwdns.' pres.
[58] Ibid. dean, faculty reg. ff. 17–18; ibid. Ch. Com., map 5.
[59] Bristol R.O., EP/A/25/1.
[60] W.R.O., Ch. Com., bpric. 37A; *Lond. Gaz.* 20 Aug. 1880, p. 4577.
[61] Inf. from the vicar, the Revd. J. T. Walker.
[62] Phillipps, *Wilts. Inst.* ii. 13; *Walker Revised*, ed. A. G. Matthews, 382.

[63] *W.A.M.* xli. 110; *Walker Revised*, ed. Matthews, 382; W.R.O., dean, reg. inst. f. 63.
[64] W.R.O., dean, vis. bk.
[65] *Vis. Queries, 1783* (W.R.S. xxvii), pp. 122–3.
[66] *Alum. Oxon. 1715–1886*, iii. 813; W.R.O., dean, reg. inst. ff. 165v., 174v.; *Educ. of Poor Digest*, 1019; *Rep. Com. Eccl. Revenues*, 824–5; P.R.O., HO 129/250/2/1/1.
[67] P.R.O., HO 129/250/2/1/1.
[68] *Endowed Char. Wilts.* (N. Div.), 63, 69.
[69] Char. Com. file; inf. from Mr. Walker.
[70] W.R.O., dean, Chaundler's reg. f. 60.
[71] See plate facing p. 192.
[72] The font was restored in 1882: Bristol R.O., EP/J/6/2/16; Wilts. Cuttings, xvii. 185.
[73] Bristol R.O., EP/J/6/2/16; Wilts. Cuttings, xxviii. 209.
[74] *Endowed Char. Wilts.* (N. Div.), 63.
[75] Ibid. 62, 64, 66.
[76] Char. Com. file; inf. from Mr. Walker.
[77] W.R.O., dean, Chaundler's reg. f. 81.
[78] Nightingale, *Wilts. Plate*, 175–6.
[79] Walters, *Wilts. Bells*, 27.

There was a peal of eight in 1794.[80] The oldest was said to be dated 1602.[81] In 1891 the bells, including three of 1796 cast by Robert and James Wells of Aldbourne and given under his will by Thomas Goddard, were destroyed by fire. A new peal of eight was cast in that year by Mears & Stainbank, the tenor from the fragments of the old bells.[82]

The registers date from 1573: entries for the period 1573–93 are transcripts, those for 1594–1602 are missing.[83]

NONCONFORMITY. A parishioner was presented in 1624 for failing to receive Holy Communion.[84] It is likely that several houses in Bishopstone were licensed for nonconformist worship in the early 19th century,[85] and in 1829 there was a congregation of Independents in the parish.[86] A chapel for Primitive Methodists was opened in the south-east part of the village in 1833.[87] It was said to hold a congregation of 130 and to be full at the evening service on Census Sunday in 1851.[88] It was replaced by a chapel at the south end of High Street in 1886.[89] That chapel was closed c. 1970.[90]

EDUCATION. By will dated 1703 Thomas Goddard of Lockeridge in Overton gave some of his books to the school at Bishopstone.[91] By deed of 1778 Thomas Coker gave 5 a. at Purton, subject to a rent charge of 30s. for Little Hinton school, and £200 for a school for poor children at Bishopstone, and by will proved 1796 Thomas Goddard gave £600 for a similar purpose.[92] From c. 1803 to c. 1840 the school was held in the manor house, which was leased to the schoolmaster.[93] In 1818, when there was another boarding and day school, the charity school was open to all poor children of the parish and attended by nearly 40.[94] Attendance had risen to 83 by 1833 when there were 65 charity pupils.[95] The school was then held by the master and an assistant. Coker's charity kept eighteen children there and Goddard's provided £4 10s. for books and £23 10s. for the master.[96] It had been resolved in 1821 not to distinguish Coker's and Goddard's pupils[97] and in 1834 they were being taught together; the remaining pupils were taught at the opposite end of the large schoolroom.[98] In 1849 the school was in a two-room cottage, but in 1850 a new National school was completed on a site

beside the mill pond.[99] Attendance in 1859 was c. 70,[1] and the school was enlarged in 1872.[2] Numbers fell steadily from 83 in 1908 to 51 in 1938 although from 1920 the older children of Little Hinton were sent to Bishopstone.[3] In 1980 there were 31 children on roll.[4]

By an invalid will dated 1867 Christopher Edmonds intended to give £100 to the school. After his death his family gave the money to the Sunday school.[5] In 1872 the school received £50 from Coker's and Goddard's charities and in 1960 £52 from all three charities.[6] Income was still received in 1980.[7]

CHARITIES FOR THE POOR. By will proved 1658 Gilbert Keate gave £600 to the Grocers Company of London for life pensions of £4 a year to four old people of Bishopstone.[8] Pensioners were chosen in 1665 but, because much of the company's property was destroyed in the Great Fire of London, payments were not made until c. 1680. In 1706 the company compounded for the arrears for the period 1665–80 in £150, £100 of which was invested and used for extraordinary relief in cash or kind.[9] In 1903 there were only women pensioners.[10] In 1680 Christopher Willoughby gave the great tithes of Clench in Milton Lilbourne for various charitable purposes, including two life pensions of £3 10s. a year to poor parishioners of Bishopstone and four similar pensions from the residue of the charity's income.[11] The pensions of £3 10s. were paid to women; the four variable, and usually more valuable, pensions were paid to men. Payments were suspended 1814–21 because of a dispute among the trustees. In 1900 the men's pensions were each of £7 2s.[12] By will dated 1819 Stephen Goddard gave the income from £200 as a life pension to a poor widow or widower.[13] In the 19th century successive pensioners received c. £5 a year.[14]

A copyhold stone quarry in Bourton (Berks., later Oxon.) was held for the poor of Bishopstone before 1658, presumably to provide stone for building in Bishopstone. Stone was sold to the G.W.R. c. 1840 for £213 which was invested. The quarry was later leased to inhabitants of Bourton, c. 1903 for £5 14s. a year.[15] At inclosure in 1813 the poor of Bishopstone were allotted 1 a. for clothing or fuel to replace their right to cut furze on lands then inclosed. The land, called the Forty Gardens, was let as allotments, some of

80 *Endowed Char. Wilts.* (N. Div.), 62.
81 Wilts. Cuttings, xxviii. 209.
82 Ibid.; Walters, *Wilts. Bells*, 27–8.
83 W.R.O. 1364/1–10.
84 Ibid. prebend, chwdns.' pres.
85 Ibid. bishop, certs. dissenters' meeting hos., including some possibly for Bishopstone in Downton hund.
86 *Educ. Enquiry Abstract*, 1029.
87 W.R.O., bishop, return of cert. places; O.S. Map 6″, Wilts. XVI (1887 edn.).
88 P.R.O., HO 129/250/2/1/2.
89 Date on bldg.
90 Local inf.
91 *W.A.M.* xlix. 360.
92 *Endowed Char. Wilts.* (N. Div.), 60–2.
93 Above, manors; W.R.O., Ch. Com., bpric. 472; Wilts. Cuttings, xvii. 185.
94 *Educ. of Poor Digest*, 1019.
95 *Educ. Enquiry Abstract*, 1029.

96 *Endowed Char. Wilts.* (N. Div.), 61–2.
97 W.R.O. 1364/17.
98 *Endowed Char. Wilts.* (N. Div.), 62.
99 W.R.O. 1364/30.
1 *Acct. of Wilts. Schs.* 6.
2 P.R.O., ED 7/130, no. 22.
3 Ibid. ED 21/42124; Bd. of Educ., *List 21* (H.M.S.O.).
4 Inf. from Mr. C. H. Gwyther, headmaster.
5 *Endowed Char. Wilts.* (N. Div.), 74.
6 P.R.O., ED 7/130, no. 22; Char. Com. file.
7 Inf. from Mr. Gwyther.
8 *Endowed Char. Wilts.* (N. Div.), 62.
9 W.R.O. 1364/3; 1364/23–4.
10 *Endowed Char. Wilts.* (N. Div.), 68.
11 Ibid. 63.
12 W.R.O. 1364/15; 1364/26–7.
13 *Endowed Char. Wilts.* (N. Div.), 63.
14 W.R.O. 1364/15.
15 *Endowed Char. Wilts.* (N. Div.), 71.

which were built on. In 1903 there were seven cottages on the land and rents yielded £8 10s. The Bourton quarry and Forty Gardens charities were then used to buy coal for some 60 people.[16]

The five Bishopstone eleemosynary charities were united by a Scheme in 1931. The incomes from Keate's, Willoughby's, and Goddard's were used to form a pension fund. In 1960 pensions of 4s. a week were paid to each of five parishioners. The incomes from the Bourton quarry and Forty Gardens charities were used for the general benefit of the poor. Percy James Stone (d. 1972) gave by will £5,835 to the united charities.[17] In 1980 pensions were still given.[18]

RAMSBURY

RAMSBURY is 9 km. east of Marlborough.[19] Before the Norman Conquest it was the seat of bishops whose hundred of Ramsbury was the second largest non-royal estate in Wiltshire.[20] The hundred lay east and west along the Kennet valley and was attenuated northwards to include the modern parishes of Baydon on the downs and Bishopstone in the Cole valley. Both parts of the hundred were in areas which in 1066 were remarkable for the many royal, episcopal, and monastic estates in them.[21] Before the Conquest there was at Ramsbury a church of which the whole episcopal estate and hundred may have been the parish.[22] Bishopstone, where there was a church in the 12th century, was in the 13th century a distinct parish.[23] Baydon became a poor-law parish but its church, standing in the early 12th century, remained dependent on Ramsbury church until the 1790s.[24] This history of Ramsbury parish therefore embraces Baydon, but most aspects of the histories of Axford and Baydon, the largest villages in the parish apart from Ramsbury, are dealt with separately under the names of those places.

Ramsbury parish was roughly the shape of a boot with Axford in the toe, Littlecote in the heel, and Baydon in the leg. It measured 8 km. from toe to heel, 12 km. from top to heel; and it contained 12,358 a. (5,002 ha.) which was reduced to 9,873 a. (3,996 ha.) when Baydon was excluded. The parish has otherwise remained unaltered. The whole, including Baydon, is in the Kennet valley and on chalk.[25] The Kennet flows from west to east across its southern part without a southern tributary valley. North of the river the steep sides of the valley have been broken into many ridges and valleys now dry, and a tributary still flows from Aldbourne through Preston and Whittonditch. Only Hens Wood in the south-west corner of the parish and the northern slopes of Bailey Hill at the north end drain to the Kennet through tributaries in other parishes. The unbroken southern side of the valley, called Spring Hill near Ramsbury, rises sharply from 122 m. to 168 m.: above it the highest points on an almost flat summit are above 183 m. South-west of Spring Hill part of the down was called Ramsbury Plain in 1820.[26] The broken and complex relief of the parish north of the Kennet is typical of the Wiltshire downs. From its highest points, over 229 m. at Baydon, the land slopes south-eastwards, the heights of the ridges, 216 m. at Marridge Hill, over 198 m. along the boundary with the southern part of Aldbourne, and over 183 m. at Eastridge, decreasing nearer to Littlecote, which lies near the river at 107 m. The parish boundary followed a Roman road north-west of Baydon, the tributary between Preston and Aldbourne, and dry valleys between Aldbourne and Baydon, near Axford, and near Rudge in Froxfield, but for most of its length was neither straight nor responsive to relief. The boundaries with Aldbourne in Love's Copse and with Aldbourne, Little Hinton, and Bishopstone on the remote downs north-west of Baydon were first marked in 1778.[27]

Deposits of clay-with-flints, valley gravel, and alluvium overlie the chalk, follow the contours, and are very extensive for a Wiltshire parish. There is clay-with-flints on all the ridges, gravel in all the valleys. Most of the down south of the Kennet is covered by clay-with-flints and a broad tongue covers the ridge from Marridge Hill through Baydon to Bailey Hill. The high ground on the boundaries with Lambourn (Berks.) and Chilton Foliat between Membury fort and Foxbury Wood and the ridges between Burney Farm and Crowood House are similarly covered. The strip of alluvium deposited by the Kennet is 200–400 m. wide in the parish. Except near Ramsbury Manor there is a narrow strip of valley gravel south of it. North of it the band of gravel is wider, and near Ramsbury, Whittonditch, and Knighton there are extensive gravel deposits. The gravel extends in long tongues between Whittonditch and Preston and in the dry valleys between Marridge Hill and Membury and north of Axford, Preston, and Bailey Hill.[28] Leland aptly

---

[16] *Endowed Char. Wilts.* (N. Div.), 71–2.
[17] Char. Com. file.
[18] Inf. from the vicar, the Revd. J. T. Walker.
[19] This article was written in 1981. Maps used include O.S. 1″, sheet 13 (1830 edn.), sheet 14 (1817 edn.), sheet 34 (1828 edn.); 1/50,000, sheet 174 (1974 edn.); 1/25,000, SU 26 (1961 edn.), SU 27 (1960 edn.), SU 28 (1960 edn.), SU 36 (1961 edn.), SU 37 (1960 edn.); 6″, Wilts. XVII (1883 edn.), XXIII (1887 edn.), XXIV (1887 edn.), XXIX (1889 edn.), XXX (1887 edn.).
[20] *V.C.H. Wilts.* ii, pp. 27–30, 49.

[21] Ibid. pp. 115–17, 119–20, 124, 146; *V.C.H. Berks.* iv. 187, 207, 253.
[22] Below, church.
[23] Above, Bishopstone.
[24] W.R.O. 656/1; below, Baydon, church.
[25] Geol. Surv. Maps 1″, drift, sheet 266 (1974 edn.), sheet 267 (1947 edn.).
[26] C. Greenwood, *Map of Wilts.* (Lond. 1820).
[27] W.R.O. 154/2.
[28] Geol. Surv. Maps 1″, drift, sheet 266 (1974 edn.), sheet 267 (1947 edn.).

described the parish as fruitful of wood and corn,[29] and the normal sheep-and-corn husbandry of the Wiltshire chalklands has predominated in the usual pattern of meadows on the alluvium, arable on the gravel and chalk, and permanent pasture on the steepest slopes of the chalk. The highest land, covered by clay-with-flints, has been wooded, arable, and pasture.[30]

In 1086 woodland at Ramsbury, 16 furlongs long and 4 broad, was possibly in that part of the parish south of the Kennet in which the lords of Ramsbury and Littlecote manors later had woodland in their parks and which was in Savernake forest in the Middle Ages.[31] That area was well wooded with little agriculture in the 16th century.[32] On the downs north of the Kennet there was by then tillage on most of the chalk and clay-with-flints, but large islands of woodland remained.[33] A north wood of Axford and 46 a. of coppice on Axford copyholds may have been north of the village.[34] A wood called Shortgrove south of Baydon, 86 a. in 1567, was mentioned from c. 1260.[35] There were woods at Membury, Eastridge, Whittonditch, and Marridge Hill, the largest of which was Witcha Wood, later Marridge Hill Wood, over 90 a.[36] In the late 16th century there may have been over 1,000 a. of woodland in the parish, perhaps equally divided between the downs north and south of the Kennet.[37] In the north part of the parish Shortgrove was the only woodland known to have been cleared for agriculture, possibly in the later 17th century.[38] In the south part the lords of Axford, Ramsbury, and Littlecote manors have preserved the largest woods, Hens Wood, 333 a., Blake's Copse and adjoining woods, c. 125 a., Park Coppice and Lawn Coppice, a total of 190 a., and Foxbury Wood, Oaken Coppice, and neighbouring woods, a total of 150 a.[39] The Plantation south of Ramsbury Manor and Staghorn Copse and Bolstridge Copse respectively south and east of Hilldrop were grown between 1773 and 1828.[40] All those woods remained in 1981 when more than 1,000 a. were wooded.

The north part of the parish is crossed by ancient and modern downland roads. The Roman road, Ermin Street, from Speen (Berks.) to Gloucester follows the Ridge Way between the Kennet and its tributary, the Lambourn.[41] The London and south Wales motorway, opened across the parish in 1971,[42] follows a parallel course. The other main roads have followed the valleys and are presumably as old as the settlements in them. That linking the villages beside the Kennet between Hungerford and Marlborough may long have rivalled the London–Bath road over the downs between those places.[43] Between Ramsbury and Axford the road presumably followed the river, as it did elsewhere, with Ramsbury Manor and Axford Farm near its course. East of Ramsbury Manor a road diverged from it and led through Sound Bottom across the downs to Ogbourne St. Andrew. That road may have been diverted northwards when the north park of Ramsbury manor was enlarged in the 15th century, and the riverside road between Ramsbury and Axford was stopped, possibly at the same time. In the late 17th century and early 18th, when it was called the Marlborough road and the London road, the road through Sound Bottom may have been the main Hungerford–Marlborough road through Ramsbury.[44] Its course round the park was diverted eastwards and northwards when the park was further enlarged c. 1775. Afterwards the circuitous route between Ramsbury and Axford was made easier by a cutting at White's Hill and shorter by a new north–south road north-west of Axford Farm,[45] and the road through Axford became the main Ramsbury–Marlborough route. The road through Sound Bottom has never been made up. The road which diverges from the Hungerford–Ramsbury road at Knighton, and which links Aldbourne and Hungerford, was turnpiked from Knighton across the downs to Liddington in 1814,[46] was moved westwards to a new course between Knighton and Whittonditch in the mid 19th century,[47] and in the 20th century has developed into a main road serving Swindon. South of the Kennet the steepness of the valley side and imparking have restricted southward egress from the parish to a single steep lane. North of the Kennet, however, the more broken relief allows many lanes to link the settlements.

There are barrows and ditches near Whittonditch, Marridge Hill, and Membury and a field system on the downs north of Axford, but archaeological discoveries and earthworks indicate no concentration of prehistoric settlement or activity in what became Ramsbury parish.[48] Membury fort on the downs, partly in

[29] Leland, *Itin.* ed. Toulmin Smith, v. 79.
[30] Below, econ. hist.
[31] Ibid.; *V.C.H. Wilts.* ii, p. 121; iv. 417–18.
[32] Leland, *Itin.* ed. Toulmin Smith, v. 79; *Survey of Lands of Wm., First Earl of Pembroke*, ed. C. R. Straton (Roxburghe Club, 1909), i. 175.
[33] *First Pembroke Survey*, ed. Straton, i. 148–79.
[34] Ibid. 163–7; P.R.O., SC 2/208/11.
[35] *First Pembroke Survey*, ed. Straton, i. 177; D. & C. Sar. Mun., press IV, box C 3/Ramsbury/9. The location is suggested by *Andrews and Dury, Map* (W.R.S. viii), pl. 15.
[36] P.R.O., SC 12/22/90; ibid. E 318/Box 7/241; *First Pembroke Survey*, ed. Straton, i. 177; map of Ramsbury, E. div., *penes* Mrs. B. Croucher, 25 Ashley Piece.
[37] P.R.O., SC 12/22/91; W.R.O. 1883/62, bargain and sale, Trenchard to White. The area of woodland in Axford and Littlecote manors can be estimated only from later evidence: below.
[38] W.R.O. 130/46/20.
[39] Ibid. 1883/95; 1650, Popham Mun., map, 1775; *Andrews and Dury, Map* (W.R.S. viii), pls. 12, 15; inf. from

Maj. F. R. D. Burdett-Fisher, Harbrook Farm; maps in Littlecote Estate Off., Littlecote Ho.
[40] *Andrews and Dury, Map* (W.R.S. viii), pls. 12, 15; O.S. Map 1″, sheet 34 (1828 edn.).
[41] *W.A.M.* xxxiii. 327.
[42] *Rep. Co. Surveyor*, 1971–2 (Wilts. co. council), 3.
[43] J. Ogilby, *Brit.* (1675), p. 20. The downland road was roughly on its present course in the early 13th cent. and the early 18th: *V.C.H. Wilts.* iv. 448; W.R.O. 1300/372, no. 7.
[44] *Andrews and Dury, Map* (W.R.S. viii), pl. 12; map of Ramsbury manor, 1676, *penes* Lady (Marjorie) Burdett-Fisher, Axford Farm: microfilm copy in W.R.O.; Axford inclosure award: W.R.O., TS. transcript in 154/2. For the park *Cal. Pat.* 1452–61, 471.
[45] *Andrews and Dury, Map* (W.R.S. viii), pl. 12; W.R.O. 154/3; O.S. Map 1″, sheet 34 (1828 edn.).
[46] *V.C.H. Wilts.* iv. 257; *L.J.* xlix. 883.
[47] O.S. Maps 1″, sheet 13 (1830 edn.), sheet 34 (1828 edn.); 6″, Wilts. XXX (1887 edn.).
[48] *V.C.H. Wilts.* i (1), 37, 98–9, 143, 188, 258, 278.

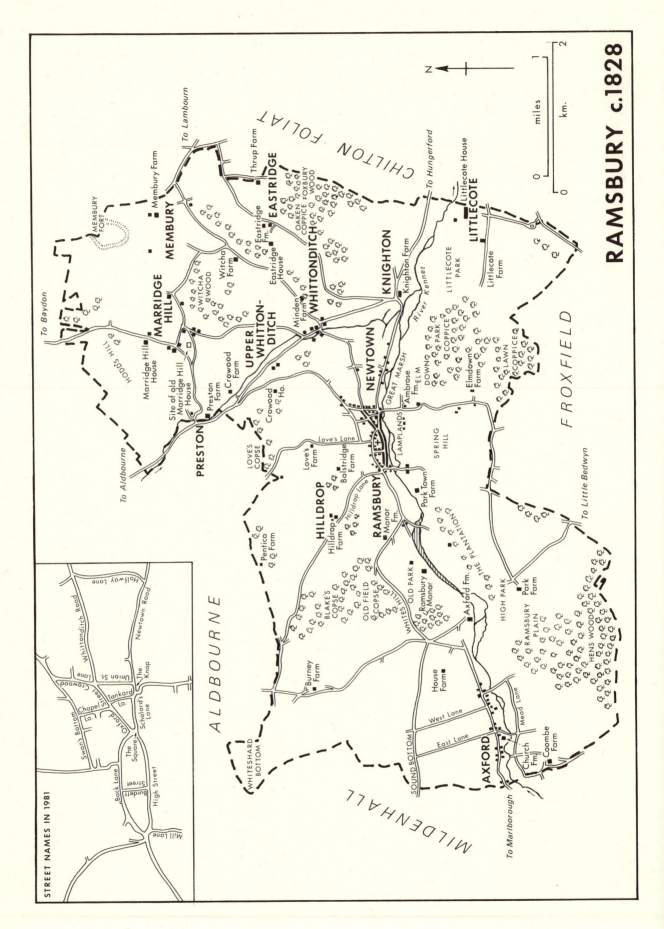

RAMSBURY c.1828

STREET NAMES IN 1981

Lambourn, was strongly fortified in the Iron Age,[49] and near Botley Copse in Ashbury (Berks., later Oxon.) there was a Roman settlement, partly in Baydon, near which Romano-British artefacts have been found in a field system north of Bailey Hill.[50] An apparently luxurious Roman villa stood near the Kennet between Knighton and Littlecote: its site was discovered c. 1728, afterwards obscured, rediscovered in 1977, and since excavated.[51]

Two downland settlements in the north part of the parish possibly preceded the many Saxon settlements of its valleys. Its site on a Roman road and, unusual for a Wiltshire village, on a ridge covered by clay-with-flints supports the suggestion that Baydon has survived as a settlement from Roman times;[52] Membury's site near an Iron-Age fort and the British element in its name suggest pre-Saxon settlement.[53] Later settlement near the Kennet was on the extensive gravel deposits north of the river where a line of seven settlements at intervals of 1 km. was strung across the parish. Ramsbury seems likely to have been the largest of them in the 11th century when its name was that of a 90-hide estate,[54] and has remained so; Axford, the westernmost, may for long have rivalled Baydon as the second largest village of the parish;[55] and between Ramsbury and Axford were the hamlet called Park Town, a palace of the bishop of Salisbury, afterwards Ramsbury Manor, and the farmstead and manor house of Axford manor. East of Ramsbury, Knighton and Thrup were hamlets whose names suggest Saxon origins.[56] Thrup was called East Thrup to distinguish it from Hilldrop or West Thrup in the Middle Ages when it presumably stood beside the Kennet near the boundary with Chilton Foliat.[57] Also near the boundary with Chilton Foliat the manor house and farmstead of Littlecote were built south of the river. A further four settlements, Whittonditch, Upper Whittonditch,[58] near which Crowood House stands, Preston, and Ford, grew at intervals of 1 km. in the tributary valley between Knighton and Aldbourne, apparently decreasing in size up the valley. Other small valley settlements developed in the 19th century near Witcha Farm north-east of Whittonditch, as a hamlet called Burney or Upper Axford around Burney Farm north of Axford,[59] and at Gore Lane north of Bailey Hill. The only downland settlement likely to be of Saxon origin is Hilldrop whose name suggests it.[60] There were hamlets on the downs at both Marridge Hill and Eastridge, apparently in

the 16th century when farms were based there,[61] and presumably much earlier. Elsewhere on the downs farmsteads including, north of the Kennet, Bailey Hill Farm, Thrup Farm, and House Farm near Axford, and, south of the Kennet, Park Farm, Darrell's Farm on the border with Froxfield, Elmdown Farm, and Littlecote Park Farm, were built in different periods, apparently following inclosure, changes in land use, or the adoption of new methods of farming.

So large a parish containing so many settlements was, as might be expected, populous and wealthy, notably so beside the Kennet, but in the early 14th century perhaps not remarkably so for its size. There were 413 or 431 poll-tax payers in 1377.[62] In 1773 there was a total of 456 men living in five of the six tithings:[63] those in the sixth and least populous, Park Town, may have been counted with the men of Ramsbury. Almost certainly more than 300 men were living in the settlements beside the Kennet.[64] In 1801 the populations of Ramsbury and Baydon parishes totalled 2,253 of whom 1,963 lived in Ramsbury parish.[65] The population of Ramsbury parish had risen to a peak of 2,696 by 1851. It had fallen to 2,164 by 1891 and, with only slight fluctuations, to 1,504 by 1921 and 1,390 by 1971.[66] In 1981 its concentration in Ramsbury village was clearly even greater than it had been in 1773.[67]

Although Ramsbury developed on the gravel near the Kennet, apart from mills at its east and west ends there has been no building beside the river. A leat carrying water to the meadows between the mills has long been a clear southern boundary.[68] High Street, in which a Saxon iron foundry has been discovered,[69] and the church presumably mark the site of earliest settlement. If the bishops of Ramsbury had a house near their cathedral in the 11th century it may have been in the village rather than on the site 2 km. east on which the bishops of Salisbury had a palace. The medieval street names Castle Wall,[70] afterwards Whitehouse Lane and Burdett Street,[71] and Old Garden, later Old Orchard and Free Orchard,[72] and the shape of the village, in which the church and vicarage house are within an ellipse, formed by High Street and Back Lane and crossed by Burdett Street, and most settlement is on the periphery, may be evidence of such a house. The names and the shape, however, could be attributed to factors other than the existence of a large house. The straightness of the middle part of High Street, the long narrow plots on its south side,[73] and several 15th-century references to

[49] V.C.H. Wilts. i (1), 269; W.A.M. xxvii. 110-11.
[50] V.C.H. Wilts. i (1), 37, 273.
[51] W.A.M. xli. 426; Wilts. Cuttings, xxviii. 255, 274-5; V.C.H. Wilts. i (2), 453; S.R.O., DD/POt 165, letter from Hartford; inf. from Mr. D. S. Wills, Littlecote Ho. The site is incorrectly marked on O.S. Map 1/50,000, sheet 174 (1974 edn.).
[52] W.A.M. lxi. 35.
[53] V.C.H. Wilts. i (2), 482.
[54] Ibid. ii, p. 121.
[55] Cf. ibid. iv. 340, 356; First Pembroke Survey, ed. Straton, i. 163-73.
[56] V.C.H. Wilts. ii, p. 81; E. Ekwall, Dict. Eng. P.N. 468; below.
[57] Cat. Anct. D. i, C 536; P.R.O., E 40/14748.
[58] O.S. Map 1", sheet 34 (1828 edn.).
[59] Ibid.; 6", Wilts. XXIX (1889 edn.).

[60] P.N. Wilts. (E.P.N.S.), 288.
[61] P.R.O., SC 12/22/90; ibid. E 318/Box 7/241.
[62] V.C.H. Wilts. iv. 301, 310. Eighteen taxpayers attributed to Preshute may have been of Preston.
[63] Approximate tithing boundaries are marked on the map of Ramsbury hund.: above, p. 2.
[64] W.R.O. 1883/3; 1883/14, list of residents.
[65] V.C.H. Wilts. iv. 340, 356.
[66] Ibid. 356; Census, 1961, 1971.
[67] Andrews and Dury, Map (W.R.S. viii), pl. 12.
[68] W.R.O. 154/3 (1778).
[69] Wilts. Cuttings, xxvii. 242-3.
[70] Cat. Anct. D. vi, C 6755.
[71] W.R.O. 154/3.
[72] Cat. Anct. D. iii, C 3292; vi, C 5946; W.R.O., bishop, Liber Niger, ff. 99v.-100.
[73] W.R.O. 154/3.

burgages[74] may be evidence of a planned expansion of the village. It is more likely, however, that it grew naturally east and west from its origin near the church along a street which followed the line of the river and may have been a market street from the early 13th century or before.[75] Ramsbury had grown eastwards from High Street by the early 14th century when Oxford Street, its north-east continuation, was so called.[76] Oxford Street had been built up by the mid 15th century. Burgages and shops then gave Ramsbury characteristics of a small town.[77] Its urban appearance may have been enhanced by the fact that, possibly because there was little agriculture south of the Kennet, and because settlement was dispersed north of it, there have been few farmsteads in it.[78] The junction of High Street and Oxford Street and Back Lane and Scholard's Lane formed a small square.[79]

The village continued to grow eastwards. Tankard Lane and Blind Lane, later Union Street, had been built up by the 18th century.[80] In 1778 there were several buildings beside and south of Scholard's Lane and in Crowood Lane. There were also houses east of the village at Newtown, so called in 1781.[81] In the later 19th century Crowood Lane, then called Andrews Lane, and Union Street still clearly marked the eastern edge of the village,[82] but in the 20th century 27 pairs of council houses and other houses and bungalows in Whittonditch Road, and 83 private houses in Ashley Piece and the Paddocks north and south of Whittonditch Road, have been built further east. North of Oxford Street council houses in Chapel Lane and private houses in Swan's Bottom, and north of Back Lane private houses in Orchard Close, are also 20th-century.

In contrast with its eastern end, the village's west end has not grown beyond High Street, possibly because the owners of Ramsbury Manor and park, the palings of which may have reached the village in the Middle Ages,[83] encouraged growth eastwards. There were houses in Mill Lane and at the west end of Back Lane in the 17th century, and in the 18th century Bodorgan House, afterwards Ramsbury Hill, and cottages north of the church stood on the south side of Back Lane near the house later called Parliament Piece.[84] North of Back Lane at its west end estates of some 70 council dwellings in Knowledge Crescent and Hilldrop Close have been built in the 20th century.

Street names in Ramsbury which have survived from the Middle Ages are High Street, Oxford Street, and Crows, later Crowood, Lane. Those lost include Castle Street, Free Orchard, Nolbit Street, and Cock's Lane.[85] Back Lane was first so called in 1663, Tankard Lane in 1677,[86] Mill Lane in 1724,[87] and Blind Lane in 1762.[88]

There were presumably coaching inns in Ramsbury in the 17th century.[89] By the mid 18th century the Bell and the Bleeding Horse had been established at the east and west junctions of High Street and Back Lane.[90] The Angel, in High Street, the Castle, later the Windsor Castle, in the Square, and the Swan were also inns in the 18th century.[91] The Burdett Arms and the Malt Shovel, both in High Street, were so called in the early 19th century:[92] the Crown, at the junction of Crowood Lane and Whittonditch Road, was so called in 1878, the Crown and Anchor afterwards.[93] Of those inns only the Angel and the Swan, which may have been succeeded by the Burdett Arms and the Malt Shovel, were not among the seven open in 1880, the eight in 1939.[94] The Halfway at the junction of Halfway Lane and Whittonditch Road and the Boot in Scholard's Lane had been opened respectively by 1839 and 1892.[95] The Burdett Arms, the Malt Shovel, the Bell, and the Crown and Anchor were open in 1981.

West of Ramsbury the bishops of Salisbury had in the 13th century or earlier a park and a palace[96] and there was a hamlet or village called Park Town. The bishop presumably had staff permanently resident in the palace. Some bishops possibly used the palace more than others but there is no evidence of neglect, and in the later 15th century and the earlier 16th the bishops spent much time there.[97] The household numbered over 100, including 12 grooms and 27 servants, c. 1523,[98] presumably as many as 300 including wives and children. Later owners of Ramsbury Manor may have had smaller households, but the successive houses on the site of the bishop's palace remained appreciable centres of population until the 19th century: there were 29 occupants in 1851.[99] Park Town, mentioned as a hamlet or village in the 1290s,[1] was beside the Kennet. In the Middle Ages and the 16th century a mill in the park, farmsteads, and cottages were said to stand at Park Town. One of the buildings, which were possibly neither numerous nor closely grouped, was near the eastern outer gate of the manor house.[2] Later the name Park Town

[74] e.g. W.R.O., bishop, Liber Niger, ff. 99–100.
[75] Below, econ. hist.
[76] D. & C. Sar. Mun., press I, box 8, no. 12A.
[77] W.R.O., bishop, Liber Niger, ff. 99v.–100.
[78] Ibid. 154/3; *Andrews and Dury, Map* (W.R.S. viii), pls. 12, 15; below, econ. hist.
[79] See plate facing p. 48.
[80] W.R.O. 1883/59, deed poll of Harris; 154/3.
[81] Ibid. 154/3; 1883/169, lease, Jones to Orchard.
[82] O.S. Map 6″, Wilts. XXX (1887 edn.).
[83] *Cat. Anct. D.* vi, C 6194.
[84] P.R.O., CP 43/796, rott. 165–6.
[85] Ibid. C 146/9336; W.R.O., bishop, Liber Niger, ff. 99v.–100.
[86] W.R.O. 1883/93A–B, deeds, Freeman and Deighton, Freeman and Harris.
[87] Ibid. 130/46/26.
[88] Ibid. 732/3.
[89] Ogilby, *Brit.* pl. 10.
[90] W.R.O. 1883/1, cts. held 13 Apr. 1753, 10 Oct. 1758.
[91] Ibid. 732/1, lease, Tatt to Dismore; 154/2–3; map of Ramsbury, W. div., *penes* Mrs. Croucher.
[92] Pigot, *Nat. Com. Dir.* (1830), 809½.
[93] O.S. Map 6″, Wilts. XXX (1887 edn.); *Kelly's Dir. Wilts.* (1880).
[94] *Kelly's Dir. Wilts.* (1880, 1939).
[95] Map of Ramsbury, E. div., *penes* Mrs. Croucher; W.R.O. 1883, rental; inf. from Mr. C. E. Blunt, Ramsbury Hill.
[96] *Reg. Ghent* (Cant. & York Soc.), i–ii, *passim*.
[97] *W.A.M.* xxv. 173.
[98] *L. & P. Hen. VIII*, iii (2), p. 1490; P.R.O., E 179/197/161.
[99] P.R.O., HO 107/1686.
[1] D. & C. Sar. Mun., press IV, box C 3/Ramsbury/13.
[2] Ibid.; B.L. Add. Ch. 54988; W.R.O., bishop, Liber Niger, f. 95v.; ibid. Ch. Com., bpric. 460, f. 42 and v.

was apparently applied to the hamlet consisting of Hales Court Farm and of those buildings in the park which in 1676 stood some 300 m. east of Ramsbury manor house near the junction of the drive of the house and the road round the park. Hales Court Farm was beside the Kennet and apparently outside the eastern boundary of the park.[3] In 1773 only Hales Court Farm, possibly a mill near it, and the mill in the park were standing. Buildings then north-east of Ramsbury Manor may have included a farmstead or the house called the Lodge in 1681.[4] About 1775 the mill or mills and Hales Court Farm were demolished when an ornamental lake was formed with water from the Kennet, and the farmstead or the Lodge was apparently demolished when the park was extended eastwards and northwards. A new farmstead incorporating Manor Farm, a house with an octagonal centre and short wings, was built beside the new road round the park.[5] A farmstead called Park Town Farm, later Harbrook Farm, has stood on the south bank of the Kennet between Ramsbury Manor and Ramsbury since the later 17th century. West of it three pairs of houses called New Cottages were built between 1958 and 1964 for employees of the owner of Ramsbury Manor.[6] South-west of them Manor Cottage is a small house of flint and thatch possibly built in the late 18th century. East of Harbrook Farm are two thatched cottages of the late 18th and early 19th centuries.

South of the Kennet in Ramsbury and Park Town tithings, Ambrose Farm, an early 19th-century farmhouse, is on the site of a farmstead which seems to have originated in the Middle Ages.[7] Several cottages west of it at Lamplands were built in the mid 19th century.[8] On the downs Elmdown Farm may have been the only farmstead in the 16th century.[9] A farmstead, later called Park Farm, had been established in the parkland by the late 17th century.[10] In the Second World War the flat land between those two downland farmsteads was used as an airfield, before 1943 as a satellite station of R.A.F. Andover (Hants) and from 1943 by No. 11 Troop Carrier Command of the United States Air Force. Hangars and a camp were built at its south-east corner and east of the Ramsbury–Froxfield lane and in Froxfield. After the war the airfield was used for short periods by Transport Command and Fighter Command of the R.A.F., became a sub-station of R.A.F. Yatesbury, and was disposed of by the state in 1955. In 1981 most of the runways survived but by then most of the buildings had been removed.[11] Bridge Farm, incorporating some of the buildings, and Darrell's Farm, partly in Froxfield, have been built near what was the south-east perimeter of the airfield.

In 1773 there were 246 men living in Rams-

bury and, apparently, Park Town.[12] There was a population of 1,759 in 1841.[13]

Red brick was used in three of the largest houses to survive in the parish, Littlecote House, Ramsbury Manor, and Parliament Piece, as facing or as the main walling, in the later 16th century and the 17th:[14] in the 18th century red brick superseded timber framing in nearly all new building. Red brick has remained the predominant building material, but in the smaller houses was often used in bands or as dressings with flints. Timber-framed and thatched cottages of the 17th century survive at the west ends of High Street and Back Lane, in Burdett Street, and in Oxford Street, and there are a few houses with apparently 17th-century origins, some timber-framed, in Mill Lane, Scholard's Lane, Newtown Road, and Whittonditch Road. The Bleeding Horse, which has east and west extensions, may also be 17th-century. It is not clear where a serious fire in 1648 was most destructive.[15]

The main block of Ramsbury Hill in Back Lane was built in the early 18th century, possibly incorporating part of an older building in its north-east corner, and a new south-east block was added in the 19th century: an early 18th-century staircase and fittings and decorations resulting from early 19th-century alterations remain in the house. The Cedars in Scholard's Lane was built in the 18th century and enlarged in the 19th, and Kennet House on the south side of High Street is an 18th-century house refronted c. 1830. Apart from those houses and the Old Mill the largest houses in Ramsbury were built in the earlier 20th century, particularly north of Newtown Road and south of Whittonditch Road.

Most 18th-century buildings to survive are houses and cottages of red brick, with which blue brick and flint were often used, in High Street. Thatched cottages of that period, of brick, sometimes perhaps encasing timber frames, and flint, are in Oxford Street and Union Street at its junction with the Knapp and Newtown Road. There is an 18th-century house with later additions in Chapel Lane, and an 18th-century house and Knapp House, built c. 1800, stand in the Knapp. Fire is said to have destroyed 40 dwellings in 1781. Several cottages north of the church in Back Lane were among them and were not replaced.[16] Few new sites were used for building in the 19th century and most of the many 19th-century cottages and small houses in the village are replacements of earlier buildings, especially in High Street, the Square, and Oxford Street, some perhaps successors to houses or cottages burnt in 1781.[17] The Malt Shovel and the Bell are 18th-century, the Burdett Arms and the Crown and Anchor are 19th-century: all except the Malt

[3] W.R.O., microfilm copy of map, 1676; *Andrews and Dury, Map* (W.R.S. viii), pl. 12.
[4] *Andrews and Dury, Map* (W.R.S. viii), pl. 12; W.R.O. 1883/60, lease, Jones to Hillman.
[5] W.R.O. 154/2–3; O.S. Map 6″, Wilts. XXIX (1889 edn.).
[6] Local inf.
[7] W.R.O., bishop, Liber Niger, f. 99; below, manors.
[8] O.S. Maps 1″, sheet 34 (1828 edn.); 6″, Wilts. XXX (1887 edn.); map of Ramsbury, W. div., *penes* Mrs. Croucher.

[9] *First Pembroke Survey*, ed. Straton, i. 150.
[10] Below, manors.
[11] Inf. from Air Hist. Branch, Lond.; local inf.
[12] W.R.O. 1883/14, list of residents.
[13] *V.C.H. Wilts.* iv. 356.
[14] Below, manors.
[15] *W. Circuit Ass. Orders* (Camd. 4th ser. xvii), p. 285.
[16] Wilts. Cuttings, iii. 23; P.R.O., CP 43/796, rott. 165–6.
[17] W.R.O. 154/3; O.S. Map 6″, Wilts. XXX (1887 edn.); personal observation.

Shovel have been much altered in the 20th century. A gabled house of *c.* 1900 stands in the Square and an earlier 19th-century flint cottage with brick dressings in Tudor style in Crowood Lane. While the village expanded eastwards and northwards in the 20th century there has also been new building in the older parts. In High Street 29 council houses and old people's homes were built in 1952 and the 1970s, and 20th-century houses and bungalows have replaced earlier buildings and are on new sites in Back Lane, Tankard Lane, Crowood Lane, and elsewhere.

Ramsbury Building Society was started as the Provident Union Building & Investment Society in 1846. It took its present name in 1928. In 1976 it had assets of £50 million and fifteen branch offices in Wiltshire, Berkshire, Dorset, and Hampshire, in 1981 assets of over £100 million and 26 branch offices.[18] Its headquarters were moved to Marlborough in 1982.[19] Until then they had been in Ramsbury in houses on the south side of the Square. The 'great tree' at Ramsbury growing in 1751 is presumably the wych-elm in the Square in 1981[20] which the society adopted as a symbol at its incorporation in 1893.[21]

None of the settlements beside the Kennet east of Ramsbury has been large. At Knighton, where the river was crossed by Deep bridge in the Middle Ages,[22] there may then have been several small farmsteads, but from the 16th century apparently only Knighton Farm.[23] The farmhouse was replaced in the mid 19th century and west of the new house a pair of cottages was built. There were extensive farm buildings there in the late 19th century:[24] none older than the 19th century, they survived, but not in use, in 1981. South of the Kennet, Littlecote House and the buildings associated with it, some in Chilton Foliat, have long been the only dwellings. There were 20 in the household of Littlecote House in 1523:[25] the house remained a small centre of employment in the later 20th century when it was open to the public. South of it Littlecote Park Farm, of banded flint and brick, replaced a farmstead nearer the house between 1839 and 1878.[26] Nothing remains to mark the medieval site of the manor house and hamlet of Thrup which may have been near the river and the boundary with Chilton Foliat.[27] Thrup Farm had been built on the downs possibly by 1712, certainly by 1773:[28] in 1981 the only one of its buildings to remain was a derelict 19th-century barn.

Whittonditch was clearly not a large village in the Middle Ages.[29] It was apparently a village of medium sized farmsteads in the 16th century,[30] and may not have been closely grouped. Its nucleus was beside the stream at the junction of Whittonditch Road and the Knighton–Aldbourne road,[31] where a pair of 18th-century thatched cottages are the oldest buildings to survive. Nearby is a 19th-century thatched house and farm buildings and other houses of the 19th and 20th centuries. In the late 18th century Whittonditch House was built north of the junction. Upper Whittonditch, formerly Minden, Farm is north-east of the junction, beside the Whittonditch–Membury lane. Witcha Farm, further north, is an 18th-century farmhouse with modern farm buildings and an older timber-framed granary. Near it in the later 19th century were several cottages and a nonconformist chapel which survive.[32] Farm buildings, a house, and a bungalow were built west of the Whittonditch–Membury lane in the mid 20th century. In the late 18th century a hamlet called Upper Whittonditch was east of Crowood House,[33] the name of which may echo Ramsbury (possibly Raven's *burg*).[34] The hamlet was no more than a farmstead in the early 19th century. The 19th-century farmhouse had become the Fox and Hounds inn by the late 19th century. The farm buildings have been replaced in the 20th century and the farmhouse has been altered to become two cottages. Farm buildings stood further north in the early 19th century: near them Crowood Farm was built in the mid 19th century and extended in the 20th century.[35] A second farmhouse was built in the mid 20th century. Most of the farm buildings are also 20th-century. Preston in 1377 may have had eighteen poll-tax payers: it was clearly a hamlet of small farmsteads in the Middle Ages and was possibly so in the 16th century.[36] It remained a hamlet, partly in Aldbourne, in the 20th century. In 1981 Preston Farm and a pair of 18th-century cottages of brick, flint, and thatch and a similar barn were the only buildings there in Ramsbury parish. No more than eighteen men lived in Whittonditch tithing, at Whittonditch, Upper Whittonditch, and Preston, in 1773.[37] In 1841 there were 135 inhabitants.[38]

The hamlet near Eastridge Farm was called Eastridge in 1773:[39] extensive 19th- and 20th-century farm buildings, a pair of 19th-century cottages, and a pair of 20th-century cottages were there in 1981. Eastridge House was built west of it. In the Middle Ages a castle and a manor house, remains of which have been excavated, stood at

---

[18] *First Fifty Million* (Ramsbury Bldg. Soc. 1977); inf. from Mr. A. F. Farmer, General Manager and Secretary, Ramsbury Bldg. Soc.

[19] *Wilts. Gaz.* 15 Apr. 1982.

[20] W.R.O. 212A/27/27, fines for renewing estates; see plate facing p. 48.

[21] Inf. from Dr. R. J. Phillips, Lichfield, Moreton-on-Lugg, Herefs.

[22] P.R.O., JUST 1/1006, rot. 42d.; W.R.O., bishop, Liber Niger, f. 99v.

[23] *Cat. Anct. D.* ii, C 2467; vi, C 7492.

[24] O.S. Map 6″, Wilts. XXX (1887 edn.); W.R.O. 1650, Popham Mun., mem. 1892.

[25] *L. & P. Hen. VIII*, iii (2), p. 1490.

[26] Map of Ramsbury, E. div., *penes* Mrs. Croucher; O.S. Map 6″, Wilts. XXX (1887 edn.).

[27] P.R.O., E 40/14748.

[28] W.R.O. 1883/69/3; *Andrews and Dury, Map* (W.R.S. viii), pl. 15.

[29] e.g. *V.C.H. Wilts.* iv. 310.

[30] Wilton Ho. Mun., survey, 1550s, pp. 288–91.

[31] *Andrews and Dury, Map* (W.R.S. viii), pls. 12, 15.

[32] O.S. Map 6″, Wilts. XXIV (1887 edn.).

[33] *Andrews and Dury, Map* (W.R.S. viii), pl. 15.

[34] Ekwall, *Dict. Eng. P.N.* 380.

[35] Map of Ramsbury, E. div., *penes* Mrs. Croucher; O.S. Maps 1″, sheet 34 (1828 edn.); 6″, Wilts. XXX (1887 edn.).

[36] Above, n. 62; D. & C. Sar. Mun., press I, box 8, no. 12B; P.R.O., SC 12/22/90.

[37] W.R.O. 1883/3.

[38] *V.C.H. Wilts.* iv. 356.

[39] *Andrews and Dury, Map* (W.R.S. viii), pl. 15.

Membury south of Membury fort.[40] Their site may have been deserted in the late 13th century.[41] There was a chapel,[42] and possibly a hamlet,[43] at Membury in the Middle Ages. From the 16th century or earlier there was almost certainly no more than a single farmstead,[44] presumably near the site of the present manor house. In 1773 there were several buildings at Membury south of the road leading north-east from Witcha Farm.[45] In the 19th century one was the Bottle and Glass inn:[46] none survives. Nine Oaks Farm west of Membury had been built by 1830:[47] a barn remains on the site. Farmsteads said to be at Marridge in the 15th and 16th centuries may have been at Marridge Hill, which has been so named from the 17th century or earlier and was a hamlet in 1773.[48] Baydon Manor, formerly Marridge Hill House, was built there, and all the buildings standing in 1773 have been replaced. A pair of estate cottages in Tudor style was built in the early 20th century. A second pair of cottages, a bungalow, and extensive farm buildings on both sides of the Marridge Hill to Baydon lane have since been built, and a small 19th-century house, possibly converted from farm buildings, survives. South of Marridge Hill an earlier Marridge Hill House was built, and north-west and south-east of it there were farmsteads in 1773 and 1839.[49] The north-western farmstead was replaced by Marridge Hill Farm, a small 19th-century house with 20th-century farm buildings, near which is another 19th-century house. Nothing remains of the south-eastern farmstead, but east of its site Balak Farm is a late 19th-century cottage with 20th-century extensions. In Eastridge tithing, which included Membury, Knighton, Littlecote, and possibly Marridge Hill there were 49 men in 1773: the population was 173 in 1841.[50]

In the late 13th century Hilldrop, sometimes West Thrup, was described as a hamlet.[51] There is no evidence that it ever comprised more than a manor house, in which there was a household of fourteen in 1523,[52] and a farmstead. The manor house may not have survived the 17th century. It was replaced much later by Hilldrop Farm, west of which is a small house partly of the 17th century and south of which are extensive 19th- and 20th-century farm buildings. Love's Farm north-east of Hilldrop is possibly on the site of a farmstead so called from the 13th century.[53] Bolstridge Farm stood east of Hilldrop in the 19th century.[54] North of Hilldrop, Pentico Farm,

near the boundary with Aldbourne, and buildings called Staples and Lattimore were standing in 1773.[55] Pentico Farm was demolished in the mid 20th century.[56] Of the others none in Ramsbury was standing in 1981.

MANORS AND OTHER ESTATES. It is very likely that Ramsbury belonged to the bishops of Ramsbury in the 10th and 11th centuries, and that their successors kept it after the see was moved to Salisbury between 1075 and 1078.[57] The bishop of Salisbury held Ramsbury in 1086, when five burgesses of Cricklade were attached to it,[58] and the manor of *RAMSBURY* passed with the see. The manor and parish were conterminous. Several freeholds, possibly originating in the total of 22 hides held by Otbold, Herbert, and Quintin in 1086, became or were reputed manors, but the bishops kept demesne and customary lands in all parts of the parish.[59] Their lands in Baydon and Axford were frequently named in the title of the manor, as if there was a single manor called Ramsbury, Baydon, and Axford, but were sometimes referred to as if there were three separate manors.[60] In 1545, under an Act of exchange, Bishop Salcot granted the manor to Edward Seymour, earl of Hertford, protector of the realm 1547-9, and from 1547 duke of Somerset.[61] After Seymour's execution and attainder in 1552 it was granted to William Herbert, earl of Pembroke.[62] It passed with the earldom of Pembroke to Philip, earl of Pembroke and Montgomery, who in 1676-7 sold it to the lawyer and politician Henry Powle.[63] Powle, who borrowed the money to buy it on the security of his manors of Williamstrip, in Coln St. Aldwyns, and Quenington (both Glos.), was apparently speculating. Named in the conveyances with the lenders' trustees, between 1677 and 1681 he sold nearly all the leaseholds and most of the copyholds, in most cases to the tenants, and in 1681 sold those remaining and the manor house and the parks and woods around it to Sir William Jones (d. 1682), attorney-general 1675-9.[64] Jones was succeeded by his son Richard (d.s.p. a minor in 1685) and by his brother Samuel (d. 1686) whose heir was his son Richard.[65] In 1736 Richard was succeeded by his brother William (d. 1753) whose heir was his son William (of age in 1764, d. 1766).[66] That William was succeeded by his sister Elizabeth, wife of William Langham (d. 1791) who assumed the additional name

[40] *V.C.H. Wilts.* i (1), 269; Pevsner, *Wilts.* (2nd edn.), 345.
[41] Below, manors.
[42] *Reg. Martival* (Cant. & York Soc.), i. 304.
[43] *Cal. Pat.* 1429-36, 320.
[44] *First Pembroke Survey*, ed. Straton, i. 158-9.
[45] *Andrews and Dury, Map* (W.R.S. viii), pl. 15.
[46] O.S. Maps 1″, sheet 13 (1830 edn.); 6″, Wilts. XXIV (1887 edn.).
[47] O.S. Map 1″, sheet 13 (1830 edn.).
[48] W.R.O., bishop, Liber Niger, f. 100v.; P.R.O., SC 12/22/90; ibid. STAC 8/213/11; *Andrews and Dury, Map* (W.R.S. viii), pl. 15.
[49] *Andrews and Dury, Map* (W.R.S. viii), pl. 15; map of Ramsbury, E. div., *penes* Mrs. Croucher.
[50] W.R.O. 1883/3; *V.C.H. Wilts.* iv. 356.
[51] Deed *penes* Mr. C. E. Eliot-Cohen, Hilldrop Farm; *Rot. Hund.* (Rec. Com.), ii (1), 265.
[52] *L. & P. Hen. VIII*, iii (2), p. 1490.
[53] Below, manors.
[54] O.S. Maps 1″, sheet 34 (1828 edn.); 6″, Wilts. XXX (1887 edn.).
[55] *Andrews and Dury, Map* (W.R.S. viii), pl. 15.
[56] Cf. O.S. Maps 1/25,000, 41/27 (1948 edn.); 1/50,000, sheet 174 (1974 edn.).
[57] *V.C.H. Wilts.* ii, pp. 20-1, 27-30; v. 45.
[58] Ibid. ii, p. 121.
[59] Ibid.; *First Pembroke Survey*, ed. Straton, i. 148-78.
[60] Below, Axford, manors; Baydon, manor.
[61] *L. & P. Hen. VIII*, xx (2), p. 411; W.R.O. 1883/59, copy of Act; *Complete Peerage*.
[62] *Cal. Pat.* 1550-3, 358.
[63] *Complete Peerage*; W.R.O. 212B/5656; *D.N.B.*
[64] W.R.O. 212B/5656; 1883/59, bargain and sale, Pembroke to Whitley and Cratford; bargain and sale, Powle to Jones; articles, Powle and Jones; *D.N.B.*
[65] W.R.O. 1003/1; *V.C.H. Berks.* iv. 160.
[66] *Musgrave's Obit.* (Harl. Soc. xlvi), 341, 343; Wilts. Cuttings, xxvi. 110.

Jones and in 1774 was created a baronet.[67] After Lady Jones's death in 1800[68] Ramsbury manor passed to her nephew Sir Francis Burdett, Bt. (d. 1844), and afterwards to Sir Francis's son Sir Robert. In 1880 Sir Robert was succeeded by his cousin Sir Francis Burdett, Bt. (d. 1892), whose heir was his son Sir Francis.[69] In the 18th, 19th, and 20th centuries the Joneses and Burdetts recovered by purchase some of the lands sold 1677–81, especially of those at Axford and Ramsbury.[70] In 1880 Ramsbury manor was a compact estate of c. 4,000 a. encompassing nearly all the west part of the parish and including little land in the east and north.[71] From between 1939 and 1943 until after 1945 c. 400 a. south and south-west of Spring Hill were held by the state for Ramsbury airfield,[72] and in 1944 Hens Wood, 333 a., was leased to the Forestry Commission for 999 years.[73] After the death in 1951 of Sir Francis Burdett[74] the airfield land, Park farm, nearly all of Park Town farm,[75] and Ramsbury Manor and c. 350 a. around it were bought by Seymour William Arthur John Egerton, earl of Wilton. In 1958 Lord Wilton sold the manor house and its surrounding land to Sir William Rootes (Baron Rootes from 1959, d. 1964):[76] they were sold in 1964–5 to Mr. H. J. Hyams, the owner in 1981.[77] Hilldrop farm, which had belonged to Sir Francis Burdett (d. 1951), was sold in 1957.[78] The remainder of Burdett's estate passed to his stepdaughter Marjorie Frances, wife of Sir Bertie Drew Fisher (Burdett-Fisher from 1952, d. 1972), who with her son Maj. F. R. D. Burdett-Fisher owned c. 2,200 a. in the west part of the parish, mainly at Axford, in 1981.[79]

Ramsbury throughout the Middle Ages was one of the bishop of Salisbury's principal and, especially in the later 15th century and the early 16th, most often lived in palaces.[80] The house stood beside the Kennet in a park which has been extended more than once.[81] The bishops had at the house a chapel dedicated to the Virgin and a cloister was mentioned in 1320.[82] Licences were granted to crenellate in 1337 and to wall and crenellate in 1377.[83] Leland described the house c. 1540 as 'fair' and 'old'.[84] Between 1552 and 1567 William, earl of Pembroke, spent over £2,000 on building work at the site. His house had a main symmetrical east front of two storeys with attics and nine gables. In 1676 it was at the centre of a series of enclosures bounded by high walls and covering 6 a.: it was approached from

the north-east along a formal avenue. The plan of the house was nearly a square of 60 m., but it included three irregularly placed internal courts possibly vestiges of the bishops' palace, parts of which may have been incorporated in the house. There was a cupola over or behind the central gable in 1676.[85] In the 16th century the earls may have used the house as much as they used Wilton, but as Wilton's importance grew in the 17th century Ramsbury's declined.[86] In 1644 the house was said to be a 'fair square stone house . . . though not comparable to Wilton'. It was some-times lived in by Mary, dowager countess of Pembroke (d. 1650), and Anne, Baroness Clifford, wife of Philip, earl of Pembroke and Montgomery (d. 1650).[87] It was leased to Charles Dormer, earl of Carnarvon (d. 1709), the grand-son of Philip, earl of Pembroke and Montgomery (d. 1650), and afterwards to John Seymour, duke of Somerset (d. 1675).[88] A new house, Ramsbury Manor, was begun for Sir William Jones c. 1681 on the site of the old.[89]

Ramsbury Manor is of brick with dressings of stone and decoration of carved and painted wood. It has a symmetrical double-pile plan, nine bays by six, and two storeys with attics and basements. The architect was almost certainly Robert Hooke.[90] If, as is likely, building began in 1681, it may not have been far advanced when Jones died in 1682. Jones directed his executors to complete the house:[91] rainwater heads bear the date 1683 and there are many fittings of the 1680s inside the house. Some of the rooms were then finished to a high standard, but it is doubtful whether all were. The rooms which retain their 17th-century panelling include the entrance hall, in the middle of the east side, the dining room, and the saloon, which is panelled with oak and has carved mouldings, an enriched overmantel attributed to Grinling Gibbons,[92] and painted panels above the doorways. The secondary staircase is in the middle of the south side and runs from basement to attics. The principal staircase, in the middle of the north side, served only the two main floors and has not survived. No 17th-century ceiling remains in the house. The basement, which at its south end is at ground level, has a brick-vaulted room below the hall. There and in the central corridor of the basement are stone architraves which, like the early 17th-century panelling reset at the bottom of the south staircase, seem to have been re-used from the earlier building.

[67] Burke, *Ext. & Dorm. Baronetcies* (1844), 284.
[68] W.R.O. 500/7.
[69] Burke, *Peerage* (1949), 299.
[70] Below; below, Axford, manors.
[71] W.R.O. 1883, rent bk.
[72] Inf. from Maj. F. R. D. Burdett-Fisher, Harbrook Farm; Defence Land Agent, Durrington.
[73] Inf. from Forestry Com., Flowers Hill, Brislington, Bristol.
[74] *Who Was Who*, 1951–60, 157.
[75] For their descents: below.
[76] Inf. from Maj. Burdett-Fisher; *Country Life*, 21 Dec. 1961; Wilts. Cuttings, xxii. 312; *Who Was Who*, 1961–70, 975–6.
[77] Inf. from Mr. H. J. Hyams, Ramsbury Manor.
[78] Below.
[79] Inf. from Maj. Burdett-Fisher.
[80] *Reg. Ghent* (Cant. & York Soc.), i–ii, *passim*; *Reg. Martival* (Cant. & York Soc.), i–iv, *passim*; *W.A.M.* xxv. 173.
[81] Below, econ. hist.

[82] *Reg. Ghent* (Cant. & York Soc.), ii. 657; *W.A.M.* xliv. 389; *Reg. Martival* (Cant. & York Soc.), iii, p. 68.
[83] *Cal. Pat.* 1334–8, 498; 1377–81, 9.
[84] Leland, *Itin.* ed. Toulmin Smith, v. 79.
[85] *First Pembroke Survey*, ed. Straton, i. 148 (which shows a ho. of 5 bays), 174; W.R.O. 84/47, partic. of Ramsbury manor; map of Ramsbury manor *penes* Lady (Marjorie) Burdett-Fisher, Axford Farm: microfilm copy in W.R.O. (which shows a ho. of 9 bays).
[86] e.g. Hist. MSS. Com. 77, *L'Isle*, ii, pp. 400, 419, 425, 435, 472–3; cf. *V.C.H. Wilts.* vi. 6.
[87] *Complete Peerage*, x. 414; *W.A.M.* xviii. 98; *Diary of Ric. Symonds* (Camd. Soc. [1st ser.], lxxiv), 153.
[88] W.R.O. 84/47, partic. of Ramsbury manor; *Complete Peerage*, s.vv. Carnarvon, Somerset.
[89] *Country Life*, 23 Jan. 1975; W.R.O., microfilm copy of map, 1676.
[90] *Country Life*, 23 Jan. 1975; see below, plates facing p. 32.
[91] *Country Life*, 23 Jan. 1975; W.R.O. 1883/5, accts.
[92] *Country Life*, 9 Oct. 1920.

RAMSBURY: THE EAST FRONT OF THE EARL OF PEMBROKE'S HOUSE, c. 1567

The first floor is planned as six bedrooms with closets accessible from the stairs or the central corridor, which is lit by a lantern passing through the attic floor.

The fitting or refitting of the inside of the house continued throughout the 18th century. Between 1766 and 1791 Sir William Langham Jones repaired and improved it and landscaped the grounds around it.[93] Most woodwork in the attics is of the early and mid 18th century and several bedrooms have mid and late 18th-century cornices, fireplaces, and panelling. On the principal floor the library was redecorated in the late 18th century and new fireplaces were installed in all the other rooms except the hall. The north-west room and its closet on that floor and one or more bedroom were then decorated with Chinese wallpaper. The last major alteration inside the house was c. 1800 when a new principal staircase was built. The Joneses lived in the house, but the Burdetts did not often live there until 1914 and in the 19th and 20th centuries only minor additions were made.[94] It has been extensively restored by its present owner.

North-east of the house stables were built in the mid 17th century.[95] By analogy with stables at Wilton House their design has been attributed to Isaac de Caux.[96] They have a south front with a central pedimented entrance bay, on each side of which are four bays: all the windows are vertical ovals each with a keystone at top and bottom. The building now houses a swimming pool and domestic accommodation. North of it a stable court was built in the late 18th century or early 19th. The late 17th-century walled kitchen garden is 350 m. west of the house and is now a rose garden. It was extended westwards in the 19th century for an orchard. Beside the house, but at a lower level south of it, a court of cottages for servants was built in the mid 18th century. Alterations were made to the park c. 1775.[97] The artificial lake was made with an ornamental bridge at its east end, and in 1775 a conservatory was built to adjoin the servants' court to the south.[98] The park was extended northwards and eastwards: the drive was lengthened and at the east end a new pair of lodges was built with late 17th-century gatepiers presumably reset from an earlier forecourt. A belt of trees was planted

[93] W.R.O. 212A/27/27, Jones Estate Act.
[94] *Musgrave's Obit.* (Harl. Soc. xlvi), 341, 343; *Country Life*, 10 Aug. 1907; 2 Oct. 1920; 9 Oct. 1920; 7 Dec. 1961; 14 Dec. 1961; 21 Dec. 1961.
[95] Cf. W.R.O., microfilm copy of map, 1676.

[96] O. Hill and J. Cornforth, *Eng. Country Hos.: Caroline, 1625–85*, 183.
[97] *Andrews and Dury, Map* (W.R.S. viii), pl. 12; W.R.O. 154/3.
[98] Date on bldg.; see plate facing p. 32.

round the new boundary of the park and the Plantation south of the house may have been planted then.[99] Near the kitchen garden a rustic fishing lodge was built in the late 18th century or early 19th.

The tithes of Ramsbury parish belonged to the chapter of Salisbury cathedral until in the mid 12th century or earlier they were given to endow the prebend of Ramsbury.[1] In 1226 *RAMS-BURY PREBEND* had a yearly value of 40 marks, all of which presumably came from within the parish.[2] At 50 marks it was clearly under-valued in 1291 since c. 1290 the prebendary's income from Baydon alone was leased for 25 marks a year.[3] The prebendary was entitled to tithes of corn, wool, and lambs from the whole parish, and various other tithes and oblations, some of which were given to the vicars of Ramsbury.[4] In 1341 he had a manor house, 2 carucates, 12 a. of meadow, 30 a. of several pasture and feeding for 100 sheep, 40 a. of woodland, a mill, and lands held by villeins whose rents and works were worth 31s. 4d. yearly.[5] The prebend was valued at £52 gross in 1535.[6] As Ramsbury prebend the endowments were given to Edward, earl of Hertford, in 1545 as part of the exchange between him and Bishop Salcot.[7] The estate was given to the Crown by exchange in 1547.[8] In 1590 Elizabeth I granted the tithes from the site of Ramsbury manor house and its surrounding parkland and woodland through trustees or agents to Henry, earl of Pembroke, and they were merged with those lands.[9] The remainder of the estate was similarly granted to William, earl of Pembroke, for a fee-farm rent of £44 13s. 4d. in 1609–10.[10] The rent had been granted by the Crown before 1639 when it was conveyed, apparently between trustees,[11] and since it was not afterwards mentioned was presumably acquired by an earl of Pembroke before 1677. The land seems to have been absorbed by Ramsbury manor. The prebendal tithes descended with that manor. After the Reformation they were leased in portions, those of Axford for £5 13s. 4d. c. 1610,[12] of Baydon for £20 in 1585,[13] and of Knighton for £60 c. 1675.[14] In 1676–7 they were sold to Henry Powle, who broke up Ramsbury manor by sales between 1677 and 1681.[15] The sales included the majority of the tithes, sold in portions with, or to the owners of, the estates from which they arose.[16] In those cases the tithes were merged. In other cases tithes arising from lands in Baydon and Ramsbury Town tithings became separate estates: they are referred to among the descents of lands in those places.[17] The remaining tithes were sold to Sir William Jones and, as Ramsbury prebend, passed with Ramsbury manor.[18] In 1778 those arising from land in Baydon, Park Town, Ramsbury Town, and Whittonditch tithings and from land in part of Eastridge tithing were exchanged for allotments of land totalling 150 a.[19] The remainder, mainly arising from Coombe farm in Axford and from the lands of the Littlecote estate at Thrup and Knighton in Eastridge tithing, 1,160 a., were commuted for a rent charge of £348 awarded to Sir Francis Burdett in 1841.[20]

Three notable estates in Park Town tithing were created by sales of the parkland around Ramsbury manor house by Henry Powle 1677–9. North of the Kennet the north-east part of the park, 108 a. including Old field and Old Field Copse, was bought in 1679 by Edward Stafford (d. c. 1688) whose relict Anne held it in 1710.[21] The Staffords had four daughters, Elizabeth, wife of John Jennings, Mary, Anne, wife of John Hall, and Susannah. In 1720 the Jenningses, Susannah, and the executor of Mary sold the land to Francis Hawes, a director of the South Sea Company. After that company collapsed the land was confiscated by parliamentary trustees who in 1725 sold it to Richard Jones, lord of Ramsbury manor.[22] Most of the land was again imparked c. 1775.[23]

South of the Kennet the estate called *PARK* farm possibly originated in the purchase by Robert Gilmore of over 100 a. in the high park in 1677.[24] That land seems to have belonged to a Mrs. Gilmore in 1705[25] but its later descent is obscure. Before 1771 it was reunited with Ramsbury manor.[26] Until the Second World War Park farm included c. 800 a. south of the Plantation and west of the Ramsbury–Froxfield lane.[27] The eastern end of it became part of Ramsbury airfield.[28] All of it passed with Ramsbury Manor to Seymour, earl of Wilton, who in 1953 sold it to R. A. Chamberlain and Mr. G. W. Wilson.[29] In that year they sold the western end of it as Park farm to J. E. Sandell who in 1969 sold the farm, 232 a., to Mr. F. Clothier, the owner in 1981.[30] Park Farm is a house of c. 1830 near which are some contemporary and later farm buildings.

[99] Above, introduction.
[1] *V.C.H. Wilts.* iii. 5; below, church.
[2] *Reg. St. Osmund* (Rolls Ser.), ii. 70.
[3] *Tax. Eccl.* (Rec. Com.), 182; D. & C. Sar. Mun., press I, box 4, no. 13.
[4] *Inq. Non.* (Rec. Com.), 175; below, church.
[5] *Inq. Non.* (Rec. Com.), 175.
[6] *Valor Eccl.* (Rec. Com.), ii. 151–2.
[7] *L. & P. Hen. VIII*, xx (2), p. 411; W.R.O. 1883/59, copy of Act.
[8] *Cal. Pat.* 1547–8, 190.
[9] W.R.O. 1883/94, copy of letters patent, f. 17; 84/47, abstr. of title; partic. of manor.
[10] Ibid. 84/47, abstr. of title.
[11] P.R.O., CP 25(2)/511/14 Chas. I Trin.
[12] Ibid. REQ 2/5/155.
[13] Ibid. C 2/Jas. I/S 33/29.
[14] W.R.O. 84/47, partic. of manor.
[15] Ibid. 1883/59, bargain and sale, Pembroke to Whitley and Cratford; above.

[16] W.R.O. 1883/59, bargain and sale, Powle to Jones.
[17] Below; below, Baydon, manor.
[18] e.g. W.R.O. 1883/69/3.
[19] Ibid. 154/2. [20] Ibid. tithe award.
[21] Ibid. 1883/75, bargain and sale, Powle to Stafford; mortgage, Stafford to Jennings; ibid. microfilm copy of map, 1676.
[22] Ibid. 1883/75.
[23] Ibid. microfilm copy of map, 1676; ibid. 154/2–3.
[24] Ibid. 1883/59, bargain and sale, Pembroke to Whitley and Cratford; 1883/65/38; below, econ. hist., for the high park.
[25] W.R.O. 1883/13.
[26] Ibid. 212A/27/27, acct. of rents.
[27] Map of Ramsbury, W. div., *penes* Mrs. B. Croucher, 25 Ashley Piece.
[28] Inf. from Defence Land Agent.
[29] Above; inf. from Mr. G. W. Wilson, Rudge Manor Farm, Froxfield.
[30] Wilts. Cuttings, xxiii. 246; inf. from Mr. Wilson; Mr. F. Clothier, Park Farm.

There has been a house on the site from 1676 or earlier.[31]

Alexander Dismore was lessee of over 100 a. in Ramsbury high park which in 1677 he bought from Henry Powle.[32] Buildings and a further 15 a. in the high park, which Powle sold to Thomas Gilmore in 1677, were bought from Gilmore by Richard Dismore in 1682.[33] Those two estates, which together made up *PARK TOWN* farm, were still held by the two Dismores in 1705.[34] They passed, apparently added to by several purchases, to Richard's grandson Richard Dismore whose heirs were his four daughters.[35] The farm passed after 1752 to his daughter Martha and her husband Edward Francis who owned it in 1780.[36] From c. 1790 to 1831 or later it belonged to a Miss Francis and in 1839, when it was a rectangle of 260 a. south of Ramsbury, mostly south of the Kennet with Park Town Farm in its northwest corner, the estate belonged to Ambrose Lanfear (d. 1864).[37] It apparently belonged to Charles Lanfear from 1865 to 1918, when it was bought by Sir Francis Burdett.[38] Nearly the whole farm, including the flat land above Spring Hill which was part of Ramsbury airfield,[39] passed with Ramsbury Manor to Seymour, earl of Wilton, who in 1953 sold it to R. A. Chamberlain and Mr. G. W. Wilson. The steep slopes of Spring Hill belonged to Mr. Wilson in 1981.[40] Park Town Farm, then called Harbrook Farm, and some meadow land remained part of the Burdett-Fishers' estate in 1981.[41] The house, bought by Richard Dismore in 1682 and later described as 'under the hill',[42] has walls of rubble and a central stack in which is a stone bearing various initials and a date, possibly 1668. The stone appears to have been reset but a later 17th-century date for the building of the house is likely. It has a small 19th-century north extension and in recent years has been greatly enlarged westwards to incorporate many fittings from other buildings.

Ramsbury airfield, c. 400 a. in Ramsbury which had been parts of Park and Park Town farms,[43] was divided by R. A. Chamberlain and Mr. G. W. Wilson in 1953. Chamberlain was allotted the eastern part which he added to other land he owned west of the Ramsbury–Froxfield lane and called Bridge farm. In 1970 he sold Bridge farm, c. 125 a., to G. S. Wills and it has since been part of the Littlecote estate.[44] Mr. Wilson was allotted the western part. In 1976 he sold most of it, 300 a., to Mr. R. T. Candy, the owner in 1981, and retains the rest.[45]

In 1327 William of Baldonshall and Walter of Warneford were Ramsbury taxpayers.[46] In 1331 Walter held an estate called Baldonshall which in 1347 John of Baldonshall settled on himself, his wife Eleanor, and their son William.[47] Thomas Hungerford and his son Thomas gave it by exchange to John Lillebon in 1368.[48] In 1412 the estate belonged to William Winslow (d. 1414) whose relict Agnes (fl. 1441) and her husband Robert Andrew (d. 1437) held it in 1416.[49] Agnes was succeeded by her son Thomas Winslow, one of whose four daughters, Joan, married Henry Hall.[50] About 1450 an elder Henry Hall shared title to the estate with Winslow who conveyed it to him in 1456, presumably as a settlement on the marriage of Joan and the younger Henry Hall.[51] The estate consisted of more than 100 a. in Park Town tithing and of many tenements in Ramsbury.[52] The Halls had daughters Elizabeth and Agnes who married respectively the brothers Nicholas and Maurice Filiol: all four were defendants in a dispute over the estate among the heirs of Winslow's daughters c. 1500.[53] The estate passed to the Filiols' nephew Sir Thomas Trenchard (d. before 1559) and came to be called the manor of *RAMSBURY TRENCHARD*.[54] It included land in several parts of the parish, mostly in Park Town tithing, and cottages in Ramsbury.[55] Sir Thomas was succeeded by a son Thomas and that Thomas's son Thomas whose son George (knighted in 1588) held the manor in 1575.[56] Sir George was succeeded in 1630 by his son Sir Thomas[57] who in 1632 sold part of the manor, Hales Court farm, c. 185 a. in Park Town tithing north of the Kennet between Ramsbury, Hilldrop, and the park of Ramsbury Manor, to the tenant Daniel White. In 1649 White sold the farm to Richard King of Upham in Aldbourne. In 1669 King's executor conveyed it to Nicholas King who in 1682 sold it to Henry Nourse of Woodlands in Mildenhall.[58] It passed with Mildenhall manor to Nourse's daughter Sarah, countess of Winchilsea, and her husband William Rollinson.[59] They sold it in 1731 to Charles Bruce, Lord Bruce, who in the same year sold it to Richard Jones, lord of Ramsbury manor.[60] It was absorbed by that manor. The remainder of Ramsbury Trenchard manor was sold in 1631 to Thomas Freeman (d. 1637), a

[31] W.R.O., microfilm copy of map, 1676.
[32] Ibid. 1883/59, bargain and sale, Pembroke to Whitley and Cratford; 1883/65/36.
[33] Ibid. 130/46/22.
[34] Ibid. 130/46/30A; 1883/13.
[35] Ibid. 130/46/30A.
[36] Ibid.; ibid. Park Town land tax.
[37] Ibid. Park Town land tax; ibid. 500/17; map of Ramsbury, W. div., *penes* Mrs. Croucher.
[38] W.R.O. 1883/285; 1883, rentals, 1918–19.
[39] Inf. from Defence Land Agent.
[40] Above; inf. from Mr. Wilson.
[41] Inf. from Maj. Burdett-Fisher.
[42] W.R.O. 130/46/22.
[43] Above.
[44] Inf. from Mr. Wilson; Mr. D. S. Wills, Littlecote Ho.; below.
[45] Inf. from Mr. Wilson.
[46] P.R.O., E 179/196/7.

[47] W.R.O., bishop, Liber Niger, f. 95; *Feet of F.* 1327–77 (W.R.S. xxix), p. 86.
[48] *Cal. Pat.* 1367–70, 106.
[49] *Feud. Aids*, vi. 533; P.R.O., CP 25(1)/291/63, no. 39; *V.C.H. Oxon.* vi. 340.
[50] *V.C.H. Oxon.* vi. 340; P.R.O., C 1/240/18.
[51] W.R.O., bishop, Liber Niger, ff. 242v.–243; P.R.O., CP 25(1)/257/64, no. 37.
[52] *Cal. Pat.* 1452–61, 471; W.R.O., bishop, Liber Niger, f. 99v.
[53] P.R.O., C 1/240/18; J. Hutchins, *Dors.* iii. 152.
[54] Hutchins, *Dors.* iii. 326; B.L. Add. Ch. 24440; P.R.O., CP 25(2)/509/7 Chas. I Hil.
[55] *First Pembroke Survey*, ed. Straton, i. 151.
[56] Burke, *Commoners* (1833–8), iv. 77; P.R.O., CP 25(2)/239/17 Eliz. I Hil.
[57] Hutchins, *Dors.* iii. 326.   [58] W.R.O. 9/20/36.
[59] Below, Mildenhall, manors.
[60] W.R.O. 1883/62, deed, Bruce to Jones; 9/20/36.

Ramsbury tanner. Freeman was apparently succeeded by another Thomas Freeman, a bankrupt in 1688 when his lands were sold. Most of what had been Ramsbury Trenchard manor was acquired by Richard Jones before 1700.[61]

BLAKE'S farm in Park Town tithing was in 1328 settled by Walter Blake on the marriage of his son Ralph (fl. 1341).[62] The farm descended in the Blake family, possibly with East Hayes manor in Ogbourne St. Andrew.[63] Thomas Blake held it in 1462[64] and it descended to William Blake (d. *c.* 1550).[65] It belonged to the owners of East Hayes until, in the 18th century, it was acquired by one of the Pophams of Littlecote. Dorothy Popham, relict of Francis Popham (d. 1780), held it in 1780 when, as Ambrose farm, it was said to be in Ramsbury Town tithing.[66] The land has since remained part of the Littlecote estate.[67]

The manor of *HILLDROP* in Ramsbury Town tithing possibly originated in the gift by Bishop Bohun to Everard of Hurst of 5 hides at Ramsbury, which had been held by Alexander nephew of Everard and was part of Ramsbury manor. The land passed with Membury and Bishop Poore confirmed Everard's son Roger's free tenure of it in 1196.[68] Land at Hilldrop, rated as $\frac{1}{2}$ knight's fee and held in the mid 13th century by Reynold of Ramsbury, was possibly the same.[69] Reynold still held it in 1275[70] and as Hilldrop manor it had passed by 1278 to his son Reynold, a minor, who in 1310 settled it on his daughter Elizabeth and her husband Reynold son of Peter.[71] Elizabeth, then a widow, conveyed it in 1329.[72] In 1333 the manor was settled on Sir William Everard and his wife Elizabeth, presumably the same woman, and it seems to have passed to Thomas, son of Simon of Ramsbury, and his wife Margaret, daughter of Sir William Everard.[73] Thomas and Margaret had no issue and in 1386 John of Ramsbury, son of Simon of Ramsbury, claimed to have inherited the manor from them and from Elizabeth.[74] Between 1392 and 1394 John settled it on himself and his wife Maud with remainder to Sir Thomas Brook and his wife Joan.[75] The land possibly belonged to Nicholas Read in 1412.[76] It passed to Nicholas Wootton who was said to be of Ramsbury in 1417 and to whom Joan, relict of Sir Thomas Brook,

conveyed or confirmed it in 1423.[77] In 1446 Wootton (d. 1454) settled the manor on himself and his wife Elizabeth for their lives and on his daughter Agnes and her husband William York in tail.[78] The Yorks entered on it in 1454.[79] William (d. 1476) was succeeded by his son John (d. 1512) who gave the manor to his son Thomas in 1509.[80] Thomas, who was thrice sheriff of Wiltshire,[81] was succeeded in 1542 by his nephew Roger Bodenham, but Roger's mother Joan and her husband Stephen Parry possibly held the manor until *c.* 1556.[82] In 1566 it belonged to Henry Bodenham,[83] who is more likely to have been a son of Parry than a close relative of Roger Bodenham. Afterwards it descended in the Bodenham family. Roger (d. 1579) had sons Thomas (d. 1583) and Sir Roger (d. 1623) who was his brother's heir. Hilldrop passed to Sir Roger's son William (d. 1641) and to William's son Roger (fl. 1689) who had sons Edward, Walter, William, and probably Roger.[84] A Roger Bodenham held the manor in 1699.[85] One of the Bodenhams sold most of it to one Hawkins who in 1704 sold that portion to William Davies. One of the Bodenhams sold the remainder to Davies in 1714.[86] Davies's heir was his son Thomas who in 1701, at the death of his grandfather Thomas Batson, had taken the surname Batson. Thomas was succeeded in 1759 by his brother Edmund who then changed his name to Thomas Batson. After his death in 1770 Batson's relict Elizabeth held Hilldrop manor until her own death in 1808. She devised it for life to her nephew Henry Maxwell and afterwards to members of a branch of the Batson family distantly related to Edmund Davies (Thomas Batson) and herself.[87] Maxwell may have held it until 1824, but it may have belonged to Robert Batson in 1819 and to E. Batson from 1825 to 1830 or later.[88] It passed to Robert Batson's brother Alfred who held it until his death in 1856. Alfred's heir was his son Alfred (d. 1885) who was succeeded by his son Francis Cunninghame Batson (d. 1931).[89] Hilldrop farm was sold in 1921 to George Wilson and Henry Wilson: in 1937 Henry Wilson and George Wilson's relict, Mrs. M. M. Wilson, sold it to Sir Francis Burdett, lord of Ramsbury manor.[90] In 1957 the farm was sold to Bertram Ede who in that year

[61] W.R.O. 1883/93A–B; *Wilts. Inq. p.m.* 1625–49 (Index Libr.), 372.
[62] B.L. Add. Ch. 54987; *Inq. Non.* (Rec. Com.), 175.
[63] Below, Ogbourne St. Andrew, manors.
[64] W.R.O., bishop, Liber Niger, f. 99.
[65] P.R.O., REQ 2/189/60; below, Ogbourne St. Andrew, manors.
[66] W.R.O., Ramsbury land tax; Burke, *Land. Gent.* (1952), 2056; cf. *Andrews and Dury, Map* (W.R.S. viii), pl. 12; O.S. Map 6″, Wilts. XXX (1887 edn.).
[67] Below; inf. from Mr. Wills.
[68] Hist. MSS. Com. 55, *Var. Coll.* i, pp. 363–5; *Sar. Chart. and Doc.* (Rolls Ser.), 57–8; below.
[69] W.R.O., bishop, Liber Niger, f. 237v.
[70] *Rot. Hund.* (Rec. Com.), ii (1), 265.
[71] *Feet of F.* 1272–1327 (W.R.S. i), p. 63; B.L. Harl. Ch. 55 C. 2.
[72] B.L. Harl. Ch. 55 B. 43.
[73] *Feet of F.* 1327–77 (W.R.S. xxix), p. 41. The transcript of the fine there edited may be incomplete: B.L. Eg. Ch. 6692.
[74] P.R.O., C 148/56; ibid. CP 40/699, rot. 525.
[75] Ibid. C 146/3557; B.L. Harl. Ch. 56 E. 32.

[76] *Feud. Aids*, vi. 533.
[77] *Cal. Fine R.* 1413–22, 220; P.R.O., C 146/10464.
[78] P.R.O., C 146/2963; C 139/154, no. 27.
[79] *Cal. Close*, 1454–61, 10–11.
[80] P.R.O., C 140/56, no. 42; C 142/28, no. 135.
[81] *W.N. & Q.* viii. 176.
[82] P.R.O., C 142/70, no. 42; C 1/946/37; ibid. CP 25(2)/46/323/34 Hen. VIII East.; CP 25(2)/81/694/3 & 4 Phil. and Mary Mich.; Wilton Ho. Mun., survey, 1550s, p. 279.
[83] B.L. Add. Ch. 24441; *First Pembroke Survey*, ed. Straton, i. 149.
[84] This acct. of the Bodenhams is based on Burke, *Commoners* (1833–8), iv. 85; pedigree compiled by Mrs. R. Pinches, Parliament Piece.
[85] W.R.O. 270/29/2.
[86] Ibid. 1883/292; P.R.O., CP 25(2)/1077/2 Geo. I Mich.
[87] Pedigree compiled by Mrs. Pinches; W.R.O., Ramsbury land tax.
[88] W.R.O., Ramsbury land tax; map of Hilldrop farm, 1819, *penes* Mr. C. E. Eliot-Cohen, Hilldrop Farm.
[89] Pedigree compiled by Mrs. Pinches; *Kelly's Dir. Wilts.* (1848 and later edns.).
[90] W.R.O. 1883/285; inf. from Mr. G. W. Wilson.

sold it to Mr. C. E. Eliot-Cohen, the owner in 1981.[91]

The lords of Hilldrop manor may have lived in a house on it in the 13th and 14th centuries, and Nicholas Wootton and nearly all later owners have done so.[92] Its name suggests that Hilldrop manor house was on the downs north of Ramsbury.[93] The house presumably on its site, Hilldrop Farm, is a brick house of c. 1820 extended north and east in the later 19th century. A house called the Rookery in 1880,[94] Parliament Piece in 1981, was built beside Back Lane in Ramsbury in the early 17th century, presumably for one of the Bodenhams, and was later lived in by the Batsons. It had a central chimney stack with rooms on both sides and was of two storeys with attics and cellars. Late in the 17th century a rear north wing, containing a staircase and a room on each floor, was added at the west end. The new, and some of the old, rooms were then fitted to a high standard. Possibly at the same time the gatepiers, surmounted by urns, were built and the early 17th-century barn was encased in brick and converted into a coach house. The house was extended at the east end of the south front c. 1800 and in the late 19th century service rooms in 17th-century style were built in the angle between the 17th-century ranges. It was separated from Hilldrop farm in the earlier 20th century and in 1981 belonged to Mr. J. H. Pinches.[95]

An estate in Ramsbury Town tithing called *LOVE'S* passed in the Love family for more than two centuries. Walter Love held land in Ramsbury in 1241;[96] Alice Love was mentioned in 1249, William Love and Ralph Love in 1258, an elder Robert Love in 1299, and elder and younger Robert Loves in 1305.[97] In 1331 Walter of Warneford held land which had been a Robert Love's but Robert Love (fl. 1341) may still have held a substantial estate.[98] John Love (fl. c. 1390) was possibly succeeded by Walter Love who conveyed the estate in 1432.[99] Walter's relict Joan Love held it in 1462 when it was rated as 1 carucate.[1] About 1510 the estate seems to have been acquired by John York, presumably by purchase, from Harry Henley otherwise Love whose wife Joan then sold her claim to dower.[2] Love's thereafter descended with Hilldrop manor.[3] In the early 18th century, however, one of the Bodenhams may have sold it separately from the manor because in 1780 Love's farm

belonged to John Barnes. It passed to Thomas Barnes c. 1791. It was apparently sold by Barnes to William Parsons in 1807 and by him c. 1813 to Edward Graves Meyrick (d. 1839), vicar of Ramsbury.[4] In 1839 the farm, 50 a., belonged to Meyrick's relict.[5] Meyrick had sons James, Henry Howard, Charles, and Frederick but the descent of the farm is obscure.[6] In 1892 some of its land was part of Ramsbury manor.[7] In 1981 Love's farm was owned by Mr. E. F. M. Talmage.[8] The farmhouse is a brick building of the 18th century.

John Helm (fl. 1249) possibly held land in Ramsbury which may have passed to his son William (fl. 1286).[9] In 1331 a William Helm held an estate in Ramsbury Town tithing, then rated as 2 yardlands, later called Bacon's and afterwards *ELMDOWN* farm.[10] Its descent in the Bacon family before 1462, when it was held by Joan, relict of John Stampford, and already called Bacon's,[11] is not clear. John Bacon held it c. 1556,[12] Richard Bacon in 1559 and 1567.[13] It passed like the Bacons' estate in Upavon to Nicholas Bacon (fl. 1598) and his daughter Joan Noyes who died holding it in 1622 leaving a son William Noyes as heir.[14] William presumably sold the farm, which was apparently John Gilmore's in 1661.[15] Catherine Gilmore, a widow, held it in the late 1670s.[16] It was possibly conveyed to Richard Francis c. 1713.[17] Between 1722 and 1726 Elmdown farm was apparently acquired by Francis Popham of Littlecote.[18] It has since been part of the Littlecote estate.[19] Elmdown Farm is a timber-framed house of 1654[20] with a three-room plan. It was encased in brick in the early 19th century when a west kitchen was added behind the north end. The house was extensively restored c. 1970, when many old fittings were introduced, and has since been extended southwards.

In 1778 the Revd. Daniel Boreman owned an estate of c. 85 a. in Ramsbury Town tithing based on buildings on the north side of Oxford Street.[21] About 1787 it was bought by Henry Read and added to the Crowood estate.[22]

The tithes arising from Hilldrop manor were bought from Henry Powle by Roger Bodenham in 1677 but were not merged with the land.[23] They were apparently not sold with either part of the manor in the early 18th century.[24] They were twice conveyed in 1720, and in 1722 were

[91] Inf. from Mr. Eliot-Cohen.
[92] e.g. *L. & P. Hen. VIII*, xv, p. 380.
[93] *P.N. Wilts.* (E.P.N.S.), 288.
[94] *Kelly's Dir. Wilts.* (1880).
[95] Inf. from Mrs. Pinches.
[96] P.R.O., CP 25(1)/251/12, no. 7.
[97] *Civil Pleas, 1249* (W.R.S. xxvi), p. 55; W.R.O., bishop, Liber Niger, f. 81v.; *Feet of F. 1272–1327* (W.R.S. i), p. 44; *Gaol Delivery 1275–1306* (W.R.S. xxxiii), p. 167.
[98] W.R.O., bishop, Liber Niger, f. 95; *Inq. Non.* (Rec. Com.), 175.
[99] *Cat. Anct. D.* vi, C 5105; P.R.O., C 146/9860.
[1] W.R.O., bishop, Liber Niger, f. 99.
[2] *Cat. Anct. D.* vi, C 4682.
[3] P.R.O., C 142/28, no. 135; C 142/70, no. 42; above.
[4] W.R.O., Ramsbury land tax; ibid. 500/10.
[5] Map of Ramsbury, W. div., *penes* Mrs. Croucher.
[6] F. J. Meyrick, *Life in the Bush*, 21.
[7] W.R.O. 1883, rental.   [8] Local inf.
[9] *Civil Pleas, 1249* (W.R.S. xxvi), p. 55; *Cal. Close, 1279–88*, 411.

[10] W.R.O., bishop, Liber Niger, f. 95.
[11] Ibid. f. 99.
[12] Wilton Ho. Mun., survey, 1550s, p. 280.
[13] B.L. Add. Ch. 24440; *First Pembroke Survey*, ed. Straton, i. 150.
[14] *V.C.H. Wilts.* x. 165; P.R.O., C 3/257/35; *Wilts. Inq. p.m. 1625–49* (Index Libr.), 124–6.
[15] W.R.O. 1883/297.
[16] Ibid. 1883/59, bargain and sale, Pembroke to Whitley and Cratford; 1883/9; J. A. Williams, *Catholic Recusancy in Wilts.* (Cath. Rec. Soc.), p. 305.
[17] W.R.O. 589/1, quitclaim, Gilmore to Francis; 130/46/26.
[18] S.R.O., DD/PO 25, acct. 1726; DD/POt 125.
[19] Below; inf. from Mr. Wills.
[20] Date on bldg.
[21] W.R.O. 154/2–3.
[22] Ibid. Ramsbury land tax; ibid. bishop, pet. for faculties, drafts, iii, no. 28; below.
[23] W.R.O. 1883/66/55.
[24] Above.

acquired by William Davies from Richard Savors and others.[25] They were then merged.

The tithes of Elmdown farm were conveyed by Thomas Abbot and his wife Martha to James Carrant in 1715.[26] They belonged to a Miss Anne Carrant, apparently from 1780 or earlier to 1831 or later, and were acquired in 1835 by Edward William Leyborne-Popham who owned the farm.[27] In 1841 the tithes were valued at £21 15s. and commuted.[28]

Most of the copyholds and leaseholds in Whittonditch tithing, all part of Ramsbury manor, were sold by Henry Powle between 1677 and 1681.[29] Most of what remained in Ramsbury manor was called *PRESTON* farm in 1778.[30] It was sold as two farms c. 1785. Thomas Rogers (d. c. 1801) bought that called Preston farm. By 1804 William Hillier had acquired it, and it passed to James Hillier who held the farm, 84 a., in 1839.[31] After Hillier's death in 1840 Preston farm was apparently bought by Sir Francis Burdett (d. 1844) and it was again added to Ramsbury manor.[32] Sir Francis Burdett sold it in 1912, probably to Moses Woolland, and it became part of the Baydon Manor estate. As a farm of 300 a. it was sold with the estate in 1947 and c. 1949.[33] It was retained by Sidney Watts, after whose death in 1961 it was sold.[34] In 1981 most of the land belonged to Maj. H. O. Stibbard and was in his Marridge Hill estate. The eastern part of it then belonged to the executors of G. B. Smith as part of Whittonditch farm.[35] Preston Farm is an 18th-century house extended in the 19th century.

The remainder of the 18th-century Preston farm, 96 a. between Whittonditch and Preston, was bought by Anthony Woodroffe c. 1785, passed to Sarah Woodroffe c. 1815, and c. 1826 was acquired by William Atherton who owned the land in 1839.[36] Sir Francis Burdett (d. 1844) may have bought the land, which before 1899 had been added to the Crowood estate.[37]

In 1677 Henry Read bought from Henry Powle an estate in Whittonditch tithing based on a copyhold called *CROWOOD* and including land which became Witcha farm.[38] The estate had been held as tenants by members of the Banks family, to whom Read (d. 1706) was apparently related.[39] It descended, presumably from father to son, to Henry Read (d. 1756) and to Henry Read (d. 1786) whose heir was his son Henry (d. 1821).[40] That Henry devised the

Crowood estate, 1,050 a., to his daughter Mary Ann, wife of John Richmond Seymour (d. 1848).[41] The Seymours were succeeded in turn by their sons Henry Richmond Seymour (d. 1876) and the Revd. Charles Frederick Seymour (d. 1897), whose son Charles Read Seymour apparently sold the estate in 1915 to Frederick Charles Giddins, the owner until 1945.[42] Later owners were the politician Sir Oswald Ernald Mosley, Bt., from 1945 to 1951; Lord George Francis John Montagu-Douglas-Scott, 1951–60; Edward Henry Berkeley Portman, 1960–6; Mark George Christopher Jeffreys, Baron Jeffreys, 1966–9; and Philip Chetwode, Baron Chetwode, 1969–79.[43] In 1979 the estate, 1,059 a. including land in Baydon and Aldbourne, was sold by Lord Chetwode to Mr. J. F. Dennis, the owner in 1981.[44] Crowood House has a recessed north-east entrance front of five bays. The centre of the house has walls partly of timber framing and possibly 17th-century, and on the ground floor contains much reset early 17th-century panelling. It was apparently heightened in the late 17th century. Unequal wings which project north-eastwards from its ends are also 17th-century.[45] In the late 18th century large north and west additions were built to provide more service rooms and a new staircase and dining room. More new rooms were built at the south corner of the house in the early 19th century when most of the older rooms were refitted: a stable and a cottage north of the house were also built then. In the late 18th century there were extensive formal gardens south-west of the house and beyond them a small park with a boundary plantation.[46]

WITCHA farm, 335 a., was sold in 1949 by Sir Oswald Mosley to Mr. A. E. Jones who later halved it into Witcha farm and Woodlands farm. In 1981 Mr. Jones's sons Mr. D. J. Jones and Mr. P. E. Jones owned respectively Witcha and Woodlands farms.[47]

A holding of more than 5 yardlands, *WHITTONDITCH* farm, was bought from Henry Powle by Jonathan Knackstone in 1677. Knackstone (fl. 1689) had sons Thomas and Stephen, both of whom held land in Whittonditch tithing in 1705.[48] Whittonditch farm passed to Stephen's son Jonathan (fl. 1736). In 1752 that Jonathan's son Jonathan was foreclosed from the estate which passed to his principal mortgagee, Henry Read of Crowood.[49] Whittonditch farm was part of the Crowood estate until in 1949

[25] P.R.O., CP 25(2)/1078/6 Geo. I Hil.; CP 25(2)/1078/7 Geo. I Mich.; CP 25(2)/1078/8 Geo. I Trin.
[26] Ibid. CP 25(2)/1087/2 Geo. I Mich.
[27] W.R.O., Ramsbury land tax; S.R.O., DD/POt 41, sched. of purchases.
[28] W.R.O., tithe award.
[29] Ibid. 1883/59, bargain and sale, Pembroke to Whitley and Cratford; bargain and sale, Powle to Jones; 1883/66.
[30] Ibid. 154/2.
[31] Ibid. Whittonditch land tax; map of Ramsbury, E. div., *penes* Mrs. Croucher.
[32] W.R.O., wills, dean, 1841, no. 1; ibid. 1883, rent bk., 1880; key to maps of Ramsbury *penes* Mrs. Croucher.
[33] W.R.O. 1883, rentals, 1912–13; 1008/25; below.
[34] Inf. from Mr. R. T. Walton, New Ho., Manor Lane, Baydon.
[35] Inf. from Maj. H. O. Stibbard, the Park, Ogbourne St. Geo.; below.
[36] W.R.O., Whittonditch land tax; map of Ramsbury, E.

div., *penes* Mrs. Croucher.
[37] Key to maps of Ramsbury *penes* Mrs. Croucher; W.R.O. 1001/11; below.
[38] W.R.O. 1883/66/72.
[39] Wilton Ho. Mun., ct. roll 1632; mon. in church.
[40] Mon. in church; W.R.O. 1883/100, abstr. of title.
[41] W.R.O. 1883/100, copy will; *V.C.H. Berks.* iv. 257; maps of Ramsbury *penes* Mrs. Croucher.
[42] Mon. in church; *Harrow Sch. Reg. 1800–1911*, 144, 428; *Kelly's Dir. Wilts.* (1911 and later edns.); inf. from Mr. J. F. Dennis, Crowood Ho.
[43] Inf. from Mr. Dennis.
[44] Ibid.; *Wilts. Gaz.* 10 May 1979; sale cat. (copy in N.M.R.).
[45] Painting in the Bell, Ramsbury; see plate facing p. 96.
[46] *Andrews and Dury, Map* (W.R.S. viii), pl. 15.
[47] Inf. from Mr. D. J. Jones, Witcha Farm.
[48] W.R.O. 1883/66/78; 1883/13; *W.N. & Q.* viii. 419.
[49] P.R.O., C 78/1887, no. 5.

it was sold by Sir Oswald Mosley to a Mr. Day. It was later bought by G. B. Smith whose executors owned it in 1981.[50]

In 1567 Ramsbury Trenchard manor included 6½ yardlands in Whittonditch and Eastridge tithings of which most was at Marridge Hill.[51] Sir Thomas Trenchard may have sold those lands *c.* 1632, when he sold Hales Court farm in Park Town tithing.[52] Two freeholds in Whittonditch tithing were held *c.* 1556 by John Goddard of Upham and William Moore.[53] Moore's was bought by Thomas Seymour *c.* 1562.[54] In those estates and in sales of other copyholds and leaseholds by Henry Powle 1677–81 two later 18th-century freeholds at Marridge Hill and others at Whittonditch and Preston presumably originated.

Thomas Shefford or Shelford, possibly in 1760, owned an estate at Marridge Hill which James Lovegrove bought in 1785.[55] From Lovegrove the estate passed *c.* 1800, presumably by will, to either his brother-in-law Cheyney Waldron or to Waldron's son and namesake:[56] the son held it at his death in 1819. Waldron devised his *MARRIDGE HILL* estate to his nephew John Waldron, a minor, who entered on it *c.* 1827.[57] John held the estate, 325 a. in 1839, until 1851 or later.[58] It was held from 1867 or earlier to 1880 or later by Stephen Waldron and from 1895 or earlier until his death in 1901 by James Lovegrove Waldron, John Waldron's son,[59] whose relict sold the estate, 554 a., in 1904.[60] It was apparently bought by Arthur Edward White but in 1911 belonged to Moses Woolland (d. 1918), under whose will its name was changed to *BAYDON MANOR* estate.[61] It passed to Woolland's son Walter who in 1947 sold the estate, then over 3,000 a. in Ramsbury, Baydon, and elsewhere, to Edwards & Sons (Inkpen) Ltd., timber merchants. That company sold it *c.* 1949 to a group of farmers, John White, Sidney Watts, and Albert Pembroke, who immediately divided it.[62] The land north of Baydon Manor which had been John Waldron's in 1839 was part of Marridge Hill farm in 1947.[63] It was bought *c.* 1950 by Maj. H. O. Stibbard, the owner of over 600 a. at Marridge Hill in 1981.[64] Baydon Manor, formerly Marridge Hill House, is a red-brick house of *c.* 1820 with an east entrance front of three bays. A water tower was added to the north side of the house in the late 19th century, and the house was extended westwards for A. E. White in 1905–6. West of it a large detached winter garden was built *c.* 1900 mainly of cast iron, glass, and wood.

George Moore (d. 1729) possibly owned the estate at Marridge Hill which descended in the Moore family with Riverside farm in Axford.[65] The land, 144 a., belonged to George Pearce Moore in 1839.[66] It was later part of the Baydon Manor estate, was part of Marridge Hill farm in 1947, and was part of Maj. Stibbard's estate in 1981.[67]

In 1753 a Roger Spanswick owned an estate in Whittonditch tithing which, with land in Eastridge tithing, was called *MINDEN*, later Upper Whittonditch, farm.[68] Roger was succeeded between 1778 and 1784 by his son Roger. After Roger's death *c.* 1810 the farm, 165 a. in 1839, was acquired by Robert Nalder who owned it in 1842.[69] The lessee in 1839 was Lovegrove Waldron: before 1909 he or one or more of his successors acquired the freehold, and thereafter the estate, which was enlarged, descended with Eastridge manor.[70] Upper Whittonditch Farm is a house of 18th-century origin.

Thomas Lovegrove (d. 1778) bought a farm at Preston *c.* 1777 and devised it to his nephew, the younger Cheney Waldron, who held it until his death in 1819. Waldron devised it to his nephew Lovegrove Waldron, a minor, who owned the land, 102 a., in 1839.[71] Its later descent is obscure until 1947 when it was in the Baydon Manor estate as part of Preston farm.[72]

Several large freeholds were created early in Eastridge tithing and became manors: only a small proportion of the land in the tithing, most of it at Marridge Hill, was held by copy or lease from Ramsbury manor.[73] The three estates in the tithing at Marridge Hill in the later 18th century presumably originated in sales of such copyholds and leaseholds by Henry Powle 1677–81 and in earlier 17th-century sales of the land there which was part of Ramsbury Trenchard manor.[74]

In 1677 Stephen Banks bought 2 yardlands in Eastridge tithing from Powle. His estate passed to one Crouch, possibly Stephen Crouch (fl. 1735), and later belonged to the two Roger Spanswicks in turn.[75] It passed with the Spanswicks' land in Whittonditch tithing as part of Minden farm.

[50] Local inf.
[51] *First Pembroke Survey*, ed. Straton, i. 151.
[52] Above.
[53] Wilton Ho. Mun., survey, 1550s, p. 279.
[54] *W.N. & Q.* iv. 561.
[55] W.R.O., Q. Sess. enrolment, jurors bk. 1760; ibid. Whittonditch land tax; ibid. 1883/2, presentments, 1770; P.R.O., CP 25(2)/1447/25 Geo. III Hil.
[56] P.R.O., PROB 11/1048 (P.C.C. 500 Hay).
[57] W.R.O., wills, dean, 1819, no. 10; ibid. Whittonditch land tax.
[58] P.R.O., HO 107/1686; map of Ramsbury, E. div., *penes* Mrs. Croucher.
[59] *Kelly's Dir. Wilts.* (1867 and later edns.); W.R.O. 500/8; 500/20.   [60] Wilts. Cuttings, iii. 133.
[61] *Kelly's Dir. Wilts.* (1907 and later edns.); W.R.O. 1008/25.
[62] W.R.O. 1008/25; inf. from Mr. Walton; Mr. F. Newman, Wentworth Cottages, Baydon Ho. Farm, Baydon.
[63] Map of Ramsbury, E. div., *penes* Mrs. Croucher; W.R.O. 1008/25.

[64] Inf. from Maj. Stibbard.
[65] W.R.O. 1883/166, lease, Jones to Moore; below, Axford, manors.
[66] Map of Ramsbury, E. div., *penes* Mrs. Croucher.
[67] W.R.O. 1008/25; inf. from Maj. Stibbard.
[68] W.R.O. 1883/1, ct. held 15 Oct. 1753; ibid. bishop, pet. for faculties, drafts, iii, no. 28.
[69] Ibid. Whittonditch land tax; P.R.O., CP 43/803, Carte rott. 26–7; map of Ramsbury, E. div., *penes* Mrs. Croucher; S.R.O., DD/POt 41, sched. of purchases.
[70] Map of Ramsbury, E. div., *penes* Mrs. Croucher; W.A.S. Libr., sale cat. xxviiib, no. 36; below.
[71] P.R.O., PROB 11/1048 (P.C.C. 500 Hay, will of Thos. Lovegrove); W.R.O., Whittonditch land tax; ibid. wills, dean, 1819, no. 10; map of Ramsbury, E. div., *penes* Mrs. Croucher.
[72] W.R.O. 1008/25; above.
[73] *First Pembroke Survey*, ed. Straton, i. 148–79; for Membury: below.
[74] Above.
[75] Ibid.; W.R.O. 1883/66/70; 1883/165/47.

In 1773 John Whitelocke, lord of a manor in Chilton Foliat, owned Marridge Hill House, a large house surrounded by a park.[76] It passed at his death in 1787 to Sarah Liddiard or Whitelocke, who c. 1791 sold it to Henry Read.[77] The house was demolished before 1828.[78] The land, with more of Read's at Marridge Hill, passed, as a farm of 122 a. in 1839, with the Crowood estate of which it remained part in 1899.[79] In 1981 the site of the house and some of the land were part of Maj. H. O. Stibbard's Marridge Hill estate. Most of the remaining land was part of Witcha farm.[80]

A large estate at Marridge Hill, including 80 a. of pasture called Broad Breaches formerly demesne of Ramsbury manor,[81] was accumulated after 1677, possibly by the Mildenhall family, and belonged to Thomas Mildenhall in 1780. Mildenhall apparently sold the Breaches to Cheyney Waldron, presumably the younger, c. 1788.[82] At his death in 1819 the younger Cheyney Waldron devised the land to his nephew Thomas Waldron, a minor, with remainder to his nephew John Waldron, also a minor.[83] Trustees held it until 1830 or later, but by 1839 it was apparently John's and was absorbed by his main Marridge Hill estate.[84] Mildenhall sold the remainder of his estate to Henry Read shortly before Read's death in 1821, and it was added to Read's other land at Marridge Hill.[85]

The manor of *LITTLECOTE* seems to have belonged to Robert of Durnford in 1182 and to have passed in 1189–90 to Roger of Durnford, whose right was disputed by Ralph de Brewer and his wife Muriel but confirmed by them in 1198.[86] Brewer was possibly lord of Axford manor and the overlordship of Littlecote manor, rated as 1 knight's fee, belonged in the 13th and 14th centuries to the lords of Axford.[87] It was still claimed in 1404[88] but in the mid 15th century the lords of Littlecote themselves acquired Axford manor.

Despite a claim by Peter de Percy against Roger in 1202[89] Littlecote manor remained in the Durnford family. It was held by Roger's son Richard of Durnford in 1219 and 1241 and possibly by a Sir Richard of Durnford in 1258.[90] The manor was later held by Roger of Calstone who c. 1292 died holding it and leaving as heir a year-old son Roger.[91] In 1328 Roger (d. c. 1342)

settled Littlecote on his marriage, and in 1356 the manor was held by his son Laurence.[92] By 1385 it had passed to Laurence's son Thomas (d. between 1412 and 1419) whose heir was his daughter Elizabeth, wife of William Darell (d. between 1439 and 1453).[93] At Elizabeth's death in 1464 the manor descended to her son Sir George Darell (d. 1474),[94] who was succeeded by his son Sir Edward (d. 1530).[95] Sir Edward's heir was his grandson Sir Edward Darell (d. 1549),[96] much of whose estate was devised for life to his mistress Mary Daniel. Littlecote manor, however, passed to his son William, then aged nine.[97]

As a result of a dispute with Sir Henry Knyvet, William Darell was imprisoned in the Fleet in 1579 for slandering the queen. He had been the co-respondent in Sir Walter Hungerford's action for divorce against his wife Anne 1568–70, and was or had been at law with many of his neighbours including Henry and Edward Manners, earls of Rutland, over Chilton Foliat 1563–5, William Hyde over Uffington (Berks., later Oxon.) 1573–4, Edward Seymour, earl of Hertford, over manors in Great Bedwyn and Burbage, and Hugh Stukeley over Axford, litigation arising partly from his father's will and his own minority. Accusations, almost certainly groundless, of infanticide and murder were made against him.[98] The expenses incurred by his imprisonment, incessant litigation, building,[99] and attendance at court led him to sell the reversion, for a term of years if he had male issue, of Littlecote to Sir Thomas Bromley (d. 1587), Lord Chancellor, apparently in the early 1580s.[1] About 1586 the reversion seems to have been transferred on similar terms to Darell's lawyer and adviser John Popham.[2] Darell was indicted at Marlborough assizes in 1588, again for slandering the sovereign.[3] The survival of many documents illuminating his affairs[4] has led to much speculation about his life and motives.[5] He died without male issue in 1589 and Popham entered on Littlecote manor.[6]

The manor descended from father to son in the Popham family, from John (d. 1607), Lord Chief Justice and a knight from 1592, to Sir Francis (d. 1644), Alexander (d. 1669), Sir Francis (d. 1674), and another Alexander.[7] At that Alexander's death in 1705 Littlecote passed to his uncle Alexander Popham (d. 1705), and the manor

[76] *V.C.H. Berks.* iv. 193; *Andrews and Dury, Map* (W.R.S. viii), pl. 15.
[77] W.R.O. 500/7; ibid. Eastridge land tax; *D.N.B.* s.v. John Whitelocke.
[78] O.S. Map 1″, sheet 34 (1828 edn.).
[79] Map of Ramsbury, E. div., *penes* Mrs. Croucher; W.R.O. 1001/11.
[80] Inf. from Maj. Stibbard; Mr. Jones.
[81] *First Pembroke Survey*, ed. Straton, i. 159.
[82] W.R.O., Eastridge land tax.
[83] Ibid.; ibid. wills, dean, 1819, no. 10.
[84] Ibid. Eastridge land tax; map of Ramsbury, E. div., *penes* Mrs. Croucher.
[85] W.R.O., Eastridge land tax; above.
[86] *Pipe R.* 1182 (P.R.S. xxxi), 87; 1189 (P.R.S. n.s. i), 118; P.R.O., CP 25(1)/250/1, no. 15; *Cur. Reg. R.* viii. 390–1.
[87] Below, Axford, manors; W.R.O., bishop, Liber Niger, ff. 95–8, 237v.; *Cal. Close, 1296–1302*, 249.
[88] *Sir Chris. Hatton's Bk. of Seals*, ed. L. C. Loyd and D. M. Stenton, pp. 263–4.
[89] *Pipe R.* 1202 (P.R.S. n.s. xv), 126.
[90] Ibid. 1219 (P.R.S. n.s. xlii), 19; *Cur. Reg. R.* viii. 390–1;

P.R.O., CP 25(1)/251/12, no. 36; W.R.O., bishop, Liber Niger, f. 81 and v.
[91] *Cal. Inq. p.m.* iii, pp. 6–7.
[92] Ibid. viii, p. 241; *Feet of F.* 1327–77 (W.R.S. xxix), p. 17; B.L. Harl. MS. 1623, f. 10v.; *Cat. Anct. D.* v, A 13602.
[93] *Cal. Close, 1385–9*, 79; *Sir Chris. Hatton's Bk. of Seals*, pp. 263–4; *Cat. Anct. D.* ii, C 2492; iii, C 3341; v, A 13602; P.R.O., SP 46/45, f. 65.
[94] P.R.O., C 140/12, no. 13; *V.C.H. Wilts.* xi. 121.
[95] P.R.O., C 142/51, no. 2; B.L. Harl. MS. 1500, ff. 1–2.
[96] P.R.O., C 142/92, no. 111.
[97] Hubert Hall, *Soc. in Elizabethan Eng.* 4, 6, 192.
[98] For Darell's career see especially ibid. *passim*; P.R.O., SP 46/44–5.
[99] Below.   [1] P.R.O., SP 46/45, f. 208.
[2] Ibid. CP 43/15, rot. 154 and d.
[3] Hall, op. cit. 256.   [4] P.R.O., SP 46/44–5.
[5] e.g. Hall, op. cit.; *W.A.M.* iv. 209–25; vi. 201–14, 390–6; Wal. Scott, *Rokeby*, canto v. xxvii.
[6] P.R.O., SP 46/44, f. 120.
[7] Burke, *Land. Gent.* (1952), 2056; *D.N.B.* s.vv. Sir John and Sir Francis Popham.

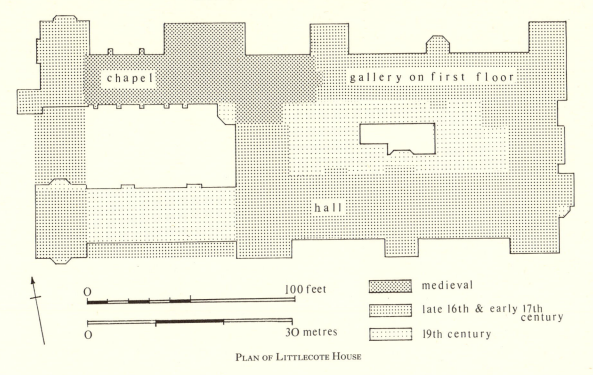

O _____ 100 feet

O _____ 30 metres

▨ medieval

▤ late 16th & early 17th
century

▦ 19th century

PLAN OF LITTLECOTE HOUSE

again passed from father to son to Francis (d. 1735), Edward (d. 1772), and Francis (d. 1780), whose relict Dorothy Popham held it until her death c. 1797 and devised it to her husband's reputed son Francis Popham. At that Francis's death without issue in 1804 the manor passed to the nephew of Francis (d. 1780), Edward William Leyborne-Popham (d. 1843), who devised it to his son Francis (d. 1880).[8] Littlecote passed in turn to that Francis's sons Francis William Leyborne-Popham (d.s.p. 1907)[9] and Hugh Francis Arthur Leyborne-Popham, who sold it in 1929 to Sir Ernest Salter Wills, Bt. (d. 1958).[10] It descended to Wills's second son G. S. Wills (d. 1979), whose son Mr. D. S. Wills was the owner in 1981.[11]

In the early 14th century, when he had a chapel there, it seems likely that Roger of Calstone lived at Littlecote.[12] Apart from a late medieval range of building containing a chapel Littlecote House was rebuilt in the later 16th century for William Darell.[13] The new building was around two courts: the chapel range became the north side of the west court. The principal rooms and the entrance porch and hall are on the south side of the east court. The north side of that court, the contract to build which is dated 1583,[14] contains a long gallery on the first floor. Possibly because, when the court was built, older building survived at its north-west corner, the north and south sides are not on the same north–south axis. Most of the house was of flint rubble but the south

front was faced with brick. A gatehouse, aligned with the porch, and garden walls were built of brick in 1585.[15] Most of the work on the house had presumably been done by then, but the fittings inside may not have been finished for several years.[16] In the mid 17th century an east pulpit and a west gallery extending along both sides were built in the chapel.[17] In the mid 18th century the south side of the west court, until then of a single storey, was rebuilt to full height, and about then the adjacent drawing room was altered and several windows in the house were sashed.[18] Other 18th-century work included the alteration of several fireplaces and the decoration of the 'Dutch' room with a painted ceiling and reset painted panelling. In 1810 the south side of the west court was again demolished and was rebuilt as a conservatory with tall Gothic windows. The west side was also demolished then and left open. There were alterations to several rooms including the drawing room and, to designs by John Robson,[19] the library. In the late 19th century the four service rooms east of the main entrance were made into a dining room and a study, in which there is a fine, presumably reset, chimneypiece dated 1592 and panelling in early 17th-century style in which the date 1896 has been carved. Both rooms have ribbed ceilings. The adjacent main staircase is also of the late 19th century. A ribbed ceiling was made in the long gallery in 1899,[20] but the original frieze incorporating the Darell arms was retained.

[8] F. W. Popham, *W. Country Fam.: the Pophams from 1150*, 66–9; S.R.O., DD/PO 3J; DD/PO 3M; W.R.O., Eastridge land tax.
[9] The date of d. is misprinted in Burke, *Land. Gent.* (1952), 2056; cf. *W.A.M.* xxxv. 321.
[10] Popham, op. cit. 70.
[11] Burke, *Peerage* (1959), 2396; *Wilts. Gaz.* 22 Mar. 1979; inf. from Mr. Wills.

[12] *Feet of F.* 1327–77 (W.R.S. xxix), p. 17.
[13] See plates facing p. 33.
[14] P.R.O., C 146/8318.
[15] Ibid. SP 46/45, ff. 310, 313.
[16] A chimneypiece is dated 1592.
[17] See plate facing p. 49.
[18] J. Buckler, watercolour in W.A.S. Libr., vol. x. 13.
[19] Drawings at Littlecote Ho.   [20] Date on ceiling.

Several other decorated plaster ceilings are possibly of similar date, but it is not clear when the sashes in the front were replaced by mullions and transoms. In the 19th century single-storeyed service rooms were built over most of the east courtyard and a staircase was built at its south side.

Walled gardens and yards surrounded the house in the later 17th century and included a west raised walk from which there were views across the adjoining park.[21] Most of those features and formal gardens apparently survived in the later 18th century but by then the gate-house had been demolished.[22] South of the house the walls were apparently demolished before 1806 and the park was brought up to the house,[23] but early walls survive north of it. The main feature of the park in the late 18th century was Park Coppice, on the high ground in the west part, which had a central clearing and eleven radiating vistas.[24] There are extensive 18th- and 19th-century farm buildings east of the house, mostly in Chilton Foliat.

In the 15th and 16th centuries the Darells were active in county government: from 1420 to 1519 a Darell was sheriff one year in six.[25] Littlecote House presumably became busier and more celebrated as a result of such activity. In the 17th century it was the home of a nationally important family, frequently visited by politicians,[26] and in 1688 was visited by William of Orange after meeting James II's commissioners at Hungerford.[27]

Jocelin de Bohun, bishop of Salisbury 1142–84, granted land at MEMBURY, presumably part of Ramsbury manor until then, to Everard of Hurst, to whom he may have granted Hilldrop.[28] After Everard's death Bishop Bohun conveyed it to Everard's son Roger.[29] The grant to Roger was confirmed by the king in 1175 and by Bishop Herbert Poore in 1196.[30] Gerard of Membury seems to have held the land in the 1220s[31] and Sir Peter of Membury did so in the 1240s and 1250s when it was rated as 1 knight's fee.[32] Between 1256 and 1262 Peter gave the manor of Membury to Giles of Bridport, bishop of Salisbury, in exchange for a life interest in the bishop's demesne land in Baydon.[33] Membury thus again became part of Ramsbury manor.[34] In 1678 Henry Powle sold the land as Membury farm to Thomas Seymour (d. c. 1717). Sey-

mour's heirs were his daughters Anne, wife of Toby Richmond, Jane, who granted the land which she inherited from her father to Anne's and Toby's son Seymour, and Frances, wife of John Walford.[35] Seymour Richmond (d. c. 1784) held the farm in 1720. His heir was his daughter Alethea (d. 1786), whose husband Joseph Gabbit held it until c. 1790.[36] It was then sold to the tenant Thomas Bacon.[37] It was acquired, presumably by purchase, c. 1803 by Richard Townsend, who may have been succeeded c. 1815 by a younger Richard Townsend, the owner in 1839.[38] Thereafter the descent of the farm is obscure until 1903 when the Revd. Theodore de Lanulph Sprye owned it. Sprye held it until 1919 or later.[39] From 1922 or earlier it was part of Walter Woolland's Baydon Manor estate and as a farm of 363 a. was sold in 1947 and c. 1949.[40] Noel Bechely Crundall bought it in 1949 and after his death in 1968 it was sold to Mr. A. A. Horne, the owner in 1981.[41] The 12th-century keep of a castle at Membury was the site of a house built in the Middle Ages south of Membury fort.[42] The site was possibly deserted after the manor was reunited with Ramsbury manor in the mid 13th century. A farmhouse later stood further south. Membury House was built on its site in the 1960s following the destruction by fire of its predecessor.[43] West of the house 19th- and possibly early 20th-century outbuildings and stables are now dwellings, east of the house is a walled garden, and at the end of the drive south of the house is a 19th-century lodge.

The endowment of Membury chapel was granted as an appurtenance of Ramsbury manor to Edward, earl of Hertford, in 1545,[44] but in 1574, valued at 20s., was claimed by the Crown from the tenant of Membury farm as the concealed land of a dissolved chantry.[45] In 1575 it was granted to agents or speculators and later it was again part of Membury farm.[46]

The land of THRUP or East Thrup descended in a family which took its name from the place. Before 1249 it possibly belonged to Osmund Geraud, otherwise Osmund of Thrup, and in the mid 13th century it was Adam of Thrup's.[47] In 1275, when it was rated as 1 knight's fee, it was held by Adam's heirs,[48] one of whom may have been John of Eastrop (d. before 1300). John's brother Roger held the land in 1300.[49] Roger died before 1308 leaving as heir a son Roger, a minor,

[21] Painting ascribed to T. Wyck at Littlecote Ho.; see plate facing p. 33.
[22] *Andrews and Dury, Map* (W.R.S. viii), pl. 12; W.R.O. 1650, Popham Mun., map, 1775.
[23] Buckler, watercolour in W.A.S. Libr., vol. x. 13.
[24] W.R.O. 1650, Popham Mun., map, 1775.
[25] M. M. Condon, 'Wilts. sheriff's notebook', *Medieval Legal Rec.* ed. R. F. Hunnisett and J. B. Post, 411.
[26] e.g. Hist. MSS. Com. 78, *Hastings*, ii, p. 384.
[27] *V.C.H. Wilts.* v. 168.
[28] Hist. MSS. Com. 55, *Var. Coll.* i, pp. 363–4; above.
[29] D. & C. Sar. Mun., press II, box 5.
[30] Hist. MSS. Com. 55, *Var. Coll.* i, pp. 365–6.
[31] D. & C. Sar. Mun., press IV, box C 3/Ramsbury/2; *Pat. R. 1216–25*, 310; *Sar. Chart. and Doc.* (Rolls Ser.), 174 n.
[32] *Sar. Chart. and Doc.* (Rolls Ser.), 274–5; *Crown Pleas, 1249* (W.R.S. xvi), p. 263; W.R.O., bishop, Liber Niger, f. 237v.; *Rot. Hund.* (Rec. Com.), ii (1), 240.
[33] D. & C. Sar. Mun., press IV, box C 3/Ramsbury/9.
[34] Above.
[35] W.R.O. 1883/66/69; 1883/13; *V.C.H. Berks.* iv. 257.

[36] P.R.O., CP 25(2)/1088/6 Geo. I Hil.; W.R.O. 212B/5658; ibid. Eastridge land tax; H. I. Richmond, *Richmond Fam. Rec.* iii. 48–50.
[37] W.R.O., Eastridge land tax.
[38] Ibid.; map of Ramsbury, E. div., *penes* Mrs. Croucher.
[39] *Kelly's Dir. Wilts.* (1903), where Sprye's forenames are apparently wrongly given: cf. *Crockford* (1896 and later edns.); W.A.S. Libr., sale cat. xxviiiD, no. 36.
[40] Sale cat. map *penes* Mrs. V. Wills, Eastridge Ho.; W.R.O. 1008/25; above.
[41] Wilts. Cuttings, xxiii. 199, 230; sale cat. (1982).
[42] *V.C.H. Wilts.* i (1), 269; Pevsner, *Wilts.* (2nd edn.), 345.
[43] Local inf.
[44] *L. & P. Hen. VIII*, xx (2), p. 411.
[45] P.R.O., E 178/2410.
[46] *Cal. Pat. 1572–5*, p. 409; W.R.O. 130/46, lease, Powle to Seymour.
[47] *Crown Pleas, 1249* (W.R.S. xvi), pp. 173–4, 263; W.R.O., bishop, Liber Niger, f. 237v.
[48] *Rot. Hund.* (Rec. Com.), ii (1), 265.
[49] D. & C. Sar. Mun., press IV, box C 3/Ramsbury/4.

whose heir was his daughter Evelyn, wife of David of Witchampton.[50] She held the land in 1376.[51] In 1392 she released her right to it, and in 1394 trustees settled it on her son Robert of Thrup and his wife Agnes.[52] Robert died in the period 1408–11 and was succeeded by his daughter.[53] The land was possibly sold c. 1419 to Robert Andrew to whom Alice Witchampton, granddaughter of Evelyn Witchampton, possibly Robert of Thrup's daughter, and relict of John Upton, then released her right.[54] Andrew held Thrup in 1428 when, for reasons that are obscure, it was said to have been formerly held by John of Coventry (fl. 1327).[55] It was afterwards acquired, presumably by purchase, by William Darell of Littlecote or his relict Elizabeth, who died seised of Thrup manor in 1464.[56] As Thrup farm and as part of Knighton farm it passed with Littlecote manor until in 1896 it was sold to V. J. Watney.[57] It was later reunited with Littlecote manor, presumably by Sir Ernest Salter Wills in 1929.[58] In 1979 Thrup farm, 178 a., was sold to Mr. R. A. Pearce.[59]

Another estate at Thrup, the origin of which is obscure, belonged in 1780 to a Revd. Mr. Topping, presumably Thomas Topping, vicar of Iwerne Minster (Dors.) from 1783 to 1822 or later. Francis Popham (d. 1804) apparently bought it from him c. 1804 and it became part of Thrup farm.[60]

In 1291 Poughley priory in Chaddleworth (Berks.) held an estate in Ramsbury parish, in 1331 expressly described as in Eastridge and later called the manor of EASTRIDGE.[61] In 1428 it was rated as ½ knight's fee.[62] It belonged to the priory until in 1525 the priory was dissolved so that its revenues could be used by Cardinal Wolsey for Cardinal College, Oxford. Eastridge was granted to Wolsey in 1526.[63] After Wolsey's death in 1530 the college's endowments reverted to the Crown and in 1531 the endowments of Poughley priory, including Eastridge, were granted to Westminster Abbey.[64] They were again taken by the Crown at the Dissolution.[65] Eastridge was granted to John Carlton in 1541.[66] Carlton was succeeded after 1559 by Anthony Carlton, who in 1564 was licensed to convey the estate to Richard Pocock.[67] Carlton was named as owner in 1566 and 1567 but the land passed to Pocock (d. c. 1596), who in 1582 settled it on the marriage of his son Giles.[68] In 1624 Giles was succeeded by his son Richard (d. c. 1654), whose

son Richard (d. 1694) devised his Eastridge estate to his own son Richard (d.s.p. 1718). The estate passed to that Richard's sister Sarah (d. 1733) and her husband Christopher Capel (d. 1740). After Christopher's death it apparently passed to his brother William (d. c. 1779), whose heir was his cousin William Capel.[69] Eastridge was sold by Capel c. 1791 to Cheyney Waldron, presumably the elder,[70] whose son John held the estate from c. 1791 to c. 1819.[71] John (d. before 1820) was succeeded by his eldest son Lovegrove (a minor in 1819, d. 1867) who devised his lands to his sons Thomas White (d. 1903), Lovegrove, and Walter Brind (d. 1913) as tenants in common.[72] Eastridge was apparently held by T. W. Waldron whose executors sold it to V. J. Watney in 1909.[73] Watney sold it in 1919 to Gerard Lee Bevan, who sold it in 1922 to Sir Ernest Salter Wills. From 1929 Eastridge has been part of the Willses' Littlecote estate.[74] Eastridge House was built in the style of a villa c. 1815. Its south front is of three bays with a central Doric porch. The gardens contain some trees which may be as old as the house, but the long entrance avenue, the lodge, and landscaping were created in the 1930s.

Ramsbury manor seems to have included little land in Knighton which, before the 15th century, may have been divided among several small estates.[75] William Darell and his wife Elizabeth bought an estate called Hopgrass in Knighton from William Horshill in 1426, and another from John Eastbury in 1432.[76] The Darell family built up a large estate there which in the 1470s was called KNIGHTON manor.[77] As Knighton farm it has passed with Littlecote manor.

In 1300 William of Wantage apparently acquired a small estate in Membury.[78] A carucate there later belonged to John of Wantage and descended to his son William (d. before 1369) and his brother Thomas of Winterbourne. In 1369 John's daughter Joan conveyed it to John of Eastbury (d. 1374), escheator of Berkshire, his wife Catherine, and their son Thomas. The validity of the conveyance was challenged in 1374 because Joan (d. 1392) was found to be of unsound mind and in John of Eastbury's keeping, but was upheld.[79] In 1406 John Wodhay and his wife Joan claimed the land from Thomas of Eastbury as Joan's descendants.[80] The claim apparently failed, but later owners of the carucate are unknown.

Gerard of Membury may have held land in

[50] Ibid. press IV, box C 3/Ramsbury/14; P.R.O., C 146/536.
[51] W.R.O., bishop, Liber Niger, f. 240.
[52] Cat. Anct. D. ii, C 2633; P.R.O., C 146/536.
[53] B.L. Add. Ch. 54988; Cat. Anct. D. v, A 10884.
[54] Cat. Anct. D. ii, C 2380.
[55] Feud. Aids, v. 268; P.R.O., E 179/196/7.
[56] P.R.O., C 140/12, no. 13.
[57] Above; below; S.R.O., DD/PO 99.
[58] Cf. Eastridge: below.
[59] Inf. from Mr. Wills.
[60] W.R.O., Eastridge land tax; Clergy List (1822).
[61] Tax. Eccl. (Rec. Com.), 192; W.R.O., bishop, Liber Niger, f. 95; Cat. Anct. D. ii, C 2467.
[62] Feud. Aids, v. 268.
[63] V.C.H. Berks. ii. 86; L. & P. Hen. VIII, iv (1), p. 849.
[64] L. & P. Hen. VIII, v, p. 286; P.R.O., C 142/77, rot. 53.
[65] P.R.O., E 318/Box 7/241.
[66] L. & P. Hen. VIII, xvi, p. 505.
[67] B.L. Add. Ch. 24440; Cal. Pat. 1563–6, p. 141.
[68] B.L. Add. Ch. 24441; First Pembroke Survey, ed. Straton, i. 150–1; P.R.O., C 142/247, no. 68.
[69] V.C.H. Berks. iv. 57; P.R.O., PROB 11/418 (P.C.C. 43 Box, will of Ric. Pocock).
[70] W.R.O., Eastridge land tax.
[71] Ibid.; P.R.O., PROB 11/1048 (P.C.C. 500 Hay, will of Thos. Lovegrove).
[72] W.R.O., wills, dean, 1819, no. 10; Princ. Regy. Fam. Div., 1867, Sar. 913; mon. in church.
[73] W.R.O., wills, 1903/225; Wilts. Cuttings, iii. 118.
[74] W.A.S. Libr., sale cat. xxviiib, no. 36; sale cat. map in Eastridge Ho.; inf. from Mr. Wills.
[75] Below.   [76] Cat. Anct. D. i, C 832, C 1456.
[77] Ibid. C 1484; ii, C 2872; vi, C 5696.
[78] Feet of F. 1272–1327 (W.R.S. i), p. 45.
[79] Ibid. 1327–77 (W.R.S. xxix), p. 135; Cal. Close, 1374–7, 4; Cal. Pat. 1370–4, 418–19; Cal. Inq. p.m. xiv, pp. 25–6.
[80] Cal. Pat. 1405–8, 207–8; Cat. Anct. D. vi, C 5936.

Eastridge in 1221, and in the mid 13th century Sir Peter of Membury conveyed an estate there to Nicholas Eustace.[81] In 1275 John de Cornialles held ½ knight's fee there.[82] Maud, daughter of John Fleming, conveyed 1 carucate in Eastridge to John Bacon, his wife Sarah, and his son John in the late 13th century.[83] Sarah and the younger John Bacon conveyed it to Ellis Farman in 1319.[84] Nothing is known of the later descent of those estates.

Robert at the green possibly held land in Knighton in 1327.[85] Lands conveyed by his son Roger in 1364 presumably included it.[86] In 1399 trustees conveyed to Joan at the marsh, with remainder to John son of Robert at the marsh, land in Knighton which had been Robert's.[87] Poughley priory's Eastridge manor included land in Knighton which in 1439 was leased to William and Elizabeth Darell for 90 years.[88] The freehold was never again said to belong to the priory and the land presumably became part of Knighton manor; but a quitrent apparently paid for it passed to the dean and canons of Westminster, successors to the abbot of Westminster to whom the revenues of the priory had been granted, and was still paid by the lord of Littlecote manor in 1789.[89]

ECONOMIC HISTORY. AGRICULTURE.

The bishop of Salisbury's estate of Ramsbury was assessed at 90 hides in 1084 and 1086.[90] The estate almost certainly included all of what became Ramsbury parish, including Axford and Baydon, which were later parts of Ramsbury manor, and Bishopstone, which was not mentioned in Domesday Book and was the bishop's in the early 13th century. It included five burgages in Cricklade and almost certainly nothing else.[91] The bishop's demesne of 30 hides, on which there were only 8 ploughteams and 9 serfs,[92] was presumably distributed among all four places, excluding Cricklade. Free tenants, who held a total of 27 hides, had demesne lands on which there were 11 ploughteams. The presence on the bishop's lands of 68 villeins and 43 bordars and on the free tenants' lands of 31 bordars all with a total of 35 teams suggest that villeins and bordars held most of the cultivated land. That, the low ratio of teams to hides on the bishop's demesne, and the fact that later most of the bishop's demesne land used for husbandry was at Bishopstone and Baydon[93] indicate that little of the bishop's land at Ramsbury was cultivated in

1086, and that, even if it was not then imparked, it was already reserved for sport and to keep animals for the bishop's household.[94] At £52 15s., compared to £17 5s. for the land held by others, the bishop's demesne was highly valued.[95]

Ramsbury was not among the bishop's manors leased in the late 12th century.[96] In the early 13th century, when it may still have included Bishopstone, assized rents totalled £31 12s. 4d.[97] Bishopstone had been separated from it by the late 13th century.[98] Thereafter the composition of the manor changed little: apart from the parks, woods, meadows, and pastures surrounding the bishop's palace at Ramsbury there was a demesne farm at Baydon and, except between c. 1160 and c. 1260, another at Membury.[99] Extensive demesne lands at Axford and Hilldrop may have been granted freely by a bishop before the late 12th century.[1] From the later Middle Ages there were free and customary tenants in all the tithings, more freeholders in Eastridge where the manors of Littlecote, Thrup, and Eastridge were located, and more customary tenants in Baydon, Axford, and Whittonditch.[2] The demesne lands of Baydon were leased for a short period c. 1260[3] but in the 14th century those at both Baydon and Membury were kept in hand.[4] In 1331 there were, including cottagers, some 100 customary tenants. Many labour services from them, and even some from some freeholders, were required and, in addition to normal agricultural labour, when the bishop left Ramsbury the customary tenants had to cart his victuals to Potterne, Sonning (Berks.), or Salisbury. By then, however, labour services from a few holdings had been commuted for higher rents.[5] By 1396 the demesne land at Membury had been leased and labour services from 11½ yardlands in Axford, 14½ in Whittonditch, 5 in Preston, 6 in Ford, and 6 yardlands and various smaller holdings in Ramsbury had been commuted.[6] Assized rents were £36 5s. 10d. in 1404. By then more demesne land had been leased and a moderately sized farm at Baydon was then the bishop's only directly exploited agricultural land. Many labour services from holdings at Baydon had been commuted but 1,100 could be called upon from the tenants of 18½ yardlands and 8 'cotsetlands' there.[7] That farm was afterwards leased and in the 16th century the bishops' income from the manor outside the parks was nearly all from rents. In 1535 a total of £67 11s. 11d. was paid:[8] the customary tenants of Ramsbury paid £13 4s. 10d., of Axford £8 8s. 11½d., Whittonditch £4 4s. 8d.,

[81] *Pat. R.* 1216-25, 310; D. & C. Sar. Mun., press IV, box C 3/Ramsbury/5.
[82] *Rot. Hund.* (Rec. Com.), ii (1), 265.
[83] P.R.O., E 40/4624.
[84] *Cat. Anct. D.* iii, A 4617, A 4620, A 4622.
[85] P.R.O., E 179/196/7. [86] *Cat. Anct. D.* i, C 178.
[87] Ibid. C 1769. [88] Ibid. ii, C 2467.
[89] S.R.O., DD/PO 27, acct. bk. 1788-9; above.
[90] *V.C.H. Wilts.* ii, pp. 121, 183.
[91] Below; Axford, manors; Baydon, manor; above, Bishopstone, manors; *V.C.H. Wilts.* ii, p. 121. There is no reason to suppose that Little Hinton was included: as stated ibid. p. 183.
[92] Cf. Potterne and Cannings: *V.C.H. Wilts.* ii, p. 121.
[93] *Sar. Chart. and Doc.* (Rolls. Ser.), 364; D. & C. Sar. Mun., press I, box 31, no. 11; press I, box 8, no. 12D; above, Bishopstone, econ. hist.

[94] Below.
[95] *V.C.H. Wilts.* ii, p. 121.
[96] *Pipe R.* 1186 (P.R.S. xxxvi), 166.
[97] *Interdict Doc.* (Pipe R. Soc. N.S. xxxiv), 19.
[98] *Sar. Chart. and Doc.* (Rolls Ser.), 364.
[99] D. & C. Sar. Mun., press IV, box C 3/Ramsbury/9; press IV, box C 3/Ramsbury/18; above, manors.
[1] Below; below, Axford, econ. hist.
[2] W.R.O., bishop, Liber Niger, ff. 95-8; below.
[3] D. & C. Sar. Mun., press IV, box C 3/Ramsbury/9; press IV, box C 3/Ramsbury/18.
[4] Ibid. press I, box 8, no. 12A; press I, box 31, no. 11.
[5] W.R.O., bishop, Liber Niger, ff. 95-8.
[6] D. & C. Sar. Mun., press I, box 8, no. 12B.
[7] Ibid. press I, box 8, no. 12D; press I, box 31, no. 11; below, Baydon, econ. hist.
[8] *Valor Eccl.* (Rec. Com.), ii. 70.

Ramsbury Manor from the north-east

Ramsbury Manor from the south

RAMSBURY

The north front of Littlecote House in 1806

Littlecote House from the south in the later 17th century

RAMSBURY

Marridge Hill £2 0s. 4d., Park Town £2 18s., and Baydon some £9.[9] About 1556 some 29 yardlands were held by copy in Baydon, 17 in Whittonditch, 6 in Eastridge, 22 in Axford, and 4 in Ramsbury: Baydon and Membury remained the principal demesne farms held on leases.[10] The tenures and distribution of the lands of the manor were little changed until holdings in all parts of the parish were sold between 1677 and 1681.[11] After 1681 tenants remained in all parts and a century later were a mixture of copyholders and lessees.[12]

Ramsbury manor and Ramsbury prebend were the only estates to extend throughout the parish, within which distinct agrarian economies evolved in several places. Those of Axford and Baydon are discussed below with other aspects of the histories of those places. The remainder of the parish was divided roughly by the Kennet, south of which there was for long little agriculture. There the steep side of the valley, close to the river and unbroken by a tributary valley, and the high flat land south of it were predominantly woodland and grassland imparked by the lords of Ramsbury and Littlecote manors and valued chiefly for sport. Several farms have been established there but only Elmdown shared in the common husbandry practised north of the Kennet.[13] The relief north of the Kennet is broken but few of the slopes between the ridges and dry valleys are steep enough to prevent ploughing, and arable farming predominated. In the 16th century cultivation there was in both open fields and inclosures.[14] In the Middle Ages there were evidently groups of open fields at Ramsbury, Park Town, Whittonditch, Preston, Eastridge or Marridge Hill, and Membury. They presumably developed in the early Middle Ages for use by those with holdings based at those places.[15] Inclosed land was principally at Littlecote, Thrup, Knighton, Hilldrop, and, later, Membury. The dates and circumstances of the inclosures seem to have been different.[16] Although it seems likely that they had been earlier, in the 16th century the groups of open fields were not self contained. As parts of each were attached to holdings based elsewhere in the parish, and as farms in most parts of the parish, becoming fewer and larger, encompassed land in several places, individual groups of fields were losing their identities.[17] Many open fields were still named after, and holdings located by, the places, but, even before general inclosure in 1778, separate agrarian economies in the main part of the parish could no longer be distinguished.[18]

The open fields of Ramsbury itself were in an arc north of the village, bounded on the west by Park Town, north by the inclosed lands of Hilldrop manor and Love's farm, and north-east and east by the fields of Whittonditch.[19] North, South, West, and Henley fields were mentioned in the Middle Ages.[20] There was also an East field in 1567 but neither South nor East field then seems to have been large.[21] North had been renamed Middle field by the late 17th century.[22] In 1778 the fields, West, 50 a. west of Hilldrop Lane, Middle, 69 a. east of Love's Lane, East, 60 a. south of Crowood Lane, and two smaller fields, Knowledge between West and Middle and Lower east of East, were inclosed under an Act of 1777.[23] The meadows and pastures beside the Kennet south of High Street and Scholard's Lane and bounded on the south by Royal ditch at the bottom of Spring Hill seem to have been part of the demesne of Ramsbury manor in the Middle Ages.[24] Oad marsh, meadow south of High Street, was floated c. 1642.[25] Wood marsh, demesne land leased to the tenants of Ramsbury manor in 1404 or earlier, was presumably what was later called Great marsh east of Oad marsh.[26] The yearly rent of 6s. 8d. was respited when 7 a. of the tenants' land was imparked, possibly in the late 15th century.[27] The tenants used the marsh in common and the right to feed a cow there was attached to cottages in the village.[28] In the later 18th century the leazetellers marked every beast on it at 1d. a head.[29] Although Wood marsh was reckoned no more than 20 a. in 1567, when it was inclosed in 1778 Great marsh was 44 a. On the northern slopes of Spring Hill south of Great marsh Elm down, 20 a., was a common cattle pasture in summer but at other times was used exclusively by the occupant of Elmdown farm.[30] Sheep seem to have been generously stinted on the open fields[31] but there was no upland sheep pasture at Ramsbury. Land there has been attached to large farms at Whittonditch, Park Town, and Hilldrop[32] but there has apparently never been a large farm at Ramsbury. In the Middle Ages customary holdings were small and they seem to have remained so even when there were only four of ½ yardland or more in 1567.[33] Many smallholdings were worked from buildings in the village, but the largest farm to have developed seems to have been Daniel Boreman's, c. 85 a. at inclosure. Because there were many smallholdings the arable and meadow land nearest Ramsbury continued to be worked in small parcels after inclosure.[34]

References to Park field and Bishop's field possibly suggest open fields in Park Town tithing,

[9] P.R.O., SC 12/22/90; Wilton Ho. Mun., survey, 1550s, pp. 279–301.
[10] Wilton Ho. Mun., survey, 1550s, pp. 279–301.
[11] Above, manors.
[12] W.R.O. 1883/59, bargain and sale, Powle to Jones; 154/2.   [13] Below.
[14] First Pembroke Survey, ed. Straton, i. 149–63.
[15] Below.   [16] Ibid.
[17] First Pembroke Survey, ed. Straton, i. 149–63.
[18] W.R.O. 154/2.   [19] Ibid.; 154/3.
[20] Ibid. bishop, Liber Niger, f. 101v.; Cat. Anct. D. iii, C 3308; P.R.O., C 146/10500; D. & C. Sar. Mun., press I, box 8, no. 12B.
[21] First Pembroke Survey, ed. Straton, i. 152–6.
[22] W.R.O. 130/46/30A.   [23] Ibid. 154/2–3.

[24] Ibid.; Sar. Chart. and Doc. (Rolls Ser.), 192; D. & C. Sar. Mun., press I, box 8, no. 12D.
[25] W.R.O. 212A/27/27, lease, Gilmore to Stone.
[26] Ibid. 154/2–3; D. & C. Sar. Mun., press I, box 8, no. 12D.
[27] First Pembroke Survey, ed. Straton, i. 156–7; below.
[28] First Pembroke Survey, ed. Straton, i. 150–1.
[29] W.R.O. 1883/2, ct. held 30 Oct.
[30] Ibid. 154/2–3; First Pembroke Survey, ed. Straton, i. 156.
[31] e.g. First Pembroke Survey, ed. Straton, i. 152–6.
[32] Ibid. 149, 153–5; below.
[33] D. & C. Sar. Mun., press I, box 8, no. 12B; First Pembroke Survey, ed. Straton, i. 152–6.
[34] W.R.O. 154/2.

but if such existed they were eliminated early by the expansion of the bishop's parks.[35] The right of the tenant of the lord's mill in Park Town to feed cattle and sheep in a marsh and in Blake's Lane *c.* 1600 may be a vestige of common pasture.[36] Nearly all the land of the tithing outside the parks was in a leasehold of Ramsbury manor, in Ambrose, formerly Blake's, farm, and in Hales Court farm, so called in 1584, the demesne of Ramsbury Trenchard manor.[37] In 1416 that manor included 3 carucates, most presumably in Park Town, and 24 messuages, some let for lives and most of them presumably smallholdings in Ramsbury.[38] The land in Park Town was reckoned as 7 yardlands in 1567.[39] In 1632 Hales Court farm measured 185 a. including 60 a. of meadow and pasture, 42 a. of woodland, and 83 a. of arable of which 11 a. were in the common fields of Ramsbury.[40] The farm buildings were near the Kennet between Ramsbury and Ramsbury Manor on land flooded or imparked *c.* 1775 when they were demolished.[41] In 1567 the lands of Ramsbury manor held by lease amounted to *c.* 30 a. and Blake's farm to *c.* 70 a. including 30 a. of woodland, presumably Blake's Copse.[42]

Meadow land at Whittonditch was presumably beside the stream flowing from Aldbourne to Knighton. Open fields were on both sides of the stream.[43] In the Middle Ages Whittonditch lands were used by the lord of Ramsbury manor in demesne, by his customary tenants at Whittonditch and later by others elsewhere, and by possibly three free tenants.[44] In the 14th century apparently all the demesne was pasture, sold yearly or leased, or woodland. By the 16th century the pasture, Witcha down, 30 a., had been appended to a copyhold.[45] There were ten or more customary tenants holding 14½ or more yardlands in 1396: in the mid 16th century they were fewer and their holdings were larger and extended into other parts of the parish. Thomas Seymour then held 60 a., John Goddard 18 a., and the lord of Ramsbury Trenchard manor 1½ yardland in Whittonditch tithing, but where their lands lay is obscure. No more than two or three copyholds then seem to have been based there: the largest, 154 a. including Witcha down, was possibly the later Whittonditch farm. Those and copyholds based elsewhere in the parish included some 215 a. of arable at Whittonditch.[46] In the late 17th century land was apparently being worked as Whittonditch, Crowood, and

Witcha farms.[47] Whittonditch farm measured 209 a. in 1737.[48] In the mid 18th century all three farms belonged to Henry Read who in 1755 was accused of removing merestones and of ploughing linches in the open fields.[49] In 1778 those fields were called Lower and Middle: they were possibly of roughly equal size and separated by the Aldbourne–Hungerford road. Of some 250 a. at Whittonditch inclosed in that year more than 200 a. were in Whittonditch and Witcha farms and imparked around Crowood House; 20 a. were in Minden, later Upper Whittonditch, farm; and land at Upper Whittonditch was in Preston farm.[50]

In 1396 four or more customary tenants held 5 yardlands or more at Preston.[51] In the later Middle Ages copyholds at Preston and Ford may have been merged: in the mid 16th century, when 7 yardlands said to be at Preston were held by four tenants, some of whom held land elsewhere in the parish, and when those tenants' lands were in Preston, Ford, and other fields, the two were not distinguished.[52] As a result there was uncertainty about what was Preston land and what was Ford land until the inclosure commissioners resolved it in 1778.[53] In the 16th century a common pasture, 16 a., on Hodd's Hill was for the ewes of the Preston copyholders.[54] There may have been no more than two farms based at Preston in the 16th century, and in the late 18th century there were only two. At inclosure the fields of Preston were apparently North field, *c.* 230 a. extending north-west of Marridge Hill and Hodd's Hill, and Little field, *c.* 75 a. nearer Preston. Some 200 a. were allotted in respect of farms based elsewhere. Preston farm was possibly of more than 100 a. including its land at Whittonditch and Marridge Hill and on Hodd's Hill. The second farm was smaller.[55]

There was demesne, freehold, and customary land of Ramsbury manor at Marridge Hill.[56] In the 16th century there were open fields, presumably on the flat land at the summit of the hill, and Marridge heath, 100 a., was a common pasture for sheep and cattle.[57] Before 1462, however, 40 a. of the demesne land, called Broad Breaches, had been inclosed and attached to a customary holding.[58] In the mid 16th century five copyholders held a total of 7½ yardlands and other land at Marridge Hill: 3½ of 4 freely held yardlands were part of Ramsbury Trenchard manor. Most of the copyholders also held land in Preston and elsewhere and it seems unlikely that more than

[35] D. & C. Sar. Mun., press I, box 8, no. 12C; below.
[36] W.R.O. 1883/6.
[37] *First Pembroke Survey*, ed. Straton, i. 151, 157–8; *W.N. & Q.* viii. 541.
[38] P.R.O., CP 25(1)/291/63, no. 39.
[39] *First Pembroke Survey*, ed. Straton, i. 151.
[40] W.R.O. 1883/62, bargain and sale, Trenchard to White.
[41] Cf. ibid. 154/2–3; *Andrews and Dury, Map* (W.R.S. viii), pl. 12.
[42] *First Pembroke Survey*, ed. Straton, i. 151, 157–8.
[43] W.R.O. 154/2–3.
[44] D. & C. Sar. Mun., press I, box 8, no. 12B; *First Pembroke Survey*, ed. Straton, i. 149, 151–6, 160–3; above, manors.
[45] D. & C. Sar. Mun., press I, box 8, no. 12B; *First Pembroke Survey*, ed. Straton, i. 160.
[46] D. & C. Sar. Mun., press I, box 8, no. 12B; P.R.O., SC

12/22/90; *First Pembroke Survey*, ed. Straton, i. 149, 151–6, 160–3.
[47] W.R.O. 1883/66/72; 1883/66/78.
[48] P.R.O., C 78/1887, no. 5.
[49] Above, manors; W.R.O. 1883/1, ct. held 10 Nov.; 1883/2, ct. held 14 Nov.
[50] W.R.O. 154/2–3; cf. map of Ramsbury, E. div., *penes* Mrs. B. Croucher, 25 Ashley Piece.
[51] D. & C. Sar. Mun., press I, box 8, no. 12B.
[52] P.R.O., SC 12/22/90; Wilton Ho. Mun., survey, 1550s, pp. 289–91; *First Pembroke Survey*, ed. Straton, i. 153–6, 159–63. [53] W.R.O. 154/2.
[54] *First Pembroke Survey*, ed. Straton, i. 155.
[55] Ibid. 155–6, 159–63; W.R.O. 154/2; ibid. Whittonditch land tax; cf. map of Ramsbury, E. div., *penes* Mrs. Croucher.
[56] W.R.O., bishop, Liber Niger, ff. 99, 100v.
[57] *First Pembroke Survey*, ed. Straton, i. 155–6, 162–3.
[58] W.R.O., bishop, Liber Niger, f. 100v.

three or four farms were based at Marridge Hill. The largest apparently included 120 a. of inclosed lands, among them Broad Breaches then said to be 80 a.[59] Marridge heath was inclosed in the 17th century but farmers in Marridge Hill, Preston, and Whittonditch cultivated Upper Marridge field, *c.* 100 a., in common until inclosure in 1778.[60] Three farms then seem to have been based at Marridge Hill. Most of Upper Marridge field and Broad Breaches made up Thomas Mildenhall's farm based at buildings south-east of the earlier Marridge Hill House. Other land, including much of the North field of Preston, was worked from Marridge Hill Farm and from buildings on the site of the later Marridge Hill House (Baydon Manor).[61]

In the Middle Ages there may have been common husbandry at Eastridge. References in 1567 to arable land in an apparently open field at Eastridge called Minden, possibly near what became Minden Farm, and to a common sheep pasture called Eastridge heath, 40 a., are evidence of it.[62] Land at Eastridge was held of Ramsbury manor but by the 16th century had apparently been attached to a copyhold based at Ramsbury.[63] Eastridge manor, 6 yardlands, then consisted of two farms.[64] The larger presumably included most of the land of Eastridge and may have been mainly several. In the late 18th century it was based at Eastridge Farm on the summit of the down. Minden farm then included more land at Whittonditch than at Eastridge. Other land was apparently worked in farms based at Ramsbury and Marridge Hill.[65]

At Knighton in the 16th century there were vestiges of common husbandry similar to those at Eastridge. A copyholder of Ramsbury manor held land in Knighton field, took hay from a common meadow, possibly that near Deep bridge mentioned in 1462, and had rights to feed beasts on Jacket marsh, 8 a., and Knighton marsh.[66] By then, however, most other estates in Knighton had apparently been absorbed by Knighton farm. At Thrup, however, even in the Middle Ages there seems to have been only a single estate, the lands of which were bounded by the Kennet and by those of Knighton and Chilton Foliat.[67] There is no evidence that any of Thrup manor, reckoned as 3 carucates in 1331,[68] was held customarily, and none of common husbandry. As parts of the Littlecote estate the lands of Knighton and Thrup may have been linked in the late 15th century,[69] but only from the mid 16th is it clear that Knighton farm encompassed Thrup. For a fine of £50 paid in 1545 the farm, including Thrup, was leased for 20 marks a year from 1550.[70] By 1712 a new Thrup farm had been created, possibly with a farmstead on the downs,[71] but it may not often have been leased separately.[72] In 1773 the buildings of Knighton farm were on their present site beside the Aldbourne-Hungerford road.[73]

In the Middle Ages there were open fields at Membury called East and South, possibly both south of the hamlet, and later evidence refers to a pasture which may previously have been common.[74] Those lands were presumably shared by the lord of Membury manor as demesne, by his customary tenants, and by the two freeholders with land there. The bishops of Salisbury may have exploited the demesne directly in the early 14th century. In 1330 three poor tenants of Membury were mentioned and it is unlikely that they or others held much land customarily.[75] John of Eastbury's estate was reckoned as 1 carucate in 1374:[76] some land in Membury was part of Pig's Court estate in Baydon, but how much is obscure.[77] By 1396 the demesne, Membury farm, had been leased.[78] The farm presumably absorbed Eastbury's and the customary tenants' lands, and in the 16th century all Membury land was inclosed. About 1556 Membury farm included 114 a. of arable, 9 a. of meadow, 98 a. of pasture, and Membury heath, 30 a., which was divided by ditches from Eastridge common pasture. The farmer also had pasture for 240 sheep and 28 beasts on Eastridge heath.[79] For much of the 16th century and in the early 17th century members of the Ballard family were lessees. The rent in 1567 was £4 13s. 4d.[80] In 1678 the farm included land on Membury fort which had been wooded and was then arable, almost certainly that encircled by the woodland still covering the banks and ditches called Membury walls.[81] The farm, 275 a. in 1721 when it included land in Baydon, was held by members of the Bacon family from before 1721 until *c.* 1803.[82]

There is no evidence of open field or common pasture at Hilldrop, nor of any other farm there but Hilldrop. The fact that the land, mainly north-west of Hilldrop,[83] was on the downs and near the bishop of Salisbury's palace at Ramsbury suggests that the inclosed farm originated in a grant of episcopal demesne pasture over

[59] P.R.O., SC 12/22/90; *First Pembroke Survey*, ed. Straton, i. 149, 151, 155-6, 159-60, 162-3.
[60] W.R.O. 1883/66/72; 1883/74, release, George to Shute; 154/2.
[61] Ibid. 154/2; ibid. Whittonditch land tax; Eastridge land tax; *Andrews and Dury, Map* (W.R.S. viii), pl. 15; cf. map of Ramsbury, E. div., *penes* Mrs. Croucher.
[62] *First Pembroke Survey*, ed. Straton, i. 155, 160.
[63] Ibid. 153-5; D. & C. Sar. Mun., press IV, box C 3/Ramsbury/6 (1309).
[64] *First Pembroke Survey*, ed. Straton, i. 150-1; *Cat. Anct. D.* ii, C 2467; P.R.O., E 318/Box 7/241.
[65] W.R.O. 154/2; ibid. Whittonditch land tax; Eastridge land tax.
[66] *First Pembroke Survey*, ed. Straton, i. 154-5, 160; W.R.O., bishop, Liber Niger, ff. 99v., 101v.
[67] D. & C. Sar. Mun., press IV, box C 3/Ramsbury/4; P.R.O., E 40/14748.
[68] W.R.O., bishop, Liber Niger, f. 95.
[69] Above, manors; P.R.O., C 146/1484.
[70] *Cat. Anct. D.* vi, C 7492.
[71] W.R.O. 1883/69/3; *Andrews and Dury, Map* (W.R.S. viii), pl. 15.   [72] S.R.O., DD/POt 125-7.
[73] *Andrews and Dury, Map* (W.R.S. viii), pl. 12.
[74] D. & C. Sar. Mun., press I, box 8, no. 12A; Wilton Ho. Mun., survey, 1550s, p. 304.
[75] D. & C. Sar. Mun., press I, box 8, no. 12A.
[76] *Cal. Inq. p.m.* xiv, p. 25.
[77] *Feet of F.* 1272-1327 (W.R.S. i), p. 42; W.R.O. 130/46/18.
[78] D. & C. Sar. Mun., press I, box 8, no. 12B.
[79] Wilton Ho. Mun., survey, 1550s, pp. 303-4; *First Pembroke Survey*, ed. Straton, i. 158-9.
[80] Wilton Ho. Mun., survey, 1550s, p. 303; *First Pembroke Survey*, ed. Straton, i. 158; *W.A.M.* xix. 263.
[81] W.R.O. 130/46, lease, Powle to Seymour.
[82] Ibid. 212B/5658; ibid. Eastridge land tax.
[83] Ibid. 154/2-3.

which any common right had previously been extinguished.[84] In the Middle Ages the farm may not have been leased.[85] In the 16th century its extent was estimated at 400 a. and in the late 18th century, when members of the Rawlins family were tenants, was over 500 a.[86] Love's farm between Hilldrop and Ramsbury was possibly reckoned as 1 carucate in 1462 and in the early 16th century may have been c. 100 a.[87] It may then and later have been worked with Hilldrop farm but in the late 18th century was separate.[88]

After the mid 1780s there is no evidence of a farm of more than 50 a. with buildings in Ramsbury village, nor of much copyhold land of Ramsbury manor. The land north of the village between Hilldrop and Whittonditch, which after inclosure in 1778 remained in small pieces with various owners, was gradually absorbed by the larger farms.[89] After inclosure there were in Ramsbury north of the Kennet, excluding Axford, between fifteen and twenty farms of more, most much more, than 50 a. In the west Ramsbury Manor farm, encompassing Hales Court farm and based at new buildings, was of 355 a. including 253 a. of arable in 1839, 329 a. in 1880. Bolstridge was a mainly arable farm of 67 a. in 1839, 144 a. in 1880, part of Ramsbury manor with buildings south-east of Hilldrop. In 1839 Hilldrop farm measured 530 a. including 370 a. of arable, and Love's was a wholly arable farm of 50 a. with buildings north-east of Hilldrop. In the centre in 1839 were Whittonditch farm, 248 a. worked from buildings beside the Aldbourne–Hungerford road, Witcha farm, 236 a. worked from buildings on the west side of the Whittonditch–Membury lane, William Atherton's farm of 100 a. with buildings at Upper Whittonditch, 220 a. of agricultural land south and west of Crowood House, and Minden, later Upper Whittonditch, farm, 165 a. worked from buildings on the east side of the Whittonditch–Membury lane. Those farms included a total 840 a. of arable. The land around Crowood House was presumably worked from Crowood Farm from the mid 19th century. In the north in 1839 Marridge Hill was a compact farm of 144 a. north-west of its buildings and including Large's barn, and the farm based at the later Marridge Hill House measured 325 a.; the third farm at Marridge Hill included 122 a. In Preston farm, 84 a., were 65 a. of arable, and Waldron's farm at Preston, 102 a., included 84 a. of arable. Membury was then a compact farm of 300 a. In the east Knighton and Thrup farms were being leased together in 1806 and in 1839 were a single farm of 570 a. including 458 a. of arable and 74 a. of

permanent grass. Eastridge farm then measured 377 a. of which 268 a. were arable.[90]

The concentration on arable farming evident in that whole area in the earlier 19th century has persisted, with little evidence of dairy farming at any time. In the mid 20th century most of the land of Ramsbury manor in the west was brought in hand and worked from Axford: in 1981 only Ramsbury Manor farm, 85 a., was held by lease.[91] The imparked land, which was leased for grazing in the 19th century and earlier 20th,[92] was not used for agriculture in 1981. Hilldrop was then a corn and sheep farm of over 600 a. including land in Aldbourne: Love's remained a separate small farm.[93] Most of the land of the Crowood estate in the centre had been brought in hand by the 1940s when there was mixed farming on it.[94] In 1981, including its land in Baydon and Aldbourne, the Crowood estate of over 1,000 a. was in hand and worked from Crowood Farm and buildings at Upper Whittonditch where there was a dairy.[95] Witcha farm measured 335 a. in 1949 including much of the land which had been in the third farm at Marridge Hill in 1839, the land north-west of the Whittonditch–Membury lane formerly in Upper Whittonditch farm, and land formerly in Whittonditch farm. In 1981 its halves, Witcha and Woodlands, were pasture farms respectively for cows and sheep.[96] Whittonditch was then a mixed farm with c. 200 a. at Whittonditch and Preston and additional land in Aldbourne.[97] As part of the Baydon Manor estate in the north the two farms at Preston were merged before 1947 into a farm of 293 a., including 10 a. in Aldbourne, of which only 30 a. were grass.[98] In 1981 over 200 a. were part of Maj. H. O. Stibbard's farm based at Marridge Hill.[99] The two larger farms at Marridge Hill were merged before 1947 as Marridge Hill farm, then 511 a. including land in Baydon and buildings at Marridge Hill Farm.[1] In 1981 Maj. Stibbard's was an arable and pasture farm of over 600 a. with land in Baydon and large buildings, including some for cattle rearing, north of Baydon Manor, and was in hand. Other large buildings at Marridge Hill were for poultry rearing. Those at Marridge Hill Farm were not used for agriculture.[2] In 1947 Membury farm measured 363 a. including 54 a. which were part of Membury airfield and 11 a. in Lambourn:[3] with more land in Lambourn and Ramsbury it measured 561 a. in 1981 when it was worked under contract from Hilldrop Farm.[4] In the earlier 20th century A. J. Hosier used new techniques of dairy farming at Knighton farm, of which he was tenant.[5] In the later 20th century

[84] Above, manors.
[85] B.L. Harl. Ch. 49 H. 53.
[86] First Pembroke Survey, ed. Straton, i. 149; Inclosure Awards (W.R.S. xxv), p. 55; W.R.O. 154/2; ibid. Ramsbury land tax.
[87] W.R.O., bishop, Liber Niger, f. 99; P.R.O., C 142/28, no. 135.
[88] Above, manors; W.R.O., Ramsbury land tax.
[89] Cf. W.R.O. 154/2–3; maps of Ramsbury penes Mrs. Croucher.
[90] Maps of Ramsbury penes Mrs. Croucher; for acreages in 1880, W.R.O. 1883, rent bk.; for Crowood Farm, O.S. Map 6″, Wilts. XXX (1887 edn.); for lease of Knighton and Thrup, S.R.O., DD/POt 154.

[91] Inf. from Maj. F. R. D. Burdett-Fisher, Harbrook Farm.
[92] W.R.O. 1883, rentals.
[93] Inf. from Mr. C. E. Eliot-Cohen, Hilldrop Farm.
[94] O. E. Mosley, My Life, 416.   [95] Local inf.
[96] Inf. from Mr. D. J. Jones, Witcha Farm.
[97] Local inf.
[98] W.R.O. 1008/25.
[99] Inf. from Maj. H. O. Stibbard, the Park, Ogbourne St. Geo.
[1] W.R.O. 1008/25.   [2] Inf. from Maj. Stibbard.
[3] W.R.O. 1008/25.
[4] Sale cat. (1982); inf. from Mr. Eliot-Cohen.
[5] W.A.M. xlv. 388.

Eastridge farm, the land of Upper Whittonditch farm south-east of the Whittonditch–Membury lane, Thrup farm, until 1979, and Knighton farm were in hand as parts of Littlecote estate and were devoted solely to arable farming. Their buildings were given up by the estate and only those at Eastridge, where cattle were reared, were in use in 1981. The land of Thrup was then worked from Lambourn.[6]

The large area which Domesday Book suggests was neither tenanted nor ploughed in the late 11th century[7] was around the bishop of Salisbury's palace on the Kennet between Ramsbury and Axford.[8] The part of it south of the river was taken into Savernake forest, but in 1228 was disafforested.[9] In 1246 it was acknowledged to be a chase of the bishop.[10] In 1281 the bishop maintained his right to a chase but successfully denied allegations that he also claimed free warren without licence and obstructed men hunting hares and other beasts of the warren.[11] Free warren was granted in 1294.[12] The lands, which had been imparked by the 14th century, had thrice to be defended by bishops against their neighbours: in 1316 hedges and fences were broken and animals killed and removed by Henry Esturmy, warden of Savernake forest;[13] in 1347 Hildebrand of London, lord of Axford manor, forcibly entered the park and took fish from the bishop's waters, deer from the park, and hares, rabbits, pheasants, and partridges from the warren;[14] and in 1541 Sir Edward Darell, lord of Littlecote manor, hunted without licence.[15] The first two of those incursions were possibly intended as challenges to the bishops' rights.

From the 14th century the imparked land was divided between north and south parks.[16] In 1458 Bishop Beauchamp acquired by exchange 154 a., mostly from Henry Hall from what was later called Hales Court farm, and was licensed by the king to enlarge his parks by inclosing 400 a. including 100 a. of woodland.[17] It seems likely that the exchanged land was inclosed to extend the north park: an embankment extending round Old Park Wood north of the Kennet and the site of the Plantation south of the Kennet may have marked its new boundaries, and in places is still visible.[18] In the 16th and 17th centuries that park was called the little or old park, the south park was called the great, new, or high park.[19] About 1545 the little park measured 190 a., including pastures in the north called the old fields, presumably the land inclosed c. 1458.[20] The great

park, described by Leland as a 'right fair and large park hanging on the cliff of a high hill well wooded over the Kennet',[21] contained 600 a. of pasture, 300 a. of woodland, and a rabbit warren. Near his palace the bishop had some 50 a. of meadow land, the right to exclusive fishing in the Kennet, and four well stocked fishponds. Trees in the great park were valued at 2,500 marks, those in the little park at 200 marks. There were said to be 400 deer in the great park.[22] Bishops had appointed one man as keeper of the manor of Ramsbury and of its buildings, gardens, and orchards (for 40s. a year), keeper of the warren or chase and keeper of the woods and chief parkkeeper (4d. a day), overseer of swans (10s. a year), and keeper of the waters and river bank (1d. a day): a pension of £40 a year paid to Sir Edward Baynton for surrendering the offices in 1541 possibly reflects their true value.[23] Other 16th-century estimates of the area of the parks and of the woodland, pasture, and meadow within them vary, but the distinction between the great and little parks and the pattern of land use apparently continued throughout the century.[24]

Sales of wood and payments for agistment in 1330 show that fiscal profits could sometimes be taken from the parks:[25] in 1462 rabbits and meadow land were at farm.[26] The parks, however, may have been created and been used primarily for the bishop's sport, larder, and horses. In the 17th century such use declined when the owners, the earls of Pembroke, were usually absent, and leasing became more the rule. The woods were held by lease in 1633[27] and in the later 17th century Ramsbury manor house was leased.[28] Herbert Saladin held the old park, apart from its woods and the old fields, and 57 a. of meadow in 1675.[29] Parts of the high park had been leased for agriculture before 1670 when, of 265 a. so leased, some 200 a. were tilled.[30] In 1676 the boundaries of the parks, still inclosing c. 1,100 a., apparently followed the southernmost part of the parish boundary, bisected Hens Wood, crossed the Kennet near Axford Farm, extended northwards round Old Field Copse, and crossed the Kennet again east of the manor house.[31] Nearly 300 a. of the high park were sold between 1677 and 1681.[32] In 1681 the remainder, 545 a. impaled and divided into three by hedges and rails, was leased with 33 a. of water meadow for £446 a year.[33] Some of the old park was also sold in 1679: the remainder was presumably kept in hand by the Joneses to surround the new

[6] Inf. from Mr. D. S. Wills, Littlecote Ho.; for Littlecote estate, below.   [7] Above.
[8] Leland, *Itin.* ed. Toulmin Smith, v. 79.
[9] *V.C.H. Wilts.* iv. 417–18.
[10] *W.A.M.* xlviii. 376.
[11] *Plac. de Quo Warr.* (Rec. Com.), 804.
[12] *Cal. Chart. R.* 1257–1300, 454.
[13] *Reg. Martival* (Cant. & York Soc.), ii. 68–9, 84–6, 157–8; *V.C.H. Wilts.* iv. 439.
[14] *Cal. Pat.* 1345–8, 307.
[15] *L. & P. Hen. VIII*, xvi, p. 261.
[16] D. & C. Sar. Mun., press I, box 8, nos. 12A, 12E.
[17] *Cal. Pat.* 1452–61, 471.
[18] O.S. Maps 1/10,000, SU 27 SE. (1980 edn.), SU 27 SW. (1978 edn.).
[19] P.R.O., SC 12/22/90; *First Pembroke Survey*, ed. Straton, i. 174–5; W.R.O. 212B/5651.
[20] P.R.O., SC 12/22/90; cf. map of Ramsbury manor,

1676, *penes* Lady (Marjorie) Burdett-Fisher, Axford Farm: microfilm copy in W.R.O.
[21] Leland, *Itin.* ed. Toulmin Smith, v. 79.
[22] P.R.O., SC 12/22/90.
[23] W.R.O., Ch. Com., bpric. 460, ff. 50 and v., 86 and v.
[24] Wilton Ho. Mun., survey, 1550s, pp. 310–11; *First Pembroke Survey*, ed. Straton, i. 174–5.
[25] D. & C. Sar. Mun., press I, box 8, no. 12A.
[26] W.R.O., bishop, Liber Niger, f. 102.
[27] Wilton Ho. Mun., receiver's roll.
[28] Above, manors.
[29] W.R.O. 84/47, partic. of Ramsbury manor.
[30] Ibid. 212B/5651.
[31] Ibid. microfilm copy of map, 1676.
[32] Ibid. 1883/59, bargain and sale, Pembroke to Whitley and Cratford; bargain and sale, Powle to Jones.
[33] Ibid. 1883/59, articles, Powle and Jones; 1883/60, lease, Jones to Hillman.

Ramsbury Manor. The sold portion may have been imparked again in the 1720s.[34]

In the later 18th century the non-agricultural part of the high park was again in hand and c. 1775 the old park was extended eastwards.[35] Both parks seem to have been used primarily for sport and the long pasture called Horse Race between the artificial lake and the new Plantation may have had the use implied by its name.[36] The agricultural land was taken from the south and east parts of the high park and was the basis of Park and Park Town farms.[37] By 1839 most of the parkland was used for agriculture. Ramsbury Manor had been leased with only 93 a.: much of the woodland had also been leased.[38] Park was then, as in 1880, a compact farm of 807 a., including in 1839 over 500 a. of arable and extending across the flat upland from Hens Wood to Spring Hill.[39] Park Town farm, c. 150 a. in 1752, was in 1839 a rectangular farm of 260 a., of which 240 a. were arable, extending from the Kennet to Spring Hill, with its buildings, now Harbrook Farm, beside the river in its north-west corner.[40] In 1839 there was also an arable farm of 96 a. with buildings near the parish boundary south of Spring Hill.[41] Those farms survived approximately thus until c. 400 a. were taken for Ramsbury airfield c. 1939.[42] Park farm was reduced to 232 a., mostly south and west of its buildings: in 1981 it was an arable and dairy farm.[43] The large buildings housing pigs at Darrell's Farm were part of it.[44] The lowland part of Park Town farm and the steep northern slopes of Spring Hill were pasture in 1981. After the airfield was returned to agriculture after 1955 most of it was ploughed. West of the Ramsbury–Froxfield lane, in 1981 Littlecote estate included extensive buildings at Bridge Farm and c. 125 a. of arable.[45] Since the Second World War there has been commercial forestry in Hens Wood.[46] By 1981 the parkland around Ramsbury Manor had been increased to c. 350 a.[47]

It seems likely that the Darells, lords of Littlecote manor, had a park at Littlecote long before Henry VIII had 'goodly pastimes and continual hunting' there in 1520.[48] There is also evidence of sheep-and-corn husbandry on the demesne in the 16th century: in 1549 over 700 sheep were kept and in 1589 wheat was sold for £52 and barley for £25.[49] Littlecote House is beside the parish boundary, its owners have held much land in Chilton Foliat and elsewhere,[50] and it is not certain whether the greater parts of the park and agricultural land were in Ramsbury or Chilton Foliat. Later evidence suggests that more than half of each was in Ramsbury.[51]

By the late 17th century the demesne had been leased as Littlecote, later Littlecote Park, farm, apparently 364 a. in 1699.[52] The farm sometimes included the water meadows, over 50 a., south of the Kennet between Knighton and Littlecote.[53] In the 1830s it consisted only of land in the triangle formed by the south-east corner of the parish, 327 a. including 293 a. of arable, and of c. 250 a. in Chilton Foliat. Its buildings were on the north side of the east–west road which ran south of Littlecote House and was otherwise its northern boundary.[54] In the mid 19th century those buildings were replaced by a new farmstead in the south part of the triangle.[55] In 1893 the farm, 471 a. including 305 a. in Ramsbury, was still primarily arable, but the tenant, S. W. Farmer, was a leading dairy farmer who also held 65 a. of Littlecote park in Ramsbury.[56]

Sales of wood from the park and from the woods elsewhere in the parish and in Chilton Foliat and Hungerford were a source of much income to the lords of Littlecote manor in the 18th century.[57] Wood was then also taken to fuel their brick and lime kilns in Hungerford and, possibly, near Elmdown Farm.[58] In the mid 18th century deer were still regularly hunted in the park[59] which in 1775 included c. 200 a. between the gardens around Littlecote House on the east and Park Coppice, c. 60 a., on the west.[60] The park, 200 a. of woodland in the eastern part of the parish, and the water meadows were then in hand,[61] in 1839 a total of 638 a. in Ramsbury including 56 a. of meadows, 200 a. of pasture in the park, and over 300 a. of woodland.[62]

In the later 20th century Littlecote Park farm and all the other lands of the Littlecote estate, over 4,000 a. in Ramsbury, Chilton Foliat, Hungerford, and elsewhere, have been brought in hand. In 1981 farming on them was entirely arable. Fields have been enlarged, hedges removed, and all farm buildings given up except airfield buildings at Bridge Farm which have been extended and in 1981 were used to house large machinery. Some of the woodland has been cleared for tillage but the shooting has been carefully preserved for letting.[63]

[34] Above, manors.
[35] W.R.O. 154/2–3; ibid. Park Town land tax; *Andrews and Dury, Map* (W.R.S. viii), pl. 12.
[36] O.S. Map 6″, Wilts. XXIX (1889 edn.).
[37] *Andrews and Dury, Map* (W.R.S. viii), pl. 12; above, manors.
[38] Map of Ramsbury, W. div., *penes* Mrs. Croucher.
[39] Ibid.; W.R.O. 1883, rent bk.
[40] W.R.O. 130/46/30A; map of Ramsbury, W. div., *penes* Mrs. Croucher.
[41] Map of Ramsbury, W. div., *penes* Mrs. Croucher.
[42] Inf. from Defence Land Agent, Durrington; Mr. G. W. Wilson, Rudge Manor Farm, Froxfield.
[43] Wilts. Cuttings, xxiii. 246; inf. from Mr. F. Clothier, Park Farm.
[44] Inf. from Mr. Clothier.
[45] Inf. from Mr. Wills.
[46] Local inf.
[47] Inf. from Mr. H. J. Hyams, Ramsbury Manor.
[48] *L. & P. Hen. VIII*, iii (1), p. 352.
[49] P.R.O., E 154/2/36; ibid. SP 46/45, f. 292.
[50] e.g. ibid. SP 46/44–5; ibid. C 3/378/10.
[51] W.R.O. 1650, Popham Mun., lease, Leyborne-Popham to Baring.
[52] S.R.O., DD/POt 7, mortgage.
[53] Ibid. DD/POt 155, val.
[54] Ibid. DD/PO 28; map of Ramsbury, E. div., *penes* Mrs. Croucher.
[55] Map of Ramsbury, E. div., *penes* Mrs. Croucher; O.S. Map 6″, Wilts. XXX (1887 edn.).
[56] W.R.O. 1650, Popham Mun., lease, Leyborne-Popham to Baring; farm rental, 1892; *V.C.H. Wilts.* iv. 106–7.
[57] S.R.O., DD/POt 121.
[58] Ibid. DD/POt 21, lease, Popham to Harris; DD/POt 128.
[59] Ibid. DD/POt 145.
[60] *Andrews and Dury, Map* (W.R.S. viii), pl. 12; W.R.O. 1650, Popham Mun., map.
[61] W.R.O. 1650, Popham Mun., map.
[62] Map of Ramsbury, E. div., *penes* Mrs. Croucher.
[63] Inf. from Mr. Wills.

Elmdown farm had been established on the upland between Ramsbury great park and Littlecote park, presumably by the 13th or 14th century.[64] In 1567 it consisted of 30 a. which were possibly inclosed around the farmstead, Elm down which was subject to summer pasture rights of those holding land in Ramsbury, and 10 a. in the fields of Ramsbury with pasture rights in the great marsh.[65] As part of Littlecote estate in the early 18th century the farm was leased separately.[66] From the late 18th century Elmdown and Ambrose farms were held together for long periods.[67] In 1839, when they were held separately, each with its farmstead and lands east of the Ramsbury–Froxfield lane, Elmdown measured 131 a. including 113 a. of arable, Ambrose 82 a. including 66 a. of arable.[68] In the later 20th century those lands, like other parts of Littlecote estate, were worked from Bridge Farm.[69]

Robert Maisey combined the businesses of watercress growing and basket making in Ramsbury apparently from the 1890s until the First World War.[70] The watercress beds passed to members of the Wootton family who in the 1930s had more than 20 employees and sometimes sent in a week 15,000 lb. of watercress via Hungerford to London from beds in Ramsbury, Froxfield, and Shalbourne.[71] The beds at Ramsbury, 14 a., were in the waters of the Kennet near How Mill and in the tributary valley between Knighton and Whittonditch.[72] Cultivation near How Mill ceased c. 1970, but watercress was still grown in the beds between Knighton and Whittonditch in 1981.[73]

FISHING. Several fishing in the Kennet was apparently the right of the lords of each manor with land reaching to it. It was claimed as part of Thrup manor in 1411,[74] of Ramsbury manor c. 1545,[75] of Axford manor in 1601,[76] and of Ramsbury Trenchard manor in 1634.[77] Fishing rights were excluded from the sales of much of Ramsbury manor between 1677 and 1681.[78] The Kennet at Ramsbury was then already noted for its trout.[79] Grayling were introduced c. 1890. They were later found to be harmful to trout and were with pike and coarse fish taken from the river by an electrical fishing machine and other means in the 1950s.[80]

MILLS. The 80 a. of meadow and 10 mills paying £6 2s. 6d. on the bishop of Salisbury's Ramsbury estate in 1086[81] are perhaps no more than might be expected since the estate included, apart from the Kennet at Ramsbury and Axford, streams suitable for mills at Bishopstone. In the Middle Ages the bishops had a demesne mill on the Kennet near their palace and in the north park, called Park Mill in the 1290s,[82] later Porter's Mill. It was in hand in 1330.[83] By 1395 it had been converted to a fulling mill and leased.[84] It was still a fulling mill in the 1460s but in the early 16th century was again a corn mill.[85] When the bishop was at Ramsbury the tenant had to grind for him with no more reward than food and drink and to allow him half the eels taken in the waters of the mill.[86] Henry Powle sold the mill with feeding rights in Park Town marsh and Blake's Lane to the tenant Edward Kingston in 1677.[87] It was bought back by a lord of Ramsbury manor, apparently between 1705, when a widow Porter held it, and 1728: in 1728 it was said to house three grist mills under one roof.[88] The lessee of Park farm held it in 1771.[89] It was apparently demolished c. 1775 when the artificial lake was made.[90]

How Mill, mentioned between 1274 and 1284, was a corn mill on the Kennet east of Ramsbury and was held by lease of the bishops of Salisbury in the later Middle Ages.[91] It passed with the manor and in 1559 was taken in hand by the lord following a dispute arising from a lease by him and an earlier lease in reversion:[92] thereafter the mill was held by copy.[93] It was not sold between 1677 and 1681 and remained part of the manor.[94] Milling apparently stopped there in the mid 19th century.[95] The surviving mill house is 18th-century.

A water mill at Ramsbury, presumably on the Kennet and possibly that held by William at the hill in 1331, was part of Love's estate in the Middle Ages;[96] Parson's Mill, possibly at Park Town, belonged to the prebendaries of Ramsbury from c. 1300 or earlier to 1515 or later.[97] They were possibly the two mills which were part of Ramsbury Trenchard manor in 1575.[98] After that manor was broken up in the 1630s one of the mills may have been acquired by John Cooke, who was a party to a conveyance of a mill in 1636.[99] That mill was apparently bought by

[64] Above, manors.
[65] *First Pembroke Survey*, ed. Straton, i. 150, 156.
[66] S.R.O., DD/POt 126.
[67] W.R.O., Ramsbury land tax; ibid. 1650, Popham Mun., farm rental, 1892.
[68] Map of Ramsbury, E. div., *penes* Mrs. Croucher.
[69] Inf. from Mr. Wills.
[70] *Kelly's Dir. Wilts.* (1885 and later edns.).
[71] Ibid. (1927 and later edns.); *W.A.M.* xlvi. 539–40; Wilts. Cuttings, xviii. 51.
[72] O.S. Map 6″, Wilts. XXX. NW. (1925 edn.).
[73] Inf. from Mr. B. J. W. Wootton, the Beeches, Whittonditch.
[74] *Cat. Anct. D.* v, A 10884.
[75] P.R.O., SC 12/22/90.
[76] Ibid. CP 25(2)/242/43 & 44 Eliz. I Mich.
[77] Ibid. CP 25(2)/510/10 Chas. I Mich.
[78] e.g. W.R.O. 130/46/19.
[79] Aubrey, *Nat. Hist. Wilts.* ed. Britton, 62.
[80] *V.C.H. Wilts.* iv. 365.
[81] Ibid. ii, p. 121.
[82] D. & C. Sar. Mun., press IV, box C 3/Ramsbury/13.

[83] Ibid. press I, box 8, no. 12A.
[84] Ibid. press I, box 8, no. 12B.
[85] W.R.O., bishop, Liber Niger, f. 101v.; ibid. Ch. Com., bpric. 460, ff. 95v.–96.
[86] Ibid. Ch. Com., bpric. 460, ff. 95v.–96.
[87] Ibid. 1883/65/44. The location of the mill is not clearly marked on a map made of the parks in 1676: ibid. microfilm copy of map, 1676.
[88] Ibid. 1883/13; 1883/67, lease, Jones to Slaymaker.
[89] Ibid. 212A/27/27, acct. of rents.
[90] Above, introduction.
[91] D. & C. Sar. Mun., press I, box 8, no. 12A; W.R.O., bishop, Liber Niger, ff. 80v., 102.
[92] B.L. Add. Ch. 24440; P.R.O., C 1/1404/71.
[93] *First Pembroke Survey*, ed. Straton, i. 152.
[94] W.R.O. 1883/59, bargain and sale, Powle to Jones.
[95] *Kelly's Dir. Wilts.* (1848 and later edns.); O.S. Maps 1″, sheet 34 (1828 edn.); 6″, Wilts. XXX (1887 edn.).
[96] W.R.O., bishop, Liber Niger, ff. 95, 243.
[97] Ibid. f. 80v.; ibid. Ch. Com., bpric. 460, f. 42 and v.
[98] P.R.O., CP 25(2)/239/17 Eliz. I Hil.
[99] Ibid. CP 25(2)/510/12 Chas. I Mich.; above, manors.

Richard King, the owner of Hales Court farm, from Stephen Cooke and others in 1650, and passed with that farm to Nicholas King in 1669. It was apparently near Hales Court Farm at Park Town[1] and was possibly Parson's Mill or its successor. It may have been the mill acquired by Richard Jones, lord of Ramsbury manor, from Henry Shute in 1711 and called Shute's Mill in 1771.[2] If so, it seems likely to have been demolished with Porter's Mill. The descent of Love's Mill is obscure. Its successor may have been the mill on the Kennet in Mill Lane leased in 1758 by Sir Michael Ernle, Bt. (d. 1771), and later called Upper Mill. Ernle's heir was his brother the Revd. Sir Edward Ernle (d. 1787) from whom his nephew Sir William Langham Jones, lord of Ramsbury manor, bought that mill in 1783.[3] Milling continued until the earlier 20th century: the machinery remained in the building until the 1960s.[4] The surviving mill house was built in the later 17th century or earlier 18th and extended in the later 18th century or earlier 19th.

A mill belonging to Edward Jatt in 1752 was apparently that on the Kennet beside Scholard's Lane later called Town Mill.[5] Nathan Atherton owned it from 1778 or earlier to c. 1821 and Joseph Atherton from c. 1821 to 1839 or later. Afterwards it became part of Ramsbury manor.[6] There is no evidence that corn was ground there after the 1890s.[7] The Old Mill is a large house the south half of which is built in the 18th century, the north half in the 19th century.

A mill was part of Thrup manor in 1394.[8] In the late 18th century there was possibly a mill on the Kennet near Littlecote House where Mill meads were so called in 1775,[9] but no part of such a mill survives.[10] A map of 1773 perhaps mistakenly infers that there was another mill on the Kennet between Town Mill and How Mill.[11]

MARKET AND FAIRS. The bishop of Salisbury had a market at Ramsbury in 1219.[12] In 1227 the king ordered the sheriff not to prevent it and, on condition that it harmed no other market, formally granted a Tuesday market to the bishop.[13] By 1229, however, it had been found detrimental to the market at Marlborough and was prohibited.[14] It may nevertheless have continued until 1240 when the bishop agreed with the king to give up his weekly market for two yearly three-day fairs at the Invention (3 May) and Exaltation (14 September) of Holy Cross.[15] Although it seems unlikely that the market at Ramsbury was a serious rival to that at Marlborough in the mid 13th century,[16] it remained hard to eliminate. In 1275 and 1281 the Crown accused the see of prejudicing Marlborough market by raising a new Sunday market at Ramsbury for trade in merchandise of all kinds. The accusations were disproved and the bishop claimed that there was no more than the buying and selling of food and drink on feast days and Sundays as was permitted under the agreement of 1240. Such trade and the two fairs were allowed to continue providing that no one market day should become fixed.[17] By 1300 a market at Ramsbury may have been considered no danger to trade at Marlborough and in that year the king again granted the bishop a Tuesday market.[18] The market was held in 1319[19] but nothing is known of it thereafter. The lack of surviving references to it suggests that it failed to flourish and that it petered out long before the 1790s when it was expressly said to have been discontinued.[20]

The fairs at the Invention and Exaltation were held in the 17th and 18th centuries.[21] In 1830 a cattle fair was held on 14 May and a hiring fair on 11 October.[22] Later both fairs were for dealing in cattle, but after the First World War that in October was a pleasure fair. The May fair had ceased by 1939 and the October fair ceased in the 1950s.[23]

TRADE AND INDUSTRY. A fulling mill and a quilling house on the bishop of Salisbury's demesne at Ramsbury in the 14th and 15th centuries are evidence of clothmaking.[24] From the 17th century Ramsbury had many trades related to agriculture and typical of a large village. The leather trade has been the most prominent. There was a tan house at Ramsbury in the 1630s,[25] when inspectors of leather were appointed at the view of frankpledge,[26] and there were tanners, shoemakers, glovers, and collar makers throughout the 18th century.[27] In 1780 there were three or more tan yards.[28] One, on the south side of High Street, passed from the Day to the Ashley family, members of which were tanners and curriers until the 1880s.[29] The furriery of Joseph Maslin was possibly linked with the tanning and glovemaking of the Ock-

[1] P.R.O., CP 25(2)/608/1650 Hil.; W.R.O. 212A/38/117/2; above, manors.
[2] W.R.O. 212A/27/27, acct. of rents; P.R.O., CP 25(2)/980/10 Anne Trin.
[3] W.R.O. 1883/67, lease, Ernle to Gibbs; conveyance, Ernle to Jones; 154/2-3; O.S. Map 6″, Wilts. XXX (1887 edn.); Burke, *Ext. & Dorm. Baronetcies* (1838), 187.
[4] *Kelly's Dir. Wilts.* (1890 and later edns.); Wilts. Cuttings, xxi. 314.
[5] W.R.O. 130/46/30A; O.S. Map 6″, Wilts. XXX (1887 edn.).
[6] W.R.O. 154/2-3; ibid. Ramsbury land tax; map of Ramsbury, W. div., *penes* Mrs. Croucher.
[7] O.S. Map 6″, Wilts. XXX. NW. (1900 edn.); *Kelly's Dir. Wilts.* (1890 and later edns.).
[8] *Cat. Anct. D.* i, C 536.
[9] S.R.O., DD/PO 93.
[10] Inf. from Mr. Wills.
[11] *Andrews and Dury, Map* (W.R.S. viii), pl. 12.
[12] *Pipe R.* 1219 (P.R.S. N.S. xlii), 18.
[13] *Rot. Litt. Claus.* (Rec. Com.), ii. 174; *Sar. Chart. and Doc.* (Rolls Ser.), 181.
[14] *Close R.* 1227-31, 165.
[15] *Cal. Chart. R.* 1226-57, 252.
[16] Below, Marlborough, mkts. and fairs.
[17] *Rot. Hund.* (Rec. Com.), ii (1), 260-1; *Plac. de Quo Warr.* (Rec. Com.), 801; *Bracton's Note Bk.* ed. Maitland, iii, pp. 291-2.
[18] *Cal. Chart. R.* 1257-1300, 483.
[19] *Reg. Martival* (Cant. & York Soc.), iv, p. 33.
[20] *Univ. Brit. Dir.* iv (1798), 301.
[21] P.R.O., SC 12/22/91; W.R.O. 212A/27/27, acct. of rents.
[22] Pigot, *Nat. Com. Dir.* (1830), 809½.
[23] *Kelly's Dir. Wilts.* (1890 and later edns.); inf. from Mr. C. E. Blunt, Ramsbury Hill.
[24] D. & C. Sar. Mun., press I, box 8, nos. 12B, 12D.
[25] *Wilts. Inq. p.m.* 1625-49 (Index Libr.), 372.
[26] Wilton Ho. Mun., ct. rolls.
[27] *Wilts. Apprentices* (W.R.S. xvii), pp. 58, 108, 143, 175; W.R.O. 212B/5661.
[28] W.R.O., Ramsbury land tax.
[29] Ibid. 684/5; *Kelly's Dir. Wilts.* (1855 and later edns.).

wells at Cricklade in the later 19th century.[30] In addition to tanners and curriers there were seven bootmakers and shoemakers and a collar maker at Ramsbury in 1848.[31] Bootmaking was slow to die out and was continued by Hunter & Son in Oxford Street until 1981.[32] Malthouses stood in High Street and Oxford Street in 1778 and brewing was said to be successful at Ramsbury in the 1790s:[33] in 1839 London was the destination of much of the beer from the brewery south of the Square.[34] Malting and brewing ceased in the late 19th century.[35] In the 1850s S. T. Osmond established a brass and iron foundry at Newtown to make agricultural implements. There were other workers in metal in the later 19th century, and in the 1890s work similar to Osmond's was done at the Jubilee Royal Foundry. The Newtown foundry survived until the First World War.[36] Other trades at Ramsbury have included candle making (1655 and 1788),[37] clockmaking,[38] soap-making (1744),[39] hurdle making (1936),[40] and jewellery design and manufacture (1980).[41] The firm of N. Turnbull & Co. made printed electrical circuits at premises south of High Street from c. 1965 to 1981.[42]

LOCAL GOVERNMENT. Regalian rights may have originated in the acquisition of the lands of Ramsbury hundred by the bishop of Ramsbury,[43] and they were held unchallenged by the bishop of Salisbury as lord of the hundred.[44] A grant of general liberties to the bishop by Henry III in 1227 confirmed them, and may have inspired the mistaken belief of the jurors of Selkley hundred in 1255 that they were then new.[45] In 1255 the bishop was said to have return of writs, pleas of vee de naam, and view of frankpledge: gallows and the assize of bread and of ale were specified in 1275, tumbrel and pillory in 1289.[46] In the later Middle Ages the bishop held three-weekly hundred courts and exercised public jurisdiction in biannual courts called law hundreds.[47] Men of Bishopstone may have attended both. In the mid 16th century the right to hold the three-weekly hundred court, although still claimed by the lay lords of Ramsbury manor, may no longer have been exercised,[48] and the bishop retained the right to

exercise leet jurisdiction for Bishopstone, which was not subsequently represented at the Ramsbury law hundreds held by the lords of the manor.[49]

The tithings of Ramsbury parish in the Middle Ages cannot be clearly identified. The two tithings of Ramsbury named in 1289 may have been the forerunners of Ramsbury or Ramsbury Town and Park Town tithings.[50] Eastridge, Ashridge, in Axford, and Whittonditch were tithings in the 13th century.[51] In the 1550s there were eight tithings, Ramsbury, Park Town, Eastridge, Whittonditch, Axford, Ashridge, Littlecote, and Baydon, but only six tithingmen: the tithings of Littlecote, the home of the Darells who had long held Axford manor, and Ashridge shared a tithingman with Axford tithing.[52] Those three tithings were merged as Axford tithing in the 17th century but in the 18th Littlecote was transferred to Eastridge tithing.[53] Ramsbury tithing included Hilldrop,[54] Whittonditch included Preston and Marridge Hill, Eastridge included Membury, and Baydon included Ford:[55] before the 17th century Thrup and Knighton may have been in Littlecote or Eastridge tithing. Each tithing was required to have its own instruments of punishment in the late 16th century. There was a constable for Ramsbury village and another, called the hundred constable, for the remainder of the parish.[56] In the 17th century there was a second constable for Ramsbury village: a weigher of bread and taster of ale and an inspector and sealer of leather were appointed, officers later duplicated.[57] A 'constable of Baydon' named in 1703 was the Baydon tithingman,[58] but his activities presumably superseded those of the hundred constable in Baydon.

In the later 16th century the law hundred proceeded on the presentments of the six tithingmen, affirmed and added to by a jury theoretically of 12 but actually of 15–17. Offences included those of brewers, bakers, tapsters, and butchers in Ramsbury and of millers, assaults, poaching, and harbouring rogues and vagabonds.[59] In the 17th century tipplers, tapsters, and nuisances caused by muckheaps were presented under leet jurisdiction in courts called views of frankpledge,[60] but in the 18th century

[30] Kelly's Dir. Wilts. (1848 and later edns.); V.C.H. Wilts. iv. 239.
[31] Kelly's Dir. Wilts.
[32] Ibid. (1848 and later edns.); inf. from Mrs. B. Croucher, 25 Ashley Piece.
[33] W.R.O. 154/2–3; Univ. Brit. Dir. iv (1798), 301.
[34] Map of Ramsbury, W. div., penes Mrs. Croucher; Robson, Com. Dir. (1839), 82.
[35] Kelly's Dir. Wilts. (1848 and later edns.).
[36] Ibid. (1855 and later edns.).
[37] W.A.M. vi. 87; W.R.O., bishop, pet. for faculties, drafts, iii, no. 28.
[38] W.A.M. xlviii. 314.
[39] Wilts. Apprentices (W.R.S. xvii), p. 145.
[40] W.A.M. xlvii. 562.
[41] Wilts. Cuttings, xxvii. 164–5; Wilts. Gaz. 10 Apr. 1980.
[42] Wilts. Cuttings, xxvii. 164–5; inf. from Mrs. Croucher.
[43] V.C.H. Wilts. v. 45; cf. Downton: ibid. xi. 43.
[44] Ibid. v. 49–51.
[45] Cal. Chart. R. 1226–57, 24–5; Rot. Hund. (Rec. Com.), ii (1), 234.
[46] Rot. Hund. (Rec. Com.), ii (1), 231, 266; P.R.O., JUST 1/1006, rot. 42d.

[47] D. & C. Sar. Mun., press I, box 8, nos. 12A, 12D, 12E; press I, box 31, no. 19; W.R.O., bishop, Liber Niger, ff. 95–8.
[48] L. & P. Hen. VIII, xx (2), p. 411; First Pembroke Survey, ed. Straton, i. 175.
[49] Above, Bishopstone, local govt.
[50] P.R.O., JUST 1/1006, rot. 42d.
[51] Ibid. JUST 1/998, rot. 33; for Ashridge, below, Axford, introduction.
[52] Wilton Ho. Mun., survey, 1550s, p. 309; B.L. Add. Ch. 24440.
[53] W.R.O. 84/47, partic. of Ramsbury manor; ibid. Eastridge land tax.
[54] Ibid. Ramsbury land tax.
[55] First Pembroke Survey, ed. Straton, i. 154–5, 158; B.L. Add. Ch. 24440.
[56] B.L. Add. Ch. 24441.
[57] Wilton Ho. Mun., ct. rolls 1632, 1676; manor ct. bk., various par., 1633–4, ff. 11v.–12; W.R.O. 1883/2.
[58] W.R.O. 656/1.
[59] B.L. Add. Ch. 24440–1.
[60] Wilton Ho. Mun., ct. rolls; manor ct. bk., various par., 1633–4.

the appointment and listing of the officers was the only recorded business at the biannual view.[61]

In the 14th century the bishop of Salisbury held courts, in addition to the hundred courts, presumably to deal for Ramsbury manor with matters normally connected with customary tenure. Four a year were held in the 15th century.[62] The business of the courts was enrolled with that of the law hundreds in the later 16th century, under the heading of courts of the manor held on the same day as the views in the 17th century, and under the heading of courts baron in the 18th century. It was mainly the recording of presentments by the homage, orders intended to promote good husbandry, deaths of tenants, and transfers of copyholds. The condition of hedges seems to have caused concern in the later 16th century when orders were also made to ring pigs and to exclude horses and cattle from sown fields. In the 17th century bylaws promulgated at the courts regulated common husbandry at Ramsbury, Axford, and Baydon.[63] Each part of the parish in which there was common husbandry was called a homage but was not represented at the court by a separate jury.[64] In the 18th century, however, orders governing husbandry in Baydon, where hitching was closely controlled, were distinguished in the records from those for the remainder of the parish, where the ploughing of linches was an issue. The leazetellers for Ramsbury were appointed at the courts.[65]

Prebendaries of Ramsbury apparently held courts for their tenants in Ramsbury in the mid 14th century.[66] Courts to deal with the copyhold business of Trenchard manor were held in the late 16th century and early 17th.[67]

Expenditure on the poor in Ramsbury parish, excluding Baydon, rose from £807 in 1775–6 to £1,321 in 1802–3 and exceeded £3,000 in 1812–13 and 1818. The parish had a workhouse but in 1802–3, when 237 adults were permanently relieved, four fifths of relief was outdoor. There were then 36 men and women in the workhouse, a number which had been halved by 1813.[68] From 1832 to 1835, when the parish joined Hungerford poor-law union, an annual average of £2,100 was spent on the poor.[69]

CHURCH. Parts of two cross shafts and three tomb slabs, all of stone carved in the late 9th century, were found beneath Ramsbury church in 1891.[70] They suggest that before 900 there was a large and architecturally elaborate church at Ramsbury, and the creation of a bishopric of Ramsbury in the early 10th century supports the suggestion. There were bishops of Ramsbury until 1058 when the see, which comprised Wiltshire and, from the mid 10th century, Berkshire, was united with that of Sherborne (Dors.). The united see was transferred to Salisbury between 1075 and 1078. Although the bishops of Ramsbury were so called only in charters, and although they had a seat at Sonning and possibly another at Wilton, it seems likely that the setting up of a see at Ramsbury, where the bishops had a notable church and an estate of 90 hides, was more than nominal, and that the church was served by a small cathedral establishment. In the 1050s Bishop Herman complained that there was no adequate community of clerks, but in 1086 there were priests at Ramsbury who may have been a vestige of such a community.[71] Ramsbury church passed to the canons of Salisbury, possibly as heirs to those priests or as a gift of a bishop, and was among the chapter's endowments specified in its foundation charter of 1091.[72] The chapter had used the church's revenues to establish the prebends of Ramsbury and Axford by the mid 12th century. Axford prebend was then held by the succentor.[73] The prebends were replaced by the two prebends of Gillingham in 1545.[74] By 1294 a vicarage had been ordained.[75]

In 1086 the church presumably served all the places in Ramsbury hundred and possibly others. Bishopstone was later separated and Ramsbury parish and manor became conterminous.[76] The parish was within the peculiar jurisdiction of the deans of Salisbury until 1846.[77] It included Baydon where a dependent church had been built by the early 12th century.[78] In the Middle Ages there were dependent chapels at Membury and Axford, neither of which survived the 15th century. There were also private chapels at the bishop's palace, Axford, and Littlecote.[79] Baydon became independent of Ramsbury in the 1790s. Another dependent church was built at Axford in 1856.[80] In 1973 the vicarage was united with the united benefice of Aldbourne and Baydon to create the benefice of Whitton: a team ministry, led by a rector living in Ramsbury, was established. A new benefice of Whitton was created in 1976 by the addition of the rectory of Chilton Foliat and the vicarage of Froxfield to the old.[81]

The advowson of the vicarage belonged to the prebendaries of Ramsbury and until the Reformation every known vicar was presented by a prebendary.[82] In 1545 the advowson was

[61] W.R.O. 1883/1–2.
[62] D. & C. Sar. Mun., press I, box 8, nos. 12A, 12D, 12E; press I, box 31, no. 19.
[63] B.L. Add. Ch. 24440–1; Wilton Ho. Mun., ct. rolls; manor ct. bk., various par., 1633–4; W.R.O. 1883/1–2.
[64] e.g. B.L. Add. Ch. 24440; First Pembroke Survey, ed. Straton, i. 159–63.
[65] W.R.O. 1883/2.
[66] Inq. Non. (Rec. Com.), 175.
[67] W.R.O. 1883/6.
[68] Poor Law Abstract, 1804, 568–9; Poor Law Abstract, 1818, 500–1; Poor Rate Returns, 1816–21, 189.
[69] Poor Law Com. 1st Rep. 242.
[70] V.C.H. Wilts. ii, pp. 37 and n., 38–9; inf. from Mr. C. E. Blunt, Ramsbury Hill; W.A.M. xxvii. 44.
[71] V.C.H. Wilts. ii, 27–8, 30, 121.

[72] Reg. St. Osmund (Rolls Ser.), ii. 199.
[73] Sar. Chart. and Doc. (Rolls Ser.), 34; Pipe R. 1167 (P.R.S. xi), 130.
[74] V.C.H. Wilts. iii. 185.
[75] W.R.O., bishop, Liber Niger, f. 80. No vicarage was listed in 1291: Tax. Eccl. (Rec. Com.).
[76] Above, introduction, manors; above, Bishopstone, introduction, church.
[77] e.g. W.R.O., dean, Chaundler's reg.; dean, reg. inst.
[78] Ibid. dean, Chaundler's reg. f. 55; below, Baydon, church.
[79] Below; below, Axford, church; above, manors.
[80] Below, Axford, church; Baydon, church.
[81] Lond. Gaz. 30 Oct. 1973, p. 12883; 21 May 1976, p. 7284; Wilts. Cuttings, xxvii. 195.
[82] Phillipps, Wilts. Inst. (index in W.A.M. xxviii. 228).

granted with Ramsbury manor and the endowments of Ramsbury and Axford prebends to Edward Seymour, earl of Hertford, who apparently retained it when in 1547 those endowments were given to the Crown.[83] Seymour, then duke of Somerset, presented in 1548. When he was attainted in 1552[84] the advowson presumably passed to the Crown which thereafter presented.[85] The advowson was bought from the Crown in 1865 by Angela Burdett-Coutts (created Baroness Burdett-Coutts in 1871, d. 1906),[86] and passed to her widower William Burdett-Coutts-Bartlett-Coutts (d. 1921) whose executors transferred it to Sir Francis Burdett in 1922.[87] It descended to Burdett's stepdaughter Lady (Marjorie) Burdett-Fisher who in 1981 was a member of the board of patronage constituted to present the rector of the Whitton team ministry.[88]

Although the prebendaries Thomas of Bridport, William de St. John, and Simon de Montagu augmented it in 1294, c. 1323, and in 1333 respectively, the vicarage remained poor, worth £9 13s. in 1535.[89] The living was augmented by the state in 1658 and 1659.[90] The vicar's income, £115 10s. in 1756 and £219 c. 1830,[91] remained low, but, despite the large parish, no record of a complaint by a vicar has been found. The living was augmented by the proceeds from the sale of the advowson in 1865.[92]

In 1294 the vicar was given all corn tithes from the prebendary's demesne.[93] After the augmentation of c. 1323 he was entitled to various small tithes paid in kind and to those tithes paid in cash arising from calves, foals, and lambs and from hay made in Axford: oblations at the Invention and Exaltation remained the prebendary's but those on the Sunday after the Exaltation were the vicar's.[94] In 1333 oblations at both feasts and more small tithes were given to the vicar.[95] In 1405 the vicar received nothing from Baydon, the church of which he did not serve: from the remainder of the parish he was entitled to all hay tithe from Axford, all small tithes and altarage, some commuted tithes of sheep and lambs, tithes from all mills except the prebendary's, and, in place of tithe from the prebendal glebe, a meadow of 1 a. and some grain tithes. The rent from 8 a., apparently given to the church in the late 14th century, was then being witheld by a former vicar's executors.[96] In 1756 the vicar received two thirds of his income from

tithes, mostly paid in cash, the remainder from fees and offerings.[97] At inclosure in 1778 he was allotted 43 a. between Crowood Lane and Whittonditch Road, 12 a. at Ramsbury, and 14 a. near Marridge Hill to replace tithes from the land then inclosed and from other premises belonging to the owners of that land.[98] In 1784 the vicar gave tithes from land in Axford in exchange for a site in Back Lane, on which six cottages had been burned down, to enlarge his garden.[99] The vicar's remaining tithes, mostly from Axford and the Littlecote estate, were in 1841 valued at £125 and commuted for a rent charge.[1] The glebe, which included a house in High Street, was being leased for £225 in 1864, £110 in 1934.[2] The Back Lane site was used for a church room in 1907 and there were 999-year leases of small areas of glebe for council houses in Whittonditch Road in the 1930s.[3] The land near Marridge Hill and the house in High Street were sold after 1934: there were 50 a. of glebe in 1981, mostly north of Whittonditch Road.[4]

The vicarage house between the church and Back Lane was repaired by the new vicar in 1681, partly with the aid of £46 contributed by parishioners.[5] The house was refronted and partly rebuilt c. 1786 when a schoolroom was attached to it.[6] That house was replaced c. 1840 by a new square house to which a third storey, possibly raised from attics, was later added.[7] The new house was sold c. 1967 when a new glebe house was built in Back Lane.[8]

There was a chapel on the bishop of Salisbury's demesne at Membury in 1324 when the bishop gave the chaplain appointed to serve it a stipend of 50s. a year in addition to the endowment of a house and land,[9] valued at 20s. a year in the late 16th century.[10] Bishops continued to appoint chaplains until 1412 or later.[11] The chapel may have been that called St. Anne's which was said to be in ruins in 1504 when the bishop granted an indulgence for it to be rebuilt,[12] but there is no evidence that it was used after 1412.

A chapel of St. Mary was mentioned in 1405 and was presumably served by the chaplain mentioned then as appointed by the vicar and in 1409.[13] A later reference to St. Mary's guild suggests that it was an endowed chantry.[14] In 1459 William York was licensed to found a chantry with a chaplain to say mass daily at the altar of St. Mary in the parish church for the

[83] W.R.O. 1883/59, copy of Act; *Cal. Pat.* 1547-8, 190; above, manors.
[84] W.R.O., dean, reg. inst. f. 1; *Complete Peerage.*
[85] W.R.O., dean, reg. inst. ff. 20, 62, 74v., 89, 99, 140v., 159v., 190 and v.
[86] Ch. Com. file 32531; *Complete Peerage.*
[87] Ch. Com. file 32531; *Who Was Who,* 1916-28, 147; *Crockford* (1923 and later edns.).
[88] Inf. from Maj. F. R. D. Burdett-Fisher, Harbrook Farm; Ch. Com., 1 Millbank, Lond.
[89] W.R.O., bishop, Liber Niger, f. 80; bishop, reg. Wyvil, f. 14 and v.; *Reg. Martival* (Cant. & York Soc.), i. 276; ii. 490-1; *Valor Eccl.* (Rec. Com.), ii. 151.
[90] *Cal. S.P. Dom.* 1658-9, 32; W. A. Shaw, *Hist. Eng. Ch.* ii. 597.
[91] W.R.O. 500/26; *Rep. Com. Eccl. Revenues,* 844-5.
[92] Ch. Com. file 32531.
[93] W.R.O., bishop, Liber Niger, f. 80.
[94] *Reg. Martival* (Cant. & York Soc.), ii. 490-1.
[95] W.R.O., bishop, reg. Wyvil, f. 14 and v.
[96] Ibid. dean, Chaundler's reg. ff. 54v.-55, 56v.
[97] Ibid. 500/26.
[98] Ibid. 154/2-3.
[99] P.R.O., CP 43/805, rot. 63.
[1] W.R.O., tithe award.
[2] Ibid. bishop, vis. queries; Ch. Com. file 82888.
[3] Ch. Com. file 82888.
[4] Ibid.; inf. from the Secretary, Parsonages Cttee., Sar. Dioc. Bd. of Finance, Church Ho., Crane St., Salisbury.
[5] W.R.O. 500/1.
[6] Ibid. 500/5.
[7] Ibid. dean, mortgage. A plan to incorporate part of the old ho. was given up.
[8] Inf. from Lt.-Col. W. G. Hingston, the Old Vicarage.
[9] *Reg. Martival* (Cant. & York Soc.), i. 304.
[10] P.R.O., E 178/2410.
[11] *Reg. Hallum* (Cant. & York Soc.), p. 42.
[12] W.R.O., bishop, reg. Audley, f. 115v.
[13] Ibid. dean, Chaundler's reg. ff. 54v., 56v., 115.
[14] Ibid. bishop, Liber Niger, f. 100.

souls of his father John, wife Agnes, and father-in-law Nicholas Wootton.[15] The chaplain of the Wootton and York chantry, who was also required to hold no other benefice, to live in the chantry house, and to teach grammar, was serving there in 1469.[16] In 1476 John, son of William York, gave an estate in Purton and elsewhere, including several cottages in Ramsbury, to endow the chantry, and the right to nominate the chaplain passed with Hilldrop manor.[17] The foundation charter was formulated in 1478.[18] In a way and for reasons that are not clear the endowment, worth £7 12s. in 1535,[19] was recovered by Thomas York from the chaplain in 1539:[20] in 1547 it was taken by the Crown as land of a chantry dissolved without licence, and was later sold.[21] Sir Edward Darell (d. 1530) had devised money for daily masses in the chapel,[22] the north chapel now called the Darell chapel which contains monuments possibly to the lords of Littlecote manor.[23] In 1455 the bishop of Salisbury consecrated an altar dedicated to St. Catherine in the north part of the church, possibly below the easternmost window of the north aisle.[24]

Although on their visits to Ramsbury the bishops of Salisbury worshipped in the chapel in their palace, they sometimes held services in the parish church.[25] The prebendaries of Ramsbury and of Axford, like other prebendaries, were frequently pluralists and sometimes men of distinction.[26] None seems to have had a close connexion with the parish. In 1399 the parish clerk was appealing against excommunication for contumacy and he was still in office in 1405 when he was accused of misappropriation and inefficiency.[27] The vicar was accused in 1409 of condoning immorality and of saying mass in the church when he had been suspended by the dean.[28] His penance was ordered in that year.[29] Later vicars included from 1518 Richard Arch, vicar of Avebury and principal of Broadgates Hall, Oxford.[30] John Wild was vicar from 1599 to 1664.[31] He was noted for his puritanism in the 1630s but his living had been sequestrated by 1646. The intruder was Samuel Brown.[32] Wild was restored in 1660.[33] His curate then was a schoolteacher, Henry Dent, whom John Wilson, vicar 1664–80, ejected and prosecuted for nonconformist preaching.[34] Richard Garrard was vicar from 1737 to 1784 and his successors Edward Meyrick and Edward

Graves Meyrick were vicars from 1786 until 1839.[35] E. G. Meyrick, who was also rector of Winchfield (Hants), preached once a month and administered the Sacrament thrice yearly.[36] In 1851 there were congregations of 403 at the morning and 275 at the afternoon services on Census Sunday.[37] In 1864 the resident vicar employed an assistant curate: three services were held every Sunday, two with sermons; there were services on Wednesdays and Fridays and at festivals with congregations of 20–30; prayers were said in the church morning and evening on Mondays and Fridays; and the Sacrament was administered at Christmas, Good Friday, Easter, and Whitsun and monthly, respectively to some 110 and 60 communicants.[38]

The invocation of the church, called HOLY CROSS in 1405 and almost certainly in 1323,[39] may have caused or resulted from the choice of the feasts of the Invention and Exaltation for the fairs at Ramsbury granted by the king in 1240.[40] The church, of flint rubble with ashlar dressings, consists of a chancel, a north chapel, an aisled and clerestoried nave with a south porch, and a west tower. Apart from the cross shafts and tomb slabs,[41] the oldest part of the present church is the long 13th-century chancel. By the later 13th century the nave had been aisled: the easternmost bay of each aisle was distinct from the others and each was possibly a transept extending further north or south than the true aisle. The west end of the church, including the two westernmost bays of each arcade and the aisle walls, was largely rebuilt in the 14th century, and the aisles were then widened to incorporate what may have been the transepts. The tower is also 14th-century. The chapel was built in the early 15th century, and in that century new windows were inserted in the chancel and at the east end of the south aisle. In the early 16th century the clerestory and a new nave roof of lower pitch were made.[42] A west gallery was built in 1698–9 and aisle galleries in 1788 when the roofs of both aisles were remade.[43] In an extensive restoration of 1890–3 the walls of the aisles were largely rebuilt and were given stepped buttresses and embattled parapets, a new lower pitched roof on the south aisle was made, the plain south porch was replaced by an elaborate porch in a late medieval style, a porch was added to the chancel, and the galleries were removed.[44] The bowl of the font, of

[15] Cal. Pat. 1452–61, 502–3.
[16] P.R.O., E 135/17/26; Cat. Anct. D. i, C 1387.
[17] Cal. Pat. 1476–85, 11; P.R.O., E 135/17/26; above, manors.
[18] P.R.O., E 135/17/26.
[19] Valor Eccl. (Rec. Com.), ii. 150.
[20] P.R.O., C 146/3630; ibid. CP 40/1102, rot. 415.
[21] Ibid. E 301/59, no. 33; E 318/Box 43/2306.
[22] Ibid. C 142/51, no. 2.
[23] E. D. Webb, Hist. Hund. Ramsbury (Salisbury, 1890), 46–7.
[24] Ibid. 46; W.R.O., bishop, reg. Beauchamp, f. 150v.
[25] Reg. Hallum (Cant. & York Soc.), pp. 164, 179.
[26] Le Neve, Fasti, 1300–1541, Salisbury, 24–6, 78–9.
[27] Cal. Close, 1396–9, 437; W.R.O., dean, Chaundler's reg. f. 56.
[28] W.R.O., dean, Chaundler's reg. f. 115.
[29] Reg. Hallum (Cant. & York Soc.), p. 215.
[30] W.N. & Q. ii. 444.
[31] W.R.O., dean, reg. inst. ff. 24, 62; Webb, Hund. Ramsbury, 23.

[32] V.C.H. Wilts. iii. 37; Walker Revised, ed. A. G. Matthews, 383.
[33] Phillipps, Wilts. Inst. ii. 22.
[34] Calamy Revised, ed. A. G. Matthews, 162–3; W.R.O., dean, reg. inst. f. 62; ibid. 500/1.
[35] W.R.O., dean, reg. inst. ff. 99, 140v., 159v.–160, 190; ibid. 500/5, where the wrong date of Edw. Meyrick's induction is given.
[36] Rep. Com. Eccl. Revenues, 844–5; W.A.M. xlix. 140.
[37] P.R.O., HO 129/121/2/13/20.
[38] W.R.O., bishop, vis. queries.
[39] Reg. Martival (Cant. & York Soc.), ii. 491; W.R.O., dean, Chaundler's reg. f. 55.
[40] Above, econ. hist.   [41] Above.
[42] J. Buckler, watercolour in W.A.S. Libr., vol. iv. 14 (1806).
[43] W.R.O., dean, procl. for faculties; dean, faculty reg. ff. 25–6; bishop, pet. for faculties, drafts, iii, no. 28.
[44] Ibid. bishop, pet. for faculties, bdle. 32, no. 1; Wilts. Cuttings, i. 184–5; cf. Buckler, watercolour in W.A.S. Libr., vol. iv. 14.

stone carved in the shape of a pineapple, was possibly an ornament on a gateway of Ramsbury Manor replaced c. 1775. The base was carved by Thomas Meyrick c. 1842.[45]

In 1405 the church plate included a silver and gilt chalice, bearing a design illustrating the crucifixion, and two other silver and gilt chalices with patens, one of which had possibly been misappropriated.[46] The king took 3 oz. of silver in 1553 and left a chalice of 11 oz. That chalice had presumably been lost by 1719 when a flagon hallmarked 1707, a paten made in 1718, and a chalice with paten also made in 1718 were given. A copy of the chalice of 1718 was given in 1839 and a spoon of 1666 or earlier was given in 1881.[47] The church retained all that plate in 1981.[48] There were four bells in 1553. They were replaced by a ring of six cast by Abraham Rudhall of Gloucester in 1708. The tenor was recast by Warner & Sons of London in 1865.[49] Those bells hung in the church in 1981.[50] The registers are complete from 1678.[51]

NONCONFORMITY. Roger Bodenham (fl. 1689), lord of Hilldrop manor, whose lands had been sequestrated by 1646 for his papism, lived at Ramsbury as a papist for over 40 years.[52] Francis Bodenham and in the 1670s members of the Gilmore family of Ramsbury, including Paul Gilmore (d. 1748), a Benedictine monk, were also papists,[53] but their cause did not flourish in Ramsbury.

Henry Dent, ejected from Hannington vicarage and later from the assistant curacy of Ramsbury,[54] led dissent around Ramsbury. He kept a school in Ramsbury and preached there and at Lambourn and Newbury.[55] In 1669 the presbyterian conventicle at Ramsbury was attended by 50–60, and Christopher Fowler and John Clark, ejected from the vicarages of respectively Reading and Hungerford, were among the preachers.[56] Dent's was among several houses in Ramsbury licensed for presbyterian meetings in 1672.[57] The congregation apparently survived and in 1715 built a chapel on the north side of Oxford Street, possibly the 'presbyterian barn' referred to in 1716. By 1766 it had been demolished.[58] Congregationalism was revived at Ramsbury in the 1820s, and in 1830 a chapel and a private house were licensed for meetings.

They were apparently replaced by the Ebenezer chapel built in High Street in 1839.[59] The minister's house was east of it and a schoolroom south of it.[60] There were congregations of 77 at the morning and 130 at the evening services on Census Sunday in 1851.[61] By will proved 1890 Walter Samuel Chamberlain gave £100 for the chapel, the income from which was used for general expenses.[62] Services were still held in the chapel in 1981.

Three chapels built mainly of flint with brick dressings survive in Ramsbury. Services at a Wesleyan Methodist chapel, said to have been built in 1805 and rebuilt and enlarged in 1833, were attended by congregations of 130, 70, and 169 on Census Sunday in 1851.[63] The chapel is that behind buildings on the south side of High Street: it has not been used for services since 1944.[64] Another Wesleyan Methodist chapel was at Marridge Hill in 1851 when attendance at it averaged 20,[65] but it has not survived. There were Primitive Methodists in Ramsbury from the 1830s and a chapel had been built by 1839. Where it stood is uncertain but it was possibly the flint and brick chapel, on the east side of Chapel Lane, later used as a Sunday school.[66] The Primitive Methodist chapel was attended by congregations of 70, 160, and 200 on Census Sunday in 1851.[67] A new chapel was built in Oxford Street possibly in 1876.[68] Sunday services in it were held weekly in 1981. Near Witcha Farm the smallest of the three flint and brick chapels was built for Primitive Methodists in 1859.[69] It had apparently been closed long before 1981.[70]

In the early 19th century several houses in Ramsbury were registered for worship by dissenters.[71] One may have been that used by the Church of Jesus Christ of Latter-Day Saints in which 30 attended the service held on Census Sunday in 1851.[72] A hall was built on the north side of High Street for the Salvation Army in 1881.[73]

EDUCATION. In the period 1459 to 1539 chaplains of the Wootton and York chantry were charged with teaching grammar to poor scholars coming to Ramsbury from elsewhere: how conscientiously they did so is unknown.[74] In the 1660s and possibly for longer the nonconformist

45 W.A.M. liv. 203–4.
46 W.R.O., dean, Chandler's reg. ff. 56, 78 and v.
47 Nightingale, Wilts. Plate, 161–2.
48 Inf. from Mrs. B. Croucher, 25 Ashley Piece.
49 Walters, Wilts. Bells, 161, 163; W.A.M. ii. 348.
50 Inf. from Mrs. Croucher.
51 W.R.O. 500/1–26. Transcripts for several earlier periods are ibid. dean.
52 Cal. Cttee. for Compounding, ii. 1539; Cal. Cttee. for Money, ii. 842; Williams, Cath. Recusancy (Cath. Rec. Soc.), p. 115 n.; above, manors.
53 Cal. Cttee. for Money, ii. 1155; Williams, Cath. Recusancy (Cath. Rec. Soc.), p. 264.
54 Above, church; V.C.H. Wilts. iii. 37.
55 Calamy Revised, ed. Matthews, 162–3.
56 Ibid. 117, 209; V.C.H. Wilts. iii. 105, 107.
57 Cal. S.P. Dom. 1672, 199, 201, 476; cf. S. B. Stribling, Wilts. Congregational Union, 55.
58 V.C.H. Wilts. iii. 107; W.R.O. 732/1; Webb, Hund. Ramsbury, 28.
59 V.C.H. Wilts. iii. 134; Educ. Enquiry Abstract,

1045; W.R.O., bishop, return of cert. places; bishop, certs. dissenters' meeting hos.
60 Endowed Char. Wilts. (N. Div.), 855.
61 P.R.O., HO 129/121/2/13/24.
62 Endowed Char. Wilts. (N. Div.), 856.
63 P.R.O., HO 129/121/2/13/20.
64 Map of Ramsbury, W. div., penes Mrs. B. Croucher, 25 Ashley Piece; inf. from Mrs. Croucher.
65 P.R.O., HO 129/121/2/13/22.
66 Stribling, Wilts. Congregational Union, 56; key to maps of Ramsbury penes Mrs. Croucher; O.S. Map 6″, Wilts. XXX (1887 edn.).
67 P.R.O., HO 129/121/2/13/23.
68 Date on bldg.; O.S. Map 6″, Wilts. XXX (1887 edn.).
69 Inscription on bldg.
70 Inf. from Mrs. Croucher.
71 W.R.O., bishop, return of cert. places.
72 P.R.O., HO 129/121/2/13/25.
73 Stribling, Wilts. Congregational Union, 57.
74 Cal. Pat. 1452–61, 502–3; P.R.O., E 135/17/26; above, church.

Henry Dent kept a school at his house in Ramsbury, and in 1780 there was a schoolroom on the south side of High Street: nothing further is known of either school.[75] When he became vicar in 1786 Edward Meyrick moved his school from Hungerford to Ramsbury. The school was held in buildings adjoining the vicarage house and in Bodorgan House, now Ramsbury Hill, and the house now called Parliament Piece. After Meyrick resigned the vicarage in 1811 the school was kept by his son Arthur. It was a boarding school for the sons of the middle classes: there were 60–70 pupils c. 1840. It was closed in the 1840s.[76] A boarding school for girls was mentioned in the 1790s.[77]

A charity school mentioned in the 1790s may have been the predecessor of the school for 35–40 girls being supported by a Miss, possibly Mary Ann, Read of Crowood House in 1818, when there were said to be many small schools in the area.[78] In 1833 there were five day schools paid for by the parents of the 105 children attending them: one was possibly for Independents, for whom a schoolroom was built behind the Ebenezer chapel in 1839; two had been started after 1830.[79] In 1857 one was replaced by a school for girls built on the south side of Back Lane and endowed by Louisa Read of Crowood House. The school and schoolhouse are of flint and banded brick in a plain Gothic style. That school had 55–65 pupils in 1859: then the other four were a boys' school for 100–110, a school for 15–20, and two dame schools for a total of 40 children of dissenters.[80] In 1872 the parish formed a school board.[81] A school was built at Axford in 1874, and in 1875 a new boys' and infants' school on the north side of Back Lane replaced all the schools in Ramsbury except the girls' school.[82] In 1906–7 the two Ramsbury schools were attended by 84 girls, 76 boys, and 73 infants. The number of pupils at the former board school in Back Lane had declined to 97 by 1922: they were joined by those from the girls' school which, although it still had more than 70 pupils, was closed in 1925. Attendance at Ramsbury school reached 190 in 1936 after Axford school was closed, but later fell.[83] The school has remained a primary school and in 1981 there were 115 children on roll.[84]

By will Louisa Read (d. 1879) endowed Ramsbury girls' school with £60 a year and gave money for eleemosynary purposes and for bibles and other books for both the boys' and girls' schools. From 1904, when £30 was paid, the school's income was reduced.[85] The giving of

bibles and prayer books to children leaving school afterwards lapsed. It was revived by Sir Felix Pole in memory of his father Edward Robert Pole, a headmaster of the boys' school, in a trust set up in 1939 and endowed with £200. In 1960 Lady (Ethel Maud) Pole, Sir Felix's relict, gave a further £600 in memory of Sir Felix.[86] Bibles were given in 1981.[87] By deed of 1921 A. E. Oakes gave £1,000 in trust to provide yearly pleasure trips for schoolgirls. There were 40 trippers in 1936: trips are still made.[88]

CHARITIES FOR THE POOR. By will proved 1878 Mary Jane Lanfear gave £600 to apprentice boys living in Ramsbury and East Kennett, two from Ramsbury to one from East Kennett, but in the period 1895–1904 six from Ramsbury were the only boys apprenticed. In 1905 the charity had £666 capital and £23 income.[89] A separate trust for Ramsbury with two thirds of the endowment was set up in 1924. Capital continued to accumulate as income was not spent and by a Scheme of 1936 the object was extended to general help to boys learning a trade. In 1970, when the charity had £1,600 capital and £69 income, it was renamed Lanfear Educational Trust. Benefit was extended to men and women under 25 and the use of the income to general educational purposes: £163 was spent in 1975.[90]

By will proved 1887 John Osmond gave £200 to be invested for the poor. Coal was bought with the income, £4 8s. in 1904, and distributed.[91] Louisa Read (d. 1879) by will gave £3,000 for education and to perpetuate gifts of clothes and blankets to the poor. The residue of income after fixed payments to Ramsbury girls' school or £30 was to be spent on gifts. It was not clear whether £30 was intended to be a maximum or minimum. In 1904, when £20 was spent on clothing, the Charity Commissioners divided the charity.[92] From 1936 Lanfear's and Osmond's charities and Read's eleemosynary charity have been dealt with together under a Scheme. The income from Osmond's and Read's, £20 in 1960, has been used for the general benefit of the poor. In 1965 vouchers worth £21 were given at Christmas.[93]

By a deed of 1951 and a Scheme of 1953 S. G. and Lilian Chamberlain gave £1,390 stock to perpetuate their practice of giving vouchers to the poor, old, and widowed at Christmas. S. G. Chamberlain gave additional stock of £2,700 and £5,000 in 1954 and 1956 for organized activities and for the old and poor of the parish. In 1975 the three funds had a total income of £924.[94]

[75] *Calamy Revised*, ed. Matthews, 162–3; W.R.O. 684/5, deed, Ashley to Blackman.
[76] Meyrick, *Life in the Bush*, 20–1, 24, 37, 46–8; W.R.O. 31/1–2.
[77] *Univ. Brit. Dir.* iv (1798), 301.
[78] Ibid.; *Educ. of Poor Digest*, 1035.
[79] *Educ. Enquiry Abstract*, 1045; map of Ramsbury, W. div., *penes* Mrs. B. Croucher, 25 Ashley Piece.
[80] *Endowed Char. Wilts.* (N. Div.), 849; *Acct. of Wilts. Schs.* 38.
[81] P.R.O., ED 2/466.
[82] Ibid. ED 7/131, no. 228; ED 7/131, no. 230.
[83] *Bd. of Educ.*, *List 21* (H.M.S.O.).

[84] Inf. from Chief Education Officer, Co. Hall, Trowbridge.
[85] *Endowed Char. Wilts.* (N. Div.), 849–52; mon. in church.
[86] Char. Com. files.
[87] Inf. from Mrs. Croucher.
[88] Ibid.; Wilts. Cuttings, xviii. 4; Char. Com. file.
[89] *Endowed Char. Wilts.* (N. Div.), 852–4.
[90] Char. Com. files.
[91] *Endowed Char. Wilts.* (N. Div.), 854.
[92] Ibid. 850–1; mon. in church.
[93] Char. Com. file.
[94] Ibid.

AXFORD

Axford was the westernmost tithing of Ramsbury parish, with downland on both sides of the Kennet. Its north, south, and west boundaries were those of the parish. Its east boundary with Park Town tithing cannot now be precisely plotted, but it passed a short distance east of Axford, or Priory, Farm, and thence ran south-south-west through Hens Wood and north-north-west perhaps near the western edge of Blake's Copse.[95] Within such boundaries, which would have enclosed some 2,500 a., there were in the Middle Ages almost certainly two tithings, Axford to the west and Ashridge to the east.[96] Axford village was presumably in Axford tithing and on or near its present site. Ashridge tithing presumably included the manor house and farmstead of Axford manor, Axford Farm, but since the manor was never called Ashridge the tithing may have taken its name from another hamlet, possibly one on the high ground west of the valley in which Burney or Upper Axford was so called in the later 19th century.[97] The tithing included land there[98] but the existence in the Middle Ages of a hamlet there called Ashridge has not been established. The tithings were merged in the 17th century.[99]

Axford was first mentioned in 1163.[1] In the later Middle Ages and the 16th century it was apparently a village of medium sized farmsteads,[2] and it was of average wealth c. 1523.[3] Most of its buildings are beside the Ramsbury–Marlborough road which, except at the east end of the village, is on chalk,[4] but the oldest surviving, Riverside House, the south range of the Red Lion, and a pair of possibly timber-framed cottages, all apparently 17th-century, are on the gravel south of the road, a fact which suggests that the focus of the village has moved north since the 17th century. On the south side of the road Church Farm was built near the west end of the village c. 1830. It faces south and there are 19th-century farm buildings south of it. At the east end of the village is an 18th- or 19th-century thatched cottage much enlarged. The Red Lion, extended northwards in the 19th century, was an inn in 1867.[5] Also on the south side of the street are several cottages, houses, and bungalows of the 19th and 20th centuries. On the north side of the street there were a few buildings in the late

18th century and the early 19th:[6] apart from a brick and thatched cottage possibly of the 18th century at the west end, none survives. The church, the school, and two nonconformist chapels were built there in the later 19th century. Three estate cottages were built at the east end c. 1900, 24 council houses in the earlier 20th century, and a few houses and bungalows since then. Coombe Farm south-west of the village was a farmstead in the early 17th century or earlier.[7] House Barn north-east of the village was standing in 1773.[8] A house was built before 1839[9] and was enlarged in the 20th century: in 1981 most of the farm buildings at House Farm were 20th-century. Axford Street was so called in 1727 when the road south of the Kennet and parallel to it was called Mead Lane.[10] The lane linking Axford Street and Mead Lane near Church Farm crosses the Kennet on an early 19th-century brick bridge of five arches.

On the gravel near the Kennet between Axford village and Ramsbury Manor there were in the Middle Ages a manor house with a chapel and a farmstead probably with a mill.[11] The single inhabitant associated with Axford prebend in 1428 may have been the tenant of Axford Farm.[12] In the 17th century there was a larger manor house, possibly north-west of the farmstead,[13] but settlement has never grown there and no more than Axford Farm remains. A westward diversion of the Axford–Ramsbury road west of Ramsbury park between 1773 and 1828 isolated it. In 1773 there was apparently no building at Burney, where Burney Farm had been erected on the east side of the Axford–Aldbourne road by 1828.[14] In the mid 20th century additional farm buildings were erected on the west side of the road. East of Burney Farm a farmstead called Upper Axford, later New Buildings, was built between 1839 and 1885.[15] Kearsdown Farm in Sound Bottom was possibly built in the earlier 19th century: it was demolished in the mid 20th century.[16] South of the river Coombe Farm was the only house in the 20th century and possibly much earlier .

There were 62 men living in Axford tithing in 1773.[17] The population rose from 428 to 485 between 1821 and 1841.[18]

[95] Axford inclosure award: W.R.O., TS. transcript in 154/2; map of Ramsbury manor, 1676, *penes* Lady (Marjorie) Burdett-Fisher, Axford Farm: microfilm copy in W.R.O.
[96] Ashridge was first mentioned as a tithing in 1268: P.R.O., JUST 1/998, rot. 33; Axford in 1559: B.L. Add. Ch. 24440.
[97] O.S. Map 6″, Wilts. XXIX (1889 edn.).
[98] *First Pembroke Survey*, ed. Straton, i. 156.
[99] Above, Ramsbury, local govt.
[1] *Sar. Chart. and Doc.* (Rolls Ser.), 34.
[2] W.R.O., bishop, Liber Niger, f. 101 and v.; *First Pembroke Survey*, ed. Straton, i. 163–7.
[3] P.R.O., E 179/197/161.
[4] Geol. Surv. Maps 1″, drift, sheets 266 (1974 edn.), 267 (1947 edn.).
[5] *Kelly's Dir. Wilts.*
[6] *Andrews and Dury, Map* (W.R.S. viii), pl. 12; O.S. Map 1″, sheet 34 (1828 edn.).

[7] *W.A.M.* xix. 263; below, manors.
[8] *Andrews and Dury, Map* (W.R.S. viii), pl. 12.
[9] Map of Ramsbury, W. div., *penes* Mrs. B. Croucher, 25 Ashley Piece.
[10] Inclosure award: W.R.O., transcript in 154/2.
[11] Below, manors, econ. hist.
[12] *Feud. Aids*, v. 288; below, manors. *V.C.H. Wilts.* iv. 314 wrongly infers that there was then no other inhabitant of Axford.
[13] Below, manors.
[14] *Andrews and Dury, Map* (W.R.S. viii), pls. 12, 15; O.S. Map 1″, sheet 34 (1828 edn.).
[15] Map of Ramsbury, W. div., *penes* Mrs. Croucher; O.S. Maps 6″, Wilts. XXIX (1889 edn.); 1/25,000, SU 27 (1960 edn.).
[16] O.S. Map 1″, sheet 34 (1828 edn.); 1/25,000, 41/27 (1947 edn.); 1/50,000, sheet 174 (1974 edn.).
[17] W.R.O. 1883/3.　　[18] *V.C.H. Wilts.* iv. 356.

MANORS AND OTHER ESTATES. The land of Axford, although sometimes referred to as if the lord of Ramsbury manor also held a manor of Axford,[19] was all part of Ramsbury manor.[20] More than half the land was a freehold, perhaps formerly the demesne, of that manor and itself came to be reputed Axford manor.[21] The remainder, held customarily, passed as part of Ramsbury manor from the bishops of Salisbury to Edward Seymour, earl of Hertford (d. 1552), to the earls of Pembroke, and to Henry Powle who sold more than half of it between 1677 and 1681.[22] The portion then unsold remained part of Ramsbury manor: the portion sold then was bought back in parcels by the lords of Ramsbury manor in the 18th, 19th, and 20th centuries. In 1981 nearly all of both portions belonged to Lady (Marjorie) Burdett-Fisher and Maj. F. R. D. Burdett-Fisher.[23]

Between 1677 and 1681 Powle sold 13 of 22½ copyhold yardlands and 80 a. of 90 a. held by lease.[24] A holding of 2¾ yardlands, later called COOMBE farm, was bought by Thomas and Simon Appleford in 1678. Simon Appleford (d. 1727), possibly the joint purchaser, devised the land to Thomas son of Stephen Appleford.[25] Thomas (d. 1763) was succeeded by his son Thomas who in 1784 sold Coombe farm to his own son Thomas (d. 1790).[26] That Thomas Appleford devised the farm to his wife Mary for her widowhood with reversion successively to his father, his sister Mary Kemm, and Robert Vaisey, apparently a relative. In 1804 Mary Appleford and Thomas Appleford conveyed the farm to Vaisey (d. 1834).[27] Vaisey's relict Elizabeth Vaisey held the farm, 244 a., until her death in 1854 when it passed to her son Robert Vaisey.[28] In 1886 Sir Francis Burdett bought part of the farm, perhaps c. 100 a., from Vaisey and added it to his other land in Axford.[29] The descent of the remainder is not clear until 1929 when it was bought from the executors of Frederick James Leader (d. 1927) by Percival and John White. It was later assigned to Percival (d. 1977), whose relict Dorothy White owned Coombe farm, 132 a., in 1981.[30] Coombe Farm is an early 17th-century timber-framed house encased in brick in the late 18th century. The north side of the house was heightened in the later 19th century. Inside the house 16th- and 17th-century panelling has been reset. Farm buildings mostly of the 19th century are around a yard north of the house.

A holding of 2½ yardlands called STONE LANE was bought in 1678 by Thomas Crosby who by will dated 1683 devised it to his daughters Anne and Mary.[31] One of the daughters married Jonathan Knackstone (d. 1728).[32] A moiety passed to Knackstone's daughter Mary and her husband Thomas Appleford (d. 1763) and to Thomas's son Thomas, and it became part of Coombe farm. Knackstone devised the other moiety to his granddaughter Mary Appleford who in 1756 married Robert Vaisey of Stitchcombe in Mildenhall.[33] The moiety was apparently united with Coombe farm by Robert Vaisey (d. 1834).[34]

In 1677 Thomas Whityeatt (d. 1679) bought more than 3 yardlands later called RIVERSIDE farm.[35] He was succeeded by his son Thomas (d.s.p. a minor in 1691) and by his daughter Mary (d. 1731), who in 1693 married John Moore (d. 1696).[36] The estate, which was added to,[37] passed, possibly soon after John's death, to John's brother George (d. 1729). It passed from father to son in the Moore family to George (d. 1748), Jonathan (d. 1818), George (d. 1820), and George Pearce (d. 1884). By 1839 it had been reduced to 59 a.[38] It was sold after the death of G. P. Moore. In 1901 it was bought by Ellen Jane Pegler and from her in 1920 by William Berryman, who in 1927 sold it to Sir Francis Burdett.[39] The land belonged to the Burdett-Fishers in 1981.[40] Riverside House is an early 17th-century timber-framed farmhouse which had a three-room plan. A west wing incorporating a parlour and a staircase, with woodwork of high quality, was added c. 1700.

The freehold which became AXFORD manor may have belonged to Ralph de Brewer in 1198.[41] In 1200 he claimed to hold land in Dorset through a grant by Jocelin de Bohun, bishop of Salisbury 1142-84, to Richard son of Hildebrand, a claim disputed by the prebendary of Axford, and his right to his Axford estate may have arisen from a similar grant of the bishop's demesne land in Axford.[42] In 1217 Ralph forfeited that estate for rebellion and Henry III granted it to Roger de Clifford.[43] In 1250 it belonged to Robert of London and the name of his successor, Hildebrand of London,[44] suggests that it had descended to him from Jocelin's presumed

[19] Rot. Hund. (Rec. Com.), ii (1), 265.
[20] W.R.O., bishop, Liber Niger, ff. 95, 101 and v.
[21] Below; below, econ. hist.
[22] Above, Ramsbury, manor; First Pembroke Survey, ed. Straton, i. 163-7; W.R.O. 1883/59, bargain and sale, Pembroke to Whitley and Cratford; bargain and sale, Powle to Jones.
[23] Below; W.R.O., Axford land tax; inf. from Maj. F. R. D. Burdett-Fisher, Harbrook Farm.
[24] W.R.O. 1883/59, bargain and sale, Pembroke to Whitley and Cratford; bargain and sale, Powle to Jones; 1883/64.
[25] Ibid. 1574/1, abstr. of title, Coombe farm; 500/3.
[26] Ibid. 1574/1, abstr. of title, Coombe farm; abstr. of title, Knackstone's; 500/4.
[27] Ibid. 1574/1, assignment of mortgage; bond, Vaisey to Appleford; conveyance, Vaisey to Phelps.
[28] Ibid. note of succession duty; P.R.O., HO 107/1686; map of Ramsbury, W. div., penes Mrs. B. Croucher, 25 Ashley Piece.
[29] W.R.O. 1883, loose papers in rent bk. 1880; rental, 1888.

[30] Inf. from Mrs. D. White, Coombe Farm; Mr. R. T. Walton, New Ho., Manor Lane, Baydon; Mrs. J. S. Burrows, Grove Farm, Mildenhall.
[31] W.R.O. 1574/1, abstr. of title, Knackstone's.
[32] Ibid. fam. notes; 500/3.
[33] Ibid. 1574/1, abstr. of title, Knackstone's; abstr. of settlement, 1756.
[34] Ibid. Axford land tax.
[35] Ibid. 1883/59, bargain and sale, Pembroke to Whitley and Cratford; 1883/64/8.
[36] This descent of the Whityeatts and Moores has been provided by Mr. R. K. Lloyd, Riverside Ho.
[37] Inclosure award: W.R.O., transcript in 154/2.
[38] Map of Ramsbury, W. div., penes Mrs. Croucher.
[39] Inf. from Mr. Lloyd.
[40] Inf. from Maj. Burdett-Fisher.
[41] Pipe R. 1198 (P.R.S. n.s. ix), 73.
[42] Cur. Reg. R. i. 135, 347; below, econ. hist.
[43] Pat. R. 1216-25, 42.
[44] P.R.O., CP 25(1)/283/13, no. 251.

AVEBURY: SILBURY HILL

RAMSBURY: THE SQUARE

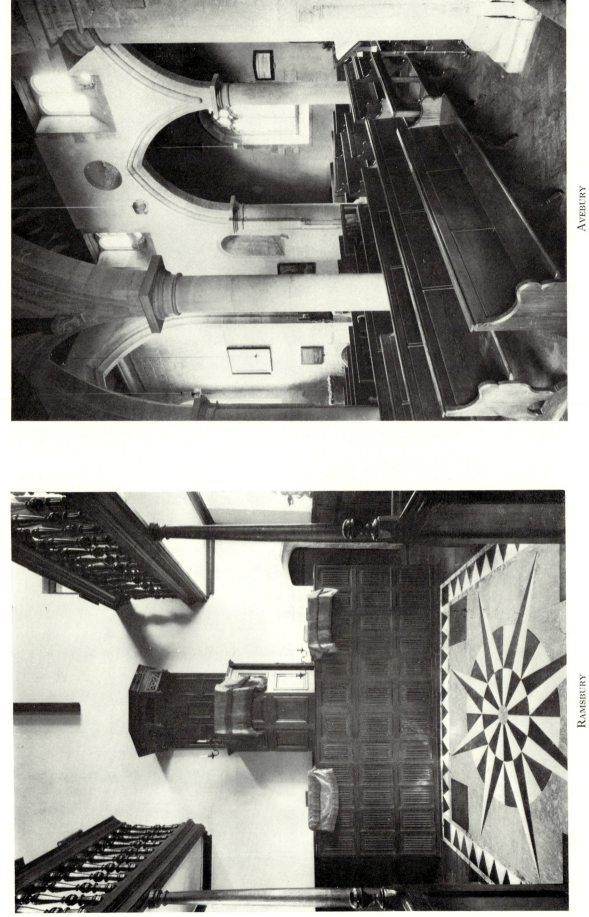

AVEBURY

The nave and north aisle of St. James's church

RAMSBURY

The chapel in Littlecote House, built in the later Middle Ages, refitted in the 17th century

grantee. The manor, rated as 2 knights' fees, was held by Hildebrand in 1275.[45] Hildebrand's son Robert of London, a minor at his father's death, entered on it in 1288.[46] His successor Hildebrand of London held it in 1315. Hildebrand, who had sons Robert and Richard and a daughter Maud, then settled the manor on himself and his wife for their lives and in succession on those three siblings in tail.[47] Robert of London succeeded his father between 1347 and 1366.[48] Richard seems to have died without issue.[49] In 1367 Robert settled the manor on himself and his wife Elizabeth for their lives with remainder to John of Ramsbury and his wife Mabel, presumably relatives of Maud who married Robert of Ramsbury.[50] In 1383, however, Robert of London (d.s.p.) conveyed the manor to trustees who in 1391 settled it on his relict Elizabeth, daughter of John Lovel, Lord Lovel (presumably him who d. 1347), with remainder to John, Lord Lovel (d. 1408), presumably her brother, and his wife Maud in tail.[51] Elizabeth died before 1403 and the Lovels entered on the manor,[52] successfully resisting a challenge by Mabel of Ramsbury:[53] Maud held the manor after her husband's death.[54] In 1414 Maud (d. 1423) and her son John, Lord Lovel, sold the manor to trustees, apparently of Sir William Esturmy (d. 1427).[55] Although in 1385 Thomas Calstone of Littlecote had quitclaimed the manor to Robert of London's trustees,[56] in the 1420s the rights of Esturmy, his trustees, and their grantee John Esturmy were disputed by Calstone's son-in-law William Darell of Littlecote, claiming his wife Elizabeth Calstone's right as the great-grand-daughter of Maud of London.[57] Arbitration was arranged but the outcome is obscure.[58]

Axford manor was acquired by the Darells, presumably by arbitration but possibly by judgement or purchase, and Elizabeth held it at her death in 1464.[59] It descended like Littlecote manor to her great-great-grandson Sir Edward Darell (d. 1549),[60] who before 1548 conveyed it to his wife's grandfather Sir William Essex as security for payment of a legacy to her father Thomas Essex (knighted in 1549).[61] Sir William (d. 1548) devised the manor to his grandson Edward Essex.[62] The death of Sir Edward Darell, having devised much land to a mistress

and leaving his son William a minor,[63] and of Sir William Essex at about the same time increased the opportunity for further dispute over title to the manor. It was later claimed that Thomas Essex had refused Sir Edward Darell's proffer of the legacy. In 1561, under duress it was claimed, Edward Essex sold the manor to his tenant Hugh Stukeley (d. c. 1588), against whom William Darell later began proceedings for its recovery.[64] Possibly to help him win the battle at law, which was long and fought partly while he was in the Fleet prison in 1579,[65] Darell seems to have offered to sell the manor on its recovery to Henry, earl of Pembroke, then owner of the copyhold lands of Axford in Ramsbury manor.[66] Darell did recover Axford manor, 'craftily' it was said.[67] He may have entered on it before 1583 when he was in dispute with Pembroke over the felling of its trees but when actions at law were incomplete.[68] In 1588, when Stukeley still hoped to recover it, Darell sold it in reversion to Sir Francis Walsing-ham on terms similar to those of his sale of Littlecote manor to Sir Thomas Bromley.[69] After Darell's death in 1589 Walsingham entered on the manor. He died in 1590 leaving as heir his daughter Frances who in that year married Robert Devereux, earl of Essex.[70] In 1601 the rights to the manor of Walsingham's relict Ursula and his daughter Frances and the claim of Hugh Stukeley's son Thomas were bought by Gabriel Pile (knighted in 1607).[71]

Axford manor passed at Pile's death in 1626 to his son Francis (created a baronet in 1628, d. 1635), and afterwards to Sir Francis's sons Sir Francis (d. c. 1649) and Sir Seymour (will proved 1681).[72] It descended from Sir Seymour to his son Sir Francis and Sir Francis's son Sir Sey-mour.[73] In 1707 a Bill to permit the sale of the manor was rejected by the House of Commons, and in 1708 a similar Bill, said to be necessary to save Sir Seymour and his family from starvation, was rejected by the Lords.[74] Sir Seymour died in 1711 leaving a son Sir Seymour no older than three. A Chancery decree of 1714 or 1715 permitted a sale, and in 1719 Sir Seymour's relict Jane, wife of Abel Griffith, and brother Gabriel sold 279 a. of woodland to Francis Hawes, a director of the South Sea Company.[75] After the company collapsed the land

[45] Rot. Hund. (Rec. Com.), ii (1), 265; a pedigree of the Londons is in B.L. Lansd. MS. 205, f. 61.
[46] Cal. Inq. p.m. ii, p. 453.
[47] Feet of F. 1272–1327 (W.R.S. i), p. 126.
[48] Ibid. 1327–77 (W.R.S. xxix), p. 131; Cal. Pat. 1345–8, 307.
[49] W.N. & Q. vii. 266.
[50] Feet of F. 1327–77 (W.R.S. xxix), p. 131; B.L. Lansd. MS. 205, f. 61.
[51] B.L. Harl. MS. 1623, ff. 10, 12v.; Lansd. MS. 205, f. 61; P.R.O., CP 25(1)/256/56, no. 13; Complete Peerage, s.v. Lovel.
[52] P.R.O., SC 2/208/11.
[53] Ibid. CP 40/574, rot. 255d.; CP 40/578, rot. 238 and d.
[54] Cal. Close, 1405–9, 414–15.
[55] B.L. Harl. MS. 1623, f. 18v.; P.R.O., CP 25(1)/256/60, no. 9; ibid. C 139/28, no. 22; Cal. Close, 1413–19, 458.
[56] Cal. Close, 1385–9, 79.
[57] W.N. & Q. vii. 265–9.
[58] P.R.O., E 326/9671.
[59] Ibid. C 140/12, no. 13; B.L. Lansd. MS. 205, f. 61v.
[60] Above, Ramsbury, manors.
[61] P.R.O., SP 46/45, f. 216; Berks. Pedigrees (Harl. Soc. lvi), 25.

[62] P.R.O., SP 46/45, f. 216; V.C.H. Berks. iv. 253.
[63] Above, Ramsbury, manors.
[64] P.R.O., SP 46/45, ff. 173, 216; ibid. CP 25(2)/239/3 Eliz. I Trin.; ibid. PROB 11/73 (P.C.C. 28 Leicester, will of Hugh Stukeley).
[65] e.g. ibid. SP 46/44, ff. 64, 158.
[66] Hall, Soc. in Elizabethan Eng. 292; above.
[67] Hist. MSS. Com. 58, Bath, iv, p. 211.
[68] P.R.O., SP 46/44, ff. 82–4.
[69] Ibid. PROB 11/73 (P.C.C. 28 Leicester, will of Hugh Stukeley); W.R.O. 1883/96/1; above, Ramsbury, manors.
[70] P.R.O., C 3/378/10; D.N.B. s.vv. Devereux, Walsingham.
[71] P.R.O., CP 25(2)/242/43 Eliz. I Hil.; CP 25(2)/242/43 & 44 Eliz. I Mich.; ibid. C 3/378/10; for the Stukeleys see Burke, Ext. & Dorm. Baronetcies (1838), 511.
[72] Wilts. Pedigrees (Harl. Soc. cv, cvi), 151; Burke, Ext. & Dorm. Baronetcies (1838), 413–14; P.R.O., PROB 11/367 (P.C.C. 122 North).
[73] Burke, Ext. & Dorm. Baronetcies (1838), 414.
[74] Ho. of Lords MSS. n.s. vii, pp. 55–6, 349–50, 561.
[75] W.R.O. 1883/95, assignment to Hawes; cf. Ho. of Lords MSS. n.s. vii, p. 349.

was confiscated by parliamentary trustees who in 1724 sold it to Richard Jones, lord of Ramsbury manor.[76] In 1744 Sir Seymour Pile sold the remainder of Axford manor to Jones's brother William.[77] The whole of it descended with the Axford part of Ramsbury manor, so that in 1981 nearly all the land of Axford belonged to the Burdett-Fishers.[78]

Hildebrand of London (fl. 1275) seems to have lived at Axford,[79] and his successors may have until the late 14th century. John Esturmy was said to be 'of Axford' in 1428.[80] In the 17th century a large house was apparently built for the Piles, presumably for Sir Gabriel Pile soon after 1601. It may have stood north-west of the Londons' house, where a field still exhibits signs of disturbance. The house, called Axford House in 1701,[81] was in 1707 said to be too large for the estate and to need repair.[82] Its demolition was commissioned after the sale of 1744.[83] Thereafter farmers lived in the Londons' house, Axford Farm, as they may have done since the earlier 15th century.[84] The site of Axford Farm, where Lady Burdett-Fisher lived in 1981, may have been moated. The main range of the house is of rubble with ashlar dressings. It has at its east end a 14th-century chapel, now divided by an inserted floor, and near its west end an elaborately moulded late medieval roof truss which was possibly at the centre of an open hall. A north wing was added in 1660,[85] and the inside of the main range has frequently been altered.

Although it was said in 1341 that tithes in Ramsbury parish were paid to none but the prebendary of Ramsbury and the vicar of Ramsbury,[86] in the later 15th century the prebend of Axford was apparently endowed with tithes arising from land in Axford.[87] The prebend was valued at 32s. in 1226, £5 in 1291, and £4 or £6 in 1535.[88] In the late 15th century it was leased to the Darells.[89] *AXFORD PREBEND*, whatever its endowment, was acquired with Ramsbury prebend by Edward, earl of Hertford, in 1545 and, since it was held by the Crown in 1567, seems to have been given to the Crown with Ramsbury prebend in 1547.[90] In 1571 Hugh Stukeley claimed, perhaps unrealistically, all tithes from Axford as part of Axford manor:[91] on the other hand, in the early 17th century all tithes of Axford were claimed as parts of Ramsbury prebend and of the vicarage.[92] The evidence suggests that the tithes arising from the land of Axford manor belonged to Axford prebend while the tithes of Ramsbury manor's land in Axford

belonged to Ramsbury vicarage and Ramsbury prebend. At his death in 1626 Sir Gabriel Pile owned Axford prebend and from then, if not earlier, the land of Axford manor and its tithes were merged.[93]

ECONOMIC HISTORY. Axford was divided lengthwise between to the west the lands of Ramsbury manor in Axford and, more extensive, to the east the lands of Axford manor:[94] until the later 18th century the two parts were nowhere merged for agriculture. Apart from woodland nearly all the Ramsbury manor land was held customarily.[95] The virtual lack of Ramsbury manor demesne land, the great size of Axford manor and its proximity to Ramsbury Manor, and the clarity of the division suggest that Axford manor originated in an early grant of a large demesne farm by a bishop of Salisbury, possibly Jocelin de Bohun, bishop 1142–84.[96] The lands of both manors south of the Kennet were within Savernake forest until 1228.[97]

The division of Axford between Axford manor and Ramsbury manor may already have been clear in the 1290s when Bishop Longespée allowed Robert of London to have a chase between their lands north of the road through Sound Bottom. Robert's surrender in exchange of his rights in a common pasture and waste[98] perhaps completed the division. The land of Axford manor was a strip, possibly as much as 1,500 a., extending from Whiteshard Bottom to Hens Wood. Its eastern boundary with the agricultural land in the north part of Park Town tithing is obscure; further south Axford manor marched with the old park north of the Kennet and with the new park south of the Kennet through Hens Wood.[99] Its western boundary with the land of Ramsbury manor began where the parish boundary makes a bend east of Mere Farm in Mildenhall, ran SSE. to the east end of Axford village, and south of the Kennet ran SSW. towards Puthall Farm in Little Bedwyn.[1] A large part of Hens Wood was apparently in Axford: the lord of Ramsbury manor had over 5,000 trees in the Axford portion in the later 16th century, and Axford manor included 279 a. of woodland, mostly presumably there, in 1701.[2]

Axford manor was assessed as 4 carucates in 1331.[3] In 1403, and presumably much earlier, it consisted of demesne and customary land. The demesne was in hand. It included sheephouses and folds said to be at Axford and Ashridge, a

[76] W.R.O. 1883/95, bargain and sale.
[77] Ibid. 1883/96/14.
[78] Above; above, Ramsbury, manors.
[79] *Cal. Inq. p.m.* ii, p. 453.
[80] *Feud. Aids*, v. 267–8.
[81] W.R.O. 1883/95, mortgage, Pile to Wall.
[82] *Ho. of Lords MSS.* N.S. vii, p. 55.
[83] W.R.O. 1883/96/12.
[84] e.g. *W.A.M.* x. 258; inf. from Mr. G. W. Wilson, Rudge Manor Farm, Froxfield.
[85] Date on bldg.
[86] *Inq. Non.* (Rec. Com.), 175.
[87] P.R.O., SP 46/45, ff. 64, 70.
[88] *Reg. St. Osmund* (Rolls Ser.), ii. 73; *Tax. Eccl.* (Rec. Com.), 182; *Valor Eccl.* (Rec. Com.), ii. 76, 152.
[89] P.R.O., SP 46/45, ff. 64, 66–70.
[90] *L. & P. Hen. VIII*, xx (2), p. 411; P.R.O., E 310/26/154; above, Ramsbury, manors.
[91] P.R.O., CP 25(2)/239/13 Eliz. I East.
[92] Ibid. REQ 2/5/155; ibid. C 2/Jas. I/A 5/63.
[93] *W.A.M.* xxxv. 490; W.R.O. 1883/95, mortgage, Pile to Wall.
[94] Inclosure award: W.R.O., transcript in 154/2; ibid. tithe award.
[95] e.g. *First Pembroke Survey*, ed. Straton, i. 163–7 (1567).
[96] Above, manors.
[97] *V.C.H. Wilts.* iv. 417–18.
[98] D. & C. Sar. Mun., press IV, box C 3/Ramsbury/16.
[99] Map of Ramsbury, 1676, *penes* Lady (Marjorie) Burdett-Fisher, Axford Farm: microfilm copy in W.R.O.
[1] Inclosure award: W.R.O., transcript in 154/2; ibid. tithe award.
[2] Ibid. 1883/95, mortgage, Pile to Wall; P.R.O., SC 12/22/91.
[3] W.R.O., bishop, Liber Niger, f. 95.

several pasture, woodland, and a rabbit warren. The customary tenants had a common pasture.[4] In the mid 16th century free fishing in the Kennet and free warren were claimed for the manor.[5] The demesne was apparently in hand in 1589 when wheat was sold for £31 and £5 2s. 2d. was paid in wages in 6 months. A reference of 1590 is the last to a copyhold of Axford manor.[6] In 1707 the woodland was in hand. All the agricultural land, possibly over 1,000 a., was then held by lease as a single farm.[7] After it was reunited with Ramsbury manor in 1744[8] Axford farm was leased to William Cox, who was ejected in 1755 for arrears of rent and for leaving the land uncultivated.[9]

The customary tenants of Ramsbury manor in Axford held the strip of land, possibly 750 a., at the west end of the parish. They cultivated it in common until it was inclosed by private agreement in 1727. The arable land was in two fields. North field, 280 a. between the Kennet and the road through Sound Bottom, included 8 a. between Axford Street and the river. South field contained 194 a. south of Mead Lane. North of North field Hillworth was a pasture for ewes and cattle in the 16th century but was later ploughed, and as the Heath, c. 63 a., became part of North field. South of South field, adjoining Hens Wood and Puthall farm, was a down, c. 74 a., apparently for cattle. Between the fields a marsh and several islands in the Kennet, c. 32 a., were commonable.[10] The meadows there may have been watered in the mid 16th century.[11] North of Sound Bottom and apparently adjoining Sound Copse in Mildenhall was the site of Kearsdown Farm, a croft called Caresden, within which there was a rabbit warren: it had been inclosed by the late 13th century. It was held customarily and in 1462, when the rabbit warren was held separately, was more than 50 a.[12] The rabbit warren was last mentioned in the earlier 16th century.[13] The copyhold was 'roofless' c. 1600: part of the land was wooded until converted then to arable.[14] Thereafter Caresden was added to the other c. 40 a. of inclosures appended to copyholds.[15]

The Axford tenants of Ramsbury manor held 22 yardlands and in the Middle Ages owed many customary services.[16] By 1396 services from half the holdings had been commuted, and it is unlikely that many of the remainder were performed since the lord of the manor then had little agricultural land nearby.[17] In 1462 rents totalled

£8 1s. 10d. There were twelve tenants and several of the holdings were large: three holdings exceeded 75 a.[18] In the mid 16th century the yardlands were nominally 24 a. with the right to feed 60 sheep and several other animals.[19] Pigs were stinted at five to a yardland in 1633.[20] In contrast with those holding in Ramsbury Town, Whittonditch, and Eastridge tithings the Axford copyholders, except one or two, held no land elsewhere in the parish.[21] They were apparently a small yeoman group of comparatively equal resources many of whom, especially in the 17th and 18th centuries, shared the name Appleford.[22] In 1567 seven held between 50 a. and 100 a., four between 25 a. and 50 a., all with pasture rights.[23] After the period 1677–81 the 13 yardlands sold by the lord of Ramsbury manor were mingled with those still held by copy and lease in farms which by 1727 had become fewer and larger. Of c. 643 a. inclosed then c. 185 a. were copyhold and leasehold, c. 458 a. freehold. There were holdings of c. 205 a. and c. 154 a. possibly worked from, respectively, the buildings near the river at the east end of Axford Street which became Riverside Farm and others near the west end of the street which became Church Farm. Coombe farm, c. 120 a., had buildings south-west of the village, but the other three holdings, each of fewer than 60 a., presumably had buildings in the street.[24]

In the later 18th century the Joneses, lords of Ramsbury and Axford manors, divided Axford farm into Burney or Upper Axford or New farm, with buildings beside the Axford–Aldbourne road, and Axford farm, and leased some land with Stock Close farm in Aldbourne.[25] Of the previously commonable land they took in hand the copyholds and leaseholds and bought some of the freeholds.[26] In 1839 Coombe, which had grown by inheritance to 244 a., Riverside, 59 a., and a holding of 60 a. were the only farms not owned and leased by their successor. Burney, 657 a., Axford, 519 a. including 117 a. of wood and buildings at Axford Farm and House Farm, and Church, 490 a. including a brick kiln near Hens Wood and 121 a. of wood, were then the principal farms in Axford: 97 a. of arable at Whiteshard Bottom, 10 a. of meadow near Ramsbury Manor, and 35 a. of Blake's Copse were separately leased, possibly still as part of Stock Close farm. Of c. 2,200 a. in Axford two thirds were arable.[27] In 1880 Church farm was 417 a. and Stock Close farm included 142 a. in Axford. From 1885 to

[4] P.R.O., SC 2/208/11.
[5] Ibid. CP 25(2)/239/3 Eliz. I Trin.
[6] Ibid. SP 46/45, f. 292; ibid. REQ 2/261/13.
[7] Ho. of Lords MSS. N.S. vii, p. 55.
[8] Above, manors.
[9] W.R.O., Q. Sess. enrolled deeds, loose deed 1.
[10] Inclosure award: ibid. transcript in 154/2; cf. First Pembroke Survey, ed. Straton, i. 163–7.
[11] Wilton Ho. Mun., survey, 1550s, pp. 292–3.
[12] D. & C. Sar. Mun., press IV, box C 3/Ramsbury/16; W.R.O., bishop, Liber Niger, f. 101 and v.
[13] P.R.O., SC 12/22/90.
[14] Ibid. REQ 2/5/155; W.R.O. 1883/6; ibid. bishop, deposition bk. 53B.
[15] W.R.O. 1883/59, bargain and sale, Pembroke to Whitley and Cratford.
[16] Ibid. bishop, Liber Niger, ff. 95v. sqq., 101 and v.; First Pembroke Survey, ed. Straton, i. 163–7.

[17] D. & C. Sar. Mun., press I, box 8, no. 12B; above, Ramsbury, econ. hist.
[18] W.R.O., bishop, Liber Niger, f. 101 and v.
[19] Wilton Ho. Mun., survey, 1550s, pp. 292–6.
[20] Ibid. manor ct. bk., various par., 1633–4, f. 15v.
[21] First Pembroke Survey, ed. Straton, i. 148–67.
[22] e.g. P.R.O., E 179/196/161; of the 12 allottees under the 1727 Axford inclosure award 7 were Applefords and 2 married Applefords: W.R.O., transcript in 154/2.
[23] First Pembroke Survey, ed. Straton, i. 163–7.
[24] Above, manors; inclosure award: W.R.O., transcript in 154/2; ibid. Axford land tax; tithe award; map of Ramsbury, W. div., penes Mrs. B. Croucher, 25 Ashley Piece.
[25] W.R.O. 212A/27/27, acct. of rents; ibid. Axford land tax.
[26] Ibid. tithe award; Axford land tax; P.R.O., CP 43/805, rott. 62 and d., 64d.–66d.
[27] Map of Ramsbury, W. div., penes Mrs. Croucher.

1929 Axford, 709 a., and Burney, still 657 a., were leased with Park farm in Ramsbury, 807 a., to Henry Wilson and his sons.[28] In the mid 20th century Burney, including New Buildings, and Axford, including House Farm and Kearsdown Farm, remained large and compact farms.[29] In the later 20th century they and Church farm were in hand: in 1981 *c.* 2,000 a. of agricultural land in Axford and more in Aldbourne were used from House Farm and Stock Close Farm for sheep-and-corn husbandry.[30] Coombe was then a separate farm.[31]

Ramsbury manor included a mill at Axford in 1330,[32] but the only mill known to have been there later was that of Axford manor at Axford Farm, referred to in the mid 16th century and in the later 16th century when it was leased.[33] It was mentioned in 1601,[34] but not afterwards until 1839 when there was apparently a mill on the site.[35] An undershot wheel survives there.

For permission to inclose given by him as lord of Ramsbury manor in 1727 those holding land in the west part of Axford gave up the right to fish in the Kennet to Richard Jones, who acquired the remainder of the fishing in Axford with Axford manor in 1744.[36]

LOCAL GOVERNMENT. Records of the courts held in 1403 for Axford manor include presentments by the homage, the bailiff, and inspectors of carcasses. The courts protected the lord's rights over his bondmen, customary tenants, and pastures by ordering the return of a bondman from Salthrop in Wroughton, binding a tenant to rebuild a house burned down because of his negligence, listing payments for pannage and agistment, and in other ways.[37] Courts held for the manor in the later 16th century possibly dealt only with copyholds since then and later common husbandry in Axford was regulated in Ramsbury manor court.[38] The Axford tithingman attended and was appointed at Ramsbury law hundred.[39]

CHURCH. A church at Axford, presumably a chapel of ease, was recorded in 1288 as having been used for baptism in 1267.[40] There is no later reference to it. In the 14th century a chapel was built at Axford Farm, presumably for private use, and in the early 15th century the lord of Axford manor paid yearly for right of burial at Ramsbury.[41]

A chapel of ease dedicated to *ST. MICHAEL* and served from Ramsbury was built at Axford in 1856.[42] In 1864 it was nearly always full for the weekly services: communion was held on the Sundays after Christmas and Easter and on Trinity Sunday. There was no right of marriage in it until 1940.[43] The chapel, designed by William White,[44] is a plain rectangular building of banded brick and flint with a slate roof. It has 19th-century plate[45] and no bell.

NONCONFORMITY. A house in Axford was registered in 1818 for worship by dissenters.[46] In 1851 an Independent congregation of 35 was served from Ramsbury on Census Sunday and by 1885 a Congregational chapel had been built north of the street near the east end of the village.[47] It had been closed and demolished by 1899.[48] A Methodist chapel west of the church was opened in 1888. It had apparently been closed by 1972.[49]

EDUCATION. Children living in Axford presumably attended Ramsbury or Mildenhall schools until 1874 when the Ramsbury school board built a school and schoolhouse in the east part of Axford village.[50] Average attendance at the school was 59 in 1906–7. It had fallen steadily to 28 by 1927 and in 1931 the school was closed.[51]

BAYDON

The chapelry and tithing of Baydon was in Ramsbury parish. It relieved its own poor, apparently in the early 18th century,[52] and achieved full parish status in the 1790s when its church became independent of Ramsbury church.[53] The parish is shaped like an hourglass.

Its boundaries, especially that with Ramsbury, are irregular, except the part of the western boundary marked by the Roman road Ermin Street. They enclose the summit of the downs, marked by the 229 m. contour, and correspond with the relief. Baydon village is on the summit at

[28] W.R.O. 1883, rent bk. 1880; letter bk. 115.
[29] Ibid. 1883, misc. plans.
[30] Inf. from Maj. F. R. D. Burdett-Fisher, Harbrook Farm.
[31] Local inf.
[32] D. & C. Sar. Mun., press I, box 8, no. 12A.
[33] B.L. Add. Ch. 24440; P.R.O., CP 25(2)/239/3 Eliz. I Trin.; ibid. SP 46/45, f. 208.
[34] P.R.O., CP 25(2)/242/43 & 44 Eliz. I Mich.
[35] Map of Ramsbury, W. div., *penes* Mrs. Croucher.
[36] Inclosure award: W.R.O., transcript in 154/2; P.R.O., CP 25(2)/1233/17 & 18 Geo. II Trin.
[37] P.R.O., SC 2/208/11.
[38] Ibid. REQ 2/261/13; ibid. C 3/378/10; B.L. Add. Ch. 24440–1; Wilton Ho. Mun., manor ct. bk., various par., 1633–4, ff. 13v., 15v.
[39] Above, Ramsbury, local govt.
[40] *Cal. Inq. p.m.* ii, p. 453.
[41] W.R.O., dean, Chaundler's reg. f. 126 and v.; above, manors.
[42] W.R.O., bishop, consecrations, bdle. 5, no. 58.
[43] Ibid. bishop, Ramsbury vis. queries, 1864; inf. from Dioc. Registrar, Minster Chambers, Castle St., Salisbury.
[44] Pevsner, *Wilts.* (2nd edn.), 103.
[45] Nightingale, *Wilts. Plate*, 162–3.
[46] W.R.O., bishop, return of cert. places.
[47] P.R.O., HO 129/121/2/11/19; O.S. Map 6″, Wilts. XXIX (1889 edn.).
[48] O.S. Map 6″, Wilts. XXIX. SE. (1900 edn.).
[49] Ibid.; date on bldg.; *Statistical Returns* (Dept. for Chapel Affairs), i. 49.
[50] P.R.O., ED 7/131, no. 230; O.S. Map 6″, Wilts. XXIX (1889 edn.).
[51] *Bd. of Educ., List 21* (H.M.S.O.).
[52] *Poor Law Com. 1st Rep.* 242; W.R.O. 656/1.
[53] Below, church.

the neck of the hourglass. Ford and Gore Lane are valley settlements in respectively the extreme south-west and north parts of the parish. In 1934, when the boundary with Aldbourne was moved from the stream flowing from Aldbourne to Knighton to the Aldbourne–Knighton road to exclude Ford Farm, the area of the parish fell from 2,485 a. (1,006 ha.) to 1,001 ha. (2,473 a.).[54]

Although the village site suggests an ancient origin, the earliest reference to Baydon is of 1196.[55] Baydon was of average wealth in the early 14th century and there were 59 poll-tax payers in 1377.[56] It may have been less prosperous in the 16th century but may not have deserved to be called a hamlet as it was in 1621.[57] There were 81 men living in the parish in 1773.[58] The population was 290 in 1801. It had risen to 380 by 1861 but had declined to 213 by 1921. Since the Second World War the population, 365 in 1971, more in 1981, has more than doubled as the village has become a dormitory of Swindon.[59]

The village is bisected by a Roman road, there called Ermin Street and Baydon Road, but most settlement in it has been away from the road in the network of lanes which, with no clear pattern, lie north and south of the road. No large manor house has stood there. What was presumably the largest farmhouse was derelict in the mid 16th century and was replaced by Bailey Hill Farm[60] 1 km. north of the village. In the 16th century and until the 19th Baydon was a village of medium sized farmsteads, from the late 18th century or earlier all in the lanes:[61] Downs House, Tubbs Farm, Westfield Farm, and Finches Farm were north of Ermin Street, and south of it were Manor Farm, Walrond's Farm, Baydon House Farm, and Paine's Farm. The church, the former vicarage house, and the school are north of the road; most of the later 20th-century houses are south of it. The Green Dragon was an inn on the south side of Baydon Road in 1715.[62] It was converted into cottages in 1771 and later demolished. The Plough, which replaced it, was converted into cottages between 1848 and 1855.[63] The Red Lion, an inn in 1772,[64] also on the south side of Baydon Road, survives as a much altered building possibly of the 17th century.

East of the church Westfield Farm and a cottage are possibly 17th-century. Buildings of the 18th century include Tubbs Farm and the east half of Downs House north of the Roman road and, south of it, several thatched and other cottages beside Aldbourne Road and near Baydon House Farm at the south end of the village,

in Manor Lane, and on the south side of Ermin Street. Baydon House Farm was built in 1744 and later extended.[65] There was little rebuilding in Baydon in the 19th century: between 1875 and 1890 the wealthy philanthropist Angela, Baroness Burdett-Coutts, then patron of the living, replaced several cottages with 'model' cottages,[66] but it is not clear whether the replacements are the seven flint and brick late 19th-century cottages in Gothic style near the church or Model Cottages in Aldbourne Road, of similar date and with arch-braced eaves. In the earlier 20th century three pairs of council houses were built beside Ermin Street, three pairs in Manor Lane, and eight in Aldbourne Road. The growth of housing in the village since 1945 has, however, been by the building of small houses and bungalows beside the lanes and of a total of 61 in Ermin Close south of Ermin Street and in Downsmead west of Aldbourne Road. In 1973 a water tower, with the tank clasped by tapering concrete piers, was built to designs of Scherrer & Hicks east of the village beside the London and south Wales motorway.[67]

Ford may have been a hamlet in the Middle Ages, but in the mid 16th century and later there was apparently no more than a single farmstead there.[68] In the later 18th century the Aldbourne–Knighton road passed between the buildings and the stream.[69] By 1828 it had been remade on a straighter and higher course north-east of them.[70] In 1981 Ford Farm consisted of extensive farm buildings and a large 19th-century house.

In 1773 there was no building in the inclosures called Gore Lanes. Gore Lane Farm was built on the west side of the road there before 1828, and farm buildings were built on the east side before 1878.[71] Hazelbury Farm, south of Gore Lane Farm on the west side, was built in the mid 20th century, and there are several other 20th-century dwellings in the hamlet.

MANOR AND OTHER ESTATES. Almost certainly in 1086 as later, all the land of Baydon was part of the bishop of Salisbury's Ramsbury estate.[72] The bishop's demesne and the freely and customarily held land at Baydon were part of Ramsbury manor, but together were often referred to as if they formed a separate manor of BAYDON.[73] The bishop was granted free warren in his demesne lands in 1294.[74] Most of Baydon manor, the demesne, two thirds of the yardlands held by copy, and two thirds of the

[54] O.S. Map 6″, Wilts. XXIV (1887 and later edns.); V.C.H. Wilts. iv. 340; Census, 1971.
[55] Above, Ramsbury, introduction; Feet of Fines (Pipe R. Soc. xvii), pp. 63–4.
[56] V.C.H. Wilts. iv. 301, 310.
[57] Taxation Lists (W.R.S. x), 93; P.R.O., C 2/Jas. I/S 33/29.
[58] W.R.O. 1883/3.
[59] V.C.H. Wilts. iv. 340; Census, 1971.
[60] Wilton Ho. Mun., survey, 1550s, p. 302; below, econ. hist.
[61] First Pembroke Survey, ed. Straton, i. 167–73; Andrews and Dury, Map (W.R.S. viii), pl. 15.
[62] W.R.O. 212B/131; 700/166, conveyance, Baverstock to Haggard.

[63] Ibid. 700/166, deed, Banning to Hill; conveyance, Baverstock to Haggard.
[64] Ibid. 242/9.   [65] Date on bldg.
[66] Wilts. Cuttings, i. 184.
[67] Pevsner, Wilts. (2nd edn.), 105; plaque on bldg.
[68] V.C.H. Wilts. iv. 310; D. & C. Sar. Mun., press I, box 8, no. 12B; Wilton Ho. Mun., survey, 1550s, pp. 288–91.
[69] Andrews and Dury, Map (W.R.S. viii), pl. 15.
[70] O.S. Map 1″, sheet 34 (1828 edn.).
[71] Andrews and Dury, Map (W.R.S. viii), pl. 15; O.S. Maps 1″, sheet 34 (1828 edn.); 6″, Wilts. XXIV (1887 edn.).
[72] V.C.H. Wilts. ii, p. 84.
[73] Valor Eccl. (Rec. Com.), ii. 70; First Pembroke Survey, ed. Straton, i. 167–74.
[74] Cal. Chart. R. 1257–1300, 454.

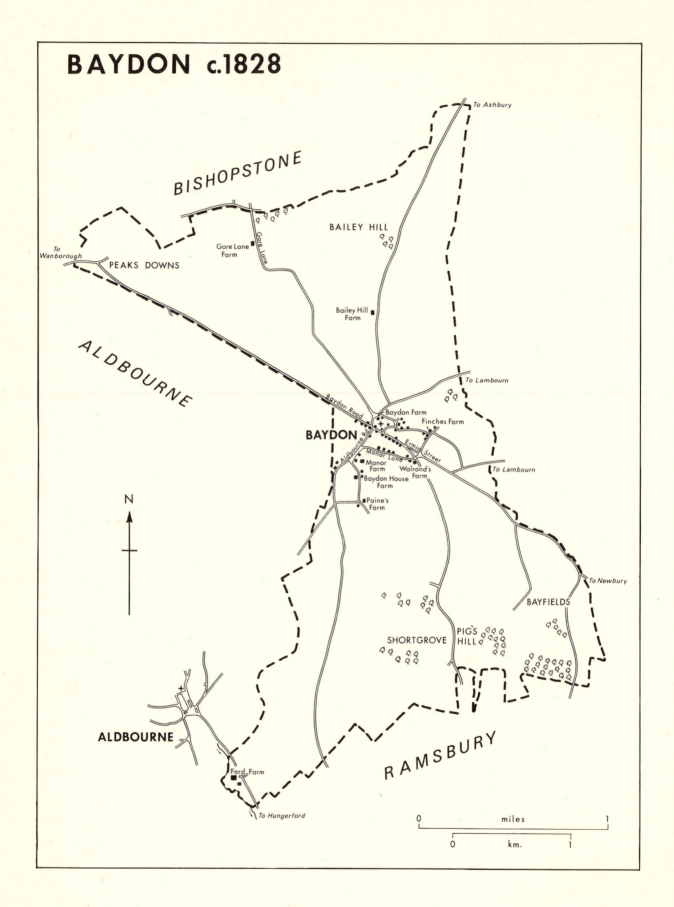

BAYDON c.1828

BISHOPSTONE

To Ashbury

BAILEY HILL

Gore Lane
Farm

Gore Lane

To
Wanborough

PEAKS DOWNS

Bailey Hill
Farm

ALDBOURNE

To Lambourn

Baydon Road

Baydon Farm

Finches Farm

BAYDON

Ermin Street

Aldbourne Rd

Manor Lane

Manor
Farm

Walrond's
Farm

To Lambourn

Baydon House
Farm

Paine's
Farm

N

To Newbury

BAYFIELDS

SHORTGROVE

PIG'S
HILL

ALDBOURNE

RAMSBURY

Ford Farm

To Hungerford

0   miles   1

0   km.   1

land held by lease, was sold by Henry Powle between 1677 and 1681.[75] The remainder, perhaps 500 a., held by copy and lease in 1778, passed with Ramsbury manor through the Jones family to Sir Francis Burdett (d. 1844).[76] By 1827 most of that land had been merged in Manor farm, which Burdett then sold to John Williams (d. c. 1854).[77] Williams was succeeded by another John Williams who in 1884 sold the farm, 495 a. including land in the north and south parts of the parish.[78] Francis James Simpkins owned it from 1885 to 1890. It passed before 1899 to William James Phelps, who owned it until 1913.[79] Nearly all the land south of Ermin Street and Baydon Road was afterwards acquired, presumably by purchase, by Moses Woolland (d. 1918) and passed with his Marridge Hill, later Baydon Manor, estate in Ramsbury to his son Walter, who in 1947 owned and sold nearly all the agricultural land in Baydon south of the Roman road, c. 1,200 a.[80] Over 200 a. of it in the south-east corner of the parish were part of Maj. H. O. Stibbard's Marridge Hill estate in 1981.[81] The land north of the Roman road and buildings and some land south of it were sold in 1955 by Edwin Smith as Manor farm, 284 a.[82] In 1981 most of the land north of the road was part of Finches farm.[83]

Land at Gore Lane remained part of Ramsbury manor until c. 1804 when it passed, presumably by sale, from Sir Francis Burdett to Henry Read of Crowood. A John Williams, possibly he who bought Manor farm, acquired it from Read c. 1812.[84] It was apparently sold in 1872, and in the late 19th century was used for racehorse training, presumably from the stables at Russley Park in Bishopstone. In 1917, after the death of Henry Challoner Smith who seems to have owned it, the land was sold as Gore Lane farm, 125 a.[85] In 1981 that farm belonged to Mr. J. D. Wright.[86]

The demesne land of Ramsbury manor in Baydon, Bailey Hill farm, was bought by Robert Gilmore in 1681.[87] Gilmore (fl. 1705) devised the land to his wife Mary and his sister Catherine. They conveyed it to Catherine's son John Miller (d. 1707) whose relict Mary seems to have sold it to its mortgagees, Alexander and William Goodall, the executors of Alexander Goodall, c. 1718.[88] The farm seems to have been acquired by Alexander Goodall (fl. 1721), whose daughter and executor Anne Goodall died seised in 1734.[89] She devised it to her uncle William Godfrey and

his wife Mary for their lives, and afterwards to her cousins Jane (d. 1789), Mary, Anne, and Sarah Godfrey. Her cousin Mary was the wife of Sir John Crosse, and Sarah was the wife of the Revd. William Goodsalve. Bailey Hill farm, 427 a., seems to have passed to Sarah's son John Goodsalve Crosse (d. 1793) and to his son John Crosse Goodsalve Crosse, who in 1800 sold it to William Craven, Lord Craven.[90] It passed with the Craven title until 1947 when it was sold twice, the second time to Mr. E. P. Geary, the owner in 1981.[91] Bailey Hill Farm was built in the 17th century to an L-shaped plan. The angle between the ranges was filled in the 18th century when the older part of the house was largely refitted. West of the house a large aisled barn, much of which had collapsed by 1981, was built in the 17th century.

Of the other leaseholds and the copyholds sold by Powle, George Adams bought in 1677 what was apparently the largest holding, and others were later added to it.[92] Adams had a son George who may have held the land in the early 18th century.[93] In 1721 it apparently belonged to John Adams.[94] Other Adamses lived in Baydon in the later 18th century,[95] but the descent of the land is obscure. It was apparently that acquired, presumably by purchase, by Peter Delme before 1778.[96] Delme sold his land to George Boughey c. 1785.[97] Boughey was succeeded in 1788 by his infant cousin John Fenton Fletcher (John Fenton Boughey from 1805), who succeeded his father Thomas Fletcher as a baronet in 1812.[98] The estate, 440 a., was sold as two farms in 1796.[99] Baydon farm, including land in the north and south parts of the parish and buildings north of the church now Downs House, was bought by John Williams (d. c. 1828). Williams devised it to his grandson John Allin Williams who sold the farm, 242 a., in 1871.[1] Thereafter the descent of that land is again obscure. The part south of the Roman road was later acquired by one of the Woollands and in 1947 was part of Walter Woolland's Baydon Manor estate.[2] That north of the road may have been acquired by Thomas Arkell who held land there in 1899; Arkell's executors held his land in the early 1920s;[3] and in 1981 much of it was part of Finches farm.[4] Ford farm, 237 a., was bought by John Hancock in 1796, and after his death in 1817 was held by a Mrs. Hancock until c. 1826. John's heir was his daughter Anne, wife of T. B. M. Baskerville (d. 1864),[5] but the descent of Ford farm is

[75] W.R.O. 1883/59, bargain and sale, Pembroke to Whitley and Cratford; bargain and sale, Powle to Jones.
[76] Ibid. 1883/59, mortgage, 1806–7; 154/2.
[77] Ibid. 1883/223; *Endowed Char. Wilts.* (N. Div.), 31–2.
[78] W.A.S. Libr., sale cat. vii, no. 57.
[79] *Kelly's Dir. Wilts.*
[80] Ibid. (1920 and later edns.); W.R.O. 1008/25; above, Ramsbury, manors; below.
[81] Inf. from Maj. H. O. Stibbard, the Park, Ogbourne St. Geo.
[82] W.A.S. Libr., sale cat. xxixc, no. 30.
[83] Inf. from Mr. R. B. Day, Finches Farm; below.
[84] W.R.O., Baydon land tax.
[85] W.A.S. Libr., sale cat. xxvi, no. 7; above, Bishopstone, econ. hist.
[86] Local inf.
[87] W.R.O. 1883/106/17.
[88] Ibid. 1883/13; 212A/27/22/1, Ambrose's bond; 212A/27/22/2, copy of decree.
[89] Ibid. 1883/215; 212A/27/22/2, Goodall's administration.

[90] Ibid. 212A/27/22/2, deed poll, Crosse and Godfrey; release, Crosse to Craven.
[91] *Complete Peerage*; inf. from Mr. E. P. Geary, Bailey Hill Farm.
[92] W.R.O. 1883/59, bargain and sale, Pembroke to Whitley and Cratford; 1883/106/28; 1883/13; 1577/2.
[93] Ibid. 1883/106/28; 1883/13.
[94] Ibid. 1883/215.
[95] e.g. *W.N. & Q.* ii. 23.
[96] W.R.O. 154/2.
[97] Ibid. Baydon land tax; cf. *V.C.H. Wilts.* xi. 244.
[98] Burke, *Peerage* (1949), 231.
[99] W.A.S. Libr., sale cat. ix, no. 32; P.R.O., C 12/976/9.
[1] W.A.S. Libr., sale cat. ix, no. 32; iii, no. 13.
[2] W.R.O. 1008/25.
[3] *Kelly's Dir. Wilts.* (1899 and later edns.).
[4] Inf. from Mr. Day; below.
[5] W.A.S. Libr., sale cat. ix, no. 32; W.R.O., Baydon land tax; below, Aldbourne, manors.

obscure. It apparently belonged to Henry James Puckeridge between 1872 and 1902 and was later part of Baydon Manor estate.[6] When that estate was broken up 1949–50 Ford farm was bought by A. G. Palmer,[7] who in 1963 sold it to E. H. B. Portman. It has since remained part of the Crowood estate.[8]

Lands bought by Anthony Stroud in 1677 were held by his relict in 1705.[9] They apparently passed to John Stroud (fl. 1714) and in 1721 may have belonged to another Anthony Stroud (fl. 1760).[10] In 1778 Thomas Stroud held the lands, over 100 a. in the north part of the parish.[11] A Thomas Stroud held them until 1831 or later.[12] They seem to have passed to members of the Tubb family, possibly to William Tubb (fl. 1848–90) or to T. Tubb (fl. 1875) and James Tubb (fl. 1884).[13] The Tubbs' lands were apparently sold in portions in 1897.[14]

In 1677 Robert Walrond bought the land which became Walrond's farm, more than 80 a. in the south part of the parish in 1778. It passed to his son Robert and to a succession of Robert Walronds until c. 1788.[15] From c. 1789 to c. 1805 it belonged to John Andrews and his relict and from c. 1810 to c. 1830 to John Walrond. In 1831 it was Robert Walrond's and in 1871 James Walrond's.[16] In 1923 it was bought from Annie Pembroke, William Pembroke, and P. M. Puckeridge, apparently by the representatives of Moses Woolland. It was added to the Baydon Manor estate and was sold in 1947 and c. 1949.[17] It was retained by John White who c. 1960 sold the farm, then c. 195 a., to his nephew Mr. R. T. Walton. In 1973 Mr. Walton sold it to Mr. J. S. Brunskill, the owner in 1981.[18]

In 1678 John Finch bought a farm which passed to Stephen Finch (fl. 1705–26) and to another Stephen Finch (fl. 1736).[19] The farm, c. 100 a. in the south part of the parish in 1778, was then John Finch's.[20] It remained in the Finch family until 1831 or later[21] but afterwards seems to have been absorbed by other farms.

A farm in the south part of the parish with buildings at Baydon House Farm presumably originated in land sold by Henry Powle between 1677 and 1681. John Brown owned the farm, over 80 a., in 1778.[22] From 1780 to 1831 or later

Thomas Brown, or a succession of Thomas Browns, owned it and from 1867 to 1899 it was Thomas Pearce Brown's.[23] Reginald Pearce Brown owned the farm from 1903 to 1907, but by 1911 it had apparently been bought by Moses Woolland.[24] As part of Walter Woolland's Baydon Manor estate it was merged with the lands of Manor farm and Baydon farm south of the Roman road as Baydon House farm, 440 a. when it was sold in 1947 and c. 1949.[25] Baydon House farm was retained by John White and c. 1950 sold by him to Crosby Dawson who soon afterwards sold it to Mary Dempster, Walter Woolland's sister and later wife of Raymond Lomax. At Mary Lomax's death c. 1956 the farm passed to her son Ian Lomax, who sold it in 1965 to Mr. L. H. Smith, the owner in 1981.[26]

Michael de Werlton (d. before 1227) held 1 carucate freely in Baydon and it may have passed to his son Walter.[27] From 1241, when they were conveyed by fine, there were two freeholds in Baydon.[28] Adam Pig's was the basis of an estate later called Pig's Court in the south-east. It may have passed to Richard Pig, who in 1295 seems to have conveyed the reversion to Richard of Highway.[29] A Richard of Highway and his wife Scholace held the estate in 1323[30] and in 1339 conveyed it to Robert of Ramsbury, who died seised of it in 1361.[31] Robert's heir was his son John of Ramsbury who apparently held the land in 1376.[32] It is uncertain how John disposed of the estate which in 1499 belonged to William Temse (d. 1502) of Netheravon.[33] It passed like Temse's Netheravon estate to his sister Joan (d. 1531), wife of Nicholas Wardour, and descended in turn to William Wardour, Mary Wardour, and Chidiock Wardour, who in 1582 sold it to Thomas Smith.[34] The estate, rated as 4 yardlands in 1567,[35] seems to have belonged to Henry Smith in 1597 and to his son Thomas in 1630.[36] The second freehold conveyed in 1241 was John Stroud's.[37] It possibly descended to Sir Hugh Stroud (fl. 1315) and Henry Stroud (fl. 1332).[38] Another Hugh Stroud held it in 1376 and another Henry Stroud in 1412.[39] It belonged c. 1556 to William Bush who sold it in 1561 or 1562 to Thomas Stephens.[40] After Stephens's death c. 1571 the descent of the land, rated as 4 yardlands in 1567, and later

[6] Reading Univ. Libr., hist. farm rec., WIL 11/3/15; W.A.S. Libr., sale cat. vii, no. 83; W.R.O. 1008/25.
[7] Above, Ramsbury, manors; inf. from Mr. R. T. Walton, New Ho., Manor Lane.
[8] Sale cat. (1979, copy in N.M.R.); local inf.
[9] W.R.O. 1883/106/25; 1883/13.
[10] Ibid. 1883/215; ibid. Q. Sess. enrolment, jurors bk. 1760; P.R.O., CP 25(2)/980/13 Anne East.
[11] W.R.O. 154/2.
[12] Ibid. Baydon land tax.
[13] Kelly's Dir. Wilts. (1848 and later edns.); W.A.S. Libr., sale cat. vii, nos. 57, 83.
[14] Wilts. Cuttings, vii. 113.
[15] W.R.O., Q. Sess. enrolment, jurors bk. 1760; ibid. Baydon land tax; ibid. 154/2; 1883/106/18; 1883/13; Q. Sess. 1736 (W.R.S. xi), p. 145.
[16] W.R.O., Baydon land tax; W.A.S. Libr., sale cat. iii, no. 13.
[17] W.R.O. 1008/25; above, Ramsbury, manors.
[18] Inf. from Mr. Walton.
[19] W.R.O. 1883/106/20; 1883/13; P.R.O., CP 25(2)/1079/12 Geo. I Trin.; Q. Sess. 1736 (W.R.S. xi), p. 145.
[20] W.R.O. 154/2.
[21] Ibid. Baydon land tax.
[22] Ibid. 154/2.

[23] Ibid. Baydon land tax; Kelly's Dir. Wilts. (1867 and later edns.).
[24] Kelly's Dir. Wilts.
[25] W.R.O. 1008/25; above, Ramsbury, manors.
[26] Inf. from Mr. Walton; Mr. F. Newman, Wentworth Cottages, Baydon Ho. Farm; Mr. L. H. Smith, Baydon Ho. Farm.
[27] P.R.O., CP 25(1)/250/5, no. 28.
[28] Ibid. CP 25(1)/251/13, no. 61.
[29] Feet of F. 1272–1327 (W.R.S. i), p. 42.
[30] Ibid. p. 110.
[31] Ibid. 1327–77 (W.R.S. xxix), p. 59; Cal. Inq. p.m. xi, p. 209.
[32] Cal. Fine R. 1356–68, 242; W.R.O., bishop, Liber Niger, f. 240.
[33] Extents for Debts (W.R.S. xxviii), p. 44; Cal. Inq. p.m. Hen. VII, ii, p. 425.
[34] V.C.H. Wilts. xi. 169; W.R.O. 130/46/4.
[35] First Pembroke Survey, ed. Straton, i. 167.
[36] P.R.O., CP 25(2)/242/39 Eliz. I East.; W.R.O. 212B/127.
[37] P.R.O., CP 25(1)/251/13, no. 61.
[38] Cat. Anct. D. i, C 1067; B.L. Harl. Ch. 49 H. 53.
[39] W.R.O., bishop, Liber Niger, f. 240; Feud. Aids, vi. 429.
[40] Wilton Ho. Mun., survey, 1550s, p. 281; W.N. & Q. v. 23.

called Baydon farm, is uncertain.[41] By 1630 it had been acquired by Thomas Smith, and it afterwards passed with Pig's Court as a single estate.[42] In 1633 a Thomas Smith, possibly Thomas's son, conveyed the estate to Philip Smith, who sold part of it in 1638, dealt with it by fine in 1645, but retained a large estate in 1663.[43] Before 1676 it seems to have passed to Philip's relict Theodosia, wife of Stephen Tracy, and his children Theophilus and Theodosia.[44] Tracy apparently held the land in 1680: one Smith did so in 1705, possibly John Smith (fl. 1713) who before 1721 sold it to Paul Calton.[45] As Baydon farm it belonged to Henry Dawkins from 1778 or earlier until c. 1795.[46] From c. 1796 to c. 1809, at which time there was another Baydon farm, it was John Finch's and was renamed Finches farm. William Finch owned it from c. 1810 to c. 1814 and William Brown from c. 1815 to 1831 or later.[47] Afterwards its descent is obscure. The farm, 122 a. east of the village, was bought by Moses Woolland in 1918.[48] In 1944 Walter Woolland sold it to Mr. R. N. Day whose son Mr. R. B. Day owned the farm, 265 a., in 1981.[49]

Several estates consisting only of tithes were created between 1677 and 1681. The largest seems to have been that bought by Thomas Kingston in 1677.[50] It was possibly that sold by Thomas Abbot and his wife Martha to Richard Jones, lord of Ramsbury manor, in 1705,[51] and may have been that belonging to William Williams which was exchanged for allotments of land totalling 76 a. at inclosure in 1778.[52] Tithes from the Bayfield area of Baydon belonged to the owners of Membury farm from the 1720s or earlier.[53] They were valued at £9 10s. and commuted in 1845.[54]

ECONOMIC HISTORY. The owners and tenants of the two freeholds and of the demesne and customary lands of Ramsbury manor in Baydon shared nearly all the land in the chapelry. They practised sheep-and-corn husbandry in common until inclosures in the 18th century.[55] In the Middle Ages the land of Ford was possibly used in common only by customary tenants of Ramsbury manor who had holdings based at Ford.[56] By the 16th century, however, the distinction between the lands of Ford and Preston had been blurred because, it seems, most land in both was then in the hands of men holding in

both.[57] When the line between Preston in Whittonditch tithing and Baydon was drawn in 1778 Ford field but no common pasture was counted part of Baydon.[58]

In the late 12th century and the early 13th the bishop of Salisbury leased for lives a messuage and 5½ yardlands of his demesne land, including 57½ a. of possibly several land, feeding for eight oxen in a common pasture, and woodland at Pax down in the south-east corner of the chapelry.[59] The land, later rated as 1 hide and as 1 carucate and worth 4 marks in 1246, remained at farm in 1249.[60] All the demesne lands, including rights to wood from Shortgrove, and the rents and services of ten Baydon bondmen were leased c. 1258 to Sir Peter of Membury for his life in exchange for Membury manor: by 1263 Sir Peter had surrendered the arable land, and apparently the pasture or right to feed sheep, for a yearly pension of 40 qr. of wheat, 50 qr. of dredge, 20 qr. of oats, and 100s. to be paid at Baydon.[61] The bishop's demesne lands made a moderately sized farm, in hand in 1405 when 70 a. were sown and 391 wethers were kept on pastures which included a several down at Shortgrove. The land may still have been cultivated largely by the tenants doing customary works although many works had been commuted.[62] It had been leased by the earlier 16th century.[63] The customary holdings were rated as yardlands and 'cotsetlands' in the 15th century.[64] Three-field cultivation is suggested by the statement in 1362 that two thirds of an estimated 100 a. of arable in the Pig's Court estate could be sown yearly.[65]

In the 14th and 15th centuries the bishop's income from Ford was counted with that from Ramsbury rather than Baydon manor. Customary works due from 6 yardlands had been commuted by 1396, suggesting by analogy with other places that Ford land was rated as 12 or more yardlands. Much of it was then in the bishop's hand and by 1425 four crofts in Ford field had been leased.[66]

In the mid 16th century it seems that more than 1,200 a. in the chapelry were arable. Apart from that at Ford the principal open fields were West in the north-west corner of the chapelry, Cossetel, later Costern, in the north-east corner, and in the southern half South field and the field 'on the west side of the wood'; there were two apparently open fields of fewer than 50 a. West down, 90 a., now called Peaks Downs, was a

[41] W.N. & Q. v. 415; First Pembroke Survey, ed. Straton, i. 168.
[42] W.R.O. 212B/127.
[43] Ibid. 130/46/8–10; W.A.S. Libr., Wilts. Misc. MSS. i, no. 6.
[44] W.R.O. 130/46/14; 130/46/18; Wilton Ho. Mun., ct. roll 1676.
[45] W.R.O. 1883/10; 1883/13; 1883/215; 212A/27/22/1, lease, Smith to Collins.
[46] Ibid. 154/2; ibid. Baydon land tax.
[47] Ibid. Baydon land tax; cf. Andrews and Dury, Map (W.R.S. viii), pl. 15; W.A.S. Libr., sale cat. xii, no. 18; above.
[48] W.A.S. Libr., sale cat. xii, no. 18.
[49] Inf. from Mr. Day.
[50] W.R.O. 1883/106.
[51] P.R.O., CP 25(2)/979/4 Anne Trin.
[52] W.R.O. 154/2.
[53] Ibid. 212B/5658; ibid. Baydon land tax; Eastridge land tax; P.R.O., CP 25(2)/1088/6 Geo. I Hil.
[54] W.R.O., tithe award.

[55] e.g. D. & C. Sar. Mun., press I, box 8, no. 12D; First Pembroke Survey, ed. Straton, i. 167–78; below.
[56] D. & C. Sar. Mun., press I, box 8, no. 12B.
[57] First Pembroke Survey, ed. Straton, i. 160–2, 169–72.
[58] W.R.O. 154/2; above, Ramsbury, econ. hist.
[59] D. & C. Sar. Mun., press IV, box C 3/Ramsbury/2; press IV, box C 3/Ramsbury/19; Civil Pleas, 1249 (W.R.S. xxvi), pp. 77–8; Hist. MSS. Com. 55, Var. Coll. i, p. 366.
[60] P.R.O., CP 25(1)/250/7, no. 87; Cal. Inq. Misc. i, pp. 11, 20; Close R. 1247–51, 205.
[61] D. & C. Sar. Mun., press IV, box C 3/Ramsbury/9; press IV, box C 3/Ramsbury/18; W.R.O., bishop, Liber Niger, f. 81 and v.; Close R. 1261–4, 203.
[62] D. & C. Sar. Mun., press I, box 31, no. 11.
[63] Wilton Ho. Mun., survey, 1550s, p. 302.
[64] D. & C. Sar. Mun., press I, box 31, no. 11.
[65] Wilts. Inq. p.m. 1327–77 (Index Libr.), 316.
[66] D. & C. Sar. Mun., press I, box 8, nos. 12B, 12E; cf. above, Axford, econ. hist.

common pasture for the tenants' sheep; their cattle and horses were, except in spring, pastured together on the Furnett, 100 a. east of the village; and there were six pastures, 35 a., for various uses in common. Almost alone among Wiltshire villages Baydon is dry and lacks riverside meadow land: *c.* 50 a. in small common fields near the village may have been mown. There were 120 a. or more of woodland, most of it in five coppices at Shortgrove apparently separating Baydon and Ford lands. The two freehold farms, Pig's Court and that formerly Stroud's, were each 4 yard-lands and included rights to use the common pastures. Baydon manor demesne farm measured 214 a. and the assignee of the lease also held 40 a. of pasture on Pax down, presumably merged with the farm. The farmer held 140 a. of arable in the open fields and 60 a. severally: he could pasture 400 sheep and 30 avers in common.[67] Although not mentioned before 1800, *c.* 200 a. of pasture on Bailey Hill were clearly an additional and several part of the farm.[68] The farmhouse no longer served its purpose and the farm, which had been occupied in the earlier 16th century by Harry Precy of Bishopstone and included land in the north part of the chapelry adjoining Bishopstone, may have lacked the usual farm buildings.[69] At Gore Lane inclosures totalling 26 a. had possibly been demesne.[70] The copyholders of Ramsbury manor held 24½ yardlands at Baydon, each nominally 26 a. with feeding for 60 sheep and each including 1 a. or more of presumably inclosed coppice.[71] The assignee of the demesne farm held 1 yardland and Thomas Stephens, who owned the freehold formerly Stroud's and held the land at Gore Lane, held 1½ yardland and may thus have had a composite farm of nearly 200 a. and feeding rights. The holdings of the remaining fourteen tenants were from 26 a. to 83 a. and averaged 50 a.: most tenants held no other land in Ramsbury parish.[72] Four tenants with holdings based at Preston and Marridge Hill held 124 a. in Ford field in 1567. A Baydon tenant, who also held land in Preston, then held 3¼ yardlands apparently based at Ford and the forerunner of Ford farm.[73]

Possibly in the late 17th century some of the woodland at Shortgrove was broken up,[74] but the system of common husbandry was little altered. In the period 1677–81 the lord of Ramsbury manor sold 17¾ of the 27¼ copyhold yardlands, 130 a. of 200 a. held by leases, and the demesne farm in Baydon: if most of those holding the lands which were sold also occupied them, the average size of farms had not increased and had possibly decreased in the preceding century.[75]

The demesne was called Bailey Hill farm in 1650 by which time a farmstead had been built on the site of the present one.[76] Pig's Court and the farm formerly Stroud's were mentioned in 1633 and 1676 but thereafter may have been merged as Baydon, later Finches, farm.[77] At the southern end of the chapelry there were upper and lower fields at Ford in 1713[78] but almost certainly no more than a single farmstead. At the northern end Gore Lane was apparently a small pasture farm in the later 17th century.[79]

Baydon Furnett east of the village and north and south of Ermin Street was inclosed by agreement in 1721, apparently with the other common grasslands near the village: 192 a. were allotted at a little over 1 a. for the right to feed one beast.[80] In the mid 18th century the regulations governing the use of the open fields were flexible. The growing of crops out of rotation, 'hitching', was frequent, but accompanied by a compulsory abatement of feeding rights for sheep, three for every acre sown with spring corn out of course in 1755.[81] The open fields and remaining common pasture were inclosed by Act in 1778. The four principal fields were still West, 350 a., Costern, 125 a., South, 213 a., and the field 'behind the wood', 108 a. apparently south of South field. Near the village were some 60 a. in smaller fields. The common pasture on Peaks Downs was then *c.* 200 a. In the south-west corner of the chapelry Ford field measured 268 a. At the time of inclosure *c.* 500 a. were held by copy and lease as part of Ramsbury manor, *c.* 1,400 a. were freehold: several farms were composite.[82] After the land was allotted Bailey Hill was a farm of 427 a. in the north-east corner of the chapelry, in 1800 half arable and half pasture.[83] Manor farm, more than half copyhold and leasehold, was mainly in the north-west corner and was worked from farm buildings in the south part of the village: its tenant owned land in the southern half of the chapelry worked from Paine's Farm south of the village, 365 a. in all.[84] Baydon, later Finches, farm included 120 a. or more and buildings east of the village and on the Furnett and was already a largely inclosed farm before 1778.[85] The second Baydon farm, 204 a. including 166 a. of arable in 1795, was worked from buildings north of the church.[86] Gore Lane, which in the early 18th century may have been part of the Russley Park estate in Bishopstone, was in the late 18th century an apparently separate farm of 37 a.[87] Ford, a largely arable farm of 237 a. in 1795, included 198 a. of Ford field.[88] There were four other farms of over 75 a., Stroud's, Finch's, Walrond's, with buildings at the east end of

[67] *First Pembroke Survey*, ed. Straton, i. 167–74, 177–8.
[68] W.R.O. 212A/27/22/2, release, Crosse to Craven.
[69] Wilton Ho. Mun., survey, 1550s, p. 302; *First Pembroke Survey*, ed. Straton, i. 173.
[70] *First Pembroke Survey*, ed. Straton, i. 173–4.
[71] Ibid. 168–72; Wilton Ho. Mun., survey, 1550s, pp. 282–8.
[72] *First Pembroke Survey*, ed. Straton, i. 168–74.
[73] Ibid. 160–2, 170–1.
[74] W.R.O. 1883/106/18; 1883/106/20.
[75] Ibid. 1883/59, bargain and sale, Pembroke to Whitley and Cratford; bargain and sale, Powle to Jones.
[76] Ibid. 212A/27/22/1, deed poll of Hawles.
[77] Ibid. 130/46/8; 130/46/14.

[78] Ibid. 212A/27/22/1, lease, Smith to Collins.
[79] Ibid. 492/41, deed, Clidesdale to Willoughby.
[80] Ibid. 1883/215.
[81] Ibid. 1883/1–2.
[82] Ibid. 154/2.
[83] Ibid. 212A/27/22/2, release, Crosse to Craven.
[84] Ibid. 154/2; 1883/223; O.S. Map 6″, Wilts. XXIV (1887 edn.).
[85] *Andrews and Dury, Map* (W.R.S. viii), pl. 15; W.R.O. 154/2.
[86] W.R.O. 154/2; 212A/38/117/14; W.A.S. Libr., sale cat. iii, no. 13.
[87] W.R.O. 154/2; 492/41, deed, Clidesdale to Willoughby; above, Bishopstone, manors.
[88] W.R.O. 212A/38/117/14; 154/2.

Manor Lane, and Brown's, worked from the farmstead later called Baydon House Farm, and several smaller farms.[89]

In the 19th century there apparently remained about ten farms in the parish. Arable farming clearly predominated. Two early pioneers of steam ploughing, J. A. Williams and A. Brown, farmed there, and Williams made many changes on his land to use machinery efficiently.[90] In the 20th century the number of farms seems to have decreased, especially in the south part of the parish where by 1947 nearly all the land had been absorbed by a single estate: Baydon House was a farm of 440 a., including 157 a. of pasture, worked from Baydon House Farm and Paine's Farm, Walrond's was a farm of 125 a. including 50 a. of pasture, and Ford an arable and dairy farm of 291 a.; 132 a. were part of Marridge Hill farm based in Ramsbury and 63 a. in East Leaze farm based in Aldbourne.[91] In 1981 Baydon House farm, 402 a., was devoted to cereal and beef production.[92] Walrond's farm measured 215 a. in 1973 and since then has been worked from outside the parish.[93] The land of Ford farm was worked as part of the arable and dairy farm based at Crowood Farm and Upper Whittonditch.[94] In the north part of the parish Bailey Hill, a corn and sheep farm of 400 a.,[95] Gore Lane, a dairy farm of c. 125 a.,[96] and Finches, an arable and beef farm of 265 a.,[97] were the only large farms based in the parish in 1981. Other arable and pasture land, especially at Peaks Downs, was worked from outside the parish.[98]

LOCAL GOVERNMENT. Leet jurisdiction over Baydon was exercised at Ramsbury law hundred, where the Baydon tithingman or constable was appointed, and Ramsbury manor court dealt with copyholds and the rules for agriculture in Baydon.[99] Before it first appears to be one in 1702–3 Baydon may have long been a poor-law parish.[1] It spent £119 on its poor in 1775–6, over £300 in 1802–3, and over £400 in 1818 and 1819.[2] Average expenditure in the early 1830s was £268 a year. In 1835 Baydon joined Hungerford poor-law union.[3]

CHURCH. A church had been built at Baydon by the early 12th century.[4] In the early 13th century it was presumably served by the chaplain of Baydon murdered before 1249.[5] It had a grave-yard in the late 13th century and in 1405 all rights, but remained dependent on Ramsbury as a chapel. All the tithes of the chapelry were owed to the prebendary of Ramsbury, who appointed and remunerated chaplains.[6] The chaplain's yearly stipend was £6 in the 16th century.[7] The right to appoint and the duty to pay the chaplain apparently passed with the tithes to Edward Seymour, earl of Hertford, in 1545 and to the Crown in 1547. The stipend remained a charge on the prebendal estate which passed with Ramsbury manor from 1590.[8] The lowness of the stipend may have inhibited separate appointment and the Crown charged vicars of Ramsbury with serving the chapel.[9] In the mid 17th century the vicar sometimes did so, but there was a chaplain in 1661.[10] Although the Crown continued its charge to the vicars, in the 18th century chaplains were appointed and given the stipend by the lords of Ramsbury manor.[11] In 1757, however, the vicar was serving the chapel and receiving the stipend.[12] In 1781 members of the Jones family, lords of Ramsbury manor, formally claimed the right to appoint.[13] In 1793 Lady Jones and Queen Anne's Bounty endowed the chapel with money which was used in 1796 to buy 34 a. at South Marston. The conveyance of the patronage from the Crown to Lady Jones was completed in 1798.[14]

The advowson of the perpetual curacy created by the endowment of Baydon church passed with Ramsbury manor to Sir Francis Burdett who in 1827 sold it with Manor farm in Baydon to John Williams.[15] In 1828 Williams conveyed it to the Revd. Arthur Meyrick (d. 1855) of Ramsbury, and it passed to Meyrick's son Edwin, vicar of Chiseldon.[16] In 1875 Meyrick conveyed the advowson, presumably by sale, to Angela, Baroness Burdett-Coutts, who settled it on her marriage in 1881 and on her husband in 1903. Her widower William Burdett-Coutts-Bartlett-Coutts transferred it to the bishop of Salisbury in 1908.[17]

The perpetual curacy was worth £147 a year c. 1830.[18] A glebe house east of the church was built in 1857–8 to designs by T. H. Wyatt.[19] The living was augmented by Baroness Burdett-Coutts and Queen Anne's Bounty in 1876.[20] In 1919 the land in South Marston, in 1925 1 a. beside Baydon Road, and in 1954 the vicarage house were all sold.[21]

The benefices of Aldbourne and Baydon were held in plurality from 1957 and united in 1965.[22]

[89] Ibid. 154/2; O.S. Map 6″, Wilts. XXIV (1887 edn.).
[90] V.C.H. Wilts. iv. 85, 87.
[91] W.R.O. 1008/25.
[92] Inf. from Mr. F. Newman, Wentworth Cottages, Baydon Ho. Farm.
[93] Inf. from Mr. R. T. Walton, New Ho., Manor Lane.
[94] Local inf.
[95] Inf. from Mr. E. P. Geary, Bailey Hill Farm.
[96] Local inf.
[97] Inf. from Mr. R. B. Day, Finches Farm.
[98] Local inf.
[99] Above, Ramsbury, local govt.
[1] W.R.O. 656/1.
[2] Poor Law Abstract, 1804, 568–9; Poor Rate Returns, 1816–21, 189.
[3] Poor Law Com. 1st Rep. 242.
[4] Below.
[5] Crown Pleas, 1249 (W.R.S. xvi), p. 173.

[6] P.R.O., JUST 1/1004, rot. 99d.; W.R.O., dean, Chaundler's reg. f. 55.
[7] Cal. Pat. 1569–72, pp. 124–5.
[8] Ibid.; above, Ramsbury, manors.
[9] Ch. Com. file F 320.
[10] V.C.H. Wilts. iii. 37; Hist. MSS. Com. 55, Var. Coll. i, p. 125.
[11] Ch. Com. file F 320.   [12] W.R.O. 500/26.
[13] Ibid. 500/5.   [14] Ch. Com. file F 320; K 6895.
[15] Ibid. 11257; above, manor.
[16] Ch. Com. file 11257; Alum. Oxon. 1715–1886, iii. 949.
[17] Ch. Com. file 11257.
[18] Rep. Com. Eccl. Revenues, 824–5.
[19] W.R.O., bishop, mortgages, 130.
[20] Ch. Com. file F 320.
[21] Ibid. 19832; inf. from Mr. P. Mather, Barley Mead.
[22] Lond. Gaz. 18 Dec. 1956, p. 7175; 22 Mar. 1965, p. 3048; Crockford (1961–2).

That united benefice was united with the vicarage of Ramsbury in 1973 and Baydon has since been served by the Whitton team ministry.[23]

In 1405 the inhabitants of Baydon failed to provide a mass book for the church and the incumbent was accused of adultery:[24] in 1571 the churchwardens failed to provide a surplice and the chaplain admitted fornication.[25] Before the Reformation 9 a. were given for Sunday prayers in the church. They were taken and granted by the Crown as concealed chantry land.[26] The vicar held services in the church once a month in the later 18th century: c. 1830, however, the perpetual curate employed an assistant curate.[27] On Census Sunday in 1851 congregations of 40 and 50 attended the morning and afternoon services.[28] In 1864 the incumbent held morning and afternoon services with congregations of 50–60, read prayers in the church on Wednesdays and Fridays, and administered the Sacrament at Christmas, Easter, and Whitsun or Trinity to 15–20 communicants and once a month to 8–10 communicants.[29]

The dedication of the church to *ST. NICHOLAS* is recorded only from the 19th century.[30] The church is built of flint rubble, chalk, and limestone and consists of a chancel with north vestry, an aisled and clerestoried nave with south porch, and a west tower. The nave and the two-bay south arcade are both of the early 12th century: the narrowness of the nave suggests that they were built about the same time. The nave was presumably lengthened in the 13th century when the three-bay north arcade was built.[31] The tower arch is 14th-century but the tower was largely rebuilt in the 15th century when there was much reconstruction of the nave, the aisles were widened and refenestrated, and the clerestory was made. In the early 17th century the chancel was restored: the arch was rebuilt, the windows renewed,[32] and the interior refitted. The vestry was built in 1853.[33] The east window was again replaced in 1854. In 1858–9, to designs of G. E. Street, the porch, which may have been 18th-century, and part of the north aisle were rebuilt.[34] The church was also restored in 1876 and, to designs of J. A. Reeve, in 1892.[35] In 1628 Thomas Hayne of Aldbourne conveyed the reversion of a chantry house and of a cottage and 3 a. in Aldbourne for repairs and maintenance of Baydon church. The cottage was burned down

in 1817 and two cottages at Baydon were bought in 1818 to replace it. In 1834 the charity's income was £4, £12 c. 1868. The premises were sold in 1877 and the proceeds invested. Income in 1904 was £9 7s.[36] In 1981 the income was still used for church repairs.[37]

In 1553 the king took 6 oz. of silver and left a chalice of 6 oz. A new chalice and paten were given c. 1848.[38] There were three bells in 1553. They have been replaced by bells (i) 1744, John Stares of Aldbourne; (ii) 1670, Henry Knight of Reading; (iii) 1650, William and Roger Purdue of Bristol.[39] The bells were rehung in 1891.[40] The registers date from 1673 and, except for 1692–4, are complete.[41]

NONCONFORMITY. The Independent congregation based on Ramsbury after the Restoration possibly included members at Baydon where Daniel Burgess, an evangelist from Marlborough, preached in a conventicle in 1681,[42] but there is no further evidence of dissent at Baydon before the 19th century. The Providence chapel for Particular Baptists was built in the village on the east side of Aldbourne Road in 1806. Congregations averaged no more than seventeen at the three services on Census Sunday in 1851. The chapel was closed between 1885 and 1922,[43] and the building has been demolished. A Wesleyan Methodist chapel was built on the south side of Ermin Street at the east end of the village in 1823.[44] Congregations of 7, 30, and 36 at the three Sunday services were said to be average in 1851.[45] In 1939 the chapel, now a private house, was superseded by one on the west side of Aldbourne Road at which weekly services were held in 1981.[46]

EDUCATION. Two day schools for a total of 28 children were started at Baydon between 1818 and 1833.[47] They were replaced by a National school and schoolhouse built of chequered stone and flint in plain Tudor style near the church in 1843.[48] In 1858 some 50–60 children were taught there: boys left when they were nine, girls at eleven or twelve.[49] Average attendance had fallen to 33 by c. 1906–7 and was c. 40 until the Second World War.[50] From 1940 the older children were sent to Lambourn.[51] The school was en-

[23] *Lond. Gaz.* 30 Oct. 1973, p. 12883; above, Ramsbury, church.
[24] W.R.O., dean, Chaundler's reg. ff. 56–7.
[25] Ibid. dean, act bk. 3, f. 45.
[26] P.R.O., E 310/26/153, f. 41.
[27] Ch. Com. file F 320; *Rep. Com. Eccl. Revenues*, 824–5.
[28] P.R.O., HO 129/121/3/2/6.
[29] W.R.O., bishop, vis. queries.
[30] *W.A.M.* xv. 100.
[31] See plate facing p. 80.
[32] J. Buckler, watercolour in W.A.S. Libr., vol. iv. 14.
[33] Date on bldg.
[34] M. Child, *St. Nicholas, Baydon* (priv. print. 1975); Buckler, watercolour in W.A.S. Libr., vol. iv. 14; W.R.O., bishop, pet. for faculties, bdle. 8, no. 15.
[35] Child, op. cit.; W.R.O., bishop, pet. for faculties, bdle. 32, no. 13.
[36] *Endowed Char. Wilts.* (N. Div.), 28–30.
[37] Inf. from Mr. Mather.
[38] Nightingale, *Wilts. Plate*, 154–5.

[39] Walters, *Wilts. Bells*, 18, 20.
[40] Wilts. Cuttings, i. 184.
[41] Inf. from Mr. K. H. Rogers, Co. Archivist, Co. Hall, Trowbridge. There are transcripts for various periods after 1578: W.R.O., dean.
[42] Above, Ramsbury, nonconf.; *Cal. S.P. Dom.* 1680–1, 563.
[43] P.R.O., HO 129/121/3/2/8; O.S. Maps 6″, Wilts. XXIV (1887 edn.), XXIV. NW. (1925 edn.).
[44] W.R.O., bishop, return of cert. places; O.S. Map 6″, Wilts. XXIV (1887 edn.).
[45] P.R.O., HO 129/121/3/2/7.
[46] *Statistical Returns* (Dept. for Chapel Affairs), ii. 72; date on bldg.
[47] *Educ. of Poor Digest*, 1018; *Educ. Enquiry Abstract*, 1028.
[48] *Endowed Char. Wilts.* (N. Div.), 30.
[49] *Acct. of Wilts. Schs.* 5; W.R.O., bishop, vis. queries, 1864.
[50] *Bd. of Educ., List 21* (H.M.S.O.).
[51] P.R.O., ED 21/63163.

larged in 1968.[52] There were 57 children on roll in 1981.[53]

CHARITIES FOR THE POOR. By will proved 1854 John Williams gave £300 for blankets and clothing for the poor of Baydon at Christmas. In the period 1900-3, when the yearly income of the charity was £8, clothing was given to more than 30 families: in 1951 clothing worth £7 4s. 5d. was given to ten recipients.[54] The income in 1981 was £15.[55] By Scheme of 1959 Aldbourne and Baydon Aid in Sickness Fund for the general benefit of the sick poor was set up with the proceeds of the sale of a district nurse's house. In 1965 income was £79 10s. and £163 was spent.[56]

[52] Wilts. Cuttings, xxiii. 160.
[53] Inf. from Chief Education Officer, Co. Hall, Trowbridge.
[54] *Endowed Char. Wilts.* (N. Div.), 31-2; Char. Com. file.
[55] Inf. from Mr. P. Mather, Barley Mead.
[56] Char. Com. file; below, Aldbourne, charities.

SELKLEY HUNDRED

ELKLEY hundred as constituted in 1841 comprised nine complete ancient parishes and five tithings in other parishes. The complete parishes were Aldbourne, Avebury including the tithings of Beckhampton and West Kennett, East Kennett, Mildenhall including the tithings of Poulton and Stitchcombe, Ogbourne St. Andrew including the tithings of Ogbourne Maizey and Rockley, Ogbourne St. George, Preshute including the tithings of Elcot, Clatford, Manton, Langdon Wick, and Temple Rockley, Winterbourne Bassett including the tithing of Richardson, and Winterbourne Monkton. The tithings in other parishes were Broad Hinton in Broad Hinton parish, West Overton, Lockeridge, and Shaw in Overton parish, and Catcomb in Hilmarton parish.[1] This volume contains the history of Broad Hinton parish because the parish church was in Broad Hinton tithing. Apart from that tithing the parish contained Uffcott and Bincknoll tithings in Blackgrove, later Kingsbridge, hundred, and part of Broad Town tithing in Kingsbridge hundred. The histories of the whole tithing of Broad Town and of the civil parish of Broad Town created in 1884 from that and part of Bincknoll tithing have been given with that of Clyffe Pypard.[2] Accounts of West Overton, Lockeridge, and Shaw have been given under Overton.[3] Catcomb was in Selkley hundred because it was part of Avebury manor from the 12th century until the 17th,[4] though it has not been found recorded as part of Selkley hundred before 1736;[5] its history is dealt with under Hilmarton.[6]

Estates at Avebury, Beckhampton, West Kennett, Broad Hinton, Uffcott, East Kennett, Mildenhall, Poulton, Ogbourne including lands later in Ogbourne St. Andrew and Ogbourne St. George, Rockley, East Overton, West Overton, Fyfield, Lockeridge, Shaw, Preshute, Clatford, Manton, Winterbourne Bassett, Rabson, Stanmore, and Winterbourne Monkton were in the hundred in 1084.[7] The tithings of East Overton and Fyfield in Overton were detached from the hundred in the early 13th century.[8] Aldbourne may have been in Thornhill hundred in 1084 and Stitchcombe was then in Kinwardstone hundred: both were in Selkley hundred in 1242–3.[9] Although then geographically at its centre, the king's estate in Preshute parish was not part of the hundred in the 13th century and earlier. It consisted of the tithings of Elcot and Langdon Wick, the king's tithing of Manton, and possibly the tithing of Temple Rockley, and was called the honor of Marlborough and hundred of the barton.[10] As Elcot tithing all those tithings were in Selkley hundred in the later 18th century.[11]

The hundred was on the Marlborough Downs and surrounded Marlborough. The later addition Aldbourne protruded on the north-east and Berwick Bassett parish in Calne hundred intruded on the west. The river Kennet and its tributary the Og divided the downs into three chalk masses overlain on the heights by clay-with-flints. Hackpen Hill, the wide and steep north-west scarp face of the downs,

[1] *Census*, 1841.
[2] Below, Broad Hinton, introduction; *V.C.H. Wilts.* ix. 23–43.
[3] *V.C.H. Wilts.* xi. 181–203.
[4] Ibid. ix. 57; below, Avebury, local govt.
[5] *Q. Sess. 1736* (W.R.S. xi), p. 145.
[6] *V.C.H. Wilts.* ix. 49–65.
[7] Ibid. ii, pp. 200–1.
[8] Ibid. xi. 105.
[9] Ibid. ii, p. 200; *Bk. of Fees*, ii. 748.
[10] Below, Preshute, local govt.
[11] W.R.O. 9, Selkley hund. ct. bk. 1734–1861.

overlooks an extensive semicircular terrace of Lower Chalk. The Kennet flows south through Broad Hinton, Winterbourne Bassett, Winterbourne Monkton, and Avebury where, south of the London–Bath road, it turns east. The Og, which took its name from the settlements of Ogbourne St. Andrew, Ogbourne St. George, and Ogbourne Maizey, flows southwards into it on the Marlborough–Mildenhall boundary. Nearly all settlement in the hundred has been in the valleys of the Kennet and its tributaries. Except south of the Kennet in Mildenhall there was little woodland in the area in 1982. Selkley hundred was an agricultural area where a sheep-and-corn economy typical of downland has always predominated. There was additionally some industry at Aldbourne where fustians were manufactured and bells founded. Warrens were maintained on tracts of rough downland in Preshute and Aldbourne. In the 19th and 20th centuries racehorses have been trained on the downs, chiefly at Beckhampton, Manton, Ogbourne Maizey, and Rockley, and in the 20th century at Hightown in Aldbourne.[12]

There has been settlement, probably continuous, on the land of the hundred from prehistoric times. Avebury may have been an important cult centre in the Neolithic Period and Bronze Age. Silbury Hill south of Avebury and the mound which formed the motte of Marlborough Castle were both raised beside the Kennet in prehistoric times. The Roman town of Cunetio stood south of the Kennet in Black Field south-east of Mildenhall village. Of the many prehistoric tracks which cross the hundred, the Ridge Way ran north-east across Hackpen Hill, and Harepath Way was part of the main road from Devizes through the Winterbournes to Swindon in 1982. Cunetio, upon which several Roman roads converged, was afterwards replaced by Marlborough as the focus of routes. That which ran west to Bath and east to London has, in spite of alterations to its course, always been a main road. Ermin Street became a part of the northern boundary of the hundred between 1084 and 1243.[13]

The hundred belonged to the king and was administered by the constable of Marlborough Castle.[14] With the borough of Marlborough, the hundred was assigned as dower in 1273 to Queen Eleanor, to whom in 1262 Marlborough Castle and the hundred of the barton had been granted, in 1299 to Queen Margaret, in 1318 to Queen Isabel, who was deprived of it in the years 1324–7, and in 1330 to Queen Philippa, on whose death in 1369 it reverted to the Crown.[15] In 1403 the reversion was granted to Humphrey, duke of Gloucester, and from 1415 or earlier until 1621 the lordship of Selkley, like that of the borough, descended with the site of Marlborough Castle, from 1621 to 1779 with Barton manor in Preshute, and from 1779 with both.[16]

In 1255 and 1275 the hundred was worth £10.[17] It was leased for terms of years at £14 yearly from 1450 or earlier and was still so leased in the earlier 16th century.[18] In 1525 the profits of waifs, felons' goods, deodands, and treasure trove were expressly excluded from the farm and reserved to the queen.[19] Cert money paid at the Michaelmas tourn amounted to £3.[20] Quitrents payable c. 1740 amounted to £10 10s. 2d.[21]

'Selk', supposedly a place near Woodlands Farm in Mildenhall, is unlikely to have

---

[12] Para. based on introductions and econ. hist. sections of par. hists. below.

[13] Para. based on introductions of par. hists. below.

[14] *Pipe R.* 1195 (P.R.S. n.s. vi), 150–1; *Cal. Lib.* 1226–40, 17, 206; *Rot. Hund.* (Rec. Com.), ii (1), 234.

[15] *Cal. Pat.* 1266–72, 737; 1272–81, 27; 1292–1301, 451–4; 1317–21, 115; 1327–30, 556; 1330–4, 55; 1367–70, 301, 452; *Cal. Close*, 1272–9, 31; M. McKisack, *Fourteenth Cent.* 81,

97, 102.

[16] Below, Preshute, manors.

[17] *Rot. Hund.* (Rec. Com.), ii (1), 234, 270.

[18] e.g. P.R.O., SC 6/1055/19; SC 6/1094/1–2; SC 6/Hen. VII/885; SC 6/Hen. VIII/3805; ibid. DL 29/724/11800–1.

[19] Ibid. E 326/6379.

[20] Ibid. DL 30/127/1908.

[21] W.R.O. 9, survey bk. of Selkley hund. etc. 1734– , pp. 239–43.

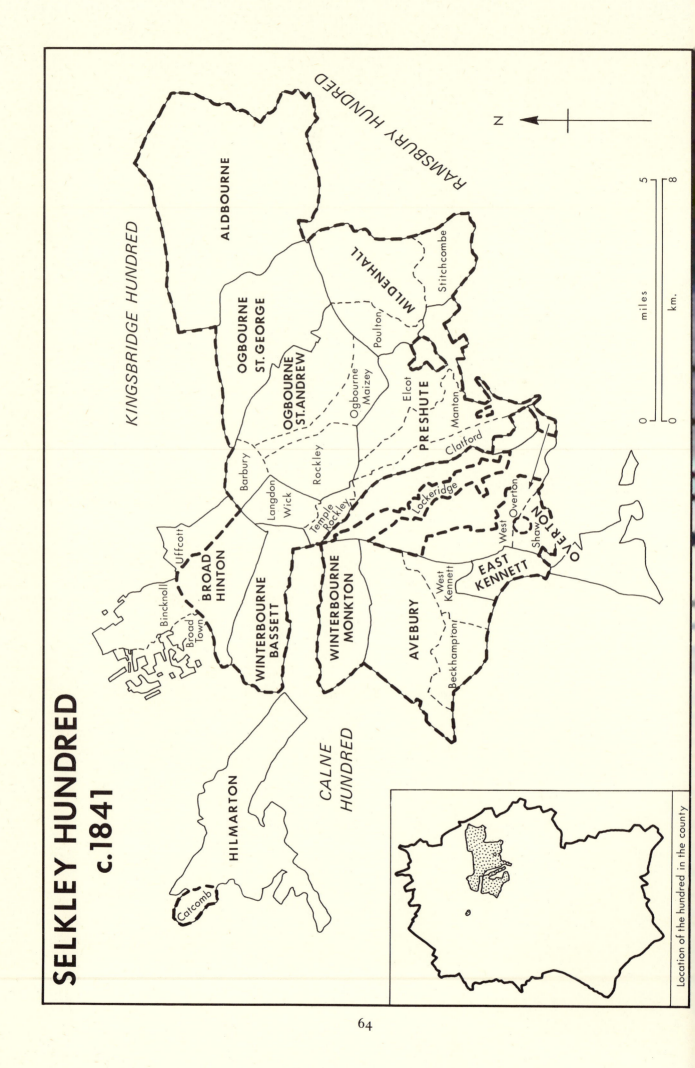

SELKLEY HUNDRED c.1841

KINGSBRIDGE HUNDRED

RAMSBURY HUNDRED

ALDBOURNE

MILDENHALL

Stitchcombe

OGBOURNE ST.GEORGE

OGBOURNE ST.ANDREW

Poulton

Ogbourne Maizey

Elcot

PRESHUTE

Manton

Barbury

Rockley

Clatford

Langdon Wick

Temple Rockley

Lockeridge

West Overton

OVERTON

Uffcott

BROAD HINTON

WINTERBOURNE BASSETT

WINTERBOURNE MONKTON

AVEBURY

West Kennett

Shaw

EAST KENNETT

Bincknoll

Broad Town

Beckhampton

HILMARTON

CALNE HUNDRED

Catcomb

miles

km.

Location of the hundred in the county

64

named the hundred.[22] The name of the hundred seems to have come from Selkley wood, mentioned in the 13th century, near East Overton and Fyfield,[23] and possibly north of West Woods. In the earlier 16th century pasture for sheep near Lockeridge was called Selkley.[24] The hundred possibly met at Marlborough Castle in the Middle Ages. From 1781 to 1784 courts met at the Bull inn at Marlborough and from 1785 to 1861 at the Castle and Ball.[25] There was a hundred constable from 1230 or earlier.[26] From the 16th century a constable was elected at the Michaelmas views. From 1736 or earlier two constables were elected yearly.[27] A hundred bailiff was mentioned from 1255.[28]

The suit owed by the tenants of Aldbourne manor was withdrawn from the hundred courts possibly between 1257 and 1268,[29] certainly before 1289 when views of frankpledge and other liberties in Aldbourne were claimed.[30] The abbess of Lacock withdrew the suit of her tenants at Upper Upham c. 1258.[31] Although the men of Avebury were accustomed to attend hundred courts in 1255,[32] they claimed in 1275 that their suit had been withdrawn between 1216 and 1272. A tumbrel and gallows may have been used in Avebury from c. 1235.[33] In 1281 the abbot of Cirencester showed charters issued by Henry I and Henry III to support his claim to view of frankpledge, assize of bread, and infangthief in Avebury manor.[34] The abbot's right to hold views was confirmed in 1360.[35] Although Mildenhall was considered exempt from hundred jurisdiction in 1249,[36] its suit at the hundred courts does not seem to have been finally withdrawn until c. 1260.[37] The king had a prison at Mildenhall in 1265[38] and in 1272-3 James de Audeberg raised a gallows there.[39] The abbot of Bec-Hellouin (Eure) was granted quittance from suit of shire and hundred and other liberties in Ogbourne St. Andrew and Ogbourne St. George c. 1178.[40] Under a grant of 1239-40 to William de Cauntelo of quittance from suit of shire and hundred for his men and the right to take view of frankpledge,[41] the suit of Rockley was withdrawn c. 1252.[42] In 1275 Selkley was entitled to return writs concerning its affairs addressed to the constable of Marlborough Castle and to hear pleas *de vetito namio*.[43] Between 1173 and 1182 Henry II granted to the monks of St. Victor quittance from suit of shire and hundred in their lands, which included Clatford.[44] After the alien priories were suppressed in 1414 Clatford again followed the hundred.[45] Manton tithing was a member of the honor of Wallingford (Berks., later Oxon.) and withdrew from Selkley c. 1259.[46] The men of the abbot of Glastonbury at Winterbourne Monkton apparently withdrew in the early 13th century. A tumbrel and gallows were claimed there in 1275.[47] In 1280 the abbot was granted return of writs, and other liberties in the early 14th century.[48]

Although Philip Basset was said to have withdrawn his men of Winterbourne Bassett c. 1260, the tithing attended hundred courts and views from 1481. Similarly,

[22] *W.A.M.* x. 306; below, Mildenhall, introduction.
[23] *Rot. Litt. Claus.* (Rec. Com.), ii. 52, 94; *Cal. Chart. R.* 1300-26, 1; P.R.O., JUST 1/1005, rot. 117d.; *P.N. Wilts.* (E.P.N.S.), pp. xl, 291.
[24] P.R.O., C 1/1082/31.
[25] W.R.O. 9, Selkley hund. ct. bk. 1734-1861.
[26] *Pipe R.* 1230 (P.R.S. n.s. iv), 3.
[27] W.R.O. 192/12c; 9, Selkley hund. ct. bk. 1734-1861; *Q. Sess. 1736* (W.R.S. xi), p. 89.
[28] *Rot. Hund.* (Rec. Com.), ii (1), 240; P.R.O., DL 30/127/1908; Hist. MSS. Com. 58, *Bath*, iv, p. 207.
[29] *Rot. Hund.* (Rec. Com.), ii (1), 270; for the date *Complete Peerage*, vii. 681-2; xi. 384.
[30] P.R.O., JUST 1/1011, rot. 47d.
[31] Ibid. JUST 1/998A, rot. 27d.
[32] *Rot. Hund.* (Rec. Com.), ii (1), 234.   [33] Ibid. 270.

[34] P.R.O., JUST 1/1005, rot. 119d.
[35] *Cirencester Cart.* ed. C. D. Ross and M. Devine, ii, pp. 353-7.
[36] *Crown Pleas, 1249* (W.R.S. xvi), pp. 62, 224.
[37] *Rot. Hund.* (Rec. Com.), ii (1), 270.
[38] *Close R.* 1264-8, 69.
[39] *Rot. Hund.* (Rec. Com.), ii (1), 270.
[40] A. A. Porée, *Histoire de l'Abbaye du Bec*, i. 471-3.
[41] P.R.O., JUST 1/1005, rot. 119d.
[42] *Rot. Hund.* (Rec. Com.), ii (1), 234.   [43] Ibid. 270.
[44] *Cal. Chart. R.* 1327-41, 67-8.
[45] Below, Preshute, manors; P.R.O., DL 30/127/1908; W.R.O. 192/12A-K; 9, Selkley hund. ct. bk. 1734-1861.
[46] *Rot. Hund.* (Rec. Com.), ii (1), 263.
[47] Ibid. 234, 270.
[48] *Cal. Chart. R.* 1327-41, 260; B.L. Eg. MS. 3321, f. 251.

although the suit owed for land at Richardson was withdrawn *c.* 1245, Richardson tithing followed the hundred from 1481.[49] Besides those from Winterbourne Bassett and Richardson, tithingmen from Hinton Columbers and Hinton Wase, which from the early 18th century were merged as Hinton or Broad Hinton, Beckhampton, 'Kennett', which from the 18th century and earlier included both East Kennett and West Kennett, West Overton, Shaw, Clatford, Ogbourne Maizey, Rockley, Poulton, and Stitchcombe attended the hundred courts and views from 1481. For unknown reasons tithingmen from Aldbourne attended in 1544, Avebury in 1544 and from 1822, and Elcot from 1775. That part of the liberty of Savernake which afterwards became the civil parish of North Savernake Park was represented between 1784 and 1812. Lockeridge for unknown reasons did not attend in the 17th and 18th centuries and Catcomb was never represented, possibly because Avebury's quittance extended to it.[50]

Records of views and courts for the hundred survive, with gaps, from the 15th century until 1861. The courts were held, usually every three weeks, on Tuesdays in the 15th and 16th centuries. At the hundred court lists of free suitors were made and the tithingmen presented matters, more properly the concern of the view, such as infringements of the assize of ale and pleas of assault and trespass. The courts may also have heard pleas of debt. In 1577 the tithings were divided into a south-west group made up of Beckhampton, East and West Kennett, West Overton, Clatford, and Shaw, and a north-east group comprising Broad Hinton, Ogbourne Maizey, Rockley, Poulton, and Stitchcombe. Separate courts were held for each group in that year but in 1579 all the tithings again attended the same court.[51] The views, which were recorded separately, were held twice a year, at Hocktide and Michaelmas, and, in the 16th century, on the same day as the hundred court.[52] From *c.* 1600 the hundred courts and views were merged and, called views of frankpledge of the hundred, were biannual.[53] They were called views of frankpledge with courts baron in the later 17th century and from 1734 courts leet and views of frankpledge. They were held twice a year until 1820, afterwards less often, and from 1844 irregularly. At the views tithingmen were elected at Michaelmas, cert money, afterwards called quitrents, was paid, and matters such as default of suitors, millers who took excessive tolls, and pounds, stocks, bridges, watercourses, hedges, and highways in need of repair were presented by the tithingmen.[54]

[49] *Rot. Hund.* (Rec. Com.), ii (1), 234, 270; P.R.O., DL 30/127/1908; W.R.O. 192/12A–K; 9, Selkley hund. ct. bk. 1734–1861.

[50] P.R.O., DL 30/127/1908; W.R.O. 192/12A–K; 9, Selkley hund. ct. bk. 1734–1861.

[51] P.R.O., DL 30/127/1908; W.R.O. 192/12A–B; 192/12E.

[52] P.R.O., DL 30/127/1908; W.R.O. 192/12A; 192/12C–D; 192/12F.

[53] W.R.O. 192/12G–J.

[54] Ibid. 192/12K; 9, Selkley hund. ct. bk. 1734–1861.

ALDBOURNE

ALDBOURNE, a downland parish north-east of Marlborough and south-east of Swindon, includes Aldbourne village, the hamlets of Upper Upham and Woodsend and part of that of Preston, and the deserted hamlet of Snap.[1] It measures 3,441 ha. (8,502 a.)[2] and forms a rough square with an extension at its north-west corner. The parish's northern boundary, later also the hundred boundary, had for its western two thirds apparently been established by the mid 11th century along Rogues or Sugar Way, which is said to have run approximately east and west *c.* 4 km. north-west of Aldbourne village.[3] The parish was largely conterminous with a single estate, Aldbourne manor, on which there was a church in the late 11th century.[4] In the 16th century the manor's boundary closely resembled that of the modern parish, excluding the north-western extension.[5] That extension was included in the parish at an unknown but probably early date. Aldbourne's western boundary is marked by the Roman road from Cirencester to Cunetio, now in Mildenhall; another Roman road, Ermin Street, crosses Sugar Way and forms the east end of the northern boundary of the parish. Some 250 m. west of Baydon village the boundary turns south across downland and follows a dry valley to the Swindon–Hungerford road. Until 1934 it crossed the road and ran south along a small stream to Preston, where it turned south-westwards. The boundary was then moved east to the road north and south of Ford Farm and 6 a. were thus transferred from Baydon to Aldbourne.[6] The southern boundary is marked by few natural or man-made features until it reaches Whiteshard Bottom, where it turns north-west along a dry valley for 2 km. It continues north and north-west for another 2 km. and then turns due west to the Roman road from Cirencester.

Much of the parish lies above 152 m. and the chalk which outcrops over it is covered on the higher downland by clay-with-flints, which extends in a broad band across the southern part of the parish and in an east-facing arc between Woodsend and Upper Upham.[7] The highest land in the parish, above 259 m., is west of Woodsend. Westwards from there it descends steeply, flattening out towards the western boundary. Valleys, some of them steep-sided, converge on the south-east corner of the parish. The boundary stream, flowing south-east to the Kennet, rises *c.* 200 m. east of Aldbourne church.

The other valleys are dry but gravel has been deposited in all of them. Prehistoric cultivation took place near Upper Upham and Snap, near North Farm in the north-east corner of the parish, and near the farmstead called Stock Lane.[8] Some of the clay in the central and southern parts of the parish continued to be ploughed in historic times and there was also arable land in the valleys around Aldbourne village and probably on the level chalk west of Lower Upham Farm. Land near the southern and south-western boundaries, much of it wooded, formed Aldbourne Chase. The chalk downs were mostly pasture and those in the middle of the parish, probably between Dudmore Lodge and Sugar Hill, were used as a warren in the Middle Ages and until the 18th century.[9]

Part of a ditch extending from Liddington Hill in Liddington to Church Hill in Ogbourne St. George marks the western extent of archaeological discoveries within the parish, and there is little evidence of prehistoric activity south of Aldbourne village. Elsewhere, artefacts of the Neolithic Period and later have been found, and there are numerous barrows, especially on the downs north and west of the village, and earthworks south of Woodsend.[10] There was a substantial settlement at Upper Upham; Iron-Age and Romano-British finds have been made there and an associated field system covers 113 ha.[11] Smaller field systems lie east of Snap, north of Stock Lane Farm, and on Peaks Downs. Other Romano-British finds have been made at North Farm, North Field Barn, and the farmstead called Hillwood, north of Stock Lane. Lewisham Castle, east of Stock Lane Farm, is a circular medieval earthwork.[12]

Whereas the parish is apparently bounded on its west, north, and north-east sides by ancient roads, the only early routes to cross it are the track from Liddington to Mildenhall along the ridge east of Lower Upham Farm and another ridge way, which may have existed in the 11th century or earlier, along the crest of Sugar Hill.[13] The principal route through the parish is the Swindon–Hungerford road, turnpiked in 1814,[14] which runs in a dry valley north-west of Aldbourne village and beside the stream south-east of it. Another road runs parallel to that one, joining roads from Mildenhall to Ramsbury and from Aldbourne to Ogbourne St. George. In the late 18th century as in 1982 most other roads led

[1] This article was written in 1982. Maps used include O.S. Maps 1″, sheet 34 (1828 edn.); 1/50,000, sheet 173 (1974 edn.), sheet 174 (1974 edn.); 1/25,000, SU 17 (1960 edn.), SU 27 (1960 edn.); 6″, Wilts. XXIII (1887 and later edns.), XXIV (1887 and later edns.), XXIX (1889 and later edns.), XXX (1887 and later edns.); 1/10,000, SU 27 NW. (1980 edn.), SU 27 SE. (1980 edn.), SU 27 SW. (1978 edn.).
[2] *Census,* 1971.
[3] *W.A.M.* lvii. 207–8.
[4] Below, manors; *V.C.H. Wilts.* ii, p. 117.

[5] *W.A.M.* vi. 188–9.
[6] *Census,* 1931.
[7] Geol. inf. is from Geol. Surv. Maps 1″, drift, sheet 266 (1964 edn.), sheet 267 (1947 edn.).
[8] *V.C.H. Wilts.* i (1), 272.
[9] Below, econ. hist.
[10] *V.C.H. Wilts.* i (1), 21–3, 147–8, 206, 216, 249, 261.
[11] Ibid. 22–3, 272; i (2), 480, 484.
[12] Ibid. i (1), 22–3, 261, 272.
[13] *W.A.M.* lvii. 207–8.
[14] *L.J.* xlix. 883.

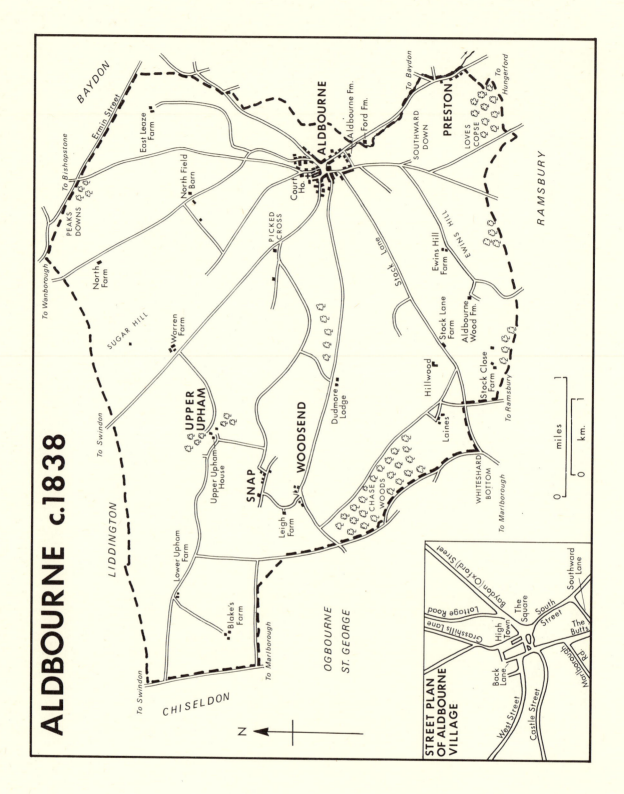

ALDBOURNE c.1838

STREET PLAN OF ALDBOURNE VILLAGE

from the village.[15] North from Aldbourne roads led over the downs to Baydon and along a dry valley via North Farm to Wanborough: that to Wanborough was called Port Street in the 15th century and the 16th.[16] Another road, perhaps in the 17th century and certainly in the 19th called Grasshills Lane, led north to Bishopstone[17] and had become a track by the 20th. A road to Ogbourne St. George ran west from Aldbourne and turned south-west at Woodsend. Another, called Stock Lane, led south-west to Marlborough in the 18th century and the early 19th[18] but, west of Stock Lane Farm, that road was later neglected in favour of the road via Axford and Mildenhall and by 1982 it had there become a track. South of Aldbourne village tracks fanned out to Ramsbury via Love's Copse, to Hilldrop in Ramsbury, and to Stock Close Farm. Others from Picked Cross to Upham and Snap had become footpaths by the 20th century.[19] In 1982 Upper Upham was reached by a drive from Warren Farm. A track from Upper Upham to Lower Upham was still in use in the mid 20th century, but was little used thereafter.[20] The farmstead called East Leaze was approached by a track from the Aldbourne–Wanborough road in the late 18th century as later.[21]

Medieval tax assessments show Aldbourne to have been the wealthiest parish in the hundred and in 1377, when there were 332 poll-tax payers, the most populous.[22] Tax assessments were still high in the 16th century when totals were inflated by assessments of wealthy individuals.[23] Between the mid 16th century and the mid 17th the population may have doubled; there were c. 400 adults in 1549[24] and c. 800 in 1637 and 1676.[25] In 1801 the population was 1,280. Numbers had increased to 1,622 by 1851 but fell thereafter to 1,117 in 1901 and 980 in 1921. The population had grown to 1,024 by 1931[26] and increased considerably after the Second World War. In 1971 there were 1,459 inhabitants.[27]

The main centre of population, Aldbourne village, lies near the eastern boundary at the junction of five dry valleys, where the tributary stream of the Kennet rises, flowing south-east in a sixth valley. Preston lies further downstream in that valley and the site of the deserted hamlet of Snap, 4 km. west of Aldbourne, is also near the bottom of a steep-sided valley. On the hills above Snap are the hamlets of Upper Upham, 700 m. north of it, and Woodsend, 400 m. south. Also on the downs are scattered farmsteads, some occupying sites in use since the Middle Ages but most dating from the 17th century or the 18th.[28]

In the Middle Ages much of the wealth of the parish was concentrated in Aldbourne village, where there was a market, then apparently thriving. Tax assessments for the village were high and in 1377 there were 253 poll-tax payers.[29] Aldbourne prospered as an industrial centre in the 18th century but in 1826 was said to be decaying.[30] A fire in 1760 which destroyed 72 houses and some other buildings, another in 1770 in which 80 houses and 20 barns were burned down, and a third in 1817 in which 15 cottages, 3 barns, and 2 malthouses were lost,[31] all contributed to its decline. There was rebuilding or new building after the fires, however, and it seems unlikely that the extent of the village changed much.[32] Its population was 1,233 in 1851.[33] There was a new expansion in the 20th century when the village became a dormitory for workers from Swindon and elsewhere.

Earliest settlement in the village may have been on gravel near the stream which surfaces beside Lottage Road, the road to Wanborough, and flows south-east beside the Swindon–Hungerford road, there called South Street. The church was built on chalk on higher ground north-west of the stream, and north of the church is Court House which was occupied in the 16th century by tenants of the demesne farm of Aldbourne manor, and in the 19th century was the vicarage house.[34] The central part of the house is of the late 16th century: it has thick walls with stone-mullioned windows, and ceiling beams in the principal rooms have been covered in heavily moulded cases. A small addition was made on the east side of the house in the 18th century and rooms were added along the west side during the 19th. The rectangular green south of the church may have been the market place in the Middle Ages as it probably was in the late 18th century. The market cross, restored after the fire of 1760 and again later, has stood on the Green since the early 19th century or earlier.[35] It is possible, however, that the Green may occupy the site of houses destroyed in one of the fires. Most of the buildings around it date from the late 18th century or the early 19th and were perhaps rebuilt after the fires. In the 18th century and the early 19th the Green was called High Town[36] but in the 20th century Hightown was the name of a house at its south-east corner, to which racing stables were attached.[37] The streets bordering the Green are the north-eastern section of a grid formed by streets running almost north and south and almost east and west; the grid extends south to the Swindon–Hungerford road. That road may have run continuously south-east through the village and have been diverted by new, planned building on the grid

[15] *Andrews and Dury, Map* (W.R.S. viii), pl. 15.
[16] *Cal. Inq. p.m. Hen. VII*, iii, p. 560; W.R.O. 1064/18.
[17] M. Crane, *Aldbourne Chron.* (Aldbourne, 1980), 34; W.R.O., tithe award.
[18] *Andrews and Dury, Map* (W.R.S. viii), pl. 15; W.R.O., tithe award.
[19] O.S. Map 6″, Wilts. XXIII (1887 and later edns.).
[20] Inf. from Mr. T. Dewis, Eyre's Barn, Upper Upham.
[21] *Andrews and Dury, Map* (W.R.S. viii), pl. 15; W.R.O., tithe award.
[22] *V.C.H. Wilts.* iv. 301, 310.
[23] *Taxation Lists* (W.R.S. x), 22–3, 101.
[24] *W.A.M.* xii. 379.
[25] *Cal. S.P. Dom. 1637*, 121–2; *W.N. & Q.* iii. 537.

[26] *V.C.H. Wilts.* iv. 339.
[27] *Census*, 1971.
[28] Below.
[29] *V.C.H. Wilts.* iv. 301, 310; below, econ. hist.
[30] Below, econ. hist.; W. Cobbett, *Rural Rides*, ed. G. D. H. and M. Cole, ii. 455.
[31] Wilts. Cuttings, i. 106; xxvi. 40, 117.
[32] *Andrews and Dury, Map* (W.R.S. viii), pl. 15; W.R.O., inclosure award; tithe award.
[33] P.R.O., HO 107/1686.
[34] Below, manors, church.
[35] *Wilts. Inq. p.m. 1242–1326* (Index Libr.), 382–3; *W.A.M.* li. 453–4; below, econ. hist. and plate facing p. 80.
[36] W.R.O. 212A/15; ibid. inclosure award.
[37] Below, econ. hist.

pattern. Its modern route, turning sharply south and east as part of the western edge of the grid and its southern boundary, had probably been established by the 17th century, the date of the oldest buildings within the grid, and may be much older. North of the road Back Lane marks the western edge of the grid and leads north to the school. At the south-western corner of the grid the major routes into the village meet. North-east of the junction the road from Baydon opens out as the Square, an irregularly shaped space at the modern centre of the village. Within it is the pond, which dates from the 18th century or earlier[38] and for which a concrete base was provided in the late 20th. Although a house on the north side of the Square is probably 17th-century, most of the buildings within the grid date from the late 18th century or the early 19th and were probably rebuilt like those around the Green.

Building spread along the roads radiating from the village centre. The earliest extension may have been along Lottage Road; the name Lottage was in use in the mid 13th century.[39] Beside the stream at the southern end of the road are cottages of the 17th century or earlier. Further north are 19th-century houses, including Alma Cottage, once isolated at the northern end of the village.[40] Beside Grasshills Lane west of Lottage Road is Beech Knoll, a large early 19th-century brick house. Oxford Street, which leads north-east from the Square, was called Baydon Street from the 17th century or earlier until the late 19th.[41] In the late 18th century and the early 19th, as in 1982, there were houses along its eastern side to a point 250 m. north-east of the Square, where a steep bank, perhaps the edge of a former chalk pit, rises above the street.[42] Many of the buildings there are small cottages of the 18th and 19th centuries. In 1809 there were a few houses west of the street south of its junction with Lottage Road; by 1837 more had been built north of the junction.[43] Other new building west of the road in the 19th century included a chapel south of the junction.[44] Until 1900 a windmill 300 m. north of the junction marked the edge of the village.[45]

Until the 19th century many of the farmsteads of Aldbourne stood beside the north-western or south-eastern arms of the Swindon–Hungerford road, West Street and South Street. In the late 18th century and perhaps earlier the principal farmstead of Aldbourne manor stood south-west of South Street, straddling Southward Lane.[46] In 1809 and 1837 it was the largest farmstead in the village;[47] an early 19th-century farmhouse survives. Other former farmhouses include the Old Malthouse and Glebe Farm, both 18th-century buildings, which stand respectively north-east and south-west of South Street, and

the Old Rectory, a red-brick house of the early 19th century, south of the Square. Industrial buildings in South Street included the malthouse, a fustian factory north-east of the street in the 18th century and the 19th, and a chair factory south-west of it in the 19th.[48] In the early 19th century a workhouse stood at the north-western end of the street[49] and Yew Tree House, a villa in Gothic style, was built near the fustian factory. There were farmsteads beside West Street in the 16th century[50] and probably earlier. Rose Cottage, north of that street, and a thatched farmhouse and barn further west are of the 17th century or earlier. East of St. Michael's Close, which leads north from the street, there are 18th-century houses. In the early 19th century cottages, including a row of four leading south from the street, and Manor Farm, a red-brick house with a Gothic front at the western end of the village, were built. Between the junctions with Back Lane and with Castle Street and Marlborough Road, the lower part of Stock Lane, 18th- and 19th-century cottages, mostly small and of brick, line the western side of the street.

There were houses in Castle Street in the 16th century[51] but most surviving cottages are 19th-century, thatched, and built of stone rubble. A row of flint cottages stands on higher ground some 400 m. west of the junction with Marlborough Road. Along Marlborough Road the buildings are larger and more scattered. East of the road stands a thatched timber-framed house, west of it are 19th-century houses. The road turns sharply west 200 m. from the junction with Castle Street. South of the bend the Butts is a row of small thatched cottages, apparently built on waste ground in the late 18th century and the early 19th. Other cottages of similar date are further south.

In the early 20th century there was some infilling in the centre of the village, including the Memorial Hall in Oxford Street: private houses were built further north beside that road and beside Lottage Road, and council houses beside Southward Lane. The greatest expansion of the village, especially northwards, took place in the 1960s and 1970s. Bungalows were built east of Lottage Road and there was a large development of private houses west of it in Cook Road, Cook Close, and Grasshills Lane. A small factory was built near the southern end of Lottage Road. Private houses were built on the site of Hightown stables, bungalows in St. Michael's Close, and council houses north of Castle Street and south and east of the Butts.

There is said to have been an inn at Aldbourne in 1516 and one in or near Grasshills Lane in 1617.[52] The Crown, in the Square, was recorded in 1735.[53] A house south of the Green was the

[38] Andrews and Dury, Map (W.R.S. viii), pl. 15.
[39] P.N. Wilts. (E.P.N.S.), 292.
[40] W.R.O., tithe award.
[41] Ibid. 691/1; 838/16.
[42] Ibid. tithe award; Andrews and Dury, Map (W.R.S. viii), pl. 15; O.S. Map 1/25,000, SU 27 (1960 edn.).
[43] W.R.O., inclosure award; tithe award.
[44] Below, nonconf.
[45] Ibid. econ. hist.
[46] Andrews and Dury, Map (W.R.S. viii), pl. 15.
[47] W.R.O., inclosure award; tithe award.
[48] M. Crane and C. Newton, Map of Aldbourne (Aldbourne, n.d.); below, econ. hist.
[49] Below, local govt.
[50] P.R.O., DL 43/9/24.
[51] Ibid.
[52] Crane, Aldbourne Chron. 34.
[53] Ct. bks., 1732–1903, penes Mr. W. A. Brown, Manor Ho.

George inn in the early 18th century; the inn was closed in the early 19th.[54] The Bell, open in 1809, stood north of the junction of Castle Street and Marlborough Road.[55] It was closed in 1958.[56] The Blue Boar east of the Green was open in 1822,[57] closed in 1911, but reopened in or before 1931.[58] The Queen inn, east of the Swindon–Hungerford road between Back Lane and Castle Street, opened between 1837 and 1848.[59] Known as the Queen Victoria from 1855,[60] it was closed c. 1970.[61] Across West Street from it was the Mason's Arms, opened in or before 1920.[62] West Street House, adjoining the inn, was apparently once part of it.[63] The Crown, the Blue Boar, and the Mason's Arms were open in 1982.

Of the outlying farmsteads that with the longest history of occupation may be Laines, perhaps on the site of the medieval farmstead called Pickwood.[64] A farmhouse stood there in 1773.[65] That or a later house was replaced in 1938[66] by a stone house with, at each end of a central north-facing block, circular extensions from which led a long north-east wing and a shorter north-west wing. New farm buildings were then built 1 km. north-west of the house. A house called Dudmore Lodge was built in the early 16th century.[67] The early 19th-century farmhouse so called may be on its site. There was a farm and probably also a farmstead called Stock Close c. 1700.[68] Stock Close Farm was standing in 1773;[69] the surviving buildings may be of that date or a little later. The farm buildings were replaced after a fire in 1874.[70] Cottages stood east of the farmstead in the late 19th century but were demolished in the mid 20th.[71] In the late 18th century other farmsteads included that called Stock Lane, a little east of the junction of the lane and the road from Ramsbury, Aldbourne Wood, c. 800 m. south-east, Ewins Hill, 1.5 km. east, and Hillwood, c. 300 m. north of the junction.[72] Only that at Ewins Hill survived in 1982. Most of the buildings of Stock Lane Farm were disused in the early 20th century;[73] a 19th-century cottage remains. Farm buildings were erected beside the lane c. 1 km. north-east of the old farmstead in the late 20th century. Hillwood was also deserted between 1900 and 1910[74] but a bungalow and stables were built there after the Second World War. North of Aldbourne village East Leaze, a 19th-century farmhouse, stands on the site of a farmstead of the late 18th century or earlier. White Pond is a 20th-century house beside earlier farm buildings. Warren Farm is also on a

site of the 18th century or earlier[75] although the large farmhouse is of the early 19th century. East of it are cottages of a slightly later date. North Farm and cottages south of it were built between 1809 and 1837.[76] At North Field Barn are farm buildings and cottages of the late 19th century east of the Aldbourne–Wanborough road and an early 20th-century house west of it.

In the 14th century Snap was the smallest settlement in the parish, and one of the poorest in the county; there were 19 poll-tax payers in 1377.[77] In the early 17th century there was a row of five cottages along the southern side of the valley.[78] There may have been a cottage nearby at Woodsend in the early 16th century.[79] In 1773 there were between 5 and 10 houses at Snap, about half as many at Woodsend, and Leigh Farm between them.[80] Woodsend expanded in the early 19th century; c. 1850 it included sixteen cottages, and a chapel and a school were built. The population in 1851, including that of Leigh Farm, was 84; at Snap there were 41 inhabitants.[81] Agricultural changes led to the desertion of Snap soon after 1900.[82] In 1909 there were only two residents. Most of the houses were destroyed by Army gunnery practice during the First World War, although an uninhabited farmhouse still stood in the 1930s.[83] Rubble marked the sites of houses in 1982. At Woodsend the school and chapel were closed and several cottages abandoned in the early 20th century. Later there was some new building for which materials from Snap were used.[84] In 1982 there were cottages scattered on the north side of the road from Aldbourne to Ogbourne St. George and beside the track to Leigh Farm, then called Snap Farm.

Early settlement at Upper Upham may have continued into historic times.[85] In the 14th century Upham was a small village, having 40 poll-tax payers in 1377, and was poorer than the average community in the hundred.[86] There may have been some six houses at Upper Upham in the 16th century.[87] In the first decade of the 17th century there were two large and recently built houses; Upper Upham House north of the lane leading to Lower Upham and another south of it. Between Upper Upham House and the lane were two cottages.[88] Only Upper Upham House, its farmstead, and a cottage, later High Clear House, south-east of them, were standing in the late 18th century and the early 19th.[89] In 1851 the population of the hamlet was 34, of whom 18 lived in

54 Crane, *Aldbourne Chron.* 35; W.R.O., inclosure award.
55 W.R.O., inclosure award.
56 Crane, *Aldbourne Chron.* 35.
57 W.R.O., reg. alehousekeepers' recognizances, 1822–7.
58 *Kelly's Dir. Wilts.* (1911, 1931).
59 Ibid. (1848); W.R.O., tithe award.
60 *Kelly's Dir. Wilts.* (1855 and later edns.).
61 Crane, *Aldbourne Chron.* 35; I. Gandy, *Heart of a Village* (Bradford-on-Avon, 1975), 22.
62 *Kelly's Dir. Wilts.* (1920).
63 Gandy, *Heart of a Village*, 22.
64 Below, manors, econ. hist.
65 *Andrews and Dury, Map* (W.R.S. viii), pl. 15.
66 Sale cat. of Laines farm, 1982 (copy in N.M.R.).
67 P.R.O., DL 1/3, no. E 2; below, econ. hist.
68 Below, manors, econ. hist.
69 *Andrews and Dury, Map* (W.R.S. viii), pl. 15.
70 W.R.O. 1883, estate papers, letter, Smith to Burdett.
71 O.S. Map 6″, Wilts. XXIX (1889 and later edns.).

72 *Andrews and Dury, Map* (W.R.S. viii), pl. 15.
73 Below, econ. hist.   74 Ibid.
75 *Andrews and Dury, Map* (W.R.S. viii), pl. 15.
76 W.R.O., inclosure award; tithe award.
77 *V.C.H. Wilts.* iv. 296, 301, 310.
78 P.R.O., MPC 5 (DL 31/5).
79 Ibid. DL 43/9/24.
80 *Andrews and Dury, Map* (W.R.S. viii), pl. 15.
81 P.R.O., HO 107/1686; W.R.O., return of regns.; ibid. 526/15.
82 Below, econ. hist.
83 Wilts. Cuttings, xi. 22; *W.A.M.* lvii. 389–90; inf. from Mr. G. W. Wilson, Rudge Manor Farm, Froxfield.
84 *W.A.M.* lvii. 390.   85 Above.
86 *V.C.H. Wilts.* iv. 301, 310.
87 P.R.O., DL 43/9/24.
88 Ibid. MPC 5 (DL 31/5).
89 *Andrews and Dury, Map* (W.R.S. viii), pl. 15; W.R.O., inclosure award; tithe award.

Upper Upham House and its outbuildings.[90] West of the house Eyre's Barn, later a house, had been built by 1900[91] and extensive outbuildings were added in the early 20th century. They were altered and extended, and new farm buildings and Summerdale Cottages, a crescent of large houses, were built in the 1960s.[92] Lower Upham was never more than a farmstead. The stone-walled farmhouse is of the late 16th century or the early 17th, extended southwards in the early 19th century. In 1982 there were two groups of cottages of the 19th century and the 20th west of the house. There was a farmstead called Blake's 800 m. south-west of Lower Upham in 1773;[93] some buildings survived in 1960[94] but they had been demolished by 1982.

Preston stands at the junction of the road from Marridge Hill in Ramsbury with the Swindon–Hungerford road. Only the buildings west of the stream are in Aldbourne parish. Of those only Preston Old House, the most southerly, was standing in 1773.[95] A round, thatched tollhouse was built east of the Swindon–Hungerford road in the early 19th century.[96] Little Orchard and Alma Farm west of the road are also 19th-century buildings.

In 1643 a parliamentary army marching from Gloucester to London was attacked by Prince Rupert's cavalry north of Dudmore Lodge, driven thence into Aldbourne village, and forced to withdraw to Hungerford.[97] In April 1644 a muster of some 10,000 royalist troops was held in Aldbourne Chase, and there is said to have been another skirmish near the village a month later.[98]

A brass and reed band was formed in Aldbourne in 1835. It later became an orchestra and afterwards a silver band. New instruments were given for the band in 1925.[99] Thereafter the band had many successes in competitions and it still flourished in 1982.[1] Charles McEvoy, a dramatist, converted the former malthouse in South Street into a theatre and in 1910 his play *A Village Wedding* was performed there by village residents before an audience which included George Bernard Shaw. The production was successfully taken to Devizes and to Manchester but failed in London. The theatre was closed in 1912.[2]

MANORS AND OTHER ESTATES. By will of c. 970 Alfheah devised *ALDBOURNE* to his

brother Alfhere.[3] Gytha or her son Earl Harold held the estate in 1066. It passed to William I[4] and after 1086 was granted to a count of Perche. Aldbourne was held c. 1135 by Rotrou, count of Perche (d. 1144), and passed with the title to his son Rotrou (d. 1191) and to the younger Rotrou's son Geoffrey (d. 1202).[5] The manor was confiscated in 1217 after the death of Geoffrey's son Thomas, count of Perche, at the battle of Lincoln. In the same year the king granted it to William Longespée, earl of Salisbury. Another grant to Longespée, perhaps confirming the king's, was made by William, bishop of Châlons and count of Perche, Thomas's uncle and heir.[6] After Longespée's death in 1226 Aldbourne passed to his wife Ela, countess of Salisbury, but in 1229 seisin was granted to their son Sir William and in 1230 Ela was ordered to release the manor to him.[7] Sir William (d. 1250) was succeeded in turn by his son Sir William (d. 1257) and by that William's daughter Margaret, countess of Salisbury and wife of Henry de Lacy, earl of Lincoln (d. 1311).[8] Aldbourne descended with Trowbridge manor to John of Gaunt, duke of Lancaster (d. 1399), and it was held by the Crown as part of the duchy of Lancaster from the accession of Henry IV.[9] In 1467 the manor was settled on Queen Elizabeth for life. It was confiscated in 1483–4 and may not have been restored with her other estates in 1486.[10] In 1547 it was granted to Edward Seymour, duke of Somerset, and it reverted to the Crown on Somerset's attainder in 1552.[11] The manor was settled for 99 years on trustees for Charles, prince of Wales, in 1617 but the remainder of the term and the reversion were conveyed in 1627 to trustees for the City of London.[12]

Until the 17th century Aldbourne manor was unusually large and much of the parish was demesne or copyhold land of the manor. Between 1627 and 1631 the demesne lands were broken up and they and the warren were sold. By the end of the century hunting rights in the chase and many copyholds had also been sold or granted away.[13]

In 1632 the City sold the lordship of the manor, apparently with land tenanted by copyholders, to Thomas Bond who at his death in or before 1653 also held those parts of the demesne lands later called Aldbourne farm and East Leaze farm. His estate kept the name Aldbourne manor. In 1686 Bond's son George sold it to Richard Kent (d. 1690), who devised it to his nephew John Kent.[14] In 1691 George's relict Elizabeth

[90] P.R.O., HO 107/1686.
[91] O.S. Map 6", Wilts. XXIII. NE. (1900 edn.).
[92] W.A.S. Libr., sale cat. xxviii, no. 173; O.S. Map 1/10,000, SU 27 NW. (1980 edn.).
[93] *Andrews and Dury, Map* (W.R.S. viii), pl. 15.
[94] O.S. Map 6", SU 27 NW. (1960 edn.).
[95] *Andrews and Dury, Map* (W.R.S. viii), pl. 15.
[96] See plate facing p. 145.
[97] *W.A.M.* xxiii. 262–7; Clarendon, *Hist. of the Rebellion*, ed. W. D. Macray (1888), iii. 172–3.
[98] S. R. Gardiner, *Hist. of the Civil War* (1965), i. 331; Gandy, *Heart of a Village*, 30.
[99] Gandy, *Heart of a Village*, 99.
[1] Inf. from Mr. J. W. Jones, 29 Severn Avenue, Swindon.
[2] Gandy, *Heart of a Village*, 99; Wilts. Cuttings, xiii. 82, 185; xvi. 23.
[3] Finberg, *Early Wessex Chart.* p. 98.
[4] *V.C.H. Wilts.* ii, pp. 117, 200, 207.

[5] Ibid. p. 117; L. Bart des Boulais, *Receuil des Antiquitéz du Perche*, ed. H. Tournoüer (Mortagne, 1890), 110, 115, 129, 151; *Lewes Cart. Supplt. Wilts. portion* (Suss. Rec. Soc. xl), p. 23.
[6] Bart des Boulais, *Antiquitéz du Perche*, ed. Tournoüer, 169–72; *Rot. Litt. Claus.* (Rec. Com.), i. 311; *Rot. Hund.* (Rec. Com.), ii (1), 269.
[7] *Rot. Litt. Claus.* (Rec. Com.), ii. 110; *Close R. 1227–31*, 223, 307.
[8] *Complete Peerage*, vii. 686; xi. 382–4; *Bk. of Fees*, ii. 748; *Rot. Hund.* (Rec. Com.), ii (1), 269.
[9] *V.C.H. Wilts.* vii. 128–9.
[10] *Rot. Parl.* v. 628; vi. 288; Resumption Act, 1 Ric. III, c. 15; *Cal. Pat.* 1485–94, 75–7.
[11] *Cal. Pat.* 1547–8, 121; *Complete Peerage*, xii (1), 63.
[12] *W.N. & Q.* iii. 271–2; *W.A.M.* xlii. 576.
[13] Below.
[14] *W.A.M.* xlii. 579–80; *W.N. & Q.* vii. 234–5.

Bond recovered the manor because the financial conditions of the sale had not been met.[15] By will proved 1728 she devised it to her daughter Frances Hulbert for life, with remainder to her nephew William Hoskins.[16] William's son William sold the manor in 1750 to Peckham Williams, who by 1801 had been succeeded by his son John. In 1804 John sold it to John Hancock (d. 1817),[17] whose daughter and heir Anne was wife of T. B. M. Baskerville (d. 1864). The manor passed to Baskerville's son W. T. M. Baskerville (d. 1897).[18] In 1904 Aldbourne farm was sold by the son's trustees[19] and dispersed. The lordship of the manor, the copyhold land, and East Leaze farm had been sold in 1875.[20] The lordship passed to S. Pattison (fl. 1880)[21] and F. E. Pocock and Mrs. H. M. F. Hancock, who sold it in 1892,[22] probably to William Brown. Land called Manor farm, presumably including the copyholds and perhaps also lands from Aldbourne farm, passed from Brown (d. 1908) to his son William (d. 1953) and that William's son Mr. W. A. Brown, who owned it in partnership with members of his family in 1982.[23] W. C. Maisey bought East Leaze farm in 1911 and sold it in 1917 to Moses Woolland.[24] It passed with the Baydon Manor estate in Ramsbury to John White, Sidney Watts, and Albert Pembroke. It was assigned to Pembroke c. 1949 and his relict owned most of it c. 1982.[25] Part was sold after 1968 to Mr. R. N. Lawton who owned that part in 1982.[26]

The right to hunt deer over the 1,400 a. of the CHASE was, as part of Aldbourne manor, settled for a term of 99 years on trustees for the prince of Wales in 1617.[27] The remainder of the term was granted in 1674 to Charles Sackville, Baron Buckhurst, later earl of Middlesex and Dorset (d. 1706).[28] No later reference to the right has been found.

In 1631 the City of London sold to Edward Nicholas demesne lands of Aldbourne manor in the south part of the parish, later PICKWOOD or LAINES and STOCK CLOSE farms. Nicholas sold them in 1634 to Philip Herbert, earl of Pembroke and Montgomery (d. 1650).[29] The lands passed with the earldoms to Philip's son Philip (d. 1669) and to that Philip's sons William (d. 1674) and Philip.[30] In 1682 Philip sold them to Sir William Jones (d. 1682), who

was succeeded by his son Richard (d. 1685), his brother Samuel (d. 1686), and Samuel's son Richard.[31] In 1718 Richard sold some of the lands, known as Pickwood farm, to Sir Anthony Sturt.[32] The farm passed from father to son in the Sturt family, to Humphrey (d. 1740), Humphrey (d. 1786), and Humphrey[33] who sold it in 1791.[34] It was probably bought by Thomas Baskerville, the owner in 1809.[35] Baskerville was succeeded in 1817 by his cousin T. B. M. Baskerville,[36] and thereafter the farm passed with Aldbourne farm to W. T. M. Baskerville and was sold in 1904 as Pickwood Laines farm.[37] It was bought then or soon afterwards by Henry Wilson (d. 1911) who devised it to one of his daughters. James Bomford was owner from 1938 until 1959[38] and c. 1960 much of the farm was sold to Mr. J. D. Owen, the owner in 1982; it was then part of Chase Woods farm.[39]

Land retained by Richard Jones in 1718 passed as Stock Close farm in the Jones and Burdett families with Ramsbury manor and land in Axford to Marjorie Frances, Lady Burdett-Fisher, and her son Maj. F. R. D. Burdett-Fisher, the owners in 1982.[40]

Aldbourne warren was part of Aldbourne manor. In 1631 the City of London sold it to Philip, earl of Pembroke and Montgomery.[41] Lands allotted when it was diswarrened, later called Warren farm and Dudmore Lodge farm, passed with Pickwood farm.[42] In 1904 WARREN farm was sold to Henry Brown,[43] who sold it in 1919 to James White.[44] After White's death in 1926 it was bought by J. B. Joel, who sold it in 1946 to V. S. Bland. Bland's sons, Mr. H. V. Bland and Mr. J. V. Bland, were owners in 1982.[45] DUDMORE LODGE farm was bought, probably in 1791, by Robert Church[46] (d. 1804). He was succeeded by Robert Church (d. 1852) and Robert Church (d. 1861).[47] In 1863 Theodosia Church sold the farm. It was later bought by T. B. M. Baskerville (d. 1864) and sold by his son W. T. M. Baskerville in 1875,[48] probably to A. L. Goddard (d. 1898). In 1918 Goddard's son F. P. Goddard sold the farm to the Dudmore Farm Co. The company sold it in 1927 to F. C. Gentry. In 1952 Gentry sold c. 200 a. and at his death in 1968 the remaining lands, 280 a., passed to his daughters Miss Elizabeth Gentry and Miss Margaret Gentry, the owners in 1982.[49]

[15] P.R.O., C 5/120/5; C 33/277, f. 250v.
[16] Ibid. PROB 11/624 (P.C.C. 281 Brooke).
[17] W.A.M. xlii. 581-2; Williams's Estates Act, 42 Geo. III, c. 53 (Local and Personal); W.R.O., land tax.
[18] Burke, Land. Gent. (1906), i. 85.
[19] Reading Univ. Libr., hist. farm rec., WIL 11/3/18.
[20] W.A.S. Libr., sale cat. vii, no. 83.
[21] Kelly's Dir. Wilts. (1880).
[22] Reading Univ. Libr., hist. farm rec., WIL 11/3/6.
[23] Kelly's Dir. Wilts. (1903); inf. from Mr. W. A. Brown, Manor Ho.
[24] Notes on Aldbourne hist. penes Mr. M. A. Crane, 20 Oxford St.
[25] Above, Ramsbury, manors; inf. from Mr. R. T. Walton, New Ho., Manor Lane, Baydon.
[26] Inf. from Mr. R. N. Lawton, North Farm.
[27] Above; W.R.O. 84/47/21.
[28] Cal. Treas. Bks. 1672-5, 500; Complete Peerage, iv. 425-6.
[29] W.R.O. 84/47/21; P.R.O., DL 43/9/24; Complete Peerage, x. 418.
[30] Complete Peerage, x. 420-2.

[31] W.A.M. xlii. 584; above, Ramsbury, manors.
[32] W.R.O. 1883/102, deed, Jones to Sturt.
[33] Burke, Land. Gent. (1846), ii. 1326-7.
[34] Wilts. Cuttings. xxiv. 72.
[35] W.R.O., inclosure award.
[36] Burke, Land. Gent. (1906), i. 85.
[37] Above; Reading Univ. Libr., hist. farm rec., WIL 11/3/18.
[38] Inf. from Mr. G. W. Wilson, Rudge Manor Farm, Froxfield.
[39] Inf. from Mr. J. D. Owen, Chase Woods Farm; below.
[40] W.R.O. 1883/102; above, Ramsbury, manors.
[41] W.A.M. xlii. 576; W.R.O. 84/47/21.
[42] W.R.O. 1883/102; above; below, econ. hist.
[43] Reading Univ. Libr., hist. farm rec., WIL 11/3/18.
[44] Ibid. WIL 11/4/24.
[45] Inf. from Mr. H. V. Bland, the Warren.
[46] W.R.O., land tax; Wilts. Cuttings. xxiv. 72.
[47] W.A.S. Libr., sale cat. vii, no. 83; notes penes Mr. Crane.
[48] W.A.S. Libr., sale cat. vii, no. 83.
[49] V.C.H. Wilts. ix. 120; inf. from Miss E. Gentry, Dudmore Lodge Farm.

Demesne lands of the manor in Upham and Snap were sold by the City to Obadiah Sedgewick in 1631.[50] Other demesne lands there were acquired by Sedgewick before his death and by will proved 1657 he devised the whole estate to his wife Priscilla for sale. A capital messuage and 70 a. of arable called Heydon were sold to Gabriel Martin (fl. 1681).[51] The land was probably that later known as *SNAP* farm, held in 1800 by John Neate (d. 1812).[52] Neate was succeeded by Stephen Neate (d. 1843), perhaps his brother,[53] and by S. J. Neate (fl. 1867). The farm was sold to B. Hayward in 1900[54] and to Henry Wilson in 1905.[55] At Wilson's death in 1911 the farm passed to one of his daughters. It was sold in 1938 to James Bomford and, after 1959, to Dr. J. A. E. Hobby, the owner in 1982.[56]

Another portion of Sedgewick's estate was sold in 1657 to Richard King (fl. 1663).[57] That land may be identified with *LOWER UPHAM* farm, owned in 1780 by John Stone[58] (d. 1814). The farm passed to Stone's son John (d. 1858), who was succeeded in turn by his daughters Maria (d. 1858) and Catherine, wife of William Warry. Catherine (d. 1861) was succeeded by her son W. J. E. Warry who took the additional name Stone in 1886. He was succeeded after 1942 by his cousin Mrs. R. Buchan.[59] Mr. R. Brinkworth bought Lower Upham in 1958 and sold it in 1982 to Mr. C. R. Peplow.[60]

Land called Lyes and 66 a. at Snap, also part of Sedgewick's estate, were sold in 1657 to Edward Goddard.[61] *LEIGH* farm, probably derived from that land, was held by William Brown in 1809,[62] by John Brown as owner or tenant *c.* 1825,[63] and by William Brown in 1837.[64] By 1875 it had passed to Thomas Brown (d. *c.* 1900)[65] and it was sold *c.* 1905 to Henry Wilson (d. 1911). Thereafter it passed with Snap farm.[66]

Copyhold lands of the manor were sold by Elizabeth Bond in small portions in 1694 and were merged in the 18th century and the early 19th as *NORTH* farm.[67] The farm was held in 1809 by James Wells,[68] who sold it to John Brogden in 1828.[69] Brogden was succeeded in or before 1837 by his son the Revd. James Brogden,[70] who sold the farm to Thomas Hicks Chandler in 1848.[71] Chandler (d. 1867) was succeeded by his son Thomas on whose death in 1902 the farm was inherited jointly by his children Richard, William, Thomas, and Anne. In 1903 her brothers conveyed their interests to Anne Chandler who by will proved 1910 devised the farm to trustees for sale.[72] It may have been bought by her brother William who was owner or tenant of the farm at his death in 1915 and was succeeded there by his son Thomas.[73] The farm was sold *c.* 1921; some of the land was bought by William Brown (d. 1953) and was merged with Manor farm.[74] A. W. Lawrence owned the remainder, still called North farm, in 1929, and that farm was sold by Frederick Butcher to Albert Pembroke in 1935. In 1947 John Lawrence owned the farm and in 1968 he sold it to Mr. R. N. Lawton, the owner in 1982.[75]

Oliver Cor settled the lands which he held by copy of Aldbourne manor on his son Robert in 1699. Robert (will proved 1716) was succeeded by his son Robert (d. 1724) and that Robert's son Robert[76] who sold those and other lands to William Brown in 1739. Most of the lands were then held freely.[77] In 1799 *COR'S* was settled on another William Brown who held it in 1809.[78] A William Brown held Cor's and *WEST STREET* farm, probably also a former copyhold, *c.* 1825.[79] He was succeeded in 1835 by his son William[80] and the two farms passed in the Brown family to William Brown (d. 1908). Thereafter they passed with the lordship of Aldbourne manor and in 1982 they were part of Manor farm.[81]

By will proved 1743 John Brown devised to his son Richard lands at Lottage, probably a former copyhold, which he had bought from Thomas Mott.[82] Richard was succeeded by Mark Brown, perhaps his son, who held *LOTTAGE* farm in 1780.[83] From Mark (will proved 1829) the farm passed to Thomas Brown (fl. 1851), perhaps his son, and it was sold in 1888.[84] At his death in 1908 William Brown held the farmhouse and a few acres but most of the lands had apparently been dispersed.[85]

Rotrou, count of Perche (d. 1191), gave Aldbourne church to the priory of Nogent-le-Rotrou (Eure-et-Loir). The *RECTORY* had been appropriated by 1228.[86] It may have been granted to Amesbury priory in or before 1289 and was certainly held by that priory in 1315.[87] It passed to the Crown at the Dissolution and in 1541 the rectory or rectory manor, an estate of land and tithes, was granted to the dean and

[50] Public Libr., Swindon, Goddard MS. 722.
[51] *W.A.M.* xlii. 583; W.R.O. 130/46/13; *Cal. S.P. Dom.* 1680–1, 563.
[52] W.R.O., land tax; mon. in church.
[53] W.R.O., land tax; mon. in church.
[54] Reading Univ. Libr., hist. farm rec., WIL 11/3/13.
[55] *W.A.M.* lvii. 389.
[56] Inf. from Mr. Wilson; Mr. Owen.
[57] W.R.O. 130/46/13; W.A.S. Libr., Wilts. Misc. MSS. i, no. 6.
[58] W.R.O., land tax.
[59] Burke, *Land. Gent.* (1937), 2165; (1952), 2649.
[60] Inf. from Mr. and Mrs. R. Brinkworth, Lower Upham Farm.
[61] *W.A.M.* xlii. 583.
[62] W.R.O., inclosure award.
[63] Wilts. Cuttings, xvii. 194.
[64] W.R.O., tithe award.
[65] W.A.S. Libr., sale cat. iv, no. 36.
[66] *W.A.M.* lvii. 389; above.
[67] W.R.O. 212A/6/2–5; 212A/6/7; 212A/36/37–40; 700/86.
[68] Ibid. inclosure award.

[69] Ibid. 212A/36/40; deed, Wells to Brogden, *penes* Mr. Lawton.
[70] W.R.O., tithe award.
[71] Deed, Brogden to Chandler, *penes* Mr. Lawton.
[72] Abstr. of title of Anne Chandler, *penes* Mr. Lawton.
[73] Wilts. Cuttings, xvi. 23.
[74] Inf. from Mr. Brown.
[75] Inf. from Mr. Lawton.
[76] *W.N. & Q.* iv. 410–11.
[77] W.R.O. 700/83.
[78] Ibid. 700/111; ibid. inclosure award.
[79] Ibid. tithe award; Wilts. Cuttings, xvii. 194.
[80] Val. of goods of Wm. Brown, 1835, *penes* Mr. Brown.
[81] Above; inf. from Mr. Brown.
[82] W.R.O. 526/13.
[83] Ibid. land tax; list of quitrents, 1786–96, *penes* Mr. Brown.
[84] W.A.S. Libr., sale cat. v, no. 30; P.R.O., HO 107/1686.
[85] Reading Univ. Libr., hist. farm rec., WIL 11/3/22.
[86] P.R.O., DL 25/3394.
[87] Aubrey, *Topog. Coll.* ed. Jackson, 199; *V.C.H. Wilts.* iii. 250.

chapter of Winchester.[88] The rectorial tithes were replaced by a rent charge of £1,475 in 1837.[89] In 1861 the estate passed to the Ecclesiastical Commissioners. The land was sold then or soon afterwards to F. W. Neate[90] and by him in 1869 to H. J. Puckridge.[91] It was sold again in 1885[92] and afterwards apparently dispersed.

Sir William Longespée gave land in Upham to Lacock abbey c. 1249.[93] The abbey held *UPPER UPHAM* at the Dissolution and in 1540 the Crown sold the manor to John Goddard (d. 1557).[94] It passed to his son Thomas (d. 1598) and grandson Richard Goddard (d. 1614),[95] whose relict Elizabeth and her husband Richard Digges held it in 1626.[96] Upper Upham may have passed with Swindon manor in the Goddard family during the late 17th century but had apparently been sold by the early 18th.[97] In the mid 18th century it passed from John Grove to Francis Grove, perhaps his son,[98] and in 1780 it belonged to Timothy Caswell,[99] who was succeeded in 1802 by his daughter Diana (fl. 1831).[1] The manor was sold c. 1834, probably to John Round, the owner in 1837,[2] and sold again in 1847.[3] In 1870 it was bought by A. L. Goddard (d. 1898). His son F. P. Goddard[4] sold it in 1909 to Hilda Hambury, later wife of Sir James Currie. Lady Currie died in 1939.[5] R. Peplow owned Upper Upham c. 1945 and sold it in 1961 to Martin Summers. Upper Upham farm was sold several times between 1965 and 1976, and in 1977 it was bought by the Electricity Supply Nominees on behalf of Mr. R. N. Lawton.[6]

Upper Upham House, built in the late 16th century of coursed flint and sarsen rubble with ashlar dressings, has been much altered and extended since 1909.[7] The older part, dated 1599,[8] has a symmetrical south front with a projecting porch and oriels. The hall lies behind the central and eastern portions of the front. Behind the hall were the parlour and staircase, and west of it were the service rooms. The attic on the south side of the house may have served as a long gallery. The house fell into disrepair in the late 19th century and was restored between 1909 and 1922 by Biddulph Pinchard for Lady Currie.[9] New panelling and ceilings in an early 17th-century style were introduced and a west wing, housing more extensive service rooms and

nursery accommodation, and a gatehouse north of the new wing were added. Formal gardens were laid out east of the house and a walled court and a double avenue were made north and south of it respectively. Between 1961 and 1965 many interior fittings were replaced, including the hall ceiling and the library fittings in the former parlour, 18th-century French panelling was introduced in the dining room, and a new staircase was built.[10] After 1965 the house was divided into three and the outbuildings, most of which were built for Lady Currie, were sold for conversion into separate houses.[11]

A farm, apparently held freely of Aldbourne manor and called *WALROND'S* in the 16th century, descended with the keepership of the chase. Both were held before 1311 by William Walrond[12] and were settled in 1326 on William or his namesake with remainder to his or the namesake's son John.[13] In 1350 John Ellis granted them to his son Roger,[14] whose son Robert held them in 1358.[15] They were conveyed to John Newbury in 1365[16] and to Thomas Restwold in 1379.[17] Restwold conveyed them in 1406 to John Gerard who granted them in 1410 to Lewis John.[18] In 1417 Lewis conveyed them to Sir William Esturmy (d. 1427).[19] In the 15th century or the early 16th the lands again passed to members of the Walrond or Waldron family. Ingram Walrond was succeeded by his son William (fl. 1527)[20] and later by Thomas Walrond (fl. 1532).[21] Thomas was succeeded c. 1553 by his son Thomas[22] (will proved 1558) and later by that Thomas's son Thomas[23] (will proved 1569).[24] The farm and keepership passed to the youngest Thomas's son George (fl. 1611).[25] In 1622 another Thomas Walrond and Alexander Thistlethwaite, perhaps trustees, sold the keepership and probably the farm to William Herbert, earl of Pembroke (d. 1630). They passed to William's brother Philip, earl of Pembroke and Montgomery,[26] and the lands were probably absorbed into Philip's other holdings in Aldbourne. The keepership and Dudmore Lodge, which belonged to the keeper, descended with the lands which became Pickwood farm to Richard, son of Samuel Jones. In 1689 the keepership and other rights were replaced by an allotment of 260 a.[27] That and the lodge became

[88] *L. & P. Hen. VIII*, xvi, p. 417.
[89] W.R.O., tithe award.
[90] Ch. Com., survey, 1861; Reading Univ. Libr., hist. farm rec., WIL 11/3/4.
[91] W.A.S. Libr., sale cat. xxi, no. 1.
[92] Reading Univ. Libr., hist. farm rec., WIL 11/3/4.
[93] *Lacock Chart.* (W.R.S. xxxiv), p. 78; *V.C.H. Wilts.* iii. 305.
[94] P.R.O., E 318/Box 11/488; *L. & P. Hen. VIII*, xv, pp. 293, 296; *W.N. & Q.* ii. 66.
[95] P.R.O., C 142/351, no. 115; *V.C.H. Wilts.* ix. 120, which is corrected here. See plate facing p. 193.
[96] *Wilts. Inq. p.m.* 1625-49 (Index Libr.), 395; P.R.O., E 36/157, pp. 76-7.
[97] *V.C.H. Wilts.* ix. 120; P.R.O., PROB 11/476 (P.C.C. 106 Ash, will of Thos. Goddard).
[98] List of quitrents, 1786-96, *penes* Mr. Brown.
[99] W.R.O., land tax.   [1] Ibid.; *W.A.M.* xlii. 583.
[2] *Endowed Char. Wilts.* (N. Div.), 1; W.R.O., tithe award.
[3] Sale notice, *penes* Mr. Lawton.
[4] *W.A.M.* xlii. 110; *V.C.H. Wilts.* ix. 120.
[5] Wilts. Cuttings, xvi. 22; *W.A.M.* xlix. 104-5.
[6] Inf. from Mr. Lawton.

[7] See plate facing p. 96.
[8] Date stone above porch.
[9] *Country Life*, 1 July 1922.
[10] Inf. from Mrs. J. Atwater, Upham Ho.
[11] Inf. from Mr. T. Dewis, Eyre's Barn, Upper Upham.
[12] P.R.O., E 326/7482.
[13] *Feet of F.* 1272-1327 (W.R.S. i), p. 121.
[14] P.R.O., E 326/7479.
[15] Ibid. E 326/11806.
[16] *Feet of F.* 1327-77 (W.R.S. xxix), p. 128.
[17] P.R.O., E 326/11812.
[18] Ibid. E 326/11809.
[19] Ibid. E 326/8253; *V.C.H. Wilts.* x. 78.
[20] P.R.O., DL 1/3, no. E 2.
[21] Ibid. DL 3/20, no. B 8.
[22] Ibid. DL 1/35, no. W 8; DL 1/39, no. P 8.
[23] Ibid. DL 1/36, no. W 5; ibid. PROB 11/40 (P.C.C. 35 Noodes).
[24] Ibid. PROB 11/51 (P.C.C. 16 Sheffelde).
[25] Ibid. PROB 11/118 (P.C.C. 81 Wood, will of Roger Walrond); ibid. DL 4/54, no. 51.
[26] W.R.O. 84/47/21; *Complete Peerage*, x. 414-15.
[27] W.R.O. 1883/288; above.

part of the estate from which Warren and Dudmore Lodge farms were derived.[28]

Lands in Aldbourne, later *CHASE WOODS* farm, probably belonged to Ogbourne priory and passed with Ogbourne St. Andrew manor to King's College, Cambridge, in the 15th century.[29] In the mid 16th century the college held woods in Aldbourne called Priors Woods,[30] and in the 19th century its estate there included between 160 a. and 200 a. of wood and arable.[31] The holding was sold with land in Ogbourne St. George as Cowcroft farm to a Mr. Shields in 1927 or 1928. Thereafter the farm was sold several times. In 1959 it was bought by Mr. J. D. Owen and as Chase Woods farm he owned it in 1982.[32]

CHURCH'S freehold and copyhold estate, formerly John Bacon's, was held by Robert Church in 1790.[33] The estate may have been that held by Thomas Church in 1809[34] and by Robert Church in 1837.[35] It probably passed with Dudmore Lodge farm to Robert Church (d. 1861).[36] In 1875 Thomas Church held the farm,[37] which later became part of Manor farm.[38]

Henry Southby (d. 1796) devised *SOUTHBY'S* farm to his nephew Thomas Hayward (d. 1799), who was succeeded in turn by his wife Catherine and daughter Elizabeth (d. 1801), wife of Thomas Perfect (fl. 1817).[39] Perfect's son Thomas Hayward apparently took the surname Southby and he or another T. H. Southby held the farm *c.* 1825, in 1837, and in 1888.[40] By 1892 it had passed to Elizabeth Hayward Southby,[41] who devised it to her nephew F. S. Walker. In 1920 Walker sold it to Thomas Illingworth, who sold part to William Brown in 1922. That land became part of Manor farm.[42] The descent of Illingworth's other land has not been traced.

The origins of *HILLWOOD* farm and *STOCK LANE* farm are obscure. Hillwood farm was sold in 1798,[43] probably to George Church who held it in 1801.[44] He or his namesake owned both farms in 1851.[45] By 1855 they had passed to Thomas Church[46] and in 1901 they were sold by W. E. N. Brown and Mary Brown, probably to Henry Wilson.[47] Thereafter they passed with Snap farm.[48]

William Woodman bought small holdings of land in Aldbourne in the 1820s and in 1837 held a farm of 171 a.[49] In 1852 he conveyed the farm to

H. D. Woodman, presumably his son, who sold *WOODMAN'S* in 1893 to Sir Francis Burdett, Bt.[50] Thereafter it became part of Stock Close farm.[51]

A gift by Hugh of Upham to Bradenstoke priory of 2 a. in Upham was confirmed in 1207.[52] After the Dissolution the land was granted, in 1541, to Richard Ingram who sold it to John Goddard (d. 1557), the lord of Upper Upham manor.[53]

William Longespée, probably William, earl of Salisbury (d. 1226), confirmed a grant made by a count of Perche to the priory of Southwick (Hants) of 20s. rent in Aldbourne.[54] The priory held lands there in 1291.[55] They were sold to Richard Ingram in 1540 and to John Goddard in 1541. Thereafter they probably passed with Goddard's Upper Upham estate.[56]

Lands in Aldbourne which had belonged to the fraternity of St. Mary in Aldbourne before the Dissolution were sold by the Crown to Edward Clinton or Fiennes, earl of Lincoln, in 1575.[57] Other fraternity lands were held by Thomas Walrond by lease from the Crown in 1606 but later as a freehold.[58] In 1628 Thomas Hayne gave a messuage called the chantry house and 3 a., probably fraternity land, for the maintenance of Baydon church. That house and land were sold by trustees in 1877.[59]

Rents from Aldbourne or Wanborough granted by Rotrou, count of Perche, to the priory of Lewes (Suss.) *c.* 1135 were probably from Wanborourgh.[60]

ECONOMIC HISTORY. In 1086 Aldbourne was assessed at 40 hides. The size of the demesne, 18 hides, may have been exaggerated to avoid paying geld.[61] In 1084 there were probably 15 hides in demesne,[62] and in 1086 only 10 plough-teams, with 25 serfs and 14 'coliberts', were assigned to the demesne. There were 26 teams shared by 73 villeins and 38 'cozets'. Some of those teams may also have worked on the demesne, but the estate, which had land for 45 teams, was not fully exploited.[63] There was pasture measuring 1 league by ½ league, and one of the largest areas of meadow in the county, measuring 1 league by 5 furlongs, much of which probably lay outside Aldbourne parish.[64] The

[28] W.R.O. 1883/102, deed, Jones to Sturt; above.
[29] Below, Ogbourne St. Andrew, manors.
[30] P.R.O., DL 3/61, no. W 2.
[31] King's Coll., Camb., Mun., survey, 1803; W.R.O., tithe award; W.A.S. Libr., sale cat. xxxii, no. 39.
[32] Inf. from Mr. Owen.
[33] List of quitrents, 1786–96, *penes* Mr. Brown.
[34] W.R.O., inclosure award.
[35] Ibid. tithe award.
[36] *Kelly's Dir. Wilts.* (1855); above.
[37] *Kelly's Dir. Wilts.*
[38] Inf. from Mr. Brown.
[39] Notes *penes* Mr. Crane; Reading Univ. Libr., hist. farm rec., WIL 11/3/1.
[40] Notes *penes* Mr. Crane; Wilts. Cuttings, xvii. 194; W.R.O., tithe award; W.A.S. Libr., sale cat. vii, no. 83; v, no. 30.
[41] W.R.O. 1883/285.
[42] Notes *penes* Mr. Crane.
[43] W.R.O. 212A/36/37.
[44] Ibid. land tax.
[45] P.R.O., HO 107/1686.

[46] *Kelly's Dir. Wilts.*
[47] W.A.S. Libr., sale cat. xxviiiG, no. 32.
[48] Above.
[49] W.R.O. 1883/285; ibid. tithe award.
[50] Ibid. 1883/285.
[51] Above.
[52] *Rot. Chart.* (Rec. Com.), 170.
[53] *L. & P. Hen. VIII,* xvi, p. 638; above.
[54] B.L. Add. MS. 33280, f. 35v.
[55] *Tax. Eccl.* (Rec. Com.), 192.
[56] *L. & P. Hen. VIII,* xv, p. 407; xvi, p. 638; above.
[57] P.R.O., E 318/Box 45/2421.
[58] Ibid. DL 43/9/24; W.R.O. 405/3.
[59] *Endowed Char. Wilts.* (N. Div.), 28–30; above, Baydon, church.
[60] *Lewes Cart. Supplt. Wilts. portion* (Suss. Rec. Soc. xl), p. 23; *V.C.H. Wilts.* ix. 179.
[61] *V.C.H. Wilts.* ii, p. 117; cf. ibid. p. 51.
[62] Ibid. p. 200.
[63] Ibid. p. 117; cf. ibid. pp. 49, 51.
[64] Ibid. pp. 56 and n., 117; *Wilts. Inq. p.m. 1242–1326* (Index Libr.), 382–3.

estate was assessed for payment of £70 by weight but the English, presumably a local jury, claimed that only £60 by tale should be paid. The church had an estate of 2 hides, on which there was land for 2 ploughteams. It was valued at 40s.[65]

Although most of the parish lay within Aldbourne manor,[66] the open fields and common pastures of Aldbourne and of Upham and Snap were distinct in the early 13th century.[67] In Aldbourne, a 16th-century surveyor distinguished between the fertile meadows and arable lands of the southern part and the barren soil of the north-western part, including the warren, good only for sheep pasture. The open fields, North, East, South, West, and Windmill, lay in the valleys converging on Aldbourne village.[68] Uneven ground near Stock Close Farm and on Ewins Hill, referred to as ancient furrows in the 17th century, was probably part of the several arable land of Pickwood farm in the 15th century and perhaps earlier.[69] There was common pasture for sheep on East Down, in the north-east corner of the parish, and for sheep and cattle in Southwood and on South Hill, parts of Southward Down.[70] The warren provided several pasture for the demesne flock.[71] Tenants of Ogbourne St. George manor had grazing rights in Priors Wood.[72]

Upham and Snap were once separate agricultural units but demesne lands of Aldbourne manor there were held and perhaps worked together from the 13th century.[73] In the 16th century and perhaps earlier Snap Upper or Snap field lay in the valley north-west of Snap; Upham Upper or Upham field adjoined it on higher ground further north. Lower field, at the western end of the parish, was then worked by tenants from both hamlets but may formerly have been divided.[74] The tenants also shared Snap common, north-east of Round Hill Downs in Ogbourne St. George, and Upham common, east of Lower Upham Farm, but their grazing rights differed slightly.[75]

In 1311 the demesne of Aldbourne manor included 306 a. of arable, 80 a. of meadow in Wanborough, several pasture for 24 oxen, and pasture for 500 sheep.[76] The sheep pasture may have been several; there was presumably also common pasture as the demesne flock usually numbered over 1,000 during the 14th century and the early 15th.[77] In the late 13th century and the early 14th most of the corn produced on the demesne was sold,[78] and in 1280 sheep, poultry, and other produce were sent to London, presumably to market.[79] Services of carrying corn, wool, and cheese for distances up to 20 leagues

were required of customary tenants in the 14th century.[80] In 1311 there were 21 yardlanders and 8 ½-yardlanders, owing services valued at £5 6s. 1d.[81] The yardlanders' services included ploughing in winter a strip for each beast, ploughteam, and yardland they held and in spring a strip for each beast and yardland. Each yardlander owed seven boonworks of reaping and services of hoeing and shearing. Half-yardlanders were to plough three strips and owed services of washing and shearing sheep. Hay in the lord's meadows in Wanborough was cut by tenants of Wanborough manor but carried by those of Aldbourne.[82] The area of demesne arable was assessed at no more than 200 a. in 1347.[83] In the late 14th century there were 38 yardlanders and 11 ½-yardlanders. Many held 'sonderland', probably newly cultivated land, in addition to that in the open fields.[84] Most labour services had been commuted, probably by the late 14th century and certainly by the 15th, although some, including those required of Wanborough tenants, were referred to in the 16th century.[85] Demesne lands of Aldbourne manor in Upham and Snap, comprising 4–5 yardlands and pasture for 100 sheep, and the services of seven customary tenants, presumably with holdings in Upham and Snap, were at farm c. 1215.[86] Those lands and other demesne lands were leased in the 15th century. In 1426 most of the arable in Aldbourne was leased to a single tenant and others held small parcels of arable and pasture.[87] Pickwood was held by tenants in 1436 and perhaps earlier as a several farm.[88] The demesne flock remained in hand until c. 1450,[89] and in the early 15th century the purchase and sale of sheep and wool on the duchy of Lancaster's estates, including Aldbourne, was organized centrally. There were few exchanges of stock between the estates but wool from Collingbourne Ducis and Everleigh was sometimes collected at Aldbourne where the flock was kept mainly for wool.[90]

Other medieval estates included the rectory estate, consisting of land and tithes, and Upper Upham manor, which were valued at £20 and £1 10s. respectively in 1291.[91] In 1476 Upper Upham was at farm.[92]

In the mid 16th century Court farm, the demesne farm of Aldbourne manor, was worked from Court House and included 209 a. of arable in North and West fields. There were 70 a. of several pasture called East Leaze, another several pasture in Leaze Park or Old Park, and others called Middle ridge, Nether ridge, and Summer leaze. There was common pasture for 600 sheep.[93] In 1509 c. 1,700 a. of arable were held by 44

[65] V.C.H. Wilts. ii, pp. 43, 117.
[66] Above, manors.
[67] Rot. Chart. (Rec. Com.), 170.
[68] P.R.O., DL 42/115, ff. 30–1; W.R.O., inclosure award.
[69] P.R.O., MR 13 (DL 31/99); see plate facing p. 81; below.
[70] P.R.O., DL 3/63, no. A 1; ibid. E 36/157, p. 80.
[71] Ibid. DL 42/108, f. 81v.   [72] Ibid. DL 44/47.
[73] Ibid. DL 36/1/8.   [74] Ibid. MPC 5.
[75] Ibid. DL 4/41, no. 37; ibid. MPC 263; W.R.O., inclosure award.
[76] Wilts. Inq. p.m. 1242–1326 (Index Libr.), 382–3.
[77] P.R.O., DL 29/682/11058; DL 29/728/11981.
[78] Ibid. DL 29/1/1–3.
[79] Ibid. DL 28/32/11.
[80] Ibid. DL 29/682/11058; W.R.O. 212A/27/3.

[81] Wilts. Inq. p.m. 1242–1326 (Index Libr.), 382–3.
[82] P.R.O., DL 29/682/11058; W.R.O. 212A/27/3.
[83] Wilts. Inq. p.m. 1327–77 (Index Libr.), 181.
[84] W.R.O. 212A/27/3.
[85] P.R.O., DL 5/28, f. 171v.; DL 29/682/11058.
[86] Ibid. DL 36/1/8.
[87] Ibid. DL 29/682/11058.
[88] Ibid. DL 29/683/11069; ibid. E 326/8248.
[89] Ibid. DL 29/684/11078; DL 29/684/11089.
[90] Ibid. DL 29/683/11068–9; R. C. Payne, 'Agrarian conditions on the Wilts. estates of the duchy of Lanc. etc.' (Lond. Univ. Ph.D. thesis, 1940), 171–4, 211.
[91] Tax. Eccl. (Rec. Com.), 189, 192.
[92] P.R.O., WARD 2/28/94c/9.
[93] Ibid. DL 42/108, f. 81.

copyholders; no copyholder held more than 5 yardlands, c. 120 a.[94] The area of copyhold arable had fallen to c. 1,000 a. by the early 17th century,[95] probably because copyholds were taken in hand and leased. There were 18 copyhold yardlands in Upham and Snap in 1509 but only 6 in 1553.[96] In the early 17th century lessees held Court farm, 867 a., the demesne lands of Aldbourne manor in Upham and Snap which comprised 276 a. and were known as Heydon farm, a farm of 140 a. probably in Upham and Snap, and Pickwood farm, 206 a.[97] Walrond's farm measured 183 a. c. 1610; its lands presumably lay in the open fields of Aldbourne. A farm of 248 a., of which 70 a. lay in small inclosures, was probably Upper Upham. Another farm, of 1 yardland and 60 a. in Snap, may have included land formerly demesne of Upper Upham manor.[98] The lands of the rectory estate, c. 80 a. mainly in the Aldbourne fields, were leased.[99]

The lord of Aldbourne manor had a park and rights of free chase and warren at Aldbourne in 1307;[1] in 1311 the park was said to be worthless.[2] The park, which was near Snap, contained a herd of fallow deer until the early 16th century when the fences were destroyed and the deer allowed into better woodland.[3] Leaze Park or Old Park thereafter provided demesne pasture. In 1659 there were hunting rights over 1,400 a. of woodland and pasture, extending from the southern boundary to Snap and from Priors Wood to Southward Down. The open fields and perhaps other arable lands were exempt from the rights of chase. It was said that the deer herd, destroyed during the Civil War, had numbered 400,[4] but in the late 16th century there were 120–200 deer.[5] No lease of the chase is known. The title of forester, keeper, or ranger passed with Walrond's farm[6] but other keepers and officers were also appointed. The distinction between the offices is not clear. In 1463 Sir George Darell was appointed master of the hunt of Aldbourne Chase, receiving yearly a buck and a doe and other unspecified profits.[7] His son Sir Edward Darell was appointed master in 1499.[8] In 1545 Sir William Herbert (created earl of Pembroke in 1551) was appointed lieutenant of the forests and chases of Aldbourne and Everleigh.[9] The rights of chase apparently lapsed in the late 17th century, and in 1689 the keepership was replaced by an allotment of land.[10]

Woods within the chase yielded a considerable income in the 15th century; timber and underwood were sold for £17 8s. 10d. in 1425–6.[11] In the 16th and 17th centuries a woodward, who had rights to underwood, brushwood, and the cutting of stakes, was appointed.[12] In the early 16th century there were 239 a. of coppices and 585 a. of 'shere' woods, perhaps strips of woodland, in the chase.[13] Unlicensed cutting of timber and damage by deer, rabbits, and cattle were blamed for the decline of the woods, but sufficient timber, mainly oak and ash, was cut to send some to Everleigh and Marlborough in the 1580s.[14] No later reference to the 'shere' woods has been found and early 17th-century surveys of the chase mention c. 200 a. of woodland, chiefly coppices. The woods were then leased in two portions.[15] One, including Hillwood, Snap, Park, and Upper Witchell coppices, was held in 1668 by the keeper of the chase in the right of his office.[16] When the keeper's rights were replaced in 1689 those coppices were allotted to the freeholders and tenants of Aldbourne manor to be held in common.[17] By the late 18th century most woods of the chase had been felled and common pasture rights had apparently replaced those in the woods.[18]

In the later Middle Ages the lord of Aldbourne manor had free warren over the whole parish except Upper Upham manor and certain lands mostly in the northern part. In the mid 15th century his right of warren was divided into three parts. The two larger included rights over lands divided by the road from Aldbourne to Upper Upham, the third comprised rights over Southwood and Pickwood.[19] Within those divisions lay the three 'walks' into which the warren itself had been divided by the 17th century, Dudmore walk west of the village, North walk north of it, and Southwood walk south of it.[20] In the 16th century Upper Upham manor also included rights of warren.[21] Between 1390 and 1430 the sale of rabbits from Aldbourne warren produced approximately £40 a year, sometimes half the profit from the demesne of Aldbourne manor, of which it was part.[22] Between Michaelmas and Lent 1357–8, however, rabbits valued at only £5 were caught[23] and in 1435–6, after two hard winters had almost destroyed the warren, none was taken.[24] In the 14th century rabbits were sold to a London poulterer or supplied to the lord's household. In 1372 the warrener was ordered to send six dozen rabbits to the palace of the Savoy

94 P.R.O., DL 42/108, f. 84; DL 43/9/24.
95 Ibid. E 36/157, pp. 69–71.
96 Ibid. DL 42/108, ff. 75v.–80; DL 43/9/24.
97 Ibid. E 36/157, p. 71.
98 Ibid. pp. 74–8.
99 D. & C. Winton. Mun., Chase's bk., f. 97; act bk. 1622–45, f. 48v.
1 Cal. Pat. 1301–7, 544.
2 Wilts. Inq. p.m. 1242–1326 (Index Libr.), 382–3.
3 P.R.O., DL 1/3, no. E 2.
4 Ibid. E 317/Wilts. 19.
5 Ibid. DL 42/115, f. 30v.; ibid. SC 12/25/14.
6 Above, manors.
7 Cal. Pat. 1461–7, 274.
8 R. Somerville, Duchy of Lanc. i. 633; above, Ramsbury, manors.
9 L. & P. Hen. VIII, xx (2), p. 182; Complete Peerage, x. 406–7.
10 Above, manors; W.R.O. 1883/102.

11 P.R.O., DL 29/682/11058; Payne, 'Agrarian conditions', 323.
12 P.R.O., DL 3/20, no. B 8; DL 5/22, pp. 917–21; DL 44/47.
13 Ibid. SC 12/1/3.
14 Ibid. DL 1/187, no. A 49; DL 3/63, no. A 1; DL 42/115, f. 30; ibid. SC 12/25/14.
15 Ibid. DL 43/9/24; ibid. E 36/157, pp. 75, 78.
16 Ibid. DL 4/111, no. 30.   17 W.R.O. 1883/288.
18 Ibid. inclosure award; Andrews and Dury, Map (W.R.S. viii), pl. 15.
19 P.R.O., DL 29/684/11078; DL 29/685/11089; DL 29/686/11133.
20 Ibid. DL 4/53, no. 64; DL 5/124, f. 241; ibid. STAC 8/302/25.
21 Ibid. E 318/Box 11/488.
22 Payne, 'Agrarian conditions', 328.
23 Wilts. Inq. p.m. 1327–77 (Index Libr.), 181.
24 P.R.O., DL 29/683/11069.

and fifteen dozen to Hertford Castle during Christmas.[25] Rights of warren were leased in the early 15th century,[26] and in the mid 15th century the three portions of rights of warren were held by different tenants.[27] They were again leased to a single tenant c. 1470.[28]

In 1378 the abbess of Lacock had the right to four dozen rabbits from Aldbourne warren in compensation for damage done to her lands adjoining it.[29] In the 16th and 17th centuries there were frequent complaints about the increasing numbers of rabbits, and lessees of the warren were sued for damage to crops and woods.[30] Burrows in West field were destroyed before 1609, although rabbits were allowed on fallow fields adjoining the warren.[31] In 1659 the keeper stopped up burrows within the chase, while allowing rabbits to graze there.[32] In the mid and late 16th century keepers of the chase and warreners of Aldbourne frequently engaged in litigation with the tenants of the demesne of Ogbourne St. George manor who claimed rights of free warren and chase in Priors Wood.[33] In 1622 Henry Martin claimed free warren in Hay Leaze in Upham, adjoining the warren. He was accused in return of enticing rabbits from the warren to new burrows, so reducing the number sent by the warrener to the London markets.[34]

In 1652 Philip, earl of Pembroke and Montgomery, who held the right of warren, and the tenants of Aldbourne manor agreed that Dudmore and Southwood walks should be diswarrened. The earl was compensated with a several holding of 571 a. and parts of the warren were ploughed soon afterwards. By 1657 the agreement had broken down; the earl again claimed rights of warren and the resulting litigation continued until 1671 or later.[35] The diswarrening of Southwood walk may have taken effect; no further reference to the walk has been found. Another agreement to diswarren Dudmore walk was made in 1689. Lands which were part of the walk were divided between the earl and the tenants and freeholders of Aldbourne. A several holding of 180 a., and 80 a. in the open fields, were also allotted to the earl in place of the right of warren and the keepership of the chase.[36] North walk remained a warren. In the late 17th century John Aubrey described rabbits from Aldbourne as the best, sweetest, and fattest in England,[37] and in the 1720s they were prized for both their flesh and their fur. There was then a stock of 8,000 rabbits, increasing annually to 24,000. They grazed on the poor grass of the downs in summer, and in winter were fed on hay and hazel cuttings.[38]

By the early 19th century approximately half the parish had been inclosed, including land diswarrened in 1689, much of Upper Upham, and Lower Upham, Leigh, and Snap farms. New farmsteads were established on the downs, from which several holdings were worked.[39] Before 1700 Pickwood and Heydon farms had been divided. Heydon became the later Lower Upham, Leigh, and Snap farms.[40] The meadow and pasture lands of Pickwood became Stock Close farm, part of which was ploughed in the late 17th century. The arable was worked as Pickwood Laines farm.[41] By 1773 each of them had a farmstead. By the late 18th century also the demesne of Aldbourne manor had been divided into two farms, that worked from Aldbourne Farm, beside Southward Lane, which perhaps included most of the arable in the open fields, and land, probably several, worked from East Leaze Farm. The diswarrened lands were then parts of Warren farm and Dudmore Lodge farm, worked from farmsteads north-west and west of the village.[42]

Most of the many small farms which survived in the 18th century were probably worked from the village and had arable in the open fields and common pasture on the downs.[43] In 1724 the common pastures were judged inadequate for the stock entitled to graze there, and c. 60 parishioners agreed to reduce their feeding rights by a third for the next four years.[44] The shortage may have resulted in part from the state of the summer cattle pasture in the south part of the parish, previously within the chase, which was said c. 1800 to be much overgrown.[45] Copyholds of Aldbourne manor, sold in the 1690s and 1700s, were amalgamated into farms of c. 100 a. of arable in the 18th century. Cor's farm, which comprised 71 a. with common for 160 sheep in 1739, and North farm, c. 120 a. in 1770, were so formed.[46] The origin of Hillwood farm, 179 a. with common for 360 sheep in 1798, was perhaps similar.[47] Other copyholds may have become leasehold, although c. 220 a. remained copyhold in the late 19th century.[48] Copyholds of the rectory manor were apparently taken in hand in the late 18th century or the early 19th.[49]

In 1809 the open fields and downs, 3,933 a., were inclosed. That area included c. 2,200 a. of open fields, 800 a. in the North walk of the warren, and 1,000 a. of common pasture on Southward Down and within the former chase.

[25] *John of Gaunt's Reg.* i (Camd. 3rd ser. xx), pp. 113–14; ii (Camd. 3rd ser. xxi), p. 109.
[26] P.R.O., DL 29/682/11058.
[27] Ibid. DL 29/684/11078; DL 29/685/11089; DL 29/686/11133.
[28] Ibid. DL 29/688/11156.
[29] *Lacock Chart.* (W.R.S. xxxiv), p. 78.
[30] P.R.O., DL 5/22, pp. 917–21; DL 42/108, f. 83; ibid. E 36/157, p. 78.
[31] Ibid. DL 4/54, no. 51.
[32] Ibid. E 317/Wilts. 19.
[33] Ibid. DL 1/36, no. W 5.
[34] Ibid. STAC 8/212/6.
[35] *Cal. S.P. Dom.* 1660–85, 279–81; Hist. MSS. Com. 5, *8th Rep., H.L.* pp. 162–3.
[36] W.R.O. 1883/288.

[37] Aubrey, *Nat. Hist. Wilts.* ed. Britton, 59.
[38] Gandy, *Heart of a Village*, 27–8.
[39] W.R.O., tithe award.
[40] Ibid. 130/46/13; Public Libr., Swindon, Goddard MS. 722; *W.A.M.* xlii. 583.
[41] P.R.O., E 134/28 Chas. II East./13.
[42] W.R.O., land tax; *Andrews and Dury, Map* (W.R.S. viii), pl. 15.
[43] W.R.O., land tax; inclosure award.
[44] Ibid. 526/21.
[45] Gandy, *Heart of a Village*, 26; *W.A.M.* xxiii. 260.
[46] W.R.O. 212A/6/11; 212A/36/36–8; 700/84.
[47] Ibid. 212A/36/37.
[48] Reading Univ. Libr., hist. farm rec., WIL 11/3/2.
[49] W.R.O., inclosure award; tithe award; D. & C. Winton. Mun., box 104, ct. rolls, 1740, 1755–60.

Most allotments were small.[50] In 1837 there were eighteen farms of over 100 a. in the parish. Five were over 500 a.: Warren, 790 a., Dudmore Lodge, 637 a., Lower Upham, 627 a., Upper Upham, 577 a., and North, 515 a., were compact farms on each of which more than half the land was arable. Aldbourne farm, 480 a., East Leaze, 410 a., and Snap, 412 a., were also principally arable, and on most remaining farms, including Stock Close, 354 a., Hillwood, 346 a., Laines, 184 a., and Leigh, 120 a., there was very little pasture. The exception was the vicar's glebe, 421 a., of which 321 a. were pasture in the former chase. The only extensive meadow land was that near Snap and surrounding Upper Upham House, 90 a., parts of Snap and Upper Upham farms.[51]

By 1851 the acreage of most of the larger farms had increased, probably by the absorption of holdings of less than 100 a. Approximately a third of the lands of the parish were then in hand, rather more than in 1837. Most of the farms worked by their owners were of medium size but Dudmore Lodge farm was also in hand in 1837 and 1851.[52] In 1830 protesters, mainly from Ramsbury, smashed newly introduced threshing machines in Aldbourne.[53] In 1878 an early steam plough was in use in the parish but there is no evidence that its introduction led, as has been suggested, to the extension of arable lands.[54] The absorption of lands into larger holdings continued in the late 19th century and the 20th; in the late 20th century there were few small farms in the parish. Land from Aldbourne farm, 362 a. in 1904, was later merged with other farms, although some was still worked from Southward, formerly Aldbourne, Farm in 1982.[55] The rectory estate, 117 a. in 1885, and vicarial glebe, 362 a. in 1919, were apparently also absorbed into other farms.[56] Much of Laines farm, c. 200 a. in 1904, became part of Chase Woods farm after 1959.[57] After 1905 Snap, Leigh, Hillwood, and Stock Lane farms, totalling c. 900 a. in the south and west parts of the parish, were laid to grass and used as sheep runs by Henry Wilson, a butcher and sheep dealer.[58] In 1982 the combined farm, c. 1,000 a., was a mixed farm, including a stud farm at Hillwood.[59] Manor farm, also created by the amalgamation of smaller farms, was 535 a. in 1915; it included 472 a. of arable and had a flock of 500 sheep.[60] By 1982 it had grown to a farm of 950 a., on which sheep and store cattle were kept

and cereals produced.[61] Warren farm remained a mixed arable and livestock farm of c. 800 a. in the 20th century. In 1982 sheep and poultry were kept and there were c. 400 a. of arable.[62] Dudmore Lodge was a farm of c. 600 a. until after 1927; in 1982 it was a chiefly arable farm of c. 300 a.[63] Lower Upham farm, which had changed little in size since the mid 19th century, was an arable and beef farm in the late 20th.[64] Upper Upham farm, 654 a., East Leaze farm, 422 a., and North farm, 534 a., were then worked together. Much of the land was arable but beef cattle were also kept and there was a dairy at North Farm.[65] The lands of Stock Close were worked with land at Axford in Ramsbury as a sheep and corn farm.[66] On Cowcroft, later Chase Woods, farm, of which c. 200 a. lay in Aldbourne, a Merino flock was kept after 1928, and later a private airfield was built; both ventures were unsuccessful. Sheep were again kept in the 1950s but in 1982 the farm, c. 300 a., was principally arable.[67] Land in the south-east corner of the parish was then worked from Hilldrop Farm in Ramsbury and as part of the Crowood estate in Ramsbury.[68]

In 1086 there was woodland measuring 2 leagues by ½ league at Aldbourne.[69] In the Middle Ages much of the woodland lay within the chase, but Priors Wood may also have been of medieval origin. That wood, known from the 19th century as Chase Woods, was usually leased to the tenant of the demesne farm of Ogbourne St. George manor.[70] Its area declined from c. 180 a. in 1751[71] to c. 100 a. in 1858.[72] Some 60 a. of woodland were cleared in the 1970s, and in 1982 Chase Woods, surrounding Chase Woods Farm, and Wildings Copse, 400 m. south-east of the farmstead, amounted to 40 a., mostly in Aldbourne parish.[73] Love's Copse, in the south-east corner of the parish, included c. 50 a. in Aldbourne in the 16th century and the late 20th.[74]

There were racing stables at the Old Rectory, probably in the early 20th century,[75] and at Lottage in 1910, when they were let to a Capt. Barnett.[76] Gallops, probably on Sugar Hill, were let to James White of Foxhill in Wanborough in 1919.[77] There was a racing stable at Hightown before 1921, when the buildings were burned down. In 1924 they were rebuilt and about that time the stable was bought by J. B. Powell, under whom it became very successful. The stable was closed in the 1970s.[78]

[50] W.R.O., inclosure award. Slightly different figures are given by J. R. Ellis, 'Parl. Enclosure of Aldbourne', W.A.M. lxviii. 98.
[51] W.R.O., tithe award.
[52] Ibid.; P.R.O., HO 107/1686.
[53] Gandy, Heart of a Village, 77.
[54] V.C.H. Wilts. iv. 97.
[55] Reading Univ. Libr., hist. farm rec., WIL 11/3/18; local inf.
[56] Reading Univ. Libr., hist. farm rec., WIL 11/3/4; W.A.S. Libr., sale cat. xxi, no. 1; above, manors.
[57] Reading Univ. Libr., hist. farm rec., WIL 11/3/18; above, manors.
[58] Reading Univ. Libr., hist. farm rec., WIL 11/3/12-13; W.A.S. Libr., sale cat. xxviiiG, no. 32; W.A.M. lvii. 389-90.
[59] Inf. from Mr. G. W. Wilson, Rudge Manor Farm, Froxfield; local inf.
[60] Reading Univ. Libr., hist. farm rec., WIL 11/7/1.
[61] Inf. from Mr. W. A. Brown, Manor Ho.
[62] Reading Univ. Libr., hist. farm rec., WIL 11/4/24; inf.

from Mr. H. V. Bland, the Warren.
[63] Inf. from Miss E. Gentry, Dudmore Lodge Farm.
[64] Inf. from Mr. R. Brinkworth, Lower Upham Farm.
[65] Inf. from Mr. R. N. Lawton, North Farm.
[66] Inf. from Maj. F. R. D. Burdett-Fisher, Harbrook Farm, Ramsbury.
[67] Inf. from Mr. J. D. Owen, Chase Woods Farm.
[68] Above, Ramsbury, econ. hist.
[69] V.C.H. Wilts. ii, p. 117.
[70] P.R.O., DL 44/47; King's Coll., Camb., Mun., survey, 1816; below, Ogbourne St. Geo., econ. hist.
[71] King's Coll., Camb., Mun., survey, 1751.
[72] W.A.S. Libr., sale cat. xxxii, no. 39.
[73] Inf. from Mr. Owen.
[74] P.R.O., DL 42/108, f. 73; ibid. E 36/157, p. 74; O.S. Map 6", SU 27 SE. (1960 edn.).
[75] Gandy, Heart of a Village, 53.
[76] Reading Univ. Libr., hist. farm rec., WIL 11/3/22.
[77] Ibid. WIL 11/4/24.
[78] Gandy, Heart of a Village, 53.

ALDBOURNE: THE CHURCH OF ST. MICHAEL

BAYDON: THE CHURCH OF ST. NICHOLAS

ALDBOURNE

Ewins Hill and land in the south part of the parish *c.* 1608

MILLS. There were four mills, valued together at 16s. 8d., on the royal estate of Aldbourne in 1086.[79] A mill valued at 33s. 4d. in 1295[80] was perhaps the windmill which was part of Aldbourne manor in 1311 and 1347.[81] Its site may have been south of Aldbourne village, where there was a Windmill field.[82] By the early 15th century the windmill had been destroyed but there was a water mill.[83] That mill was burned down in 1472.[84] A new one had been built by 1509 but has not been traced after 1553.[85] A windmill, built beside Baydon Street before 1851,[86] was still working in 1880,[87] but was demolished in 1900.[88]

MARKETS AND FAIRS. A Thursday market was worth £1 6s. 8d. a year to the lord of Aldbourne manor in 1311.[89] The market tolls were leased in the late 14th century,[90] and in the early 17th century they were received by a bailiff as lessee.[91] Markets were held on Tuesdays in the mid 16th century but none was held for 10 years or more after 1571[92] and the market was characterized as poor in the early 17th century.[93] It revived in the late 17th century in response to the growth of the fustian trade but was discontinued after the fire of 1760.[94]

In 1581 fairs were said to be held annually on St. Edward's day, 18 March, and St. Mary Magdalene's day, 22 July.[95] In the early 17th century there were said to be three fairs a year.[96] They had apparently been discontinued by the mid 18th century.[97]

INDUSTRIES. The weaving of fustian, a heavy mixture of cotton and linen, probably started in Aldbourne in the later 17th century,[98] although a weaver was recorded in the parish in 1633.[99] Employers who may have been fustian makers issued trade tokens in the 1650s[1] and Edward Witts, perhaps a Dutchman, made fustian in Aldbourne in 1666.[2] Several other families were fustian makers in the late 17th century and in the early 18th,[3] when a factory was built in South Street.[4] Materials and finished goods were sent from and to London;[5] in 1709 the inhabitants of Aldbourne supported a proposal to make the Kennet navigable between Reading and New-

bury, because it would ease the carriage of goods for the industry.[6] In the fire of 1760 warehouses and looms were destroyed,[7] a waggon loaded with candlewick was lost in 1777,[8] and a weaver's shop was burned down in 1817.[9] Edward Read, a fustian weaver and dealer, was declared bankrupt in 1762.[10] The industry continued to flourish until the 1790s or later: the number of manufacturers fell from seven c. 1791[11] to five in 1809[12] and one in 1830.[13] Only four fustian weavers lived in Aldbourne in 1851,[14] and only two in 1881.[15]

Although silk was said to have been produced in Aldbourne during the 18th century,[16] no record of silk weaving has been found. There was a woollen weaver in the parish in 1711.[17]

The brothers William and Robert Cor established a bell foundry in the grounds of Court House, probably in 1694. By 1724 the foundry had produced 88 bells.[18] Complicated family settlements and perhaps declining trade forced the sale of the foundry c. 1741 to John Stares,[19] who was succeeded in 1757 by Edward Read. The foundry probably closed when Read was declared bankrupt in 1762.[20] Members of the Cor family may have continued as bell founders,[21] and in 1760 Robert Wells, a relative of the family by marriage, opened a new foundry at Bell Court, a house at the south-west corner of the Green.[22] He produced both church and small bells and mill brasses.[23] Between 1781 and 1825 Wells's sons Robert and James made 200 church bells but in 1825 James was declared bankrupt. The foundry was bought and closed by Thomas Mears who transferred some of the workers to his foundry at Whitechapel (Mdx.).[24] One of them, James Bridgeman, returned to Aldbourne in 1829 to start a new foundry at High Town, perhaps at the house later called Hightown. It was working in 1851 but was probably closed after Bridgeman's death in 1858.[25] Most of the bell founders also engaged in other trades. The Cors made wooden buttons, Edward Read and Robert Wells (d. 1799) were fustian makers, and James Wells was a corn dealer.[26]

Straw plaiting was said to have been introduced to Aldbourne in the 1790s by the society for the betterment of the poor.[27] The plaited

[79] V.C.H. Wilts. ii, p. 117.
[80] P.R.O., DL 29/1/1.
[81] Wilts. Inq. p.m. 1242–1326 (Index Libr.), 382–3; 1327–77 (Index Libr.), 181.
[82] P.R.O., DL 42/115, ff. 30–1; above.
[83] Ibid. DL 29/682/11058.
[84] Ibid. DL 29/689/11171.
[85] Ibid. DL 42/108, f. 79v.; DL 43/9/24.
[86] Ibid. HO 107/1686.
[87] Kelly's Dir. Wilts.
[88] M. Watts, Wilts. Windmills (Wilts. Libr. and Mus. Service, 1980), 16–17.
[89] Wilts. Inq. p.m. 1242–1326 (Index Libr.), 382–3.
[90] P.R.O., DL 29/728/11981.
[91] Ibid. E 36/157, p. 82.
[92] Ibid. DL 42/115, f. 30v.
[93] Ibid. E 36/157, p. 82.
[94] Below; Univ. Brit. Dir. ii (1793), 73.
[95] P.R.O., DL 42/115, f. 30v.
[96] Ibid. E 36/157, p. 82.
[97] Kelly's Dir. Wilts. (1848).
[98] V.C.H. Wilts. iv. 179.
[99] P.R.O., DL 4/81, no. 11.
[1] W.A.M. vi. 79.
[2] V.C.H. Wilts. iv. 179.

[3] W.R.O. 212A/6/1; 212A/6/7–8; 212A/15.
[4] Gandy, Heart of a Village, 38.
[5] V.C.H. Wilts. iv. 179.
[6] C.J. xvi. 68.
[7] W.N. & Q. ii. 117.
[8] Wilts. Cuttings, xxvi. 40.
[9] Pigot, Nat. Com. Dir. (1830), 809½.
[10] W.R.O. 212A/36/38.
[11] Univ. Brit. Dir. ii (1793), 73.
[12] W.R.O., inclosure award.
[13] Pigot, Nat. Com. Dir. (1830), 809½.
[14] P.R.O., HO 107/1686.
[15] V.C.H. Wilts. iv. 180.
[16] Ibid. 176 n.
[17] W.R.O. 212A/6/13.
[18] V.C.H. Wilts. iv. 253.
[19] Ibid.; W.R.O. 212A/36/36.
[20] W.R.O. 212A/36/38.   [21] W.A.M. ii. 50.
[22] V.C.H. Wilts. iv. 253; W.N. & Q. ii. 450.
[23] W.A.M. ii. 48 n.
[24] V.C.H. Wilts. iv. 253; W.A.M. xlviii. 437.
[25] Crane, Aldbourne Chron. 35–6.
[26] V.C.H. Wilts. iv. 253; W.R.O. 212A/36/38.
[27] Gandy, Heart of a Village, 44; Crane, Aldbourne Chron. 17.

material, known locally as 'tuscin', was supplied to milliners.[28] A straw-hat maker working in Aldbourne in 1830[29] was probably William Pizzie, described in 1842 as a willow-bonnet manufacturer.[30] Hatmaking ended soon afterwards but the weaving of willow squares for millinery flourished until the 1880s. In 1851 Pizzie and five others employed c. 140 workers, mostly women and children, in willow weaving.[31] The industry was said in 1864 to be expanding[32] but in each of the years 1867, 1875, and 1880 there were four willow square manufacturers in the village. By 1903 willow weaving had ceased but there were two willow cutters.[33]

In 1851 two chairmakers lived in Castle Street.[34] Thomas Orchard began making chairs c. 1855,[35] and in 1887 opened a factory in South Street. In the late 19th century he had 40 employees. Local ash, birch, and beech were used to produce about a hundred chairs a week c. 1915. There were only twelve workers in the factory in 1921, and by 1927 it had been closed.[36] Some furniture was produced in the village in 1982.[37]

Malthouses and brewhouses were destroyed in the fire of 1760,[38] another malthouse in that of 1777,[39] and two more in 1817.[40] There was a maltster in Aldbourne until c. 1900, probably working in South Street.[41] An iron foundry and agricultural engineering business, begun by W. T. Loveday in 1911 or earlier, was known from 1939 as the Aldbourne Engineering Co.[42] In 1949 an egg packing factory was built north of Stock Lane for Wiltshire Poultry Farmers Ltd.,[43] later Thames Valley & Wiltshire Poultry Producers. The building was extended in 1960.[44]

LOCAL GOVERNMENT. Before 1257 the bailiff, freemen, and tithingmen of Aldbourne, accompanied by four others 'to strengthen the court', attended the hundred court. In or after 1257 their suit was withdrawn, although it was said to be still owed in 1275.[45] In 1289 Henry de Lacy, earl of Lincoln, claimed the right to hold a view of frankpledge and other liberties in Aldbourne.[46] Later the parish was a single tithing and there is no evidence that it was divided, other than for manorial administration, in spite of its size and large population. Courts leet and views of frankpledge for Aldbourne manor were held twice a year in the 15th century.[47] The earliest surviving court records are of the mid 18th

century, when a court baron and a view were held each autumn. A tithingman, two constables, and breadweighers and aletasters were elected at the view and presentments concerning repairs to roads and buildings were made by a jury. The court baron, at which the homage presented, regulated the use of open fields and pastures and dealt with tenurial matters. Courts and views were held until 1903.[48]

The suit owed by the abbess of Lacock's men of Upper Upham to the hundred court was withdrawn c. 1260 but it is not clear whether they attended the Aldbourne view.[49] Courts were apparently held for Upper Upham manor in the late 18th century.[50] Infringements of rights of chase were tried at a court of vert and venison at Aldbourne c. 1375[51] but no later chase court is known. Records of a court baron held for the rectory manor between 1740 and 1760 relate only to tenurial matters.[52]

Poor relief in Aldbourne was applied by three overseers. Under an Act of 1800 a building near the junction of Oxford Street and South Street was used as a workhouse and a fourth overseer was appointed. The workhouse was burned down c. 1819.[53] Poor rates in Aldbourne were high compared with those in neighbouring parishes in 1803.[54] The amount spent on poor relief fell from £1,658 in 1812–13 to £810 in 1814–15. The number of adults receiving permanent relief fell from 174 to 105, apparently excluding those in the workhouse.[55] Expenditure on the poor fluctuated thereafter;[56] in the early 1830s the average annual sum was £1,172. In 1835 Aldbourne became part of Hungerford poor-law union.[57]

CHURCH. There was a church belonging to Aldbourne manor in 1086.[58] It was given by Rotrou, count of Perche (d. 1191), to the priory of Nogent-le-Rotrou and in 1228 a vicarage was ordained.[59] In 1260 the advowson of the vicarage was claimed both by the priory and by Queen Eleanor, wife of Henry III, in the right of her ward Margaret Longespée, lord of Aldbourne manor. Judgement was given in the priory's favour[60] but the Longespée claim persisted. In 1296 Margaret and her husband Henry, earl of Lincoln, granted the advowson to Amesbury priory, then or a little later holder of the impropriate rectory by grant from Nogent-le-Rotrou priory.[61] From 1302, however, the bishop of Salisbury collated the

[28] W.A.M. xliv. 287.
[29] Pigot, Nat. Com. Dir. (1830), 809½.
[30] Gandy, Heart of a Village, 45.
[31] P.R.O., HO 107/1686.
[32] W.R.O., bishop, vis. queries.
[33] Kelly's Dir. Wilts.
[34] P.R.O., HO 107/1686.
[35] Gandy, Heart of a Village, 49.
[36] W.A.M. xliv. 288; Crane, Aldbourne Chron. 38.
[37] Local inf.
[38] Wilts. Cuttings, i. 106.
[39] Ibid. iii. 17–18.   [40] Ibid. xi. 152.
[41] Kelly's Dir. Wilts. (1848 and later edns.); Reading Univ. Libr., hist. farm rec., WIL 11/3/21.
[42] Kelly's Dir. Wilts. (1911 and later edns.).
[43] Wilts. Cuttings, xxii. 92.
[44] W.A.M. lviii. 48.
[45] Rot. Hund. (Rec. Com.), ii (1), 270.
[46] P.R.O., JUST 1/1011, rot. 47d.

[47] Ibid. DL 29/682/11058; DL 29/684/11078; DL 29/689/11171.
[48] Ct. bks. 1732–1903, penes Mr. W. A. Brown, Manor Ho.
[49] Rot. Hund. (Rec. Com.), ii (1), 270.
[50] W.R.O. 105/7.
[51] John of Gaunt's Reg. i (Camd. 3rd ser. xx), p. 287.
[52] D. & C. Winton. Mun., box 104, ct. rolls, 1740, 1755–60.
[53] 39 & 40 Geo. III, c. 48 (Local and Personal); Crane, Aldbourne Chron. 17.
[54] King's Coll., Camb., Mun., survey; Poor Law Abstract, 1804, 569.
[55] Poor Law Abstract, 1818, 500–1.
[56] Poor Rate Returns, 1816–21, 189.
[57] Poor Law Com. 1st Rep. 242.
[58] V.C.H. Wilts. ii, p. 117.
[59] P.R.O., DL 25/3394; above, manors.
[60] P.R.O., DL 25/3387.
[61] Feet of F. 1272–1327 (W.R.S. i), p. 42 and n.

vicars.[62] Aldbourne was held in plurality with Baydon vicarage from 1957[63] and in 1965 the benefices were united.[64] In 1973 Aldbourne and Baydon benefice was combined with Ramsbury vicarage and a team ministry was established: a vicar lived at Aldbourne.[65]

In 1291 the vicar received £8 13s. 4d., rather less than most incumbents in Marlborough deanery,[66] but in the 15th century and the early 16th his yearly income, c. £25 including £2 a year from Amesbury priory, was probably higher than most.[67] After the Dissolution the pension was paid by the dean and chapter of Winchester.[68] In the early 1830s the vicar's net annual income was £367, about average for Salisbury diocese.[69]

In 1609 all tithes from the rectorial glebe and Pickwood farm, and wool and lamb tithes, tithes of underwood, and lesser tithes from the rest of the parish, were due to the vicar.[70] By the 1670s tithes of rabbits from the North walk of the warren and of herbage from part of Stock Close farm had been commuted to payments of £3 and £4 a year respectively.[71] In the late 17th century the dean and chapter of Winchester, owners of the rectory estate, granted to the vicar a third of the hay and corn tithes from land called Sandridge to compensate for vicarial tithes lost at its inclosure.[72] In 1809 the vicar's tithes on c. 3,950 a. were replaced by allotments of land. He remained entitled to tithes from 2,172 a., which were valued at £210 15s. in 1837 and commuted.[73]

The vicar's glebe was 1 yardland in 1412.[74] A vicar, John Stone (will proved 1524), gave a garden and a small area of land to be held by his successors.[75] In 1609 the glebe was 24 a. with pasture rights for 60 sheep.[76] The land and rights and some tithes were replaced by an allotment of 421 a. in 1809.[77] Of that land 362 a. were sold in 1919 and 54 a. in 1920.[78] There was no house on the glebe in 1412; it was then estimated that necessary repairs and building a house would cost £40.[79] The vicar had a two-storeyed house in the late 16th century,[80] and in the 18th century a three-storeyed house built of rough cast and timber on the north side of West Street was given as a vicarage house.[81] The vicar was allotted Court House by exchange in 1809.[82] It was used as the vicarage house until 1956 when it was sold[83] and replaced by a house beside the Green.[84] That house was sold in 1974 and a new one built.[85]

A chantry priest of Aldbourne who died in 1508 probably served the fraternity of St. Mary, which had endowments valued at £5 17s. 4d. at its dissolution in 1548.[86] In the late 15th century, early 16th, and early 17th many vicars were pluralists. Among them were Simon Elvyngton, vicar 1474–8, who served as suffragan bishop in Salisbury diocese,[87] John Edmunds, vicar c. 1524 to 1544 and master of Peterhouse, Cambridge,[88] and Richard Steward, vicar 1629–39, who was also provost of Eton College (Bucks.) and rector of Mildenhall.[89] In 1548 there were 400 communicants in the parish and the vicar was said to need an assistant.[90] Several parishioners who still held church goods were referred to the ecclesiastical commissioners in 1556,[91] and in the 1580s Richard Cook, the vicar, was accused of preaching unsound doctrine and of immorality. The accusations were denied by Cook, who claimed that he had enjoyed the friendship and approval of Bishop Jewell.[92] In the early 17th century the parish was served by curates.[93] In 1637 the curate was ordered by Bishop Davenant to celebrate communion on four successive Sundays at each of the three great festivals, dividing the communicants into four groups so that no more than 200 should attend each celebration. The bishop also ordered the communion table to be replaced against the east wall of the chancel from which it had been removed by parishioners, either to accommodate large numbers at communion or because its position was considered popish.[94] A group of parishioners, perhaps those who had moved the table, were prosecuted in 1638 for leaving their parish church to hear William Wyld preach at Baydon.[95] A minister from Aldbourne subscribed to the Concurrent Testimony in 1648 and another was a member of the Wiltshire Association in 1655.[96] Curates, who apparently received the pension paid by the dean and chapter of Winchester, served the parish in the 18th century, when most vicars were again non-resident pluralists, and in the 19th, although most incumbents were then resident.[97] In 1883 the Ecclesiastical Commissioners, to whom the rectory estate had passed, granted the vicar an

[62] Reg. Ghent (Cant. & York Soc.), ii. 610; Phillipps, Wilts. Inst. (index in W.A.M. xxviii. 211).

[63] Lond. Gaz. 18 Dec. 1956, p. 7175; above, Baydon, church.

[64] Ibid. 26 Mar. 1965, p. 3048.

[65] Ibid. 30 Oct. 1973, p. 12883.

[66] Tax. Eccl. (Rec. Com.), 189.

[67] Reg. Hallum (Cant. & York Soc.), pp. 149–50; Valor Eccl. (Rec. Com.), ii. 94, 151.

[68] W.R.O., bishop, glebe terrier, 1609.

[69] Rep. Com. Eccl. Revenues, 822–3.

[70] W.R.O., bishop, glebe terrier.

[71] Ibid. bishop, glebe terrier, 1670; ibid. 211/19/8.

[72] Ibid. bishop, glebe terriers, 1677, 1705.

[73] Ibid. inclosure award; tithe award.

[74] Reg. Hallum (Cant. & York Soc.), pp. 149–50.

[75] P.R.O., E 36/157, p. 75; W.N. & Q. viii. 537–8.

[76] W.R.O., bishop, glebe terrier.

[77] Ibid. inclosure award.

[78] W.A.S. Libr., sale cat. xxi, no. 1; xxvi, no. 1.

[79] Reg. Hallum (Cant. & York Soc.), pp. 149–50.

[80] P.R.O., C 2/Eliz. I/P 11/57.

[81] W.R.O., bishop, glebe terrier, 1783.

[82] Ibid. inclosure award.

[83] Inf. from Mr. R. Fitch, Court Ho.

[84] Gandy, Heart of a Village, 15.

[85] Inf. from Mr. J. Wilson, Glebe Ho.

[86] W.A.M. i. 332; P.R.O., E 301/58, no. 56.

[87] Phillipps, Wilts. Inst. i. 153, 163; P.R.O., C 1/405/23.

[88] L. & P. Hen. VIII, iv (3), pp. 2840–1; Phillipps, Wilts. Inst. i. 211; D.N.B.

[89] D.N.B.; W.N. & Q. viii. 83; Walker Revised, ed. A. G. Matthews, 10; below, Mildenhall, church.

[90] W.A.M. xii. 379.

[91] W.R.O., bishop, detecta bk.

[92] P.R.O., C 2/Eliz. I/P 11/57; Phillipps, Wilts. Inst. i. 231.

[93] Subscription Bk. (W.R.S. xxxii), p. 14; W.R.O. 526/2.

[94] Cal. S.P. Dom. 1637, pp. 121–2.

[95] W.R.O., archd. Wilts., act bk. 1632–42.

[96] Calamy Revised, ed. A. G. Matthews, 558; W.A.M. xxxiv. 162.

[97] Short Acct. of Aldbourne Church (priv. print. 1925); Rep. Com. Eccl. Revenues, 822–3; W.A.M. xxxvii. 468; W.R.O. 526/2; ibid. bishop, vis. queries, 1864; D. & C. Winton. Mun., ledger bk. XXVII, f. 8v.; acct. bk. 1850–76, p. 53.

additional stipend of £60 on condition that a curate was employed.[98] In 1783 sermons were preached at the morning service and at the afternoon service, attended mainly by servants, held each Sunday. Services were also held during the octaves of the three great festivals, on Ash Wednesday, Good Friday, and some other holy days. Some poor parishioners would not attend because they had no suitable clothes. Communion was celebrated monthly and at the great festivals. Through the efforts of James Neale, a classical scholar, the number of communicants had risen from 30 in 1772 when he became curate to 100 by 1783.[99] In 1815, however, only fifteen people received communion at the monthly celebrations.[1] On Census Sunday in 1851 the congregation numbered 350 at morning service and 400 at afternoon service.[2] From 1855 services were held in the school at Woodsend,[3] which was licensed but not consecrated. In 1864 two services with sermons were held each Sunday in the church and one at Woodsend. Additional services were held at festivals, in Lent, and in Advent. Communion was celebrated at festivals and monthly in the church and at Woodsend. The average congregation in the church was 400.[4] Services at Woodsend had ceased by 1913.[5]

The church of *ST. MICHAEL*, so called in the 15th century but perhaps earlier known as St. Mary Magdalene's,[6] is built of rubble and ashlar and has a chancel with north and south chapels, an aisled and clerestoried nave with transepts, south chapel, and south porch, and a west tower.[7] By the mid 12th century a church with an aisled nave and perhaps a central tower had been built. The south doorway and some masonry survive from it. Some of the stonework is discoloured, apparently by fire, and a fire may have prompted the rebuilding of the church in the early 13th century. Its plan was then cruciform, with a long chancel, almost certainly a central tower, transepts, and an aisled nave of four bays. Any late 13th- and 14th-century alterations were probably destroyed in the 15th century when a west tower was built, the central tower presumably removed, and the crossing arches rebuilt. Chapels were then added to the chancel, porches and an embattled clerestory were added to the nave, the roofs were renewed, and most windows enlarged. In the early 16th century a small chapel was added between the south porch and transept.

In the restoration of 1867 by William Butterfield a more steeply pitched roof was placed over the nave and chancel, the 15th-century roof being retained as a ceiling. A north porch was apparently removed, as was the stair turret from the south porch, the east window was replaced by three lancets, and the south windows of the south chancel chapel were altered.[8]

By will proved 1935 Rachel Goldsmith left the income from £300 for repairs to the church. The income was c. £40 in 1982.[9]

In 1524 the vicar, John Stone, bequeathed a chalice to the church.[10] A chalice weighing 8½ oz., perhaps that given by Stone, was left in the parish in 1553 when 1½ oz. of plate was confiscated. Two new chalices, a paten cover, paten, and flagon were given in the late 17th century;[11] in 1685 the earlier plate was sold.[12] The late 17th-century plate and two chalices and a paten of the 20th century were held by the parish in 1982.[13] There were four bells and a sanctus bell in 1553. Two early 16th-century bells hung in the church in 1982. There were also two 17th-century bells and four bells cast in Aldbourne in the 18th century. One 18th-century bell was recast in 1915.[14] Monuments include that of William Walrond (d. 1614) and Edward Walrond (d. 1617), and one of Richard Goddard (d. 1614) and his wife and children.[15]

The parish registers begin in 1637. There are gaps in those for marriages and burials for the years 1639–46.[16]

NONCONFORMITY. In the late 1660s a conventicle at Aldbourne was led by Christopher Fowler who had been ejected from his living in 1662.[17] Noah Webb and Robert Rogers, also ejected ministers, were fined for preaching at Aldbourne in 1673.[18] Webb rode from Sandhurst (Berks.) to attend the Aldbourne conventicle every Sunday for almost a year.[19] In 1669 a congregation of 200–300 met on Thursdays and Sundays at Court House.[20] Of those, between 20 and 30 adults were probably Aldbourne residents; 20 parishioners were presented for failure to attend church in 1674[21] and there were 28 nonconformists in the parish in 1676.[22] In 1672 the house of Charles Gilbert, a Presbyterian, was licensed for meetings[23] and another conventicle was held at Gabriel Martin's house at Upper Upham in 1681. Daniel Burgess, a dissenting minister, preached at Upham and at Aldbourne in the early 1680s.[24] Houses in Aldbourne were licensed for dissenters' meetings in 1704 and 1706.[25] There was an Independent minister in 1715,[26] and the Independent congregation survived until 1760 when its meeting house was

[98] *Lond. Gaz.* 15 June 1883, p. 3100.
[99] *Vis. Queries, 1783* (W.R.S. xxvii), pp. 19–20; *D.N.B.*
[1] *W.A.M.* xli. 129.
[2] P.R.O., HO 129/121/3/1/1.
[3] Wilts. Cuttings, xi. 22.
[4] W.R.O., bishop, vis. queries.
[5] Ibid. 526/15.
[6] *W.A.M.* xxviii. 156–7; *W.N. & Q.* viii. 537–8.
[7] See plate facing p. 80.
[8] Wilts. Cuttings, xvi. 47.
[9] Char. Com. file; inf. from Mr. Wilson.
[10] *W.N. & Q.* viii. 538.
[11] Nightingale, *Wilts. Plate*, 153–4.
[12] W.R.O. 526/9.
[13] Inf. from Mr. Wilson.
[14] Ibid.; Walters, *Wilts. Bells*, 6–8.

[15] *W.A.M.* xxviii. 157; Pevsner, *Wilts.* (2nd edn.), 82; above, manors; see below, plate facing p. 193.
[16] W.R.O. 526/2. Bishops' transcripts for 1607–8, 1615, 1605–19, and of an undated reg. from the Interregnum are ibid.
[17] Ibid. bishop, chwdns.' pres., 1668; *Calamy Revised*, ed. Matthews, 209.
[18] Hist. MSS. Com. 55, *Var. Coll.* i, p. 152.
[19] *Calamy Revised*, ed. Matthews, 516.
[20] *Trans. Salisbury Field Club*, i. 36.
[21] W.R.O., bishop, chwdns.' pres.
[22] *W.N. & Q.* iii. 537.   [23] *Cal. S.P. Dom.* 1672, 299.
[24] Ibid. 1680–1, 563; Hist. MSS. Com. 55, *Var. Coll.* i, p. 157.
[25] W.R.O., bishop, certs. dissenters' meeting hos.
[26] *V.C.H. Wilts.* iii. 107 n.

burned down.[27] In 1737 Presbyterians met in a newly built house in West Street.[28]

Houses were licensed for Methodist meetings in 1772, 1798, and 1802.[29] In 1783, however, there was said to be no meeting house and ten or twelve people who met regularly to hear readings by a Methodist weaver all attended the parish church.[30] A Wesleyan Methodist chapel was built in 1807,[31] probably on the site of that in Lottage Road said to have been built in 1844.[32] Afternoon and evening services there on Census Sunday in 1851 were each attended by c. 250 people.[33] By will proved 1913 William Cuss left the income from £50 to provide bibles and hymn books for children attending the Sunday school. The income from the charity was £1 10s. in 1962.[34] In 1968 the chapel was replaced by a hall to be used in conjunction with the Primitive Methodist chapel.[35] A house at Woodsend was licensed for Methodist meetings in 1798 and a Wesleyan Methodist chapel was built there c. 1845.[36] The chapel was closed c. 1910.[37]

Cottages in West Street were converted into a Primitive Methodist chapel, apparently in 1840.[38] In 1851 afternoon and evening services were held; the average congregation numbered 160.[39] A new chapel was built on the same site in 1906 and extended in 1936.[40] It was in use in 1982.

Strict Baptist prayer meetings were started by Thomas Barrett, whose house was licensed for meetings in 1833. Cottages in Back Lane were converted into Little Zoar chapel c. 1841.[41] On Census Sunday in 1851 there was an afternoon service attended by 87 people and an evening service attended by 40 people.[42] A new Zoar chapel was built in 1868.[43] By will proved 1894 William Taylor gave £120 to provide a minister to officiate there once a month. The chapel may already have been in decline; in 1904 it was reported that only two or three services had been held in the last six years and that Taylor's bequest had not been used.[44] The chapel was demolished after 1931;[45] the later use of Taylor's bequest is not known.

A house on Ewins Hill was licensed for meetings in 1832 and a cottage near Stock Lane Farm in 1843.[46]

EDUCATION. A dissenter may have kept a school in Aldbourne in 1668.[47] A schoolmaster lived there in 1736,[48] and before 1783 a room over the church porch was used for a school. The school had been closed by 1783 and the building of a new school for the poor, begun by the curate James Neale, had been left unfinished, probably for lack of money.[49] In 1833 there were five day schools in Aldbourne attended by 84 children; none was free and most had recently opened.[50] One may have been the dame school taught by a dissenter which survived until 1858 or later. It was attended by fifteen children in 1858.[51] A National school with two schoolrooms was built in 1839;[52] the pupils were taught by two masters and two mistresses in 1848.[53] In 1856 the schoolrooms were extended or replaced by a brick and flint building in Gothic style to which a master's house was attached.[54] There were between 80 and 100 pupils in 1858.[55] A schoolroom for infants was added in 1873. Average attendance had risen to 185 by 1898[56] and was usually 160 or more until 1914. Thereafter attendance fell; there were 103 pupils in 1938.[57] In 1963 the school buildings were replaced[58] and in 1972 the new building was extended.[59] There were 139 pupils on roll in 1981.[60]

In 1812 Jane Bridgeman paid for a school for sixteen children at Snap.[61] In 1855 a National school was opened at Woodsend in a converted cottage also used as a chapel.[62] There were c. 20 pupils in 1858.[63] The school had been closed by 1913.[64]

By will proved 1856 John Brown bequeathed £200 to be given after the death of his wife to the National schools of the parish. The money was invested in 1872 and the income, £5 8s. in 1904 and £5 10s. in 1962, was used for the maintenance of the schools.[65]

CHARITIES FOR THE POOR. By will proved 1598 Thomas Goddard left £2 a year from Upper Upham manor to the poor of Aldbourne parish.[66] In the 18th century and the early 19th the income was often allowed to accumulate for several years.[67] In the 1830s it was spent on coal or blankets for the poor; in 1904 it was paid in

[27] Vis. Queries, 1783 (W.R.S. xxvii), p. 20.
[28] W.R.O., bishop, certs. dissenters' meeting hos.
[29] Ibid. bishop, return of cert. places.
[30] Vis. Queries, 1783 (W.R.S. xxvii), p. 19.
[31] P.R.O., HO 129/121/3/1/2.
[32] W.R.O., inclosure award; tithe award; Crane, Aldbourne Chron. 19.
[33] P.R.O., HO 129/121/3/1/2.
[34] Char. Com. file.
[35] Crane, Aldbourne Chron. 19.
[36] W.R.O., bishop, return of cert. places; ibid. return of regns.
[37] W.A.M. lvii. 389.
[38] Crane, Aldbourne Chron. 29.
[39] P.R.O., HO 129/121/3/1/4.
[40] Crane, Aldbourne Chron. 29; Statistical Returns (Dept. for Chapel Affairs), ii. 72.
[41] W.R.O., return of regns.; R. W. Oliver, Strict Bapt. Chapels Eng. (Strict Bapt. Hist. Soc.), v. 16.
[42] P.R.O., HO 129/121/3/1/5.
[43] Oliver, op. cit. 16; Lond. Gaz. 7 Mar. 1873, p. 1414.
[44] Endowed Char. Wilts. (N. Div.), 7.
[45] Oliver, op. cit. 16.
[46] W.R.O., bishop, return of cert. places.
[47] Ibid. bishop, chwdns.' pres.
[48] Q. Sess. 1736 (W.R.S. xi), pp. 93, 99, 114.
[49] Vis. Queries, 1783 (W.R.S. xxvii), pp. 19, 21.
[50] Educ. Enquiry Abstract, 1026.
[51] Acct. of Wilts. Schs. 3.
[52] P.R.O., ED 7/130.
[53] Kelly's Dir. Wilts.
[54] W.R.O. 782/1.
[55] Acct. of Wilts. Schs. 3.
[56] Kelly's Dir. Wilts. (1898).
[57] Bd. of Educ., List 21 (H.M.S.O.).
[58] Wilts. Cuttings, xxii. 189.
[59] Crane, Aldbourne Chron. 23.
[60] Inf. from Chief Education Officer, Co. Hall, Trowbridge.
[61] Crane, Aldbourne Chron. 23; Gandy, Heart of a Village, 62.
[62] W.R.O. 526/15; above, church.
[63] Acct. of Wilts. Schs. 3.
[64] W.R.O. 526/15.
[65] Endowed Char. Wilts. (N. Div.), 6; Char. Com. file.
[66] Endowed Char. Wilts. (N. Div.), 1; P.R.O., PROB 11/91 (P.C.C. 40 Lewyn).
[67] W.R.O. 526/9.

cash.[68] By a Scheme of 1968 the charity was merged with others as the Goddard, Brown, and Hill charity; the combined income was between £5 and £10.[69] In 1982 the income was used with that from the Poor's Furze to give fuel or cash to elderly parishioners at Christmas.[70]

By will proved 1785 Lawrence Brown bequeathed the income from £200, half of which was to buy coats for three poor men of the parish and half to buy gowns for five poor women every year. Preference in the choice of beneficiaries was to be given to Brown's kinsmen.[71] Coats and gowns were bought in 1834. In the late 19th century and the early 20th the yearly income, £5 or £6, was still spent on clothing.[72] The charity became part of the Goddard, Brown, and Hill charity by the Scheme of 1968.[73]

At inclosure in 1809 an allotment of 50 a. of furze was made for the poor. The land was partly cleared and was leased from 1829 until 1854. The income from rents, c. £35 in 1834 and £14 17s. in 1850, was used to buy coal. Furze was again grown over the whole area in 1892[74] but by 1916 it had been cleared and rents were then used to buy fuel.[75] In 1982 the income, c. £1,000, was used with that of the Goddard, Brown, and Hill charity.[76]

By a deed of 1834 Hester Hill gave the income from £100 to buy material for gowns for poor women of the parish. The income was £3 2s. 5d. in 1875, and £2 12s. in 1904, when material for eight gowns was bought.[77] By the 1968 Scheme the charity became part of the Goddard, Brown, and Hill charity.[78]

By will proved 1884 Joseph Wentworth left the income from £200 to the two oldest agricultural labourers who were born and resident in Aldbourne and who had never received poor relief. The income, £5, was distributed in 1904,[79] but in the 1980s, when it was c. £20 a year, there were few suitable beneficiaries.[80]

Rachel Goldsmith bequeathed much of her estate to the poor of Aldbourne by will proved 1935. The income from it, £206 12s. 9d., was spent in grants to 233 people for outings, fuel, and other goods in 1959.[81] In the 1980s the income, c. £250 a year, was added to that from other parish charities.[82]

By a Scheme of 1959 the assets of the Aldbourne and Baydon nursing association, including the profits from the sale of the district nurse's house belonging to the association, were transferred to the Aldbourne and Baydon Aid in Sickness Fund.[83] In 1982 the income, c. £200, was spent on home nursing, equipment, and hospital treatment.[84]

AVEBURY

THE PARISH of Avebury, at the head of the river Kennet some 8 km. west of Marlborough, measures 1,898 ha. (4,690 a.) and has the shape of an elongated lozenge, indented at the south-eastern corner where East Kennett has been taken from it.[85] On its longer axis, from south-west to north-east, it measures 8 km.; on the shorter, between Windmill Hill and Overton Hill, 4 km. Within the parish are Avebury, some 2,780 a. north of the London–Bath road in 1845, including the villages of Avebury and Avebury Trusloe, Beckhampton, then 790 a., which lies to the south, and West Kennett, c. 930 a., to the south-east.[86] The name Avebury is first recorded in Domesday Book.[87] Lands in the valley of the upper Kennet earlier shared the name of the river. In 972 the lands of Kennett were divided; an estate east of the Ridge Way became part of Overton and the lands to the west, then perhaps a

single unit extending south to the downs, later formed the parishes of Avebury and East Kennett, divided by the river.[88] Much of what was later part of Avebury was probably still known as Kennett in 1086, as were East and West Kennett. There was, however, a church at Avebury.[89] By the 12th century it had established rights over Beckhampton, also mentioned in Domesday Book, as it had over West Kennett by the 13th.[90]

Apart from the river which divides East Kennett and Avebury, no natural physical feature marks the extent of the parish. The Ridge Way and the course of a Roman road respectively form the east and south-west boundaries. Chalk downland above 152 m. occupies much of the west, south, and east parts of the parish.[91] Heights of 229 m. and 254 m. are reached in the south-western and north-eastern corners on West and

[68] Endowed Char. Wilts. (N. Div.), 1–3.
[69] Char. Com. file.
[70] Inf. from Mr. J. Wilson, Glebe Ho.
[71] W.R.O. 526/13.
[72] Endowed Char. Wilts. (N. Div.), 1–3.
[73] Char. Com. file.
[74] Endowed Char. Wilts. (N. Div.), 1–5.
[75] F. S. Thacker, Kennet Country, 264.
[76] Inf. from Mr. Wilson.
[77] Endowed Char. Wilts. (N. Div.), 5–6; Kelly's Dir. Wilts. (1875).
[78] Char. Com. file.
[79] Endowed Char. Wilts. (N. Div.), 6–7.
[80] Inf. from Mr. Wilson.
[81] Char. Com. file.
[82] Inf. from Mr. Wilson.   [83] Char. Com. file.

[84] Inf. from Mr. Wilson.
[85] This article was written in 1979; maps used include O.S. Maps 1/50,000, sheet 173 (1974 edn.); 1/25,000, SU 06 (1961 edn.), SU 07 (1959 edn.), SU 16 (1961 edn.), SU 17 (1960 edn.); 6″, Wilts. XXVIII (1889 and later edns.), XXXV (1889 and later edns.).
[86] W.R.O., tithe award.
[87] V.C.H. Wilts. ii, p. 119.
[88] Finberg, Early Wessex Chart. p. 98; Arch. Jnl. lxxvi. 240–7; Rep. Marlborough Coll. Natural Hist. Soc. lxxxvii. 118–25; V.C.H. Wilts. xi. 189.
[89] V.C.H. Wilts. ii, pp. 119, 143.
[90] Ibid. p. 147; Cirencester Cart. ed. C. D. Ross and M. Devine, ii, pp. 423, 427–8.
[91] Geological inf. in this para. is based on Geol. Surv. Map 1″, drift, sheet 266 (1964 edn.).

Avebury Downs. South of Avebury village Waden Hill rises to 191 m. There was cultivation on the eastern and southern downland in prehistoric times[92] but from the 16th century and presumably before then the downs and Waden and Windmill Hills were used mainly for pasture.[93] Since the mid 19th century there have been training gallops for racehorses in the northeast and west parts of the parish on Avebury Down and on West and Knoll Downs.[94] Near the centre of the parish is the confluence of the two head streams of the Kennet which enter it from the north skirting Windmill Hill in broad gently sloping valleys. From the confluence the river flows in a narrower valley south for some 1.5 km. to Swallowhead Springs and then eastwards south of Overton Hill. Narrow strips of valley gravel adjoin the alluvial banks of the river. Gravel also extends along dry tributary valleys east of the eastern head stream, west from Swallowhead Springs, and north of West Kennett village. Arable lands on the lower ground have been extended since the 18th century by ploughing the neighbouring down.[95] There were meadows in the river valleys, including water meadows at the foot of Silbury Hill.[96] Willows were planted south of West Kennett Manor in the late 18th century[97] and there were withy beds west of Avebury Manor in the early 20th century.[98] There were 7 a. of woodland in West Kennett in 1086[99] and in the late 18th century the parish was sparsely wooded.[1] Small plantations had been established by 1886 on the western and southern boundaries, on West Down, and north of the confluence.[2] Sarsen stones were apparently abundant in the area in prehistoric times. Stones from Waden Hill were used for building c. 1700[3] but from the late 18th century sarsens were to be found principally on Avebury Down and south of West Kennett long barrow.[4]

The prehistoric remains of Avebury have become famous.[5] The earliest evidence of human activity in the parish was found on Windmill Hill, where an early Neolithic settlement was replaced c. 3250 B.C. by a causewayed camp covering some 8.4 ha. Greatest interest has, however, been aroused by the complex of ceremonial monuments of the Neolithic Period and the Bronze Age, said to be one of the most extraordinary prehistoric cult centres in England. At its centre is the Circle on a broad chalk plain east of the confluence of the two head streams of the Kennet. A ditch and outer bank between 4 m. and 6 m. high surround an enclosure of nearly 12 ha., within which stand the surviving undressed sarsens of the Great Circle and the inner circles. Similar stones, some of which still stand in pairs, formed the Kennett Avenue which led 2 km. south-east from the southern entrance of the Circle to the Sanctuary, concentric rings of stones and wooden posts on Overton Hill. A similar avenue is thought to have led from the western entrance to Beckhampton.[6] Standing apart from that complex but of a similar period is Silbury Hill, a man-made mound 1.2 km. to the south rising some 39 m. from a base covering an area of 2.2 ha.[7] The importance of Avebury as a centre is indicated by the number of earthworks and barrows in the vicinity, the most notable of which is the West Kennett long barrow, a stone-chambered collective tomb south-west of West Kennett.[8] The continued occupation of the area into historic times is well attested. Iron-Age and Romano-British field systems have been identified beside the Kennett Avenue, on West and Knoll Downs, and near the boundaries with West Overton and Winterbourne Monkton. The Roman road from Bath to Mildenhall runs from west to east across the parish through the village of West Kennett, deflected from its straight course only by Silbury Hill, and there was a Roman villa south of Windmill Hill. Later remains include Pagan Saxon material within the Circle and in Avebury high street, and an intrusive Viking interment on Silbury Hill.

Stones from the Circle were buried during the Middle Ages, perhaps in recognition of their connexion with pre-Christian religion.[9] The ditch and bank, known from the 13th century as Wallditch,[10] were used as a common pound in the 16th century and were still common in part in 1754.[11] Although 'camps and sepulchres of men of war' at Avebury were noticed by John Leland c. 1540,[12] serious interest in the archaeological sites was first shown by John Aubrey in the mid 17th century.[13] William Stukeley made several visits to Avebury between 1719 and 1724 and published his findings and theories in *Abury, a Temple of the British Druids* in 1746.[14] Archaeological work was resumed in the late 18th century and continued at intervals throughout the 19th.[15] In 1908 systematic investigations were begun and the excavation of Windmill Hill was undertaken in the 1920s. Alexander Keiller who had worked on Windmill Hill[16] began the excavation and restoration of the Kennett Avenue and the Circle in the 1930s.[17] The Sanctuary was investigated in 1930 and further work was carried

[92] Below.
[93] P.R.O., E 134/40 & 41 Eliz. I Mich./7; W.R.O. 184/4; 415/45.
[94] *Kelly's Dir. Wilts.* (1848 and later edns.); W.A.S. Libr., sale cat. ii, no. 17; iv, no. 3; Wilts. Cuttings, xvi. 48.
[95] W.R.O., inclosure award; tithe award; *W.A.M.* liii. 311.
[96] W.R.O., inclosure award.   [97] Ibid. 118/88.
[98] W.A.S. Libr., sale cat. iv, no. 3.
[99] *V.C.H. Wilts.* ii, p. 143.
[1] *Andrews and Dury, Map* (W.R.S. viii), pl. 11.
[2] O.S. Map 6″, Wilts. XXVIII (1889 edn.).
[3] *W.A.M.* xl. 354.
[4] *Andrews and Dury, Map* (W.R.S. viii), pl. 11; O.S. Map 6″, SU 17 SW. (1960 edn.), SU 16 NW. (1961 edn.).
[5] The arch. of Avebury is described in *V.C.H. Wilts.* i (1), 31–5; i (2), 317–26, on which this para. is based.

[6] F. de M. Vatcher and L. Vatcher, *Avebury Mons.* 38.
[7] See plate facing p. 48.
[8] *V.C.H. Wilts.* i (2), 312.
[9] S. Piggott, *Wm. Stukeley,* 111.
[10] *W.A.M.* lv. 60; *Cirencester Cart.* iii, p. 1051.
[11] P.R.O., E 134/40 & 41 Eliz. I Mich./7; W.R.O. 212A/31/4.
[12] Leland, *Itin.* ed. Toulmin Smith, v. 81.
[13] *W.A.M.* iv. 310–13.
[14] Piggott, *Stukeley,* 41–50.
[15] Vatcher, *Avebury Mons.* 5; B.L. Add. MS. 33,648; *W.A.M.* x. 209–16; xxiii. 65.
[16] Vatcher, *Avebury Mons.* 5; A. Burl, *Prehistoric Avebury,* 61.
[17] E. Storey, *Rep. and Analysis of the Survey for the Development Plan for Wilts.* (priv. print. Nov. 1952), 95.

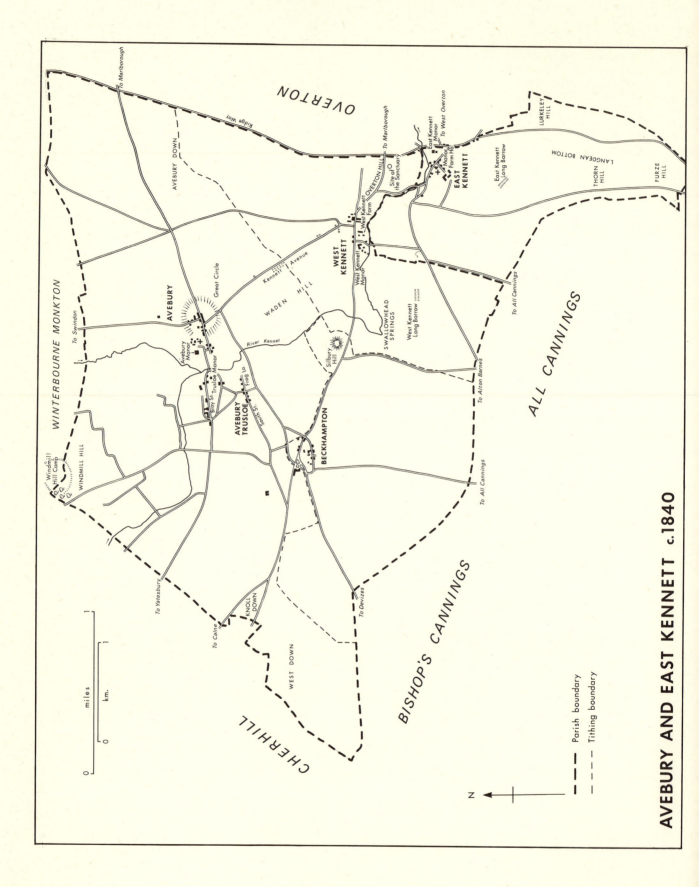

OVERTON

To Marlborough

To Marlborough

Ridge Way

AVEBURY DOWN

LURKELEY HILL

East Kennett Manor

To West Overton

Manor Farm Ho.

West Kennett Farm

East Kennett Long Barrow

LANGDEAN BOTTOM

Site of the Sanctuary

THORN HILL

FURZE HILL

OVERTON HILL

EAST KENNETT

WINTERBOURNE MONKTON

Kennett Avenue

Great Circle

WADEN HILL

WEST KENNETT

West Kennett Manor

West Kennett Manor

West Kennett Long Barrow

ALL CANNINGS

To Swindon

AVEBURY

River Kennet

SWALLOWHEAD SPRINGS

To All Cannings

Avebury Manor

Silbury Hill

Bray St. Trusloe Manor

Frog La.

To Alton Barnes

To Yatesbury

South St.

AVEBURY TRUSLOE

BECKHAMPTON

To All Cannings

Windmill Hill Camp

WINDMILL HILL

To Calne

KNOLL DOWN

To Devizes

BISHOP'S CANNINGS

miles

km.

WEST DOWN

CHERHILL

N

Parish boundary

Tithing boundary

AVEBURY AND EAST KENNETT c.1840

out at Windmill Hill, West Kennett long barrow, and Silbury Hill after the Second World War.[18]

Archaeological interest was accompanied by concern for the preservation of the monuments which were particularly threatened by the proximity of Avebury village and its eventual intrusion into the Circle. Stukeley and others reported that standing stones from the Circle, the Avenues, and the Sanctuary were removed, usually for building, in the late 17th century and the 18th.[19] Part of the Beckhampton Avenue was destroyed in the 18th century on the orders of turnpike trustees because horses shied at the stones.[20] Stones were still being removed in the mid 19th century[21] but in the 1870s Sir John Lubbock, Bt., later Baron Avebury, bought Silbury Hill and certain lands within or near the Circle in order to prevent further damage.[22] The Circle, Silbury Hill, the entrenchment on Windmill Hill, the Roman road, and several barrows were recognized under the Ancient Monuments Act of 1913 and recognition was extended to the Sanctuary in 1933.[23] Between 1924 and 1939 Alexander Keiller purchased Windmill Hill and much of the Circle.[24] Those sites and that of the Kennett Avenue were part of the estate bought in 1943 by the National Trust and passed into the custodianship of the Ministry of Works.[25] The Trust later bought other lands and buildings in the parish.[26] Work on a general preservation scheme began in 1934 and in 1952 a special scheme to safeguard the monuments was adopted by the county planning authorities. New building, apart from that for agricultural purposes on the downs, was limited to a specified area. The demolition of houses within the Circle as they became vacant, which had begun in the late 1930s, was to continue. In 1960 the policy became one of gradual clearance and in 1976 it was recommended that the remaining buildings be allowed to stand.[27]

Three ancient roads ran through the parish, the Ridge Way, the Roman road, and Harepath Way, the path of which has been traced for 1 km. along the edge of West Down. In the 18th century the London–Bath road ran through West Kennett to Beckhampton, crossing the Kennet south-east of Silbury Hill. At Beckhampton the road forked. One branch continued north-westwards to Cherhill, the other led south-westwards, reaching Bath via Sandy Lane in Calne. Both were turnpiked in 1742.[28] The more northerly branch became the modern London–Bath road, the principal route through the parish. West of Beckhampton its path was moved slightly to the south in 1790[29] but it had returned to its original course by 1889.[30] In the early 18th century a coach road led over the downs from Marlborough towards Avebury village. It entered the Circle from the east and apparently turned south-west across the Kennet to Beckhampton.[31] The downland route fell out of use after the London–Bath road was turnpiked[32] and was marked only by a track in 1979. In 1675 a road to Devizes left the London–Bath road near Silbury Hill.[33] In the 18th century the main route to Devizes within the parish was part of the Bath road via Sandy Lane. The road from Beckhampton to Avebury was turnpiked in 1742 and that north of Avebury in 1767 to form the Swindon–Devizes road.[34] Another turnpike road linked Avebury and West Kennett. The lane leading from the London–Bath road to East Kennett was turnpiked in 1840 as part of the West Kennett to Amesbury road, one of the last roads in England to be turnpiked.[35] The bridge over the Kennet between Avebury and Beckhampton was replaced in 1950[36] and a roundabout built at Beckhampton c. 1960.[37]

Few changes occurred in the pattern of secondary roads between the late 18th century and the 20th. A path which skirted Avebury village to the north and west in the 18th century had, however, disappeared by 1979. The main street of Avebury village was linked by a footbridge with the network of lanes west of the river which connected the farms and houses of Avebury Trusloe. From a point on the old road to Marlborough some 700 m. east of the Circle, tracks radiated to Winterbourne Monkton, Chiseldon, and West Overton. In the 19th century new or improved tracks were made to South Farm on Avebury Down, Windmill Hill, and Beckhampton Penning south of Beckhampton. An older path led from Beckhampton village to Tan Hill in All Cannings. Further east a path ran from the London–Bath road at West Kennett to East Kennett across a bridge perhaps built in the late 18th century.[38]

AVEBURY village was one of the larger settlements in Selkley. Its assessment for taxation was the third highest in 1334, and in 1377 there were 134 poll-tax payers, again the third highest number in the hundred.[39] Avebury may have lost some ground by 1576 when sixteen inhabitants were assessed for taxation at £6 5s.[40] Between 1801 and 1841 its population fell from 590 to 488. Later figures refer to the whole parish, in which the population remained c. 750 between 1851 and 1881, then declined to 588 in 1901. Numbers rose above 600 again only in 1911,[41] perhaps as a result of the expansion of Beckhampton racing stables,

[18] *W.A.M.* xliv. 302–17; Vatcher, *Avebury Mons.* 5.
[19] *W.A.M.* xvii. 333; xlv. 321; lxiv. 100–5; R. Colt Hoare, *Anct. Wilts.* i (1), 87.
[20] *W.A.M.* iv. 238–9.   [21] Wilts. Cuttings, v. 11.
[22] *W.A.M.* xiii. 221–2; xix. 21.
[23] Ibid. xliii. 176–9; W.R.O. 271/10, map.
[24] *W.A.M.* xliii. 42, 215; Storey, *Rep. and Analysis*, 95.
[25] Nat. Trust, Wessex Regional Off., Stourton, Avebury deeds; Storey, op. cit. 95.
[26] Nat. Trust, Wessex Regional Off., Avebury deeds.
[27] Storey, op. cit. 93–5; Nat. Trust, Wessex Regional Off., Avebury mem.
[28] *V.C.H. Wilts.* iv. 256, 268.
[29] W.R.O. 473/352.
[30] O.S. Map 6″, Wilts. XXVIII (1889 edn.).

[31] W. Stukeley, *Abury*, frontispiece.
[32] J. Nichols, *Illustrations*, iv. 855–6.
[33] J. Ogilby, *Brit.* (1675), pl. 11.
[34] *Andrews and Dury, Map* (W.R.S. viii), pl. 11; *V.C.H. Wilts.* iv. 256, 268.
[35] *V.C.H. Wilts.* iv. 257, 264; W.R.O., Q. Sess. enrolled deeds, turnpike plans 40, 40A.
[36] Date on bridge.
[37] O.S. Map 1/25,000, SU 06 (1961 edn.).
[38] O.S. Maps 1/50,000, sheet 173 (1974 edn.); 6″, Wilts. XXVIII (1889 edn.); *Andrews and Dury, Map* (W.R.S. viii), pl. 11; W.R.O., inclosure award map; tithe award map.
[39] *V.C.H. Wilts.* iv. 301, 310.
[40] *Taxation Lists* (W.R.S. x), 103–4.
[41] *V.C.H. Wilts.* iv. 340.

and in 1961 when there were 631 inhabitants. In 1971 there were 537 people living in the parish.[42]

The village of Avebury grew up around the church and the principal houses of Avebury and Avebury Trusloe manors on the gravel east of the confluence of the head streams of the Kennet.[43] By the early 18th century the settlement had spread into the Circle. It was drawn eastwards along the high street, following the line of the coach road to Marlborough. That road and the road from Swindon met in the centre of the Circle, easily accessible through the northern, southern, and eastern entrances, at a staggered crossroads which became a secondary centre of the village.[44] In the late 18th century houses also lined the narrow lanes west of the Circle between the high street, the church, and the grounds of Avebury Manor. Several houses stood either side of Bray Street which led west from the river on the same line as the high street.[45] By 1773 a separate village, known in 1889 and probably before as Avebury Trusloe, had grown up on the chalk some 700 m. south-west of Avebury church.[46]

In 1979 the pattern of settlement differed little from that of the late 18th century; the cottages demolished within the Circle were presumably of the 19th century.[47] Many buildings shown on Stukeley's plan of the Circle of 1724 could still be identified in 1979, although all had apparently been substantially altered or completely rebuilt. The centre of the village was characterized by the large number of small cottages, some of which incorporated sarsen walling. More substantial buildings included the old school, the former vicarage house, and Manor Farm west of the Circle. Within it was the former farmhouse of Norris's, which stood at the north-east corner of the junction in 1724 and has been altered, probably in the later 18th century. Between the church and the ditch was a group of farm buildings, including a 16th-century pigeon house and a late 17th-century barn,[48] owned by the National Trust and leased in part to the Wiltshire Folk Life Society. The buildings were being restored in 1979 for use as a museum and tourist information centre.[49] In 1938 Alexander Keiller converted the coach house and stables of Avebury Manor into a museum for archaeological finds from Windmill Hill.[50] It passed to the National Trust in 1943 and was named the Alexander Keiller Museum in 1966 when Mrs. Gabrielle Keiller presented the contents to the nation.[51] A few houses of the 19th and 20th centuries stood outside the Circle on the old road to Marlborough and on the Swindon–Devizes road. West of the Kennet, in the angle formed by the river and Bray

Street, were Avebury Trusloe Manor and Avebury Trusloe Manor Farm. The former farmhouses of Bannings, a house of five bays with an 18th-century front of chequered brick, and Westbrook, a thatched building probably of 17th-century origin with mullioned windows, stood north of the street. The older part of the village of Avebury Trusloe consisted of a few 18th- and 19th-century buildings along Frog Lane and South Street, which led east and west from a crossroads. Trusloe Farm and its out-buildings, all of the 19th century, stood at the corner of Frog Lane. Council houses were built north of South Street in the late 1930s and after the Second World War to replace those demolished in Avebury village under the preservation scheme.[52]

The Catherine Wheel inn, patronized by Stukeley in the 1720s, stood north-east of the crossroads in the Circle.[53] Trade declined after the London–Bath road was turnpiked and the inn was closed in the late 18th century.[54] The building became a farmhouse in the 19th century and was eventually demolished.[55] West of the junction is the Red Lion, built in the 19th century and extensively modernized since.[56]

BECKHAMPTON. The medieval settlement of Beckhampton was less populous than Avebury; assessed at 39s. for taxation in 1334, it had 31 poll-tax payers in 1377.[57] The assessment of £9 11s. 8d., higher than that for Avebury in 1576, suggests that some residents were wealthy.[58] Beckhampton village stands at the foot of a dry valley c. 2 km. south-west of Avebury. The older farmsteads and houses lie on the gravel south of the roundabout along a lane which runs from the London–Bath road south-west and west to the Swindon–Devizes road. In 1724 there may have been only four houses in the village[59] but by 1773, as in 1979, buildings lined both sides of the lane.[60] Stones from the Sanctuary were used in the early 18th century for farm buildings in Beckhampton,[61] possibly those of Galtee More Farm at the eastern end of the lane. The population of Beckhampton rose from 99 to 155 between 1801 and 1841,[62] the last date for which separate figures are available, but numbers probably rose again c. 1900 with the expansion of the racing stables. Willonyx, a house north of the lane from the London–Bath road, was built on the site of an earlier farmhouse c. 1900,[63] and probably incorporates part of the original building. In the early 20th century the village expanded north of the London–Bath road across the tithing boundary. Most of the new buildings were connected with racing stables; they included estate cottages and

[42] Census, 1961, 1971.
[43] e.g. P.R.O., E 134/40 & 41 Eliz. I Mich./7; see plate facing p. 97.
[44] Stukeley, Abury, frontispiece.
[45] W.R.O., inclosure award map.
[46] Andrews and Dury, Map (W.R.S. viii), pl. 11; O.S. Map 6", Wilts. XXVIII (1889 edn.).
[47] Storey, Rep. and Analysis, 95.
[48] P.R.O., E 134/41 Eliz. I Hil./8; W.N. & Q. viii. 321.
[49] Inf. from Maj. L. Vatcher, Hon. Director, Avebury Barn Project, Great Barn.
[50] W.A.M. xlviii. 389–90.
[51] Vatcher, Avebury Mons. 42–3.

[52] Storey, Rep. and Analysis, 95.
[53] Stukeley, Abury, frontispiece; Piggott, Stukeley, 63.
[54] Nichols, Illustrations, iv. 855–6.
[55] W.A.M. x. 212.
[56] W.R.O., alehousekeepers' recognizances, 1822–7.
[57] V.C.H. Wilts. iv. 301, 310.
[58] Taxation Lists (W.R.S. x), 104.
[59] W.A.M. xlii. 52.
[60] Andrews and Dury, Map (W.R.S. viii), pl. 11.
[61] W.A.M. xlv. 321; Hoare, Anct. Wilts. i (1), 87.
[62] V.C.H. Wilts. iv. 340.
[63] S. Darling, Reminiscences, 230; W.R.O., inclosure award map; O.S. Map 6", Wilts. XXVIII (1889 edn.).

stables on both sides of the Swindon-Devizes road and west of them the Grange.[64]

The Waggon and Horses, north of the London-Bath road and east of the crossroads, was built in 1669 as the Bear and had lands attached for resting fat cattle travelling to the London markets.[65] Known as the Hare and Hounds in 1724 and as the Waggon and Horses in 1823,[66] it was much altered or rebuilt in the 19th and 20th centuries. The keeper of the Catherine Wheel at Avebury apparently built another inn of the same name in the western angle of the crossroads in 1745 to serve the new turnpike road.[67] In 1796 it was also known as the Beckhampton House inn.[68] The Beckhampton club, a political association of local gentlemen, met there in the early 19th century.[69] The innkeeper also trained racehorses in 1848, and in 1855 the inn was closed.[70] Since 1880 or earlier the house and its outbuildings have been used as a racing stable.[71] The house has a symmetrical front with the public rooms at the north end and domestic quarters to the south.

Stanmore, 5 km. north-west of Avebury, was held with lands in Beckhampton from the 11th century and in 1700 was said to be a detached but tithable part of Beckhampton.[72] The eastern part of Stanmore then became part of Winterbourne Bassett parish and the western part was then or later absorbed into Clyffe Pypard parish.[73] From the 12th century to the 16th there was a village or farmstead a little east of the boundary of the modern parish of Winterbourne Bassett. The last inhabitants were said to have left within living memory c. 1700.[74]

WEST KENNETT. The small village of West Kennett, some 2 km. south-east of Avebury, lies on valley gravel between Waden and Overton Hills north of the Kennet. It was always the least prosperous and populous settlement in the parish. In 1334 it was assessed for taxation at 30s. and in 1377 there were 24 poll-tax payers.[75] In 1576 the combined assessment of West and East Kennett for taxation was only £6 11s. 6d., below the average for the hundred.[76] In the late 18th century the few houses, most of which incorporated stones from the Kennett Avenue, stood south of the London-Bath road.[77] The village expanded in the 19th century when a brewery and a number of houses were built on both sides of the road.[78] In 1841, the only date for which a

figure is available, there were 108 inhabitants.[79] Several buildings were demolished c. 1960 when the road was widened[80] and in 1979 there were a few cottages and four substantial houses. West Kennett House, a three-storey house of the mid 19th century, stood north of the road on a steep slope. West Kennett Farm, opposite the house, has a main range of the 17th century, which preserves a cross-passage ground plan, and an 18th-century service wing. West of the farm-house are Tan Hill House, the only postwar building in the village, and West Kennett Manor. There was a White Hart inn at West Kennett between 1736 and 1827 but nothing is known of its later history.[81]

MANORS AND OTHER ESTATES. The estates in Kennett which Alfred of Marlborough held in 1086 may have included lands now in Avebury but no certain identification can be made.[82] Among them may have been an estate which, in or before 1114, escheated to the Crown and was granted by Henry I to William de Tancarville, his chamberlain.[83] In that year William granted the estate to the abbey of St. Georges de Boscherville near Rouen.[84] Geoffrey son of Pain also gave lands in Avebury to the abbey in 1114 and a priory was established there soon afterwards.[85] The possessions of the alien priory, including *AVEBURY* manor, were granted to Fotheringhay college (Northants.) in 1411.[86] In 1545 the college conveyed Avebury to the Crown in exchange for other lands[87] and in 1547 the manor was granted to Sir William Sharington.[88]

Sharington was attainted in 1549 but his lands were restored in 1550.[89] In 1551 he conveyed the manor to William Dunche,[90] who settled it on his son Walter in 1582. Walter (d. 1595) was succeeded by his son William[91] who sold the manor to Sir John Stawell in 1640.[92] Stawell's estates were sequestrated after the Civil War and in 1652 Avebury manor was sold to George Long.[93] Between 1651 and 1657 it was occupied by Sir Edward Baynton as tenant and possibly as owner.[94] It was recovered at the Restoration and Stawell (d. 1662) was succeeded by his sons George (d. 1669) and Ralph, created Baron Stawell in 1683. Ralph's son John, Lord Stawell, inherited the manor in 1689[95] but after his death in 1692 it was sold to Sir Richard Holford.[96]

[64] Darling, *Reminiscences*, pl. facing p. 40; *Kelly's Dir. Wilts.* (1903, 1911).
[65] W.R.O. 184/1; 529/185.
[66] Ibid. 529/185; ibid. alehousekeepers' recognizances.
[67] Ibid. 184/1; 473/227.
[68] Ibid. 473/45.
[69] *V.C.H. Wilts.* v. 200-1, 205; *W.A.M.* lviii. 385.
[70] *Kelly's Dir. Wilts.* (1848, 1855).
[71] Darling, *Reminiscences*, 20-1.
[72] *V.C.H. Wilts.* ii, p. 147; P.R.O., E 134/11 & 12 Wm. III Hil./8.
[73] *V.C.H. Wilts.* ix. 32; below, Winterbourne Bassett, introduction, manors.
[74] *W.A.M.* lxxi. 138; P.R.O., E 134/11 & 12 Wm. III Hil./8.
[75] *V.C.H. Wilts.* iv. 301, 310.
[76] *Taxation Lists* (W.R.S. x), 103-4.
[77] *W.A.M.* xvii. 333; *Andrews and Dury, Map* (W.R.S. viii), pl. 11.
[78] W.R.O., tithe award.

[79] *V.C.H. Wilts.* iv. 340.
[80] Inf. from Mr. W. J. Osmond, W. Kennett Farm.
[81] *Q. Sess. 1736* (W.R.S. xi), 125; W.R.O., alehouse-keepers' recognizances.
[82] *V.C.H. Wilts.* ii, p. 143; above, introduction; below.
[83] *Rot. Hund.* (Rec. Com.), ii (1), 269.
[84] *Cal. Doc. France*, ed. Round, p. 66.
[85] Ibid.; *V.C.H. Wilts.* iii. 392.
[86] *Cal. Pat.* 1408-13, 358.
[87] *L. & P. Hen. VIII*, xx (1), p. 624.
[88] *Cal. Pat.* 1547-8, 401-2.
[89] Ibid. 1549-51, 188-9.
[90] Ibid. 1550-3, 84.
[91] P.R.O., C 142/238, no. 84.
[92] W.R.O. 184/4.
[93] *Cal. Cttee. for Compounding*, ii. 1429.
[94] W.R.O. 473/52.
[95] *Complete Peerage*, xii (1), 265-8.
[96] P.R.O., C 5/166/23.

Holford (d. 1718) left a life interest in the manor to his wife Susanna,[97] from whom it passed to their son Samuel in 1722. On Samuel's death in 1730 his nephew Richard Holford inherited. The manor passed c. 1742 to Richard's brother Staynor (d. 1767) who devised it to his half-brother Arthur Jones[98] (d. 1789). Jones's heir was his niece Ann, wife of Adam Williamson (d. 1798). Williamson, who was knighted in 1794 and became governor of Jamaica and St. Domingo,[99] devised the manor to his wife's nephew Richard Jones.[1] That Richard and his namesakes held it until 1873.[2] The manor was then sold to Sir Henry Meux, Bt., and passed in 1883 to his son Sir Henry (d. 1900).[3] The younger Sir Henry's widow sold it in 1907 to L. C. D. Jenner.[4] In 1920 Manor farm was bought by J. Peake Garland[5] who sold it after 1939 to A. T. Farthing. The farm, 651 a., was purchased from Farthing in 1943 by the National Trust, the owners in 1979.[6]

The monks of Avebury priory had a manor house on their demesne in 1294.[7] A later house was retained by Jenner on the sale of Manor farm in 1920 and sold c. 1935 to Alexander Keiller.[8] It was bought in 1955 by Sir Francis Knowles, Bt. (d. 1974), and in 1976 by Michael Brudenell-Bruce, marquess of Ailesbury.[9] Avebury Manor extends round three sides of a courtyard with the hall occupying the central southern range. That part of the house which is earlier than a reconstruction of c. 1600 is east of the hall. A single room in 1979, it was formerly two small rooms and a passage, probably the screens passage of a medieval house, the hall range of which was in much the same position as the present one. The hall was rebuilt c. 1600[10] as a ground floor room with a principal chamber above and a new screens passage across its west end. Beyond the screens were new service rooms, and a parlour was built as a southern continuation of the medieval service end. By the late 17th century there was a service passage behind the hall. The old service range was continued northwards by a kitchen, probably on the site of, and perhaps incorporating parts of, its 16th-century predecessor, beyond which was a structurally later brewhouse.[11] In the mid 18th century the hall, the chamber above it, and the main staircase were elaborately refitted and further service rooms were built along the north side of the hall range.[12] New gatepiers and wrought-iron gates were then placed in the southern boundary wall. Thereafter the house was little altered until the early 20th century. Jenner carried out a thorough reconstruction of the surviving features of the old house, introduced a number of old fittings from elsewhere, and enlarged some windows. He reconstructed the interior of the west range to make new principal rooms and added a library wing to its north end.

AVEBURY MANOR FROM THE SOUTH IN THE 18TH CENTURY

In 1086 Rainbold the priest held Avebury church and 2 hides.[13] In 1133 Henry III granted to Cirencester abbey all the estates formerly Rainbold's, including the reversion of Avebury church, then held for life by Roger (d. 1139), bishop of Salisbury.[14] Thereafter the abbey held the *RECTORY* estate consisting of lands, the rectorial tithes of Avebury and West Kennett, and some dues from Beckhampton.[15] Between 1195 and 1275 the vicarial tithes of Avebury and West Kennett were also due to the abbey.[16] In 1183, 1240, 1253, and 1336 agreements were reached with the prior of Avebury for the payment of tithes from the demesne of Avebury manor but no major concession was made by the abbey.[17] In 1540 the abbey's possessions in Avebury were said to have included the rectory estate and a manor; of the two the lands of the rectory estate were probably more extensive.[18]

After the Dissolution the rectory estate remained in the hands of the Crown until 1604 when it was granted to Maria, relict of William Dunche.[19] The lands were probably absorbed into those of Avebury manor, then also held by members of the Dunche family. In 1628 the tithes were held by William Dunche, Maria's grandson, who sold those arising from Avebury manor with the manor to Sir John Stawell in 1640.[20]

[97] P.R.O., PROB 11/564 (P.C.C. 119 Tenison).
[98] W.R.O. 271/2.
[99] *W.N. & Q.* viii. 273–4; *D.N.B.*
[1] *W.A.M.* lvi. 368.
[2] *Kelly's Dir. Wilts.* (1848); *W.N. & Q.* viii. 278.
[3] W.R.O. 271/11; *Kelly's Dir. Wilts.* (1875); Burke, *Peerage* (1907), 1150.
[4] *W.A.M.* lvi. 368.
[5] Ibid. xli. 163.
[6] *Kelly's Dir. Wilts.* (1939); Nat. Trust, Wessex Regional Off., Stourton, Avebury deeds.
[7] P.R.O., E 106/2/2.
[8] *Kelly's Dir. Wilts.* (1927, 1935, 1939); *W.A.M.* lvi. 370.
[9] *Avebury Man. Guide* (1978).
[10] The date 1601 and initials I.M.D. are above the main doorway. Sir Jas. Mervyn married Deborah, relict of Walter

Dunche (d. 1595), and lived in the ho. c. 1600: P.R.O., E 134/40 & 41 Eliz. I Mich./7.
[11] Cf. plan of 1695: W.R.O. 184/9.
[12] A stone on a gable is inscribed S.H. 1750.
[13] *V.C.H. Wilts.* ii, p. 119.
[14] *Cirencester Cart.* i, pp. 21–4.
[15] *Inq. Non.* (Rec. Com.), 158; below, church.
[16] *Cirencester Cart.* i, pp. 153–4; iii, pp. 1052–4.
[17] Ibid. ii, pp. 420, 423–7; iii, pp. 1047–9. *V.C.H. Wilts.* iii. 392 wrongly gives 1253 as the date of the earliest agreement.
[18] P.R.O., E 310/26/153; E 134/40 & 41 Eliz. I Mich./7; E 134/41 Eliz. I Hil./8.
[19] *Cal. S.P. Dom.* 1603–10, 128.
[20] P.R.O., CP 25(2)/508/3 Chas. I Mich.; *W.N. & Q.* viii. 221.

The remaining tithes passed with Avebury Trusloe manor to Robert Baynton.[21] Those of West Kennett were sold to Charles Tooker in 1676[22] and descended with East Kennett manor until they were sold by Benjamin Price to William Tanner in 1791.[23] The tithes on West Kennett farm were then merged. William Tanner received tithes from 331 a. of West Kennett which were commuted in 1845.[24]

Tithes on lands which passed to George Popham and Henry Baynton may have been merged while they were in Robert Baynton's hands: the lands were tithe free in 1845.[25] Other tithes were sold with lands in 1681:[26] the estates of John Griffen, Richard Phelps, and Mary Stevens were probably tithe free.[27] The remaining tithes with those arising from Avebury Trusloe manor, afterwards considered merged, were sold to John White in 1704.[28] They descended to J. W. Hopkins, who in 1845 held the tithes on 136 a. for which a rent charge was then substituted.[29]

From the early 14th century the abbot of Cirencester had a house at Avebury. It stood near the Circle and the manor house of Avebury manor, and is perhaps to be identified with that on the rectory estate in the mid 16th century.[30]

The manor formerly held by Cirencester abbey was granted by the Crown to Anselm Lane in 1558, to William Allen in the same year,[31] and to John Cutt and Richard Roberts in 1560.[32] In 1563 Roberts conveyed it to Joan Trusloe,[33] who was succeeded in 1568 by her son John Trusloe. John (d. 1593) devised it to a relative, Richard Trusloe of Teffont Evias.[34] In 1614 Richard was succeeded by his son John[35] who conveyed the manor to William Smith in 1623.[36] In 1628 the manor of *AVEBURY TRUSLOE* was held by William Dunche.[37] In 1633 Dunche sold it to Sir Edward Baynton,[38] whose son Robert inherited it in 1657.[39] Robert sold the estate in several portions. John Griffen bought one portion in 1681.[40] In 1704 Griffen's estate was sold to John White (d. 1712),[41] vicar of Avebury. It passed to White's son William who sold it before 1755 to Robert Rose.[42] The estate was held by William Simkins in 1780, and in 1795 by Charles

Simkins who sold it c. 1797 to a Mr. Hopkins,[43] possibly John Hopkins (fl. 1779).[44] John William Hopkins held it in 1845.[45] It was sold in 1877, probably to G. Ruddle.[46] In 1904 it was bought by William Grose[47] who sold the Avebury Trusloe Manor estate to William Greader in 1923.[48] Between 1935 and 1939 it was purchased by Butler Bros., the owners in 1979.[49] A house attached to the Trusloes' estate stood near Avebury manor house in the mid 16th century.[50] It cannot be identified with any later building. Manor Farm at Avebury Trusloe was built on the estate in the 19th century. It is surrounded by farm buildings of similar and later date.

Another part of the Bayntons' estate was bought in or before 1675 by George Popham (d. 1687).[51] It was sold by George's son John to William Norris in 1691.[52] Norris (d. 1717) was succeeded by his son John (d. 1758) and grandson William Norris (d. 1794).[53] The estate, known in the late 18th century as Popham's or Little Avebury farm, was held in 1806 by George William Norris (d. 1811)[54] who devised it to his brother James.[55] James sold the farm in 1816 to John Brown (d. 1839). In 1845 and 1875 it was held by George Brown[56] and in 1897 by S. Brown.[57] Another George Brown, the owner in 1911, sold it c. 1930 to William Greader,[58] who sold the farm between 1935 and 1939 to Butler Bros., the owners in 1979.[59] Trusloe Manor, in 1795 the farmhouse of Popham's farm, is a small 17th-century house which has a tall east front with mullioned and transomed windows.

Lands formerly held of Avebury Trusloe manor by copy of court roll were sold in 1681 by Robert Baynton in three portions. One portion was conveyed to John Griffen (d. 1715)[60] and passed in turn to his son John (d. 1733) and daughter Mary, wife of John Banning (d. 1772). Banning was succeeded by his son John[61] and the property passed to members of the Banning and Griffen families in the early 19th century.[62] It was held by J. Banning in 1873,[63] by J. S. Banning in 1877,[64] and was sold in lots in 1894.[65]

A second portion passed to Richard Phelps in 1681[66] and was inherited by his son John (d.

[21] P.R.O., E 112/535/164; below.
[22] W.R.O. 371/2.
[23] Ibid. 1366/8; below, E. Kennett, manor.
[24] W.R.O., tithe award.
[25] Ibid.; below.   [26] W.R.O. 184/4.
[27] Ibid. 529/125; 212A/36/1, no. 1; 435/24; ibid. tithe award; below.
[28] P.R.O., CP 25(2)/979/3 Anne Mich.
[29] W.R.O., tithe award.
[30] *Cirencester Cart.* iii, pp. 1050-1; P.R.O., E 134/40 & 41 Eliz. I Mich./7.
[31] P.R.O., E 318/Box 41/Phil. and Mary/2188; B.L. Harl. MS. 608, f. 50v.
[32] *Cal. Pat.* 1558-60, 464-5.
[33] P.R.O., CP 25(2)/289/4 Eliz. I East.
[34] *W.N. & Q.* v. 546; P.R.O., C 142/237, no. 132.
[35] P.R.O., C 142/333, no. 29.
[36] Ibid. CP 25(2)/372/20 Jas. I Trin.
[37] Ibid. CP 25(2)/508/3 Chas. I Mich.
[38] W.R.O. 184/4.
[39] Burke, *Commoners* (1833-8), iv. 685.
[40] W.R.O. 184/4.
[41] P.R.O., CP 25(2)/979/3 Anne Mich.; W.R.O. 435/24/1/8. Sir Ric. Holford was said to be lord of Avebury Trusloe manor in 1710, but the grounds for the claim are not clear: ibid. 184/1.
[42] W.R.O. 435/24/1/8.

[43] Ibid. land tax; inclosure award.
[44] Ibid. 212A/31/4.
[45] Ibid. tithe award.
[46] W.A.S. Libr., sale cat. ii, no. 17; viii, no. 6.
[47] Ibid. sale cat. iv, no. 3; *Kelly's Dir. Wilts.* (1911).
[48] W.A.S. Libr., sale cat. xvii, no. 38; *Kelly's Dir. Wilts.* (1923).
[49] *Kelly's Dir. Wilts.* (1935, 1939); inf. from Mr. P. S. Layley, Manor Farm, Avebury Trusloe.
[50] P.R.O., E 134/40 & 41 Eliz. I Mich./7.
[51] Herts. R.O. 27240.
[52] Norris Estate Act, 31 Geo. II, c. 19 (Priv. Act); Burke, *Commoners* (1833-8), ii. 199.
[53] W.R.O. 415/134.
[54] Ibid. 473/73.
[55] Ibid. 473/352; mon. in church.
[56] W.R.O., tithe award; *Kelly's Dir. Wilts.* (1875).
[57] W.A.S. Libr., sale cat. ii, no. 17.
[58] *Kelly's Dir. Wilts.* (1911, 1927, 1931).
[59] Ibid. (1935, 1939); inf. from Mr. and Mrs. A. Titcombe, 10 Trusloe Cottages.
[60] W.R.O. 435/24.
[61] Ibid. 464/56.
[62] Ibid. 212B/119; ibid. land tax.
[63] W.A.S. Libr., sale cat. ii, no. 20.
[64] Ibid. viii, no. 6.
[65] Wilts. Cuttings, v. 189.   [66] W.R.O. 529/125.

1731) and grandson Richard Phelps (d. 1744). On the death of Richard's widow Mary it passed to his sisters and coheirs.[67] John Savage (d. before 1770), husband of Richard's sister Eleanor, acquired the reversion of the estate in 1757. The estate was sold in 1770 to Richard Bailey, James Thring, and John Nalder as joint owners.[68] It was held in 1802 by Richard Thring (d. c. 1826)[69] who devised it to his grandson Edward Phipson (d. 1869) and Edward's sisters Mary Ann (d. 1875) and Elizabeth Thring Phipson (d. c. 1907). Edward's portion passed to his daughter Irene Jane, later wife of James Bernard Wall. His sisters' portions passed to Irene and to Sarah Lydia Selby, also their niece, later wife of Thomas Lockwood Heward.[70] The farm inherited by Irene and Sarah, called Norris's farm, was sold in 1920 to J. Peake Garland.[71] It was later bought by Alexander Keiller. In 1943 Keiller sold the farm and an additional 70 a. at Windmill Hill which he had purchased in 1924–5 to the National Trust.[72]

A smaller portion of lands was sold in 1681 to Mary Stevens, later wife of Walter Stretch. Their son George held the land in 1725[73] and his daughter Mary and her husband James Hitchcock sold it in 1755 to Richard Bailey, James Thring, and John Nalder.[74] It may have been part of an estate, held by Robert Nalder in 1780, which passed, probably by sale, to another Hitchcock c. 1803. That estate was held by P. Hitchcock in 1828[75] and by trustees for M. P. Hitchcock in 1845.[76] It had been absorbed into Avebury Manor estate by 1873 but Hitchcocks farm was still so called in 1875.[77] The farmhouse was later known as Manor Farm.[78]

Brunsden's farm, probably also the successor of a copyhold of Avebury Trusloe manor, passed, presumably with that manor, from John Trusloe (fl. 1623) to William Dunche (d. 1666) and from Dunche to the Baynton family.[79] It was retained by Robert Baynton when he sold the manor and passed to his nephew Henry Baynton, who sold it in 1691 to William Norris.[80] As Great farm, it passed with Little Avebury farm until 1796 when it was purchased by John Brown.[81] The farms descended together in the Brown family from 1816 until 1924 when William May bought Trusloe, including part of Great, farm.[82] He sold it c. 1930 to William Greader and thereafter it passed with Greader's other holdings.[83]

In 1194 John of Calstone and his wife Margaret were ordered to return 1 yardland in Avebury, part of the dowry of Maud, wife of Sewel del Broc.[84] Philip of Calstone gave 4 a. of meadow there to Stanley abbey in 1227, and in 1228 his nephew and heir Walter of Calstone confirmed the grant and made a further gift of meadow to the abbey.[85] Stanley mead, perhaps those lands or the meadow west of the river occupied by John of Stanley in 1307,[86] was sold by Richard Smith and his son Thomas to Daniel Dyke in 1713.[87]

Lands at Avebury which had been given for the maintenance of a lamp in the church were held by the Crown from the Dissolution until 1575 or later and in 1547 were on lease to John Chesterman.[88] Some 3 yardlands, called Higdens, were bought from Thomas and Catherine Henslow by Richard Smith (d. 1633).[89] Chestermans, c. 35 a., and Higdens passed with West Kennett manor to Richard Smith and his son Thomas who together sold them to Daniel Dyke in 1713.[90] By will dated 1729 Dyke devised his estates to his sister Margery with reversion to his niece Sarah Walter.[91] In 1751 they were held by Sarah, then wife of Henry Howson.[92] Sarah (d. c. 1787) devised them to her son Henry for life and then to her nephew Daniel Dyke.[93] Daniel's brother Thomas Webb Dyke (d. c. 1822) held the estate in 1795[94] and he devised a life interest to John Skinner, husband of his sister Susan. In 1830 the estate was sold by the heirs of Daniel's mother, Mary Dyke, to Thomas Merriman.[95] In 1873 it was held as owner or occupier by E. Combley[96] and in 1877 by J. E. Combley.[97] It was sold in 1904 with Avebury Trusloe Manor estate to William Grose[98] and has since passed with that estate.

In 1494 Richard Beauchamp, Lord St. Amand, his wife Anne, and Sir Roger Tocotes were licensed to assign lands in Avebury to the chaplain of Bromham.[99] Rents due to the lord of Avebury were extinguished under Edward VI when both manor and chantry were held by the Crown.[1] The possessions of the chantry were granted to Edward Carey in 1564[2] and in 1582 the lands in Avebury, Rowses farm, were held by John Shuter.[3] Shuter (d. 1591) devised the farm to his grandson John Shuter, who sold it to John Goldsmith after 1611.[4] Goldsmith (d. 1640) devised Rowses to his son Thomas.[5] The later history of the estate is not clear but it may have been that held in 1780 by one Warner, in 1783 by

---

[67] W.R.O. 212A/31/2.
[68] Ibid.; 212A/31/4.
[69] Ibid. 212A/31/4; 137/14/6.
[70] Princ. Regy. Fam. Div., 1869, will of Edw. Phipson; 1875, will of Mary Ann Phipson; 1907, will of Eliz. Thring Phipson.
[71] W.R.O. 1102/6.
[72] Nat. Trust, Wessex Regional Off., Avebury deeds.
[73] W.R.O. 212A/36/1, no. 1.
[74] Ibid. 212A/31/4.
[75] Ibid. land tax.
[76] Ibid. tithe award.
[77] Ibid. 271/11; Kelly's Dir. Wilts. (1875).
[78] Nat. Trust, Wessex Regional Off., Avebury deeds.
[79] P.R.O., PROB 11/321 (P.C.C. 114 Mico, will of Wm. Dunche); ibid. E 134/40 & 41 Eliz. I Mich./7; above.
[80] W.R.O. 415/134, abstr. of title of Wm. Norris.
[81] Ibid. 473/352.
[82] Above; W.A.S. Libr., sale cat. xix, no. 59.
[83] Inf. from Mr. and Mrs. Titcombe.
[84] Abbrev. Plac. (Rec. Com.), 12.

[85] P.R.O., CP 25(1)/250/6, no. 68.
[86] Cirencester Cart. iii, p. 1052.
[87] W.R.O. 212A/36/11.
[88] P.R.O., E 301/58, f. 85; E 178/2863.
[89] Wilts. Inq. p.m. 1625–49 (Index Libr.), 183.
[90] W.R.O. 568/5; below.
[91] W.R.O. 700/115.
[92] Ibid. 184/3.
[93] Ibid. 700/115.
[94] Ibid. inclosure award.
[95] Ibid. 700/115.
[96] W.A.S. Libr., sale cat. ii, no. 20.
[97] Ibid. viii, no. 6.
[98] Ibid. iv, no. 3.
[99] Cal. Pat. 1485–94, 471.
[1] Ibid. 1566–9, 94.
[2] Ibid. 1563–6, 80.
[3] P.R.O., REQ 2/92/35.
[4] Ibid. STAC 8/269/32.
[5] Wilts. Inq. p.m. 1625–49 (Index Libr.), 375–6.

William Crook,[6] and in 1813 by R. Crook, possibly William's son. Crook sold the estate to James Kemm in 1843.[7] Westbrook farm, the successor to Kemm's estate, was held between 1903 and 1920 by George Farley, perhaps as tenant until 1909 and then as owner.[8] It had passed to J. Farley by 1923. Between 1935 and 1940 it was sold several times and some of the land was absorbed into Avebury Trusloe Manor estate.[9]

BECKHAMPTON was held by Edric in 1066 and by Ansfrid of Gilbert of Breteuil in 1086.[10] The overlordship passed with that of Clyffe Pypard to the Reviers family and in 1242–3 was held by Baldwin de Reviers, earl of Devon (d. 1245).[11] He was succeeded in turn by his son Baldwin, earl of Devon (d. 1262), and daughter Isabel de Forz, countess of Aumale and Devon.[12] Walter Marshal, earl of Pembroke (d. 1245), held Beckhampton of the earl of Devon in 1242–3 and his five sisters and coheirs held it of Isabel de Forz in 1275.[13] No mention has been found of the Marshal or de Forz lordships after that date. A second intermediate lord, Matthew Columbers, held Beckhampton in 1242–3 and later.[14] His interest passed with the manor of Clyffe Pypard to the Cobham family. In 1315 Beckhampton was said to be held of John Cobham, although by that date he had been succeeded by his son Henry, created Lord Cobham c. 1335.[15] The lordship then passed in the Cobham and Wroughton families with the manor of Broad Hinton, of which it was said to be part in 1374.[16] Beckhampton manor was held of John Wroughton in 1463.[17] Before 1485 the lordship passed to Fotheringhay college, the overlord in 1495.[18]

Hilary of Beckhampton held Beckhampton c. 1190,[19] as did Hamon of Beckhampton c. 1235 and in 1242–3.[20] John, son of Richard of Beckhampton, had a manor there in 1268.[21] Before 1302 a moiety of it passed to Joan, wife of Sir Henry le Moyne,[22] and after her death in 1340 it descended with the manor of Shipton Moyne (Glos.) to their son John, grandson Sir Henry le Moyne, and great-grandson John le Moyne (d. by 1381).[23] John's heir, then a minor, was probably Sir John Moyne who held the moiety in 1428.[24] It passed to John Stourton (created Baron Stourton in 1448), son of Sir John's daughter

Elizabeth. Lord Stourton was succeeded in 1462 by his son William, Lord Stourton (d. 1478).[25] In 1467 the estate was settled on William's son John, Lord Stourton (d. 1485), and John's wife Catherine.[26] After Catherine's death in 1494 the moiety passed in turn to her husband's brothers William, Lord Stourton, and Edward, Lord Stourton, who both died in 1524.[27] Edward's son William, Lord Stourton, sold the moiety to William Button[28] (d. 1549), who was succeeded by his grandson William Button (d. 1591)[29] and great-grandson Ambrose Button. Ambrose sold the estate in 1596 to Richard Trusloe,[30] who was succeeded by his son John in 1614.[31] A portion of the estate was sold to Thomas Smith c. 1638 and the remainder passed to John's son John, who held it in 1692, and grandson Richard Trusloe. In 1702 Trusloe sold it to Charles Tooker who also acquired the other moiety of Beckhampton manor.[32] Both moieties were sold as Griffens, Trusloes, or Beckhampton farm and Goddards farm to Sir Richard Holford in 1710.[33] The estate passed with Avebury manor to his grandson Richard Holford, who conveyed it to his uncle Robert Holford in 1731.[34] Robert was succeeded by his sons Robert and Peter (d. 1803).[35] The estate passed to Peter's sons Robert (d. 1838) and George (d. 1839), grandson Robert Staynor Holford (d. 1892), and great-grandson George Lindsay Holford.[36] It was sold in 1897 to Samuel Darling, the racehorse trainer.[37] After his death in 1921[38] his estate, some 1,200 a.,[39] was broken up. His son Frederick retained some 670 a. which were sold to J. A. Dewar in 1947 and to Mr. H. G. Blagrave in 1950. Mr. Blagrave sold all but 20 a. to Beckhampton Estates in 1969.[40] In 1926 Galtee More farm, some 206 a., was bought by C. N. Hues. He was succeeded in 1956 by his sons Robert and Roger Hues, joint owners until Robert's death in 1979.[41] Galtee More Farm, a two-storey brick house, was enlarged or rebuilt in the 19th century.[42] Lower Galtee More farm, 287 a., was sold in 1923 to C. D. Butler & Co.[43] and in 1926 to William Vines. It was bought c. 1959 by Mrs. Elizabeth Westropp, the owner in 1979, when it was known as Durran farm.[44]

The second moiety of Beckhampton manor was held by Richard Casterton in 1316 and by Geoffrey Casterton in 1428.[45] With the manor

[6] W.R.O., inclosure award; land tax.
[7] Ibid. 212B/119.
[8] *Kelly's Dir. Wilts.* (1903, 1911, 1915, 1920); Wilts. Cuttings, viii. 126. Trustees of J. Banks were said to be owners in 1904: W.A.S. Libr., sale cat. iv, no. 3.
[9] *Kelly's Dir. Wilts.* (1923 and later edns.); local inf.
[10] *V.C.H. Wilts.* ii, p. 147.
[11] Ibid. ix. 27; *Bk. of Fees*, ii. 749.
[12] *Complete Peerage*, iv. 318–22.
[13] Ibid. x. 376; *Rot. Hund.* (Rec. Com.), ii (1), 269.
[14] *Bk. of Fees*, ii. 749; *Rot. Hund.* (Rec. Com.), ii (1), 269.
[15] *V.C.H. Wilts.* ix. 27; *Cal. Inq. p.m.* v, p. 285.
[16] Below, Broad Hinton, manors; *Cal. Inq. p.m.* xiv, p. 76.
[17] P.R.O., C 140/8, no. 18.
[18] *Cal. Inq. p.m. Hen. VII*, i, pp. 60–1, 478–9.
[19] *Cirencester Cart.* ii, pp. 429–30.
[20] Ibid. pp. 430–1; *Bk. of Fees*, ii. 749.
[21] *Abbrev. Plac.* (Rec. Com.), 164–5, 168.
[22] *Reg. Ghent* (Cant. & York Soc.), ii. 614; *Wilts. Inq. p.m. 1242–1326* (Index Libr.), 398.
[23] *V.C.H. Glos.* xi. 249.
[24] Ibid.; *Feud. Aids*, v. 269.
[25] *Complete Peerage*; P.R.O., C 140/8, no. 18.

[26] *Cal. Inq. p.m. Hen. VII*, i, pp. 60–1.
[27] Ibid. pp. 478–9; *Complete Peerage*, xii (1), p. 306.
[28] P.R.O., CP 25(2)/46/322, no. 37.
[29] Ibid. C 142/87, no. 101; C 142/239, no. 123.
[30] *V.C.H. Wilts.* x. 218; B.L. Add. Ch. 40086; W.R.O. 184/4, abstr. of title to Griffens farm.
[31] P.R.O., C 142/133, no. 29.
[32] W.R.O. 184/4; below.
[33] W.R.O. 184/4; 371/1; P.R.O., C 5/355/32.
[34] W.R.O. 371/1.   [35] Ibid. 271/2.
[36] Burke, *Land. Gent.* (1906), i. 839; W.R.O., tithe award.
[37] W.A.S. Libr., sale cat. xix, no. 17; Darling, *Reminiscences*, 21.
[38] *W.A.M.* xli. 438.
[39] Darling, *Reminiscences*, 240.
[40] Inf. from Mr. H. G. Blagrave, the Grange, Beckhampton.
[41] Inf. from Mr. Roger Hues, Galtee More Farm.
[42] W.R.O., inclosure award; O.S. Map 6″, Wilts. XXVIII. SW. (1900 edn.).
[43] W.A.S. Libr., sale cat. xix, no. 17.
[44] Inf. from Mrs. E. Westropp, Durran Farm.
[45] *Feud. Aids*, v. 205, 269.

of Wheathampstead (Herts.) it passed in the Casterton family until 1445 when Richard Casterton was succeeded by his daughter Elizabeth, wife of Nicholas Freton. It was probably held in 1503 and in 1547 by John Colville (d. 1552).[46] William Saville and his wife Anne, perhaps Colville's relict or daughter, sold the moiety in 1561.[47] John Mitchell sold it to Thomas Goddard of Upham in Aldbourne in 1573[48] and thereafter it descended like the manors of East and West Swindon from father to son in the Goddard family until 1702, when Thomas Goddard sold the farm to Charles Tooker.[49]

The portion of Trusloe's estate purchased by Thomas Smith c. 1638 passed with West Kennett manor to his great-grandson Thomas Smith who sold it to Daniel Dyke in 1713.[50] Probably before 1743 it was acquired by John Beake who sold it in 1749 to Prince Sutton (d. 1779).[51] Sutton was succeeded by his son James whose daughters Eleanor, wife of Thomas Grimston Bucknall Estcourt, and Sarah, wife of James Matthews, inherited in 1801. Sarah and James Matthews conveyed their rights in the farm in Beckhampton to Estcourt in 1804.[52] The farm was held by Anthony Guy between 1815 and 1828 and by Thomas Pinnegar in 1829.[53] It remained in the Pinnegar family at least until 1897 when it was held by Thomas Lord Pinnegar.[54] It was bought c. 1900 by Samuel Darling[55] and was part of his estate divided in the 1920s.[56]

Coles Bargain, a farm of 180 a. held by Francis Hawes, a director of the South Sea Company, was sold by trustees in 1726 to Sarah Churchill (d. 1744), duchess of Marlborough. The farm descended with the Marlborough title until sold in 1823 by the trustees of George Spencer (d. 1817), duke of Marlborough, to Robert Holford.[57] It was then absorbed into Beckhampton manor.[58]

At the Dissolution, the estate attached to Beckhampton chapel included all tithes on two farms in Beckhampton except those on sheep, a messuage, 1 a. of pasture, and 1 yardland in Beckhampton and Stanmore.[59] In 1549 it was granted to John Warner, Regius Professor of Medicine in the university of Oxford and former chaplain of Beckhampton.[60] Warner sold it in 1561 to Thomas Browne,[61] who granted it to Reynold Howse in 1569. In 1570 Howse settled it

on Robert Howse and Robert's son Robert who both sold it in 1584 to John Trusloe (d. 1593). It passed to Richard Trusloe (d. 1614) and Richard's son John who sold the estate to William Dunche. It descended with Avebury Trusloe manor to Robert Baynton who sold it to Charles Tooker (d. 1700).[62] Tooker's son Charles sold the estate to Sir Richard Holford in 1710[63] and thereafter it descended with Beckhampton manor. In 1845 the tithes of Beckhampton were commuted.[64]

Hilary of Beckhampton (fl. c. 1190) granted an annual rent of 8s. from the tithes of his demesne to Malmesbury abbey.[65] The rent was still paid in 1535[66] and in 1588 was granted with other pensions to Edward Hobbs and others.[67]

Alfred of Marlborough held Kennett in 1086.[68] The overlordship passed with his manor of Lydiard Tregoze and was held by John Tregoze in 1275.[69] In 1518 the manor of *WEST KENNETT* was held of Sir John Leigh and in 1529 of his heirs.[70]

In 1066 Uluiet, Edmar, Leuric, Alnod, and Ulmar held lands in Kennett later Alfred's. All but Alnod and Ulmar, who had been replaced by Nicholas and Turstin, were his tenants in 1086.[71] No certain identification can be made of holdings derived from theirs. There was a number of estates in West Kennett between the 11th century and the 15th, the descent and eventual coalescence of which have not been fully traced.

Thomas of Kennett had demesne lands in the parish in 1239.[72] In 1242–3 he was one of four tenants of Robert Tregoze[73] and in 1275 he held a moiety of West Kennett.[74] In 1227 Walter de Indingeburg granted lands there to John Barbost[75] which John held of Robert Tregoze in 1242–3.[76] In 1275 Geoffrey Barbost held the second moiety of West Kennett.[77] Adam Barbost and his wife Alice granted lands there to trustees in 1334.[78] Walter son of John, the third of the tenants in 1242–3,[79] may have been the Walter of Berwick to whom Reynold of Berwick and his wife Edith confirmed lands in East or West Kennett in 1250.[80] In 1281 Walter of Berwick granted 10 yardlands in West Kennett to John of Berwick,[81] who still held them in 1327.[82] William Crispin held lands there in 1242–3 and in 1288.[83] His estate may have been that held by William Wroughton and his wife Isabel in 1365,[84] and by Isabel alone in 1393.[85] Its later descent is obscure.

[46] *V.C.H. Herts.* ii. 309; P.R.O., E 301/58, f. 77.
[47] *V.C.H. Herts.* ii. 309; P.R.O., CP 25(2)/239/3 & 4 Eliz. I Mich.
[48] W.R.O. 184/4.
[49] Ibid.; *V.C.H. Wilts.* ix. 120.
[50] Below; W.R.O. 248/75.
[51] W.R.O. 212A/31/3; 184/1; 248/75.
[52] Ibid. 248/75; *V.C.H. Wilts.* x. 115, 290.
[53] W.R.O., land tax.
[54] Ibid. tithe award; W.A.S. Libr., sale cat. ii, no. 17.
[55] Darling, *Reminiscences*, 230.   [56] Above.
[57] P.R.O., CP 25(2)/1079/12 Geo. I East.; W.R.O. 371/1; *Complete Peerage*.
[58] W.R.O., tithe award.   [59] P.R.O., E 301/58, f. 77.
[60] Ibid.; *Cal. Pat. 1549–51*, 53; *Alum. Oxon. 1500–1714*, iv. 1574.
[61] *Cal. Pat. 1560–3*, 202.
[62] W.R.O. 184/4, abstr. of title; below, E. Kennett, manor.
[63] W.R.O. 184/4, abstr. of title.
[64] Ibid. tithe award.
[65] *Reg. Malmsburiense* (Rolls Ser.), i. 443–4; *Cirencester*

Cart. ii, pp. 429–30.
[66] *Valor Eccl.* (Rec. Com.), ii. 133.
[67] P.R.O., E 310/26/154, f. 6.
[68] *V.C.H. Wilts.* ii, p. 143.
[69] Ibid. ix. 78; *Rot. Hund.* (Rec. Com.), ii (1), 269.
[70] P.R.O., C 142/34, no. 15; C 142/50, no. 65.
[71] *V.C.H. Wilts.* ii, p. 143.
[72] *Cirencester Cart.* ii, pp. 427–8.
[73] *Bk. of Fees*, ii. 748.
[74] *Rot. Hund.* (Rec. Com.), ii (1), 269.
[75] P.R.O., CP 25(1)/250/6, no. 63.
[76] *Bk. of Fees*, ii. 748.
[77] *Rot. Hund.* (Rec. Com.), ii (1), 269.
[78] *Feet of F. 1327–77* (W.R.S. xxix), p. 29.
[79] *Bk. of Fees*, ii. 748–9.
[80] P.R.O., CP 25(1)/251/17, no. 3.
[81] *Feet of F. 1272–1327* (W.R.S. i), p. 17.
[82] Ibid. *1327–77* (W.R.S. xxix), p. 15.
[83] Ibid. *1272–1327* (W.R.S. i), p. 29; *Bk. of Fees*, ii. 749.
[84] *Feet of F. 1327–77* (W.R.S. xxix), p. 128.
[85] P.R.O., C 136/78, no. 31; *Cal. Close 1392–6*, 161.

ALDBOURNE

The south front of Upper Upham House

RAMSBURY

Crowood House from the north-east *c.* 1800

OGBOURNE ST. ANDREW: OGBOURNE MAIZEY MANOR

OGBOURNE ST. GEORGE: THE MANOR HOUSE

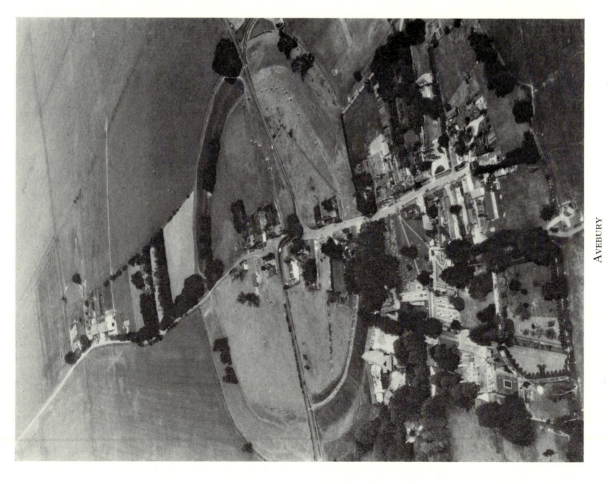

AVEBURY

View of the village and circle from the west, 1956. The church and Avebury Manor are in the left foreground.

In 1412 William Sparsholt held lands to be identified with the later manor of West Kennett.[86] The lands passed to John Benger (d. 1518), son of William's daughter Eleanor.[87] John was succeeded by his grandson Richard Benger (d. 1524) and granddaughter Anne Benger, later wife of Thomas Smith.[88] After Thomas's death *c.* 1558, the manor was settled on Anne (fl. 1573) for life with remainder to Ralph Henslow and his wife.[89] In 1594 Thomas Henslow, Ralph's son, and his wife Catherine sold the manor, then known as Barborscourt and perhaps therefore derived from the holding of the Barbost family, to Thomas Smith[90] (d. *c.* 1597). It passed to Thomas's son Richard (d. 1633) and grandson Thomas Smith.[91] The younger Thomas's son Richard settled the manor on his son Thomas in 1666.[92] Thomas was succeeded in or before 1713 by his brother Richard, whose son Thomas held the manor in 1719.[93] Although Thomas devised the manor by will dated 1750 to his cousin Thomas Smith of Marlborough,[94] in 1755 West Kennett was held jointly by his brother-in-law Samuel Martyn and Staines Chamberlain.[95] In 1780, after Martyn's death, his wife Hannah held the manor.[96] It was inherited *c.* 1807 by their daughter Thermuthis, wife of Robert Ashe (d. 1829). The Ashes were succeeded by their son the Revd. Robert Ashe (d. 1855) and grandson the Revd. Robert Martyn Ashe (fl. 1907).[97] In 1911 the manor was held by Robert Martyn Ashe's daughter Thermuthis Mary Ashe,[98] who sold it to F. E. Shipp in 1921. West Kennett Manor farm was bought by Mr. H. G. Blagrave *c.* 1940. He sold it to C. N. Hues whose son Mr. Roger Hues was owner in 1979.[99] The back range of West Kennett Manor is part of a 17th-century house, to which a principal front was added in the early 18th century. The house has been further altered on several occasions, notably in the early 19th century when a new staircase was inserted and in the late 19th century when the windows were rearranged.

Lands in West Kennett were held in 1682 by Walter Grubbe (d. 1715)[1] and passed to William Grubbe. He was succeeded *c.* 1753 by William Hunt, who took the additional surname Grubbe,[2] by that William's son Thomas (d. *c.* 1772), and grandson William Hunt Grubbe.[3] William Tanner bought the estate *c.* 1784 and it was held by his descendants until offered for sale as West Kennett farm in 1900.[4] In 1911 the farm was held

by William Pullen.[5] It was sold to the Olympia Agricultural Co. in 1920, to J. W. Osmond *c.* 1925, and to Balanter Estates *c.* 1937. Mr. W. J. Osmond, son of J. W. Osmond, bought the farm *c.* 1950.[6]

ECONOMIC HISTORY. AVEBURY. In the 16th century and probably earlier Avebury and Avebury Trusloe formed a single agrarian unit.[7] The open fields, called East and West, were probably divided by the Kennet and its eastern head stream in the 13th century.[8] In the 16th and 17th centuries copyhold lands were said to be held in Eastbrook and Westbrook,[9] a division which may originally have corresponded to that of the open fields. In the 17th century and the 18th open fields, called West and North, were apparently west of the river and north of Avebury village; South field was smaller and probably lay between the village and Waden Hill.[10] The demesne of Avebury manor had been consolidated east of the village by the late 18th century.[11] Common pasture on East down, which probably included Avebury Down, and on West Down[12] may have been allotted to those with holdings in Eastbrook and Westbrook respectively. Inclosures of pasture were made on West Down in the 16th century and on Windmill Hill and Knoll Down in the 17th. Meadow beside the river near Avebury village and near the northern boundary of the parish had been divided into small closes by the mid 17th century, although there was still a common meadow.[13]

In 1114 Avebury manor was valued at £42.[14] The prior of Avebury held 322 a. of arable land in demesne and 15 a. of meadow in 1294. There were then 36 customary tenants of the manor, including 5 yardlanders, 5 ½-yardlanders, and 22 cottagers, who paid rents totalling £4 11s. 9½d. The greater part of the manorial flock was pastured at Catcomb in Hilmarton, a detached part of the manor. In 1294 there was grazing for 300 sheep at Catcomb and for 100 at Avebury.[15] The number of sheep on the manor rose from 250 *c.* 1210 to 800 in 1324.[16]

Little is known of other medieval estates in the tithing. The 2 hides held with the church were worth 10s. in 1086[17] and probably remained a single estate until the 16th century. The abbot of Cirencester held 5 messuages and 3 carucates in 1360.[18] Four free tenants of Avebury manor held

[86] *Feud. Aids*, vi. 534.
[87] P.R.O., C 142/34, no. 15.
[88] Ibid. C 142/50, no. 65.
[89] Ibid. CP 25(2)/239/1 Eliz. I Trin.; *V.C.H. Wilts.* x. 218.
[90] W.R.O. 568/4.
[91] *W.N. & Q.* viii. 468; *Wilts. Inq. p.m.* 1625-49 (Index Libr.), 183.
[92] W.R.O. 568/5.
[93] Ibid.; 118/88.
[94] Ibid. 118/88.
[95] Ibid. 568/7.
[96] Ibid.; ibid. land tax.
[97] Ibid. land tax; Burke, *Land. Gent.* (1871), i. 29.
[98] Burke, *Land. Gent.* (1871), i. 29; *Kelly's Dir. Wilts.* (1911); W.A.S. Libr., sale cat. xiv, no. 33.
[99] Inf. from Mr. W. J. Osmond, W. Kennett Farm.
[1] W.R.O., bishop, glebe terrier; Burke, *Land. Gent.* (1846), i. 511.
[2] Grubbe Estate Act, 26 Geo. II, c. 40 (Priv. Act).
[3] P.R.O., PROB 11/981 (P.C.C. 329 Taverner).

[4] W.R.O., land tax; tithe award; Wilts. Cuttings, xvi. 48.
[5] *Kelly's Dir. Wilts.*
[6] Inf. from Mr. Osmond.
[7] P.R.O., E 134/40 & 41 Eliz. I Mich./7; E 134/41 Eliz. I Hil./8.
[8] Ibid. E 310/26/155; *Cirencester Cart.* iii, p. 1054.
[9] P.R.O., E 134/41 Eliz. I Hil./8; W.R.O. 435/24; 529/125.
[10] P.R.O., E 134/8 Chas. I Mich./53; W.R.O., bishop, glebe terrier, 1682; ibid. 473/274; Herts. R.O. 27240.
[11] W.R.O., inclosure award.
[12] Ibid. 473/52, ff. 15v.-16, 49, 72.
[13] Ibid. 473/274; 529/125; 435/24; P.R.O., E 134/40 & 41 Eliz. I Mich./7.
[14] *Cal. Doc. France*, ed. Round, p. 66.
[15] P.R.O., E 106/2/2.
[16] Ibid. E 106/8/26; *Interdict Doc.* (Pipe R. Soc. N.S. xxxiv), 29.
[17] *V.C.H. Wilts.* ii, p. 119.
[18] *Cirencester Cart.* ii, p. 353.

a total of 6½ yardlands and paid rents totalling 67s. 8d. in 1294.[19] In the 14th century the abbot of Cirencester received rents and services from several free tenants.[20]

The demesne lands of Avebury manor were leased to John Shuter and his son John for lives c. 1535.[21] William Dunche (d. 1666) took the demesne in hand[22] but from 1690 until the mid 18th century the farm was again leased.[23] There were 160 a. of arable and 1,300 sheep on the farm c. 1620.[24] It probably then included the lands of the rectory estate, absorbed in the early 17th century.[25] Higdens is the only former copyhold of Avebury manor of which record has been found after the Middle Ages. In 1633 it consisted of three messuages and 85 a.[26] In 1713, when it was sold, it was said to include common pasture for 160 sheep.[27]

In the mid 16th century the estate later called Avebury Trusloe manor was said to be worth 64s. and a yearly rent of £36 16s. was paid for the rectory estate of tithes and some 60 a. of land.[28] Both estates were leased c. 1533 for 60 years to Thomas Trusloe, his wife Joan, and son John (d. 1593).[29] The lease of Avebury Trusloe manor was converted to a freehold in 1563;[30] that of the rectory estate ran its full term.[31] Tenants of the two estates pastured sheep in common at the rate of 40 for every yardland on West Down and 50 on East down.[32] Two tenements kept in hand by the Trusloes may have formed the basis of Avebury Trusloe manor farm and were perhaps divided in the late 17th century into the farms which passed to John White and George Popham.[33] In 1675 Popham's farm, held on lease for a term of years, was of 139 a. of arable in the open fields, 13 a. of meadow, pasture for 320 sheep on the stubble of the West field, and unrestricted pasture on Knoll Down.[34] The lands which passed with the tithes were merged with Avebury manor farm after 1604.[35] The farm buildings on them east of Avebury Manor were mentioned in 1640.[36]

Five tenants held of Avebury Trusloe manor by copy in the late 16th century. They owed services of reaping and mowing, works allegedly due in place of tithes; it was disputed whether the services were due to the lord of the manor or the holder of the rectory.[37] In 1681 there were five copyholds, each of which included 30–70 a. of arable land and common pasture for 100–120 sheep.[38] A sixth perhaps formed the basis of Brunsden's, in 1702 a freehold of 300 a. of arable and meadow land and 87 a. of several pasture on Windmill Hill and Knoll Down.[39]

In 1750 Staynor Holford, lord of Avebury manor, John Norris, owner of Great (Brunsden's) and Little Avebury (Popham's) farms, and certain small landowners including the vicar agreed to an exchange of lands in North and West fields.[40] Much of the arable north of the London–Bath road and west of the eastern head stream of the Kennet was thus brought into several cultivation, although Great and Bannings farms continued as fragmented holdings.[41] The remaining common arable and down, 1,516 a., were inclosed and allotted in 1795 under an Act of 1792.[42]

In 1756 an agreement concerning the employment of threshers and other day labourers was reached between seven Avebury and two Beckhampton farmers. Hours of work were laid down and the time allowed for meals, said formerly to have been to the farmers' 'great detriment', sharply reduced.[43]

After 1795 most of Avebury Manor farm formed a consolidated holding of some 640 a. east and south of the village extending from the river a little north of Silbury Hill to the north-east corner of the parish.[44] The area of arable land was increased by inclosure, by ploughing the downland to the north and east, and by amalgamation with other farms, from 180 a. in 1791 to 457 a. in 1873.[45] Before 1873 Hitchcocks, in the early 19th century a farm of 194 a., had been added to Avebury Manor farm.[46] Norris's, 129 a. in 1813, was added to the estate in 1920.[47] Avebury Manor farm was brought in hand by Staynor Holford c. 1760 but was held on lease for much of the 19th century.[48] A lessee, Mr. Denham, introduced straw plaiting into Avebury c. 1805. It continued as a cottage industry supplying material for hatmaking.[49] Norris's was also leased[50] until that farm and Avebury Manor farm were brought in hand c. 1920.[51] Since 1943 tenants of the National Trust have farmed 716 a., parcel of those farms.[52] In 1873 Avebury Manor farm was worked from the former farmstead of Hitchcocks, now Manor Farm.[53] A new farmstead was built outside the Circle c. 1955.[54]

In the early 19th century other farms included Avebury Trusloe Manor, a scattered holding of c. 400 a., Bannings, c. 120 a. mainly of arable land,

[19] P.R.O., E 106/2/2.
[20] *Cirencester Cart.* ii, p. 353; *Inq. Non.* (Rec. Com.), 158.
[21] P.R.O., SC 6/Hen. VIII/3931, rot. 1.
[22] Ibid. C 2/Jas. I/D 10/58.
[23] W.R.O. 184/4, leases to Skeate and Rose; 435/24/1/7, lease to Griffen.
[24] P.R.O., C 2/Jas. I/D 10/58.
[25] Below.
[26] *Wilts. Inq. p.m.* 1625–49 (Index Libr.), 183.
[27] W.R.O. 212A/36/11.
[28] B.L. Harl. MS. 608, f. 50v.; P.R.O., E 310/26/153.
[29] P.R.O., E 318/Box 43/2324; ibid. C 142/237, no. 132.
[30] Ibid. CP 25(2)/289/4 Eliz. I East.
[31] Ibid. E 134/41 Eliz. I Hil./8.
[32] Ibid.; E 134/40 & 41 Eliz. I Mich./7.
[33] Ibid. E 134/41 Eliz. I Hil./8; above, manors.
[34] Herts. R.O. 27240.
[35] *Cal. S.P. Dom.* 1603–10, 128.
[36] *W.N. & Q.* viii. 221.
[37] P.R.O., E 134/40 & 41 Eliz. I Mich./7.
[38] W.R.O. 529/125; 212A/31/2.

[39] Ibid. 473/274.
[40] Ibid. 184/1; 184/4.
[41] Wilts. Cuttings, v. 189; W.A.S. Libr., sale cat. viii, no. 6.
[42] W.R.O., inclosure award.
[43] *W.A.M.* xxix. 181–2.
[44] W.R.O., inclosure award.
[45] Ibid. 184/4; W.A.S. Libr., sale cat. ii, no. 20.
[46] W.R.O. 212B/119; W.A.S. Libr., sale cat. ii, no. 20.
[47] W.R.O. 212B/119; 1102/6; *Kelly's Dir. Wilts.* (1920 and later edns.).
[48] W.R.O. 184/1; ibid. land tax; tithe award; *Kelly's Dir. Wilts.* (1855 and later edns.); *W.A.M.* xxx. 278.
[49] Wilts. Cuttings, v. 191; *W.A.M.* xlvii. 281.
[50] W.R.O., land tax; tithe award; *Kelly's Dir. Wilts.* (1855 and later edns.).
[51] *Kelly's Dir. Wilts.* (1923 and later edns.); W.R.O. 271/1.
[52] Inf. from Mr. S. C. Garnier, Land Agent, Nat. Trust, Wessex Regional Off., Stourton.
[53] W.A.S. Libr., sale cat. ii, no. 20.
[54] Nat. Trust, Wessex Regional Off., Avebury mem.

Higdens (later Combley's), *c.* 140 a. mostly on West Down, Great (Brunsden's), 410 a., and Little Avebury (Popham's), 236 a.;[55] Westbrook, then *c.* 120 a. of arable land and 10 a. of meadow intermingled with other farms west of the river, measured 147 a. in 1909.[56] Combley's was united with Avebury Trusloe Manor farm between 1877 and 1904. Over 200 a. of downland, including training gallops on West Down leased to Samuel Darling, were sold separately in 1904.[57] In the 1920s Avebury Trusloe Manor farm, 425 a., was principally arable, with a small dairy housed in buildings north of Bray Street which had formerly belonged to Combley's and Bannings farms.[58] The lands of Bannings had been dispersed in 1894.[59] Great and Little Avebury farms were worked together in 1867[60] and the latter was absorbed into Avebury Trusloe Manor farm in the 1930s.[61] In 1924 a farm called Trusloe farm, 210 a. of arable land and 65 a. of pasture scattered in the north-west of the parish, was held with 185 a. of arable and down on West and Knoll Downs formerly parcel of Great farm. Most of the holding had been merged with Avebury Trusloe Manor farm by 1979.[62] The area of arable on that farm was increased after 1945 when part of Knoll Down was ploughed.[63] In 1979 Butler Bros. held *c.* 1,000 a. in the west of the parish worked from Avebury Trusloe Manor Farm. Corn then predominated but there were also a flock of 600 ewes with lambs and 100 beef cattle.[64]

There were two mills, worth together 26*s.* 8*d.*, on Avebury manor in 1294[65] but it is not known whether they stood within the parish. In 1620 there was said to be a mill on Avebury Trusloe manor.[66]

BECKHAMPTON. Lands held by Edric were assessed for geld at 2 hides in 1066. There was said to be land for 3 ploughteams in 1086 but there were 2 teams on the demesne of 1 hide and 4 villeins, 7 bordars, and 3 cottars had another 2 teams. The whole estate, which included 8 a. of meadow and 40 a. of pasture, was then worth £6 as it had been in 1066.[67]

The boundaries of Beckhampton were West Down, the London–Bath road, except near Silbury Hill, and a line running almost due south from that hill. North of the hill were water meadows belonging to the tithing which were held in common until the 18th century.[68] The open field of Beckhampton lay between the village and the downs to the south.[69] Part of the downland was held in severalty in the late 18th century.[70]

In the 1230s there was demesne pasture and

meadow of Beckhampton manor east of Silbury Hill. Each of at least seven tenants then kept between 30 and 70 sheep.[71] On the Moyne moiety of the manor there was in 1315 a capital messuage worth 6*s.* 8*d.* yearly, 100 a. of land valued at 6*d.* an acre, 2 a. of meadow at 2*s.* an acre, and several pasture worth 13*s.* 4*d.* Rents totalling 55*s.* were paid by villeins and there was a free tenant.[72] That moiety was worth £10 in 1494,[73] the other £20 in 1595.[74]

At their reunion in the early 18th century, each moiety consisted of a single farm worth £60 with pasture for 250 sheep. There were 86 a. of arable land on Trusloes farm and 97 a. on Goddards. They were leased together from 1709. In 1720 the tenants were said to prosper in spite of the poverty of the soil.[75]

The yearly value of the Beckhampton chapel estate, which consisted of tithes, 28 a. of land, and pasture for 160 sheep, was set at £90 in 1710. Thereafter, the whole estate was apparently combined with Trusloes and Goddards farms.[76]

The portion of the manor sold to Thomas Smith *c.* 1638 was in the early 18th century a farm of 4 yardlands, 17 a. of several and common meadow, and pasture for 240 sheep and 50 lambs.[77] In 1788 it included 88 a. of downland pasture, *c.* 13 a. of meadow, and 106 a. in the common field. The farm had profited from small exchanges of land but its value was thought likely to increase if it were in severalty.[78]

After inclosure in 1795, under the Act of 1792 for Avebury and Beckhampton, there were three several farms, each extending from the arable lands south of the village southwards and westwards to the downs. Rights to the water meadows around Silbury Hill and obligations for their maintenance were divided between the three farms. For Goddards and Trusloes farms and the lands of the chapel estate, then amalgamated as one farm, Peter Holford was allotted 419 a. including 13 a. of meadow. An allotment of 163 a. of arable and down and 6 a. of meadow was made to George, duke of Marlborough. James Sutton's farm consisted of 187 a. and 8 a. of meadow.[79] Before 1897 Holford's and Marlborough's lands were merged as a farm of 623 a. including 191 a. of pasture on the down and 404 a. of arable land.[80] With the holding formerly Sutton's and lands outside Beckhampton they were worked as a single farm of some 1,200 a. from the farmsteads called Galtee More and Willonyx *c.* 1900.[81] Galtee More farm, *c.* 200 a., was later worked with West Kennett Manor farm; half of the combined holding was arable

[55] W.R.O. 212B/119; ibid. inclosure award; tithe award; W.A.S. Libr., sale cat. viii, no. 6.
[56] W.R.O. 212B/119; ibid. tithe award; Wilts. Cuttings, viii. 26.
[57] W.A.S. Libr., sale cat. iv, no. 3; viii, no. 6.
[58] Ibid. xvii, no. 28.
[59] Wilts. Cuttings, v. 189, 195.
[60] *Rep. on Employment of Women and Children in Agric.* [4202], p. 239, H.C. (1868–9), xiii.
[61] Above, manors.
[62] W.A.S. Libr., sale cat. xix, no. 59; inf. from Mr. P. S. Layley, Manor Farm, Avebury Trusloe.
[63] *W.A.M.* liii. 311.
[64] Inf. from Mr. Layley.
[65] P.R.O., E 106/2/2.

[66] Ibid. CP 25(2)/371/17 Jas. I East.
[67] *V.C.H. Wilts.* ii, p. 147.
[68] Herts. R.O. 27240; W.R.O., inclosure award.
[69] *Andrews and Dury, Map* (W.R.S. viii), pl. 11.
[70] W.R.O. 248/195.
[71] *Cirencester Cart.* ii, pp. 430–1.
[72] *Wilts. Inq. p.m. 1242–1326* (Index Libr.), 398.
[73] *Cal. Inq. p.m. Hen. VII*, i, pp. 478–9.
[74] *Extents for Debts* (W.R.S. xxviii), p. 104.
[75] P.R.O., C 5/355/32; W.R.O. 184/1.
[76] P.R.O., C 5/355/32.
[77] W.R.O. 212A/36/1.
[78] Ibid. 248/195.   [79] Ibid. inclosure award.
[80] W.A.S. Libr., sale cat. ii, no. 17.
[81] Darling, *Reminiscences*, 230, 240.

and half used for beef and dairy cattle.[82] In the 1920s Lower Galtee More, later Durran, farm became a separate farm of 287 a. laid to permanent pasture.[83] Until 1938 it was used as off-lying land. A house and buildings were then added and the land has since been worked as a mixed farm.[84] In 1979 other lands were leased to several local farmers.[85]

In 1599 Thomas Goddard's moiety of Beckhampton manor was said to include mills[86] but no further reference to them has been found.

There have been racing stables at Beckhampton since the mid 19th century[87] with training gallops on the western downs of Beckhampton and Avebury tithings and in the northeastern corner of Bishop's Cannings.[88] At least between 1848 and 1855 William Treene trained horses at Beckhampton House.[89] The house and stables were bought from Henry Woolcott in 1880 by Samuel Darling who greatly extended them before his retirement in 1914. Darling leased part of West Down as a training course and in 1897 bought Beckhampton manor to ensure continued access to it.[90] Galtee More and Willonyx farms were both named after classic winners.[91] The stable's reputation was built up by Darling's son Frederick who trained nineteen classic winners. It was bought in 1947 by J. A. Dewar and managed by Noel Murless until 1950. It was then sold to Mr. H. G. Blagrave.[92] Mr. Blagrave had established another stable at the Grange c. 1930 which he still maintained in 1979.[93] He let Beckhampton House and part of the gallops to Sir Gordon Richards until 1956 and the remainder of the gallops to Mr. Jeremy Tree, who occupied Beckhampton House in 1979.[94] Under Mr. Tree the stable had further classic successes.[95]

WEST KENNETT. The 13½ hides and 2 a. held of Alfred of Marlborough had been worth £4 10s. when he received them but were worth £8 10s. in 1086. They were divided into five holdings, two of 3½ hides, two of 2 hides, and one of 2½ hides and 2 a. There were 11 a. of meadow, 106 a. of pasture, and land for 6 ploughteams; 1 villein and 15 bordars had 4 teams.[96] That estate was probably much more extensive than the later tithing of West Kennett. The boundaries of the tithing followed a line north from the parish boundary with All Cannings to a point a little east of Silbury Hill, and north-east to the boundary with West Overton a little south of the old Marlborough road.[97] Little is known of agriculture

there before the late 17th century. The pattern was probably similar to that elsewhere in the parish of cultivation on the lower land around the village and pasture on the downs. There was pasture on Waden Hill in the 1690s[98] but whether common or several is not known.

West Kennett manor was valued at £12 in 1520,[99] perhaps an overestimate. In 1635 when an additional ½ yardland called Georges was part of the estate it was valued at £8.[1] After the owner of the manor acquired Hardings, 2 yardlands, in 1696,[2] the manor farm was one of only two farms in the tithing. Their lands were then partly commonable and partly several. In the late 17th century an inclosure of pasture near the Kennett Avenue was made for Walter Grubbe as part of what became West Kennett farm.[3] The separation of the two farms was completed by an agreement of 1703, confirmed in 1714. To West Kennett manor were allotted 41 a. of arable, 18 a. of meadow, and 115 a. of pasture.[4] No detail survives of the allotment to West Kennett farm.

West Kennett Manor farm comprised 400 a. in 1719.[5] In the mid 19th century and the early 20th it was a farm of some 350 a. south of the London–Bath road and west of West Kennett village. The downs near the boundary with All Cannings remained pasture but more land was brought under the plough in the late 19th century. The area of arable increased from 163 a. in 1845 to 195 a. in 1919.[6] In the 1920s the farm was taken in hand by F. E. Shipp.[7] In 1979 it comprised 500 a. and was worked with Galtee More farm in Beckhampton by Mr. Roger Hues.[8]

West Kennett farm consisted of 231 a. of arable, 68 a. of meadow, and 275 a. of down in 1813.[9] In 1900 it was used chiefly for sheep and corn but 192 a. of its down were let to Thomas and Alexander Taylor of Manton House in Preshute as training gallops.[10] The farm was kept in hand for much of the 19th century.[11] Between 1923 and 1939 it was worked by J. W. Osmond, who was succeeded by his son Mr. W. J. Osmond. In 1979 Mr. Osmond worked a mixed farm of 609 a.[12]

In 1745 an interest in a malthouse was leased with the lands of West Kennett Manor farm.[13] In 1845 the buildings of George Butler's brewery, possibly the descendant of that malthouse, were north and south of the London–Bath road east of West Kennett Farm.[14] Butler was succeeded by W. S. Butler and Stephen Butler, probably his son and grandson, c. 1890 and in 1920.[15] In 1921

82 Inf. from Mr. Roger Hues, Galtee More Farm.
83 W.A.S. Libr., sale cat. xix, no. 17.
84 Inf. from Mrs. E. Westropp, Durran Farm.
85 Inf. from Mr. H. G. Blagrave, the Grange, Beckhampton.
86 P.R.O., C 142/252, no. 53.
87 Kelly's Dir. Wilts. (1848 and later edns.).
88 W.A.S. Libr., sale cat. ii, no. 17; O.S. Map 6″, Wilts. XXVIII (1889 edn.); V.C.H. Wilts. vii. 187.
89 Kelly's Dir. Wilts.
90 Darling, Reminiscences, 20–3; W.A.S. Libr., sale cat. ii, no. 17; iv, no. 3.
91 Darling, Reminiscences, 21, 230.
92 V.C.H. Wilts. iv. 382.
93 Kelly's Dir. Wilts. (1931); inf. from Mr. Blagrave.
94 V.C.H. Wilts. iv. 382; inf. from Mr. Blagrave.
95 Whitaker's Almanack (1956 and later edns.).
96 V.C.H. Wilts. ii, p. 143.
97 W.R.O., Avebury inclosure award (1795).
98 W.A.M. xl. 354.
99 P.R.O., C 142/34, no. 15.
1 Wilts. Inq. p.m. 1625–49 (Index Libr.), 183.
2 W.R.O. 118/88.   3 W.A.M. iv. 327.
4 W.R.O. 568/5.   5 Ibid.
6 Ibid. tithe award; W.A.S. Libr., sale cat. xiv, no. 33.
7 Kelly's Dir. Wilts. (1927, 1931).
8 Inf. from Mr. W. J. Osmond, W. Kennett Farm.
9 W.R.O. 212B/119.
10 Wilts. Cuttings, xvi. 48; V.C.H. Wilts. iv. 382.
11 W.R.O., tithe award; land tax; Kelly's Dir. Wilts. (1855).
12 Inf. from Mr. Osmond.
13 W.R.O. 568/7, lease to Lanfear.
14 Ibid. tithe award.
15 Kelly's Dir. Wilts. (1855 and later edns.).

Kennett Brewery, which had several tied houses in the area, was sold to the Stroud Brewery Co.[16] There was a branch of the Stroud Brewery at West Kennett in 1931[17] but it was closed shortly afterwards.[18] A former malthouse and beer store stood south of the road in 1979.

In 1086 12s. was paid for a mill in Kennett.[19] A medieval post mill may have stood on Overton Hill south of the Sanctuary.[20] A mill on the lands of John of Berwick in 1327 may have been in West Kennett.[21]

LOCAL GOVERNMENT. A tumbrel and gallows were said to have been used in Avebury from c. 1235.[22] In 1281 the abbot of Cirencester claimed the right to a view of frankpledge and other liberties at Avebury, granted by charters of Henry I and Henry III.[23] The view was said in 1360 to be held at Michaelmas and Hocktide each year.[24] In the 16th century the view and a manor court were held yearly at Avebury Trusloe manor house.[25] A court baron was held for Avebury manor in the 1630s in the house attached to the rectory estate.[26] Views of frankpledge and manor courts were held for Avebury and Avebury Trusloe manors between 1651 and 1657 for Sir Edward Baynton, lord of Avebury and possibly of Avebury Trusloe.[27] By the early 17th century Avebury had been divided into Avebury Trusloe, Eastbrook, and Westbrook tithings.[28] Between 1651 and 1653 business from Avebury (presumably Avebury Trusloe), Eastbrook, and Westbrook came before views and courts held twice a year. From 1654 to 1657 a separate view and court was held for Avebury Trusloe manor. Business from Eastbrook and Westbrook, with Catcomb in Hilmarton, the constituent parts of Avebury manor, still came before the court and view of that manor. Tithingmen were elected for Avebury, Eastbrook, and Westbrook between 1651 and 1653, and for the two latter tithings and Avebury Trusloe from 1654. Other business before the views and courts was similar for the two manors. Attendance at the courts, questions of tenure, and manorial custom, for example in the pasturing of sheep on West Down, were considered. Orders were also made for the maintenance of highways, landmarks, and, for Avebury Trusloe, a common pound and stocks. The repair of houses and removal of fire hazards were required.[29] The latest reference to Avebury Trusloe and Westbrook as tithings dates from 1713:[30] Eastbrook was mentioned as such in the late 18th century.[31] Little is known of the manorial courts after 1657; a court leet and view for Avebury manor, at which a hayward was appointed, met in 1813.[32]

A tithingman from Beckhampton attended the hundred court in the late 15th century.[33] There is no record of any court held for Beckhampton or West Kennett.

Removal of dangerously dilapidated buildings and the appointment of schoolmasters were among the responsibilities of the parish officers and vestry in the 18th century.[34] The parish joined Marlborough poor-law union in 1835.[35]

CHURCH. The church held by Rainbold the priest in 1086 was probably newly built.[36] In 1139 it passed to Cirencester abbey, which held the church and advowson until the Dissolution.[37] A vicar served the church c. 1190[38] and in 1195 the abbot of Cirencester was licensed to appropriate the vicarage and to institute a canon of Cirencester to the living when it fell vacant.[39] By 1275, when a new vicarage was ordained, the abbot presented his candidate to the bishop for institution.[40] As patron of Avebury and of the vicarage of Winterbourne Monkton, described in the 13th and 14th centuries as a chapel of Avebury,[41] the abbot petitioned for the union of the benefices in 1431, apparently without success.[42] The livings were united in 1747[43] and separated in 1864.[44] In 1923 the united benefice of Avebury with East Kennett was formed.[45] That union was dissolved in 1929 when Avebury was again joined with Winterbourne Monkton.[46] The benefice was served in plurality with Berwick Bassett from 1952[47] and the two livings and three parishes were united in 1970.[48] In 1975 the benefice of Upper Kennet was created by the union of Avebury with Winterbourne Monkton and Berwick Bassett, Broad Hinton, Overton with Fyfield and East Kennett, and Winterbourne Bassett. A team ministry was established.[49] After the Dissolution the advowson was held by the Crown[50] until it was sold to a Mr. Dunston in 1865.[51] It was again offered for sale in 1882[52] and in 1894 was held by trustees of Elizabeth, wife of W. H. Davies who was presented to the vicarage in that year.[53] In 1923 Elizabeth Davies retained the advowson of the

[16] W.A.S. Libr., sale cat. xvii, no. 78.
[17] Kelly's Dir. Wilts.
[18] Inf. from Mr. Osmond.
[19] V.C.H. Wilts. ii, p. 143.
[20] W.A.M. xlv. 317.
[21] Feet of F. 1327–77 (W.R.S. xxix), p. 15.
[22] Rot. Hund. (Rec. Com.), ii (1), 270.
[23] P.R.O., JUST 1/1005, rot. 119d.
[24] Cirencester Cart. ii, p. 353.
[25] Valor Eccl. (Rec. Com.), ii. 466; P.R.O., E 134/41 Eliz. I Hil./8.
[26] P.R.O., E 134/9 & 10 Chas. I Hil./1.
[27] W.R.O. 473/52; above, manors.
[28] Wilts. Inq. p.m. 1625–49 (Index Libr.), 375.
[29] W.R.O. 473/52.
[30] Ibid. 568/5.
[31] Ibid. 212A/31/4; 529/185; P.R.O., CP 25(2)/1447/26 Geo. III Mich.
[32] W.R.O. 271/8.
[33] P.R.O., DL 30/127/1908.   [34] W.R.O. 184/9.

[35] Poor Law Com. 2nd Rep. 559.
[36] V.C.H. Wilts. ii, p. 119; below.
[37] Cirencester Cart. i, pp. 21–4; P.R.O., SC 6/Hen. VIII/1240, rott. 61d.–62; above, manors.
[38] Cirencester Cart. ii, pp. 429–30.
[39] Ibid. i, pp. xxix–xxx, 153–4.
[40] Ibid. iii, pp. 1052–4.
[41] Ibid. pp. 1054–5, 1059.
[42] W.R.O., bishop, reg. Nevill, f. 47.
[43] Vis. Queries, 1783 (W.R.S. xxvii), p. 26.
[44] Ch. Com. file 28250.
[45] Lond. Gaz. 1 June 1923, pp. 3843–4.
[46] Ibid. 10 May 1929, pp. 3114–17.
[47] Crockford (1955–6).
[48] Lond. Gaz. 22 Oct. 1970, p. 11580.
[49] Ibid. 21 Mar. 1975, p. 3845.
[50] Phillipps, Wilts. Inst. (index in W.A.M. xxviii. 212).
[51] Ch. Com. file 28250; Wilts. Cuttings, xvi. 11.
[52] Wilts. Cuttings, i. 289.
[53] Wilts. Tracts, clxxix, no. 18.

united benefice for two turns; the bishop of Salisbury was to present at the third.[54] The bishop became sole patron of the living in 1929.[55]

Before 1275 the so called vicar received less than 7 marks a year, probably as a stipend from Cirencester abbey.[56] In 1291 the vicarage was valued at £4 6s. 8d., one of the lower figures for Avebury deanery.[57] Although the value in 1535, £8 9s. 5½d., was closer to the average for the deanery,[58] in the early 17th century the vicar complained of poverty, alleging that he received a clear yearly income of less than £20.[59] The united benefice of Avebury with Winterbourne Monkton was of moderate value, worth on average £178 a year between 1829 and 1831.[60]

In 1275 the vicarage was endowed with all tithes of the parish, except those on grain and sheep, and with the wheat crop from 1 a. of the prior of Avebury's demesne.[61] Grain tithes from 4 a. of demesne in Beckhampton and West Kennett were confirmed to the vicar in 1337.[62] Those from West Kennett were possibly from 2 a. of demesne, the crop from which was claimed by the rector of Overton in the early 13th century in return for the burial of unfree men of West Kennett at Overton. The rector's claim was successfully contested by the abbot of Cirencester on the vicar's behalf.[63] In 1682 the vicar claimed the wheat crop from 1 a. of land in West Kennett and from 1 a. in Beckhampton; otherwise his rights to tithes had remained unchanged since the 13th century.[64] In 1845 the vicarial tithes were commuted for a rent charge of £90 2s.[65] At the Dissolution the vicar also received a yearly stipend of £4 from Cirencester abbey.[66] The stipend, derived from the rectory estate, was confirmed in 1572.[67] In 1682 the payment, which had been increased to £12, was made by the owners of the rectorial tithes.[68] There was a vicarage house before 1275 and provision was made in that year for its replacement by one nearer the church. The vicarage was also endowed with ½ yardland.[69] In 1682 the vicar had a house and c. 14 a. of glebe with pasture rights for 20 sheep.[70] The vicarage house, which was much altered and extended in 1841,[71] was sold in 1976;[72] a new house was built south-west of the old in 1974.[73]

In the late 12th century the monks of Avebury priory were permitted an oratory in their manor house on condition that all tithes were paid to the parish church and no parishioner was admitted to the services.[74] Both conditions were broken and they were reimposed in 1336 at the instigation of the abbot of Cirencester whose rights had been infringed.[75] In the 14th century keepers and farmers of the alien priory were required to find a secular chaplain to perform divine service, an obligation which suggests that the priory bore some spiritual responsibility in the parish.[76]

Chapels attached to Avebury church, included in the reversionary grant of the church to Cirencester abbey of 1133, were probably those at Winterbourne Monkton, mentioned above, Beckhampton, and West Kennett. In the late 12th century the lord of Beckhampton and his household attended the free chapel of St. Vincent in Beckhampton. The status of the chapel was agreed c. 1190 by the vicar of Avebury and the chaplain of Beckhampton. On appointment the chaplain was to take an oath of fidelity to the vicar. The inhabitants of Beckhampton were to have all services in the chapel and all parishioners were free to attend there on St. Vincent's day. At great festivals, however, the lord of Beckhampton was to attend the parish church and his children were to be baptized there. The chaplain was entitled to all dues from Beckhampton, except the offerings made by the lord's family at marriage and purification.[77] From the early 14th century the advowson of the chapel descended with the moieties of Beckhampton manor.[78] The holders of the moieties did not, however, always present on alternate occasions; Richard Casterton, for example, presented in 1310, 1313, and 1314.[79] The chapel was valued at £4 8s. at its dissolution. In 1545 the farmer of the chapelry received all tithes from Beckhampton, except half of those on sheep, and held a messuage and 1 yardland in Beckhampton and Stanmore.[80] The chapel passed to the Crown at the Dissolution but in the late 17th century the inhabitants of Stanmore were said to bury their dead in the graveyard of the ruined building.[81]

Freemen of West Kennett were described in 1239 as founders of a chapel there.[82] No further reference to the chapel has been found.

Avebury was probably served by canons of Cirencester between 1195 and 1275.[83] Perhaps because the vicarage was poor, few pre-Reformation incumbents are known to have been pluralists or men of distinction. An exception was Richard Arch, principal of Broadgates Hall, Oxford, presented in 1520.[84] There was no cover for the communion table and no preaching in 1553,[85] and in 1554 the vicar was deprived, probably as a married priest.[86]

[54] Lond. Gaz. 1 June 1923, p. 3843; 4 May 1923, pp. 3209–10.
[55] Ch. Com. file 2859.
[56] Cirencester Cart. iii, p. 1052.
[57] Tax. Eccl. (Rec. Com.), 189.
[58] Valor Eccl. (Rec. Com.), ii. 129.
[59] Cal. S.P. Dom. 1635, 544.
[60] Rep. Com. Eccl. Revenues, 822.
[61] Cirencester Cart. iii, pp. 1052–4.
[62] Ibid. p. 1059.   [63] Ibid. ii, pp. 427–8.
[64] W.R.O., bishop, glebe terrier.
[65] Ibid. tithe award.
[66] P.R.O., SC 6/Hen. VIII/1240, rott. 61d.–62.
[67] Ibid. E 178/2406.
[68] W.R.O., bishop, glebe terrier.
[69] Cirencester Cart. iii, pp. 1052–4.
[70] W.R.O., bishop, glebe terrier.

[71] Ibid. bishop, mortgages, 85.
[72] Wilts. Cuttings, xxvii. 315.
[73] Inf. from Mr. H. E. Smith, Butlers Cottage, Beckhampton.
[74] Cirencester Cart. ii, p. 423.
[75] Ibid. iii, pp. 1047–9.
[76] e.g. Cal. Fine R. 1377–83, 83; 1391–9, 87; V.C.H. Wilts. iii. 393.
[77] Cirencester Cart. i, pp. 21–4; ii, pp. 429–30.
[78] Phillipps, Wilts. Inst. i (index in W.A.M. xxviii. 213).
[79] Phillipps, Wilts. Inst. i. 10, 12.
[80] P.R.O., E 301/58, f. 77.
[81] Ibid. E 134/11 & 12 Wm. III Hil./8; above, manors.
[82] Cirencester Cart. ii, pp. 427–8.
[83] Ibid. i, pp. 153–4.   [84] W.N. & Q. ii. 444.
[85] W.R.O., bishop, detecta bk.
[86] Phillipps, Wilts. Inst. i. 216; V.C.H. Wilts. iii. 31.

Between 1712 and 1851 the vicars of Avebury were James Mayo, his son, grandson, and great-grandson, all of the same name. All but the first were pluralists and also held teaching posts.[87] From the mid 18th century to the mid 19th there was usually a curate resident at Avebury.[88] Charles Lucas, curate 1791–1816 and author of several religious poems and novels,[89] was the first of a number of clergy who served in the parish in the 19th and 20th centuries to take an active interest in its archaeology.[90]

Reading of the homilies was revived in the 1740s to counter nonconformist evangelism. In 1783 a service was held on alternate Sundays at Avebury and Winterbourne Monkton. The Sacrament was administered four times a year at Avebury, where there were some 40 communicants. Additional services were held on weekdays following the great festivals and on other holy days.[91] In 1864 services were held at the two churches alternately on Sunday morning and Sunday afternoon; there was a weekly evening service at Avebury. Communion was celebrated at Avebury monthly, at the great festivals, and occasionally in the early morning. Morning and evening prayer were sometimes said on weekdays and services were regularly held on saints' days, Wednesdays, and Fridays. The average Sunday congregation was 200, of whom between 16 and 22 were communicants.[92] Bryan King, vicar 1863–94, obtained the living by exchange for that of St. George's in the East (Mdx.), where his incumbency had been marked by riots against high church practices. He introduced similar practices at Avebury but his immediate successors were low churchmen.[93]

The church, known as All Saints' in the 13th century[94] but later as *ST. JAMES'S*,[95] is built partly of ashlar and partly of sarsen and flint with ashlar dressings, and consists of chancel and nave with north and south aisles and a west tower. The nave is of the 11th century and footings of a probably contemporary chancel were found beneath the present chancel in the 19th century.[96] In the later 12th century openings were made in the north and south walls of the nave, presumably to give access to the aisles.[97] The chancel arch was enlarged and the chancel rebuilt and extended in the late 13th century. Both aisles appear to have been rebuilt and widened in the 15th century; a 12th-century doorway was reset in the south aisle and 13th-century windows were incorporated in the rebuilding. The tall ashlar

tower and its tower arch were added in the 15th century. In 1812 the 12th-century arcades were removed and replaced by tall pointed arches on Doric columns. The chancel was partly rebuilt and the western gallery removed in a restoration of 1878–84, principally designed by C. E. Ponting.[98] The nave roof may be of that date; the aisle roofs are apparently later. There is a tub font, possibly of Saxon origin, with carvings of the early 12th century. The 15th-century rood loft was uncovered in 1810 and restored under the direction of C. E. Ponting in the late 19th century, when the rood screen was set up.[99]

In 1553 2½ oz. of plate were confiscated and a chalice of 9 oz. was left in the parish. A chalice and paten of 1606, altered in 1874, and a silver paten given in 1636 were still held in 1979.[1] A 16th-century pax, apparently of latten, was found in 1872.[2] There were four bells in 1553. In the 17th and 18th centuries five new bells were cast.[3] They hung in the church in 1979.[4] The registers of burials begin in 1678, of baptisms in 1697, and of marriages in 1705.[5]

NONCONFORMITY. Some 30 people attended conventicles of different persuasions held at two houses in Avebury in 1669. Their teachers were John Baker, who had been deprived of the vicarage of Chiseldon *c.* 1662, and Thomas Mills of Calne.[6] Another ejected minister, Thomas Rashley, formerly rector of Barford St. Martin, lived in Avebury in the 1660s.[7] A chapel was built *c.* 1670, probably that which in the early 18th century stood south of the high street and east of the Swindon–Devizes road.[8] Noah Webb, a deprived Presbyterian minister, was said to travel from Upton Grey (Hants) every week to preach at Avebury in the 1670s. In the early 18th century the chapel was served by Presbyterian and Independent ministers.[9] Shortly after its foundation the chapel had a congregation of 25, including in 1695 the lessee of Avebury manor.[10] In the 1720s more than 130 people attended the services.[11] Numbers declined later in the century and in 1772 the one Sunday service was taken by a visiting Presbyterian minister.[12] The survival of the chapel, attended by only three families of Independents in 1783, was ascribed by the vicar of Avebury to support received from the fund established by Caleb Bailey of Berwick Bassett to promote the preaching of Dissent in the area.[13] There was a revival in the 19th century; on

[87] C. H. Mayo, *Gen. Acct. of Mayo and Elton Fams.* (priv. print. 1882), 42–57; *Alum. Oxon. 1715–1886*, iii. 937.
[88] Mayo, op. cit. 52; *Educ. of Poor Digest*, 1018; *Rep. Com. Eccl. Revenues*, 822; *Kelly's Dir. Wilts.* (1848).
[89] *D.N.B.*
[90] e.g. *W.A.M.* x. 209–16; xii. 243; xiii. 221–2; xix. 21.
[91] *Vis. Queries, 1783* (W.R.S. xxvii), pp. 26–7.
[92] W.R.O., bishop, vis. queries.
[93] W. Crouch, *Bryan King and the Riots at St. George's in the East* (Lond. 1904), *passim*.
[94] *Cirencester Cart.* ii, p. 423.   [95] *W.A.M.* xv. 100.
[96] Ibid. xix. 21; see above, plate facing p. 49.
[97] Measured elevation of arches by J. Buckler, watercolour in W.A.S. Libr., vol. viii. 55 (1803).
[98] W.R.O., bishop, pet. for faculties, bdle. xii, no. 2 (1); bdle. viii, no. 26; *W.A.M.* xxi. 188–93.
[99] *W.A.M.* xlvii. 282–3; liii. 463–4; *Guide to Avebury Ch.* (Swindon, priv. print.).

[1] Nightingale, *Wilts. Plate*, 134; inf. from Mr. Smith.
[2] Nightingale, *Wilts. Plate*, 134.
[3] Walters, *Wilts. Bells*, 16.
[4] *Guide to Avebury Ch.*
[5] W.R.O. 1179/1–10. There are a few transcripts for earlier periods: ibid. bishop.
[6] G. L. Turner, *Orig. Rec.* i. 109; *Calamy Revised*, ed. A. G. Matthews, 23, 50.
[7] *Calamy Revised*, ed. Matthews, 403.
[8] S. B. Stribling, *Wilts. Congregational Union*, 23; Stukeley, *Abury*, frontispiece.
[9] Dr. Williams's Libr., Wilson MS. F ii.
[10] *W.N. & Q.* iii. 536; W.R.O. 184/1.
[11] Dr. Williams's Libr., Wilson MS. F ii; ibid. MS. 34.4 (Evans MS.), p. 124.
[12] Ibid. Wilson MS. F ii.
[13] *Vis. Queries, 1783* (W.R.S. xxvii), p. 27; *V.C.H. Wilts.* iii. 123.

Census Sunday in 1851 there were 30 people at morning and 25 at afternoon service.[14] A number of Anglicans seceded to the free church, as it was known from the 1860s, during the incumbency of Bryan King. The organization of the church remained congregational but the usage of the Book of Common Prayer was thereafter adopted at one of the Sunday services.[15] The chapel, extended in the 19th century, was still open in 1979, when it was known as Avebury United Reformed Church.[16]

James Mayo (d. 1788), vicar of Avebury, professed himself concerned by the growth of Methodism from the 1740s but it is not clear whether the movement had any success in the parish at that time. A group of dissenters, identified by Mayo as Methodists, was established there through the ministry of Cornelius Winter, who was active in the 1760s and 1770s. Membership had declined by 1783 and the group, like others under Winter's leadership, was probably absorbed into the free or Congregational church.[17]

A Baptist congregation was established in Avebury as an outpost of the church at Calne.[18] Services were held from c. 1826 in a mud-walled building, from 1828 called a chapel. A Strict Baptist church was formed in 1830.[19] On Census Sunday in 1851 there was a congregation of 150 at both morning and afternoon services.[20] A new chapel was built in 1873,[21] and in 1877 a fund was established to promote the preaching of Strict Baptist principles within a radius of 30 miles from Avebury parish church.[22] The chapel lacked a pastor between 1890 and 1905 and was closed in 1928. It was reopened in the 1930s[23] but closed again c. 1953. In that year the building, which stood in the high street, west of the Swindon–Devizes road, was sold and the proceeds added to the preaching fund. The annual income from the fund was thought to be between £10 and £25 in 1965.[24]

Mary Amor's house in Beckhampton was licensed for dissenters' meetings in 1844.[25]

EDUCATION. By will dated 1722 Susanna, relict of Sir Richard Holford, left £200 for the education of poor children of Avebury.[26] Part of the bequest was received in 1733[27] and by 1736 a schoolmaster had been appointed and dismissed for irregularity. In 1739 the appointment of a new master depended on the payment of interest on the full bequest, about which there was some doubt.[28] Four cottages in South Street were purchased as an endowment and in 1783 the school, attended by sixteen children, had an income from rents and subscriptions of £8.[29] In 1805 the remainder of the Holford legacy and £20 bequeathed in that year by Hannah, relict of Samuel Martyn, were invested for the school.[30] Between 10 and 50 pupils, according to the season, were taught in the church in the early 19th century.[31] A National school was built in 1844 and rebuilt in 1849.[32] By a Scheme of 1856 income from Holford's and Martyn's charity was diverted to that or any other school in the parish. Two of the cottages were destroyed by fire in the late 19th century but rents from the remaining pair accounted for £6 of the total of £11 given to the school in 1908.[33] Those cottages were sold in 1952.[34] Avebury school received £13 from the charity in 1962.[35]

In 1859 the National school received a state grant and there were between 40 and 50 pupils.[36] The building was enlarged in 1873.[37] Average attendance declined from 81 in 1914 to 58 in 1927,[38] although some pupils from East Kennett were transferred to the school in 1924.[39] In 1940 children of men working on Yatesbury airfield increased the numbers to c. 80 and the Congregational schoolroom was rented to provide additional accommodation.[40] The school, which stood in the high street a little west of the Circle, was replaced in 1970. The new building stands behind its predecessor. In 1979 there were 58 children on roll and three teachers.[41]

A day school was said to be associated with the free church in 1820[42] but in 1833 the only nonconformist teaching was at a Sunday school.[43] A school was established in 1859 and a schoolroom built behind the free church.[44] There were probably seventeen pupils in 1871.[45] The school was open in 1885[46] but was closed in 1940.[47]

Two private day and boarding schools were established in 1821 but nothing is known of them after 1833.[48] There was also a private school at Avebury between 1875 and 1885.[49]

In 1877 a school in Beckhampton was refused a certificate of efficiency because the buildings

[14] P.R.O., HO 129/255/1/1/2.
[15] Stribling, Wilts. Congregational Union, 23; above, church.
[16] P.R.O., ED 7/130, no. 11; inf. from Mr. H. W. Jones, Priors Hill, Wroughton.
[17] Vis. Queries, 1783 (W.R.S. xxvii), p. 27; V.C.H. Wilts. iii. 131.
[18] V.C.H. Wilts. iii. 138–9.
[19] R. W. Oliver, Strict Bapt. Chapels Eng. (Strict Bapt. Hist. Soc.), v. 18.
[20] P.R.O., HO 129/255/1/1/3.
[21] Oliver, op. cit. 19.
[22] Char. Com. file.
[23] Oliver, op. cit. 19.
[24] Char. Com. file.
[25] W.R.O., bishop, certs. dissenters' meeting hos.
[26] Endowed Char. Wilts. (N. Div.), 25.
[27] W.R.O. 184/8.
[28] Ibid. 184/9.
[29] Endowed Char. Wilts. (N. Div.), 25; Vis. Queries, 1783 (W.R.S. xxvii), p. 29.
[30] Endowed Char. Wilts. (N. Div.), 25.
[31] Ibid.; Educ. of Poor Digest, 1018; Educ. Enquiry Abstract, 1027.
[32] Endowed Char. Wilts. (N. Div.), 27; P.R.O., ED 7/130, no. 11.
[33] Endowed Char. Wilts. (N. Div.), 26.
[34] W.R.O. 1569/27.
[35] Char. Com. file.
[36] Acct. of Wilts. Schs. 5.
[37] P.R.O., ED 21/18305.
[38] Bd. of Educ., List 21 (H.M.S.O.).
[39] P.R.O., ED 21/4221.
[40] Ibid. ED 21/63161.
[41] Inf. from the Head Teacher.
[42] A. Antrobus, Wilts. Congregational Union (1947), 31.
[43] Educ. Enquiry Abstract, 1027.
[44] P.R.O., ED 7/130, no. 11.
[45] Returns relating to Elem. Educ. 422–3, where figures for Avebury Nat. sch. and the dissenting sch. have apparently been transposed.
[46] Kelly's Dir. Wilts.
[47] P.R.O., ED 21/63161.
[48] Educ. Enquiry Abstract, 1027.
[49] Kelly's Dir. Wilts. (1875 and later edns.).

were unsuitable.[50] No further mention of the school has been found.

CHARITIES FOR THE POOR. By will proved 1718 Sir Richard Holford left £30 to provide beef for the poor. In 1786 the endowment was said to have been lost.[51]

By will proved 1856 Sarah Hawkins left £200 for clothing, food, or fuel for parishioners. Her estate was insufficient for the legacy to be paid in full and only £179 was invested. In 1908 and 1928 the income was used to buy blankets, clothing, and coal for poor women.[52]

BROAD HINTON

BROAD HINTON lies at the head of the Kennet valley 7 km. south-west of Swindon.[53] The parish included Broad Hinton, Bincknoll, Uffcott, and part of Broad Town, of which only Broad Hinton was in Selkley hundred. In the 11th century the tithings of Uffcott and Broad Town were probably parts of Kingsbridge hundred. Bincknoll tithing may have been part of either Kingsbridge or Blackgrove hundred. In the 13th century it was in Blackgrove, as Uffcott was in the 14th century. All three tithings were parts of the combined hundred of Kingsbridge and Blackgrove from the 16th century.[54] In the early 19th century the area of the parish was c. 4,400 a. (1,781 ha.).[55] In 1884 all of Broad Town and that part of Bincknoll tithing north-west of the ridge between Broadtown Hill and the earthwork called Bincknoll Castle became the civil parish of Broad Town; it was already an ecclesiastical parish. Of the total area of the new parish, 825 ha. (2,040 a.), 536 ha. (1,326 a.) were taken from Broad Hinton.[56] The modern parish of Broad Hinton, 1,260 ha. (3,114 a.),[57] lies south-east of the ridge. The history of Broad Town tithing and of Broad Town parish since 1884 has been recounted with that of Clyffe Pypard[58] but that of Bincknoll tithing is described below.

The watershed between the Kennet and the Bristol Avon divided the ancient parish into two contrasting parts. The division runs from south-west to north-east, approximately following a line from Cockroost Farm to Quidhampton Wood in Wroughton. South-east of the line is the Kennet valley, 4 km. wide between the watershed and Hackpen Hill, which reaches 269 m., the highest point in the parish, and marks the boundary. Most of the arable land of the parish was in the valley and streams there were used to float water meadows.[59] One stream rises outside the parish north of Uffcott, another near the farmstead called the Weir; they meet 900 m. south of that farmstead. Chalk outcrops both in

the valley and on the downland of Hackpen Hill, which was used for pasture. Settlement in the south-east part of the parish was concentrated in the nucleated villages of Broad Hinton and Uffcott. North-west of the watershed the parish extended halfway across the Avon valley, sharing a straight boundary with Wootton Bassett. A little west of the watershed Broadtown Hill and the ridge which extends north-east of it reach heights above 198 m. and mark the north-western limit of the chalk; a white horse was cut above Little Town in 1864.[60] On the western slopes of the hills are bands of Upper Greensand and Gault. Beyond them the Kimmeridge Clay forms level ground below 107 m.[61] A stream west of Broad Town Lane is fed by tributaries and flows north into Brinkworth Brook. The plain and the hills west of the watershed were used mainly for pasture[62] and settlement there was in scattered farmsteads. In the 11th century there were 4 a. of woodland at Bincknoll, probably on the ridge, and in the 14th century Bincknoll Wood was of 25 a.[63] The wood stretched east beyond the parish boundary and west to Little Town in 1766[64] but it has since contracted and in 1981 extended 1.5 km. south-west from Bincknoll Castle.

Broad Hinton township, which included Hinton Columbers and Hinton Wase tithings,[65] and Uffcott tithing lay south-east of the watershed and Bincknoll and Broad Town tithings north-west of it. Uffcott, Bincknoll, and Broad Town were townships in the 11th century[66] and had probably been absorbed into Broad Hinton parish by the 13th. Tithes from Uffcott were then paid to the vicar of Broad Hinton and a chapel at Bincknoll may have been dependent on the church. Grants made during the century of lands in Broad Town to the impropriator of Broad Hinton and of tithes there to the priory of Wallingford (Berks., later Oxon.), owner of other tithes in Clyffe Pypard, probably contributed to

[50] P.R.O., ED 21/18305, which may refer to the free church sch., for which a certificate was sought that year: ED 7/130, no. 11.
[51] Endowed Char. Wilts. (N. Div.), 25.
[52] Ibid.; inf. from Mrs. A. Titcombe, 10 Trusloe Cottages.
[53] This article was written in 1981. Maps used include O.S. Maps 1″, sheet 157 (1958 edn.); 1/50,000, sheet 173 (1974 edn.); 1/25,000, SU 07 (1959 edn.), SU 08 (1959 edn.), SU 17 (1960 edn.), SU 18 (1959 edn.); 6″, Wilts. XV (1889 and later edns.), XXII (1888 and later edns.).
[54] V.C.H. Wilts. ii, p. 198; ix. 3–4.
[55] W.R.O., Elcombe and Uffcott inclosure award; Broad Hinton tithe award.

[56] Lond. Gaz. 21 July 1846, p. 2669; V.C.H. Wilts. ix. 23, 26.
[57] Census, 1971.
[58] V.C.H. Wilts. ix. 23–43.
[59] Below, econ. hist.
[60] W.A.M. xxv. 64.
[61] Geol. Surv. Map 1″, drift, sheet 266 (1964 edn.).
[62] Below, econ. hist.
[63] V.C.H. Wilts. ii, p. 147; P.R.O., CP 25(1)/255/52, no. 23.
[64] W.R.O. 305/11.
[65] Below, local govt.
[66] V.C.H. Wilts. ii, pp. 146–7, 163.

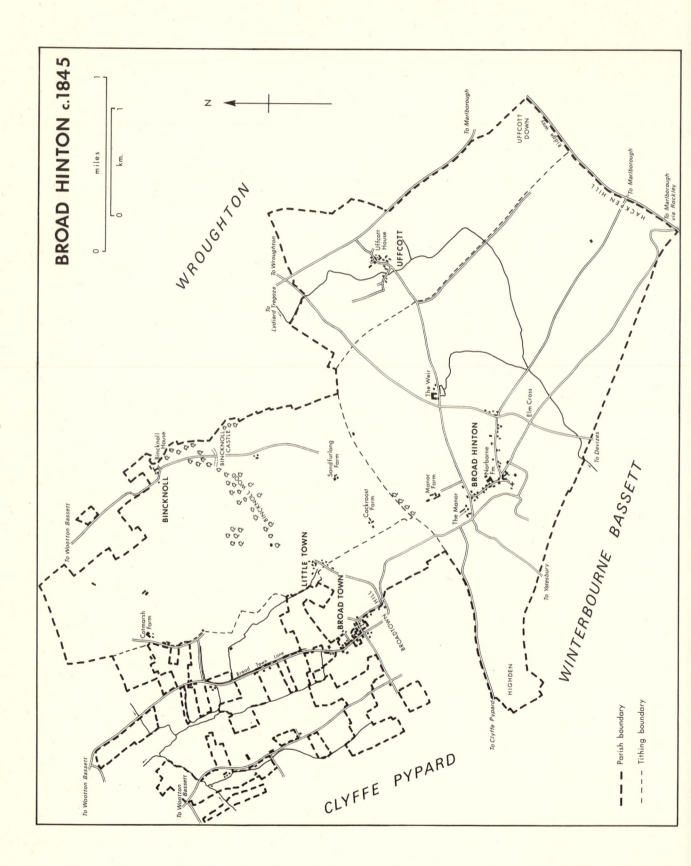

BROAD HINTON c.1845

WROUGHTON

To Marlborough

UFFCOTT DOWN

To Marlborough

To Marlborough

HACKPEN HILL

To Marlborough via Rockley

To Wroughton

Uffcott House

UFFCOTT

To Lydiard Tregoze

The Weir

Elm Cross

To Devizes

BROAD HINTON

Norborne Fm.

Bincknoll House

BINCKNOLL CASTLE

Sandfurlong Farm

BINCKNOLL WOOD

BINCKNOLL

Manor Farm

The Manor

Cockroost Farm

To Wootton Bassett

LITTLE TOWN

To Yatesbury

BROAD TOWN

BROADTOWN HILL

HIGHDEN

WINTERBOURNE BASSETT

Colmarsh Farm

Broad Town Lane

To Wootton Bassett

To Clyffe Pypard

To Wootton Bassett

CLYFFE PYPARD

——— Parish boundary
‒ ‒ ‒ Tithing boundary

N

miles
km.

the division of the tithing between the parishes.[67] The boundary created by that division crossed and recrossed Broad Town Lane, leaving detached parts of Broad Hinton west of the lane. More than half of Broad Town tithing, c. 450 a. of c. 750 a. in the 19th century, was included in Broad Hinton parish. The boundary between Broad Town and Bincknoll tithings ran parallel with and 200 m. east of the road from Broad Hinton to Broadtown Hill. North-east of the hill it followed the ridge to Little Town and then wound crookedly to the northern parish boundary.[68] The north-eastern boundary of Bincknoll was also irregular, perhaps because land there had been exchanged between Lydiard Tregoze and Bincknoll manors in the 16th century or later, when they were jointly owned.[69] In 1845 the tithing measured 1,150 a. Broad Hinton was the largest township, c. 1,850 a. in 1845; Uffcott tithing measured only c. 450 a. in 1797. Between them was a straight boundary leading 3.5 km. north-west from a point on Hackpen Hill 2 km. north-east of the road from Broad Hinton to Rockley in Ogbourne St. Andrew.[70]

The area of the parish richest in archaeological evidence is Hackpen Hill. There are several barrows and a rectangular earthwork on the downs and some supposed eoliths were found there. East of the Weir is the site of burials and perhaps also of a house of the Romano-British period.[71] Bincknoll Castle, a fortified enclosure of 3½ a. in a commanding position on the north-facing ridge near the eastern parish boundary, may be of Romano-British origin but was re-used in the early Middle Ages.[72]

In the 18th century and probably earlier roads crossed the Kennet and Avon valleys but few crossed the watershed and the most important routes in the parish led from south-west to north-east.[73] The oldest such route is the Ridge Way, along the crest of Hackpen Hill. Another ancient road may have crossed the Ridge Way west of Barbury Castle in Wroughton and followed a course now marked by the eastern parish boundary and the modern road from Uffcott to Salthrop in Wroughton and to Lydiard Tregoze.[74] South of Uffcott it was a track in 1981. A path which linked the churches of Broad Hinton, Winterbourne Bassett, and parishes further south, may also have been in use in early times but was of little importance in the late 18th century.[75] A parallel track along the foot of Hackpen Hill has disappeared since then. In the 18th century a major road through the parish ran east from Highway in Hilmarton through Broad Hinton village and past the Weir, and turned north at Uffcott to Wroughton via Red Barn. At the north-west corner of Broad Hinton village it was joined by a road which led north-east from

Yatesbury. After the mid 18th century the Highway-Wroughton road became less important; west of the village it became part of the road from Clyffe Pypard to Broad Hinton and east of Uffcott it was a footpath in the 20th century. Its decline was a result of the turnpiking in 1767 of the Swindon-Devizes road which ran south-west from Red Barn to the Weir and passed east of Broad Hinton village through Elm Cross. That was still the principal route through the parish in 1981. In the late 18th century two roads south of the Weir led westwards across the turnpike road to Broad Hinton village, one via Elm Cross, the other 250 m. further north. The northern road was only a farm track east of the Swindon-Devizes road in 1981 but the southern was part of the main road across Hackpen and Broadtown Hills which was turnpiked as a section of the road from Rockley to Wootton Bassett in 1809. North of Broadtown Hill it was known as Broad Town Lane and it was the only road of importance in the northern part of the parish. Access to Bincknoll has always been restricted. In 1773 it could be approached by road only from Salthrop. Later tracks led north from the Weir and from Manor Farm. In 1981 access for vehicles was possible only by a road running south from the road from Wootton Bassett to Swindon.[76]

Broad Hinton was both a wealthy and a populous parish by comparison with its neighbours in the Middle Ages. Taxation assessments show it to have been of moderate wealth, about the average for Selkley hundred, in the 16th century.[77] The population rose from 550 in 1801 to a peak of 714 in 1851 but fell again to 550 in 1881. In 1891, after the creation of Broad Town parish, there were 372 residents of Broad Hinton. Numbers fell in the early 20th century but rose after the Second World War as Broad Hinton village expanded as a dormitory for Swindon. In 1971 there were 368 inhabitants of the parish.[78]

BROAD HINTON village stands on rising ground in the north part of the Kennet valley where the principal roads through the parish converge. The village grew from two hamlets, Hinton Columbers and Hinton Wase. The oldest sites in the village, those of the church and of Manor Farm, 750 m. further north, may have been the centres of the two hamlets. The manor house of Hinton Columbers stood near the church in the 13th century.[79] That of Hinton Wase manor stood at the site of Manor Farm until the 17th century and was approached by a hollow way running east from the road from Wootton Bassett to Rockley.[80] No architectural or archaeological evidence suggests that there was ever more than a farmstead on that site and the main settlement may always have been that near the church. In 14th-century assessments for taxation Broad

[67] *Tax. Eccl.* (Rec. Com.), 189; *Cart. St. Nicholas's Hosp.* ed. C. Wordsworth, 62, 64, 67.
[68] W.R.O., Broad Hinton tithe award; Clyffe Pypard tithe award.
[69] Below, manors.
[70] W.R.O., Broad Hinton tithe award; Elcombe and Uffcott inclosure award.
[71] *V.C.H. Wilts.* i (1), 50, 162, 263; *W.A.M.* xlv. 178.
[72] *V.C.H. Wilts.* i (1), 263; *W.A.M.* xxiii. 190; xlv. 137.
[73] *Andrews and Dury, Map* (W.R.S. viii), pl. 14.
[74] *W.A.M.* xxv. 64.
[75] Below, Winterbourne Monkton, introduction; *Andrews and Dury, Map* (W.R.S. viii), pl. 14.
[76] *Andrews and Dury, Map* (W.R.S. viii), pl. 14; *V.C.H. Wilts.* iv. 268, 271; O.S. Map 1", sheet 34 (1828 edn.).
[77] *V.C.H. Wilts.* iv. 297, 300-1, 306, 309; *Taxation Lists* (W.R.S. x), 20-3, 101-5, 107.
[78] *V.C.H. Wilts.* iv. 350; *Census,* 1971.
[79] *Cart. St. Nicholas's Hosp.* ed. Wordsworth, 66.
[80] W.R.O. 212B/743.

Hinton was treated as a single settlement, one of the wealthiest in Selkley hundred, with 106 poll-tax payers in 1377. It was similarly prosperous in the early 16th century, although an assessment of 1576 was well below the average for the hundred.[81]

The modern pattern of settlement in the village had been established by the late 18th century.[82] Most buildings stood inside or around a triangle formed by the road from Clyffe Pypard to Uffcott, the Swindon–Devizes road, and the road from Wootton Bassett to Rockley. North of Elm Cross a lane from the downs crossed the triangle from the Swindon–Devizes road to that from Wootton Bassett. The main street is formed by the road from Wootton Bassett to Rockley which turns east and south-east at the north end of the village. The church, the vicarage house, and Broad Hinton House stand west of the street and are reached by a lane. Beside the street and north of the church are most of the older domestic buildings of the village, none of which is obviously earlier than the 18th century. Buildings of that date include thatched cottages and Comptons Farm at the junction of the street and the lane leading to the church; Marlborough House, a substantial brick house altered in the 19th century, a little further north; and cottages near the junction at which the road from Uffcott joins the street. The post office, south of those cottages, bears the date 1746, and east of them stands Church House, once used as a reading room,[83] which is probably also of the 18th century and is one of the few timber-framed buildings in the village.

In 1773 buildings were scattered along the northern road of the triangle, at the Weir at its north-east corner, and further south along the Swindon–Devizes road.[84] Of those buildings the house called the Manor, built in the late 17th century north of the junction of the northern and south-western roads of the triangle, a thatched stone cottage 1 km. further east, and a cottage east of the Weir survive. The Bell, east of the Swindon–Devizes road opposite the lane which crosses the triangle, may have been built by then but the first documentary reference to it is of 1793.[85] Some 18th- and 19th-century cottages of brick and chalk stand beside the lane. New houses and cottages were built along the village street and east of the Manor in the 19th century. The largest buildings of that date were the school and a chapel at the west corner of the triangle, and the Crown, west of the street, which was mentioned as an inn in 1903.[86] Brick estate cottages north of the Manor and a small reading room opposite the chapel were built in the late 19th century. The reading room was replaced by a village hall after the Second World War. In the 1930s the Swindon–Devizes road was straightened south of the Bell and garages were

later built nearby on either side of the road.[87] Among other 20th-century buildings are council houses of the 1930s north of the lane crossing the triangle and an estate of private houses of the 1970s within the triangle south of the road to Uffcott.

BINCKNOLL. Taxation assessments for Bincknoll from the 14th century show it to have been of moderate wealth for a township of Blackgrove hundred. It was, however, the least populous in Broad Hinton parish, having only 38 poll-tax payers in 1377 and fewer than ten households in 1428.[88] In 1576 its assessment was one of the lowest in the combined hundred of Kingsbridge, Blackgrove, and Thornhill.[89] From the 18th century or earlier settlement in the tithing has been in scattered farmsteads. At Bincknoll, on the lower slopes of the hill north of Bincknoll Castle, are Bincknoll House, several cottages, and farm buildings. Other farmsteads are linked by road with Broad Town or Broad Hinton rather than with Bincknoll. They include those at Cotmarsh, on the western boundary, which were reached from Broad Town Lane in the 18th century, and those at Little Town, at the foot of Broadtown Hill, which were in Bincknoll tithing but were outlying parts of Broad Town village. A track from the Highway–Wroughton road led to Sandfurlong Farm 1 km. north-east of Manor Farm in Broad Hinton tithing.[90] Additional farmsteads were built at Cotmarsh and at Cockroost, west of Sandfurlong Farm, in the early 19th century.[91]

UFFCOTT village stands at the head of a gently sloping valley watered by a head stream of the Kennet. The township, like Bincknoll, was of moderate prosperity in the 14th century and in 1377 had 46 poll-tax payers.[92] In the 16th century, however, assessments for tax were low compared with those of neighbouring townships.[93] The pattern of settlement at Uffcott has changed little since the 17th century.[94] The buildings of the village are gathered east of the stream and the pond which it feeds. South of the pond the old Highway–Wroughton road crosses the stream and then winds uphill through the village. A brick house east of the pond and a row of thatched cottages north of the house are probably of the 18th century or earlier. There was an inn called the Harrow at the east end of the village in the late 18th century but it was closed after 1836.[95] Most of Uffcott House, on higher ground south of the road, and most cottages are of the 19th century. A few 20th-century houses have been built at the east end of the village. Hangars belonging to Wroughton airfield were built in the parish east of Uffcott village after 1937.[96]

[81] V.C.H. Wilts. iv. 301, 309; Taxation Lists (W.R.S. x), 23, 102.
[82] Andrews and Dury, Map (W.R.S. viii), pl. 14.
[83] W.R.O. 1505/92.
[84] Andrews and Dury, Map (W.R.S. viii), pl. 14.
[85] W.R.O. 212B/878.
[86] Kelly's Dir. Wilts.
[87] Ibid. (1898); Char. Com. file; local inf.
[88] V.C.H. Wilts. iv. 297, 306, 314.

[89] Taxation Lists (W.R.S. x), 104–8.
[90] Andrews and Dury, Map (W.R.S. viii), pl. 14.
[91] W.R.O., tithe award.
[92] V.C.H. Wilts. iv. 297, 306.
[93] Taxation Lists (W.R.S. x), 20, 105.
[94] W.R.O. 631/1.
[95] Ibid. Ch. Com., chap. 125/1; Ch. Com., chap. 126; ibid. Elcombe and Uffcott inclosure award.
[96] V.C.H. Wilts. xi. 238.

MANORS AND OTHER ESTATES. An estate at Broad Hinton was held in 1066 by Ulgar and in 1086 by Humphrey Lisle.[97] Overlordship of the estate, the manor of *BROAD HINTON*, passed to Reynold de Dunstanville, husband of Humphrey's daughter Adelize, and thereafter descended with Reynold's barony of Castle Combe.[98] The overlordship was held as part of the barony by Giles de Badlesmere, Lord Badlesmere, at his death in 1338 and when his estates were divided it was allotted with Castle Combe to his sister Margaret and her husband John Tiptoft, Lord Tiptoft.[99] The manor was held of Castle Combe in 1404[1] but no later reference to the overlordship has been found.

In 1086 Ranulph held the estate.[2] It passed to members of the Wase family and was called *HINTON WASE* manor until the 14th century. John Wase (fl. after 1189) was succeeded in or before 1194 by Reynold son of Wase (d. before 1242–3).[3] Roger Wase held the manor in 1316 and 1319, as did Faith Wase, probably his relict, in 1339.[4] In 1365 Nicholas Wase sold it to William Wroughton.[5] After the death of Wroughton in 1392 and of his wife Isabel (fl. 1404)[6] the manor passed to their son William (d. 1408), grandson John Wroughton (d. *c.* 1429), and great-grandson John Wroughton (d. 1496).[7] The younger John was succeeded in turn by his son Sir Christopher (d. 1515) and great-grandson Sir William Wroughton (d. 1559).[8] Sir William's son Sir Thomas held the manor at his death in 1597.[9] His son Sir Giles sold it in 1628 to Sir John Glanville, a prominent M.P. and later a king's serjeant.[10] Glanville (d. 1661) was succeeded by his son William (d. 1680) and then by William's nephew John Glanville who in 1709 sold the manor to Thomas Bennet (will proved 1754).[11] It passed to Bennet's daughter Martha, wife of Peter Legh (d. 1792),[12] and to the Leghs' daughter Elizabeth. She married first Anthony James Keck and secondly, before 1793, William Bathurst Pye who took the additional name Bennet. Elizabeth was succeeded *c.* 1827 by her daughter Elizabeth Keck, then wife of Thomas Calley (d. 1836).[13] The Calleys' son John James sold the manor in 1839 to Arthur Wellesley, duke of Wellington (d. 1852). It was sold by Wellesley's son Arthur, duke of Wellington, to M. H. N. Story-Maskelyne in 1867[14] and by him to Sir Henry Meux, Bt., in 1869.[15] Meux (d. 1883) was succeeded by his son Sir Henry Bruce Meux (d. 1900), whose relict Valerie, Lady Meux, sold the

estate in several lots in 1906.[16] Manor farm was bought by H. J. Horton (d. 1924) and passed to his son R. W. Horton (d. 1959) and grandson Maj. R. D. Horton, the owner in 1981. Norborne farm belonged to F. Bailey in 1917 and in 1953 was sold to Mr. and Mrs. D. Jones who owned it in 1981.[17] Weir and Hackpen farms were bought in 1908 by J. H. W. Hussey, who was succeeded in turn by his son R. J. Hussey and grandson Mr. J. P. L. Hussey, the owner in 1981.[18]

Sir William Wroughton (d. 1559) had a house built at Broad Hinton, reputedly from the stones of Bradenstoke priory.[19] John Evelyn described it as a 'very fair dwelling house' and reported that it had been destroyed by Sir John Glanville to prevent the establishment of a parliamentary garrison there. According to other contemporary sources it was burned down by royalist forces in 1645.[20] The site of the house may have been close to the farmstead which stood north-east of the Manor in 1981. The older farm buildings are largely of re-used ashlar, some of it reddened by fire. North of the farmstead is a large grass platform bounded on one side by a bank. The field west of it has been much disturbed and is crossed by a hollow way. The Manor may have been the gatehouse in which Glanville was living in 1654.[21] The plan of the main range of the house is of the early or mid 17th century. Its walls of chalk block were cased in red and black brick with stone dressings probably *c.* 1700 when a short back wing of brick was added at the east end. A similar wing of ashlar was added at the west end in the mid 18th century. The main, south, front was of seven bays but was altered and given a Tuscan porch in the early 19th century. A 17th-century timber-framed stable east of the house has been largely rebuilt in brick.

Another estate held in 1066 by Ulgar became *HINTON COLUMBERS* manor. Gilbert of Breteuil held it in 1086[22] and in 1242–3 Baldwin de Reviers, earl of Devon and lord of the Isle of Wight (d. 1245), was overlord. The overlordship passed in turn to his son Baldwin, earl of Devon (d. 1262), and daughter Isabel de Forz, countess of Aumale and Devon. Isabel was overlord in 1275 but no later reference to the Devon interest has been found. Walter Marshal, earl of Pembroke (d. 1245), was intermediate lord of Hinton Columbers in 1242, and in 1275 the lordship was held by his five sisters and coheirs.[23] It probably passed, with the manor of Hampstead Marshall (Berks.) and like the lordship

[97] *V.C.H. Wilts.* ii, p. 145.
[98] G. Poulett Scrope, *Castle Combe* (priv. print. 1852), 19.
[99] *Cal. Inq. p.m.* viii, pp. 127, 137, 143.
[1] Poulett Scrope, *Castle Combe*, 157.
[2] *V.C.H. Wilts.* ii, p. 145.
[3] *Cat. Anct. D.* iii, A 4619; *V.C.H. Wilts.* iii. 270; *Rot. Cur. Reg.* (Rec. Com.), i. 115; *Bk. of Fees*, ii. 749.
[4] *Feud. Aids*, v. 206; *Feet of F. 1272–1327* (W.R.S. i), p. 104; *Cal. Inq. p.m.* viii, p. 137.
[5] *Feet of F. 1327–77* (W.R.S. xxix), p. 128.
[6] P.R.O., C 136/78, no. 4; Poulett Scrope, *Castle Combe*, 157.
[7] P.R.O., C 137/74, no. 50A; C 139/42, no. 85; *Cal. Inq. p.m. Hen. VII*, i, p. 505.
[8] P.R.O., C 142/30, no. 27; C 142/192, no. 124; mon. in church.
[9] Mon. in church.
[10] W.R.O. 212B/732–3; *D.N.B.*

[11] W.R.O. 75/1; 200/1; 212B/764; P.R.O., PROB 11/806 (P.C.C. 31 Pinfold).
[12] W.R.O. 212B/814; *W.A.M.* xxxi. 194–5.
[13] *W.A.M.* xxxi. 194; W.R.O., land tax. A different acct. of the Bennet fam. is in *V.C.H. Wilts.* xi. 241.
[14] Aubrey, *Topog. Coll.* ed. Jackson, 335; *W.A.M.* xxiv. 76; Wilts. Tracts, cviii, no. 4, p. 18.
[15] W.R.O. 106, sale cat. of Meux estates.
[16] Ibid.; Burke, *Peerage* (1904), 1069.
[17] Wilts. Cuttings, xvii. 5; xxi. 235; *W.A.M.* xliii. 106; inf. from Maj. R. D. Horton, the Manor.
[18] Inf. from Mr. J. P. L. Hussey, Weir Farm.
[19] Mon. in church; Aubrey, *Topog. Coll.* ed. Jackson, 189.
[20] J. Evelyn, *Diary*, ed. E. S. de Beer, iii. 111; *Cal. Cttee. for Money*, i. 409; *Perfect Passages*, 17 May 1645, p. 237.
[21] Evelyn, *Diary*, ed. de Beer, iii. 111.
[22] *V.C.H. Wilts.* ii, p. 147.
[23] *Bk. of Fees*, ii. 749; *Complete Peerage*, s.v. Pembroke; iv. 319–22; *Rot. Hund.* (Rec. Com.), ii (1), 269.

of Bincknoll, to Queen Joan, relict of Henry IV, who was overlord of Hinton Columbers in 1428.[24]

Richard of Hinton inherited Hinton Columbers from his father Sir Hugh of Hinton (fl. c. 1226) and in 1242–3 held it of Matthew Columbers.[25] In 1258 he exchanged it for a life interest in Matthew's manor of Bincknoll.[26] Columbers was succeeded c. 1272 by his brother Michael who granted the manor to John Cobham c. 1279.[27] In 1285 Matthew's relict Maud, then wife of John's son Henry, surrendered her dower rights in the manor to John.[28] After John's death in 1300 the manor passed in turn to his son Henry, Lord Cobham (d. 1339), grandson John Cobham, Lord Cobham (d. 1355), and great-grandson John Cobham, Lord Cobham.[29] In 1372 Cobham granted the manor to William Wroughton[30] and thereafter it passed with Hinton Wase manor.

In return for a grant of lands and rights to the rector of Broad Hinton Sir Hugh of Hinton was licensed c. 1226 to build an oratory on his estate.[31] No more is known of it.

In 1253 Broad Hinton rectory was appropriated by St. Nicholas's hospital in Salisbury. The *RECTORY* estate included 6 a. in Broad Hinton given by Richard of Hinton to the hospital in 1253, 2 a. there given by William of Calne c. 1260, and a messuage and croft in Broad Town given by Henry of Woodhay in the late 13th century.[32] The hospital had a carucate of land and demesne meadow valued at 8s. in 1341 and in 1845 it had 55 a. in Broad Hinton.[33] Grain tithes from most of the parish were due to the hospital, although those from parts of Bincknoll, Uffcott, and Broad Town passed to other owners in the 13th century or later.[34] Hay tithes from Broad Hinton and Uffcott were also part of the estate.[35] Rectorial tithes from Uffcott were replaced by an allotment of 97 a. in 1797. Those from the rest of the parish, of which some 360 a., mainly in Bincknoll, were exempt, were commuted to a rent charge of £535 in 1845.[36] The lands in Uffcott and Broad Hinton were still owned by the hospital in 1981.[37]

John Wase gave 1 yardland in Broad Hinton to Stanley abbey probably after 1189.[38] Other lands there were granted to the abbey, probably in the 12th and 13th centuries. They included 8 a. given by Nicholas Wase, 12 a. by Richard (fl. 1194) son of William of Hinton, 22 a. by Richard's son Sir Hugh (d. in or before 1243), and 1 yardland by Robert son of Samuel.[39] The lands passed to the

Crown at the Dissolution and by an exchange of 1539 to Charles Brandon, duke of Suffolk.[40] The estate was probably later merged with Broad Hinton manor.

In 1702 Constables farm, a leasehold of Broad Hinton manor, was sold by John Glanville to Thomas Andrews.[41] In or before 1725 Andrews was succeeded by his son Townsend (will dated 1734) who devised the farm to his wife Sarah.[42] It was sold c. 1766 to Peter Legh and reunited with the manor.[43]

A yardland in 'Henton' was granted by Roger of Sutton to Bradenstoke priory before 1232.[44] The identity of 'Henton' is uncertain and no later reference to lands in Broad Hinton belonging to the priory has been found.

Estates at 'Bechenhalle', probably Bincknoll, were held by Hacun and Toli in 1066; another was held by Saul and Alwin. All of them were held by Gilbert of Breteuil in 1086.[45] The overlordship of *BINCKNOLL* manor descended with that of Hinton Columbers to Isabel, countess of Aumale and Devon[46] (d. 1293). As one of her heirs Warin de Lisle claimed rights in her estates, apparently including the overlordship, in 1294; it is not known whether he entered on the estates before his death in 1296. He was succeeded by his son Robert (created Lord Lisle of Rougemont in 1311), who received livery of the inheritance in 1310. When Robert entered the Franciscan order in 1342 his estates passed to his son John, Lord Lisle (d. 1355). John's son Robert, Lord Lisle, surrendered the overlordship of Bincknoll to the Crown in 1368.[47]

Walter Marshal, earl of Pembroke, was intermediate lord of Bincknoll in 1242–3.[48] After his death in 1245 the lordship probably passed with the manor of Hampstead Marshall and in 1333 may have been granted with a life interest in that manor to William Montagu (created earl of Salisbury in 1337).[49] The lordship passed with the title to William, earl of Salisbury (d. 1397), and at the death of his relict Elizabeth in 1415 to their grandnephew Thomas, earl of Salisbury.[50] In 1428 Bincknoll manor, like Hampstead Marshall, was held of Queen Joan, relict of Henry IV.[51]

Matthew Columbers held Bincknoll in 1242–3 and in 1251 was granted free warren in his demesne there.[52] His estate was increased in 1247 by a grant of c. 80 a. from William of Calne and his wife Sarah and in 1267 by a grant of a messuage and a carucate from Imbert de Funteynes and his wife Maud.[53] In 1258 Matthew granted the manor to Richard of Hinton for life,

[24] *Feud. Aids*, v. 269; *V.C.H. Berks*. iv. 179–80; below.
[25] *Cart. St. Nicholas's Hosp*. ed. Wordsworth, 56–8, 65; *Bk. of Fees*, ii. 749.
[26] P.R.O., CP 25(1)/251/19, no. 14; below.
[27] B.L. Harl. Roll C. 28; *V.C.H. Wilts*. iv. 27.
[28] *Cal. Pat*. 1281–92, 178; *Coll. Topog. et Gen*. vii. 148.
[29] *Complete Peerage*, iii. 343–4; *Feet of F*. 1327–77 (W.R.S. xxix), pp. 65–6.
[30] *Feet of F*. 1327–77 (W.R.S. xxix), p. 141.
[31] *Cart. St. Nicholas's Hosp*. ed. Wordsworth, 65–7.
[32] Ibid. 56–60, 64–5; below, church.
[33] *Inq. Non*. (Rec. Com.), 158; W.R.O., tithe award.
[34] *Cart. St. Nicholas's Hosp*. ed. Wordsworth, 60–1; below.
[35] *Cart. St. Nicholas's Hosp*. ed. Wordsworth, 62.
[36] W.R.O., Elcombe and Uffcott inclosure award; tithe award.
[37] Inf. from Jonas & Parker, Castle St., Salisbury.

[38] *Cat. Anct. D*. iii, A 4619; *V.C.H. Wilts*. iii. 270.
[39] *W.A.M*. xv. 260–1; *Rot. Cur. Reg*. (Rec. Com.), i. 115; P.R.O., CP 25(1)/251/16, no. 89; above.
[40] *L. & P. Hen. VIII*, xiv (1), p. 258.
[41] W.R.O. 212B/787.
[42] Ibid. 212B/812. [43] Ibid. 829/3.
[44] *Cal. Chart. R*. 1226–57, 159–61.
[45] *V.C.H. Wilts*. ii, p. 147.
[46] *Rot. Hund*. (Rec. Com.), ii (1), 243.
[47] *Complete Peerage*, s.v. Lisle of Rougemont; *Cal. Close*, 1364–8, 494, 498.
[48] *Bk. of Fees*, ii. 712. [49] *V.C.H. Berks*. iv. 180.
[50] *Complete Peerage*, s.v. Salisbury; *Cal. Close*, 1396–9, 188–9; *Cal. Fine R*. 1413–22, 92, 97.
[51] *Feud. Aids*, v. 279.
[52] *Bk. of Fees*, ii. 712; *Cal. Chart. R*. 1226–57, 353.
[53] P.R.O., CP 25(1)/251/14, no. 28; CP 25(1)/251/21, no. 2.

in exchange for Hinton Columbers manor.[54] After Richard's death it passed with Hinton Columbers manor to John, Lord Cobham, and was forfeited at his attainder in 1398. It was restored before his death in 1408[55] and passed to his granddaughter Joan de la Pole, Baroness Cobham, whose husband John Oldcastle, Lord Oldcastle, was executed in 1417. The manor was then confiscated but was restored to Joan in 1418.[56] At her death in 1434 it passed to her daughter Joan, wife of Thomas Brooke, Lord Cobham. It descended with the Cobham title in the Brooke family to Edward (d. 1464), John (d. 1512), Thomas (d. 1529), George (d. 1558), and William, Lord Cobham,[57] who sold it in 1562 to John St. John.[58] Thereafter it passed with Lydiard Tregoze manor in the St. John family. John St. John (d. 1576) was succeeded by his son Nicholas (d. 1589), grandson John St. John (d. 1594), great-grandsons Walter St. John (d. 1597) and John St. John (created a baronet in 1611, d. 1648), and by Sir John's grandson Sir John St. John. The manor passed in 1656 to the younger Sir John's uncle Sir Walter St. John (d. 1708), and then to Sir Walter's son Sir Henry (created Viscount St. John in 1716, d. 1742), grandson John St. John, Viscount St. John (d. 1748), and great-grandson Frederick St. John, Viscount St. John, who inherited the viscountcy of Bolingbroke in 1751. Thereafter the manor passed with both titles from father to son to Henry St. John, Viscount Bolingbroke (d. 1899), who devised his estates to his wife Mary Emily Elizabeth.[59] She sold the Bincknoll estate in 1920.[60] Upper Bincknoll farm was bought by Henry White and Sandfurlong farm by Emily and Charlotte Humphries. Both farms were sold in the 1920s to R. W. Horton and have since passed with Manor farm in Broad Hinton. Great Cotmarsh and Little Cotmarsh farms, sold in 1920, belonged to Mr. A. H. John and Mr. T. W. Marks respectively in 1981.[61]

Bincknoll House is presumably on the site of a long thatched 'hall-house' and outbuildings, all of which were said to need repair in the late 14th century.[62] The modern house is a long brick building, probably built in 1757.[63] In the early 20th century it was divided into cottages but in 1981 it was again one house.[64]

The priory of Goldcliff (Mon., later Gwent) had an estate at Bincknoll c. 1210[65] but no later record of it has been found.

Walter, earl of Pembroke, was overlord of an estate at LITTLE TOWN in 1242–3.[66] The overlordship passed with the intermediate lordship of Bincknoll manor to Thomas, earl of Salisbury (d. 1428).[67]

In 1225 Grace de Parys, relict of Thomas de Parys, claimed $\frac{1}{3}$ yardland in Little Town as dower from Richard de Parys, probably Thomas's son.[68] Richard held Little Town in 1242–3 and it passed to Matthew Columbers in or before 1247.[69] Columbers apparently sold the lordship and lands of Little Town separately. The lordship passed with Hinton Columbers manor to members of the Cobham family. In 1496 it belonged to John Brooke, Lord Cobham,[70] but its descent has not been traced further. In 1247 Columbers granted part, if not all, of the lands of Little Town to William of Calne and his wife Sarah.[71] Nicholas Borden held Little Town, probably to be identified with William's estate, at his death in 1301.[72] It was held as dower by his relict Agnes, wife of Sir Peter Doygnel, and passed to her son Nicholas Borden in 1349.[73] Isabel, relict of William Wroughton, was granted seisin of the estate in 1393 and thereafter it passed with Broad Hinton manor.[74]

William of Calne gave lands to St. Nicholas's hospital c. 1260 to secure the master's intercession with the bishop of Salisbury for a licence to build an oratory. There is no certain evidence that a chapel was built although John the chaplain of Little Town, where William held land, died in or before 1262.[75]

Before 1291 tithes from the demesne of Bincknoll manor, reputedly the endowment of a chapel there, were granted to St. Denis's priory in Southampton.[76] The tithes passed to the Crown at the Dissolution and were sold in 1543 to Christopher Willoughby.[77] William Stumpe acquired them from Isabel Baynton in 1550 and in 1558 his son Sir James sold them to John Richmond.[78] John's son Henry sold them in 1578 to Richard Franklin (fl. 1583).[79] Before 1610 they were bought by Sir John St. John and they were afterwards merged in Bincknoll manor.[80]

An estate 'in the marsh', later known as COTMARSH, was held of Roger Bigod, earl of Norfolk, as earl marshal in 1306 and of Queen Joan, relict of Henry IV, in 1428. In 1306 and 1319 the land was held by Thomas Parys and in 1428 by William Parys.[81] Thomas Parys (d. c. 1515) held land at Cotmarsh and was succeeded by his son Christopher (fl. c. 1535).[82] Before 1610 the land or the reversion of it was sold to a St. John: Thomas Parys died in 1610,

[54] Ibid. CP 25(1)/251/19, no. 14.
[55] *Cal. Inq. Misc.* vi, p. 149; *Complete Peerage*, iii. 344–5.
[56] *Cal. Close*, 1405–9, 307–8; 1413–19, 487–8.
[57] P.R.O., CP 25(1)/292/66, no. 76; *Complete Peerage*, s.v. Cobham.
[58] P.R.O., CP 25(2)/239/4 Eliz. I Trin.
[59] *V.C.H. Wilts.* ix. 79–80.
[60] W.R.O. 305/8.
[61] Inf. from Maj. Horton; Mr. A. H. John, Great Cotmarsh Farm; Mr. T. W. Marks, Little Cotmarsh Farm.
[62] *Cal. Inq. Misc.* vi, p. 152.
[63] A stone, now loose, is inscribed 'Ld. F.B. 1757'.
[64] Inf. from Mrs. C. Spickernell, Bincknoll Ho.
[65] *Interdict Doc.* (Pipe R. Soc. N.S. xxxiv), 18.
[66] *Bk. of Fees*, ii. 725.
[67] *Cal. Fine R.* 1413–22, 97–8; *Complete Peerage*, xi. 395.
[68] *Cur. Reg. R.* xii, p. 310.

[69] *Bk. of Fees*, ii. 725; P.R.O., CP 25(1)/251/14, no. 28.
[70] *Cal. Inq. p.m. Hen. VII*, i, pp. 505–6.
[71] P.R.O., CP 25(1)/251/14, no. 28.
[72] *Wilts. Inq. p.m.* 1242–1327 (Index. Libr.), 278, 280–1.
[73] Ibid. 1327–77 (Index Libr.), 213–14.
[74] *Cal. Inq. Misc.* vi, p. 149; P.R.O., CP 25(2)/339/17 Eliz. I East.
[75] *Cart. St. Nicholas's Hosp.* ed. Wordsworth, 58; *Cal. Pat.* 1258–66, 230.
[76] P.R.O., C 146/105, no. 19; *Tax. Eccl.* (Rec. Com.), 189.
[77] *L. & P. Hen. VIII*, xviii (2), p. 281.
[78] *Cal. Pat.* 1549–51, 356; 1557–8, 329.
[79] P.R.O., CP 25(2)/240/20 Eliz. I Hil.; *Sess. Mins.* (W.R.S. iv), 84.
[80] W.R.O. 326/3/2; 305/5; ibid. tithe award.
[81] *Cal. Inq. p.m.* iv, p. 299; *Feet of F.* 1272–1327 (W.R.S. i), p. 104; *Feud. Aids*, v. 277–8.   [82] P.R.O., C 1/875/11.

holding either a life interest in or a lease of Cotmarsh of Sir John St. John. Thereafter Cotmarsh passed with St. John's Bincknoll estate.[83]

Lands at Little Town were devised by Thomas Franklin to his son Thomas in 1744.[84] In 1780 Thomas Ody held an estate there. It passed c. 1784 to a Mr. Collins and c. 1791 to Benjamin Tarrant, whose relict held it in 1813. The estate passed c. 1820 to Robert Smith[85] and before 1838 was acquired by Susanna (fl. 1845), wife of Algernon Brown.[86] In 1917 it was sold by the executors of George and Adam Twine.[87] It was bought in 1928 by R. C. Hicks who sold it c. 1945 to a Mr. and Mrs. Iles. The estate was later divided. Lands south of Broadtown Hill were bought by R. W. Horton and passed with Manor farm in Broad Hinton. The remainder was owned by Bourton & Sons in 1981.[88]

In 1838 and 1845 William Brown owned a small farm called COCKROOST.[89] In 1872 it passed to W. E. N. Brown who sold it in 1901 to Emily and Charlotte Humphries.[90] They sold it in 1936 to R. W. Horton and it has since passed with Manor farm in Broad Hinton.[91]

An estate at Uffcott held by Almar in 1066 had passed to Durand of Gloucester by 1086. Another estate there was then held by Ulvric, a king's serjeant, who had inherited it from his father after 1066.[92] The relation of those estates to the later manor of UFFCOTT is not clear. In 1361 Uffcott was part of the honor of Winchester, then in the king's hand.[93]

Uffcott was probably held with Elcombe in Wroughton by members of the Lovel family from the 13th century or earlier.[94] John Lovel, Lord Lovel, died seised of the manor in 1361[95] and it passed with the title to Francis, Viscount Lovel, on whose attainder in 1485 it was forfeited to the Crown. In 1512 it was granted to William Compton and his wife Werburgh. With Elcombe manor it passed from father to son to William, Lord Compton, who sold it in 1605 to Thomas Sutton.[96] Uffcott was among the endowments of the Charterhouse hospital founded by Sutton in 1611. The governors of the Charterhouse sold the manor in 1919 to Wiltshire county council.[97] It was bought c. 1922 by H. J. Horton and in 1981 Mr. S. J. Horton was the owner.[98]

The east portion of Uffcott House dates in part from the 17th century. A west range and a new south front were added in the early 19th century.

Arnold the falconer, apparently a servant of William I, held Uffcott church. In or before 1115 it was granted to Salisbury cathedral.[99] A confirmation made in 1146 of the grant mentions tithes among the endowments of Uffcott and other churches given to the cathedral but there is no direct evidence that the canons received tithes from Uffcott. An estate of tithes there which passed to Kington St. Michael priory, however, may previously have belonged to the cathedral.[1] Lands at Uffcott, held by the cathedral c. 1210, were attached to Shipton and Brixworth prebend and like the prebend were divided in two c. 1220.[2] One moiety became part of Shipton prebend, the other of Brixworth prebend which from 1240 was held by the chancellor of the cathedral.[3] Lands in Uffcott were also said to belong to Blewbury prebend in 1223.[4] The estates attached to Shipton and Blewbury prebends were not recorded separately after the 13th century. Lands belonging to the dean and chapter of Salisbury, presumably derived from those of both prebends, were sequestrated by parliamentary trustees and sold in 1650 to John Were or Brown. They were recovered by the dean and chapter after the Restoration[5] and in 1860 passed to the Ecclesiastical Commissioners. In 1898 the lands were sold to E. Gantlett.[6] The chancellor's estate was sold in 1859 to J. W. Brown. Both estates were later absorbed into Uffcott manor.[7]

Simon Lovel bought lands in Uffcott from Robert Toby and Walter son of Gunuld c. 1200 and gave them to the abbey of Godstow (Oxon.).[8] By the 16th century the abbey's estate had been reduced to a small close of land, which was sold by the Crown in 1553.[9]

Henry de Bohun, earl of Hereford and Essex, gave rents totalling 20s. 4d. from lands in Uffcott to Lacock abbey c. 1274. In 1280 St. John's hospital in Calne held a tenement in Uffcott of the abbey.[10] That land and the abbey's rents passed to the Crown at the Dissolution. In 1548 the land was sold to Richard Randall.[11]

Tithes from Uffcott were among the endowments of Kington St. Michael priory in 1535.[12] A member of the Brimpton family, founders of the priory, may have acquired the tithes from Salisbury cathedral and given them to the priory. Adam of Brimpton claimed rights in Shipton and Brixworth prebends, the endowments of which included Uffcott church.[13] In 1538 rever-

[83] P.R.O., C 142/682, no. 125.
[84] W.R.O. 149/17/28.
[85] Ibid. land tax.
[86] Ibid. 829/4; ibid. tithe award.
[87] Sale cat. penes Maj. Horton.
[88] Inf. from Mr. G. Grigson, Broad Town Farm; Mr. R. Bourton, Manor Farm, Broad Town; Mr. C. Banks, Little Town Farm.
[89] W.R.O. 829/4; ibid. tithe award.
[90] Ibid. 700/321.
[91] Wilts. Cuttings, xviii. 5.
[92] V.C.H. Wilts. ii, pp. 148, 163.
[93] Cal. Inq. p.m. xi, pp. 276, 278.
[94] Godstow Reg. (E.E.T.S. orig. ser. 142), 628–9; V.C.H. Wilts. xi. 240.
[95] Cal. Inq. p.m. xi, pp. 276, 278.
[96] V.C.H. Wilts. xi. 240; P.R.O., CP 25(2)/369/3 Jas. I Mich.
[97] W.A.M. xxxvii. 413; xl. 451; xli. 460.
[98] Inf. from Mr. S. J. Horton, Uffcott Ho.

[99] Reg. St. Osmund (Rolls Ser.), i. 200–1; V.C.H. Wilts. iii. 159.
[1] W. Holtzmann, Papsturkunden in Eng. (Berlin, 1935), ii, pp. 208, 210; below.
[2] Interdict Doc. (Pipe R. Soc. n.s. xxxiv), 16, 21; Sar. Chart. and Doc. (Rolls Ser.), 102–5.
[3] Fasti Eccl. Sar. ed. W. H. Jones, ii. 369.
[4] Sar. Chart. and Doc. (Rolls Ser.), 123–4.
[5] W.A.M. xxi 185–7.
[6] Ch. Com. file 14480; 27376.
[7] W.A.M. xxi. 185; inf. from Mr. Horton.
[8] Godstow Reg. (E.E.T.S. orig. ser. 142), 628–9.
[9] Valor Eccl. (Rec. Com.), ii. 195; Cal. Pat. 1553, 129, 131.
[10] Lacock Chart. (W.R.S. xxxiv), pp. 81–2.
[11] P.R.O., SC 6/Hen. VIII/3985, rot. 31; Cal. Pat. 1548–9, 44–5.
[12] Valor Eccl. (Rec. Com.), ii. 113.
[13] V.C.H. Wilts. iii. 259; Sar. Chart. and Doc. (Rolls Ser.), 102–5; above.

sion of the priory's estates was granted by the Crown to Sir Richard Long who in 1545 conveyed it to Robert Long, then lessee of the estates.[14] Robert (d. 1564) was succeeded by his brother William who sold the tithes to John Ewe in 1570.[15] They were sold in 1607 by William Woodley to Richard Constable and were held by Edmund Maskelyne at his death in 1630.[16] Before 1797 the tithes were merged into the rectory or vicarage estates.[17]

A tenement in Uffcott belonged to Tewkesbury abbey at the Dissolution.[18] In 1540 the Crown granted it to William Richmond or Webb and in 1555 Christopher Baynton granted it to Thomas, John, and William Sadler.[19] In 1590 it was held with Uffcott manor.[20]

The descent of *BROAD TOWN* manor, in Broad Hinton and Clyffe Pypard parishes, from Miles Crispin (fl. 1086) to the Despenser family and then with the earldom of Warwick has been traced elsewhere. In 1487 Anne Neville, countess of Warwick, conveyed the manor to Henry VII and in 1536 it was granted to Edward Seymour, later duke of Somerset. Thereafter it descended with the Somerset and Hertford titles until the death in 1692 of Sarah Hare, duchess of Somerset, under whose will it became the principal endowment of the Broad Town Trust.[21] Of the lands of the manor, parts of Ham and Broad Town Manor farms were in the ancient parish of Broad Hinton in the 19th century.[22] The trustees of the charity sold the estate in 1920. J. E. Price bought Broad Town Manor farm and in 1981 Bourton & Sons were the owners.[23]

Tithes from two hides of the demesne of Broad Town manor, then said to be in Broad Hinton parish, were held by Wallingford priory in the mid 13th century and descended with others in Clyffe Pypard held by the priory.[24] The lands from which they came probably became part of that parish; in 1845 there was no land in Broad Hinton parish from which tithe had formerly been paid to the priory.[25]

In 1653 Roger Spackman held lands in Broad Town tithing, which were later known as *BROAD TOWN* farm and most of which lay in Broad Hinton parish.[26] The farm was divided in or before 1698 when a third of it was conveyed to Edward Richards. Another third was conveyed by Thomas Strickland to Richards in 1700 and the residue by Sir William Strickland to John Clarke in 1704. Richards (will dated 1725) was succeeded by his daughter Ann. The Revd. William Wright sold the whole farm to Solomon Hughes and William Essington before 1787. Essington and Hughes's relict Elizabeth sold it in 1791 to John Ralph, who gave it by will proved

1807 to Robert Codrington (d. before 1845).[27] Much of the land was sold before 1917 when a house and some 30 a. were bought from the executors of George and Adam Twine by H. White.[28] Those lands were sold after 1945 to Brasenose College, Oxford.[29]

ECONOMIC HISTORY. Broad Hinton, Bincknoll, Uffcott, and Broad Town were separate agricultural units. The economic history of Broad Town has been described elsewhere.[30]

BROAD HINTON. Sheep-and-corn husbandry was probably practised in Broad Hinton township as elsewhere in the upper Kennet valley. Evidence of medieval agriculture is scanty but from the 16th century until the mid 19th century arable farming was more important than pastoral. An imbalance between arable land and pasture was commented upon in the early 17th century. The small area of downland, *c.* 50 a. in the south-east corner of the township, was several, and common grazing was restricted to the open fields after harvest.[31] The open fields were south and east of the village. East and West fields, so called, were separated by the Swindon–Devizes road. In the 18th century there was a South field, probably created from the East field.[32] There were meadows at Highden, in the west corner of the township, and near the village. In the mid 17th century the streams east of Broad Hinton were probably used to float water meadows and in the 18th century arable land near the village was converted to meadow.[33]

In 1086 there were estates in Broad Hinton of 11 hides and 10 hides with land for 5 and 4 ploughteams respectively. Of Gilbert of Breteuil's 11-hide estate 9 hides and 1 yardland were in demesne with 2 ploughteams. There were also 4 villeins and 5 bordars with 2 teams. On Humphrey Lisle's 10-hide estate the proportion of land in demesne was smaller, 6 hides with 1 team and 1 serf: another 2 teams were held by 4 villeins and 6 bordars. Gilbert's estate included 16 a. of meadow and 30 a. of pasture and had increased in value from £5 in 1066 to £7. Humphrey's was valued at £5 in 1066 and 1086 and included 12 a. of meadow and 14 a. of pasture.[34]

Although the estates derived from Gilbert's and Humphrey's were held together from the late 14th century, the lands may still have been worked separately in the late 15th century. Hinton Columbers, the larger estate, was said to include 5 carucates in 1258 and was valued at £10 in 1496.[35] Hinton Wase, 3 carucates in 1319, was

---

[14] *V.C.H. Wilts.* iii. 261; *L. & P. Hen VIII*, xiii (1), p. 488; xx (1), p. 227.
[15] P.R.O., C 142/140, no. 200; *Cal. Pat.* 1569–72, p. 140.
[16] W.R.O., Q. Sess. enrolled deeds, roll 1, rot. 11.
[17] Ibid. Elcombe and Uffcott inclosure award.
[18] *Valor Eccl.* (Rec. Com.), ii. 472.
[19] *L. & P. Hen. VIII*, xv, p. 341; *Cal. Pat.* 1554–5, 4.
[20] Charterhouse Mun. D. 5/202.
[21] *V.C.H. Wilts.* ix. 28–9.
[22] W.R.O., tithe award.
[23] Inf. from Mr. Bourton.
[24] *Cart. St. Nicholas's Hosp.* ed. Wordsworth, 67; *V.C.H. Wilts.* ix. 39.

[25] W.R.O., tithe award.
[26] Ibid. 110/7.
[27] Ibid. 1064/13; ibid. tithe award.
[28] Sale cat. *penes* Maj. Horton.
[29] Inf. from Mr. Grigson; inf. from the Land Agent, Brasenose Coll., Oxf.
[30] *V.C.H. Wilts.* ix. 34–7.
[31] W.R.O. 212B/743.
[32] Ibid. 75/2; O.S. Map 1″, sheet 34 (1828 edn.); *Cart. St. Nicholas's Hosp.* ed. Wordsworth, 58.
[33] W.R.O., bishop, glebe terrier, 1671; *W.A.M.* lv. 112.
[34] *V.C.H. Wilts.* ii, pp. 145, 147.
[35] P.R.O., CP 25(1)/251/19, no. 14; *Cal. Inq. p.m. Hen. VII*, i, p. 505.

valued at £6 13s. 4d. in 1496.[36] Of the other estates, the rectory estate had the highest value, £17 in 1341; 48s. was derived from lands, rents, and services.[37] In the 13th century Stanley abbey held 3 yardlands, of 24 a. each, and another 45 a., including 4 a. of pasture. Bradenstoke priory may have held 1 yardland.[38] Hinton Columbers manor included two freeholds in the early 14th century: one was probably of 64 a. of arable and 4 a. of meadow land, with common pasture valued at 4s. 6d. yearly.[39]

Demesne arable land east of Broad Hinton village was inclosed in the 1590s[40] and the lord of Broad Hinton or his lessee had several pasture for sheep on Hackpen Hill in the early 17th century. The demesne was then worked as one farm but leaseholds and copyholds from the constituent manors of Hinton Columbers and Hinton Wase were still distinguished. In 1636 a total of twelve copyholders held 15 yardlands. There were seventeen leaseholders, nine of whom held ½ yardland or more each and one 7 yardlands.[41] Some copyholds may have been converted to leaseholds in the late 17th century; in 1708 there were two copyholders who held a total of 95 a. and seven leaseholders who held 702¼ a. between them.[42] Constables, the farm of 7 yardlands in 1636, was a freehold of c. 200 a. in 1702. Some of its lands lay in Broad Town but most were scattered in Broad Hinton township. In the late 18th century the farm was leased with and may have been worked as part of the demesne farm.[43] By 1751 many smaller holdings had been absorbed into the demesne; a few acres were then held by copy and c. 200 a., excluding the demesne farm, by lease.[44] Common husbandry continued until the 1770s or later[45] but no inclosure award was necessary. Only the lands of the rectory estate, leased in the late 18th century and the 19th by the members of the Brown family, lay outside the manor estate.[46] In the early 19th century most of the lands of the tithing were in two farms.[47] In 1802 the larger, worked from Manor Farm and Weir Farm, consisted of 1,180 a., mostly in the east part of the tithing and including land on Hackpen Hill. The smaller included 596 a., mostly arable land west of the village, and was worked from Norborne Farm.[48] Both were leased in the late 18th century and the 19th.[49] From 1851 until 1866 Richard Stratton and his son Richard, members of a distinguished Wiltshire farming family, held Manor farm and worked it with lands at Salthrop. They kept a summer flock of 1,000 sheep but were chiefly noted for their shorthorn cattle and for technical innovations,

which were reputed to include the first steam plough in the county.[50] In the early 20th century Broad Hinton manor was divided into four large and several small farms. The largest, Manor farm, 568 a. in 1906,[51] was kept in hand from the 1920s and has since been enlarged. In 1981 it was a farm of 1,350 a., including some 200 a. in Bincknoll. Corn was grown on c. 350 a. and there was a large dairy herd.[52] After 1925 Hackpen and Weir farms, a total of 680 a., were worked together as Weir farm. In 1981 the farm measured c. 800 a., with 450 a. of arable land and a herd of 140 cows. Much of Norborne farm, 214 a. in 1906, was later divided between Manor and Weir farms.[53] The rectorial glebe was leased by local farmers in the 20th century.[54]

BINCKNOLL. Estates of 5 hides, of 3 hides and 1 yardland, and of 1¾ hide at Bincknoll were valued at 50s., 27s., and 18s. respectively in 1086. The highest value had risen from 40s. and the second from 20s. since 1066. Only the largest estate included demesne, 4 hides with 1 plough-team and 4 serfs. On that estate there were 1 villein and 3 bordars with 1 team, on the second 2 villeins and land for 10 oxen, and on the smallest 1 villein and land for 6 oxen. There were 14 a. of meadow, 18 a. of pasture, and 4 a. of woodland.[55]

The ridge which extends north-east from Broadtown Hill divided pasture in the north-west part of the tithing from the arable lands in the south-east. In the Middle Ages there were open fields south of Bincknoll Castle. Honey Hill, halfway between the castle and Broadtown Hill, and 'Lynton' and 'le Hale', neither of which can be located, provided several pasture.[56] An area of common pasture, said in the 14th century to be badly drained, may have been that at Westmarsh in the north-east corner of the tithing referred to in the 17th century. Tenants of the lord of Bincknoll who held land at Chaddington in Lydiard Tregoze then had rights of pasture for sheep and cattle at Westmarsh.[57]

In the late 14th century the demesne of Bincknoll manor included 219 a. of arable and 25 a. of meadow land, the pasture at Honey Hill, 'Lynton', and 'le Hale', another 20 a. of several winter pasture, and common pasture for 200 sheep. A flock of 300 or more sheep was usually kept. Rents totalling £8 6s. 8d. were paid by customary tenants, and two free tenants held estates of 2 yardlands and of a few acres.[58] Other estates were small. In the early 13th century that of Goldcliff priory was valued at £1 a year and was entirely let to a tenant.[59] That of Bincknoll

[36] Feet of F. 1272–1327 (W.R.S. i), p. 104; Cal. Inq. p.m. Hen. VII, i, p. 505.
[37] Inq. Non. (Rec. Com.), 158.
[38] Cal. Chart. R. 1226–57, 161; above, manors; W.A.M. xv. 260–1.
[39] B.L. Harl. Roll G. 34; Wilts. Inq. p.m. 1242–1327 (Index Libr.), 280.
[40] D. & C. Sar. Mun., press IV, misc. chapter papers, i, doc. concerning Broad Hinton advowson.
[41] W.R.O. 212B/743.
[42] W.A.M. xxxix. 382–6.
[43] W.R.O. 212B/787; 75/2; ibid. land tax; tithe award.
[44] W.A.M. xxxix. 387–90.
[45] W.R.O. 75/2.
[46] Ibid. 1672/15/6–11; ibid. tithe award; W.A.S. Libr., sale cat. ii, no. 7.

[47] W.R.O., land tax; tithe award.
[48] Ibid. 212B/836.
[49] Ibid. land tax; ibid. 75/4; Kelly's Dir. Wilts. (1848 and later edns.).
[50] W.A.M. xliv. 86–7; Wilts. Cuttings, xvi. 89; V.C.H. Wilts. iv. 86.
[51] W.R.O. 106, sale cat. of Meux estates.
[52] Inf. from Maj. R. D. Horton, the Manor.
[53] W.R.O. 106, sale cat. of Meux estates; inf. from Mr. J. P. L. Hussey, Weir Farm.
[54] Inf. from Jonas & Parker, Castle St., Salisbury.
[55] V.C.H. Wilts. ii, p. 147.
[56] Cal. Inq. Misc. vi, p. 152; W.R.O., tithe award.
[57] Cal. Inq. Misc. vi, p. 152; P.R.O., STAC 8/270/23.
[58] Cal. Inq. Misc. vi, pp. 152–3.
[59] Interdict Doc. (Pipe R. Soc. N.S. xxxiv), 18, 30.

chapel was said to include 1 yardland in 1341 but later ½ yardland.[60] In 1301 a farm at Little Town included 40 a. and 6 a. of meadow; one there in 1496 was of 4 yardlands.[61] A farm at Cotmarsh in 1319 included 1 carucate of arable land and as much meadow, 25 a., as the demesne farm.[62]

In the late 16th century 140 a. of Westmarsh were inclosed by an agreement between the lord and tenants of Bincknoll manor.[63] No other inclosure award is recorded but by 1766 the whole tithing was held in severalty.[64] In the 1690s there were two farms derived from the demesne farm of Bincknoll manor and some eleven smaller holdings. Some of the smaller holdings had apparently been merged by the late 18th century when there were two large farms, two or three of moderate size, and six or seven small estates.[65] In 1845 the lands of Bincknoll manor were in four farms. The largest, 489 a., half arable, half pasture, occupied the south and east part of the tithing and was worked from Bincknoll House and Sandfurlong Farm. The other three, of 214 a., 139 a., and 107 a., were almost entirely of pasture, including both the lowland north of Broadtown Hill and the hill's north-western slopes. They were worked from farmsteads at Cotmarsh. There were then two other farms in the tithing, Little Town, 112 a., which was worked with Bincknoll farm, and Cockroost, 62 a.[66] In the late 19th and early 20th centuries much of the arable land in the tithing was converted to pasture and in 1920 the largest farm, Bincknoll, was principally a dairy farm.[67] Before the Second World War the lands south of Broadtown Hill became part of Broad Hinton Manor farm.[68] Great Cotmarsh and Little Cotmarsh farms, which measured 170 a. and 100 a. respectively in 1981, were used for dairying and stock rearing.[69]

In 1439–40 there was a mill at Bincknoll.[70] There were possible sites for water mills at Cotmarsh and east of Bincknoll Castle and for a windmill at Broadtown Hill or between it and the castle; at which, if any, the mill stood is not known.

UFFCOTT. There were estates of 3½ hides and 1½ hide at Uffcott in the 11th century. The larger had land for 1½ ploughteam and was valued at 30s. in 1086. The smaller had land in demesne for 1 team and was valued at 15s. in 1066 and 1086.[71]

In the early 17th century and probably earlier the open fields of Uffcott occupied most of the low flat land north and south of the village. There was common pasture on Uffcott Down in the south-east part of the tithing and on Uffcott common, an area of lowland pasture in the north-west corner.[72]

The demesne farm of Uffcott manor was small. In 1361 it consisted of 70 a. of arable land and pasture for 100 sheep. Tenants paid rents totalling 6s. 8d.[73] Godstow abbey had an estate of 4½ yardlands c. 1200 and three tenants of Lacock abbey held 2 yardlands and ½ hide between them in the 14th century.[74] The estate of Salisbury cathedral was valued at £3 a year c. 1210 and was held by two tenants.[75] Their holdings may have been of 5 yardlands each as were those of the dean and chapter and the chancellor after the division of the estate.[76] In the early 17th century both were leased in moieties and the chancellor's estate was sometimes further subdivided.[77]

A map of Uffcott in 1616 shows small closes around the village. The largest several holding, 25 a. north of the Swindon–Devizes road, was part of the demesne farm and the tenant of Elcombe manor farm held a close of 20 a. in the north-east corner of Uffcott. There were two substantial farms in the tithing, the demesne farm and a copyhold farm of 6 yardlands, and three freeholds of 1 yardland each. The demesne included 108 a. of arable, 30 a. of inclosed pasture and meadow, and common pasture for 360 sheep.[78] By the mid 18th century part of the copyhold had probably been absorbed into the demesne farm, Uffcott farm, which then included 152 a. of arable land and some 50 a. of inclosed pasture and meadow.[79] Some 20 a. of Uffcott common were inclosed between 1616 and 1633[80] and by the 1790s the whole common had become part of Uffcott farm. There was then a total of some 90 a. of inclosed land but the down was still common and East, West, Middle, and Uffcott fields were open. Common husbandry was ended in 1797 under an Act of 1796. Allotments were then made of all lands in the tithing, whether newly or previously inclosed. Some 295 a., including Hackpen Hill and most of the eastern part of the tithing, were allotted to the Charterhouse. The chancellor of Salisbury's land, 58 a., lay south-west and the dean and chapter's land, 61 a., north-east of the village. An allotment of 97 a. in the west of the tithing was made in place of tithes to St. Nicholas's hospital in Salisbury.[81]

From the mid 16th century to the early 18th members of the Cleeter family were lessees of Uffcott farm.[82] In the 19th century the farm was held by members of the Brown family as tenants.[83] It was then principally arable with some sheep.[84] Wiltshire county council bought the farm

[60] Inq. Non. (Rec. Com.), 162; W.R.O. 326/3/2.
[61] Wilts. Inq. p.m. 1242–1327 (Index Libr.), 280; Cal. Inq. p.m. Hen. VII, i, p. 506.
[62] Feet of F. 1272–1327 (W.R.S. i), p. 104.
[63] P.R.O., STAC 8/270/23.
[64] W.R.O. 305/11.
[65] Ibid. 212B/777; 212B/825; ibid. land tax.
[66] Ibid. tithe award.
[67] Ibid. 305/18.
[68] Inf. from Maj. Horton.
[69] Inf. from Mr. A. H. John, Great Cotmarsh Farm; Mr. T. W. Marks, Little Cotmarsh Farm.
[70] W.A.M. xiii. 112.
[71] V.C.H. Wilts. ii, pp. 148, 163.
[72] W.R.O. 631/1.

[73] Cal. Inq. p.m. xi, p. 278.
[74] Godstow Reg. (E.E.T.S. orig. ser. 142), 628–9; Lacock Chart. (W.R.S. xxxiv), pp. 81–2.
[75] Interdict Doc. (Pipe R. Soc. N.S. xxxiv), 21.
[76] Above, manors; W.R.O., Ch. Com., bpric. 460; ibid. Ch. Com., chap. 207, pp. 295–7.
[77] D. & C. Sar. Mun., lease bks. III, pp. 9–11; IV, ff. 40–2; XIII, pp. 143–5.
[78] W.R.O. 631/1; Charterhouse Mun. M.R. 5/149B.
[79] Charterhouse Mun. M.R. 5/182.
[80] Ibid. M.R. 5/149B; M.R. 5/150A.
[81] W.R.O., Elcombe and Uffcott inclosure award.
[82] Charterhouse Mun. D. 202; D. 204–10.
[83] Ibid. D. 214–18; D. 260.
[84] Wilts. Cuttings, i. 215.

in 1919 for division into smallholdings for former soldiers[85] but *c.* 1922 Uffcott was taken in hand as a single farm. In 1981 it was of *c.* 900 a. and was chiefly arable, although a dairy herd and some beef cattle were kept.[86] The lands of the dean and chapter and the chancellor of Salisbury cathedral were leased to local farmers for much of the 19th century and eventually became part of Uffcott farm.[87] Lands belonging to St. Nicholas's hospital were leased to the owners of Uffcott farm.[88]

LOCAL GOVERNMENT. From the 15th century two tithingmen, representing Hinton Wase and Hinton Columbers, were sent from Broad Hinton to courts of Selkley hundred.[89] Courts baron with views of frankpledge were held for Broad Hinton manor in the 18th century. The homage presented tenurial matters and necessary repairs to walls and bounds. Other business before the courts included the regulation of common pastures and watercourses.[90]

Although the tenant of Uffcott farm was said to owe suit at Elcombe manor court in the early 18th century, there is no record of the transaction of business from Uffcott in the rolls of that court.[91] Records of Broad Town manor courts are described elsewhere.[92] None is known for Bincknoll manor.

Overseers and some other officers were usually appointed by tithing in the 17th century. Although two overseers were appointed for the whole parish in 1637-8, there was an overseer and a wayman for Broad Hinton township and each of the tithings of Bincknoll, Uffcott, and Broad Town in 1639. In the 1670s overseers were appointed for Broad Hinton, Uffcott, and the lands 'below the hill', presumably the northern part of Bincknoll tithing and that part of Broad Town within the parish. Their receipts are recorded separately but it is not clear whether each was responsible for the relief of the poor in his own tithing or area.[93] In 1771 there were again two overseers for the whole parish.[94] In 1632 an appeal was made to the justices that Winterbourne Bassett should contribute to the relief of Broad Hinton's numerous poor;[95] on what grounds and with what success is not known. Expenditure on the poor rose from £8 a year in the late 17th century to the same sum monthly in the 1770s.[96] In the 1830s it was £713 a year.[97] Two cottages opposite the school, used as a poorhouse in the early 19th century, were later let

at very low rents. They were sold in 1881.[98] Broad Hinton became part of Marlborough poor-law union in 1835.[99]

CHURCH. There was a church at Uffcott in the late 11th century but nothing is known of it after 1146.[1] There was probably a church at Broad Hinton in the 12th century. It was appropriated by the hospital of St. Nicholas in Salisbury in 1253 and presumably served by a chaplain until 1259 when a vicarage was ordained.[2] In 1846 the northern part of the parish became part of the ecclesiastical parish of Broad Town.[3] The remainder, as Broad Hinton parish, was served in plurality with Winterbourne Bassett from 1951 until 1975. Thereafter the living was part of the Upper Kennet team ministry.[4]

Sir Hugh of Hinton was patron of the church *c.* 1226 and in 1253 his son Richard granted the advowson to St. Nicholas's hospital.[5] The advowson was not mentioned when the vicarage was ordained and the living apparently remained in the gift of the bishop of Salisbury, patron of the hospital, until the 15th century. Probably to protect the bishop's rights a vicar admitted in 1321 was said to have been collated, although he held papal bulls of provision.[6] In 1438 the king presented *sede vacante*.[7] The bishop apparently surrendered the advowson in 1478, when the hospital was granted a new constitution. The master of St. Nicholas's first presented to Broad Hinton in that year but his candidate was judged inadequate and the patronage reverted to the bishop for that turn. Although the hospital was thereafter acknowledged as patron, others frequently presented by grant or lapse in the 16th and early 17th centuries. In 1551 a presentation made by Roland Swinburne, a canon of Salisbury, was found invalid, perhaps because of Swinburne's or his candidate's Catholicism, and the advowson was returned to the hospital. In 1576 the candidate presented by another grantee, Sir Thomas Wroughton, the lessee of the rectory estate, was rejected as inadequately educated but later collated to the vicarage on promise of improvement.[8] In 1611 the Crown presented by lapse and in 1614 Richard Pugh was patron, the advowson having been granted for a turn to Sir Giles Wroughton, the lessee of the rectory estate, by Wroughton to Richard Constable, and by Constable to Pugh. Edward Northey was patron in 1629[9] and in 1635 the next presentation

[85] *W.A.M.* xl. 451; xli. 460.
[86] Inf. from Mr. S. J. Horton, Uffcott Ho.
[87] Ch. Com. file 27376; 14480; inf. from Mr. Horton.
[88] Inf. from Jonas & Parker.
[89] P.R.O., DL 30/127/1908; W.R.O. 212B/743.
[90] W.R.O. 212B/743; 212B/800; 212B/809; 212B/816; 529/83.
[91] Charterhouse Mun. D. 5/210.
[92] *V.C.H. Wilts.* ix. 37.
[93] W.R.O. 829/13.
[94] Ibid. 1505/79.
[95] Hist. MSS. Com. 55, *Var. Coll.* i, p. 99.
[96] W.R.O. 829/13; 1505/79.
[97] *Poor Law Com. 2nd. Rep.* 559.
[98] *Endowed Char. Wilts.* (N. Div.), 564-5.
[99] *Poor Law Com. 2nd Rep.* 559.
[1] *Reg. St. Osmund* (Rolls Ser.), i. 200-1; Holtzmann, *Papsturkunden in Eng.* ii, pp. 208, 210; above, manors.

[2] Below; *Cart. St. Nicholas's Hosp.* ed. Wordsworth, 59-61, 65.
[3] *Lond. Gaz.* 21 July 1846, p. 2669.
[4] *Crockford* (1955 and later edns.); *Lond Gaz.* 21 Mar. 1975, p. 3845.
[5] *Cart. St. Nicholas's Hosp.* ed. Wordsworth, 56-8, 65.
[6] *Reg. Martival* (Cant. & York Soc.), iv, pp. xxvii, 92-6; 'Hinton', to which the Crown and others presented in 1361, 1381, and 1387, was probably not Broad Hinton: Phillipps, *Wilts. Inst.* i. 59, 65, 72.
[7] *Cal. Pat. 1436-41,* 167.
[8] *V.C.H. Wilts.* iii. 348; D. & C. Sar. Mun., press IV, misc. chapter papers, 1, doc. concerning Broad Hinton advowson; Phillipps, *Wilts. Inst.* i. 214-15; *Alum. Cantab. to 1751,* iv. 193.
[9] Phillipps, *Wilts. Inst.* ii. 6, 8, 15; D. & C. Sar. Mun., press IV, misc. chapter papers, 1, doc. concerning Broad Hinton advowson.

was granted to Edward Nicholas, the brother of the hospital's master.[10] That right was apparently not used and after the Restoration St. Nicholas's presented.[11] Between 1951 and 1975 Magdalen College, Oxford, the patron of Winterbourne Bassett, and the hospital held the advowson alternately.[12] In 1975 provision was made for the appointment of a vicar of Broad Hinton by the team rector and the bishop of Salisbury.[13]

Before 1253 the rector probably received all tithes from the parish except those paid from the demesne of Broad Town manor to Wallingford priory, and perhaps except those from Bincknoll and Uffcott which were granted to the priories of St. Denis in Southampton and of Kington St. Michael.[14] There was a glebe house c. 1226. Sir Hugh of Hinton then granted to the church the road between that house and his own, and pasture for four beasts and a palfrey.[15]

In 1291 Broad Hinton vicarage was valued at £5 6s. 8d., close to the average for vicarages in Avebury deanery.[16] The endowment was increased in 1295.[17] Broad Hinton was one of the wealthier livings in the deanery in 1535, when the vicar's clear yearly income was £14 18s. 10d., and in the early 1830s, when he received on average £322 a year.[18] From 1846 the vicar paid £10 a year towards the stipend of the curate of Broad Town.[19]

At its ordination the vicarage was explicitly endowed with all tithes from the rectorial glebe and by implication with tithes other than corn from the rest of the parish. In 1295 the vicar was entitled to hay tithes from 'below the hill', that is from lands north-west of the ridge between Broadtown Hill and Bincknoll Castle, and to 1 a. in place of certain tithes from Uffcott.[20] In 1341 the vicar's 'small' tithes were valued at 40s. a year and the hay tithes at 27s. a year.[21] By the late 17th century compositions had been made for some hay and other tithes from Broad Town and Bincknoll but the sources of the vicar's income had otherwise changed little. Although wool, lamb, and other tithes were then said to be due from the whole parish, the land of Uffcott manor remained exempt from vicarial tithes.[22] In 1797 no vicarial tithe was paid from Uffcott manor except for two small moduses. Other vicarial tithes from Uffcott were then replaced by an allotment of 22 a. and in 1845 those from the rest of the parish were valued at £382 and commuted.[23]

To the glebe of a house and 2 a. granted to the vicar in 1259 were added 16 a. and grazing for two cows on pasture belonging to the rectory estate in 1295.[24] In 1341 the glebe was 1 carucate valued at 30s. a year, demesne meadow valued at 8s., and rents and services at 10s.[25] In the late 17th century, however, the vicar held only 5 a. of arable and 2 a. of meadow land.[26] The glebe land, including that at Uffcott, was sold, apparently in the 20th century.[27] In 1783 the stone vicarage house of two storeys and nine rooms had a roof of tile and thatch.[28] It was partly rebuilt to designs by W. E. Baverstock in 1867 and was sold in 1978. A new vicarage house was built south of the church.[29]

Tithes granted to the priory of St. Denis in Southampton were said in 1291 and later to be the endowments of a chapel at Bincknoll.[30] There is no evidence that a chapel was built.

In 1459 John Parys, the vicar, was licensed to hold two additional benefices. He had earlier been outlawed for debt and in spite of his pluralism the debt remained outstanding at his death c. 1468.[31] In the 16th century the parish suffered religious upheaval and the church neglect. In 1553 parishioners refused to receive communion for fear of falling masonry. The broken stonework allowed so many birds into the chancel that the minister could not stand by the communion table and there was no seat for him during the reading of the psalms. Several parishioners were reported to the commissioners for ecclesiastical causes in 1556 for failing to return church property removed under Edward VI.[32] Marriage, protestantism, or both presumably caused the deprivation of the vicar in 1554 and the flight abroad of his successor in 1556.[33] John Buckwell, whose learning was judged insufficient at his appointment in 1576, was presented by the churchwardens in the 1580s for inability to preach, neglect of catechizing, and failure to wear the prescribed dress.[34] After the Restoration no major complaint was made about the buildings or the clergy, although some furnishings were still lacking.[35] Between 1781 and 1866 most incumbents were non-resident pluralists.[36] An exception was W. L. Rham, vicar 1804–7, who was later a leading agriculturalist.[37] In 1783, when both vicar and curate were non-resident, a service was held each Sunday, alternately in the morning and the evening, and communion was celebrated four times a year.[38] On Census Sunday in 1851 the morning

10 W.R.O. 1672/18/4; Cal. S.P. Dom. 1636–7, 488.
11 Phillipps, Wilts. Inst. ii (index in W.A.M. xxviii. 214).
12 W.R.O. 1505/92.
13 Lond Gaz. 21 Mar. 1975, p. 3845.
14 Cart. St. Nicholas's Hosp. ed. Wordsworth, 67; above, manors.
15 Cart. St. Nicholas's Hosp. ed. Wordsworth, 65–6.
16 Tax. Eccl. (Rec. Com.), 189.
17 Cart. St. Nicholas's Hosp. ed. Wordsworth, 61–2.
18 Valor Eccl. (Rec. Com.), ii. 132; Rep. Com. Eccl. Revenues, 836–7.
19 P.R.O., HO 129/255/1/5/9.
20 Cart. St. Nicholas's Hosp. ed. Wordsworth, 60–2.
21 Inq. Non. (Rec. Com.), 158.
22 W.R.O., bishop, glebe terrier, 1671; ibid. 1505/15.
23 Ibid. Elcombe and Uffcott inclosure award; tithe award.
24 Cart. St. Nicholas's Hosp. ed. Wordsworth, 60–2.
25 Inq. Non. (Rec. Com.), 158.
26 W.R.O., bishop, glebe terrier, 1671.
27 Inf. from the vicar, the Revd. B. A. Tigwell.
28 W.R.O. 1505/15.
29 Ibid. bishop, mortgages, 181; ibid. 1505/26.
30 P.R.O., C 146/105, no. 19; Tax. Eccl. (Rec. Com.), 189; Inq. Non. (Rec. Com.), 162.
31 Cal. Fine R. 1445–52, 246; Cal. Papal Reg. xi. 531; Cal. Pat. 1467–77, 146.
32 W.R.O., bishop, detecta bks.
33 Ibid.; D. & C. Sar. Mun., press IV, misc. chapter papers, 1, doc. concerning Broad Hinton advowson.
34 Above; W.R.O., bishop, detecta bk. 1584–5.
35 W.R.O., bishop, chwdns.' pres. 1662.
36 W.A.M. xxxiv. 369; Alum. Oxon. 1715–1886, ii. 713, 891; Rep. Com. Eccl. Revenues, 836–7; Kelly's Dir. Wilts. (1848 and later edns.).
37 D.N.B.
38 Vis. Queries, 1783 (W.R.S. xxvii), pp. 120–2.

and afternoon services were attended by congregations of 100 and 72 respectively; the numbers were said to be smaller than usual. In 1864 there were additional services at festivals and in Lent, and communion was celebrated eight times a year.[39] Occasional services were held at a house in Uffcott in the late 19th century.[40] In 1919 Alfred Turner gave part of the income from a house, shop, and garden to buy 1 ton of coal for the church every year. In 1960 £7 was spent on fuel.[41]

The church was called St. Mary's in the 13th century but in the 19th century *ST. PETER'S*.[42] It has a chancel with a south organ chamber, a nave with a south porch, all of coursed rubble with ashlar dressings, and a west tower faced with ashlar. Some 12th-century masonry fragments in the nave and a late 12th-century priest's doorway, which has been moved to the organ chamber, survive in it. The chancel was altered and the nave rebuilt in the 13th century. In the 15th century or early 16th century the tower was built, and also in the early 16th century a rood stair was inserted in the north wall of the nave. The nave roof was renewed in the 17th century and the east end of the chancel was altered or rebuilt in the 18th. In 1879 the church was restored by C. E. Ponting and many medieval features of the nave were renewed.[43] The chancel was restored in a uniform 13th-century style, the chancel arch was enlarged, and the original small arch reset between the chancel and the new organ chamber.

The parish had a chalice weighing 11 oz. in 1553.[44] A chalice, a paten, and two flagons, given in 1677, were stolen from the church in 1756 but were recovered soon afterwards.[45] That plate and a chalice, paten, and ciborium of the 20th century were held by the parish in 1981.[46] There were two bells in 1553.[47] Three new bells were hung in 1664 and two more in the 18th century. In 1927 there were six bells, of which (v) and (vi) were of 1664 and the rest were cast or recast in the 19th century.[48] Those bells hung in the church in 1981.[49] There are registers of baptisms, marriages, and burials from 1612. Missing are those of marriages for the years 1620–5 and 1745–57, and those of burials for the years 1678–1708 and 1743–57.[50]

NONCONFORMITY.
There were three nonconformists in the parish in 1676 but none in 1783.[51] In 1846 a house, probably in Broad

Hinton village, was licensed for dissenters' meetings.[52] That may have been the house at which a 'Bible Christian or Baptist' held meetings in 1864. There were then *c.* 50 nonconformists, including 'Baptists or Brethren', Primitive and Wesleyan Methodists, and Mormons.[53] Some may have attended chapels in Broad Town, where nonconformity flourished in the 19th century.[54] A Methodist chapel in Broad Hinton was apparently built in the late 19th century and in use in 1925.[55] It was disused in 1981. The 'Brethren' of 1864 may have been Plymouth Brethren, a group of whom met in houses in the parish in the 1920s and 1930s.[56]

EDUCATION. In the early 18th century the children of the poor were taught to read by the vicar.[57] In 1743 Thomas Bennet gave a rent charge of £20 a year from Quidhampton manor in Wroughton to pay a schoolmaster to teach poor children between the ages of six and fifteen. In 1751 he gave a house in Broad Hinton village for the school and teacher and another £2 a year from Quidhampton for its maintenance.[58] There were *c.* 50 pupils in the early 19th century but the school was short of books and in 1818 the provision for the education of the poor was said to be insufficient.[59] Another classroom was added in 1845 but in 1847 the older, thatched, part of the building was burned down. A new stone school, with two schoolrooms and a teacher's house, was immediately built.[60] Attendance rose to between 60 and 80 in the 1850s, and between 1865 and 1875 a private school with *c.* 60 pupils also flourished in the parish.[61] The buildings of the endowed school were extended in 1882 but attendance fell to between 55 and 65 in the late 19th century and the first two decades of the 20th, and to *c.* 40 in the 1930s.[62] In the mid 19th century the schoolmaster sometimes had an assistant, but there was usually only one teacher until 1919 when three were appointed.[63] In 1981 there were 58 pupils from Broad Hinton and Winterbourne Bassett parishes.[64]

In 1848 £36, the surplus of money raised for rebuilding the school, was invested and the income used to pay for fire insurance. In that year £50 given by Mary Brown to provide coals for the school was also invested. The income from both investments and the rent charge from Quidhampton were used as general school funds in the 20th century.[65]

[39] P.R.O., HO 129/255/1/5/9; W.R.O., bishop, vis. queries.
[40] Ch. Com. file 27376.   [41] Char. Com. file.
[42] *Cart. St. Nicholas's Hosp.* ed. Wordsworth, 67; *W.A.M.* xv. 100.
[43] W.R.O., bishop, pet. for faculties, bdle. 27, no. 8. The date 1634 is inscribed on the roof. A pen and wash drawing in the vestry shows the church in the late 18th cent.
[44] *W.A.M.* i. 92.
[45] Nightingale, *Wilts. Plate*, 136–8.
[46] Inf. from Mr. Tigwell.   [47] *W.A.M.* i. 92.
[48] Walters, *Wilts. Bells*, 104–5.
[49] Inf. from Mr. Tigwell.
[50] W.R.O. 1505/1–9; bishops' transcripts, including those for the periods for which there are omissions in the originals, are in W.R.O.
[51] *W.N. & Q.* iii. 536; *Vis. Queries, 1783* (W.R.S. xxvii), p. 121.

[52] W.R.O., return of regns.
[53] Ibid. bishop, vis. queries.
[54] *V.C.H. Wilts.* ix. 41.
[55] O.S. Map 6″, Wilts. XXII. NW. (1925 edn.).
[56] Inf. from Miss L. E. Knight, Broad Hinton Ho.
[57] *W.N. & Q.* iii. 377.
[58] *Endowed Char. Wilts.* (N. Div.), 558.
[59] *Educ. of Poor Digest*, 1029; *Educ. Enquiry Abstract*, 1031.
[60] W.R.O. 1505/59; 1505/64.
[61] *Acct. of Wilts. Schs.* 27; *Kelly's Dir. Wilts.* (1865, 1867, 1875); *Returns relating to Elem. Educ.* 422.
[62] W.R.O. 1505/64; *Kelly's Dir. Wilts.* (1898 and later edns.); *Bd. of Educ., List 21* (H.M.S.O.).
[63] *Acct. of Wilts. Schs.* 27; *Kelly's Dir. Wilts.* (1867); P.R.O., ED 21/42146.
[64] Inf. from the Head Teacher.
[65] *Endowed Char. Wilts.* (N. Div.), 563; Char. Com. file.

CHARITIES FOR THE POOR. In 1614 John Sherston gave 5s. a year to buy bread for the poor. Before 1834 the income was added to parish funds and 5s. was paid each year from the rates to buy loaves for children attending Sunday school. In 1850 £7 17s. 11d. was contributed by parishioners to restore the benefaction. The income of 5s. was then used to buy buns for schoolchildren at Easter.[66] By a Scheme of 1977 the charity was joined with the Broad Hinton portion of that of Henry Smith. The income of the combined charity, the Broad Hinton Relief in Need fund, was c. £170 in 1981 and was distributed among elderly residents at Christmas.[67]

By will dated 1627 Henry Smith established a charity for the poor of various places including Broad Hinton. An estate at Stoughton (Leics.) provided £220 a year, £7 of which was Broad Hinton's share.[68] In the 1770s the income was £5 but it rose to £15 in the early 19th century and was said to be £21 in 1880. It was spent on clothing and bedding for all deserving poor of the parish in turn.[69] In 1884 the income was divided between the new parishes of Broad Town, which was allotted three elevenths of the total, and Broad Hinton, which received the remainder. Between 1904 and 1961 the total income was c. £10 a year. It had risen to £56 by 1974 when Broad Hinton's share was used to buy fuel for fourteen elderly residents.[70]

Boys from the part of Broad Town manor

which lay in Broad Hinton were beneficiaries of the apprenticing charity established by Sarah, duchess of Somerset (d. 1692), and known as the Broad Town Trust. An account of the charity is given elsewhere.[71]

In 1741 Elizabeth Bennet gave rents totalling £13 8s. 2d. a year from lands in Lydiard Tregoze and Cherhill to apprentice children from Broad Hinton parish.[72] One or two boys were apprenticed every year until the 1790s and one every two years thereafter.[73] By 1834 the premium had been reduced from £20 to £15, the sum paid by the Broad Town Trust, but it was difficult to find masters willing to accept so small a payment. After 1866 £2 rent from Lydiard Tregoze was not paid: the owner of the lands later successfully claimed exemption under the Real Property Limitation Act of 1874. In the late 19th century and the early 20th the annual income of £10 was used to apprentice children from the modern parish of Broad Hinton. The needs of Broad Town parish were thought to be met by the Broad Town Trust.[74] By a Scheme of 1931 the purposes of the charity were extended to include assistance in the education or training of any poor parishioner. The income, c. £45 a year in 1981, was used to buy tools for apprentices.[75]

By will proved 1919 Alfred Turner gave part of the income from a house, shop, and garden to provide coal for farmworkers. In 1960 £1 was spent on coal.[76]

EAST KENNETT

EAST KENNETT, 319 ha. (788 a.), lies 7 km. west of Marlborough, separated from West Kennett in Avebury to the north by the river Kennet from which both take their names.[77] The name Kennett appears in records from the 10th century[78] and may have been applied to several settlements in the river valley. In Domesday Book it was used of holdings which were later in East and West Kennett.[79] The lands of Kennett then probably lay north and south of the river and west of the Ridge Way which still forms the eastern boundary of Avebury and of much of East Kennett. East Kennett was so called in the mid 12th century. In 1291 it was a separate parish[80] and its independence may have owed much to the early foundation of a church there.[81]

The separation from West Kennett and Avebury perhaps accounts for the irregular shape of the parish which extends 3 km. south from the river and 1 km. from east to west at its widest

point a little south of East Kennett long barrow. The eastern boundary runs slightly east of the Ridge Way for 1.5 km. and rejoins it north of the junction with Wansdyke in the south-east corner of the parish. The southern and western boundaries are not determined by major physical features but are marked by mounds across the crest of Furze Hill, northwards over Thorn Hill, and north-west and north from there to the river opposite West Kennett village.

Chalk outcrops over the whole parish. In the river valley, 500 m. at its widest, is a narrow strip of alluvium, and deposits of gravel extend southwards in two dry valleys, one on the east side and one on the west side of the parish.[82] That on the east side, Langdean Bottom, runs almost the length of the parish between Thorn Hill and Lurkeley Hill, both over 213 m. Only near the river is the land under 152 m., and at the southern end of the parish Furze Hill rises to 229 m. Field

[66] Endowed Char. Wilts. (N. Div.), 557, 560.
[67] Char. Com. file; inf. from the vicar, the Revd. B. A. Tigwell.
[68] Endowed Char. Wilts. (S. Div.), 733–4, 752.
[69] Ibid. (N. Div.), 557; W.R.O. 829/7; Kelly's Dir. Wilts. (1880).
[70] Endowed Char. Wilts. (N. Div.), 561, 567; Char. Com. file.
[71] V.C.H. Wilts. ix. 42–3.
[72] Endowed Char. Wilts. (N. Div.), 556.
[73] W.R.O. 829/8.
[74] Endowed Char. Wilts. (N. Div.), 558–60.

[75] Char. Com. file; inf. from Mr. Tigwell.
[76] Char. Com. file.
[77] This article was written in 1978. Maps used include O.S. Maps 1/50,000, sheet 173 (1974 edn.); 1/25,000, 41/16 (1949 edn.); 6″, Wilts. XXVIII (1889 and later edns.), XXXV (1889 and later edns.).
[78] Finberg, Early Wessex Chart. p. 98; Arch. Jnl. lxxvi. 245–6.
[79] V.C.H. Wilts. ii, pp. 151, 156.
[80] Abbrev. Plac. (Rec. Com.), 164–5; Tax. Eccl. (Rec. Com.), 189.   [81] Below, church.
[82] Geol. Surv. Map 1″, drift, sheet 266 (1964 edn.).

systems near the parish boundary 1 km. south-west of the village and on Thorn Hill date from the Iron Age and Romano-British period.[83] The downs were later used for pasture and the arable lands lay in the north and in Langdean Bottom.

Two notable signs of prehistoric activity survive in the parish. A Neolithic long barrow 1 km. south of the village is a large and fine example of its kind. Sarsens, arranged in a circle approximately 10 m. in diameter, in Langdean Bottom are thought to have formed the retaining kerb of a round barrow or a circular house site of the Bronze Age. Langdean Bottom has yielded a number of Bronze-Age finds and there are barrows on Harestone Down, mostly in Stanton St. Bernard, and west of the village.[84] The crossing of the river Kennet by the Ridge Way in the north-east corner of the parish may have been the site of the Danish defeat at the battle of 'Cynete' in 1006.[85]

The Ridge Way runs south from the bridge over the Kennet to join the road from West Kennett to Boreham Wood in West Overton for 500 m., and then continues to the south-east corner of the parish as a track. From it, other tracks lead south-west towards Thorn Hill and Langdean stone circle. The London–Bath road runs 500 m. north of the village. The lane leading from that road through East Kennett to Boreham Wood was turnpiked in 1840.[86] It was joined in the village by a road from West Overton. Earlier the principal road from West Kennett had crossed the river immediately south of that village and turned east towards East Kennett 500 m. inside the parish boundary.[87] A track still ran that way in 1978 and from it a path led along the boundary to All Cannings Down. A parallel track across the downs recorded in 1922[88] was not visible in 1978.

In the 14th century East Kennett was a small but moderately wealthy community. It was assessed for taxation at 40s. in 1334 but in 1377 there were only 30 poll-tax payers, one of the lower figures for Selkley. In 1428 there were fewer than ten households,[89] but the assessment of £2 10s. 4d. in 1545 was close to the average for the hundred.[90] In 1801 there were 102 inhabitants. The number had fallen to 85 by 1811 but had recovered to 103 by 1831. The population did not rise above 90 during the rest of the 19th century and by 1921 had declined to 44.[91] In 1961 it stood at 66 but by 1971 the number of households had fallen from 30 to 15 and there were only 45 residents.[92]

The village of East Kennett is in the north-east of the parish, where the valley gravel is widest. Most of the buildings lie on the south side of the road from West Kennett to Boreham Wood and along a lane leading south-west from the manor house, the only substantial building between the road and the river. The church and Manor Farm House, which face each other across the lane, perhaps mark the earlier centre of the village. A number of cottages in the lane appear to incorporate part of the structure of sarsen-walled buildings, probably of the 17th century, but almost all were altered in the later 18th century and the 19th. North and south of the junction of the road and the lane stand the old vicarage house and the school. A few houses, mainly of the 19th and 20th centuries, have been built along the road. Most are south-east of the manor house and several, including some older buildings, lie across the parish boundary in West Overton.

MANOR AND OTHER ESTATES. Land in Overton and Kennett granted to Wulfswyth by King Athelstan in 939 and to Alfeld by King Edgar in 972 may have included areas within the eastern boundary of the parish and near the church. The grants refer chiefly to Overton, however, and any small portion in East Kennett cannot be identified with a later estate.[93]

Lands in Kennett which later formed the manor of *EAST KENNETT* were held in 1066 by Leueclai and in 1086 by Waleran the huntsman.[94] The overlordship descended with the manor of Hamptworth to Walter Walerand (d. 1200-1) and to the heirs of two of Walter's daughters, Aubrey de Botreaux (d. 1270) and Isabel de Neville.[95] Aubrey's portion passed to the heirs of her marriage to John of Ingham. After the death of her great-grandson Oliver Ingham, Lord Ingham, in 1344, the fees which he held were divided between his daughter Joan, wife of Roger Lestrange, Lord Strange (d. 1349), and his granddaughter Mary Curzon.[96] Mary died in 1349 and her portion reverted to Joan. Joan later married Miles de Stapleton and on his death in 1365 the overlordship passed to their son Miles.[97] It descended from father to son in the Stapleton family and was said to be held by a Miles Stapleton in 1428, although Joan's grandson Miles had been succeeded by his son Brian in 1420.[98] The other portion of the overlordship was inherited by Isabel de Neville's daughter Joan (d. 1263), wife of Jordan de St. Martin. Joan was succeeded by her son William and grandson Reynold de St. Martin (d. 1315),[99] but his portion of the overlordship was not mentioned after 1300.[1]

In 1297 John Tregoze was intermediate tenant of the whole estate of East Kennett and his estates were divided after his death in 1300. The fee in East Kennett allotted to John la Warr, son of Tregoze's daughter Clarice,[2] was, however, not afterwards mentioned.

In 1086 Richard held the land in Kennett of

[83] V.C.H. Wilts. i (1), 272.
[84] Ibid. 67, 140, 172-3, 229, 243; i (2), 305, 382.
[85] W.A.M. xlii. 96; liii. 411.   [86] V.C.H. Wilts. iv. 271.
[87] Andrews and Dury, Map (W.R.S. viii), pl. 11.
[88] O.S. Map 6″, Wilts. XXXV. NW. (1926 edn.).
[89] V.C.H. Wilts. iv. 301, 310, 314.
[90] Taxation Lists (W.R.S. x), 22.
[91] V.C.H. Wilts. iv. 351.   [92] Census, 1961, 1971.
[93] Arch. Jnl. lxxvi. 242, 245-6; Finberg, Early Wessex Chart. p. 98; V.C.H. Wilts. ii, p. 85; xi. 188-9.
[94] V.C.H. Wilts. ii, p. 151.

[95] Ibid. p. 111; xi. 59; W.A.M. xxii. 253; V.C.H. Hants, iv. 521.
[96] Cal. Inq. p.m. viii, pp. 376-7; Complete Peerage, vii. 60-1; xii (1), 354.
[97] W.A.M. xxii. 255; Cal. Inq. p.m. xv, p. 20; Complete Peerage, vii. 63-4.
[98] W.A.M. xxii. 255; Feud. Aids, v. 269.
[99] Hoare, Mod. Wilts. Alderbury, 21; V.C.H. Hants, iv. 521.
[1] Wilts. Inq. p.m. 1242-1326 (Index Libr.), 254-5.
[2] Cal. Close, 1296-1302, 55, 476-7.

Waleran the huntsman.[3] William de Ringeburn held the estate in 1242–3[4] and his son Robert sued for possession in 1297.[5] Geoffrey Weston held it in 1316 and 1344[6] and in 1376 his holding was granted to Ellis Spelly, a prominent Bristol merchant. In the following year the grant was confirmed by William Weston, perhaps Geoffrey's son.[7] In 1390, about the time of Spelly's death, a licence was obtained for the alienation of the estate to the priory of St. Margaret near Marlborough.[8] The priory retained the manor until the Dissolution.

The possessions of St. Margaret's, including East Kennett, were settled on Anne of Cleves in 1539 and on Catherine Howard in 1541.[9] In 1543 the manor was granted to Henry Jones for life.[10] A fourth royal grant was made in 1553 to William Herbert, earl of Pembroke.[11] Pembroke sold the manor in 1563 to Richard Franklin (d. 1597) who was succeeded by his son Richard (d. 1634) and grandson William Franklin.[12] William Norden (d. 1638) purchased the manor in 1637 and his sons Richard (d. 1641) and John inherited in turn.[13] John Norden and his wife Elizabeth conveyed the manor to Michael Ernle in 1657.[14] In 1667 it was held by Mary, relict of Sir Edward Baynton, and passed in that year to her son Robert Baynton who sold it in 1676 to Charles Tooker.[15] In 1700 Tooker was succeeded by his son Charles (d. 1716)[16] who devised the manor to his kinsman John Saunders.[17] It passed in turn to Saunders's son John and daughter Jane.[18] In 1732 it was held by Jane, who married Sir John Guise, Bt. (d. c. 1769).[19] Their son William died in 1783; after litigation the manor passed to his sister Jane, wife of Shute Barrington, bishop of Salisbury.[20] In 1787 Barrington sold it to Benjamin Price who sold it to Joseph Mighell in 1789.[21] The manor was purchased from Mighell in 1803 by Richard Mathews,[22] after whose death in 1842 it passed in turn to his sons Richard (d. 1849) and John (d. 1879).[23] John devised East Kennett to his nephew Richard Fisher.[24] In 1911 Richard's son William held the manor[25] and in 1922 he sold it to M. J. Read. Read's son, Mr. J. M. Read, succeeded in 1972[26] and in that year sold some 500 a. in East Kennett to Mrs. C. B. Cameron, owner of the manor house.[27]

East Kennett Manor is a square red-brick house of c. 1800 with a principal south front of five bays to which balancing wings in a similar style were added c. 1925.[28] The large service courtyard north of the house has barn, dovecot, and stables of the 18th and 19th centuries and is entered through reset gatepiers of the late 17th century.

In 1066 the abbess of St. Mary's, Winchester, was tenant in chief of 1½ hide, perhaps the estate in Kennett held by the abbey of Hugh Lasne in 1086. That estate had earlier been held by Honewin.[29] In 1242–3 the estate was held of the abbey by William de Ringeburn and it may have been absorbed into his manor of East Kennett.[30] If the estate remained independent it was probably that later held by the Berwick family. Reynold of Berwick and his wife Edith granted lands in Kennett to Walter of Berwick in 1250.[31] In 1300 John of Berwick conveyed holdings in East and West Kennett to trustees; he or his namesake received a grant for life of property in East Kennett in 1327.[32]

In addition to the manor there was a large freehold in the parish in the late 17th century, possibly derived from the Berwick estate.[33] John Weston held a capital messuage and 4 yardlands in 1658. In 1703 he conveyed lands in East Kennett and Overton to William Cooper, husband of his sister Anne. Part of John's estate was apparently inherited by another sister but the holding has not been traced. William Cooper's estate was divided between his sons Samuel and William. Samuel settled his portion on his son Samuel in 1723. In 1733 the younger Samuel also acquired the estate of his uncle William Cooper. The younger Samuel's lands passed to Robert Cooper who in 1760 devised the estate to his sister Rebecca Cox and nephew Thomas Lavington or to the survivor.[34] Lavington (d. c. 1815) was succeeded by his grandson Thomas Lavington (d. 1827). In 1832 the executors of the younger Thomas sold the estate, East Kennett farm, to Elijah Lawrence[35] who sold it to John Mathews in 1863.[36] The farm was thereafter held with the manor until 1972 when the lands were retained by Mr. J. M. Read as part of Manor farm.[37] The main range of Manor Farm House, which is of sarsen rubble with ovolo-moulded windows in ashlar, has the date 1630 over the

[3] V.C.H. Wilts. ii, p. 151.
[4] Bk. of Fees, ii. 748–9.
[5] Cal. Close, 1296–1302, 55.
[6] W.A.M. xii. 18; Cal. Close, 1343–6, 272; Wilts. Inq. p.m. 1327–77 (Index Libr.), 160.
[7] Feet of F. 1327–77 (W.R.S. xxix), p. 147; Cal. Close, 1374–7, 520.
[8] Cal. Pat. 1388–92, 328; Cal. Close, 1389–92, 561.
[9] L. & P. Hen. VIII, xiv (2), p. 154; xvi, p. 716.
[10] Ibid. xviii (1), p. 550.
[11] Cal. Pat. 1547–53, 178–9.
[12] P.R.O., CP 25(2)/239/3 Eliz. I East.; ibid. C 2/Jas. I/F 3/53; Wilts. Inq. p.m. 1625–49 (Index Libr.), 190–1.
[13] P.R.O., CP 25(2)/510/12 Chas. I East.; Wilts. Inq. p.m. 1625–49 (Index Libr.), 318, 322.
[14] P.R.O., CP 25(2)/609/1657 Trin.
[15] W.R.O. 248/161; 371/2; W.N. & Q. iii. 242.
[16] Glos. R.O., D 326/T 176; dates of d. are from mons. in church.
[17] W.R.O. 1366/3.
[18] Ibid. 1366/7.
[19] Ibid. 1366/4; Burke, Ext. & Dorm. Baronetcies (1844), 230.

[20] Glos. R.O., D 326/L 19.
[21] W.R.O. 1366/5.
[22] Ibid. 1366/6.
[23] Mon. in church; P.R.O., PROB 11/2096, f. 251v.
[24] Princ. Regy. Fam. Div., will pr. 1879.
[25] Endowed Char. Wilts. (N. Div.), 583; Kelly's Dir. Wilts. (1911).
[26] Inf. from Mr. J. M. Read, E. Kennett.
[27] Inf. from Mrs. C. B. Cameron, E. Kennett Manor.
[28] Cf. sale cat. (1924) penes Mrs. Cameron.
[29] V.C.H. Wilts. ii, p. 156.
[30] Bk. of Fees, ii. 748–9.
[31] P.R.O., CP 25(1)/251/17, no. 3.
[32] Feet of F. 1272–1327 (W.R.S. i), p. 45; 1327–77 (W.R.S. xxix), p. 15.
[33] The estate formerly belonging to the Berwicks may have been that of 5 messuages and 200 a. which Edm. Ernle was said to hold of Amesbury priory at his d. in 1485: Cal. Inq. p.m. Hen. VII, i, p. 88.
[34] W.R.O. 1366/10A, abstr. of title of Thos. Lavington.
[35] Ibid.; W.A.S. Libr., sale cat. vi, no. 32.
[36] W.R.O. 1366/10B.
[37] Inf. from Mr. Read.

doorway. It contains only two principal rooms on each floor. The kitchen wing, apparently of the late 18th century, probably replaced an older building. On the south side is another short wing of the 19th century.

A gift of Henry of Kennett of 1 yardland in East Kennett to the hospital of St. John the Baptist in Marlborough was confirmed in 1215.[38] The land belonged to the hospital until its dissolution and with its other possessions was granted to the borough of Marlborough in 1550 to endow a grammar school.[39] The small estate was sold by the trustees of the school in 1920.[40]

In 1383 the priory of St. Margaret was licensed to appropriate East Kennett church[41] which it retained until the Dissolution. The rectory estate was held by the Crown until 1550 when it was granted to Sir William Herbert (created earl of Pembroke in 1551).[42] Pembroke apparently sold it with the manor to Richard Franklin (d. 1597).[43] Richard Franklin (d. 1634) devised it to his daughters Joyce and Cecily, who conveyed it to Richard Brownjohn in 1637.[44] The rectory estate had been reunited with the manor by 1676 and thereafter descended with it.[45] By 1838 most of the tithes had been merged in the lands of the manor; the remainder were valued at £58 10s. and commuted.[46]

ECONOMIC HISTORY. The field systems on and north-west of Thorn Hill indicate that cultivation took place in the parish in prehistoric times.[47] The two estates in East Kennett in 1086 were each of 1¾ hide and worth a total of 40s. Richard's was valued at 20s. in both 1066 and 1086, but the abbess of Winchester's had by 1086 doubled its value of 10s. in 1066. They had demesne each for 1 ploughteam, with a serf on Richard's demesne, and 4 a. and 6 a. of pasture respectively; each had 1 a. of meadow and 2 bordars.[48]

Although the Domesday survey made no mention of wood, the small area of the parish east of the Ridge Way lay within the forest of Savernake in the late 13th century. By 1300 it had been disafforested.[49] In that year the demesne of the manor was worth 31s. 6d. There were four free tenants, who held 5½ yardlands between them, and two cottars.[50] In 1376 there were five customary tenants and three small parcels of the manor were held on life tenancies.[51]

Meadow, arable, and pasture were used in common in the mid 16th century. Small closes of

meadow and arable were attached to certain tenements and to the demesne farm of East Kennett manor, and one copyholder was licensed to keep sheep on his own tenement rather than on the common pasture.[52] Some arable land was inclosed by the lord of the manor in the late 17th century or early 18th. An agreement for inclosure was drawn up in 1713 between the owners of the manor farm and East Kennett farm and nine others, probably their tenants. The Great West and Little West fields were to be divided. Claimants then unsatisfied were to be allotted lands in a third field between the road to West Kennett and a track leading west from the village. A division was also to be made of Longbridge mead, between East and West Kennett, and of Lords meads and the adjacent down. Had the agreement taken effect, part of the arable lands and much of the downland pasture would still have been worked in common. An endorsement on the agreement shows that the articles were not executed, for what reason is not known.[53] There is no record of any other formal agreement to end common husbandry but certain small holdings were inclosed in the early 18th century.[54] Pasture was still in common in 1832[55] but in 1838 all farms were worked in severalty.[56]

At his death in 1496 John Wroughton held the manor of St. Margaret's priory as lessee.[57] His son Sir Christopher (d. 1515) and Sir Christopher's grandson Sir William Wroughton may have succeeded him in the tenancy.[58] Several lessees and sub-lessees held the demesne of the Wroughtons between 1520 and 1539.[59] Richard Weston held the lease in 1530 and Robert Weston in 1676 but no other family seems to have had a recurring interest.[60] In the late 18th century and the early 19th the owners probably occupied the demesne themselves;[61] in 1789 Joseph Mighell, the owner, is said to have introduced into the county the Southdown sheep and their Leicestershire crosses, popular breeds in the early 19th century.[62] In the mid 16th century there were 120 a. of arable and 7 a. of meadow in demesne, with pasture in common for 400 sheep.[63] During the 17th century several copyholds and freeholds were absorbed into the demesne and in 1787 the manor consisted of a single farm which measured c. 508 a. of which 232 a. were pasture on the downs.[64]

There were four customary tenants of the manor in 1539. Together they held 2 yardlands and 4 a. and they paid between 4s. and 25s. rent each.[65] In the 1550s there were two free tenants and four copyholders. The copyholders held a

[38] Rot. Chart. (Rec. Com.), 205; V.C.H. Wilts. iii. 341.
[39] Cal. Pat. 1549–51, 226.
[40] Endowed Char. Wilts. (N. Div.), 721; inf. from Miss G. M. Marston, Headmistress, St. John's Sch., Marlborough.
[41] Cal. Pat. 1381–5, 339.
[42] P.R.O., E 318/Box 30/1687.
[43] W.R.O., bishop, detecta bk. 1585.
[44] Wilts. Inq. p.m. 1625–49 (Index Libr.), 190–1; P.R.O., CP 25(2)/510/12 Chas. I East.
[45] W.R.O. 371/2.   [46] Ibid. tithe award.
[47] V.C.H. Wilts. i (1), 272, 275.
[48] Ibid. ii, pp. 151, 156, 200.
[49] Ibid. iv. 419, 451; W.A.M. xl. 399.
[50] Wilts. Inq. p.m. 1242–1326 (Index Libr.), 254–5.
[51] Feet of F. 1327–77 (W.R.S. xxix), pp. 147–8.

[52] Wilton Ho. Mun., survey, 1550s.
[53] Glos. R.O., D 326/T 176.
[54] W.R.O. 488/11.
[55] W.A.S. Libr., sale cat. vi, no. 32.
[56] W.R.O., tithe award.
[57] Cal. Inq. p.m. Hen. VII, i, p. 505.
[58] P.R.O., C 142/30, no. 27; C 142/124, no. 192.
[59] Ibid. REQ 2/8/321; ibid. C 1/1267/37; ibid. SC 6/Hen. VIII/3985, rot. 65.
[60] Ibid. REQ 2/8/321; W.R.O. 371/2.
[61] W.R.O., land tax; tithe award.
[62] V.C.H. Wilts. iv. 71.
[63] Wilton Ho. Mun., survey, 1550s.
[64] Wilts. Inq. p.m. 1625–49 (Index Libr.), 190–1; W.R.O. 371/2; 1366/2; 1366/5.
[65] P.R.O., SC 6/Hen. VIII/3985, rot. 65.

total of 4½ yardlands and pasture for 270 sheep and paid rents of between 6s. 8d. and 25s. The two larger copyholds were of 48 a. and 50 a. with rights for 120 and 90 sheep respectively.[66]

In 1658 there were four tenants on the estate later called East Kennett farm. Their lands had been merged into a single holding by 1832.[67]

In 1838 the parish was half arable and half grassland. Most of the pasture was on the downs and there were 69 a. of meadow beside the Kennet. The manor farm measured c. 580 a., of which 280 a. were arable, and the farm later called East Kennett farm 163 a. including 91 a. of arable and 65 a. of pasture. There were three holdings of less than 30 a., including one of 24 a. belonging to the trustees of Marlborough grammar school.[68] In the 1870s William Hewitt was tenant of both the manor farm and East Kennett farm.[69] The two farms together measured c. 777 a. in 1920.[70] They were worked as East Kennett Manor farm from 1922 until 1972. Sheep farming predominated on the combined holding in the early 20th century. Dairying was introduced by M. J. Read and for a time two herds were kept. There were 200 cows on Manor farm in 1979.[71]

In the early 20th century a considerable income was said to be derived from the sale of flints underlying the East Kennett estate.[72] There were large deposits of valuable sarsen stones in Langdean Bottom and on Furze Hill, Thorn Hill, and Harestone Down. In the 1920s and 1930s the stones were worked by the Free family, local masons. They ceased work in 1939, by which time most of the usable stones in East Kennett had been cut.[73]

There were mills on the estate of the Berwick family in 1300 and 1327,[74] one of which may have been at East Kennett. A water mill was among the possessions of Richard Franklin in 1634.[75] It probably stood in Mill mead, west of the bridge carrying the new road to West Kennett across the river.[76]

LOCAL GOVERNMENT. There is no record of manorial government in East Kennett, which in 1835 formed part of Marlborough poor-law union.[77] Expenditure on the poor was £30 12s. in 1776, an average of £64 a year from 1783 to 1785.[78]

CHURCH. A 'churchstead' referred to in King Edgar's charter of 972 may have been in East Kennett. It has, however, been suggested that the charter referred to a church in Overton.[79] Architectural evidence indicates that there was a church at East Kennett in the 12th century.[80] The church was appropriated by St. Margaret's priory near Marlborough in 1383.[81] Thereafter the living was a donative curacy until the late 19th century when it became known as a vicarage.[82] In 1923 the united benefice of Avebury with East Kennett was formed[83] and in 1929 the living of East Kennett was transferred to the benefice of Overton and Fyfield with East Kennett.[84] In 1975 East Kennett was included in the benefice of Upper Kennet, served by a team ministry.[85]

In 1306 William of Bruges and his wife Alice claimed the right of presentation to the rectory but their claim was not accepted and in the same year a candidate presented by St. Margaret's priory was instituted.[86] Rectors were presented by the priory until 1383.[87] The valuation of the living at £4 6s. 8d. in 1291 was the lowest for a rectory in Avebury deanery.[88] In 1341 almost a quarter of the rector's income was derived from oblations, although he received the great and small tithes. The glebe consisted of 1½ yardland with a yearly value of 2 marks.[89]

From 1383 until at least 1445 St. Margaret's priory presented curates for admission by the bishop.[90] After the Dissolution the donation of the living descended with the rectory estate until 1923 when William Fisher transferred the patronage to the bishop of Salisbury.[91] The bishop had the right of collation of the united benefice at every third turn[92] until 1929 when the living came entirely within his gift.[93]

At the Dissolution the curate's annual stipend was set at £6 or £6 13s. 4d. to be paid by the owner of the rectory estate.[94] The stipend was later augmented by owners of the estate and lords of the manor. In 1647 Richard Brownjohn agreed to increase the minister's yearly income by £20 as part of his composition with parliament.[95] In accordance with the will of his mother Ann Tooker, dated 1706, the younger Charles Tooker increased the stipend from £40 to £55.[96] An endowment of £50 was confirmed by Bishop Barrington when he sold the manor in 1787.[97] The income of the curacy was still only £57 in 1831 when few livings in the diocese had an annual value of less than £100.[98] John Mathews added a further £50 to the stipend c. 1863, on condition that the curate kept permanent residence and took two full services on Sundays.[99] In the early 20th century the difficulty of filling so

[66] Wilton Ho. Mun., survey, 1550s.
[67] W.R.O. 1366/10A, abstr. of title of Thos. Lavington.
[68] Ibid. tithe award.
[69] Kelly's Dir. Wilts. (1875 and later edns.).
[70] W.A.S. Libr., sale cat. xvi, no. 6.
[71] Inf. from Mr. J. M. Read, E. Kennett.
[72] W.A.S. Libr., sale cat. xvi, no. 6.
[73] Ibid.; W.A.M. lxiii. 85, 89.
[74] Feet of F. 1272–1327 (W.R.S. i), p. 45; 1327–77 (W.R.S. xxix), p. 15.
[75] Wilts. Inq. p.m. 1625–49 (Index Libr.), 190–1.
[76] W.R.O., tithe award. [77] Poor Law Com. 2nd Rep. 559.
[78] Poor Law Abstract, 1804, 568–9.
[79] Arch. Jnl. lxxvi. 245; Rep. Marlborough Coll. Natural Hist. Soc. lxxxvii. 118. [80] Wilts. Cuttings, xvi. 43.
[81] Cal. Pat. 1381–5, 339.
[82] W.A.M. xxxiv. 262; Clergy List (1892).

[83] Lond. Gaz. 1 June 1923, pp. 3843–5.
[84] Ibid. 10 May 1929, pp. 3114–17.
[85] Ibid. 21 Mar. 1975, p. 3845.
[86] Reg. Ghent (Cant. & York Soc.), ii. 682.
[87] Phillipps, Wilts. Inst. i. 7, 15–16, 30, 33, 38, 46, 49, 57.
[88] Tax. Eccl. (Rec. Com.), 189.
[89] Inq. Non. (Rec. Com.), 158.
[90] W.R.O., bishop, reg. Erghum, ff. 83v., 182–3; reg. Chaundler, f. 57; reg. Nevill, ff. 70, 76; reg. Aiscough, ff. i, ix.
[91] Lond. Gaz. 4 May 1923, pp. 3209–10.
[92] Ibid. 1 June 1923, pp. 3843–5.
[93] Ibid. 10 May 1929, pp. 3114–17.
[94] L. & P. Hen. VIII, xiv (1), p. 75; P.R.O., E 318/Box 30/1687. [95] Cal. Cttee. for Compounding, ii. 1553.
[96] W.R.O. 1366/7. [97] Tablet in church.
[98] Rep. Com. Eccl. Revenues, 838–9.
[99] Wilts. Tracts, xcii, no. 6.

impoverished a living was given as a reason for the union with Avebury.[1]

In 1539 the curate had the use of a room and a garden, part of the rectorial glebe.[2] There was a glebe house in 1831.[3] It was described as a cottage in 1863 but was extensively improved during the 1860s.[4] There has been no resident incumbent at East Kennett since 1923.

For 70 years after 1383 incumbencies were numerous and often brief, presumably because of the poverty of the living.[5] A canon of St. Margaret's was presented in 1422 and at the Dissolution John Rodley was pensioned both as a former canon and as curate of East Kennett.[6] In 1556 a parishioner was prosecuted for detaining goods belonging to the church, probably vestments or ornaments removed during Edward VI's reign.[7] The living remained vacant between 1561 and 1565.[8] In 1584 the curate claimed to be an approved preacher but refused to wear the prescribed dress.[9] In 1662 it was reported that the lessee of the rectory estate had failed to provide a settled minister.[10] During the 19th century a number of curates held second appointments, often as chaplains to Marlborough prison or poor-law union.[11] Two services were held on Sundays in 1851. The average congregation was 30 in the morning and 50 in the afternoon.[12] In 1864 there were sermons at both services and the curate, W. C. Badger, intended to replace quarterly with monthly celebrations of communion and to hold additional celebrations at festivals.[13] While at East Kennett, Badger entered into controversy with Bishop Hamilton whose tractarian views he found unacceptable.[14]

CHRIST CHURCH stands on the site of an earlier church which contained 12th- and 13th-century stonework, walled in during renovations in the 15th century.[15] In the late 16th century and the 17th there were frequent reports of the decay of the church fabric through the negligence of the owner of the rectory estate.[16] In 1807 there was a nave and south porch, with a wooden bell turret at the west end.[17] The church was rebuilt in 1863 by Gane & Co. of Trowbridge.[18] The new building of chequered ashlar and knapped flint, in Early English style, has a chancel, a nave with north tower, and a south porch. The most notable surviving features from the old church are monuments of the Tooker and Mathews families. In his will proved 1879 John Mathews left the income from £300 for the upkeep of the church and churchyard. Maintenance of the church was the responsibility of the owner of

the rectory estate and he received the profits of the endowment. Between 1881 and 1905 £105 16s. was spent on the fabric and fittings.[19]

A bell given in 1704 hung in the old church. In the later 19th century five new bells were donated.[20] A cup, paten, and flagon were given in 1864.[21] The registers are complete from 1655.[22]

NONCONFORMITY. In 1676 there were three nonconformists in the parish.[23] The curate reported two Baptist chapels in 1864[24] but no other reference to either has been found. One was possibly the building east of the village in West Overton later used as a reading room.[25]

EDUCATION. Although in 1818 the poor were said to desire the means of education,[26] there is no evidence of a day school in the parish before a schoolhouse was built in 1857. Average attendance was between 20 and 25 in 1859.[27] There was accommodation for 30 children in 1872 but only fifteen places were needed by the parish.[28] In 1878 Maria Mathews gave £2,300 for the school, then known as Miss Mathews's school.[29] Part of the endowment was used in 1895 to replace the schoolroom with a new building with accommodation for 40.[30] Attendance had risen to 38 by 1919 but it declined after 1924 when the older children were transferred to schools in Avebury and West Overton. Most of the pupils at East Kennett school then came from West Overton and West Kennett.[31] In 1978 there were 54 children on roll, many of whom came from outside the parish.[32]

As it was difficult to use Maria Mathews's endowment in so small a parish, the purposes of the charity were extended by Schemes of 1910 and 1926. From 1910 the proceeds were also used to provide further training for girls taught at the school and from 1926 yearly payments were made towards the maintenance of the schools at East Kennett and West Overton. The fund was also used to help children from East Kennett receiving further education and to improve local recreational facilities. The uses of the endowment were similar in 1962 when the annual income was £81.[33]

CHARITIES FOR THE POOR. By will proved 1878 Mary Jane Lanfear left £600 to apprentice one boy each year from East Kennett or Rams-

[1] *Wilts. Cuttings*, xiv. 249.
[2] P.R.O., SC 6/Hen. VIII/3985, rot. 65.
[3] *Rep. Com. Eccl. Revenues*, 838–9.
[4] *Wilts. Tracts*, xcii, no. 6.
[5] Phillipps, *Wilts. Inst.* i. 71, 113, 116, 127–9.
[6] Ibid. 113; *L. & P. Hen. VIII*, xiv (1), p. 75.
[7] W.R.O., bishop, detecta bk.
[8] *V.C.H. Wilts.* iii. 33 n.
[9] W.R.O., bishop, detecta bk.
[10] Ibid. bishop, chwdns.' pres.
[11] Ibid. bishop, vis. queries, 1864; *Rep. Com. Eccl. Revenues*, 838–9; *Wilts. Cuttings*, xvi. 49; *Kelly's Dir. Wilts.* (1872).
[12] P.R.O., HO 129/255/1/19/40.
[13] W.R.O., bishop, vis. queries.
[14] *Wilts. Tracts*, xcii, no. 6.
[15] *Wilts. Cuttings*, xvi. 43.
[16] W.R.O., bishop, detecta bks. 1550–3, 1584, 1585; bishop, chwdns.' pres. 1662.

[17] J. Buckler, watercolour in W.A.S. Libr., vol. iv. 43.
[18] W.R.O., bishop, pet. for faculties, bdle. 12, no. 7; see plate facing p. 161.
[19] *Endowed Char. Wilts.* (N. Div.), 584–5.
[20] Walters, *Wilts. Bells*, 110–11.
[21] Nightingale, *Wilts. Plate*, 149.
[22] W.R.O. 1404/1–3. There are transcripts for 1606–9 and 1619–23: ibid. bishop.
[23] *W.N. & Q.* iii. 536.
[24] W.R.O., bishop, vis. queries.
[25] O.S. Map 6″, Wilts. XXVII (1889 edn.).
[26] *Educ. of Poor Digest*, 1030.
[27] *Acct. of Wilts. Schs.* 28.
[28] P.R.O., ED 21/18407.
[29] *Endowed Char. Wilts.* (N. Div.), 581.
[30] P.R.O., ED 21/18407.
[31] Ibid. ED 21/42221; *Bd. of Educ., List 21* (H.M.S.O.).
[32] Inf. from the Head Teacher.
[33] Char. Com. file; P.R.O., ED 49/8182.

bury. The beneficiary was to come from East Kennett every third year. In the later 19th century the charity was not used regularly because there were insufficient candidates.[34] By a Scheme of 1924 a separate trust was established for East Kennett with a third of the endowment to provide apprenticeships or other forms of training. In 1963 the annual income from the charity was £6 10s.[35] The fund was rarely used in the 1970s.[36]

In his will proved 1879 John Mathews left the income from £300 to buy clothing, food, and fuel for the poor of the parish at Christmas. In 1904 £7 10s. was spent on coal for sixteen people.[37] In 1979 £13 was used to supply fuel to four beneficiaries.[38]

A dispensary and a room for the use of parishioners of East Kennett and West Overton were built in East Kennett in the 1880s with money bequeathed by Sarah or Maria Mathews. A minimum of £1,000 was to be spent on the building. The trust was wound up in 1917 and the building has been sold for conversion to a private house.[39]

MILDENHALL

THE PARISH of Mildenhall lies north and south of the Kennet immediately east of Marlborough.[40] South of the river and closely related to it by name was the Roman town Cunetio.[41] The parish included the tithings of Mildenhall, the name of which was frequently written and is still pronounced 'Minal',[42] Poulton, and Stitchcombe. A chapel at 'Selk' is supposed to have been in the north part of the parish and to have given its name to Selkley hundred but evidence of its existence is tenuous.[43] The probable absence of any church between Mildenhall and Preshute in the Anglo-Saxon period may have prompted the early extension of the parish westwards and southwards to include the lands of Poulton and Stitchcombe. Mildenhall, Poulton, and Stitchcombe were all townships in the 11th century.[44] The compact, roughly triangular, parish has its western point at Bay Bridge on the river Og. The south-west boundary follows the Og to the Kennet, the Kennet for 1 km., turning south to the London–Bath road which it follows to the Grand Avenue in Savernake forest, and the Grand Avenue for 1 km. before turning east to the south-east point of the triangle on the London–Bath road. From there the eastern boundary is marked by stretches of a lane to Stitchcombe and runs over the downs and up a dry valley to Whiteshard Bottom, the northern point, from where the north-west boundary runs above the valley of the Og and down into it to Bay Bridge.

Of the three tithings Mildenhall, c. 2,200 a. in 1838, was the largest and occupied the north and east parts of the parish. West of a road from Marlborough to Aldbourne was Poulton tithing, c. 800 a., and south of the Kennet was Stitchcombe, c. 1,000 a.[45] The total area of the parish was 4,177 a. (1,691 ha.) in 1891.[46] In 1901 it was increased by 46 a. from Preshute, most of which lay north of the London–Bath road and east of the G.W.R. line. Much of the land then added to Mildenhall was transferred to Marlborough in 1934 and thereafter Mildenhall parish measured 1,692 ha. (4,180 a.).[47]

The parish lies above 152 m. except near the rivers and in the south-east corner; the highest point, 221 m., is on the north-western boundary. The chalk which outcrops over the whole parish is covered on the lower slopes by clay-with-flints and a broad band of clay extends east and west over much of Stitchcombe tithing.[48] Much of the chalk downland was used as pasture and there was a large rabbit warren near the site of Warren Farm. Before the 19th century most of the arable lands of the parish were on the clay. Gravel soils in Sound Bottom, Whiteshard Bottom, and the dry valley bordered by Rabley Wood may also have been tilled.[49] Meadow land, much of it floated in the 16th century and later, is provided by the alluvium of the Og and particularly of the Kennet, beside which it is c. 400 m. wide.[50] Most settlement took place on the gravel of the river valleys, and on the river banks are the sites of several mills. Much of the parish's abundant woodland is on the clay and the largest area has always been south of the Kennet. All or a large part of Stitchcombe tithing lay within Savernake forest from the 13th century or earlier.[51] There were 365 a. of wood in the parish in 1838. Then, as in 1982, broad bands of scattered woodland stretched from Warren Farm south-east to Sound Copse and Thicket Copse, and south to Rabley Wood.[52]

The chief evidence of pre-Roman activity in the parish, apart from several barrows and

[34] Endowed Char. Wilts. (N. Div.), 585, 852–4.
[35] Char. Com. file.
[36] Inf. from the vicar, the Revd. P. J. Harrison, Overton Vicarage.
[37] Endowed Char. Wilts. (N. Div.), 583–4.
[38] Inf. from Mr. Harrison.
[39] Ibid.; Endowed Char. Wilts. (N. Div.), 581.
[40] This article was written in 1982. Maps used include O.S. Maps 1/50,000, sheet 173 (1974 edn.), sheet 174 (1974 edn.); 1/25,000, SU 16 (1960 edn.), SU 17 (1960 edn.), SU 26 (1961 edn.), SU 27 (1960 edn.); 6", Wilts. XXIX (1889 and later edns.).
[41] Below.
[42] P.N. Wilts. (E.P.N.S.), 301.

[43] W.A.M. x. 306.
[44] V.C.H. Wilts. ii, pp. 124, 145, 162; below, Preshute, church; Marlborough, churches.
[45] W.R.O., tithe award.
[46] Census, 1891.
[47] Ibid. 1901, 1931; O.S. Map 6", Wilts. XXIX (1889 and later edns.).
[48] Geol. inf. in this para. is from Geol. Surv. Maps 1", drift, sheet 266 (1964 edn.), sheet 267 (1957 edn.).
[49] Below, econ. hist.
[50] W.R.O. 490/1541; W.A.M. lv. 112.
[51] Close R. 1227–31, 103–4; below, econ. hist.
[52] W.R.O., tithe award.

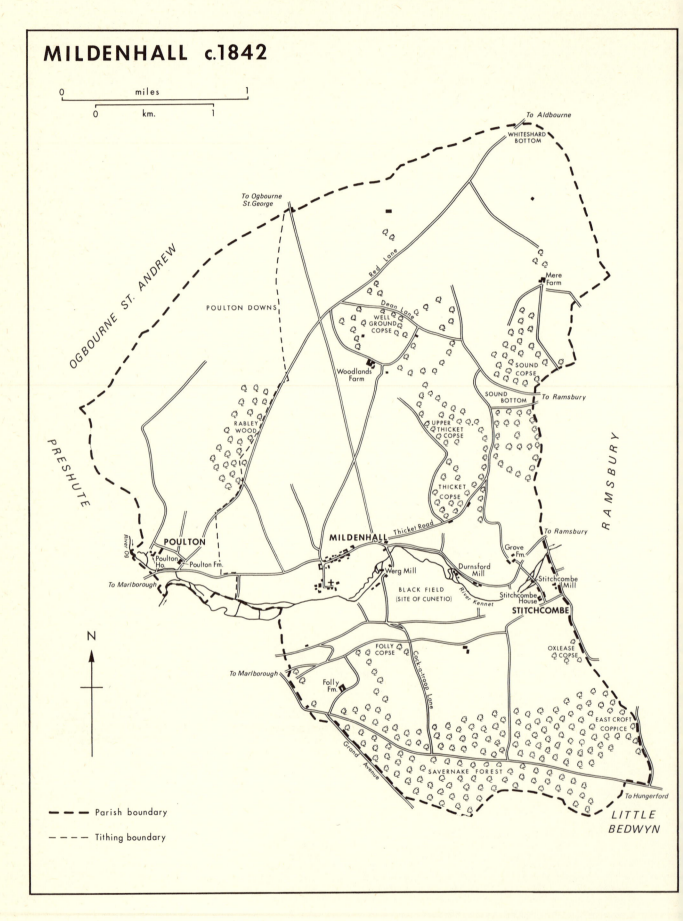

MILDENHALL c.1842

0   miles   1

0   km.   1

To Aldbourne

WHITESHARD BOTTOM

To Ogbourne St.George

OGBOURNE ST. ANDREW

Red Lane

Mere Farm

POULTON DOWNS

Dean Lane

WELL GROUND COPSE

SOUND COPSE

Woodlands Farm

SOUND BOTTOM

To Ramsbury

RABLEY WOOD

UPPER THICKET COPSE

RAMSBURY

PRESHUTE

THICKET COPSE

Thicket Road

MILDENHALL

To Ramsbury

River Og

POULTON

Grove Fm.

Poulton Ho.

Poulton Fm.

Werg Mill

Durnsford Mill

Stitchcombe Mill

To Marlborough

BLACK FIELD (SITE OF CUNETIO)

River Kennet

Stitchcombe House

STITCHCOMBE

OXLEASE COPSE

N

FOLLY COPSE

Cock-a-troop Lane

To Marlborough

Folly Fm.

EAST CROFT COPPICE

Grand Avenue

SAVERNAKE FOREST

To Hungerford

LITTLE BEDWYN

– – – Parish boundary

– – – Tithing boundary

scattered artefacts, is a cemetery, possibly a war cemetery, of the early Iron Age 250 m. south of Mildenhall church. South-east of Mildenhall village in Black Field is the site of Cunetio. The town was a trading centre at the junction of roads from Bath, Winchester, and Cirencester, and possibly from Old Salisbury and Silchester (Hants). At its foundation it was apparently un-fortified but in the 4th century it was enclosed by a stone wall, 16 ft. wide at its base, with bastions. The town probably survived as a small local market into Anglo-Saxon times, although only a few finds of that period have been made. The site of a smaller Roman settlement is 500 m. north-west of Forest Hill, formerly Folly, Farm.[53]

The course of the Roman road north from Cunetio is marked by a road from Mildenhall village which becomes a track north of Wood-lands Farm and joins the Marlborough–Swindon road at Ogbourne St. George. The roads from Cunetio to Winchester and Old Salisbury are traceable south-eastwards and south-westwards from where they fork near the northern edge of Savernake forest. The road from Bath probably ran south of the Kennet but its course is not known. Part of it may have been the Roman road, identified in the 18th century, which ran north-west and south-east across Black Field.[54] In the 13th century an east–west road followed a more southerly course through Savernake forest, probably along a route similar to that of the modern London–Bath road.[55] That road, the main route through the parish since the early 18th century or before, was turnpiked in 1726.[56] Until the late 18th century the road through Sound Bottom, Dean Lane, may have been part of a main Hungerford–Marlborough road, and it linked Ramsbury with the old Swindon–Marlborough road at the Old Eagle in Ogbourne St. Andrew.[57] In 1982 it was a track only. In 1773 and in the 20th century other principal roads were near the Kennet. North of the river is the Marlborough–Ramsbury road, south of it is that from Marlborough to Stitchcombe.[58] The two were probably linked by a bridge north of Werg Mill in the late 16th century and there was also a bridge at Stitchcombe in the early 18th century.[59] The road which leads north-eastwards from Poulton to Aldbourne was called Red Lane in the late 18th century and the 19th. Cock-a-troop Lane, 700 m. east of Forest Hill and only a path in 1982, and a steep and winding lane leading west and south from Stitchcombe linked the Marlborough–Stitchcombe and London–Bath roads.[60] From the London–Bath road rides lead north and south into Savernake forest. A section of the Swindon, Marlborough & Andover Rail-way was built across the parish near the Og and was opened in 1881. The line was closed to passengers in 1961 and for freight in 1964.[61]

In 1377 there were 122 poll-tax payers in Mildenhall parish, a little below the average for Selkley hundred. Tax assessments show the parish to have been one of the less prosperous of the hundred in both the 14th century and the 16th.[62] In 1801 there was a population of 376 and the total had risen to 501 by 1871. It had fallen to 422 by 1901 and later fluctuations followed boundary changes. Barnfield, a suburb of Marl-borough, was built on land transferred to Mildenhall from Preshute in 1901. The popula-tion of that area was then 7 and had increased to 44 by 1911 and 95 by 1934, when most of the land was transferred to Marlborough. In 1971 the parish had 421 inhabitants.[63]

MILDENHALL, which had 72 poll-tax payers in 1377, was by far the most populous tithing in the parish. It differed little in wealth from Stitch-combe tithing, however, and was less prosperous than average among the communities in the hundred.[64] The population was 281 in 1841.[65] Probably in the Anglo-Saxon period the site of settlement moved from Black Field to the north bank of the Kennet. The village spread north from Mildenhall church, near the river, along a lane leading to the crossroads at which the Marlborough–Ramsbury road and a track running north-east to Woodlands Farm meet. Beside the lane and near the church stand the oldest houses of the village, some of them timber-framed and thatched. Church Farm and Glebe House south of the church and cottages west and north of it may date from the 17th century and early 18th. The rectory house demolished in the mid 19th century stood west of the lane opposite the church[66] and in 1982 a pair of gate pillars marked the entrance to its grounds. No site of a manor house has been traced in the village but the demesne farmstead of Mildenhall manor stood north of the rectory house in the early 19th century.[67] The farmhouse was later demolished but some farm buildings remained in 1982. In the 18th century the village extended 400 m. east of the crossroads along the Ramsbury road, which thus became its principal street.[68] Surviving houses of the 18th and early 19th century beside the street include Hawthorn Cottage and Home Farm. The Horse Shoe, north of the street, was a beerhouse in the mid 19th century.[69] Many cottages date from the later 19th century and some were probably built in the 1860s when new building attracted new residents to the village.[70] In the 1880s the eastern extent of the village was marked by the school, built at the junction of the Marlborough–Ramsbury road and the Roman road to Cirencester.[71] In the 20th century council houses were built east of that junction and private houses were built at the west end of the village. Infilling included council houses built

[53] V.C.H. Wilts. i (1), 87–9, 277; i (2), 440, 447, 461, 466.
[54] Ibid. i (1), 88; i (2), 440; W.A.M. xxxviii. 289.
[55] V.C.H. Wilts. iv. 418; W.A.M. xlix. 405.
[56] V.C.H. Wilts. iv. 258; L.J. xxii. 664.
[57] Above, Ramsbury, introduction.
[58] Andrews and Dury, Map (W.R.S. viii), pl. 12.
[59] W.R.O. 490/1536; 1300/372.
[60] Andrews and Dury, Map (W.R.S. viii), pl. 12; W.R.O., tithe award.
[61] V.C.H. Wilts. iv. 289; below, Preshute, introduction.

[62] V.C.H. Wilts. iv. 301, 310; Taxation Lists (W.R.S. x), 22, 101–2.
[63] V.C.H. Wilts. iv. 354; Census, 1901, 1931, 1971.
[64] V.C.H. Wilts. iv. 301, 310.
[65] P.R.O., HO 107/1185.
[66] Below, church.   [67] W.R.O., tithe award.
[68] Andrews and Dury, Map (W.R.S. viii), pl. 12.
[69] Kelly's Dir. Wilts. (1855 and later edns.).
[70] V.C.H. Wilts. iv. 354.
[71] O.S. Map 6″, Wilts. XXIX (1889 edn.).

south of the street and a village hall, notable for its steeply pitched roof above low walls, built north of the street in 1974.[72] Mildenhall House, a former rectory house built in the 1860s, stands south of the Marlborough–Ramsbury road 400 m. west of the village.[73] Older settlement sites beside the road east of the village include those of Durnsford Mill and Lucky Lane, a former farmhouse. Of the outlying farmsteads, the earliest was at or near the modern Woodlands Farm. There was probably a farmstead at Woodlands in the 15th century, and in the 16th century tenants of the demesne farm of Mildenhall manor lived there. In the late 17th and early 18th century the lord of the manor had a house there.[74] In 1982 there were two farmhouses, one built in the 19th century, the other in the 20th. The sites of Mere Farm and Grove Farm have been in use since the 16th century or earlier.[75] A large house of unusual design was being built at Mere in 1982. Grove Farm is a red-brick house of the 18th century; another farmhouse was built north of it in 1979.[76] Warren Farm was established in the 19th century and Mildenhall Warren Farm, 500 m. north of it, in the 20th.[77]

POULTON. Medieval tax assessments show Poulton to have been the poorest of the tithings of Mildenhall and in 1377, when there were only eight poll-tax payers, it was one of the smallest communities in Wiltshire.[78] In the late 18th century the hamlet consisted of two farmsteads, later called Poulton House and Poulton Farm, which stood a little north of the confluence of the Kennet and the Og. Poulton Farm, then known as Little Poulton,[79] was rebuilt in the 19th century. There were 29 inhabitants of the hamlet in 1841 and numbers may have increased in the late 19th century and the early 20th when several cottages were built east of the Poulton–Aldbourne road.[80]

STITCHCOMBE. There were only 42 poll-tax payers in Stitchcombe in 1377.[81] In the early 18th century and in the 20th there were three small settlements in the tithing, Stitchcombe hamlet, a group of houses around Werg Mill 500 m. east of Mildenhall church, and Folly, later Forest Hill, Farm.[82] Cottages were built near the northern end of Cock-a-troop Lane in the late 18th century and the 19th.[83] In 1841 the population of the tithing was 127.[84]

The buildings of Stitchcombe hamlet stand beside a road joining the roads from Marlborough on each side of the Kennet. West of the road is the site of Stitchcombe Mill, only part of which

remains. On the steep slopes south of the mill is Stitchcombe House, a farmhouse mainly of the 19th century which may incorporate parts of an earlier building in the eastern service block. Farm buildings and cottages stand east and north of the house. In the late 18th century there were several houses near Werg Mill beside a lane leading south and west from Mildenhall village[85] but none seems to have survived. Houses of the 19th century, some of them thatched and timber-framed, include the mill house and cottages west of it. Houses and bungalows were built west and north of the mill house in the 20th century. At Forest Hill only an 18th-century lodge in Gothic style[86] and the 19th-century farmstead lay within Stitchcombe tithing.

MANORS AND OTHER ESTATES. Between 757 and 786 Cynewulf, king of Wessex, gave lands, later *MILDENHALL* manor, to Bica his thegn who granted them to Glastonbury abbey. A grant made to the abbey by King Edred between 946 and 955 probably confirmed the earlier gift.[87] The abbey held Mildenhall in 1086 and was overlord of the manor c. 1230 and in 1282.[88]

Mildenhall was held of Glastonbury abbey by Hugolin before 1086 and by Edward, probably Edward of Salisbury, in that year.[89] It apparently passed to Edward of Salisbury's son Walter (d. 1147) and Walter's son Patrick, first earl of Salisbury, and descended with the earldom to Margaret Longespée, for in 1275 Margaret's husband Henry de Lacy, earl of Lincoln, was lord of a knight's fee in Mildenhall in her right.[90] Their daughter Alice, countess of Lincoln and of Salisbury, and her husband Sir Ebles Lestrange granted the lordship to Hugh le Despenser, earl of Winchester, in 1325.[91] After Despenser's execution in 1326 the lordship passed to the Crown.[92]

William Marshal, earl of Pembroke (d. 1219), was tenant in demesne of the manor which he granted to his daughter Sibyl and her husband William de Ferrers, earl of Derby.[93] In 1241 Ferrers conveyed the manor to Gilbert Basset (d. 1241), husband of his daughter Isabel, in exchange for lands previously granted to Basset. In 1242–3 it was held by Isabel and her husband Reynold de Mohun (d. 1256).[94] Isabel was succeeded in 1260 by her son William de Mohun (d. 1282), whose relict Beatrice (fl. 1292) retained Mildenhall as part of her dower.[95] In 1294 the manor was conveyed to a trustee for William's son Reynold, after whose death while a minor in

[72] Char. Com. file; inf. from Capt. G. H. Stanning, Mildenhall Ho. [73] Below, church.
[74] P.R.O., SC 6/1056/7; below, manors.
[75] W.R.O. 442/1, ff. 251, 256.
[76] Inf. from Mrs. J. S. Burrows, Grove Farm.
[77] W.A.S. Libr., sale cat. vii, no. 76; W.R.O. 1043/2.
[78] V.C.H. Wilts. iv. 301, 310.
[79] Andrews and Dury, Map (W.R.S. viii), pl. 12.
[80] P.R.O., HO 107/1185; O.S. Map 6″, Wilts. XXIX (1889 and later edns.).
[81] V.C.H. Wilts. iv. 310.
[82] W.R.O. 1300/372.
[83] Andrews and Dury, Map (W.R.S. viii), pl. 12; W.R.O., tithe award.
[84] P.R.O., HO 127/1185.

[85] Andrews and Dury, Map (W.R.S. viii), pl. 12.
[86] See plate facing p. 145.
[87] Finberg, Early Wessex Chart. pp. 71, 90.
[88] V.C.H. Wilts. ii, p. 124; Glastonbury Cart. i (Som. Rec. Soc. lix), 200–1; Cal. Inq. p.m. ii, p. 250.
[89] V.C.H. Wilts. ii, p. 124.
[90] Complete Peerage, xi. 373–85; Rot. Hund. (Rec. Com.), ii (1), 269.
[91] Feet of F. 1272–1327 (W.R.S. i), pp. 132–3.
[92] Complete Peerage, iv. 266; Cal. Inq. p.m. x, p. 219.
[93] Complete Peerage, iv. 197; x. 263; Bk. of Fees, ii. 748.
[94] Cat. Anct. D. ii, A 3555; Bk. of Fees, ii. 748; V.C.H. Wilts. x. 163.
[95] Cal. Inq. p.m. i, p. 141; ii, p. 250; Cal. Close, 1279–88, 198; Cal. Pat. 1281–92, 468.

or before 1297 his father's estates were divided. Mildenhall was allotted to William's daughter Mary and her husband John de Meriet.[96] At John's death in 1327 it passed to Mary's kinsman John de Mohun, Lord Mohun,[97] and probably before 1330 it was granted for life to John of Mere (d. c. 1350) and his wife Eleanor (fl. 1352).[98] The reversion of the manor passed at the death of John, Lord Mohun, in 1330 to his grandson John de Mohun, Lord Mohun, who in 1352 granted it to Bartholomew Burghersh, Lord Burghersh (d. 1355).[99] Burghersh's son Bartholomew, Lord Burghersh, conveyed the manor to Sir Thomas Hungerford in 1362.[1]

Hungerford, who in 1385 received a grant of free warren in his demesne at Mildenhall,[2] was succeeded in 1397 by his son Sir Walter, later Lord Hungerford (d. 1449). The manor passed in turn to Walter's son Robert, Lord Hungerford (d. 1459),[3] and Robert's son Robert, Lord Hungerford and Moleyns, who conveyed it to his son Sir Thomas in 1460.[4] After Sir Thomas's attainder in 1469 Mildenhall was retained by or immediately restored to his relict Anne who held it later in the same year. A grant of the manor to Richard, duke of Gloucester, in 1474 was presumably without effect. In 1485 the Hungerford title to the manor was assured by the reversal of the attainder of 1469.[5] In 1493 Anne and her husband Hugh Vaughan conveyed the manor for Anne's life to trustees for her daughter Mary Hungerford, Baroness Botreaux, wife of Edward Hastings, Lord Hastings (d. 1506).[6] After Anne's death in 1522 Mildenhall was probably retained by Mary (d. 1533). In 1535 it was, like other estates belonging to the Hungerford family, a subject of litigation between Mary's son George Hastings, earl of Huntingdon, the heir general, and Sir Walter Hungerford, created Lord Hungerford in 1536, who as grandnephew of Sir Thomas Hungerford (d. 1469) was the heir male.[7] A settlement was reached by arbitration and the manor was allotted to Hungerford. On his attainder in 1540 it was forfeited to the Crown and it was granted as jointure in 1541 to Catherine Howard (d. 1542) and in 1544 to Catherine Parr (d. 1548).[8] In 1547 the reversion was granted to Edward Seymour, duke of Somerset,[9] and the manor passed to the Crown on his attainder in 1552. In 1554 it was

restored to Walter, son of Walter, Lord Hungerford (d. 1540).[10] Walter was succeeded in 1596 by his brother Sir Edward (d. 1607) who settled the manor on his grandnephew Sir Edward Hungerford.[11] In 1648 it passed to the younger Sir Edward's half-brother Anthony Hungerford (d. 1657) whose son Sir Edward sold it in 1673 to Henry Nourse.[12] Nourse (will proved 1705)[13] was succeeded by his daughter Sarah and her husband Charles Finch, earl of Winchilsea (d. 1712).[14] In 1731 Sarah and her husband William Rollinson sold Mildenhall manor to Charles Bruce, Baron Bruce, later earl of Ailesbury.[15] It passed with the Ailesbury title to George Brudenell-Bruce, marquess of Ailesbury, who offered it for sale in 1929 as two farms, each of c. 200 a.[16] Home farm was sold to D. M. Jeans and, after 1931, to A. W. Gale. In 1982 Gale & Ainslie Ltd. owned it.[17] Grove farm was sold to Mrs. L. M. Edwards (d. 1946), who was succeeded by her son R. H. Edwards (d. 1971). In 1972 Mr. G. Young bought the farm and in 1973 sold most of the lands to Mr. and Mrs. J. S. Burrows, the owners in 1982.[18]

A copyhold at Woodlands, which from the late 16th century or earlier had been held by the tenants of the demesne lands of Mildenhall manor, had been taken in hand as *WOOD-LANDS* farm by 1695.[19] Before 1742 it was sold by Charles, earl of Ailesbury, to Charles Stanhope.[20] The farm passed by sale or inheritance from Stanhope's relict (fl. 1751) to John Calcraft (d. before 1769)[21] and descended in the Calcraft family probably from father to son. It was held by Thomas Calcraft in 1769 and 1776,[22] by John Calcraft the younger in 1780, and by Thomas Calcraft the younger from 1782 until c. 1829.[23] Thomas was succeeded by his son John (will proved 1830)[24] and by his son-in-law the Revd. George Wyld. George's son the Revd. Thomas Wyld inherited the farm in 1836.[25] It was sold in 1858 to Richard Pocock, and in 1878 probably to Francis James Simpkins, the owner in 1895.[26] Further sales took place in 1896 and 1911, and in 1923 the farm belonged to C. R. E. Powell.[27] His relict Florence held it in 1932, as did W. E. Powell, presumably their son, in 1935.[28] After 1939 it was sold to a member of the Dawson family, and members of that family were owners in 1982.[29]

[96] *Cal. Pat. 1292–1301*, 67; *Cal. Close, 1296–1302*, 134.
[97] *Cal. Inq. p.m.* vii, p. 22.
[98] *Feet of F. 1327–77* (W.R.S. xxix), pp. 91–2, 98; *Feud. Aids*, vi. 574.
[99] *Complete Peerage*, ix. 23; *Feet of F. 1327–77* (W.R.S. xxix), p. 98; *Cal. Inq. p.m.* x, p. 219.
[1] W.R.O. 490/1470, f. 61v.
[2] *Cal. Chart. R. 1341–1417*, 297.
[3] P.R.O., C 136/100, no. 31; C 139/135, no. 30; *Complete Peerage*, vi. 617.
[4] *Cal. Close, 1454–61*, 439; Hist. MSS. Com. 78, *Hastings*, i, p. 241.
[5] *Complete Peerage*, vi. 621–3; *Cat. Anct. D.* ii, C 2506; *Cal. Pat. 1467–77*, 466–7.
[6] *Cal. Close, 1485–1500*, p. 213.
[7] *Complete Peerage*, vi. 622–3; P.R.O., C 1/813/60.
[8] Hist. MSS. Com. 78, *Hastings*, i, p. 292; *L. & P. Hen. VIII*, xvi, p. 241; xix (1), p. 83; *D.N.B.* s.vv. Catherine Howard, Catherine Parr.
[9] *Cal. Pat. 1547–8*, 119, 121.
[10] Ibid. 1553–4, 94–5.
[11] *Complete Peerage*, vi. 626; P.R.O., C 142/306, no. 160.

[12] P.R.O., C 142/306, no. 160; W.R.O. 9/20/31.
[13] P.R.O., PROB 11/480 (P.C.C. 13 Gee).
[14] W.R.O. 9/20/33; 9/20/144; *Complete Peerage*, xii (2), 779–80.
[15] W.R.O. 9/20/35; 9/20/37.
[16] Ibid. 9, sale cat.; Burke, *Peerage* (1959 edn.), 31.
[17] *Kelly's Dir. Wilts.* (1931 edn.); inf. from Mr. G. Young, Stitchcombe Cottage.
[18] Inf. from Mrs. J. S. Burrows, Grove Farm.
[19] W.R.O. 442/1, ff. 254, 259; 9/20/34.
[20] Ibid. 9, ct. bk. 1741–58.
[21] Ibid. 9, estate acct. bks.
[22] Ibid. 9, estate acct. bk.; ibid. inclosure award.
[23] Ibid. land tax.
[24] P.R.O., PROB 11/1768 (P.C.C. 155 Beard).
[25] W.A.S. Libr., Revd. C. Soames's notes; *Alum. Oxon. 1715–1886*, iv. 1619.
[26] W.A.S. Libr., sale cat. vii, no. 76; ibid. Soames's notes.
[27] Wilts. Cuttings, iv. 445; W.R.O. 1043/2; *Kelly's Dir. Wilts.* (1923).
[28] W.R.O., tithe award; *Kelly's Dir. Wilts.* (1935).
[29] *Kelly's Dir. Wilts.* (1939); inf. from Mr. Young.

A substantial house at Woodlands, in which Henry Nourse, lord of Mildenhall manor, lived in the late 17th century, was probably on the same site as that occupied by tenants of the demesne farm in 1586.[30] Nourse's house was standing c. 1720[31] but was demolished before 1792 when stone pillars from the entrance were used for the north portico of the central block of the building which became C House of Marlborough College.[32]

Demesne lands of Mildenhall manor, known as LOWER and later as CHURCH farm, were sold before 1742 to Charles Stanhope and passed with Woodlands farm to John Calcraft (will proved 1830).[33] Lower farm was inherited by Calcraft's sister Arabella (d. 1841), wife of William St. Quintin.[34] She was succeeded by her son the Revd. G. D. St. Quintin (d. 1873) and he by his nephew Geoffrey St. Quintin, the owner in 1895.[35] In or before 1923 the farm was bought by D. M. Jeans and thereafter it passed with Home farm.[36]

Between 801 and 805 Eahlmund, bishop of Winchester, granted an estate to Byrhtelm and received in exchange lands in various places including Mildenhall.[37] Nothing more is known of any holding there belonging to the see.

Robert de Mercinton gave lands in Mildenhall, perhaps Mildenhall in Wiltshire, for the foundation of the abbey of Netley (Hants), which took place in 1239. They were the subject of an exchange between the abbey and the Crown in 1241[38] but no further reference to them has been found.

The hospital of St. John the Baptist in Marlborough held land in Mildenhall in 1535.[39] The land was granted with the hospital's other estates to the mayor and burgesses of Marlborough in 1550 to endow the grammar school.[40] Before 1584 it was sold to Sir Walter Hungerford and was added to Mildenhall manor.[41]

In 1584 John Pearse held a farm called MERE.[42] In 1596 he settled half the farm on his son John, reserving the other half to himself and his wife Elizabeth for life.[43] The elder John died in or before 1616, the younger in or before 1642. Mere farm was held by William Pearse in 1642 and in 1650 by Thomas Pearse, who sold it in 1652 to William Blissett.[44] On Blissett's death c. 1672 it passed to Robert Blissett (fl. 1705). In 1733 John Tarren sold the farm to Nathaniel Merriman (will proved 1743) or his son Nathaniel (d. 1781).[45] The younger Nathaniel's executors

sold it in 1792 to Thomas Brudenell-Bruce, earl of Ailesbury, and it became part of the Mildenhall manor estate.[46] Mere was sold as a separate farm in 1929 to a Mr. Crook,[47] and in 1932 was bought by members of the Wight family. In 1975 it passed to Mr. G. R. Wight, the owner in 1982.[48]

POULTON was held by Toni in 1066 and by Humphrey Lisle in 1086.[49] Humphrey's estates formed the nucleus of the barony of Castle Combe, and the overlordship of Poulton passed with Broad Hinton manor and the barony to Giles de Badlesmere, Lord Badlesmere (d. 1338).[50] At the division of Badlesmere's estates in 1341 a knight's fee in Poulton was allotted to his sister Margaret and her husband John Tiptoft, Lord Tiptoft, and ½ fee there to another sister Margery and her husband William Ros, Lord Ros.[51] Margery's holding in Poulton may later have been acquired by Tiptoft or his successors; both holdings passed with Castle Combe to members of the Scrope family. The last overlord to whom reference has been found was George Scrope (d. 1604).[52]

Reynold de Dunstanville, husband of Humphrey Lisle's daughter Adelize, granted 5 hides at Poulton to Baldwin, a merchant of Wilton. A confirmation of the endowments of Tewkesbury abbey, dated 1114, mentioned tithes from Poulton given to the abbey by Adelize after Reynold's death. Adelize's gift was possibly not tithes, to which there is no later reference, but the 5 hides given to Baldwin, since the abbey is said to have compensated him for their loss.[53] LITTLE POULTON manor was held by the abbey before c. 1210 when it was confiscated by the Crown.[54] It was restored soon afterwards and after the Dissolution was apparently sold to a St. John; members of that family had formerly been tenants. In 1588 Nicholas St. John settled the manor on his son Sir John[55] and thereafter it descended with Bincknoll manor in Broad Hinton in the St. John family.[56] In 1819 George St. John, Viscount Bolingbroke, sold it to Charles Brudenell-Bruce, earl of Ailesbury.[57] It passed with the Ailesbury title and in 1929, with most other land in Poulton, was offered for sale as Poulton farm by George, marquess of Ailesbury. It was sold then or shortly afterwards to F. J. Sainsbury. In 1936 it was sold by Sainsbury's executors to E. H. North.[58] Mr. H. E. Hill bought the Poulton estate, 800 a., c. 1945 and owned c. 500 a. there in 1982.[59]

[30] W.R.O. 442/1, f. 259; 9/20/34.
[31] W.A.M. xliii. 388.
[32] Ibid. xxxiv. 141; xlii. 116; below, Preshute, manors.
[33] W.R.O. 9, ct. bk. 1741–58.
[34] W.A.S. Libr., Soames's notes.
[35] Ibid. sale cat. vii, no. 76; Burke, Land. Gent. (1906), ii. 1463.
[36] Kelly's Dir. Wilts. (1923); above.
[37] Finberg, Early Wessex Chart. p. 72.
[38] Cal. Chart. R. 1226–57, 251, 259–60; V.C.H. Hants, ii. 146.
[39] Valor Eccl. (Rec. Com.), ii. 147.
[40] Cal. Pat. 1549–51, 226.
[41] W.R.O. 442/1, f. 252.
[42] Ibid.
[43] P.R.O., C 2/Jas. I/R 7/35.
[44] W.R.O. 9/20/3; 9/20/10–12.
[45] Ibid. 9/20/17–18; 9/20/21; Burke, Land. Gent. (1937), 1580.
[46] W.R.O. 9/20/30.

[47] W.A.S. Libr., sale cat. xxviiiB, no. 17.
[48] Inf. from Mr. G. R. Wight, Wattlefield, Speen, Berks.
[49] V.C.H. Wilts. ii, p. 145.
[50] G. Poulett Scrope, Castle Combe (priv. print. 1852), 17, 19, 55; Cal. Inq. p.m. viii, pp. 127, 137–8; above, Broad Hinton, manors.
[51] Cal. Close, 1341–3, 150, 152.
[52] Poulett Scrope, Castle Combe, 55, 262, 317; P.R.O., C 142/239, no. 119.
[53] Poulett Scrope, Castle Combe, 26–7; Reg. Regum Anglo-Norm. ii, no. 1069.
[54] Interdict Doc. (Pipe R. Soc. N.S. xxxiv), 27.
[55] P.R.O., SC 6/Hen. VIII/1260, rot. 44; ibid. C 142/239, no. 119.
[56] Above, Broad Hinton, manors.
[57] W.R.O. 9/20/25.
[58] W.A.S. Libr., sale cat. xxviiiB, no. 17; Wilts. Cuttings, xviii. 100.
[59] Inf. from Mr. and Mrs. H. E. Hill, Poulton Ho.

An estate, later *GREAT POULTON* manor, was held of Humphrey Lisle's successors by Thomas de Cardeville in the late 12th century. Thomas was succeeded by his sons William (d. before 1222) and Adam (fl. 1227).[60] The estate was held by Walter de Cardeville in 1242–3 and by William de Cardeville in 1275.[61] In 1324 a messuage and 1 carucate of land, perhaps part of the estate, were settled by Roger Poulton on Thomas Poulton and his wife Isabel with remainder to John Poulton.[62] Thomas held lands in Poulton in 1338, and in 1399 an estate, probably Great Poulton manor, was conveyed to another Thomas and Isabel Poulton by trustees, with remainder to Thomas Poulton.[63] That last Thomas, later bishop of Worcester (d. 1433), was succeeded by George Poulton his nephew,[64] whose relict Isabel held the estate in 1454.[65] From Isabel it passed, by what right is not known, to John Crook (d. c. 1509), and in turn to John's son Robert and Robert's son George. George's right to part of the estate was disputed c. 1535 by William Bush, who claimed it by inheritance from his father Thomas.[66] In 1557 William's son Thomas was seised of the whole manor, which he then sold to Robert Were or Brown.[67] Robert (will proved 1570) was succeeded by his son Richard, who by will proved 1577 gave the manor to his son Robert (will proved 1592).[68] Robert was succeeded by his brother Clement (d. 1602), by Clement's son Richard,[69] and by Richard's son Alexander Brown (fl. 1665).[70] In or before 1670 Alexander devised the manor to Cornelius Cornwallis, husband of his daughter Margaret.[71] By will proved 1674 Cornwallis devised it to trustees to be sold but in 1693 the trustees conveyed it to another Cornelius Cornwallis, perhaps his son.[72] The younger Cornelius sold the manor in 1698 to William Lydiard, whose relict Elizabeth conveyed it to their son Stephen in 1712.[73] Stephen was succeeded in 1719 by his daughter Elizabeth, sometimes called Stephania Elizabeth. By will proved 1739 she devised the manor for life to her mother Elizabeth Lydiard (fl. 1748) with remainder to her sister Frances, later wife of John Hart.[74] In 1777 Frances Hart sold the manor to Thomas Brudenell-Bruce, earl of Ailesbury.[75] In 1929 it was sold with Little Poulton as a single farm.[76]

Poulton House, built in 1706,[77] is of brick with stone dressings and has a south front of seven bays. The original principal and secondary stair-cases and a moulded plaster ceiling survive, but otherwise the interior was altered, apparently in the 19th century. The principal windows were then sashed and a canted bay was added on the south-east side of the house. The rear service wing was also built in the 19th century.

In 1066 and 1086 Gode held lands which later became *STITCHCOMBE* manor.[78] In 1242–3 Stitchcombe was held of William de Beauchamp (d. 1269) and in 1275 his son William, earl of Warwick, was overlord. The heirs of Hubert Busati were then intermediate lords of the manor.[79]

Robert of Stitchcombe held lands in Stitchcombe, probably Stitchcombe manor, in 1167 and was succeeded in or before 1200 by Sir Richard of Stitchcombe.[80] In 1217 Sir Richard's lands were granted at the king's pleasure to Reynold of Whitchurch but in 1242–3 Robert of Stitchcombe held the manor.[81] Robert (fl. 1249) was succeeded by Reynold of Stitchcombe (d. in or before 1264).[82] Reynold's heir, apparently a minor in 1286, may have been Roger of Stitchcombe, who held the manor in 1316.[83] In 1325 it was settled on Roger for life with remainder to Hildebrand of London.[84] Roger died after 1332, and in 1359 Hildebrand's son Robert held the manor.[85] After Robert's death c. 1391 it was settled for life on his relict Elizabeth (d. before 1403) with remainder to John Lovel, Lord Lovel, probably her brother, and his heirs.[86] Lovel (d. 1408) held the manor jointly with his wife Maud, who apparently conveyed it to Sir William Esturmy or trustees for him in or before 1418.[87] After Esturmy's death in 1427 it passed to his grandson Sir John Seymour (d. 1464),[88] and in turn to Seymour's grandson John Seymour (d. 1491 or 1492) and that John's son John, later Sir John, Seymour. In 1536 the manor passed to the younger Sir John's son Edward, Viscount Beauchamp, later earl of Hertford and duke of Somerset.[89] With other lands forfeited at Somerset's attainder in 1552, Stitchcombe was restored to his son Edward, created earl of Hertford in 1559. It passed with the earldom of Hertford and later with the dukedom of Somerset to John Seymour, duke of Somerset,[90] and at his death in 1675 it was inherited by his sister Elizabeth (d. 1697), wife of Thomas Bruce who succeeded to the earldom of Ailesbury in 1685. Thereafter the manor passed with the Ailesbury title and between 1731 and 1929 with Mildenhall manor.[91] In 1939 George Brudenell-Bruce, marquess of

[60] *Cur. Reg. R.* x. 310–11; P.R.O., CP 25(1)/250/5, no. 18.
[61] *Bk. of Fees*, ii. 748; *Rot. Hund.* (Rec. Com.), ii (1), 269.
[62] *Feet of F. 1272–1327* (W.R.S. i), p. 113.
[63] *Cal. Inq. p.m.* viii, pp. 137–8; P.R.O., CP 25(1)/256/57, no. 33.
[64] *W.A.M.* xxvi. 53.
[65] Poulett Scrope, *Castle Combe*, 220.
[66] P.R.O., C 1/961/62; C 1/961/64.
[67] W.R.O. 9/20/74.
[68] P.R.O., PROB 11/52 (P.C.C. 37 Lyon); PROB 11/59 (P.C.C. 35 Daughtry); *W.N. & Q.* viii. 539.
[69] P.R.O., C 142/269, no. 95.
[70] Reading Univ. Libr., hist. farm rec., WIL 11/8/4.
[71] W.R.O. 9/20/79; 9/20/83; 9/20/105.
[72] Ibid. 9/20/84; 9/20/87.
[73] Ibid. 9/20/88; 130/23.
[74] Ibid. 9/20/92; 9/20/94; 9/20/98–9.
[75] Ibid. 9/20/100.
[76] Ibid. 9, sale cat.

[77] Pevsner, *Wilts.* (2nd edn.), 336; see below, plate facing p. 161.
[78] *V.C.H. Wilts.* ii, p. 162.
[79] *Bk. of Fees*, ii. 748; G. Baker, *Northants.* ii. 219; *Rot. Hund.* (Rec. Com.), ii (1), 269.
[80] *Pipe R. 1167* (P.R.S. xi), 129; *Cur. Reg. R.* i. 789.
[81] *Rot. Litt. Claus.* (Rec. Com.), i. 304; *Bk. of Fees*, ii. 748.
[82] *Civil Pleas, 1249* (W.R.S. xxvi), p. 97; *Close R. 1261–4*, 334.
[83] *Cal. Pat. 1281–92*, 219; *Feud. Aids*, v. 205.
[84] *Feet of F. 1272–1327* (W.R.S. i), p. 116.
[85] *Cat. Anct. D.* vi, C 6155; *Feet of F. 1327–77* (W.R.S. xxix), pp. 114–15.
[86] P.R.O., CP 25(1)/256/56, no. 13; above, Axford, manors.
[87] *Complete Peerage*, viii. 221; *Cal. Close, 1405–9*, 414–15; *1413–19*, 458.
[88] P.R.O., C 139/28, no. 22.
[89] Hoare, *Mod. Wilts.* Mere, 119.
[90] *Complete Peerage*, xii (1), 63–9; W.R.O. 1300/372.
[91] *Complete Peerage*, i. 59–61; above.

Ailesbury, granted a lease for 999 years to the Forestry Commission of the part of Savernake forest which lay within the tithing.[92] In 1950 he conveyed the residue of the estate at Stitchcombe to the Crown Estate Commissioners, the owners in 1982.[93]

Alice, wife of Thomas Cooke, held *HENDIS* farm in Stitchcombe tithing and was succeeded *c.* 1540 by her son John Marchant.[94] In 1573 Marchant sold the farm to John Cornwall (d. 1611), whose daughter Bridget, relict of Sir William Jordan, held it in 1629. Marchant's son Robert and his grandnephew William Gough contested the validity of that sale and Bridget's title to the farm, probably without success.[95] Her son Sir William Master held the farm in 1638 and sold it in 1649 to Alexander Staples. It was bought from Staples in 1664 by Adam Peddington or Tuck[96] who released it in 1680 to another Adam Peddington, probably his son. The younger Adam sold the farm in 1681 to William Bailey.[97] In 1701 Bailey conveyed it to his son William who sold it in 1710 to William Hillear.[98] The farm passed *c.* 1713 to Hillear's son William who sold it in 1739 to Thomas Bruce, earl of Ailesbury.[99] Thereafter, under the name of Folly farm and later of Forest Hill farm, it passed with Stitchcombe manor.[1]

A small parcel of land in Stitchcombe tithing may have been among lands granted by Robert Grafton, rector of Mildenhall, and others to St. Margaret's priory, near Marlborough, in 1412.[2] Lands near Puthall Farm in Little Bedwyn held by the priory at the Dissolution were part of the jointure of Anne of Cleves in 1539.[3] In 1542 they were granted to Edward Seymour, earl of Hertford, and added to Stitchcombe manor.[4]

ECONOMIC HISTORY. MILDENHALL. The estate of Glastonbury abbey, said to include 15 hides in the 10th century,[5] was assessed at 10 hides in 1066. In 1086 there were only 6 plough-teams, although there was land for 10. The demesne, on which there were 2 teams, was of 4 hides, and 15 villeins and 5 bordars had 4 teams. There was pasture ½ league long and 3 furlongs broad and 10 a. of meadow. The estate increased in value from £12 in 1066 to £18 in 1086.[6]

Most of the arable lands of Mildenhall tithing lay in three fields, West, Middle, and East or Thicket fields, in a band on the north side of the Marlborough–Ramsbury road. A fourth field, Wore or Oare, lay south of the road and west of the church. There was also tillage further north

again, probably in Sound Bottom; a field there may have been open in the 14th century but was partly or wholly inclosed in the 16th.[7] In the 16th century there was common pasture for sheep on Greenhill, south of Sound Bottom, and on 'Hockdown' and 'Rawdown', which presumably lay in the north and west parts of the tithing. There was also a common cow down, the location of which is not known. Burridge down provided demesne pasture, which was probably several, and was the site of a rabbit warren.[8]

In the late 13th century sheep-and-corn husbandry was extensively practised on the demesne of Mildenhall manor: in addition to the downland pastures there were arable lands assessed at 200 a. in 1282, when there were 24 a. of meadow, and 360 a. in 1297. Much of the work on the demesne may have been done by the customary tenants whose holdings, for which rents totalling over £5 were paid, may also have been large,[9] although nothing is known of their number. Some services, including boonworks of 24, 20, and 18 persons to cut, bind, and carry the demesne corn, were performed in the 15th century.[10] There was demesne pasture for 400 sheep in the late 13th century; the size of the flock rose to between 500 and 600 in the late 14th and early 15th centuries. Additional labour was often hired for shearing: 30 people were employed in 1380. From the mid 14th century Mildenhall was one of several manors of the Hungerford family which were linked in a system of sheep rearing, though it may not have been fully integrated with the others: there are only occasional references to ewes sent from Mildenhall to Farleigh Hungerford, in Norton St. Philip (Som.), or fleeces to Heytesbury, the principal collection centres for the estates.[11] From 1425 or earlier the demesne arable and meadow and small parcels of demesne pasture, presumably lowland pasture, were leased in portions and from 1439 the demesne was leased as a single farm. Among the 15th-century tenants of the farm were members of the Goddard family.[12]

The demesne warren, first mentioned in 1448,[13] was leased in 1453 to three tenants, whether jointly or in portions is not known, and thereafter the warrener was probably always a lessee. In the 16th century and the early 17th the warren was leased with the demesne farm.[14] Estimates of its size vary from 250 a. in 1673 to 400 a. in the early 18th century. By 1673 a lodge had been built for the warrener.[15] A reference to the warren of 1731 is the latest which has been found.[16]

[92] Inf. from Forestry Com., Flowers Hill, Brislington, Bristol.
[93] Inf. from Crown Estate Com., Bracknell, Berks.
[94] P.R.O., C 1/969/41–2.
[95] Ibid. C 2/Jas. 1/G 6/11.
[96] W.R.O. 9/20/52–4; Burke, *Land. Gent.* (1937), 1554.
[97] W.R.O. 9/20/56–7.
[98] Ibid. 9/20/58; 9/20/60.
[99] Ibid. 9/20/61; 9/20/64; 9/20/66.
[1] Ibid. 9, estate acct. bks.
[2] *Cal. Pat.* 1408–13, 450.
[3] *L. & P. Hen. VIII,* xiv (2), p. 154.
[4] Ibid. xvii, p. 322; W.R.O. 9/20/2.
[5] Finberg, *Early Wessex Chart.* p. 90.
[6] *V.C.H. Wilts.* ii, p. 124.

[7] W.R.O. 442/1, ff. 252–64; Hist. MSS. Com. 78, *Hastings,* i, p. 240.
[8] W.R.O. 442/1, ff. 254–5, 259–60v.; below.
[9] *Wilts. Inq. p.m.* 1242–1326 (Index Libr.), 141–2, 214–15.
[10] *V.C.H. Wilts.* iv. 38.
[11] *Wilts. Inq. p.m.* 1242–1326 (Index Libr.), 141; R. C. Payne, 'Agrarian conditions on the Wilts. estates of the Duchy of Lanc. etc.' (Lond. Univ. Ph.D. thesis, 1940), 176, 179, 196, 211, 227; P.R.O., SC 6/1056/9.
[12] P.R.O., SC 6/1056/7; SC 6/1056/10; SC 6/1056/13.
[13] Ibid. SC 6/1119/12.
[14] Ibid. SC 6/1056/13; ibid. E 126/13, f. 247; W.R.O. 442/1, f. 260v.
[15] W.R.O. 9/20/31; P.R.O., E 126/13, f. 247.
[16] W.R.O. 9/20/37.

In addition to the demesne farm and the presumably extensive customary holdings of Mildenhall manor, details survive of two medieval freeholds in the tithing. A yardland at Woodlands, called Hamstalls in 1313, had become a small several holding by the 16th century.[17] The demesne farm of the rectory estate included 1 carucate and meadow valued at 10s. a year in 1341. The rector also received rents and services valued at 16s. from four customary tenants.[18]

In the 16th century there were five principal farms in the tithing, the demesne farm of Mildenhall manor, Woodlands and Grove farms, both then copyholds of the manor, Mere farm, and the glebe. In 1586 the demesne farm was leased to William Jones, and members of that family held it until the mid 17th century.[19] It consisted of 108 a. in the open fields, 20 a. of inclosed arable land, 23 a. of meadow, and 60 a. of wood, with 200 a. of pasture, most of it on the downs in the north part of the tithing. The lessee also had pasture on the cow down from 21 December until 25 March. In the 1670s the farm included c. 850 a., of which perhaps 400 a. was the warren; the downland pasture was by then inclosed.[20] Lower farm had by then been separated from other demesne land and included 120 a. of several arable. In the late 16th century the copyholds of Mildenhall manor amounted to 18½ yardlands, including c. 800 a. of arable in the open fields and pasture in common for 1,500 sheep, in eleven holdings. Two holdings were of 4 yardlands each, the later Woodlands and Grove farms. Woodlands included 104 a. in severalty, of which 54 a. were arable land and 50 a. pasture, and pasture in common for 400 sheep. Grove farm included 82 a. of pasture in small closes, common pasture for 400 sheep, and 11 a. in the open fields, and no other arable land.[21] By 1770 Woodlands and some smaller holdings had been converted to freeholds or leaseholds.[22] Mere farm, east of Woodlands, consisted of c. 75 a., all inclosed, in 1642 and 1733.[23] The rector's estate changed little between the late 16th century and the 18th; it included some 37 a. in the open fields, 26 a. of inclosed land, and four ½-yardlands held by tenants.[24] All the principal farms were worked by tenants in the late 18th century.[25]

The demesne farm included 11 a. of watered meadow in 1586, and in 1637 permission was given in the manor court for the lessee to divert water from the Kennet to meadows 'in the curtilage of the manor', probably close to the farmstead near the church.[26] In the late 17th century there were c. 45 a. of watered meadow in the tithing.[27]

Although the northern part of the tithing was mostly several by the 1670s, there was probably still some common pasture on the downs.[28] By the late 18th century the downland had been inclosed, but no record has been found of the process of inclosure. The fields which bordered the Marlborough–Ramsbury road remained open until 1776. An agreement, confirmed by an Act of 1779, was then made for the inclosure of 476 a. Allotments, totalling 478 a., were made of 251 a. to the lord of Mildenhall manor, including c. 80 a. for copyhold land, of 165 a. to Woodlands farm, and of 62 a. to the rector, presumably for both demesne and copyhold lands.[29] By 1838 most small copyholds and leaseholds had been absorbed into the larger farms. Land had also been transferred from Mildenhall farm, the demesne farm, then c. 250 a., to the farms of the Woodlands estate, Lower farm, 593 a. with buildings south of the church, and Woodlands, 566 a. On Grove farm were c. 240 a., on Mere farm 141 a., and on Rectory farm 159 a. with buildings west of the church. Parts of the downland had by then been ploughed and the farms were mainly arable. Only Lower farm had a substantial proportion of pasture, including 174 a. on the downs.[30] In the late 19th century it was a dairy farm.[31] Arable farming in the tithing declined in the late 19th and early 20th centuries. By 1878 Woodlands had been divided into two farms, Woodlands, c. 340 a., and Warren, c. 200 a., and by 1896 most of the lands of both had been converted to pasture.[32] Mildenhall and Grove farms, which had been merged as an arable farm described as fertile but badly managed in 1867,[33] were separate in 1929. Each was then of c. 200 a. and each included c. 50 a. of pasture. Mere then measured 221 a., approximately half of which was pasture,[34] and in 1982 it included c. 100 a. of grassland.[35] After 1929 Home, formerly Mildenhall, farm, Lower farm, and part of Warren farm were merged as Church farm, a mixed farm worked from buildings south of the church and including a trout farm in 1982.[36] In the 1970s a dairy herd was established at Grove farm and 12 a. were worked as a vineyard.[37]

There was woodland ½ league long and 3 furlongs broad at Mildenhall in 1086.[38] In the Middle Ages sales of wood and underwood were an important part of the lord of Mildenhall manor's income.[39] In 1586 c. 60 a. of wood, all of hazel and ash and including Thicket Copse and Sound Copse, were in hand and farms in the tithing included a few acres of woodland each.[40] The area of demesne woodland had risen to 100 a. by 1673 and 120 a. by 1838;[41] it changed little thereafter.[42]

[17] Hist. MSS. Com. 78, *Hastings*, i, p. 240; *Feet of F.* 1272–1327 (W.R.S. i), p. 86; W.R.O. 442/1, f. 252.
[18] *Inq. Non.* (Rec. Com.), 158.
[19] W.R.O. 442/1, ff. 259–60; *Wilts. Inq. p.m.* 1625–49 (Index Libr.), 122–3; P.R.O., E 134/32 Chas. II East./14.
[20] W.R.O. 442/1, ff. 259–60; 9/20/31.
[21] Ibid. 442/1, ff. 254, 256.
[22] Ibid. 9, estate acct. bk. 1769–70.
[23] Ibid. 9/20/11; 9/20/21.
[24] Ibid. bishop, glebe terriers, 1593 × 1619, 1705.
[25] Ibid. land tax.
[26] Ibid. 442/1, f. 260; 490/1541.
[27] Ibid. 9/20/31; ibid. bishop, glebe terrier, 1671; *W.A.M.* lv. 112.   [28] W.R.O. 9/20/31.

[29] Ibid. inclosure award.
[30] Ibid. tithe award.   [31] *W.A.M.* xxx. 143.
[32] W.A.S. Libr., sale cat. vii, no. 76; Wilts. Cuttings, iv. 445.   [33] W.R.O. 9, survey.
[34] Ibid. 9, sale cat.
[35] Inf. from Mr. G. R. Wight, Wattlefield, Speen, Berks.
[36] Inf. from Mr. G. Young, Stitchcombe Cottage.
[37] Inf. from Mrs. J. S. Burrows, Grove Farm.
[38] *V.C.H. Wilts.* ii, p. 124.
[39] *Wilts. Inq. p.m.* 1242–1326 (Index Libr.), 214; P.R.O., SC 6/1056/6; SC 6/1056/9–10.
[40] W.R.O. 442/1, ff. 252–63.
[41] Ibid. 9/20/31; ibid. tithe award.
[42] O.S. Map 6″, Wilts. XXIX (1889 and later edns.).

A rent of 30s. was paid for a mill at Mildenhall in 1086,[43] and in 1453 a mill was leased by the lord of Mildenhall manor.[44] Stockham Mill, a corn and fulling mill, was leased by the lord of the manor in 1586.[45] From the early 17th century it was sometimes called Durnsford Mill.[46] Fulling apparently ceased after 1745 but in the 1790s there were still spinners at Mildenhall; they were then losing work because of the introduction of the jenny elsewhere in the county.[47] The corn mill had three pairs of stones driven by a 12-ft. water wheel in 1867, and in 1898 both water and steam power were used.[48] It ceased working between 1903 and 1911.[49]

POULTON. In 1086 Poulton was an estate of 10 hides, of which 8 were in demesne. There were only 3 ploughteams although there was land for 4; there were 2 teams and 2 serfs on the demesne and 2 villeins and 7 bordars had 1 team. There were 4 a. of meadow, 10 a. of pasture, and 8 a. of wood. The estate was valued at £8, as it had been in 1066.[50]

Little more is known of agriculture in the tithing in the Middle Ages but the location of arable land and pasture was probably similar then and in the 18th century, when Poulton Downs and a cow down east of Poulton provided common grazing. South and south-west of the downs were the open fields of the tithing.[51] The 11th-century estate was divided into moieties. In 1210 Little Poulton manor was valued at £5 10s., of which 30s. was rent paid by tenants. There were 100 sheep on the estate.[52] Great Poulton manor comprised 5 hides in 1223 and was valued at £10 in 1339.[53] The only land in the tithing not part of either manor was part of the rector's glebe, said to be ½ yardland in the late 16th century.[54]

By the late 18th century any copyhold or leasehold lands had been absorbed into the two principal farms. The two farms had equal shares in the pasture of Poulton Downs and the cow down, which measured 206 a. and 26 a. respectively.[55] Great Poulton farm apparently included the larger proportion of arable lands, c. 200 a. in 1777. Some 12 a. of meadow and 12 a. of Rabley Wood then belonged to that farm and 40 a. of the wood to Little Poulton farm.[56] Lessees worked the larger farm from 1748 or earlier and the smaller from the late 18th century.[57] Large parts of the fields and downs were still open in the late 18th century but the process of inclosure was eased c. 1810 when the same tenant leased both farms and in 1819 when the farms were held by one owner.[58] Under an Act passed in 1815 in-closure took place in or before 1819, although the formal award was not made until 1824. Two allotments were made. The larger, 569 a., was all part of Poulton farm. The smaller, 43 a., was made to the rector.[59] In 1838 Poulton farm consisted of 348 a. of arable, 293 a. of pasture, of which 220 a. were downland, and 13 a. of water meadow. Rabley Wood, 66 a., was then in hand.[60] In 1929 Poulton was a corn and dairy farm of 750 a., including some land in Preshute and in Mildenhall tithing, and was worked from buildings east of Poulton House.[61] In 1982 it was a farm of c. 500 a. and other lands in the tithing were worked with those of farms in Mildenhall tithing.[62]

In 1086 there was a mill valued at 5s. on Humphrey Lisle's Poulton estate.[63] The prior of Ogbourne had a water mill at Poulton in the 12th century, and in the 13th he claimed the right to send a cart into Marlborough to collect corn for grinding.[64] The mill was apparently working in 1342[65] but no further reference to it has been found. Its site may have been that of a mill which was part of Great Poulton manor in 1606 and which stood beside the Og west of Poulton House.[66] The mill was leased with Great Poulton farm in the 18th century but was destroyed before 1838.[67]

A royal fulling mill was said in 1215 to stand between Marlborough and Poulton. Elcot mill in Preshute was probably the one meant.[68]

STITCHCOMBE. There was said to be 1½ hide in demesne at Stitchcombe in 1084 but the whole estate was assessed at no more than 1 hide in 1086. There was then land for 3 ploughteams, of which 1 was held in demesne and 2 were held by 2 villeins and 5 bordars. The estate was valued at 50s.[69]

No pasture in Stitchcombe was mentioned in the Domesday survey and grazing was probably scarce in the Middle Ages. Common pasture for sheep may have been limited to Stitchcombe down, east of Cock-a-troop Lane, and Werg down, north-west of Forest Hill Farm, which were still open in the 18th century. Grazing rights on Stitchcombe down may have belonged to the lord or farmer and tenants of Stitchcombe manor and those on Werg down to the owners and tenants of Hendis, later Forest Hill, farm and to those living near Werg Mill, but there is no positive evidence of such a division. In the 18th century and probably earlier there was pasture for cattle of the lord and tenants of Stitchcombe manor in Savernake forest. Apart from meadows near the Kennet most land north of the forest was open arable fields.[70] In the late 13th cen-

[43] V.C.H. Wilts. ii, p. 124.
[44] P.R.O., SC 6/1056/13.
[45] W.R.O. 442/1, f. 261v.
[46] Ibid. 490/1451; 9, contract bk. 1734-49.
[47] Ibid. 9, contract bk. 1734-49; 9, letter, Francis to Ailesbury.
[48] W.R.O. 9, survey, 1867; Kelly's Dir. Wilts. (1898).
[49] Kelly's Dir. Wilts. (1903, 1911).
[50] V.C.H. Wilts. ii, p. 145.
[51] W.R.O. 143/4.
[52] Interdict Doc. (Pipe R. Soc. N.S. xxxiv), 27.
[53] Cur. Reg. R. xi, p. 243; Cal. Close, 1339-41, 280.
[54] W.R.O., bishop, glebe terrier, 1593 × 1619.
[55] Ibid. 143/4.   [56] Ibid. 9/20/97.
[57] Ibid. 9/20/94; ibid. land tax.

[58] Ibid. 9/20/97; ibid. land tax; above, manors.
[59] W.R.O., inclosure award.
[60] Ibid. tithe award.
[61] Ibid. 9, sale cat.
[62] Inf. from Mr. and Mrs. H. E. Hill, Poulton Ho.
[63] V.C.H. Wilts. ii, p. 145.
[64] Sel. Doc. Eng. Lands of Bec (Camd. 3rd ser. lxxiii), 35; Cal. Pat. 1266-72, 377; Wilts. Inq. p.m. 1242-1326 (Index Libr.), 56-7.
[65] King's Coll., Camb., Mun., acct. roll.
[66] W.R.O. 9/20/76; 9/20/91; ibid. tithe award.
[67] Ibid. 167/3; 9/20/94; ibid. land tax; tithe award.
[68] Collectanea (W.R.S. xii), 5-7; below, Preshute, econ. hist.   [69] V.C.H. Wilts. ii, pp. 162, 213-14.
[70] W.R.O. 1300/372; 1300/1840.

tury the bishop of Salisbury had rights of chase of hares and foxes in Stitchcombe, probably as an extension of his rights of chase in Ramsbury.[71]

No detail survives of the working of a demesne farm or any copyhold of Stitchcombe manor before the 18th century. In the mid 16th century Hendis farm included 20 a. of inclosed pasture and arable and probably also feeding rights on the downs.[72] Additional lands were bought and the farm included 70 a. of inclosed arable land in 1664 and 108 a. in 1680.[73] An agreement of 1703 may have completed the division of the open fields. A map of 1716 showed the whole tithing, except the downs and the forest, divided into small several fields, with those of the demesne of Stitchcombe manor, later called Stitchcombe farm, and of other holdings intermixed. Stitchcombe farm then consisted of 261 a. of arable land, 9 a. of dry meadow and 17 a. of water meadow, 40 a. of woodland, and 25 a. of pasture.[74] In 1751 there were ten copyholds and eight leaseholds, including Hendis farm. The smaller holdings had been absorbed by two larger farms by the early 19th century.[75] Folly farm, derived from Hendis, consisted of c. 200 a. in the western part of the tithing in 1838 and Stitchcombe of c. 460 a. in the eastern part. Both were principally arable, each having only c. 20 a. of downland pasture.[76] The area of grassland on each had increased slightly by 1867, and in the late 19th century arable land was probably converted to pasture in Stitchcombe as in the parish's other tithings.[77] Dairy herds were kept in the early 20th century but after 1960 both Stitchcombe and Forest Hill were arable and stock farms.[78]

There were 50 a. of wood at Stitchcombe in 1086,[79] and in the early 13th century the whole tithing lay within the boundary of Savernake forest. The tithing was disafforested north of the Marlborough–Hungerford road in 1228, except for a small triangle of land in the south-eastern corner.[80] Stitchcombe manor remained well wooded and in 1333 the keepership of its woods was leased.[81] Woodland north and south of the Marlborough–Hungerford road was part of Savernake forest in the 18th century and in the 20th. In 1838 there were c. 320 a. of woodland in the tithing. After 1939 the woods were restocked with oak and beech.[82]

In 1086 there was a mill at Stitchcombe and there may have been a fulling mill there in the 14th century.[83] The lords of Stitchcombe manor had a mill in the 16th century perhaps to be identified with Werg Mill or Stitchcombe Mill,

both of which were water-driven corn mills belonging to the manor in 1704.[84] Stitchcombe Mill was extensively repaired c. 1825 but in 1867 the building, containing two pairs of stones, was in poor condition.[85] It was demolished before 1895.[86] Werg Mill also had two pairs of stones, driven by a new 9-ft. wheel in 1867. The mill may have remained in use until the 1920s.[87]

LOCAL GOVERNMENT. Mildenhall tithing was exempt from hundred jurisdiction in 1249,[88] although in 1275 it was said that suit had been withdrawn from the hundred courts c. 1260.[89] There was a royal prison at Mildenhall in 1265, and in 1272–3 James de Audeberg raised a gallows there.[90]

In the 15th and 16th centuries and in the early 17th a combined view of frankpledge and court was held for the lord of Mildenhall manor in spring and autumn each year. Annual courts, known as courts leet and courts baron, were held in the autumn in the 18th century. In 1512–13 and in the 1590s a tithingman was elected at the autumn court and presented breaches of the peace and of the assize. In 1592 it was agreed that the tithingman should hold while in office a plot of land near Werg bridge. In the 1630s the occupier's tenure of the land lasted more than a year and he was obliged to fill the office himself or by deputy. The tithingman was then sworn at the spring court. The homage made presentments relating to customary tenures and common husbandry at the courts in the 16th century and the early 17th. In the 1590s and later a jury presented such matters as the repair of highways and of the common pound and stocks. From 1756 a brief combined presentment was made by the homage and the jury.[91]

A court for Stitchcombe manor was held in March 1580, when the homage presented and orders were issued for the use of common pastures and for the repair of tenements.[92] Annual courts were held, usually in May, from 1742 until 1757. Customary tenants were admitted and orders made for repairs.[93]

Between 1795 and 1807 and perhaps for a longer period a house was rented by the parish to accommodate some of the poor.[94] In 1796 monthly outdoor relief was provided for 25 adults.[95] Relief was given regularly to 32 adults and occasionally to another 43 in 1802–3, when £374 was spent on the poor.[96] Expenditure fluctuated in the next 30 years; it was c. £190 in 1816 and 1834–5, £443 in 1818, and £238 in

[71] *Rot. Hund.* (Rec. Com.), ii (1), 270; above, Ramsbury, econ. hist.
[72] P.R.O., C 1/969/41–2.
[73] W.R.O. 9/20/53–4; 9/20/56.
[74] Ibid. 1300/372.
[75] Ibid. 9, estate acct. bks.; ibid. land tax.
[76] Ibid. tithe award.
[77] Ibid. 9, survey; above.
[78] Inf. from Mr. Young.
[79] *V.C.H. Wilts.* ii, p. 162.
[80] Ibid. iv. 418, 448, 450; *Close R. 1227–31,* 103–4.
[81] *Cat. Anct. D.* vi, C 6155.
[82] *Andrews and Dury, Map* (W.R.S. viii), pl. 12; W.R.O., tithe award; inf. from Forestry Com., Flowers Hill, Brislington, Bristol.
[83] *V.C.H. Wilts.* ii, p. 162; *W.A.M.* xxxiii. 395.

[84] W.R.O. 9, misc. estate papers, ct. papers; ibid. bishop, glebe terrier, 1704.
[85] Ibid. 9, misc. estate papers; 9, survey, 1867.
[86] W.A.S. Libr., Soames's notes.
[87] W.R.O. 9, survey, 1867; *Kelly's Dir. Wilts.* (1920, 1923).
[88] *Crown Pleas, 1249* (W.R.S. xvi), pp. 62, 224.
[89] *Rot. Hund.* (Rec. Com.), ii (1), 270.
[90] Ibid.; *Close R. 1264–8,* 69.
[91] P.R.O., SC 6/1056/7; SC 6/1056/9–10; SC 6/1056/12; SC 2/208/64; W.R.O. 490/1536–9; 490/1541; 9, ct. bk. 1741–58.
[92] W.R.O. 9, misc. estate papers, ct. papers.
[93] Ibid. 9, ct. bk. 1741–58.
[94] Ibid. 167/10.
[95] Ibid. 167/5.
[96] *Poor Law Abstract, 1804,* 568–9.

1835–6. Mildenhall became part of Marlborough poor-law union in 1835.[97]

CHURCH. There was a church at Mildenhall in the 12th century.[98] In 1297 the advowson of the rectory was assigned with Mildenhall manor to John de Meriet and his wife Mary and it passed with the manor until 1460.[99] Between 1404 and 1422 the patronage was exercised by feoffees of Walter, Lord Hungerford.[1] After the attainder of Robert, Lord Hungerford and Moleyns (d. 1464), in 1461 the advowson was granted to Richard, duke of Gloucester, who presented in 1462.[2] It was restored to Robert's mother Margaret Hungerford, Baroness Botreaux, at whose death in 1478 it passed to her great-granddaughter Mary, Baroness Botreaux, later wife of Edward, Lord Hastings.[3] In or after 1485, however, Sir Walter Hungerford, son of Robert, Lord Hungerford (d. 1464), claimed the advowson as part of his father's entailed estates.[4] In 1486, 1487, and 1490 presentations were made by Robert's trustees. That of 1490 apparently did not take effect, perhaps because Mary, Lady Botreaux and Hastings, also claimed the advowson, and in 1491 the bishop of Salisbury presented by lapse.[5] Sir Walter presented in 1514, and after his death in 1516 his claim to the advowson presumably passed to his son Sir Edward (will proved 1522), and grandson Sir Walter Hungerford, later Lord Hungerford (d. 1540).[6] In the 1520s the union of the churches of Mildenhall and Welford (Berks.) was authorized by the pope for an incumbent of Welford[7] but the union, if it took place, was short lived. The advowson was among property allotted to Sir Walter Hungerford (d. 1540) by arbitration in 1535 and passed with Mildenhall manor until 1552.[8] A grant of the next presentation made by the queen to John Walker and others in 1546 was released by them to the Crown which presented in 1547.[9] In 1552 the advowson was granted to William Herbert, earl of Pembroke, and it passed with the Pembroke title until the late 17th century.[10] Few presentations were made by the earls. Roger Earth presented in 1575 and Gabriel Pile in 1593, both presumably by virtue of grants of a turn, and in 1630 the Crown presented on the translation of the incumbent, Walter Curle, bishop of Rochester, to Bath and Wells.[11] The

advowson was conveyed by Philip, earl of Pembroke and Montgomery, to trustees in 1675[12] and may have been sold soon afterwards. In 1684 Elizabeth Percy, countess of Northumberland, presented and in 1687 Edward and Elizabeth Ryder were patrons.[13] Charles Longueville and Henry Mompesson presented in 1727 and John Pocock, rector of Mildenhall, presented on his resignation in 1763.[14] The advowson passed to his kinsman and successor Richard Pocock, rector 1763–73, and to Richard's relict Elizabeth, who presented in 1788.[15] The patronage was divided, perhaps after her death. In 1832 George Pocock Buxton, rector of Mildenhall 1822–55, held three-fifths of the advowson, his mother, a Mrs. Buxton, a fifth, and his aunt, a Mrs. Pinnegar, a fifth. Charles Soames was patron in 1862 and was succeeded after 1867 by Charles Soames, presumably his son, rector of Mildenhall 1861–94, and the younger Charles's son Gordon, rector 1894–1934. The advowson was transferred in 1964 by Soames's executors to Miss Patricia E. G. Courtman, the patron in 1982.[16]

The rectory was of average value for a living in Marlborough deanery in both 1291 and 1535, when it was valued at £13 6s. 8d. and £18 respectively.[17] In the early 1830s the rector's average annual income, £760, was high.[18] He received tithes from the whole parish and in 1269 was also entitled to those from part of a meadow near the king's fishpond in Preshute.[19] No later reference to tithes owed from the meadow has been found. Those from Burridge warren were replaced by an annual payment of 6s. 8d. in the mid 17th century[20] and those from all the mills in the parish had also been commuted by 1705.[21] The remaining tithes were commuted and a yearly rent charge of £780 was established in 1838.[22] In 1341 the glebe formed a small manor.[23] There were 143 a. of glebe in 1671, 159 a. in 1838, and c. 130 a. in 1982.[24] There was a rectory house in 1671, perhaps that built of brick and stone which stood west of the lane leading to the church in 1776.[25] After 1862 a large new house in 18th-century style was built west of Mildenhall village.[26] A verandah on the south and west sides and an extra storey were later added to the house. The house was sold and a new one built north of the church in 1965.[27]

By will proved 1433 Thomas Poulton, bishop

[97] Poor Rate Returns, 1816–21, 189; Poor Law Com. 2nd Rep. 408–9, 559.
[98] Below.
[99] Cal. Inq. p.m. iii, p. 277; above, manors.
[1] Phillipps, Wilts. Inst. i. 36, 46, 92–3, 95–6, 110, 113.
[2] Complete Peerage, vi. 618–19; Phillipps, Wilts. Inst. i. 153.
[3] W.R.O. 490/1479; P.R.O., C 140/67, no. 40.
[4] P.R.O., C 1/139/10.
[5] Phillipps, Wilts. Inst. i. 169, 171, 174; Hist. MSS. Com. 78, Hastings, i, pp. 240, 291–2.
[6] Phillipps, Wilts. Inst. i. 191; Complete Peerage, vi. 621–5.
[7] W.R.O., bishop, reg. Campeggio, f. 7.
[8] Hist. MSS. Com. 78, Hastings, i, p. 292; above, manors.
[9] Cal. Pat. 1547–8, 192.
[10] Ibid. 1550–3, 358; Phillipps, Wilts. Inst. i. 228; ii. 10, 15; W.R.O. 212B/5652; Complete Peerage, x. 405–25.
[11] Phillipps, Wilts. Inst. i. 228, 233; ii. 10; Subscription Bk. (W.R.S. xxxii), p. 47.
[12] W.R.O. 212B/5652.
[13] Phillipps, Wilts. Inst. ii. 39; W.R.O., bishop, pet. for faculties, drafts, iii, no. 12.
[14] Phillipps, Wilts. Inst. ii. 60, 81.
[15] Ibid. 94; W.R.O., bishop, glebe terrier, 1774.
[16] Ch. Com. benefice file; inf. from Miss P. E. G. Courtman, Church Lane.
[17] Tax. Eccl. (Rec. Com.), 189; Valor Eccl. (Rec. Com.), ii. 151.
[18] Rep. Com. Eccl. Revenues, 842–3.
[19] W.R.O., bishop, glebe terrier, 1671; Close R. 1268–72, 163.
[20] P.R.O., E 134/32 Chas. II East./14.
[21] W.R.O., bishop, glebe terrier.
[22] Ibid. tithe award.
[23] Inq. Non. (Rec. Com.), 158; above, econ. hist.
[24] W.R.O., bishop, glebe terrier, 1671; ibid. tithe award; inf. from Miss Courtman.
[25] W.R.O., bishop, glebe terrier, 1671; ibid. 143/1.
[26] Ibid. bishop, pet. for faculties, bdle. 11, no. 3.
[27] Inf. from Capt. G. Stanning, Mildenhall Ho.

of Worcester, bequeathed 120 sheep to Mildenhall church for a vigil to be kept and masses to be said annually.[28]

John de Knovill, rector of Mildenhall, held two other livings and suffered sequestration of the profits of Mildenhall in 1301, probably for non-residence, and in 1319, because he had leased the rectory estate without licence.[29] Another pluralist was Richard Newport, rector 1491–1514.[30] Presentments of the 16th century reveal few serious faults in the parish: four parishioners were referred to the ecclesiastical commissioners in 1556 for detaining church goods, and quarterly sermons were not preached in 1584–5.[31] In the early 17th century incumbents were eminent pluralists and curates served the parish. Walter Curle, rector 1619–29, was elected bishop of Rochester in 1628 and held Mildenhall briefly *in commendam*.[32] Richard Steward, rector 1629–41, was later a prominent royalist exile.[33] George Morley, who was rector from 1641 until 1645 and petitioned to have the living restored in 1660, was elected bishop of Winchester in 1662.[34] Thomas Bailey, who had been intruded into the living in 1645, was ejected in 1660.[35] Most rectors from the late 17th century until the early 19th were also pluralists and often absentees. Edward Pocock, 1692–1727, and his son John, 1727–63, were both canons of Salisbury.[36] In 1783 a morning service with a sermon and an afternoon service were held each Sunday and there were additional services in Holy Week, at Whitsun, and at Christmas. Communion was celebrated at the three principal festivals.[37] In 1812 there was a fourth annual celebration of communion and the number of communicants had risen from between 20 and 30 in 1783 to between 60 and 70.[38] In 1851, on Census Sunday, 172 people attended the morning service and 163 the afternoon service but the average congregation was smaller, 125, in 1864. There were then two Sunday services and additional services at festivals and in Lent, and communion was celebrated seven times a year.[39]

The church of *ST. JOHN THE BAPTIST*, built mostly of rubble with some brick and ashlar, has a chancel, an aisled and clerestoried nave with a south porch, and a west tower. The chancel and nave were rebuilt in the late 12th century but the arcades, of which the south arcade is the earlier, probably follow the lines of earlier walls. The tower arch was probably added soon after that rebuilding and windows in the middle and lower stages of the tower, which have

an 11th-century character, may also be 12th-century. In the 13th century the west doorway and a lancet window in the south aisle were inserted, but most of the windows are of the 15th and early 16th centuries. The top storey of the tower, the clerestory, and the nave roof date from the late Middle Ages. In the early 17th century the nave roof was embellished with pendants and partly ceiled, and about the same time the coved and panelled chancel ceiling was made. Much medieval glass was destroyed during the Civil War.[40] The late 18th-century altar rails may be contemporary with the leather communion kneelers of 1796.[41] The church was restored in 1814–16 when a large window was inserted in the south clerestory and the south porch was rebuilt. The nave and aisles were refurnished in a late-Georgian Gothic style with box pews, a west gallery, and a pulpit balanced by a reading desk, all of oak.[42] Further restoration took place in 1871, 1949, and 1982.[43]

In or before 1818 the income, £1 a year, from a small piece of land near Marlborough was given for the repair of the church porch.[44] By wills proved 1821 and 1894 respectively Charles Francis, rector 1788–1821, and Charles Soames each gave £100 to be invested for the upkeep of the church. The combined income from the three charities was *c.* £6 10s. in 1905.[45] It was still used for church repairs in the 1970s.[46]

In 1553 the parish had a chalice weighing 13 oz. A paten of 1727, two chalices with paten covers of 1733, and a mug, basin, and flagon, given in 1813, 1843, and 1852 respectively, belonged to the parish in 1982.[47] There were three bells in 1553. In 1596 they were replaced by four new bells, from which five bells were cast in 1801. Those bells hung in the church in 1982.[48]

The parish registers begin in 1560. Those for marriages for the years 1644–51, 1653, and 1741, and for burials for the years 1646–52 are missing.[49]

NONCONFORMITY. Thomas Bailey, a Fifth Monarchy man, ejected from Mildenhall rectory in 1660, probably continued to preach in the area until his death in 1663.[50] A Quaker family lived in the parish in the 1660s and 1670s.[51]

EDUCATION. In 1808 some fourteen children attended a school kept by a poor woman in Mildenhall.[52] The school had been closed by

[28] *W.A.M.* xxvi. 65–6, 80.
[29] *Cal. Pat.* 1292–1301, 122; *Reg. Ghent* (Cant. & York Soc.), ii. 609, 846; *Reg. Martival* (Cant. & York Soc.), iv, p. 33.
[30] Phillipps, *Wilts. Inst.* i. 174; *W.N. & Q.* v. 83.
[31] W.R.O., bishop, detecta bks.
[32] Phillipps, *Wilts. Inst.* ii. 10; *Cal. S.P. Dom.* 1628–9, 224; P.R.O., E 134/32 Chas. II East./14.
[33] *Walker Revised*, ed. A. G. Matthews, 10.
[34] Ibid. 377–8; Hist. MSS. Com. *7th Rep., Ho. of Lords*, pp. 101, 107.
[35] *Calamy Revised*, ed. A. G. Matthews, 40.
[36] *Alum. Oxon. 1500–1714*, ii. 813; iii. 1174; *W.A.M.* xli. 129.
[37] *Vis. Queries, 1783* (W.R.S. xxvii), p. 158.
[38] Ibid.; *W.A.M.* xli. 134.

[39] P.R.O., HO 129/255/1/8/18; W.R.O., bishop, vis. queries, 1864.
[40] Aubrey, *Topog. Coll.* ed. Jackson, 339.
[41] Council for Places of Worship, survey.
[42] *W.A.M.* xli. 134; see *frontispiece*.
[43] Council for Places of Worship, survey.
[44] W.R.O. 143/6; notice in church.
[45] *Endowed Char. Wilts.* (N. Div.), 772–5.
[46] Inf. from Miss Courtman.
[47] Ibid.; Nightingale, *Wilts. Plate*, 159–60.
[48] Walters, *Wilts. Bells*, 138, 140; inf. from Miss Courtman.   [49] W.R.O. 1532/1–9.
[50] *Calamy Revised*, ed. Matthews, 40.
[51] W.R.O., bishop, chwdns.' pres. 1671, 1674; *W.N. & Q.* iii. 537; v. 226.
[52] Lamb. Palace Libr. MS. 1732.

1818 when the only provision for educating the poor was two Sunday schools and catechizing.[53] In that year, however, Charles Francis, the rector, gave land and in 1821 he bequeathed £4,000 for a school. Half the money was invested and half used to build a school and teacher's house, designed by Robert Abraham and completed in 1824. The building, in Perpendicular style, has a two-storeyed octagonal central block and a lantern roof. From alternate sides radiate single-storeyed wings, two of which were used as schoolrooms.[54] The income from investment, £100 in 1858, was used to pay a master and a mistress and for the general expenses of the school.[55] There were 28 pupils in 1833[56] and numbers rose to between 60 and 70 in the late 19th century. By 1873 the central area of the school had been divided into additional schoolrooms and in 1898 one of the original schoolrooms was enlarged. In 1906 the average attendance was 70[57] and numbers fluctuated between 50 and 75 until 1938 when they stood at 40.[58] The school was closed in 1969.[59]

CHARITIES FOR THE POOR. None known.

OGBOURNE ST. ANDREW

OGBOURNE ST. ANDREW, 2,180 ha. (5,387 a.), stretches west from the river Og across the downs north of Marlborough and Preshute.[60] An estate called Ogbourne existed c. 946[61] and in the 11th century that name was borne by several holdings near the source of the river and along its valley.[62] Most of the lands of Ogbourne west of the river became part of Ogbourne St. Andrew, known in the 12th century as Little Ogbourne and later as South Ogbourne[63] to distinguish it from Ogbourne St. George, which lay chiefly east of the Og. To the lands of Ogbourne were added those of Rockley, which formed the western part of Ogbourne St. Andrew parish. Rockley may have included much of the downland between the Ogbournes and Hackpen Hill but by 1086 it had been divided into two estates. The eastern estate became part of Ogbourne St. Andrew parish, the western became part of Preshute parish as Temple Rockley manor. Land formerly in Ogbourne may have passed to Preshute after 1086, but it is not clear when the western boundary of Ogbourne St. Andrew, presumably marking that between the two estates, was firmly established.[64]

The modern western boundary runs north and north-east from the dry valley which marks the southern extent of the parish across Temple Bottom and Dean Bottom and then turns sharply north-west to Hackpen Hill. East of the hill fort called Barbury Castle the boundary with Ogbourne St. George follows Smeathe's Ridge and crosses Coombe Down, reaching the river almost halfway between the churches of St. Andrew and St. George. East of the Og it runs along the ridge above the valley and then descends to Bay Bridge. Within the boundaries are the townships of Ogbourne St. Andrew, Ogbourne Maizey, and Rockley, and the lands of Barbury farm. The largest township, Ogbourne St. Andrew, some 2,000 a. in the mid 19th century, included lands either side of the river beside the northern boundary. Ogbourne Maizey, south and west of Ogbourne St. Andrew, then included some 1,100 a., Barbury, in the north-west corner of the parish, 590 a., and Rockley, south of Barbury and west of the Ogbournes, some 1,500 a.[65]

The downs rise steeply in the north-west corner of the parish, reaching heights of 247 m. north of Four Mile Clump and 268 m. east of Barbury Castle. The chalk which outcrops over the whole parish is covered with clay-with-flints around the earthwork. The Og valley, below 137 m., is narrowest between the villages of Ogbourne St. Andrew and Ogbourne Maizey and widens near the parish boundaries. The dry valley which extends along the southern boundary divides 2 km. west of the river. One branch leads northwards east of Rockley village, others skirt Rough Hill as Temple and Wick Bottoms. That lying east of Rockley is sometimes watered by the Hungerbourne which rises below Barbury Castle. The stream, noted by Camden in 1609, flows more frequently from a spring at Rockley House and rose every three or four years in the early 20th century. It joins the Og at Bay Bridge. Gravel has been deposited in all the valleys and there is alluvium in the wider parts of that of the Og.[66]

Although prehistoric cultivation took place on the downs in the north part of the parish,[67] the lower ground was later used for arable and most of the downland for pasture. There was some downland arable, on the clay near Barbury Castle and on the lower slopes of Coombe Down, and in

[53] Educ. of Poor Digest, 1033.
[54] Endowed Char. Wilts. (N. Div.), 771–2; Char. Com. file; see below, plate facing p. 161.
[55] Acct. of Wilts. Schs. 34.
[56] Educ. Enquiry Abstract, 1043.
[57] Acct. of Wilts. Schs. 34; P.R.O., ED 7/131; ED 21/18494.
[58] Bd. of Educ., List 21 (H.M.S.O.).
[59] Inf. from Chief Education Officer, Co. Hall, Trowbridge.
[60] This article was written in 1980. Maps used include O.S. Maps 1/50,000, sheet 173 (1974 edn.), sheet 174 (1974 edn.); 1/25,000, SU 17 (1960 edn.); 6″, Wilts. XXII (1888 and later

edns.), XXIII (1887 and later edns.), XXVIII (1889 and later edns.), XXIX (1889 and later edns.).
[61] Finberg, Early Wessex Chart. p. 88.
[62] V.C.H. Wilts. ii, pp. 119, 146, 163–4.
[63] Sel. Doc. Eng. Lands of Bec (Camd. 3rd ser. lxxiii), 20; W.R.O. 9/20/129.
[64] V.C.H. Wilts. ii, pp. 138, 142; below, manors; below, Preshute, manors.
[65] W.R.O., tithe award.
[66] Geol. Surv. Map 1″, drift, sheet 266 (1964 edn.); Rep. Marlborough Coll. Natural Hist. Soc. lxxiv. 65–8; W.A.M. xlix. 362, 492.
[67] V.C.H. Wilts. i (1), 274, 277.

the 19th century more downland was brought under the plough.[68] Few references have been found to woods in the parish before the 19th century, when fir plantations were established. Of some 60 a. of woodland in 1839, 35 a., mostly planted with young firs, were around Rockley House and north of Rockley village[69] and the distribution of wood had changed little by 1980. Hare coursing took place at Rockley c. 1800[70] and from the mid 19th century the downs east and north of that village were used as training gallops.[71]

In the 18th century the main route through the parish was the Swindon–Marlborough road, turnpiked in 1762. It entered the parish 500 m. east of Barbury Castle and ran south-east and then south to the Old Eagle, then an inn, 800 m. south-east of Rockley. Another north–south road, from Draycot Foliat to Marlborough, crossed the river a little south of the church.[72] Both were superseded by a Swindon–Marlborough road via Coate in Liddington, turnpiked in 1819, which followed the eastern bank of the Og to Bay Bridge.[73] In 1980 the two old roads survived as tracks north of the Old Eagle and of Ogbourne St. Andrew. The road from Marlborough to Wootton Bassett which ran from the Old Eagle across Rockley Down was turnpiked in 1809.[74] In the 18th and 19th centuries a road to Barbury Castle and Wroughton led north-west from that road 1 km. north of Rockley.[75] South of Barbury Castle Farm it was a track in 1980. Other tracks, most of them in the south and west parts of the parish, led from east to west across the downs in the late 18th century[76] and were still in use in the 20th century. They included the steep lane past the Old Eagle from Ogbourne Maizey to Rockley, which further west became a track leading to Top Temple in Preshute. The Swindon–Marlborough section of the Swindon, Marlborough & Andover Railway, built on the eastern slopes of the Og valley, was opened in 1881 and closed in 1964.[77]

The most notable archaeological site in the parish is the Iron-Age hill fort, Barbury Castle, the northern half of which lies in Wroughton. Near it are barrows and extensive earthworks indicating settlement continuing into historic times. The downs are generally rich in archaeological material. Late Bronze-Age earthworks and enclosures overlap the sites of field systems on Ogbourne Down and in Dean Bottom, and there are barrows on the surrounding downs. Ditches run from east to west north of Rockley and from north to south across Smeathe's Ridge and on Coombe Down. A bowl-barrow in Og-

bourne St. Andrew churchyard was re-used in Roman, Pagan Saxon, and medieval times.[78]

If the tax assessments of the constituent townships of Ogbourne St. Andrew are considered together, the parish appears to have been one of the most highly rated in Selkley hundred in 1334. Similarly the total of 172 poll-tax payers in the parish in 1377 suggests a larger population than the average.[79] Tax assessments of the 16th century also were a little higher than average.[80] In the 1660s, however, there was plague in the parish and the inhabitants petitioned for exemption from a levy for the relief of Salisbury because of their own sufferings.[81] There were 434 inhabitants in 1801 and the population had risen to 511 by 1841. It had dropped to 386 by 1891 but was again above 400 in the early 20th century. Numbers declined from 422 in 1931 to 275 in 1971.[82]

OGBOURNE ST. ANDREW village stands on the west bank of the Og 1 km. south of the parish boundary. The main street, some 400 m. long, was part of the road from Marlborough to Draycot Foliat.[83] It is joined to the Swindon–Marlborough road, to which it is roughly parallel, by lanes which turn sharply east across the river at each end of the street. In 1377 Ogbourne St. Andrew was the most populous settlement in the parish.[84] Tax assessments of the 16th century were moderate or low compared with those of other communities in the hundred.[85] The original centre of the village may have been west of the street, where the church stands on rising ground. Beside the street are cottages of 17th-century origin; most are timber-framed with brick nogging, partly replaced by sarsen. Two cottages on the west side of the street have walls partly of banded flint and stone with ashlar quoins. Substantial houses of the 18th and 19th centuries, standing opposite the lane which leads past the church, were at some time part of the principal farmstead.[86] The new turnpike road drew settlement eastward in the 19th century and infilling took place along the southern lane from the street and along the west side of the main road between Ogbourne St. Andrew and Ogbourne Maizey.[87] In 1841 the population was 166;[88] it may have increased slightly as building continued in the mid and late 19th century. Buildings of that period included the Baptist chapel, north of the southern lane, Tresco House, then the vicarage house, beside the road,[89] and the Wheatsheaf inn at the junction of the road and the lane.[90] Houses, including some council houses, were built east of the road in the 20th century.

[68] Below, econ. hist.
[69] W.R.O., tithe award.
[70] V.C.H. Berks. ii. 298.
[71] Below, econ. hist.
[72] V.C.H. Wilts. iv. 263, 270; Andrews and Dury, Map (W.R.S. viii), pls. 12, 15.
[73] V.C.H. Wilts. iv. 263; Rep. Marlborough Coll. Natural Hist. Soc. lxxiv. 47.
[74] V.C.H. Wilts. iv. 263.
[75] Andrews and Dury, Map (W.R.S. viii), pls. 12, 14–15; W.R.O., tithe award.
[76] Andrews and Dury, Map (W.R.S. viii), pls. 12, 14–15.
[77] V.C.H. Wilts. iv. 289; below, Preshute, introduction.
[78] V.C.H. Wilts. i (1), 94, 142, 186, 210, 224, 258, 286; i (2), 348–9.

[79] Ibid. iv. 301, 310.
[80] Taxation Lists (W.R.S. x), 23, 102.
[81] Hist. MSS. Com. 55, Var. Coll. i, p. 148.
[82] V.C.H. Wilts. iv. 355; Census, 1971.
[83] Andrews and Dury, Map (W.R.S. viii), pl. 12.
[84] V.C.H. Wilts. iv. 310.
[85] Taxation Lists (W.R.S. x), 23, 102.
[86] King's Coll., Camb., Mun., survey, 1751; W.R.O., tithe award.
[87] Andrews and Dury, Map (W.R.S. viii), pls. 12, 15; O.S. Map 1″, sheet 34 (1828 edn.).
[88] P.R.O., HO 107/1185.
[89] O.S. Map 6″, Wilts. XXIX (1889 edn.); below, church, prot. nonconf.
[90] Kelly's Dir. Wilts. (1855).

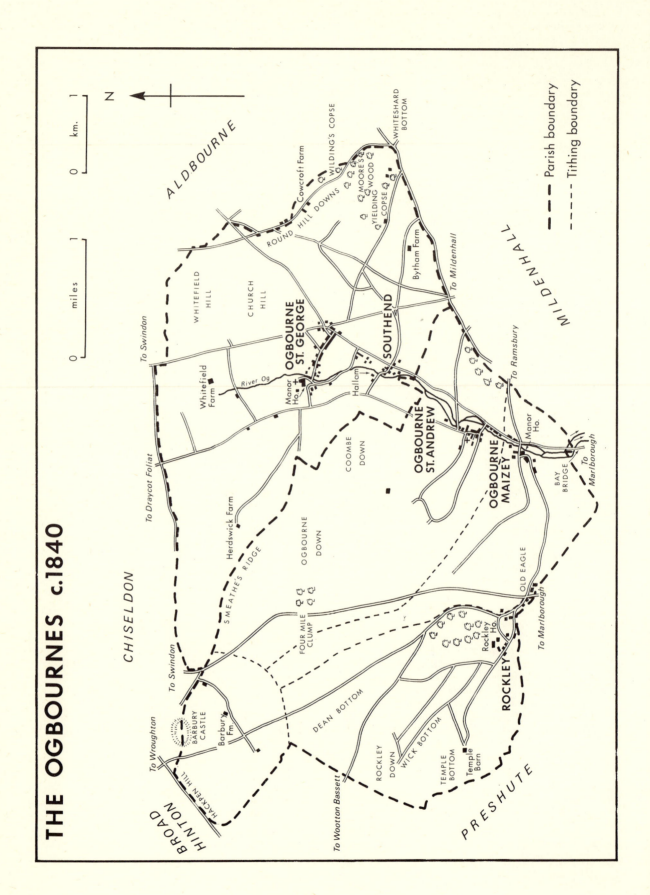

THE OGBOURNES c.1840

Other 20th-century buildings include a new farmhouse on the lane leading past the church towards Ogbourne Down, and houses beside the northern lane leading from the street.

There is little evidence that Barbury, on the downs 500 m. south of Barbury Castle, was ever much more than a single farmstead.[91] In 1841 it had a population of 44 including an innkeeper.[92] In 1980 Barbury Castle Farm, a building of the 18th century or earlier, was approached by road from Wroughton.

OGBOURNE MAIZEY stands west of the Og in the narrowest part of the river valley. In the Middle Ages it was a smaller settlement than Ogbourne St. Andrew; it was assessed for tax at 34s. in 1334 and had 50 poll-tax payers in 1377.[93] Tax assessments of the 16th century show it to have been one of the poorer communities of the hundred.[94] The older houses, including some 17th-century cottages, stand beside the lane to Rockley, which turns sharply south and west in the village. South of the lane and immediately west of the bridge over the Og is Ogbourne Maizey Manor. In the late 18th century the village was similar in size to Ogbourne St. Andrew and extended northwards beside the later Swindon–Marlborough road so that the two villages merged.[95] In 1841 the population of Ogbourne Maizey was 173 and it was the largest settlement in the parish.[96] New farm buildings south of the village were linked with the Swindon–Marlborough road by a bridge in the late 19th century[97] and c. 1900 the Bonita stables were built on steeply rising ground beside the lane to Rockley.[98] West of the village Maisey Farm was built on the crest of a hill 800 m. along the lane c. 1930.[99] Since the Second World War cottages have been demolished, there has been little new building, and the extent of the village in the 1970s was similar to that of the late 18th century.[1]

ROCKLEY. When Rockley lay close to a major north–south route, the village may have been more important than in the 20th century. It was of sufficient substance to have been appointed the meeting place for the hundred court of Dunworth in the 13th century, although that appointment, which required the men of Dunworth to travel long distances, was one of several complaints laid against the deputy sheriff responsible.[2] In both the 14th and the 16th century Rockley was more highly rated for taxation than Ogbourne St. Andrew, perhaps because assess-

ments of wealthy individuals were included.[3] There were 40 poll-tax payers in 1377.[4] The village was similar in size to Ogbourne St. Andrew and Ogbourne Maizey in the late 18th century.[5] It declined after the eastern Swindon–Marlborough road was turnpiked[6] but the population was still 128 in 1841.[7] The Old Eagle at the junction of the former Swindon–Marlborough road and the road from Marlborough to Wootton Bassett has retained its name but was no longer in use as an inn in the mid 19th century.[8] There were several houses of the 19th and 20th centuries at the junction in 1980. The main part of the village is west of the road from Marlborough to Wootton Bassett, 2.5 km. west of Ogbourne Maizey in the valley watered intermittently by the Hungerbourne. Rockley House, Rockley Farm, and cottages of the 18th century are grouped north of a curving drive which was part of the road through the village until the late 18th century. In 1776 a new road was built 100 m. further south,[9] along which stand buildings mainly of the 19th century. They include the former school, the chapel, farm buildings, and cottages, one group of which bears the date 1897. Some 2 km. north-west of Rockley a white horse was cut in the chalk west of the road from Marlborough to Wootton Bassett, probably in the early 19th century. It became overgrown and was rediscovered in 1947.[10]

MANORS AND OTHER ESTATES. Lands at Ogbourne devised by the ealdorman Athelwold to his brother Edric in 946–7 may have been in Ogbourne St. George or Ogbourne St. Andrew or both.[11]

The estate at Ogbourne held by Earl Harold in 1066 and by Miles Crispin in 1086 was probably the later manor of *OGBOURNE ST. ANDREW*.[12] On Miles's death it passed to his wife Maud of Wallingford.[13] The overlordship of the manor was part of the honor of Wallingford in 1242–3.[14] It descended with the honor until 1540 and thereafter with the honor of Ewelme.[15]

Between 1107 and 1133 Maud of Wallingford and Brian FitzCount, her second husband, gave the estate to provide clothing for the monks of the abbey of Bec-Hellouin (Eure).[16] A daughter house of Bec, Ogbourne priory, was established, probably at Ogbourne St. George, and endowed with the manor. The priory and manor were taken into royal keeping at various times in the 14th century during the wars with France.[17] In

[91] Below, econ. hist.; map of Barbury Down farm by N. Hill, 1752, temporarily deposited in W.R.O.
[92] P.R.O., HO 107/1185.
[93] V.C.H. Wilts. iv. 301, 310.
[94] Taxation Lists (W.R.S. x), 22, 102.
[95] Andrews and Dury, Map (W.R.S. viii), pls. 12, 15.
[96] P.R.O., HO 107/1185.
[97] W.R.O., tithe award; O.S. Map 6″, Wilts. XXVIII (1889 edn.).
[98] Kelly's Dir. Wilts. (1898, 1903).
[99] Inf. from Mr. R. Curnick, Maisey Farm.
[1] Inf. from Mr. A. C. Cooper, Ogbourne Maizey Manor; O.S. Map 1/50,000, sheet 173 (1974 edn.); Andrews and Dury, Map (W.R.S. viii), pls. 12, 15.
[2] Rot. Hund. (Rec. Com.), ii (1), 256; V.C.H. Wilts. v. 13.
[3] V.C.H. Wilts. iv. 301; Taxation Lists (W.R.S. x), 22, 101.

[4] V.C.H. Wilts. iv. 310.
[5] Andrews and Dury, Map (W.R.S. viii), pl. 12.
[6] O.S. Map 1″, sheet 34 (1828 edn.).
[7] P.R.O., HO 107/1185.
[8] Rep. Marlborough Coll. Natural Hist. Soc. lxxiv. 47; W.R.O., tithe award; Kelly's Dir. Wilts. (1848).
[9] W.R.O., Q. Sess. enrolled deeds, diversion of highways, no. 8.
[10] W.A.M. lii. 396; lx. 183–4.
[11] Finberg, Early Wessex Chart. p. 88.
[12] V.C.H. Wilts. ii, pp. 146, 200 n.
[13] Ibid. p. 146 n.; Sel. Doc. Eng. Lands of Bec (Camd. 3rd ser. lxxiii), 20.   [14] Bk. of Fees, ii. 149.
[15] V.C.H. Berks. iii. 523–31.
[16] Sel. Doc. Eng. Lands of Bec (Camd. 3rd ser. lxxiii), 20.
[17] V.C.H. Wilts. iii. 395; below, Ogbourne St. Geo., introduction.

1404 the keeping of the priory was granted to William de St. Vaast (d. 1404 or 1405), the last prior, Thomas Langley, dean of York, and John, duke of Bedford,[18] who was licensed to acquire the estates of the priory in 1410.[19] At the duke's death in 1435 Ogbourne St. Andrew reverted to the Crown and in 1437 it was granted to John St. Lo for life.[20] The reversion was granted to Cambridge University in 1439[21] but was restored to the Crown in 1441. In that year it was included in the foundation grant to the college of St. Nicholas, later King's College, Cambridge.[22] Edward IV resumed the estates granted by his predecessor and omitted Ogbourne St. Andrew from those restored to the college in 1461. In 1462, presumably after the death of John St. Lo, he granted the manor to the London Charterhouse.[23] A commission was appointed by parliament in 1490 to determine the title to lands claimed by King's College and subject to dispute. Probably as a result of its findings, Ogbourne St. Andrew was held c. 1500 by the college, which paid a rent to the Charterhouse.[24] A similar arrangement was made in 1504 or 1505[25] and in 1510 the college was licensed to pay £33 6s. 8d. yearly to the Charterhouse for the manors of Ogbourne St. Andrew and Ogbourne St. George.[26] The rent was extinguished at the Dissolution.[27] King's College sold its lands in Ogbourne St. Andrew in 1927. Poughcombe farm, some 405 a., was bought by W. H. Box who sold it to W. W. Saunders in 1928.[28] It was sold again in 1942 and 1959. In 1963 Mr. N. C. Naumann bought the farm, which he sold in 1977 to Hambro's Bank Executor Trustee Co. Ltd.[29] Upper Poughcombe, later New Barn, farm, 450 a., was bought in 1928 by Swindon corporation and sold to S. Maundrell c. 1935. It remained in the Maundrell family in 1980.[30]

Maud of Wallingford's gift of Ogbourne St. Andrew church to the abbey of Bec was confirmed c. 1148.[31] In 1192 or 1193 the abbey was licensed to appropriate the church[32] which became part of the endowment of the prebend of Ogbourne established in Salisbury cathedral for the abbot of Bec in 1208.[33] The prebendal estate, which included tithes and glebe in 1341 but later only tithes, passed with Ogbourne St. Andrew manor to John, duke of Bedford,[34] who granted it to the dean and canons of St. George's chapel, Windsor, in 1421.[35] The canons' tithes were commuted in 1839.[36]

Before 1147 Maud of Wallingford granted to her kinsman Richard 1 yardland in Ogbourne once held by his uncle Turga.[37] That may have been the basis of a second estate at Ogbourne St. Andrew held of the honor of Wallingford. Ralph Foliot (d. c. 1204) held an estate in Ogbourne of the honor in 1196.[38] He was succeeded by his brother Henry (d. 1233)[39] and by Henry's son Sir Sampson Foliot, mesne lord in 1242–3 and 1275.[40] After 1281 the mesne lordship passed with the manor of Draycot in Draycot Foliat to Henry Tyeys, Baron Tyeys (d. 1308).[41] On the execution of Henry's son Henry, Baron Tyeys, in 1321 it may have been forfeited to the Crown.[42] In 1231 William of Stoke had lands in one of the Ogbournes[43] and in 1242–3 he and Nicholas Crook held ½ knight's fee in Ogbourne St. Andrew of Sir Sampson Foliot.[44] By 1275 the estate had passed to Ingram de Waleys[45] who was succeeded by his son John in 1304.[46] It has not been traced further.

In 1780 Samuel Hawkes had a freehold estate of some 850 a. Its origins are obscure but it was probably formed by the consolidation and enfranchisement of copyholds of Ogbourne St. Andrew manor.[47] The estate was held c. 1796 by John Ward, husband of Hawkes's daughter Hannah.[48] It passed to their son T. R. Ward (fl. 1838) and grandson M. F. Ward (d. 1915).[49] In the 1930s the estate was bought by Whatley Bros.,[50] and C. W. Whatley sold it to Mr. R. W. Margesson in 1946. In 1978 Mr. Margesson sold it as Ogbourne St. Andrew and Ogbourne Down farms to the Cadbury Schweppes pension fund.[51]

The endowments of a chantry founded in or before the late 14th century in Ogbourne St. George church[52] included 1 yardland and common pasture in Ogbourne St. Andrew in 1549.[53] The lands were sold by the Crown in 1550.[54]

The gift by Geoffrey son of Pain of lands at Barbury to the abbey of St. Georges de Boscherville near Rouen was confirmed in 1112–13.[55] The estate became part of the endowment of a priory founded at Avebury. After the suppression of that house, the lands passed in 1411 to Fotheringhay college (Northants.) and in 1545 to the Crown.[56] In 1547 the manor of *BARBURY*

[18] *V.C.H. Wilts.* iii. 395; *Cal. Pat.* 1401–5, 466.
[19] *Cal. Pat.* 1408–13, 209.
[20] Ibid. 1436–41, 92, 126; P.R.O., C 139/77, no. 36.
[21] *Cal. Pat.* 1436–41, 296.
[22] Ibid. 522; *V.C.H. Cambs.* iii. 377.
[23] *V.C.H. Cambs.* iii. 379–80; *Cal. Pat.* 1461–7, 141.
[24] *V.C.H. Cambs.* iii. 380; *V.C.H. Mdx.* i. 161.
[25] King's Coll. Mun., D. 41.
[26] *L. & P. Hen. VIII,* i (1), p. 319.
[27] Ibid. xiv (2), pp. 99, 347.
[28] W.A.S. Libr., sale cat. xx, no. 1; Swindon corp. rec., waterworks and fire brigade cttee. file 60.
[29] Inf. from Mr. Naumann, Poughcombe Farm.
[30] Swindon corp. rec., waterworks and fire brigade cttee. files 314, 869; local inf.
[31] A. A. Porée, *Histoire de l'Abbaye du Bec,* i. 461.
[32] *Sel. Doc. Eng. Lands of Bec* (Camd. 3rd ser. lxxiii), 4.
[33] *Reg. St. Osmund* (Rolls Ser.), i. 189–90.
[34] Above; *Inq. Non.* (Rec. Com.), 158; *W.A.M.* xli. 111–12.
[35] *Cat. MSS. D. & C. Windsor,* ed. J. N. Dalton, 15.
[36] W.R.O., tithe award.

[37] *Sel. Doc. Eng. Lands of Bec* (Camd. 3rd ser. lxxiii), 24.
[38] *Boarstall Cart.* (Oxf. Hist. Soc. lxxxviii), 313.
[39] Ibid.
[40] Ibid.; *Bk. of Fees,* ii. 749; *Rot. Hund.* (Rec. Com.), ii (1), 269.
[41] *V.C.H. Wilts.* ix. 44–5; *Cal. Inq. p.m.* iii, pp. 466–7, 480; iv, pp. 144–5. [42] *V.C.H. Wilts.* ix. 45.
[43] *Cur. Reg. R.* xiv, p. 266.
[44] *Bk. of Fees,* ii. 749.
[45] *Rot. Hund.* (Rec. Com.), ii (1), 269.
[46] *Cal. Inq. p.m.* iv, pp. 144–5.
[47] W.R.O., inclosure award; below, econ. hist.
[48] W.R.O., land tax; King's Coll. Mun., survey, 1751.
[49] Burke, *Land. Gent.* (1937), 2360–1; W.R.O., tithe award; ibid. 1459/2.
[50] *Kelly's Dir. Wilts.* (1931, 1935).
[51] Inf. from Mr. R. W. Margesson, Eastholme.
[52] Below, Ogbourne St. Geo., church.
[53] P.R.O., E 301/58, f. 22v.
[54] Ibid. E 318/Box 25/1423.
[55] *Reg. Regum Anglo-Norm.* ii, app. no. lxxv.
[56] Above, Avebury, manors.

LEES was granted to Sir William Sharington (d. 1553).[57] Sharington was succeeded by his brother Henry (d. 1581).[58] The manor passed with that of Liddington to Henry's daughter Olive (d. 1646), wife of John Talbot, and to her grandson Sharington Talbot (d. 1677), whose son Sir John Talbot sold it in 1709 to John Churchill, duke of Marlborough.[59] It descended with the Marlborough title until 1877 when Barbury Castle farm was sold to Sir Henry Meux, Bt.[60] Meux was succeeded in 1883 by his son Sir Henry Bruce Meux (d. 1900),[61] whose relict sold the farm in 1906.[62] Members of the Redman family held the farm until 1936 when it was bought by J. W. W. Bridges. It was sold in 1942 to T. A. Sutton who was succeeded in 1945 by his son Mr. J. A. Sutton. Mr. Sutton was owner with his son Mr. C. A. Sutton in 1980. In 1979 some 94 a. were sold to Chiseldon Grain Dryers.[63]

Harding had lands at Ogbourne in 1066 and 1086. In 1086 Turchil held another estate there in which he had succeeded his father.[64] In 1242–3 Richard de Clare, earl of Gloucester and Hertford (d. 1262), held two estates in Ogbourne Maizey, possibly derived from those holdings.[65] They passed with the titles to Gilbert de Clare, earl of Gloucester and Hertford, on whose death in 1314 the overlordships passed to the Crown.[66] Both were held by William Poulton in 1428.[67] That of one estate belonged to the duchy of Lancaster in 1405 and to Philip Wroughton in 1462.[68] In 1242–3 Robert Marmium was mesne lord of that estate.[69]

The heirs of Robert de Maizey held *OGBOURNE MAIZEY* manor of Robert Marmium in 1242–3 and 1291.[70] In 1370 the manor was conveyed by William of Mere and his wife Catherine to William of Clyffe.[71] At his death in 1404 Peter Courteney held it in the right of his wife Margaret, daughter of John Clyvedon.[72] Margaret was succeeded in 1411 by her grandson William de Botreaux, Lord Botreaux.[73] On his death in 1462 the manor passed to his daughter Margaret, Baroness Botreaux, relict of Robert Hungerford, Lord Hungerford (d. 1459).[74] In 1469 that Margaret's granddaughter Frideswide Hungerford quitclaimed a share in the manor to Nicholas Hall.[75] The entire manor passed with Hall's manor of Bradford-on-Avon. Nicholas Hall (d. 1478) was succeeded by his sons Henry

(fl. 1481) and Thomas (d. 1515).[76] The manor passed to Thomas's son William (d. 1550) and grandson Thomas Hall (d. before 1577), whose son John sold it in 1593 to John Cornwall.[77] After Cornwall's death in 1611[78] it passed to his daughter Bridget (fl. 1629),[79] who was succeeded in or before 1638 by her son Sir William Master (d. 1662).[80] In 1712 the manor was held by Philip Ballard who sold it to John Pearce in 1717.[81] Pearce sold it in 1722 to Richard Stokes (d. 1723), whose relict Judith held it in 1740.[82] Their daughter Judith sold it to John Lydiard in 1743. Lydiard was succeeded in 1763 by his grandson the Revd. William Stratton Lydiard[83] who sold the manor in 1765 to George Spencer, duke of Marlborough.[84] It descended with the Marlborough title until 1820 when it was bought by Sir Hugh Smyth, Bt. In 1824 Smyth was succeeded by his brother Sir John (d. 1849).[85] In 1856 the manor was sold to John Tanner[86] who devised it by will proved 1859 to his son R. P. Tanner.[87] In 1893 it was bought by Frederick Lyneham who sold it before 1903 to George Edwardes, impresario of the Gaiety theatre in Aldwych, Westminster. On Edwardes's death in 1915[88] his estate was divided between his daughters Dorothy and Nora. In 1948 the manor house and 550 a. were bought from Dorothy, wife of Cuthbert Sherbrooke, by Mr. A. C. Cooper, owner of the house and some 200 a. in 1980. In 1950 Mr. Cooper sold Maisey farm, 330 a., to Mr. Robert Curnick, the owner in 1980. Nora's portion was dispersed.[89]

Ogbourne Maizey Manor was built of banded sarsen and knapped flint with later additions in brick. There is a long main range with a central pedimented doorcase dated 1636.[90] A short back range formerly housed the kitchen. Many original stone-mullioned windows and some panelling survive but in the early 18th century the interior of the central part of the house was altered, a new staircase built, and some sash windows introduced. Extensive additions, which now house kitchens and service rooms, were made at the back in the 19th century.

The earl of Gloucester and Hertford's other estate at Ogbourne became the manor of *EAST HAYES*. It was held by Bartholomew de Emneberg in 1242–3[91] and by Ellis Cotel in 1275.[92] The manor had passed to Walter Blake by

[57] *L. & P. Hen. VIII*, xx (2), p. 216; P.R.O., C 142/101, no. 121.
[58] P.R.O., C 142/193, no. 91.
[59] *V.C.H. Wilts.* ix. 67; N.R.A. list, Marlborough deeds.
[60] *Complete Peerage*; W.A.S. Libr., sale cat. iii, no. 38; W.R.O. 106/2.
[61] Burke, *Peerage* (1904), 1069.
[62] W.R.O. 106/2.
[63] Inf. from Mr. J. A. Sutton, Badbury Wick Ho., Chiseldon.
[64] *V.C.H. Wilts.* ii, pp. 163–4.
[65] *Bk. of Fees*, ii. 149; *Complete Peerage*, v. 701.
[66] *Complete Peerage*, s.v. Gloucester; *Rot. Hund.* (Rec. Com.), ii (1), 269; *Cal. Inq. p.m.* iii, p. 250.
[67] *Feud. Aids*, v. 269.
[68] *Cal. Close*, 1402–5, 440; P.R.O., C 140/7, no. 15.
[69] *Bk. of Fees*, ii. 749.
[70] Ibid.; *Cal. Inq. p.m.* iii, p. 250.
[71] *Feet of F.* 1327–77 (W.R.S. xxix), pp. 137–8.
[72] P.R.O., C 137/50, no. 38.
[73] *Cal. Close*, 1402–5, 440; P.R.O., C 137/86, no. 30.
[74] P.R.O., C 140/7, no. 15; *Complete Peerage*, vi. 618.

[75] *Cal. Close*, 1468–76, pp. 59–60; *Complete Peerage*, vi. 618.
[76] *V.C.H. Wilts.* vii. 14–15; P.R.O., C 140/66, no. 33.
[77] P.R.O., C 142/94, no. 90; C 2/Jas. I/H 2/8; ibid. CP 25(2)/242/35 Eliz. I East.
[78] Ibid. C 142/315, no. 164.
[79] Ibid. C 2/Jas. I/G 6/11; W.R.O. 9/20/52.
[80] W.R.O. 9/20/52; Burke, *Land. Gent.* (1937), 1554.
[81] W.R.O. 212B/5150; 212B/5152.
[82] Ibid. 212B/16; 9/20/139; *W.N. & Q.* vi. 49.
[83] W.R.O. 403/34.
[84] P.R.O., CP 25(2)/1445/5 Geo. III East.
[85] *Complete Peerage*, s.v. Marlborough; W.R.O. 403/34–5; Burke, *Land. Gent.* (1855), 1113.
[86] W.R.O. 403/51.
[87] Ibid. 9/20/142.
[88] W.A.S. Libr., sale cat. i, no. 16; *Kelly's Dir. Wilts.* (1898, 1903); *Oxf. Companion to the Theatre*, ed. P. M. Hartnoll, 270, 359–60.
[89] Inf. from Mr. A. C. Cooper, Ogbourne Maizey Manor.
[90] See plate facing p. 97.
[91] *Bk. of Fees*, ii. 749.
[92] *Rot. Hund.* (Rec. Com.), ii (1), 269.

1316 and to Thomas Blake by 1428 when Thomas Seymour was named as a former holder.[93] John Blake was succeeded by his son William (d. *c.* 1550) and grandson William Blake. The younger William's relict Thomasine held the manor until her death *c.* 1573. The reversion passed to Nicholas Shipreve and Ralph Crook, nephew and grandnephew of the elder William.[94] William Goddard (d. 1603) bought Crook's reversionary interest in 1561 and Shipreve's moiety of the manor in 1573.[95] He was succeeded by his sons William (d. 1604), John (d. 1635), and Vincent (d. *c.* 1644),[96] and by Thomas Goddard, probably Vincent's nephew. By will dated 1653 Thomas devised the manor to Elizabeth Smith and Lucy Clarke, daughters of John Goddard (d. 1635), for life with reversion to his kinsman Edward Goddard of Hartham in Corsham. Edward inherited East Hayes in or before 1660 and was succeeded in 1676 by his son Edward (d. 1679).[97] The manor passed to that Edward's son John (d. before 1729) and granddaughter Elizabeth Goddard. Elizabeth, who married her cousin Edmund Goddard, sold the manor to William Lydiard in 1740. In 1760 Lydiard's son the Revd. William Stratton Lydiard inherited it[98] and thereafter it passed with Ogbourne Maizey manor.

Between 1449 and 1475 Isabel Bird endowed a chantry dedicated to St. Catherine in St. Peter's church, Marlborough, with a messuage in Ogbourne Maizey.[99] A messuage and 1 yardland, parcel of the chantry, were sold by the Crown in 1557[1] and in 1558 were bought by Robert Drewe (d. 1575).[2] Nicholas Drewe (d. 1589) devised the lands to his wife Joan and daughters Joan, Dorothy, and Anne in succession.[3] The daughters, however, held them jointly. The three portions were acquired by John Hurlebatt, husband of the younger Joan, by inheritance or purchase and were sold by him to Thomas Goddard in 1614. The lands were then absorbed into East Hayes manor.[4]

The hospital of St. John the Baptist in Marlborough received 10*s.* rent for lands in Ogbourne St. Andrew in 1535.[5] The land passed to the Crown at the Dissolution and was granted to the mayor and burgesses of Marlborough in 1550 as part of the endowment of a grammar school there.[6] The holding, 26 a. in Ogbourne Maizey, was sold in 1650.[7]

Alfred of Marlborough held *ROCKLEY* in 1086.[8] The overlordship passed in the Tregoze family with the manor of Lydiard Tregoze and in 1302 it was part of the moiety of John Tregoze's estate allotted to Sir William de Grandison and his wife Sibyl.[9] Grandison (d. 1336) was succeeded by his sons Sir Peter (d. 1358) and John, bishop of Exeter.[10] In 1366 the bishop conveyed all his knights' fees in Wiltshire to Sir John Montagu.[11] Montagu was succeeded in 1390 by his son Sir John, later earl of Salisbury (d. 1400).[12] In 1538 a rent was paid for Rockley to Margaret Pole, countess of Salisbury.[13]

Hugh of Kilpeck had a house at Rockley in 1222[14] and held the manor of Rockley in 1242–3.[15] He died in or before 1244 when the manor was granted to his relict Mazire as part of her portion.[16] In 1258, probably on Mazire's death, Hugh's estates were divided and Rockley was allotted to his daughter Isabel, wife of William Walerand, on payment of a rent to her sister Joan, wife of Philip Marmium.[17] Maud de Cauntelo held Rockley, perhaps as intermediate lord, in 1255.[18] Her grandson George de Cauntelo held the manor in 1268.[19] He was succeeded in 1274 by his sister Millicent, wife of Eudes de la Zouche.[20] In 1285 Millicent granted the manor to Elizabeth de la Zouche, perhaps her daughter, in return for an annuity.[21] Before 1301 Rockley passed to Nicholas Poyntz (d. *c.* 1311), who was succeeded by his son Sir Hugh (d. 1337).[22] Sir Hugh's son Nicholas conveyed it in 1351 to Sir Robert Russell (fl. 1395).[23] In 1397 Sir Ives FitzWarren and others, perhaps Russell's trustees, granted a moiety of the manor to Gilbert Newburgh and his wife Amice.[24] John Newburgh held the other moiety in 1412[25] and the whole manor in 1428.[26] Newburgh or a descendant of the same name was succeeded in 1483 by a grandson John Newburgh.[27] On the younger John's death in 1486 the manor passed to his brother Sir Roger (fl. 1494).[28] It may have been sold in 1502[29] and in or before 1509 it passed to Simon Green, whose son William inherited it in 1511.[30] In 1604 John Green, grandson and heir of Matthew Green, sold the manor to William Jones (d. 1611).[31] It passed to William's grandson

[93] *Feud. Aids*, v. 206, 269.
[94] P.R.O., REQ 2/189/60. REQ 2/121/46 gives a different, shorter, acct. of the descent.
[95] Ibid. CP 25(2)/239/3 & 4 Eliz. I Mich.; B.L. Add. Ch. 24441.
[96] *Wilts. Inq. p.m.* 1625–49 (Index Libr.), 186–7; P.R.O., C 6/48/52; W.R.O. 130/41.
[97] *Wilts. Inq. p.m.* 1625–49 (Index Libr.), 186–7; P.R.O., C 6/182/21; Burke, *Commoners* (1833–8), iv. 328–9; W.R.O. 130/41.
[98] W.R.O. 403/34.
[99] *Cal. Pat.* 1446–52, 301; *W.A.M.* xxxvi. 564; below, Marlborough, churches.
[1] P.R.O., E 318/Box 40/2148.
[2] W.R.O. 130/41; *W.N. & Q.* v. 314.
[3] W.R.O. 130/41.
[4] Ibid. 212B/5146.
[5] *Valor Eccl.* (Rec. Com.), ii. 147.
[6] *V.C.H. Wilts.* iii. 342; *Cal. Pat.* 1549–51, 226.
[7] A. R. Stedman, *Hist. Marlborough Grammar Sch.* (Devizes, priv. print. [1946]), facing p. 104.
[8] *V.C.H. Wilts.* ii, p. 142.
[9] Ibid. ix. 78; *Cal. Close*, 1296–1302, 562.
[10] *Cal. Inq. p.m.* vii, p. 460; x, p. 347.
[11] *Cal. Pat.* 1364–7, 312.
[12] *Cal. Inq. p.m.* xvi, p. 337; *Complete Peerage*, xi. 391–3.

[13] *L. & P. Hen. VIII*, xiii (1), p. 330.
[14] *Rot. Litt. Claus.* (Rec. Com.), i. 491.
[15] *Bk. of Fees*, ii. 749.
[16] *Close R.* 1237–47, 155.
[17] P.R.O., CP 25(1)/283/14, no. 28.
[18] *Rot. Hund.* (Rec. Com.), ii (1), 234.
[19] *Close R.* 1264–8, 487–8; Burke, *Extinct Peerages*, i. 101.
[20] *Wilts. Inq. p.m.* 1242–1326 (Index Libr.), 81–2; *Cal. Fine R.* 1272–1307, 17–18.
[21] *Feet of F.* 1272–1327 (W.R.S. i), p. 25.
[22] *Cal. Inq. p.m.* iii, p. 455; v, p. 346; viii, pp. 72–3.
[23] *Feet of F.* 1327–77 (W.R.S. xxix), p. 96; P.R.O., C 136/84, no. 31.
[24] P.R.O., CP 25(1)/290/57, no. 295.
[25] *Feud. Aids*, vi. 425, 539.
[26] Ibid. v. 269.
[27] P.R.O., C 141/4, no. 41.
[28] *Cal. Inq. p.m. Hen. VII*, i, p. 18; P.R.O., SC 6/Hen. VII/115.
[29] P.R.O., CP 25(1)/257/66, no. 30.
[30] *L. & P. Hen. VIII*, i (1), p. 266; P.R.O., C 142/25, no. 16.
[31] P.R.O., CP 25(2)/369/2 Jas. I Mich.; ibid. C 142/680, no. 30.

MARLBOROUGH

St. Mary's church in 1803

PRESHUTE

St. George's church in 1803

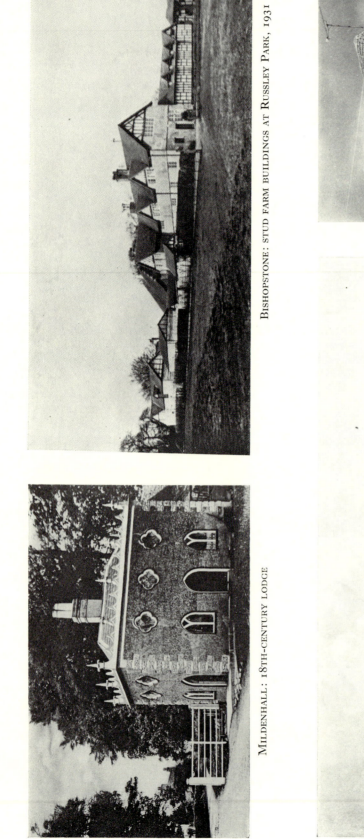

BISHOPSTONE: STUD FARM BUILDINGS AT RUSSLEY PARK, 1931

MILDENHALL: 18TH-CENTURY LODGE

ALDBOURNE: EARLY 19TH-CENTURY TOLLHOUSE

PRESHUTE: THE STABLE YARD OF MANTON HOUSE, c. 1895

William Jones (d. 1632) and great-grandson John Jones (fl. 1649).[32] In 1674 the manor was sold to William Grinfield (fl. 1685).[33] By will dated 1742 Edward Grinfield devised it to his son Steddy who sold it to the Revd. William Stratton Lydiard in 1775.[34] It passed with Ogbourne Maizey manor to John Tanner.[35] Tanner devised part of Rockley manor to his son William,[36] who apparently acquired the rest from his brother Robert.[37] William (d. before 1898) was survived by his wife Jane who sold the estate in 1911.[38] The manor house and some land were bought by H. de H. Whatton (d. 1926)[39] and passed through various hands until 1962. Mr. J. Lees-Millais then bought the house and 100 a. of land and in 1980 held 450 a.[40] In 1911 most of the land was bought by George Cowing whose executors sold it to Messrs. Hurditch and Harding of Portishead (Som., later Avon) in 1920.[41] In 1980 it was owned by Mereacre Ltd.[42]

Hugh of Kilpeck was granted timber to repair his house at Rockley in 1222, and in 1274 'certain buildings badly built' stood there.[43] Rockley Farm, a large timber-framed building of the 17th century or earlier, was derelict in 1980. It was probably superseded as the manor house by Rockley House. The east front of that house is of five bays with a central pediment and is in the style of the mid 18th century, but the decoration may be much later. The front appears to have been added to an earlier house to give symmetry; the addition may have been made when the house was extended westwards to make it almost square. The west side was probably further altered in the early 19th century when most of the roofs of the house were renewed. The many 20th-century alterations include the removal of some original fittings, extensions on the north, west, and south sides, and general restoration of the 18th-century character of the house.

Robert of Ewias, to whom the estates of Alfred of Marlborough had passed, gave a hide in Rockley to the Templars in the 12th century.[44] The land apparently became part of their manor of Temple Rockley in Preshute.[45] In 1338 payment of 20 marks was made to the prior of Ogbourne for tithes, probably owed from the land formerly held by the Templars.[46] No other such payment is recorded and the land may thereafter have been considered part of Preshute parish.

A chantry founded at Bromham in 1494 by Sir Richard Beauchamp, Lord St. Amand, and his wife Anne was endowed with lands at Rockley.[47]

They passed to the Crown at the Dissolution and were granted to Edward Carey in 1564.[48]

ECONOMIC HISTORY. OGBOURNE ST. ANDREW. There was land for 8 ploughteams on Miles Crispin's estate in 1086. The demesne was of 6 hides with 3 teams and 4 serfs. Another 3 teams were held by 11 villeins and 4 bordars. There were 8 a. of meadow and pasture ½ league long and ½ league broad. The estate was valued at £15 in 1066 and 1086.[49]

The open fields of Ogbourne St. Andrew probably lay on either side of the Og and the common pasture on the downs west of the river. There was an East field in the 16th century[50] and East, West, and South fields in the mid 17th.[51] Lord and tenants shared sheep pasture on Brinscombe, perhaps the later Coombe, Down from the 13th century to the 16th.[52] The farmer of the demesne of Ogbourne St. George had rights of pasture in Ogbourne St. Andrew and tenants from Ogbourne St. George worked lands in the Og valley south of the boundary between the parishes. Those rights probably derived from the common ownership of the manors of Ogbourne St. George and Ogbourne St. Andrew over a long period but may have predated it. Neither lord nor tenants of Ogbourne St. Andrew are known to have had equivalent rights in Ogbourne St. George.[53]

In the late 13th century the prior of Ogbourne had in hand 352 a. of arable in demesne, 8 a. of meadow, and common pasture for c. 1,000 sheep.[54] Much of the lord's income derived from corn, some £87 of the total of £114 in 1282. The income from sheep, however, may appear artificially low as some sheep were sold with those from Ogbourne St. George and their price was omitted from the total.[55] In 1294 there were 25 villeins who held 15 yardlands between them and 11 cottars who paid rents of 3s. 4d. each.[56] In the mid 13th century three cottars, all craftsmen, paid rents totalling 2s. The yardlanders then owed small money payments and three days work each week from Michaelmas to 1 August. During harvest they worked every day on the demesne. They performed the usual boonworks of ploughing and ploughed additional acres in return for herbage. Shearing and haymaking were done as the lord required. Exemption from certain works was granted for carrying services and threshing malt. Half-yardlanders owed half the services of yardlanders.[57] Labour

[32] Wilts. Inq. p.m. 1625-49 (Index Libr.), 120-4; W.R.O. 56/3.
[33] P.R.O., CP 25(2)/746/26 Chas. II Trin.; D. & C. Windsor Mun., XV. 31. 103.
[34] W.R.O. 542/12; P.R.O., CP 25(2)/1446/15 Geo. III Trin.   [35] Above.
[36] W.R.O. 9/20/142.
[37] Kelly's Dir. Wilts. (1875, 1880, 1885).
[38] Ibid. (1898, 1915); W.A.S. Libr., sale cat. xxi, no. 28.
[39] W.A.S. Libr., sale cat. xvii, no. 26; notice in church.
[40] Local inf.
[41] W.A.S. Libr., sale cat. xvii, no. 26; Wilts. Cuttings, xiv. 111.   [42] Local inf.
[43] Rot. Litt. Claus. (Rec. Com.), i. 491; Wilts. Inq. p.m. 1242-1326 (Index Libr.), 81.
[44] V.C.H. Wilts. ix. 78; Rec. Templars in Eng. ed. B. A. Lees, pp. 53, 206.
[45] Below, Preshute, manors.
[46] Knights Hospitallers in Eng. (Camd. Soc. [1st ser.], lxv), 187, 209.
[47] Cal. Pat. 1485-94, 471.
[48] Ibid. 1563-6, p. 80.
[49] V.C.H. Wilts. ii, p. 146.
[50] King's Coll., Camb., Mun., D. 36, f. 1.
[51] W.A.M. xli. 112.
[52] Sel. Doc. Eng. Lands of Bec (Camd. 3rd ser. lxxiii), 38; King's Coll. Mun., D. 36, f. 3.
[53] King's Coll. Mun., survey, 1751; below, Ogbourne St. Geo., econ. hist.
[54] P.R.O., E 106/2/2.
[55] Eton Coll. Mun., compotus roll, 1282.
[56] P.R.O., E 106/2/2.
[57] Sel. Doc. Eng. Lands of Bec (Camd. 3rd ser. lxxiii), 37-40.

services which already bore heavily upon the comparatively few tenants may have increased during the 13th century as exemptions in return for rents and special services were withdrawn.[58] In the 14th century there were repeated protests against the lord's demands. A writ was brought against the abbot of Bec in or before 1306 alleging that the manor was ancient demesne of the Crown and that yardlanders, who properly held by 5s. rent, 10d. woodgavel paid at Hocktide, and suit of court, had been compelled since the time of Edward I to do villein service including three days work each week. Although the courts found for the abbot,[59] the claim to ancient demesne was revived in 1332 and 1341.[60] In the 1330s the tenants resisted the abbot's servants by force, maintaining their cause from a common purse.[61] Rebellious tenants were fined and imprisoned and the lands of some were seized, but there were further disturbances in the 1340s, in 1389, and in 1416.[62] In the mid 15th century the demesne was leased with that of Ogbourne St. George manor.[63] Members of the Goddard family, lessees in the early 16th century, were succeeded by members of the Young and Bond families c. 1590–1685. The demesnes were still leased together in the 18th century.[64] The demesne lands of Ogbourne St. Andrew manor were known as Poughcombe farm from the 17th century.[65] In the mid 18th century that mainly several holding of 774 a. was worked from buildings on the east side of the village street, opposite the lane leading past the church. There were 221 a. of arable, mostly on the western slopes of Coombe Down. Near the river were 78 a. of meadow including Berry mead, formerly used in common. Sheep were pastured on 480 a. of Coombe Down. North-west of that pasture the farmer of Poughcombe had summer pasture for cattle on 409 a. of down, which were grazed by sheep from Ogbourne St. George in winter.[66]

Most, if not all, of the lands held by customary tenants of Ogbourne St. Andrew manor in the Middle Ages may have been shared in the 17th century between copyholders of inheritance and eleven copyholders for lives, known as corsiclemen. None of the corsiclemen had lands worth more than £4 a year. The copyholders of inheritance were more numerous and had larger holdings.[67] In the late 18th century there were no more than three copyholds. Many others had probably been absorbed into the substantial freehold estate then held by Samuel Hawkes which, with Poughcombe farm, included most of the lands of the township.[68]

In 1341 the prebendal estate included 2 yardlands, valued at 12s., and rents and services, valued at 6s. 8d.[69] The land was probably worked with the demesne land of Ogbourne St. Andrew manor[70] and may have been leased to the tenants of the demesne after 1421. In 1438 there were 28 a. of glebe arable and 2 a. of meadow.[71] From the mid 15th century the impropriate tithes of Ogbourne St. Andrew were leased with those of Ogbourne St. George. Members of the Goddard family were lessees from 1652 until c. 1680[72] and from 1714 a lease passed in the Lydiard family, from 1740 with East Hayes manor.[73] The tithes were commuted to a rent charge of £830 in 1839.[74]

Except on Poughcombe farm common cultivation continued until c. 1,280 a. were inclosed by an award of 1780. Two large allotments were made, of 895 a. to Samuel Hawkes and 354 a. to King's College. Of the lands allotted to the college, c. 110 a. were attached to copyholds.[75] Much of the remainder may have been that part of the cow down, 235 a. in 1839, which was worked with Herdswick farm in Ogbourne St. George in the 19th and 20th centuries.[76] Poughcombe farm was little affected by the award. In the 19th century and the early 20th the farm measured 800–900 a., more than half of which was pasture, and was then worked from buildings north-west of the village, although there was no farmhouse until after 1858.[77] From 1800 until 1858 the farm was leased with the lands of Ogbourne St. George manor to members of the Canning family.[78] Members of the Gale family were lessees in the late 19th century and the early 20th when the farm was sometimes sublet.[79] When the farm was divided c. 1927 the northern part, Upper Poughcombe, included some 295 a. of down, 105 a. of lowland pasture, and only 50 a. of arable. Poughcombe farm included 141 a. of arable but was also mainly of pasture.[80] The other large farm in the parish, formerly Samuel Hawkes's, comprised 521 a. of down and lowland pasture, 468 a. of arable, and 49 a. of meadow land, including 17 a. of water meadows, in 1839. The arable lay either side of the Og and included burnbaked land on the downs east of the river. The land was worked from Upper and Lower Farms in Ogbourne St. Andrew and was held by lessees in the late 18th century and the 19th.[81] In the 20th century the land was divided into Ogbourne St. Andrew farm, 471 a., and Ogbourne Down farm, 404 a. Until 1969 Ogbourne St. Andrew farm was worked as a dairy farm. In 1980 the two farms and land outside the parish

[58] M. Morgan, *Eng. Lands of the Abbey of Bec*, 81–3.
[59] *Gaol Delivery 1275-1306* (W.R.S. xxxiii), pp. 149–50; P.R.O., KB 27/207, rot. 82; *Abbrev. Plac.* (Rec. Com.), 313; *Year Bk.* 5 Edw. II (Selden Soc. xxxi), 125–9.
[60] P.R.O., SC 8/63/3133; *Cal. Pat.* 1340-3, 231.
[61] *Cal. Inq. Misc.* ii, p. 310.
[62] Morgan, *Eng. Lands of Bec*, 107; P.R.O., SC 8/63/3133; *Cal. Pat.* 1340-3, 231; 1388-92, 53; 1416-22, 50.
[63] King's Coll. Mun., compotus roll, 1456.
[64] Below, Ogbourne St. Geo., econ. hist.
[65] W.R.O., dean, glebe terrier, 1672.
[66] King's Coll. Mun., survey, 1751.
[67] Ibid. bursar's bk. 1647–65.
[68] W.R.O., inclosure award; above, manors.
[69] *Inq. Non.* (Rec. Com.), 158.
[70] W.R.O., dean, Chaundler's reg. f. 67v.; *Sel. Doc. Eng.*

Lands of Bec (Camd. 3rd ser. lxxiii), 40.
[71] D. & C. Windsor Mun., X. 4. 6.
[72] *Cat. MSS. D. & C. Windsor*, ed. Dalton, 245, 255.
[73] Ibid.; W.R.O., land tax; above, manors.
[74] W.R.O., tithe award.
[75] Ibid. inclosure award.
[76] Ibid. tithe award; W.A.S. Libr., sale cat. ix, no. 17; xx, no. 1.
[77] King's Coll. Mun., surveys, 1803, 1816; W.A.S. Libr., sale cat. ix, no. 17; ibid. Kemm papers, sale cat.
[78] W.R.O., land tax; ibid. 212B/5155; 212B/5176; W.A.S. Libr., sale cat. ix, no. 17; below, Ogbourne St. Geo., econ. hist.   [79] *Kelly's Dir. Wilts.* (1880 and later edns.).
[80] Swindon corp. rec., waterworks and fire brigade cttee. file 60; W.A.S. Libr., sale cat. xx, no. 1.
[81] W.R.O., land tax; tithe award.

were worked together. There was some arable land and sheep and cattle were reared.[82]

At Barbury the prior of Avebury had 102 a. in demesne, valued at 34s., in 1294. Rents of 41s. 8d. were paid by five villeins, who held 4 yardlands, and two cottagers paid 3s. There was pasture for 300 sheep and the whole estate was valued at £5 8s. 4d.[83] From the 16th century or earlier Barbury was leased as a single farm,[84] until taken in hand briefly c. 1900.[85] In the 18th century the farmstead was 500 m. south-east of Barbury Castle and the lands lay in a semicircle around the earthwork with the pasture on the downs at the circumference.[86] There was grazing for 600 sheep in 1585.[87] In the 18th and 19th centuries almost half the farm of 590 a. was pasture,[88] and in the early 20th century there was only a small area of arable. Part of the land was then let as training gallops.[89] Since the 1930s much of the grass has been converted to arable.[90]

The mill which stood on Miles Crispin's estate in 1086, for which 30s. a year was paid, was one of the most valuable in the county.[91] Frequent references to mills and millers occur from the late 13th century to the 16th.[92] In 1294 there was a water mill on Ogbourne St. Andrew manor;[93] it is not clear how long that mill stood or when it was replaced by a windmill. In 1296 two tenants of the manor were amerced for having millstones in their houses to the detriment of the lord's mill.[94] In 1316 the miller was charged with grinding additional corn without licence.[95] In 1589 and probably earlier a mill was held as part of a copyhold of the manor.[96] That mill was probably the windmill at the east end of the churchyard said in 1760 to have been destroyed many years earlier.[97]

OGBOURNE MAIZEY. Geld was paid for 5 hides from Harding's estate in 1066. In 1086 there was land for 3 ploughteams. On the demesne were 1 team and 1 serf, and 3 villeins and 4 bordars also had 1 team. There were 2 a. of meadow and pasture 2 furlongs long and 1 furlong broad. The estate was valued at £4. Turchil's was an estate of 2 hides, valued at 10s., with land for 1 team and 30 a. of pasture.[98]

From the 16th century or earlier open-field cultivation took place in East, South, and West fields and there was a common meadow west of the village, probably in the valley of the Hungerbourne. There was a large area of down in the township and sheep stints, reckoned at 80 to a

yardland in the 16th century, were high.[99] Grazing for sheep on part, if not all, of the downland north and west of the village may have been shared with Rockley. In 1730 the boundary between Ogbourne Maizey and Rockley sheep downs was defined. It is not clear whether that was a new division or the re-establishment or adjustment of an existing one.[1]

The demesne farm of Ogbourne Maizey manor was of 4 yardlands in the late 16th century and was valued at £40 c. 1615. East Hayes was a farm of 10 yardlands, valued at £40 c. 1550. Both were leased in the 16th and 17th centuries.[2] There were then several copyholds, at least one of which was held of East Hayes manor, and all of which were apparently small.[3]

By an agreement of 1731, confirmed in 1740, the common fields and downs, some 1,000 a., were divided in 1735.[4] The allotment for the demesne farm of Ogbourne Maizey manor was of 339 a., including 197 a. of down. That for East Hayes manor was of 413 a., including 241 a. of down. Allotments of 176 a., including 105 a. of down, and of 56 a. of arable were made to copyholders.[5] By 1760 all those holdings had been amalgamated and in the late 18th century and the early 19th the land was worked as a single farm.[6] In 1839 it comprised 460 a. of pasture, 496 a. of arable, including 66 a. of ploughed downland, and 61 a. of meadow, of which 6 a. were water meadows beside the Og.[7] In the late 19th century new farm buildings were built on the down west of Ogbourne Maizey, the area of arable was extended, and a dairy herd introduced. The farm was in hand from 1893 to the 1920s.[8] Dorothy Sherbrooke's portion of it remained in hand until c. 1937.[9] It was then leased as Manor farm, c. 200 a., which was worked from buildings in the village, and Drove Barn, later Maisey, farm, 330 a. chiefly of downland.[10] Both Manor and Maisey farms were dairy farms until the 1960s when they became mainly arable. In 1980 some beef cattle were raised and commercial egg production took place on Maisey farm. Nora Edwardes's portion of Ogbourne Maizey farm was dispersed after 1915 and the lands worked with surrounding farms.[11]

Gallops on the downs between Ogbourne Maizey and Rockley were let to the tenants of Manton House stables in Preshute in the late 19th century.[12] A training stable was established at Ogbourne Maizey Manor by Frederick Lyneham in the 1890s[13] and another, Bonita, was built

[82] Inf. from Mr. R. W. Margesson, Eastholme.
[83] P.R.O., E 106/2/2.
[84] Ibid. SC 6/Hen. VIII/3931; W.A.M. iv. 152; W.R.O. 529/93; ibid. land tax.
[85] Kelly's Dir. Wilts. (1898, 1903).
[86] Map of Barbury Down farm temporarily deposited in W.R.O.
[87] P.R.O., REQ 2/196/11.
[88] Map of Barbury Down farm; W.R.O., tithe award; W.A.S. Libr., sale cat. iii, no. 8.
[89] W.R.O. 106, pt. 2.
[90] [1st] Land Util. Surv. Map, sheet 122.
[91] V.C.H. Wilts. ii, pp. 57, 146.
[92] e.g. King's Coll. Mun., C. 15 (1321); C. 79, ff. 1–3 (1506–8); P.R.O., SC 2/212/2 (1422).
[93] P.R.O., E 106/2/2.
[94] Sel. Pleas in Manorial Cts. i (Selden Soc. ii), 47.
[95] King's Coll. Mun., C. 17.
[96] Ibid. D. 36, f. 1.

[97] Ibid. ct. bk. 1760.
[98] V.C.H. Wilts. ii, pp. 163–4.
[99] P.R.O., C 2/Jas. I/H 2/8; W.R.O. 212B/5150.
[1] W.R.O. 649/14.
[2] Ibid. 130/41; P.R.O., C 2/Jas. I/H 2/8; ibid. REQ 2/189/60.
[3] e.g. P.R.O., REQ 2/121/86; W.R.O. 130/41; 520/2.
[4] W.R.O. 9/20/137.
[5] Ibid. 9/20/139.
[6] Ibid. 403/34; 403/55; ibid. land tax.
[7] Ibid. tithe award.
[8] W.A.S. Libr., sale cat. i, no. 16; ix, no. 18; Kelly's Dir. Wilts. (1898 and later edns.).
[9] Kelly's Dir. Wilts. (1923, 1927); inf. from Mr. R. Curnick, Maisey Farm.
[10] Inf. from Mr. A. C. Cooper, Ogbourne Maizey Manor.
[11] Inf. from Mr. Curnick; above, manors.
[12] W.A.S. Libr., sale cat. i, no. 16; ix, no. 18.
[13] Kelly's Dir. Wilts. (1898).

in or before 1903 for J. D. Edwardes. The stables were combined for some years but were managed separately from the 1930s. In 1980 Mr. A. R. Turnell trained at the Manor and Mr. P. Makins at Bonita.[14] The gallops, west of the village, ran parallel with the road from Marlborough to Wootton Bassett.[15]

ROCKLEY. There was land for 6 ploughteams on Alfred of Marlborough's Rockley estate in 1086. The demesne was of 6 hides and 3 yard-lands with 1 team and 1 serf: 3 teams were held by 7 villeins and 12 bordars and there were 3 a. of meadow and pasture $\frac{1}{2}$ league long and 4 furlongs broad. The estate was valued at £8.[16]

In the 13th century much of the pasture of the township was several[17] but open-field cultivation continued until the 18th century.[18] The several pasture included 'Rothersdune', perhaps Rough Down, south of Ogbourne Maizey.[19] In the 18th century there was a common sheep down which bounded and may have been shared with Og-bourne Maizey.[20] The common arable lay in Dean and Temple Bottoms and probably in the valley of the Hungerbourne. Meadow land, much of which was divided into small closes in the 17th century, also lay in the valley.[21]

In the 13th century there was a large demesne farm and other small farms comprised 13 yard-lands. The demesne included 432 a. of arable, several pasture for 200 sheep, 16 oxen, and 2 plough beasts, and another several pasture valued at 13s. 4d. Rents totalling 54s. were paid by villeins who held 9 yardlands between them and owed 2s. at harvest, three ploughworks, and two days weeding in the lord's corn. Two cottars owed 2s. in rent and three works in autumn. The yearly value of the manor was £16 3s. 7d. Six free tenants paid 25s. 8d. in rents; four were yard-landers, two held only crofts.[22] The men of Rockley owed services including ploughing, reaping, and carrying, to the barton estate of Marlborough Castle but in 1255 were said to have refused them for three years.[23] The holding granted to Bromham chantry, 32 a. of arable and 52 a. of pasture in 1494, was leased for 13s. 4d. as 1 yardland in 1563.[24] In the 17th century there were three farms. The demesne farm was said to include 200 a. of arable, 200 a. of pasture, and 20 a. of meadow.[25] There was a copyhold farm of 2$\frac{1}{2}$ yardlands including 72 a. of arable, pasture for 300 sheep, and closes of meadow, and another of 29 a. of arable and pasture for 100 sheep.[26] The

three farms had rights on the sheep down in 1730 when the boundary was defined between the pastures of Rockley and Ogbourne Maizey.[27] The farms, which remained separate in the late 18th century, were in a single ownership and occupation in the early 19th and no inclosure award was therefore necessary.[28]

The Rockley estate was c. 1,330 a. in 1839. There were then 637 a. of downland on either side of the road from Marlborough to Wootton Bassett.[29] The proportion of pasture remained high although some downland was later ploughed.[30] From the late 18th century until the mid 19th Rockley House and between 40 a. and 80 a. were kept in hand or leased separately.[31] The remainder, 1,290 a. in 1845, was leased as Rockley farm to members of the Canning family.[32] It was in hand from c. 1867 to 1911. The land was then worked from Rockley Farm and farmsteads in Temple and Wick Bottoms.[33] The land in the western part of Rockley was later worked with land in Preshute as Temple farm, in 1980 by Mereacre Ltd. It was part of an extensive mixed farm with a principal farmstead in Rockley called Temple Farm, formerly Temple Bottom Farm.[34] In 1920 Rockley was a cattle and sheep farm of 750 a. of pasture and 133 a. of arable.[35] A farm of 450 a. was attached to Rockley House in 1980.[36]

In 1842 Rockley House and some 40 a. were leased to Edmund Jones, a racing trainer.[37] There was a racing stable adjoining the house in 1855.[38] Horses were still trained and bred there in 1911 but no later reference to the stable has been found.[39]

Spinners at Rockley were mentioned in the 18th century but nothing is known of their work.[40]

Sarsens were cut in Temple and Wick Bottoms by masons of the Cartwright family in the late 19th century. The supply of stone was exhausted c. 1905.[41]

LOCAL GOVERNMENT. Public and manorial business from Ogbourne St. Andrew township was transacted at courts held at Og-bourne St. George for the manors of Ogbourne St. Andrew and Ogbourne St. George.[42] Separate presentments from Ogbourne St. Andrew are not recorded before the 15th cen-tury. In the 15th, 16th, and 17th centuries a tithingman for Ogbourne St. Andrew was elected

[14] Kelly's Dir. Wilts. (1903); inf. from Mr. Cooper.
[15] O.S. Map 1/50,000, sheet 173 (1974 edn.).
[16] V.C.H. Wilts. ii, p. 142.
[17] Wilts. Inq. p.m. 1242–1326 (Index Libr.), 81.
[18] W.R.O. 212A/36/11.
[19] Wilts. Inq. p.m. 1242–1326 (Index Libr.), 81; V.C.H. Wilts. iv. 17.
[20] W.R.O. 212A/36/11; 649/14.
[21] Ibid. 212A/36/1; 212A/36/11.
[22] Wilts. Inq. p.m. 1242–1326 (Index Libr.), 81–2.
[23] Rot. Hund. (Rec. Com.), ii (1), 234.
[24] Cal. Pat. 1485–94, 471; P.R.O., E 310/26/153.
[25] Wilts. Inq. p.m. 1625–49 (Index Libr.), 120–4.
[26] W.R.O. 212B/5149; 212B/5161.
[27] Ibid. 649/14.
[28] Ibid. Q. Sess. enrolled deeds, diversion of highways, no. 8; ibid. tithe award.
[29] Ibid. tithe award.
[30] W.A.S. Libr., sale cat. ix, no. 18.
[31] W.A.M. xxx. 105; W.R.O. 403/55; 212B/5161; ibid. tithe award.
[32] W.R.O., land tax; tithe award; ibid. 212B/5160; 403/35; 403/45.
[33] Kelly's Dir. Wilts. (1867 and later edns.); W.A.S. Libr., sale cat. xxi, no. 28.
[34] Local inf.; below, Preshute, econ. hist.
[35] W.A.S. Libr., sale cat. xvi, no. 26; Wilts. Cuttings, xiv. 115.   [36] Wilts. Cuttings, xxi. 301; local inf.
[37] W.R.O. 212B/5161.
[38] Ibid. 403/35.
[39] W.A.S. Libr., sale cat. xxi, no. 28.
[40] J. Clark, Memoirs (Bath, 1810), 55; Trowbridge Woollen Ind. (W.R.S. vi), p. x.
[41] W.A.M. lxiii. 92.
[42] Sel. Pleas in Manorial Cts. i (Selden Soc. ii), 9, 19–20, 36, 47; King's Coll., Camb., Mun., C. 13; C. 79; Eton Coll. Mun., ct. roll, temp. Edw. I; P.R.O., E 106/2/2; below, Ogbourne St. Geo., local govt.

at the autumn court and made presentments.[43] Breaches of assize and manorial custom were the main business from the township. In 1249 the township was fined for failing to come to wash the lord's sheep.[44] Other offences included the omission of archery practice by inhabitants of the tithing in the 1590s.[45]

There is no evidence that representatives of the other townships in the parish attended the courts of Ogbourne St. Andrew manor and nothing is known of any court held for Ogbourne Maizey, Rockley, or Barbury. In 1281 quittance from suit at shire and hundred courts was claimed for Rockley manor,[46] but tithingmen from Rockley and Ogbourne, presumably Ogbourne Maizey, attended the hundred court in the 15th century.[47]

In 1776 the parish overseers bought a house to accommodate those unable to afford rents. Between 1770 and 1790 some £130 a year was spent on poor relief. In 1770 ordinary relief for 14–20 people each month cost the parish between £4 10s. and £6; another £4 a month was spent on extraordinary relief.[48] The average yearly expenditure rose to £352 in the 1830s. The parish joined Marlborough poor-law union in 1835.[49]

CHURCHES. Maud of Wallingford confirmed her gift of the church of Ogbourne St. Andrew to the abbey of Bec c. 1148.[50] After the appropriation of the church by the abbey in 1192–3 the living was served by a chaplain.[51] In 1208 a vicarage was ordained to which the abbot of Bec presented as prebendary of Ogbourne.[52] Under Edward I the prebendary received the right of archidiaconal jurisdiction in Ogbourne St. Andrew.[53] The exercise of that right by officials of the prior of Ogbourne and of the dean and canons of St. George's chapel, Windsor, or by lessees, is recorded from the 14th century to the mid 17th.[54] The Crown presented to the vicarage as keeper of Ogbourne priory in the 14th century, although the abbot of Bec sought to recover the patronage in 1335.[55] In 1421 the advowson passed with the prebendal estate to the dean and canons of St. George's chapel.[56] Grants of next presentation from the dean and canons allowed laymen to present to the living in 1565 and 1574.[57] The parish was served in plurality with Ogbourne St. George from 1951[58] until the

benefices were united in 1970 as the benefice of Ogbourne St. Andrew and St. George. In 1974 the united benefice became part of the Ridgeway team ministry. The rector of that ministry was thereafter appointed by a patronage board of five members including a representative of the dean and canons of Windsor.[59]

The vicarage of Ogbourne St. Andrew, valued at £4 13s. 4d. in 1291, was poor by comparison with others in the prebendal churches of the diocese.[60] In 1535, however, the vicar's yearly income of £15 12s. 10d. was above the average for Marlborough deanery.[61] The living was of moderate value, £160 a year, c. 1830.[62] The vicar received 2s. from the prior of Ogbourne on St. Andrew's day in the mid 13th century[63] and £20 a year in the 1660s from the dean and canons of St. George's chapel in augmentation of his income from tithes.[64] In the 15th century he held all tithes except those of corn, hay, wool, and lambs. In the 17th century, perhaps as a result of a grant from the dean and canons, the vicar also received wool and lamb tithes, except from Poughcombe and Rockley farms.[65] A yardland said to be part of the vicarage in 1588 may have been that held by the vicar as lessee from the Rockley chapel estate in 1563.[66] The vicar had no land except a garden and the churchyard in the 17th century. In 1650 he had a house with three rooms on each of its two storeys.[67] The house was described as a farm cottage, unfit for residence, in the early 19th century. A new brick vicarage house, hung with tiles above the ground floor, was built to designs by William Butterfield in 1848.[68] It was sold after 1951.[69]

In 1607 Obadiah Sedgewick, vicar of Ogbourne St. Andrew, was prosecuted for failing to wear the surplice and use the sign of the cross in baptism,[70] and Bartholomew Webb was ejected from the living in 1662.[71] In the early 19th century non-residence was common because of the condition of the vicarage house.[72] Some 100 people attended service at the parish church on Census Sunday in 1851.[73] In 1864 there were morning and afternoon services on Sundays. Communion was celebrated monthly and at the great festivals and was received by between eight and twelve communicants.[74] In the 1870s a succession of short incumbencies and unpopular clergy caused complaints from parishioners.[75]

The church had evidently been dedicated to

[43] P.R.O., SC 2/209/43–5; King's Coll. Mun., C. 79; W.R.O., dean, ct. bk. of Ogbournes.
[44] Sel. Pleas in Manorial Cts. i (Selden Soc. ii), 9.
[45] King's Coll. Mun., D. 36, ff. 1, 3.
[46] P.R.O., JUST 1/1005, rot. 119d.
[47] Ibid. DL 30/127/1908.
[48] W.R.O. 902/8.
[49] Poor Law Com. 2nd Rep. 559.
[50] Porée, Histoire du Bec, i. 460–1.
[51] Sel. Doc. Eng. Lands of Bec (Camd. 3rd ser. lxxiii), 4.
[52] Reg. St. Osmund (Rolls Ser.), i. 190.
[53] Cat. MSS. D. & C. Windsor, ed. Dalton, 42.
[54] Morgan, Eng. Lands of Bec, 139; W.R.O., dean, act bk. 1571–7; dean, presentation and ct. papers.
[55] Cal. Pat. 1334–8, 149, 302, 470; 1338–40, 346; 1396–9, 372.
[56] Cat. MSS. D. & C. Windsor, ed. Dalton, 15.
[57] W.R.O., dean, reg. inst. ff. 7v., 10v.
[58] Lond. Gaz. 29 June 1951, p. 3562.
[59] Ibid. 2 Oct. 1970, p. 10764; inf. from Ch. Com.; the vicar, the Revd. R. W. C. Jeffery, Ogbourne St. Geo.

[60] Tax. Eccl. (Rec. Com.), 181–2.
[61] Valor Eccl. (Rec. Com.), ii. 149–51.
[62] Rep. Com. Eccl. Revenues, 842–3.
[63] Sel. Doc. Eng. Lands of Bec (Camd. 3rd ser. lxxiii), 40.
[64] Cat. MSS. D. & C. Windsor, ed. Dalton, 255; W.R.O., dean, glebe terriers, 1672, 1705; ibid. 403/39.
[65] D. & C. Windsor Mun., IV. 133. 13; W.A.M. xli. 113; W.R.O., dean, glebe terrier, 1672.
[66] Below; P.R.O., C 2/Eliz. I/A 6/42.
[67] W.R.O., dean, glebe terriers, 1672, 1705; W.A.M. xli. 112.
[68] D. & C. Windsor Mun., XVII. 20. 13; Rep. Com. Eccl. Revenues, 842–3; Pevsner, Wilts. (2nd edn.), 366.
[69] Local inf.
[70] W.R.O., dean, chwdns.' pres.
[71] Calamy Revised, ed. A. G. Matthews, 516.
[72] Rep. Com. Eccl. Revenues, 842–3; D. & C. Windsor Mun., XVII. 36. 2.
[73] P.R.O., HO 129/255/1/6/13.
[74] W.R.O., bishop, vis. queries.
[75] D. & C. Windsor Mun., XVII. 20. 13.

ST. ANDREW by the late 13th century when the modern name of the parish was first used.[76] The church is built of sarsen and flint rubble with dressings of freestone and has a chancel, an aisled and clerestoried nave with a south porch, and a west tower which occupies the last bay of the nave. A new building may have been started when the church was granted to Bec abbey in the mid 12th century.[77] The nave and its arcades, which were presumably once of three bays but after the building of the tower of only two, survive from a church of that date and the reset north and south doorways were apparently built later in the 12th century, perhaps indicating slow progress in completing the aisles. A chancel arch was removed and the chancel rebuilt, presumably to align with the nave, in the early 13th century. In the early 14th century a new east window was inserted. Major alterations were made in the 15th century when the tower was built. Its intrusion into the nave was apparently necessary because the west end of the nave stood very near to the churchyard boundary. The clerestory was then added and both aisles were widened. Work of the 19th century includes the chancel roof, probably of 1873.[78] New pews were installed and the plain post-medieval south porch was rebuilt in 1914.[79]

In 1553, when 10 oz. of plate were confiscated, a chalice said to weigh 11 oz. was left in the parish.[80] In 1861 new plate was given to replace that destroyed by fire.[81] There were three bells in 1553.[82] A 15th-century bell, presumably one of them, survives. Three other bells, (i), (ii), and (iv), are of the 17th century and a fourth, (iii), of the 18th.[83] The parish registers are complete from 1538.[84]

In the 13th century there was a chapel at Rockley, the chancel of which was maintained by the prior of Ogbourne.[85] In the early 15th century it was dedicated to *ST. LEONARD* and served by a chaplain. No sacrament was administered there and the people of Rockley were required to attend the mother church at Ogbourne St. Andrew at festivals; in 1405 they were prosecuted in the prebendal court for failing to do so.[86] In 1563 the Crown granted a lease of the chapel and 1 yardland in Rockley, then held by the vicar of the parish.[87] By 1583 the building had been demolished and no later reference has been found to the land.[88] A house in Rockley served as a chapel of ease and was attended by 20 people on Census Sunday in 1851.[89] A new chapel was built in 1872 to designs by J. Baverstock of Marlborough. It is of flint and stone chequerwork with a chancel, nave, and south-west porch and was dedicated to *ALL SAINTS*. It was served by the vicar[90] until its closure in 1961, and was sold in 1973.[91] A chalice and paten of 1872 from Rockley were transferred to Ogbourne St. George church. There was one bell.[92]

ROMAN CATHOLICISM. A private chapel was built for George Edwardes at Ogbourne Maizey in 1911. It was served as a chapel of ease from St. Joseph's church, Devizes, until 1937 and then from Marlborough until 1970. The chapel, which stood opposite the Bonita stable beside the lane to Rockley, was demolished in 1970 or 1971.[93]

PROTESTANT NONCONFORMITY. Bartholomew Webb, who was deprived of Ogbourne St. Andrew vicarage in 1662, continued to preach in the area until his death *c.* 1680.[94] In the 1660s and 1670s there were two or more Quaker families in the parish.[95] John Clark, founder of the Tabernacle church at Trowbridge, preached to spinners at Rockley in 1779.[96]

Methodist meeting houses in the parish were registered in 1817 and 1835.[97] In 1864 Primitive Methodists met in a private house.[98] A house at Rockley was registered for dissenters' meetings in 1818, and in 1820 there was an Independent chapel at Ogbourne St. Andrew.[99] The chapel was probably that known as the Zion chapel in 1858,[1] which was conveyed to the Particular Baptists in 1860.[2] In 1864 it had a small regular congregation.[3] It was closed in 1903.[4]

EDUCATION. There were two private day schools in the parish in 1818[5] but in 1833 most children from Ogbourne St. Andrew were said to attend schools in Marlborough.[6] In 1858 a National school, the origin of which is unknown, was held in a thatched cottage and had between 20 and 30 pupils. Some 35 children were then taught in a schoolroom attached to the Zion chapel;[7] nothing more is known of that school. A new National school with a teacher's house was built in 1872 and extended in 1896.[8] Average

---

76 *P.N. Wilts.* (E.P.N.S.), 303.
77 Above, manors.
78 Wilts. Cuttings, xiv. 346.
79 The porch was described as modern in 1845: *W.A.M.* xlii. 279.
80 Ibid. i. 92.
81 D. & C. Windsor Mun., XVII. 7. 1; Nightingale, *Wilts. Plate*, 160.   82 *W.A.M.* i. 92.
83 Walters, *Wilts. Bells*, 150–2.
84 W.R.O. 801/1–8.
85 *Sel. Doc. Eng. Lands of Bec* (Camd. 3rd ser. lxxiii), 40.
86 W.R.O., dean, Chaundler's reg. f. 59v.
87 P.R.O., E 310/26/153.
88 Ibid. E 310/38/240.
89 Ibid. HO 129/255/1/6/14.
90 D. & C. Windsor Mun., XVII. 20. 13; Council for Places of Worship, survey.
91 Wilts. Cuttings, xxii. 30; notice in church.

92 Inf. from Dr. F. W. Hanford, Kingscot, Ogbourne St. Geo.
93 *V.C.H. Wilts.* iii. 97; inf. from Mr. W. G. Kalaugher, 3 Leaze Road, Marlborough.
94 *Calamy Revised*, ed. Matthews, 516.
95 *W.N. & Q.* ii. 288; iii. 163, 318; v. 278.
96 Clark, *Memoirs*, 55.
97 W.R.O., bishop, certs. dissenters' meeting hos.
98 Ibid. bishop, vis. queries.
99 Ibid. bishop, certs. dissenters' meeting hos.
1 *Acct. of Wilts. Schs.* 36.
2 *Endowed Char. Wilts.* (N. Div.), 799.
3 W.R.O., bishop, vis. queries.
4 *Endowed Char. Wilts.* (N. Div.), 799–800.
5 *Educ. of Poor Digest*, 1034.
6 *Educ. Enquiry Abstract*, 1044.
7 *Acct. of Wilts. Schs.* 36.
8 P.R.O., ED 7/131, no. 215; ED 21/1851.

attendance rose from 61 in 1906 to 74 in 1914, but had fallen to 47 by 1932.[9] The school was closed in 1971 and the buildings were later used for a private nursery and primary school. Children from Ogbourne St. Andrew attended the primary school in Ogbourne St. George in 1980.[10]

A school was built at Rockley in 1868.[11] Attendance rose from 25 in 1906[12] to 35 in the 1920s when some pupils came from downland farms in Preshute. Children were then sent to schools in Preshute and Ogbourne St. Andrew to relieve overcrowding at Rockley.[13] The school was closed in 1947.[14]

CHARITIES FOR THE POOR. In 1776 money given to the poor by an unknown donor was invested to produce an income of 10s. a year. The proper beneficiaries were the second poor

but in 1796, when the money was first used, food was distributed to all poor families of the parish. In the 19th century there were irregular distributions of fuel. The charity was known in 1905 as Canning's Trust or the Poor's Money.[15]

At inclosure in 1780 an allotment was made to the lord of Ogbourne St. Andrew manor of 5 a. on the downs in the north-west corner of the parish to raise furze or other fuel for poor parishioners. In the 19th century the land was leased and the annual rent of £4 was used to buy coal for poor householders, including those at Ogbourne Maizey and Rockley, or allowed to accumulate.[16] The land remained in trust for the poor. The income from the Poor's Furze and the Poor's Money was combined from the 1950s. In 1960 twelve people received 10s. each. In 1980 the money was used for any suitable charitable cause.[17]

OGBOURNE ST. GEORGE

THE PARISH of Ogbourne St. George, 1,445 ha. (3,571 a.),[18] straddles the valley of the river Og on the downs 5 km. north of Marlborough and contains the village of Ogbourne St. George and the hamlet of Southend.[19] The name Ogbourne was used in 946–7 and was shared by several estates in the Og valley in 1086.[20] In the 12th century there was a church at the most northerly settlement in the valley, then known as Great Ogbourne.[21] That name continued in use until the 16th century but the settlement was also known as North Ogbourne in the 13th century and Ogbourne St. George from the 14th.[22]

The Og rises near the centre of the parish and flows southward to the boundary with Ogbourne St. Andrew. West of the river the land rises to Coombe Down and Smeathe's Ridge. The ridge forms the south-west boundary for 3 km. and the highest point in the parish, over 259 m., is near its western end. In the north-east corner of the parish is Whitefield Hill and south of that hill are Round Hill Downs and Church Hill. Beyond the crest of the downs, which rise to 235 m., the land slopes more gently to Whiteshard Bottom at the eastern extremity of the parish. North and west of the source of the Og the land is almost flat and lies mainly between the 152 m. and 198 m.

contours. The chalk which outcrops over the whole parish is covered on the hills east of the river by clay-with-flints. In the valley the gravel deposits are 800 m. wide near Ogbourne St. George and there is alluvium near Southend.[23]

Downland near the eastern and western boundaries was ploughed during the Iron Age and the Romano-British period.[24] The downs were later used as pasture and the lower, flatter land in the north and west parts of the parish and near the river were tilled. Near the source of the Og and beside its banks were meadows.[25] Racing stables adjoined Ogbourne St. George manor house in the 18th century[26] and horses were trained there in the 1920s[27] but the location of any training course is unknown. The southern slopes of Church Hill were laid out as a golf course, and land west of the river became the site of an army camp and firing ranges in the 20th century.[28]

The woods of Aldbourne Chase extended into the south-eastern corner of the parish. In 1086 there was woodland ½ league long and 4 furlongs broad[29] and in the later Middle Ages Ogbourne St. George manor included woods in Ogbourne St. George and Aldbourne.[30] Wheldon Coppice, mentioned in the 15th century,[31] was probably

[9] *Return of Non-Provided Schs.* 832; *Bd. of Educ., List 21* (H.M.S.O.).
[10] Inf. from the vicar, the Revd. R. W. C. Jeffery, Ogbourne St. Geo.
[11] P.R.O., ED 7/131, no. 216.
[12] *Return of Non-Provided Schs.* 846.
[13] P.R.O., ED 21/42326.
[14] Wilts. Cuttings, xxii. 190.
[15] *Endowed Char. Wilts.* (N. Div.), 796–8.
[16] Ibid. 797–9.
[17] Char. Com. file; inf. from Dr. F. W. Hanford, Kingscot, Ogbourne St. Geo. [18] *Census*, 1971.
[19] This article was written in 1980. Maps used include O.S. Maps 1/50,000, sheet 173 (1974 edn.), sheet 174 (1974 edn.); 1/25,000, SU 17 (1960 edn.), SU 27 (1960 edn.); 6″, Wilts. XXII (1888 and later edns.), XXIII (1887 and later edns.), XXIX (1889 and later edns.).

[20] Finberg, *Early Wessex Chart.* p. 88; *V.C.H. Wilts.* ii, pp. 119, 146, 163–4.
[21] *Sel. Doc. Eng. Lands of Bec* (Camd. 3rd ser. lxxiii), 25.
[22] *P.N. Wilts.* (E.P.N.S.), 303; *L. & P. Hen. VIII,* i (1), p. 319.
[23] Geol. Surv. Map 1″, drift, sheet 266 (1964 edn.).
[24] *V.C.H. Wilts.* i (1), 277.
[25] Below, econ. hist.
[26] King's Coll., Camb., Mun., survey, 1751; W.R.O., inclosure award.
[27] *Country Life*, 25 Dec. 1942.
[28] Below.
[29] *V.C.H. Wilts.* ii, p. 119.
[30] e.g. *Crown Pleas, 1249* (W.R.S. xvi), p. 222; P.R.O., SC 2/209/43, rott. 1d., 7.
[31] P.R.O., SC 2/209/44, rot. 10.

the later Wilding's Copse, some 65 a. in the 18th and 19th centuries.[32] Moore's Wood, 40 a. south of Wilding's Copse in the late 16th century, probably included Yielding Copse, which was described as a separate wood to the south of it in the 19th century.[33] In 1843 there were 113 a. of woodland in the parish[34] and there has since been little change in its distribution.

Earthworks on Whitefield Hill, Church Hill, and Round Hill Downs, artefacts of the Bronze Age and later, and a ditch leading north from Church Hill indicate considerable prehistoric activity in the north-east corner of the parish. Another ditch crosses its eastern corner. Barrows are widely scattered along the northern and western boundaries and a circular enclosure west of the manor house was built over c. 1940.[35]

Major routes through the parish have long run north and south, mostly near the Og. The Roman road from Cirencester to Winchester crosses the parish boundary 500 m. north of Whitefield Farm and runs south-eastwards.[36] In the 18th century its course was followed by the principal road through the parish to a point 1 km. south-east of the church. From there the Roman road survived as a track, still visible in 1980. The main road turned south-west to approach the river at Southend, wound east and south through that hamlet, and ran south-west again to Ogbourne St. Andrew. When turnpiked in 1819 as part of the Swindon–Marlborough road, it was moved east to run directly from Ogbourne St. George to the eastern end of the lane through Southend.[37] In 1881 a railway line was opened between Swindon and Marlborough following the turnpike road and crossing it by a bridge where the road turns south-west. A station was built north of the bridge.[38] The line was closed in 1964 and the course of the road was altered to use the railway bridge. The new road rejoined the old one 1 km. south of the bridge.[39] A road from Draycot Foliat to Ogbourne St. Andrew ran parallel to the main road west of Ogbourne St. George village in the 18th century. The two roads were then connected by Ogbourne St. George village street and by the lane through Southend;[40] in the 20th century the route from Draycot Foliat was along the village street, the road between the west end of that street and Ogbourne St. Andrew having become a mere track. North of the village tracks ran east and west in the 19th and 20th centuries, among them Gipsy Lane, along the northern boundary, and Woolmer Drove, 1 km. south of that lane.[41] Other tracks led west from the former Draycot Foliat road in 1980. North of the junction of the Swindon–Marlborough road and the village

street a road to Aldbourne, Copse Drove, led north-eastwards. Old Chase Road, then a track, ran south-east to Whiteshard Bottom and was joined to the Roman road by a network of lanes which changed little from the 18th century to the 20th.[42]

Ogbourne priory, a daughter house of the abbey of Bec-Hellouin (Eure), was established in the 12th century possibly on the site later occupied by the manor house.[43] In the 13th century many of the abbey's estates in the west of England were administered from the priory.[44] The prior or proctor was the chief officer of the abbey in England and in the 14th century occupied a position similar to that of vicar-general. Evidence of the spiritual life of the priory is slight and in the late 13th century there may have been no more than a farmstead and offices at Ogbourne St. George. In the late 14th century the title 'prior of Ogbourne' was a legal fiction and the priory was frequently in royal keeping until its suppression in the early 15th century.[45]

The parish was also an administrative centre for the honor of Wallingford (Oxon., formerly Berks.). The right to hold a view of frankpledge there at Easter belonged to the honor in 1300.[46] Courts held in the 15th century and perhaps earlier were attended by representatives of Wiltshire members of the honor.[47] Courts for the honor of Ewelme (Oxon.), to which the rights of Wallingford honor had passed, were held at Ogbourne from the 16th century to the 19th. Among the business transacted was the signing of certificates of admission for new burgesses of Calne; the guild steward brought the town book to Ogbourne St. George for the purpose.[48]

Its administrative importance may reflect the size and prosperity of Ogbourne St. George in the Middle Ages. Its assessment for tax in 1334 was high for Selkley hundred and in 1377, when there were 157 poll-tax payers, it was the second largest settlement in the hundred.[49] It was still one of the wealthier communities in the hundred in the 16th century.[50] The population had risen from 406 in 1801 to 593 by 1851 but declined, with some fluctuations, to 435 in 1931. In 1951, when there was an army camp in the parish, the population was 1,381;[51] when the camp was left empty numbers fell, to 421 in 1961 and 391 in 1971.[52]

The church and manor house of Ogbourne St. George stand on the west bank of the Og 2 km. south of the parish boundary. From there settlement spread south-eastwards across a spur of gravel to the Roman road. A second, smaller, settlement called Middle Town, later Southend, grew up 1 km. south of Ogbourne St. George in

[32] King's Coll. Mun., survey, 1751; W.R.O. 379/2.
[33] P.R.O., C 142/252, no. 53; W.R.O., tithe award.
[34] W.R.O., tithe award.
[35] V.C.H. Wilts. i (1), 95, 186–7, 248–9, 258, 268, 277.
[36] W.A.M. xxxiii. 326.
[37] Andrews and Dury, Map (W.R.S. viii), pl. 15; V.C.H. Wilts. iv. 263, 271; W.R.O., tithe award.
[38] V.C.H. Wilts. iv. 289; O.S. Map 6″, Wilts. XXIII (1887 edn.).
[39] Below, Preshute, introduction; O.S. Map 1/50,000, sheet 173 (1974 edn.), sheet 174 (1974 edn.).
[40] Andrews and Dury, Map (W.R.S. viii), pl. 15.
[41] W.R.O., tithe award.
[42] Andrews and Dury, Map (W.R.S. viii), pl. 1.

[43] V.C.H. Wilts. iii. 394–5; Country Life, 25 Dec. 1942.
[44] V.C.H. Wilts. iii. 395.
[45] M. Morgan, Eng. Lands of the Abbey of Bec, 34; Jnl. Brit. Arch. Assoc. [3rd ser.], iv. 142.
[46] Wilts. Inq. p.m. 1272–1326 (Index Libr.), 274.
[47] P.R.O., SC 2/212/2; SC 2/212/9; SC 2/212/14; SC 2/212/18–20; A. A. Porée, Histoire de l'Abbaye du Bec, i. 462; below, local govt.
[48] Calne Guild Bk. (W.R.S. vii), p. xv; W.A.M. xxiv. 210–16; W.R.O. 529/180.
[49] V.C.H. Wilts. iv. 301, 310.
[50] Taxation Lists (W.R.S. x), 22, 102.
[51] V.C.H. Wilts. iv. 355; below.
[52] Census, 1961, 1971.

or before the 17th century. In the mid 18th century there were also farmsteads to the north, Whitefield, south, Bytham, and east, Cowcroft,[53] and by the late 18th century another, Buckerfields, had been built between Ogbourne St. George and Southend. Other farmsteads were built in the north and south-east parts of the parish in the 19th century.[54]

The village of Ogbourne St. George lies between the church and manor house, west of the river, and the Swindon–Marlborough road. Its position, between the possible site of the priory and the Roman road, and the straightness of the village street, which runs south-east for 500 m. from the bridge over the Og, give an impression of a medieval planned settlement, but no documentary evidence has been found to support the theory. The surviving older buildings of the village are at the western end of the street. Kemms, a timber-framed house of the 17th century, stands west of the river and south of the street, where it curves round the grounds of the manor house. East of the bridge there are cottages of the 16th and 17th centuries above the steep banks between which the street climbs for some 200 m. Newer buildings in the western half of the street include the old and new vicarage houses and, at its highest point, the school, the village hall, and a small group of council houses. Along its remaining length are farm buildings, houses, and cottages, chiefly of the 18th and 19th centuries, including Rectory Farm House and Rectory House, which bear dates of 1742 and 1755 respectively, and the Park, an 18th-century house much extended in the 19th century. Some 200 m. west of the junction of the street and the old Swindon–Marlborough road Jubbs Lane leads north to farm buildings. Another lane, 150 m. further east, runs north-east from the street linking it with the old road. On the triangle of land so formed stand cottages of the 19th and 20th centuries. East of the old road are a few buildings including bungalows built on the site of a Methodist chapel near the junction with the street.

In the 1750s there were two inns in Ogbourne St. George, probably the Three Bells and the New Inn which were licensed in the 1820s. The New Inn was known as the White Hart in 1843 but by its old name from 1855. It stands on the north side of the village street 50 m. west of its junction with the old main road. The Shoemakers' Arms stood east of the road and a little north of the junction in 1843. The Crown, first recorded in 1855, stands on the same side of the road, opposite the street.[55] The site of the Robin Hood, mentioned in 1858, is unknown.[56]

Southend consists of a group of cottages standing on both sides of the Swindon–Marlborough road and along a winding lane leading to the river. Its earlier name, Middle Town, describes its position between Ogbourne St. Andrew and Ogbourne St. George, as Southend reflects its relation to Ogbourne St. George alone. The settlement can be no younger than the 17th century, the date of most of the surviving buildings, and it was known in the mid 18th century as Middle Town. The name was probably altered in the 19th century but physically the hamlet has apparently changed little since the 1770s.[57] Of the cottages, some are timber-framed, some have walls of sarsen rubble, and some are of brick. Hallam, a larger house on the west bank of the river, is, like the cottages, of 17th-century origin, and is approached by a bridge from the lane.[58] The population of Southend was 96 in 1841.[59]

Waterworks were built for Swindon corporation 1.5 km. north of the church in 1902.[60] From 1903 deep well and surface pumps delivered water to Overtown reservoir in Wroughton. The pumping station was later enlarged and in 1980 was being renovated for Thames Water.[61]

The course for the North Wiltshire, later Swindon, golf club was opened north-east of Ogbourne St. George village in 1929. The single-storey clubhouse, beside the Swindon–Marlborough road, was replaced by a two-storey brick building completed in 1976.[62]

A hospital for sufferers from infectious diseases was built on the east side of the Swindon–Marlborough road near the northern boundary of the parish in the 1920s. It was used as a geriatric hospital during the Second World War and later as a smallpox hospital. It was demolished c. 1965.[63]

In 1940 an army camp was built north-west of the village and between 1943 and 1950 the War Department bought the site and surrounding land, some 184 a. The camp was used principally as a transit camp for British and United States forces until c. 1957. The buildings were later abandoned and the camp was used for training in battle and street fighting. There were firing ranges west of the camp.[64]

MANOR AND OTHER ESTATES. Lands at Ogbourne devised by the ealdorman Athelwold to his brother Edric in 946–7 may have been in Ogbourne St. Andrew or Ogbourne St. George or both.[65]

Land in Ogbourne formerly belonging to Wigod, probably Wigod of Wallingford, was held by the king in 1066 and 1086.[66] It passed by grant or inheritance to Wigod's granddaughter Maud of Wallingford. The overlordship of the estate descended with the honor of Wallingford

[53] King's Coll. Mun., survey, 1751.
[54] Andrews and Dury, Map (W.R.S. viii), pl. 15; W.R.O., tithe award; O.S. Map 6", Wilts. XXIII (1887 edn.).
[55] W.R.O., alehousekeepers' recognizances; tithe award; Kelly's Dir. Wilts. (1855).
[56] W.A.S. Libr., sale cat. ix, no. 17.
[57] King's Coll. Mun., survey, 1751; Andrews and Dury, Map (W.R.S. viii), pl. 15.
[58] Below, manors.
[59] P.R.O., HO 107/1185.
[60] V.C.H. Wilts. v. 328.

[61] Inf. from Mr. A. Knowler, Thames Water, Cotswold Div., Swindon.
[62] Inf. from Hon. Sec., Swindon Golf Club.
[63] Inf. from Mr. C. R. West, Area Administrator, Wilts. Area Health Authority; Mr. A. E. MacIntyre, District Administrator, Swindon Health District.
[64] Inf. from Defence Land Agent, Durrington; Army Hist. Branch, Lond.; Mr. W. Batner, Caretaker, Ogbourne St. Geo. Camp.
[65] Finberg, Early Wessex Chart. p. 88.
[66] V.C.H. Wilts. ii, pp. 61–2, 119, 199, 200 n.

until 1540 and thereafter with the honor of Ewelme.[67]

With the consent of Brian FitzCount, her husband, Maud of Wallingford conveyed the manor of *OGBOURNE ST. GEORGE* to the abbey of Bec-Hellouin for the monks' wardrobe after 1122. The grant was confirmed in 1133.[68] The manor thereafter descended with that of Ogbourne St. Andrew as part of the endowment of Ogbourne priory. In 1410 it passed to John, duke of Bedford, and on his death in 1435 reverted to the Crown. With Ogbourne St. Andrew the manor or its reversion was granted variously to Cambridge University, King's College, and the London Charterhouse between 1439 and 1462. The college and the Charterhouse both claimed the manor in the late 15th century. From c. 1500 it was held by the college.[69]

The manor was sold in 1927 in four principal lots.[70] The manor house and 173 a. were bought by H. Colemore who sold them to Mrs. W. E. Tatton in 1934.[71] Oliver Frost bought the house and 40 a. in 1937 and his son Mr. Timothy Frost owned them in 1980.[72] Little is known of the buildings of Ogbourne priory although a reference has been found to a great grange there in the late 13th century.[73] The manor house appears to have changed little in plan since 1659 when it was described as 'a very fair house of brick 60 ft. long and 40 broad'. It was then said to have been built by 'farmer Bond', perhaps George Bond who was lessee in 1663.[74] The house was probably built in two stages. The north range, which is the earlier, has a north front of five bays with stone-mullioned windows. The south range appears to have been altered in the late 17th century, the probable date of the fenestration and the roof, and on later occasions.

Herdswick farm was sold by King's College to W. Pullen in 1927.[75] It was requisitioned by the War Department from James Bomford c. 1939. After 1945 that part of the land which had not been built on was sold by Bomford as two farms. Mr. C. J. Smith succeeded his father, the purchaser of Upper Herdswick, and owned that farm in 1980. Lower Herdswick was bought by the Ormond family in 1962.[76] Swindon corporation bought part of Whitefield farm in 1928. That land was held by Mr. M. R. Walker as owner or tenant in 1978.[77] Cowcroft farm, of which 105 a. lay in Ogbourne St. George and 225 a. in Aldbourne,[78] was sold in 1927 and several times

thereafter. In 1982 the farm, called Chase Woods farm, was owned by Mr. J. D. Owen.[79]

Maud of Wallingford confirmed her gift of Ogbourne St. George church to the abbey of Bec c. 1148.[80] The church was appropriated by the abbey c. 1190[81] and was part of the endowment of the prebend of Ogbourne established in Salisbury cathedral for the abbot of Bec in 1208.[82] The prebendal estate passed with that of Ogbourne St. Andrew to John, duke of Bedford (d. 1435), and in 1421 to the dean and canons of St. George's chapel, Windsor.[83] In the 15th century the estate comprised glebe and tithes but in 1650 it was of tithes only.[84] The dean and canons of Windsor held the tithes at commutation in 1843.[85]

In 1449 Isabel, relict of John Bird, was licensed to endow a chantry in St. Peter's church, Marlborough, with property including lands and rents in Ogbourne St. George.[86] When its foundation was confirmed in 1475, however, the chantry was endowed with lands in Ogbourne Maizey in Ogbourne St. Andrew but none in Ogbourne St. George.[87] Lands in Ogbourne St. George which may have descended like the manor of Huish from Isabel Bird to the Michell family were granted by Alice Michell to her daughter Elizabeth Hall in 1494.[88] John Michell conveyed that or another holding to Thomas Bush in 1508.[89]

Lands in Ogbourne St. George were settled on Francis Goddard in 1616.[90] In 1620 part of the estate was sold to John Potter.[91] Potter sold part of his estate to William Gardiner in 1642 and settled the remainder on Thomas Potter in 1688. The residue of Francis Goddard's holding was sold to Thomas Ayres in 1621. Ayres, or another of the same name, held the lands in 1676 and in 1689 his sons John and Vincent held an estate called *WESTONTOWN*.[92] Vincent sold it to John Kemm in 1704 and it was held by James Kemm in 1746.[93] He or another James Kemm held a smaller estate in 1796. That estate had passed to William Kemm by 1843[94] and was apparently broken up in the late 19th century.

At his death in 1691 Gabriel Evans held an estate called *BYTHAM*. It passed jointly to his brothers Henry and John and sister Ellen, wife of John Launce. By conveyances of 1691 and 1693 Henry Evans acquired the whole estate.[95] In 1714 Arthur Evans conveyed it to Edward Wilson.[96] Jonathan Braithwaite owned Bytham farm in 1780 and after his death c. 1786 it remained in

[67] *Sel. Doc. Eng. Lands of Bec* (Camd. 3rd ser. lxxiii), 24–5; *V.C.H. Berks.* iii. 528; Aubrey, *Topog. Coll.* ed. Jackson, 32.
[68] *Sel. Doc. Eng. Lands of Bec* (Camd. 3rd ser. lxxiii), 24–5; Porée, *Histoire du Bec*, i. 460.
[69] Above, Ogbourne St. Andrew, manors.
[70] W.A.S. Libr., sale cat. xx, no. 1.
[71] *Country Life*, 25 Dec. 1942.
[72] Inf. from the Hon. Mrs. J. Frost, Orchard Ho.
[73] Draft hist. of Ogbourne St. Geo. manor, apparently written from mun. of King's Coll., Camb.: *penes* Mr. T. Frost, Manor Ho.
[74] Ibid.; King's Coll. Mun., bursar's bk. 1647–65, p. 129; see above, plate facing p. 97.
[75] W.A.S. Libr., sale cat. xx, no. 1.
[76] Inf. from Mr. G. D. Herbert, Home Farm Ho.
[77] Swindon corp. rec., waterworks and fire brigade cttee. file 314; local inf.
[78] W.A.S. Libr., sale cat. xx, no. 1.
[79] Above, Aldbourne, manors.
[80] Porée, *Histoire du Bec*, i. 461.
[81] *Cal. Doc. France*, ed. Round, p. 129.
[82] *Reg. St. Osmund* (Rolls Ser.), i. 189–90.
[83] Above, Ogbourne St. Andrew, manors.
[84] *Cat. MSS. D. & C. Windsor*, ed. J. N. Dalton, 17; *W.A.M.* xli. 112.
[85] W.R.O., tithe award.
[86] *Cal. Pat.* 1446–52, 301; below, Marlborough, churches.
[87] *W.A.M.* xxxvi. 564.
[88] *V.C.H. Wilts.* x. 78; *Cat. Anct. D.* ii, B 2532.
[89] P.R.O., CP 25(1)/257/66, no. 49.
[90] W.R.O. 212B/1907.
[91] Ibid. 335/175.
[92] Ibid. 184/10.
[93] Ibid. 654/1; 654/3.
[94] Ibid. inclosure award; tithe award.
[95] Ibid. 212A/38/8/17.
[96] Ibid. 212A/38/25/4.

the hands of trustees until 1831 or later.[97] Job Buckeridge was owner or tenant of the farm in 1843[98] as were John Bathe in 1885, James Groom in 1898, Edwin Habgood in 1903, and members of the Durnford family in 1911 and 1923.[99] The farm was part of an estate sold by J. E. Thorold in 1928. It was bought with some additional land by Nicholas Grove. In 1953 Bytham passed to Grove Bros., the owners in 1980.[1]

Michael Ernle sold to John Brunsden a messuage and lands called *HALLAM* which were held by John's son Henry in 1698.[2] Hallam was held by Elizabeth Brunsden in 1796 and by J. H. Gale in 1843.[3] It was sold, probably by a member of the Gale family, to Frank Courage in or before 1906 and again in 1917. Henry Hony bought the estate in 1926 and sold it to Mrs. Owen Edwards in 1944. Mrs. Edwards sold it to Lt.-Col. and Mrs. W. E. S. Whetherly in 1951.[4] The 17th-century east range of Hallam is partly timber-framed and partly of sarsen. A south front in cottage style was added in the early 19th century and the house was much enlarged by a new west range in the late 19th century.

Lands held by John Griffen in 1780 passed to John Bannings c. 1816 and to Thomas Bannings c. 1830.[5] In 1843 Rebecca Bannings held them with a large part of the holdings of Job Matthew and James Smith to whom allotments had been made at inclosure in 1796.[6] The estate passed to Stephen Bannings (fl. 1885)[7] and to S. T. Bannings before 1898. That Bannings sold the estate as *RECTORY* farm to Douglas Parfitt in or before 1923.[8] J. E. Thorold sold an estate including that farm in 1928.[9] Rectory farm passed to S. Maundrell after 1939.[10]

John Wooldridge had an estate in Ogbourne St. George, including some copyhold land, between 1780 and 1812. The estate, known as the *PARK*, passed to James Blackman who was succeeded by the Revd. Thomas Blackman Newell after 1831.[11] Newell (d. 1850) devised the estate to his wife Catherine.[12] The Park estate was held by J. H. Gale in 1885 and c. 1912 by Joseph Poole who was succeeded by F. H. Poole c. 1930.[13] Poole Bros. were owners of the estate in 1980.[14]

ECONOMIC HISTORY. Geld was paid for 30 hides at Ogbourne St. George in 1066. The hidage was perhaps an overestimate as there was said to be land for only 25 ploughteams in 1086.

That may also have been a generous assessment; if it was accurate much of the land remained uncultivated as there were only 14 teams on the estate, 4 in demesne and 10 held by 24 villeins and 14 bordars. There were also 6 serfs. The pasture was ½ league long and 4 furlongs broad and there were 6 a. of meadow. The estate was valued at £25.[15]

The open fields of the parish lay mainly north of the village in the broad valley[16] and there were meadows by the river north and, probably, south of the village and beside the main street.[17] There was common pasture on Whitefield Hill: sheep were pastured on the downs in the southern and western parts of the parish and cattle on Round Hill Downs.[18] In the 18th century and probably earlier the keeper of the cattle there received the profits from a herd's ale held in spring or summer each year.[19] Inhabitants of Ogbourne St. George exercised certain rights in Ogbourne St. Andrew which may have arisen from the long association of the capital manors. In the 18th century the tenant of Herdswick farm pastured sheep on Ogbourne St. Andrew cow down during the winter. A field in Ogbourne St. Andrew was worked in common by the men of Middle Town;[20] by 1839 they had lost their rights there and the lands had become part of Poughcombe farm in Ogbourne St. Andrew.[21] Although produce from other manors held by the abbey of Bec was collected at Ogbourne St. George during the Middle Ages, there is no evidence of interdependence with the abbey's other estates.[22]

In 1294, when the manor of Ogbourne St. George was valued at £82 13s.,[23] the demesne, in hand, was among the largest on the English manors of Bec and had recently been expanded by taking in lands previously tenanted.[24] There was said to be pasture, including some several pasture, for 700 sheep and lambs in the mid 13th century and for 1,450 sheep in 1294, but in the 14th century there was a flock of 600–700.[25] Heavy labour services were exacted to work the demesne arable, 871 a. in 1294 when 558 a. were sown. Each of the 22 yardlanders worked in the lord's fields daily except Saturdays during harvest, and for three days a week for the rest of the year. Boonworks of ploughing were required three times a year as were works of making and carrying hurdles. Other services included washing and shearing sheep, preparing malt at Christmas and Easter, and carrying to and from local markets; remission of other works was granted in

[97] Ibid. land tax.
[98] Ibid. tithe award.
[99] *Kelly's Dir. Wilts.* (1885 and later edns.).
[1] Inf. from Mr. D. Grove, Bytham Farm.
[2] W.R.O. 212A/31/3.
[3] Ibid. inclosure award; tithe award.
[4] Inf. from Lt.-Col. W. E. S. Whetherly, Hallam; Wilts. Cuttings, xiv. 108.
[5] W.R.O., land tax.
[6] Ibid. inclosure award; tithe award.
[7] *Kelly's Dir. Wilts.* (1885).
[8] Ibid. (1898 and later edns.).
[9] Inf. from Lt.-Col. Whetherly.
[10] Inf. from Mrs. Frost.
[11] W.R.O., inclosure award; land tax; King's Coll. Mun., survey, 1816.
[12] P.R.O., PROB 11/2118, f. 264.
[13] *Kelly's Dir. Wilts.* (1885 and later edns.).
[14] Inf. from Lt.-Col. Whetherly.

[15] *V.C.H. Wilts.* ii, pp. 51, 119.
[16] *Andrews and Dury, Map* (W.R.S. viii), pl. 15; *Sel. Doc. Eng. Lands of Bec* (Camd. 3rd ser. lxxiii), 29; King's Coll., Camb., Mun., survey, 1751.
[17] P.R.O., SC 2/209/43, rot. 2; King's Coll. Mun., survey, 1751.
[18] P.R.O., SC 2/209/44, rott. 3d., 5d.; King's Coll. Mun., ct. bk. 1720.   [19] *W.A.M.* ii. 200–1.
[20] King's Coll. Mun., survey, 1751; above, Ogbourne St. Andrew, econ. hist.
[21] W.R.O., Ogbourne St. Andrew tithe award.
[22] *Sel. Doc. Eng. Lands of Bec* (Camd. 3rd ser. lxxiii), 70, 129.
[23] P.R.O., E 106/2/2.
[24] Morgan, *Eng. Lands of Bec*, 46–7; *Sel. Doc. Eng. Lands of Bec* (Camd. 3rd ser. lxxiii), 35.
[25] *Sel. Doc. Eng. Lands of Bec* (Camd. 3rd ser. lxxiii), 36; P.R.O., E 106/2/2; King's Coll. Mun., acct. rolls, Bec western manors, 14th-cent.

return for preparing malt and carrying services. Some sixteen ½-yardlanders owed lesser services. A reeve was appointed from the yardlanders and a shepherd and a hayward from the ½-yardlanders. Twelve cottars held 8 a. between them in 1294, paid rents, and owed some services. A smith and harness maker, who served the manors of Ogbourne St. George and Ogbourne St. Andrew, held 2 yardlands and owed some works.[26] In the 14th century the tenants of Ogbourne St. George sought, unsuccessfully, to prove the illegality of the services exacted on behalf of the abbot of Bec, on the grounds that they held of the ancient demesne of the Crown and owed only suit of court and small money rents. They occasionally offered armed resistance to the abbot's servants and brought lawsuits against him in or before 1306, in 1311, 1332, 1341, 1389, and 1416.[27] In the early 15th century 32 tenants held 32 yardlands and paid rents totalling £8. The prior of Ogbourne's demesne, which probably included the prebendal glebe, then included 9 ploughlands, 40 a. of meadow, and pasture for 1,000 sheep.[28]

The demesne lands of Ogbourne St. George, like those of other English estates of Bec, may have been leased from the 14th century, but no record of lessees has been found before the mid 15th century.[29] Thomas Goddard became lessee of the demesne of that manor and of Ogbourne St. Andrew in 1455. He was succeeded as lessee of both whole manors by John Goddard (d. c. 1507),[30] by William Goddard (fl. 1525), and by Vincent Goddard (fl. 1553); William and Vincent may have been sublessees.[31] Members of the Young family held the lease from c. 1590 to c. 1620[32] and of the Bond family from c. 1620 to c. 1685.[33] The estate was still leased with Ogbourne St. Andrew manor in the early 18th century.[34]

The prebendal estate, held with Ogbourne St. George manor from the 12th century to the 15th, was valued at £6 12s. 3d. in 1341. It then included 1 ploughland, pasture valued at 26s. 8d. a year, and rents and services valued at 24s. a year.[35] The glebe was of 50 a. of arable, 20 a. of pasture, and 2 a. of meadow in the mid 15th century.[36] The tithes were commuted to a rent charge of £698 in 1843.[37]

There were still many small farms in the 16th and 17th centuries. Twelve 'acremen' held copyholds of the manor for lives; none of their holdings included more than 20 a. of arable. There were also copyholds of inheritance, the size and number of which is unknown.[38] Larger farms included John Moore's, 3 yardlands in 1567,[39] and Hallam, which had 43 a. of arable in 1698.[40]

Substantial areas of land, including downland, had probably been inclosed by the late 17th century. Bytham, a farm of 147 a. with a new farmstead on the downs in 1690, may have consisted mainly of newly inclosed land and in 1796 was a compact holding near the south-eastern boundary.[41] The demesne lands of the manor were worked in severalty as three farms in the mid 18th century. Herdswick, which was worked from the manor house, comprised 745 a. north and west of Ogbourne St. George village, almost half of which was pasture, including 263 a. of down. New farmsteads had been built for Whitefield, 313 a. in the north-east corner of the parish, and Cowcroft, 147 a., south of Whitefield.[42] Small inclosures were made on other holdings during the 18th century and open-field cultivation was ended under an Act of 1792.[43] An award of 1,609 a. was made in 1796. John Wooldridge's allotment of 254 a. in various parts of the parish later became Park farm. Four other allotments of more than 100 a. were made and the remaining land was distributed in small parcels.[44]

During the 19th century the lands of the parish were consolidated into farms of 100 a. or more and three of over 500 a., Herdswick, the Park, and Rectory; those farms were still the major holdings in the early 20th century. The largest was Herdswick, which in 1803 was a farm of over 1,000 a. including downland in Ogbourne St. Andrew. It was mainly of pasture, 580 a., and meadow, 140 a. The soil of the downs was then considered too poor for crops[45] but between 1843 and 1858 some 150 a. of downland were brought under the plough.[46] About that time a farmstead, later called Lower Herdswick, was built 1 km. west of Whitefield Farm; that at the manor house may then have been given up.[47] In the 19th century, as in the 18th, Herdswick farm was leased. Lessees included members of the Canning family from 1800 to 1858[48] and of the Gale family from 1858 to 1910.[49] In 1927 Herdswick was a farm of 969 a.; 422 a. of arable and 241 a. of down in Ogbourne St. George, the remainder in Ogbourne St. Andrew.[50] After 1945 the downland was worked separately, from Upper Herdswick, a farmstead in the north-east corner of the parish. Lower Herdswick was a dairy and arable

[26] P.R.O., E 106/2/2; *Sel. Doc. Eng. Lands of Bec* (Camd. 3rd ser. lxxiii), 29–36.
[27] Above, Ogbourne St. Andrew, econ. hist.; *Year Bk.* 5 Edw. II (Selden Soc. xxxi), 125–9; *Cal. Pat.* 1330–4, 299, 347, 501; 1388–92, 53; 1416–22, 50.
[28] D. & C. Windsor Mun., IV. B. 1.
[29] Morgan, *Eng. Lands of Bec*, 117; draft hist. of Ogbourne St. Geo. manor *penes* Mr. T. Frost, Manor Ho.
[30] King's Coll. Mun., compotus roll, 1456; ledger bk. 1, ff. 172v.–173v.; *Cal. Pat.* 1494–1509, 510.
[31] P.R.O., C 2/Eliz. I/H 14/2; C 1/1389/40; draft hist. of manor *penes* Mr. Frost.
[32] King's Coll. Mun., D. 36; W.A.S. Libr., notebook of F. A. Carrington.
[33] *Cal. S.P. Dom.* 1631–3, 311; *Cal. Cttee. for Money*, ii. 1048; King's Coll. Mun., D. 116; *W.A.M.* xliii. 579–80.
[34] W.A.S. Libr., notebook of Carrington.
[35] Above, manor; *Inq. Non.* (Rec. Com.), 158.
[36] *Cat. MSS. D. & C. Windsor*, ed. Dalton, 17.
[37] W.R.O., tithe award.
[38] King's Coll. Mun., bursar's bk. 1647–65.
[39] P.R.O., C 2/Jas. I/G 4/31.
[40] W.R.O. 212A/31/3.
[41] Ibid. 212A/38/8/17; ibid. inclosure award.
[42] King's Coll. Mun., survey, 1751.
[43] Ibid. ct. bks. 1720, 1760; W.R.O., inclosure award.
[44] W.R.O., inclosure award.
[45] King's Coll. Mun., survey, 1803.
[46] *Kelly's Dir. Wilts.* (1848, 1855); W.R.O., tithe award; W.A.S. Libr., sale cat. ix, no. 17.
[47] W.R.O., tithe award; O.S. Map 6″, Wilts. XXIII (1887 edn.).
[48] Draft hist. of manor *penes* Mr. Frost; W.R.O., land tax; tithe award; W.A.S. Libr., sale cat. ix, no. 17.
[49] W.A.S. Libr., sale cat. ix, no. 17; *Kelly's Dir. Wilts.* (1865 and later edns.).
[50] W.A.S. Libr., sale cat. xx, no. 1.

farm of some 500 a. worked with lands in Draycot Foliat in 1980.[51] Between 1796 and 1843 three holdings were merged as a farm of 554 a. The lands, which lay east and south of Ogbourne St. George, were then worked from Blue Barn Farm, 500 m. north of Bytham Farm, and later from Rectory Farm in the village.[52] Park farm lay in scattered parcels north and south of the village in the late 18th century and the 19th and was of 636 a. in 1843. Rectory and Park farms together were of over 1,000 a. in the 20th century.[53]

Whitefield and Cowcroft farms were often sublet by the lessees of Herdswick farm in the 18th and 19th centuries.[54] In the mid 19th century they were worked from Whitefield Farm as a single farm of 420 a., most of which was arable land.[55] By the 1920s they were again separate. Whitefield was then a farm of 660 a.:[56] Cowcroft, later Chase Woods, of which c. 100 a. lay in Ogbourne St. George, was a mainly arable farm in 1982.[57] Bytham farm, which was tenanted in the late 18th century and the 19th, was of 145 a., including 117 a. of arable, in 1843.[58] It had grown to 263 a. by 1928 and to 348 a. by 1960, since when it has included some 200 a. of arable, a flock of 250 sheep, and a dairy herd.[59] Hallam was a mainly arable farm of 113 a. west of Southend in 1843.[60] It was probably worked from the Park with other holdings of the Gale family in the late 19th century but was a separate pasture farm of 52 a. in 1917.[61] A further 40 a. were added in the 1920s when Hallam was taken in hand as a dairy farm. Dairying continued until 1967 since when the farm has been used for rearing young stock.[62]

The prior of Ogbourne had a windmill and a water mill, valued at 4 marks and 20s. respectively, at Ogbourne St. George in the mid 13th century.[63] In 1294 and 1341 there was only a windmill.[64]

John Goddard (d. c. 1507) and Thomas Bush, his executor, were described as 'woolmen' of Ogbourne St. George and had connexions with wool merchants from Oxfordshire and Gloucestershire.[65] John Savery, a woollen weaver of Ogbourne St. George, died in 1638.[66] No other evidence has been found of the manufacture of or trade in wool in the parish.

There was a brick kiln 1.5 km. east of the junction of the Swindon–Marlborough road and Ogbourne St. George street in the 1840s.[67] Brickmakers are recorded in the parish in 1855 and 1875. Lime was quarried at or near the site of the kiln by Thorold's Pure Lime and Hydrate Co. Ltd. in 1927 and by National House Building Materials Ltd. in 1931.[68] The lime works were leased to Perry & Hawkins, later the Marlborough Lime Co., between 1941 and 1963. A liquid fertilizer plant installed by Soil Fertility Ltd. was in operation in 1973. In 1980 the quarries were being filled and landscaped.[69]

LOCAL GOVERNMENT. By a charter of c. 1178 the abbot of Bec was granted sac and soc, toll and team, infangthief, and quittance from shire and hundred courts in all his lands.[70] The charter was confirmed and rights to felons' chattels and amercements of the abbot's tenants before the king's judges were added in 1253.[71] Exemption from attendance at views of frankpledge held for the honor of Wallingford was also confirmed in 1253, although the bailiff of the honor was to attend the abbot's view once a year to ensure respect for royal rights.[72] No record has been found of attendance by the bailiff at the courts of the abbots and their successors.

Courts were held at Ogbourne St. George for Ogbourne St. George and Ogbourne St. Andrew manors from the mid 13th century.[73] In the 13th century and the early 14th courts met once or twice a year at dates determined by the arrival of the itinerant officials of Bec. Offences against public order, including assault and housebreaking, and breaches of manorial customs, such as the failure to perform boonworks, were brought before the courts. Presentments were made by two or three chief men or by jury.[74] In the 15th and 16th centuries courts with view of frankpledge, variously described as for the manor of Ogbourne St. George and St. Andrew, or for the manor of Ogbourne St. George and its members, were held in spring and autumn; in the 17th century they were sometimes held only once a year.[75] Additional courts were held at need, as in 1464 and 1468 when courts summoned for the prior of the Charterhouse were directed by royal writ to hear pleas of novel disseisin. Two tithingmen and a constable were elected for Ogbourne St. George at the autumn court. Presentments were made by a tithingman and by the homage in the late 15th century and the early 16th. In the late 16th century and the 17th the homage presented. Business before the courts then included breaches of manorial custom, repair of tenements, bridges, and roads, disputes over

[51] Inf. from Mr. G. D. Herbert, Home Farm Ho.
[52] W.R.O., inclosure award; tithe award; Kelly's Dir. Wilts. (1865 and later edns.).
[53] W.R.O., inclosure award; tithe award; local inf.
[54] W.A.S. Libr., sale cat. ix, no. 17; Kelly's Dir. Wilts. (1865 and later edns.).
[55] W.A.S. Libr., sale cat. ix, no. 17; W.R.O., tithe award.
[56] Swindon corp. rec., waterworks and fire brigade cttee. minutes, Nov. 1926.
[57] W.A.S. Libr., sale cat. xx, no. 1; above, Aldbourne, econ. hist.
[58] W.R.O., land tax; tithe award.
[59] Inf. from Mr. D. Grove, Bytham Farm.
[60] W.R.O., tithe award.
[61] Kelly's Dir. Wilts. (1855 and later edns.); Wilts. Cuttings, xiv. 108.
[62] Inf. from Lt.-Col. W. E. S. Whetherly, Hallam.
[63] Sel. Doc. Eng. Lands of Bec (Camd. 3rd ser. lxxiii), 36.

[64] P.R.O., E 106/2/2; Inq. Non. (Rec. Com.), 158.
[65] Cal. Pat. 1494–1509, 510, 551; L. & P. Hen. VIII, i (1), p. 245.
[66] W.N. & Q. vi. 80.
[67] P.R.O., HO 107/1185; W.R.O., tithe award.
[68] Kelly's Dir. Wilts.
[69] Inf. from Mr. J. Liming, Old Lime Works.
[70] Porée, Histoire du Bec, i. 471–3.
[71] Cal. Chart. R. 1226–57, 430–1.
[72] Porée, Histoire du Bec, i. 462.
[73] Sel. Pleas in Manorial Cts. i (Selden Soc. ii), 9–10, 19–20, 36, 47.
[74] Ibid.; Eton Coll. Mun., ct. roll, temp. Edw. I; King's Coll., Camb., Mun., C. 11, 13–17, 22; Morgan, Eng. Lands of Bec, 61.
[75] Except where indicated, the rest of this para. is based on P.R.O., SC 2/209/43–5; King's Coll. Mun., C. 79; D. 36, 116; W.R.O., dean, ct. bk. of Ogbournes.

common rights, and orders for the use of commons and the marking of boundaries. Those involved in brawls or guilty of defamation were amerced. A court baron for the manor of Ogbourne St. George and Ogbourne St. Andrew was still held for the admittance of copyholders in the early 19th century.[76]

In the 15th century a tithingman of Ogbourne, probably Ogbourne St. George, and in the 16th century a tithingman and the constable attended the view of frankpledge held there for the honor of Wallingford. Cert money was paid and offences similar to those dealt with at the view for Ogbourne were brought before the court.[77]

Some decisions of the parish vestry, for example about the repair of bridges, were recorded with the churchwardens' accounts in the late 18th century[78] but separate records were kept of the vestry minutes and surveyors' accounts in the 19th century.[79] In the 1790s between 25 and 30 people received monthly poor relief at an average cost to the parish of £17 a month.[80] The number and level of monthly doles rose in the early 19th century and between 1833 and 1835 the average yearly expenditure on the poor was £489. Ogbourne St. George became part of Marlborough poor-law union in 1835.[81]

CHURCH. Her gift of Ogbourne St. George church to the abbey of Bec was confirmed by Maud of Wallingford c. 1148.[82] The church was appropriated c. 1190 by the abbey, which undertook to provide a chaplain to serve the cure.[83] At the establishment of the prebend of Ogbourne in 1208 a vicarage was ordained; the abbot of Bec, as prebendary, was patron.[84] From the time of Edward I the prebendaries had the right of archidiaconal jurisdiction in the parish as they did in Ogbourne St. Andrew.[85] As keeper of Ogbourne priory the Crown presented to the vicarage on five occasions between 1326 and 1401.[86] The advowson passed with the estates of the priory to John, duke of Bedford, and in 1421 was granted by him to St. George's chapel, Windsor.[87] In 1549 and 1589 presentations were made to the vicarage by virtue of grants of the advowson from the dean and canons; in 1589 the patron was one of the canons.[88] Ogbourne St. George and Ogbourne St. Andrew were served in plurality from 1951[89] and were united as the benefice of Ogbourne St. Andrew and St. George in 1970.[90] Ogbourne St. George became part of the Ridgeway team ministry in 1974 and a representative of the dean and canons of Windsor was one of five members of the patronage board which thereafter appointed the team rector.[91]

The vicar received £4 6s. 8d. in 1291, a poor income compared with that from other prebendal churches of Salisbury.[92] In 1535, however, the clear value of the vicarage, £14 5s. 8d., was above average for Marlborough deanery.[93] Nevertheless, the dean and canons of Windsor paid the vicar £20 a year from 1666 or earlier, presumably in augmentation of his income.[94] In the early 19th century the living, valued at £244 c. 1830, was moderately prosperous.[95] Small tithes, not otherwise defined, were paid to the vicar from the whole parish except the prior's demesne in the 13th century.[96] In the 15th century the vicar's tithes were described as all but great and hay tithes[97] but he probably received then, as in the 17th century, all tithes except those of grain and of hay and wool and lambs from the demesne farm.[98] In 1843 the vicarial tithes were replaced by a rent charge of £249 14s.[99] In 1650 the vicarage house was of two storeys with three rooms on each.[1] In the mid 18th century it was a building of three bays with a wing at the west end.[2] The house, said to be fit for residence in 1831,[3] was described as a long thatched building in 1870.[4] In 1884 another house was built on higher ground immediately north of the old one which was demolished in 1885.[5] The new house was sold c. 1976 when another was built in its grounds.[6]

A chapel dedicated to All Saints, mentioned in the 13th century, was perhaps attached to Ogbourne priory. In return for saying mass there once a week the vicar held a croft and its hay tithes from the prior.[7] In 1589 a former chapel dedicated to St. Sitha on the west side of the 'west streetway' was sold by the Crown.[8] A chantry in the parish church was known as the chantry of the Holy Trinity or of St. George in the 14th century. In 1376 the Crown presented to the chantry in the right of the prior of Ogbourne, whose property was then in royal keeping, and c. 1395 the prior presented.[9] The advowson descended with Ogbourne St. George manor to King's College, Cambridge, but there was no chantry priest after c. 1543.[10] The chantry may

[76] W.R.O. 212A/16; 267/3; 654/15.
[77] P.R.O., SC 2/212/2; SC 2/212/9, rot. 3; SC 2/212/14, rot. 1; SC 2/212/19, rot. 12; SC 2/212/24, rot. 1.
[78] W.R.O. 862/10.
[79] Ibid.; 862/16.
[80] Ibid. 862/18.
[81] Ibid. 862/19; *Poor Law Com. 2nd Rep.* 559.
[82] Porée, *Histoire du Bec*, i. 461.
[83] *Cal. Doc. France*, ed. Round, p. 129.
[84] *Reg. St. Osmund* (Rolls Ser.), i. 189–90.
[85] *Cat. MSS. D. & C. Windsor*, ed. Dalton, 42; above, Ogbourne St. Andrew, church; W.R.O., dean, Chaundler's reg. f. 67v.
[86] *Cal. Pat.* 1324–7, 213; 1338–40, 241; 1370–4, 203; 1396–9, 578; 1399–1401, 537.
[87] Ibid. 1401–5, 466; 1416–22, 441–2.
[88] W.R.O., dean, reg. inst. ff. 1, 16.
[89] *Lond. Gaz.* 29 June 1951, p. 3562.
[90] Ibid. 2 Oct. 1970, p. 10764.
[91] Inf. from the vicar, the Revd. R. W. C. Jeffery; inf. from Ch. Com.

[92] *Tax. Eccl.* (Rec. Com.), 182.
[93] *Valor Eccl.* (Rec. Com.), ii. 151.
[94] *Cat. MSS. D. & C. Windsor*, ed. Dalton, 255; W.R.O., dean, glebe terriers, 1672, 1705; ibid. 403/39.
[95] *Rep. Com. Eccl. Revenues*, 842–3.
[96] *Sel. Doc. Eng. Lands of Bec* (Camd. 3rd ser. lxxiii), 35.
[97] D. & C. Windsor Mun., IV. B. 1.
[98] *W.A.M.* xli. 113; W.R.O., dean, glebe terriers, 1672, 1705.   [99] W.R.O., tithe award.
[1] *W.A.M.* xli. 113.
[2] King's Coll., Camb., Mun., survey, 1751.
[3] *Rep. Com. Eccl. Revenues*, 842–3.
[4] D. & C. Windsor Mun., XVII. 20. 10.
[5] Ibid. III. F. 1; notice in church.
[6] Inf. from Dr. F. W. Hanford, Kingscot.
[7] *Sel. Doc. Eng. Lands of Bec* (Camd. 3rd ser. lxxiii), 35.
[8] P.R.O., C 66/1322, m. 15.
[9] *Cal. Pat.* 1374–7, 245, 257; W.R.O., dean, Chaundler's reg. f. 67v.
[10] Above, manor; King's Coll. Mun., ledger bk. 1, f. 172; P.R.O., E 301/58, f. 22v.

have received additional endowments from Adam Greenfield and from a member of the Beke family in the early 16th century. In 1545–6, when it was described as a chantry of Adam Greenfield, and in 1548, when it was called St. George's or Beke's, the chantry was valued at 30s.[11] The endowment included 1 yardland in Ogbourne St. George and a house for the priest, which were granted to John Barwick by the Crown in 1549.[12] Another chantry, also Adam Greenfield's and valued at £6 7s., may have been ascribed to the parish in error in 1545–6.[13]

Before the Dissolution there was a guild or fraternity in the parish but no detail of it survives.[14] From the 17th century assistant curates were sometimes appointed to the parish,[15] although there is no evidence of non-residence before the 19th century. In the late 18th century and the 19th minor canons of St. George's chapel, Windsor, were presented to the living.[16] One of them, Benjamin Pope, vicar 1826–71, was a pluralist and non-resident.[17] Perhaps as a result, only a small proportion of the population attended the parish church in the mid 19th century. On Census Sunday in 1851 40 people attended service in the morning, 30 in the afternoon.[18] The average congregation had grown, but only to between 80 and 100, by 1864. There were then 40 communicants. Two services with sermons were held on Sundays and there were additional services at festivals and in Lent. Holy Communion was celebrated monthly and at festivals.[19]

The church had been dedicated to ST. GEORGE by the later 13th century.[20] It is built of sarsen and rubble with freestone dressings and has a chancel with north and south chapels, an aisled and clerestoried nave with a south porch, and a west tower. The chancel arch, some of the chancel walling, and the south arcade are of the early 13th century and show that there was then a building of the present length. The two eastern bays of the north arcade are of the late 13th century and probably opened into a short aisle or chapel. Alterations were made to the chancel in the 14th century and to the whole church in the 15th century or the early 16th. A priest's doorway and chapels were added to the chancel, the nave was reroofed and the clerestory made, and the tower added. Both aisles appear to have been largely rebuilt, perhaps wider than before, and the old doorways were reset. The north aisle was extended westwards, and one bay added to its arcade, and the south porch was built. Fittings of

that period include the font, the north chapel screen, and a brass to Thomas Goddard (d. 1517), which was formerly in that chapel. In the 19th century the roofs were restored and the chancel rebuilt with the renewal of most of the tracery.

In the early 17th century the church lacked even a pewter jug for the communion wine.[21] A chalice and paten cover of 1729, an almsdish hallmarked 1814 and presented in 1857, and a chalice and paten of 1910 are held by the parish. A chalice and paten of 1872 from the chapel of All Saints at Rockley in Ogbourne St. Andrew are used at festivals.[22] There were four bells in 1553. Five new bells were hung in the 17th century and are still in the church.[23]

Registers of baptisms survive from 1639 and from 1663; those of burials and marriages survive from 1664.[24]

NONCONFORMITY. Bartholomew Webb, who was ejected from Ogbourne St. Andrew vicarage in 1662, led a conventicle at Ogbourne St. George until his death in 1681.[25]

Between 1816 and 1819 there was a meeting house at Ogbourne St. George and in 1823 a building was registered for use by Independents.[26] An Independent chapel was built south of the road to Aldbourne at its junction with the Roman road in 1842. On Census Sunday in 1851 there were 75 people attending service there in the afternoon and 71 in the evening. A lay preacher officiated[27] and the teachings followed those of the Independent congregation at Marlborough. Independent services ceased in the late 19th century.[28]

Meetings were held at the house of Joseph Phelps from 1837, and in 1847 a chapel was built on his land.[29] Phelps used it for non-denominational preaching and in 1851 there were 12 people at the morning and 50 at the evening service.[30] The chapel was probably that bought by the vicar and churchwardens in 1882 for use as a reading room and was presumably on the site of the present village hall.[31]

A Wesleyan Methodist chapel was built north of the junction of the village street and the Swindon–Marlborough road in 1864[32] and the former Independent chapel was used by Primitive Methodists in the late 19th century.[33] In 1888 the congregations of both chapels were drawn from ten families, half of whom also attended the parish church.[34] The Primitive

[11] W.A.M. xii. 375; P.R.O., E 301/58, f. 22v.
[12] P.R.O., E 318/Box 25/1423; ibid. CP 25(2)/239/1 & 2 Eliz. I Mich.
[13] W.A.M. xii. 375.
[14] P.R.O., E 310/26/153.
[15] Subscription Bk. 1620–40 (W.R.S. xxxii), p. 77; Cat. MSS. D. & C. Windsor, ed. Dalton, 255; Rep. Com. Eccl. Revenues, 842–3; Kelly's Dir. Wilts. (1855 and later edns.).
[16] e.g. Alum. Cantab. 1752–1900, ii. 6; Rep. Com. Eccl. Revenues, 842–3.
[17] Rep. Com. Eccl. Revenues, 842–3; D. & C. Windsor Mun., XVII. 20. 10.
[18] P.R.O., HO 129/255/1/7/15.
[19] W.R.O., bishop, vis. queries.
[20] P.R.O., JUST 1/998A, rot. 27.
[21] W.R.O., dean, chwdns.' pres. 1607–9.

[22] Nightingale, Wilts. Plate, 160; inf. from Dr. Hanford.
[23] Walters, Wilts. Bells, 152–3; inf. from Dr. Hanford.
[24] W.R.O. 862/1–5; transcripts for 1579–97, 1605–14, 1620–33, 1636–9 are in W.R.O., bishop.
[25] Cal. S.P. Dom. 1680–1, 562–3.
[26] W.R.O., return of regns.; ibid. bishop, certs. dissenters' meeting hos.
[27] P.R.O., HO 129/255/1/7/16; O.S. Map 6″, Wilts. XXIII (1887 edn.).
[28] Endowed Char. Wilts. (N. Div.), 806.
[29] W.R.O., bishop, certs. dissenters' meeting hos.
[30] P.R.O., HO 129/255/1/7/17.
[31] D. & C. Windsor Mun., III. F. 1.
[32] Kelly's Dir. Wilts. (1898).
[33] Endowed Char. Wilts. (N. Div.), 806.
[34] W.R.O. 1156/3.

Methodist chapel was disused in 1911, that of the Wesleyan Methodists was closed c. 1950.[35]

A Baptist congregation which flourished in the 1860s may have held services in Joseph Phelps's chapel.[36]

EDUCATION. Four day schools in Ogbourne St. George established by Mr. Gosling, a Marlborough banker, were attended by 41 children, some from poor families, in 1818.[37] There was a day school in 1833,[38] and in 1850 a schoolroom and teacher's house were built. In 1858 c. 30 children attended that school and 20 a dame school.[39] The school buildings of 1850, perhaps including the house, were replaced in 1862 and another classroom was added in 1875.[40] The school was affiliated to the National Society and attended by 40 children in 1871. There was then also a private school of twelve children.[41] Attendance at the National school had risen to 96 by 1906[42] but fell from 83 to 53 between 1922 and 1936.[43] A new school was built in 1975 and in 1980 there were 53 pupils drawn from the Ogbournes and Chiseldon.[44]

CHARITIES FOR THE POOR. By will dated 1782 William Wooldridge gave £50 to buy bread for the poor. In 1786 another £66 given by various donors was held in trust for the poor of the parish. In 1795 only £35 of it remained. That and Wooldridge's money were invested in 1797 and the income, £6 a year in 1867, was used to buy bread for the second poor at Christmas in alternate years. Peter Thomegay gave £50 by will in or before 1786. The income was not used before 1834 but after 1847 £1 10s. was distributed annually. Under a Scheme of 1901 the income from Wooldridge's and Thomegay's charities was applied to any form of relief except the reduction of the poor rate. Bread was distributed in the early 20th century[45] but from 1956 money payments were made. Between 1971 and 1974 the average yearly income was £8 and payments were made to 25 people in 1973.[46]

Under the Inclosure Act of 1792 King's College, Cambridge, as lord of the manor, was allotted 20 a. north of Bytham Farm for furze for the poor.[47] The land was leased until 1867 or later and the rent, £5 yearly, used to buy bread and fuel. After 1876 furze was taken and coal bought with the accumulated rents from the shooting rights.[48] Under a Scheme of 1950 the income, c. £13 in 1979, was allowed to accumulate for several years and then distributed.[49]

PRESHUTE

THE HISTORY of Preshute, which adjoins Marlborough on the south, north, and west, has been closely involved with that of the borough from earliest times.[50] The prehistoric earthwork called the Mount which stands in Preshute and later formed the motte of Marlborough Castle, built by 1070, may have given the name Marlborough ('barrow of Maerla') to the surrounding area, which was a royal estate by the 11th century.[51] A church, most likely that built west of the mound, was, with the land encircling it, said in 1086 to be in Marlborough.[52] That church and its lands acquired the name Preshute ('priest's cell'). The name, not recorded until 1186, may have been given to the parish formed when the borough acquired its own churches in the late 11th century.[53] The area surrounding the castle, which by the 12th century formed the castle's barton or demesne farm, was the nucleus of the new parish and was later divided between Elcot tithing and that called in the 13th century the king's tithing in Manton township, which possibly contained Preshute church.[54] The westerly township of Clatford and a second tithing in Manton township were added to the new parish. Two tracts of downland to the north, the one in the Crown's hands and the other held by the Templars, had been added by the 12th century and formed the tithings of Langdon Wick and Temple Rockley.[55] Marlborough Common north of the borough was given by King John to the burgesses of Marlborough to provide the borough with pasture land, and Port field was acquired as arable land between 1216 and 1272.[56] Both, however, remained part of Preshute parish.[57] The portion of Elcot tithing east of Blowhorn Street and Rawlingswell Lane was 'new land' of Marlborough before 1252,[58] and was later built

[35] Kelly's Dir. Wilts. (1911 and later edns.); inf. from Dr. F. W. Hanford, Kingscot.
[36] Kelly's Dir. Wilts. (1867); W.R.O., bishop, vis. queries, 1864.   [37] Educ. of Poor Digest, 1034.
[38] Educ. Enquiry Abstract, 1066.
[39] Acct. of Wilts. Schs. 36.
[40] P.R.O., ED 7/131, no. 217; ED 21/18512.
[41] Returns relating to Elem. Educ. 422.
[42] Return of Non-Provided Schs. 832.
[43] Bd. of Educ., List 21 (H.M.S.O.).
[44] Inf. from the Head Teacher.
[45] Endowed Char. Wilts. (N. Div.), 801–5.
[46] Char. Com. file.
[47] W.R.O., inclosure award.
[48] Endowed Char. Wilts. (N. Div.), 802–6.
[49] Char. Com. file; inf. from Dr. F. W. Hanford, Kingscot.

[50] This article was written over the period 1979–81. Thanks are offered to Mr. E. G. H. Kempson, Sun Cottage, Hyde Lane, Marlborough, for help.
[51] The origins of Preshute par. are discussed by H. C. Brentnall in W.A.M. liii. 295–310; cf. ibid. xlviii. 140–3; P.N. Wilts. (E.P.N.S.), 297–8. See plate facing this page.
[52] V.C.H. Wilts. ii, p. 119.
[53] P.N. Wilts. (E.P.N.S.), 307–8, where the date is wrong; Pipe R. 1186 (P.R.S. xxxvi), 165; Reg. St. Osmund (Rolls Ser.), i. 199.
[54] Pipe R. 1199 (P.R.S. n.s. x), 178; Rot. Hund. (Rec. Com.), ii (1), 263.
[55] Below, manors; above, Ogbourne St. Andrew, introduction.   [56] Rot. Hund. (Rec. Com.), ii (1), 263.
[57] P.R.O., IR 29/38/188; IR 30/38/188.
[58] Sar. Chart. and Doc. (Rolls Ser.), 320–1.

The Castle inn in 1772. St. Peter's church, Marlborough, is on the right.

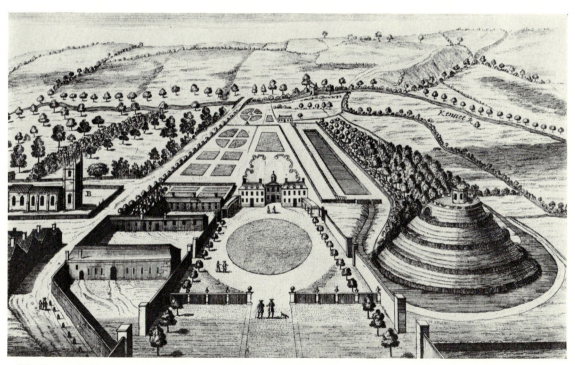

Marlborough House in 1723. St. Peter's church, Marlborough, is on the left and the Mount on the right.

PRESHUTE

MILDENHALL: SCHOOL BUILT IN 1824, CLOSED IN 1969

MILDENHALL: POULTON HOUSE, BUILT IN 1706

EAST KENNETT
Christ Church, built in 1863

on. As the chapelry of St. Martin the area, still called St. Martin's in the later 20th century, remained in Preshute parish until it was transferred to St. Mary's parish, Marlborough, *c.* 1548.[59]

From the mid 16th century, when its boundaries crystallized, until 1901 Preshute comprised 5,358 a. (2,168 ha.) stretching 10 km. from north-west to south-east across the Kennet valley and at no point as much as 5 km. wide.[60] The eastern boundary was marked partly by a short stretch of the Kennet, the Og, the Og's western head stream called the Hungerbourne,[61] and the Marlborough–Salisbury road, the southern by the Wansdyke for 1 km., and the north-western by the Ridge Way on Hackpen Hill for 750 m.; elsewhere the boundaries pursued arbitrary courses across the Marlborough Downs and north of Savernake forest.

In 1901 Preshute was divided for civil purposes into the parishes of Preshute Without and Preshute Within. Preshute Without, 4,834 a. (1,956 ha.), comprised Clatford and Manton tithings, the northern part of Elcot tithing including most of Marlborough Common, and the western part of Elcot. Preshute Within, 400 a. (162 ha.) which included Preshute church and land south-west of the borough, land on the western edge of Marlborough Common, and St. Margaret's district, became a civil parish within the borough of Marlborough. At the same date the extreme south-eastern angle of Preshute was apportioned between Mildenhall, which received 46 a. (19 ha.), and North Savernake to which 78 a. (32 ha.) were transferred.[62] Preshute Without was renamed Preshute in 1925 and Preshute Within merged with the two Marlborough parishes.[63] In 1934 a further 824 a. (333 ha.), including Manton village and the rest of Marlborough Common, were transferred to the borough, leaving Preshute with 1,624 ha. (4,012 a.).[64]

Most of Preshute is on the chalk of the Marlborough Downs.[65] From the extreme northern boundary on Hackpen Hill at 269 m. the land inclines south-eastwards to the Kennet, south of which it rises to above 183 m. on Granham Hill. The figure of a horse was cut on Granham Hill in 1804 by boys from a private school in Marlborough.[66] The chalk is overlain by clay-with-flints north of the Kennet near Manton House and on Marlborough Common. Similar deposits occur south of the river on Granham Hill. Scatters of hard siliceous sand-

stones called sarsen stones, or grey wethers from their sheep-like appearance at a distance, occur near the Devil's Den at the north-western end of Clatford Bottom.[67] There are gravel deposits in Clatford Bottom and in the dry valleys in the north-west. The wider gravel terrace south of the Kennet provides sites for the principal settlements. Lush meadows cover the alluvial deposits of the Kennet and Og.

Preshute was inhabited at least from Neolithic times. The most notable prehistoric remains are the Neolithic mound which later formed the motte of Marlborough Castle, the Manton bowl-barrow which contained many articles illustrative of the rich Wessex culture of the Bronze Age, and the 'Marlborough bucket' found in an area of early Iron-Age settlement south-east of Marlborough.[68] There were Roman settlements on Barton Down north of Field Barn near Manton House, and in St. Margaret's district on the outskirts of the Roman town of Cunetio (Mildenhall).[69] The London–Bath road crosses the parish. The possible course of the road east of Marlborough is marked by the part of the London road called Newbury Street in the 14th century and in 1678 but London Road in 1752.[70] Between *c.* 1706 and *c.* 1752 the road was diverted from Marlborough high street to run along George Lane, so called in 1752 but London Road in 1706.[71] At the west end of George Lane the Bath road turned north-westwards across the Kennet at Castle, later Cow, Bridge,[72] followed the south-western boundary of Marlborough, and at its junction with Marlborough high street took a north-westerly course through the borough east of the castle mound. That section was diverted eastwards into the borough *c.* 1705 to accommodate a new house being built on the site of Marlborough Castle.[73] In 1706 it was called the Bristol road west of Marlborough.[74] The road was turnpiked east of Marlborough in 1726 and west of it in 1743.[75] All the major roads which converged upon Marlborough crossed Preshute. The Salisbury–Swindon road by way of Rockley in Ogbourne St. Andrew was turnpiked in 1762.[76] Its course across Marlborough Common was lined in 1910 with trees given by Thomas Free, mayor of Marlborough, and thereafter called Free's Avenue.[77] North of Marlborough it was replaced as the main road to Swindon when the more easterly low lying route through Ogbourne St. George was turnpiked in 1819. That entered Preshute at Bay Bridge, mentioned from the 16th century, and crossed

[59] P.R.O., C 3/189/78.
[60] Maps used include O.S. Maps 1″, sheets 14 (1817 edn.), 34 (1828 edn.), 157 (1968 edn.); 1/50,000, sheets 173 (1974 edn.), 174 (1974 edn.); 1/25,000, SU 16 (1961 edn.), SU 17 (1960 edn.), SU 26 (1961 edn.); 6″, Wilts. XXII (1888 edn.), XXVIII (1889 edn.), XXIX (1889 edn.), XXXV (1889 edn.), XXXVI (1888 edn.), 1/10,000, SU 16 NE. (1961 edn.), SU 17 SW., NW., SE. (1960 edn.), SU 26 NW. (1961 edn.).
[61] *Andrews and Dury, Map* (W.R.S. viii), pl. 12.
[62] *Census*, 1901.
[63] Ibid. 1931; *V.C.H. Wilts.* iv. 353.
[64] *Census*, 1931.
[65] Para. is based on Geol. Surv. Map 1″, drift, sheet 266 (1964 edn.).
[66] *W.A.M.* xiv. 27.
[67] The sarsen ind. of the area is referred to in *V.C.H. Wilts.* xi. 198.
[68] Ibid. i (1), 85, 142; i (2), 314, 437; *W.A.M.* xlviii. 140–3.

[69] *V.C.H. Wilts.* i (1), 85, 97; i (2), 465.
[70] *P.N. Wilts.* (E.P.N.S.), 299 where the site of Newbury Street is wrongly identified as 'outside St. Mary's' in Marlborough; P.R.O., PROB 11/374 (P.C.C. 103 Drax, will of Geoffrey Daniell); Blenheim Mun., map of St. Margaret's, 1752.
[71] Blenheim Mun., map of St. Margaret's, 1752; W.S.R.O., PHA 3565.
[72] Blenheim Mun., map of St. Margaret's, 1752; J. E. Chandler, *Hist. Marlborough* (priv. print. 1977), 15.
[73] Alnwick Castle Mun., X.II.11, box 14, enquiry concerning new road, 1705; W.S.R.O., PHA 3565; *Rep. Marlborough Coll. Natural Hist. Soc.* xcviii, map at pp. 44–5.
[74] W.S.R.O., PHA 3565.
[75] *V.C.H. Wilts.* iv. 258; *L.J.* xxii. 664; xxvi. 241.
[76] *V.C.H. Wilts.* iv. 262; *L.J.* xxx. 205.
[77] Wilts. Cuttings, xxviii. 87.

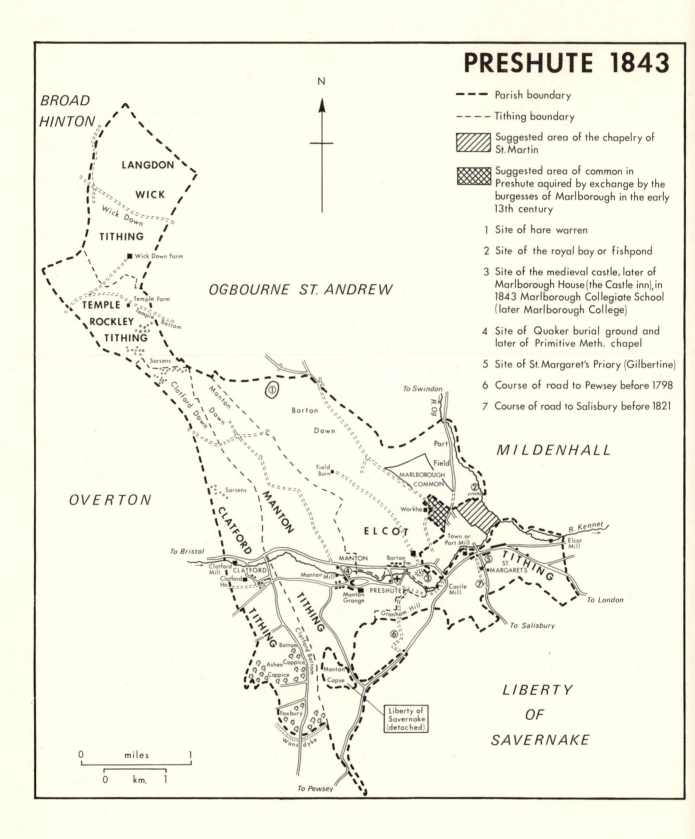

PRESHUTE 1843

- - - Parish boundary
- - - Tithing boundary

Suggested area of the chapelry of St. Martin

Suggested area of common in Preshute aquired by exchange by the burgesses of Marlborough in the early 13th century

1 Site of hare warren
2 Site of the royal bay or fishpond
3 Site of the medieval castle, later of Marlborough House (the Castle inn), in 1843 Marlborough Collegiate School (later Marlborough College)
4 Site of Quaker burial ground and later of Primitive Meth. chapel
5 Site of St. Margaret's Priory (Gilbertine)
6 Course of road to Pewsey before 1798
7 Course of road to Salisbury before 1821

BROAD HINTON

LANGDON

WICK

TITHING

Wick Down

Wick Down Farm

Temple Farm

TEMPLE

ROCKLEY

TITHING

Temple Bottom

Sarsens

OGBOURNE ST. ANDREW

Clatford Down

Manton Down

Barton Down

To Swindon

R. Og

Port Field

MARLBOROUGH COMMON

MILDENHALL

OVERTON

Sarsens

CLATFORD

MANTON

Field Barn

Workho

ELCOT

R. Kennet

Town or Port Mill

Elcot Mill

To Bristol

Clatford Mill

CLATFORD

Clatford Ho.

Manton Mill

MANTON

Barton Fm.

TITHING

ST. MARGARETS

Manton Grange

PRESHUTE

Castle Mill

To London

TITHING

TITHING

Clatford Bottom

Granham Hill

To Salisbury

Bottom

Ashen Coppice

Coppice

Manton Copse

LIBERTY

OF

SAVERNAKE

Foxbury

Liberty of Savernake (detached)

Wansdyke

0   miles   1
0   km.   1

To Pewsey

162

Marlborough Common.[78] South-east of Marlborough the part of Salisbury Road called Daniell's Lane in 1752 and Station Road in 1900 was diverted eastwards to its present course through St. Margaret's in 1821.[79] The portion of the road from Marlborough to Wootton Bassett across Wick Down was turnpiked in 1809.[80] In the 18th century a road ran westwards from the Bath road as a continuation of George Lane linking Preshute church and the villages of Manton and Clatford. It ran south of the Kennet along the footpath called Treacle Bolly. Between Preshute church and Manton it was called Frog Lane in the 18th century and Preshute Lane in 1981.[81] The stretch west of Clatford was, like Treacle Bolly, no more than a footpath by 1981. Treacle Bolly was in 1773 part of the Marlborough-Pewsey road, the old course of which was marked by a footpath from Treacle Bolly to Granham Farm in Savernake in 1981.[82] That road was diverted eastwards to a less steep route over Granham Hill from Castle Bridge in 1798.[83]

Like other amenities provided for Marlborough in the 19th century, the railway stations which served the town were in Preshute. In 1864 the Marlborough Railway was opened and ran from a station west of the Salisbury road in St. Margaret's in a westerly loop to join the Berks. & Hants Extension Railway at Savernake station in Burbage. The line was worked by the G.W.R., in which it was vested in 1896.[84] In 1881 the Swindon, Marlborough & Andover Railway, from 1884 the Midland & South Western Junction Railway, was opened and from a station east of the Salisbury road ran in an easterly loop round Marlborough northwards to Swindon. The M. & S.W.J.R. was extended south-eastwards in 1898 by the construction of the Marlborough & Grafton Railway. The M. & S.W.J.R. worked the line from its opening and acquired it in 1899.[85] That railway merged with the G.W.R. in 1923 and from 1924 the G.W.R. and M. & S.W.J.R. stations were called High Level and Low Level respectively. Alterations between 1926 and 1933 reduced the former Marlborough & Grafton line to a single track and provided a second by the partial rerouting of the G.W.R. line. The original G.W.R. track, except a short stretch south-west of High Level station, was removed. The new route was first fully used, and High Level station closed, in 1933.[86] Passenger services were withdrawn from Low Level station in 1961.[87] Freight services were

withdrawn, and the station and line finally closed, in 1964.[88]

Preshute, represented by Marlborough barton, Manton, and Clatford, was in 1334 taxed fourth highest of the ten parishes in Selkley hundred. There were 139 poll-tax payers in 1377.[89] In 16th- and 17th-century taxation assessments Preshute appears one of the more prosperous parishes in Selkley hundred.[90] In 1801 there were 618 people in the parish.[91] The number had declined to 583 by 1811 but thereafter rose steadily until 1851. An increase from 898 to 1,227 between 1841 and 1851, although like the 1831-41 rise attributed to the opening in 1837 of a union workhouse on Marlborough Common, is more likely to be accounted for by the growth of Marlborough College. The population was 1,209 in 1861 but the expansion both of the college and of training stables on Manton Down had resulted in an increase to 1,374 by 1871.[92] In 1881 the population was 1,837 but by 1891 had declined inexplicably to 1,311. Numbers had risen to 1,622 by 1901. Preshute Without, later Preshute, parish had 559 inhabitants in 1911, 556 in 1921, and 615 in 1931. The population of the parish, from which Manton had been transferred in 1934, was 216 in 1951, 194 in 1961, and 132 in 1971.[93]

The village of ELCOT gave its name to the tithing which was conterminous with the royal barton. In the 14th century another village grew up along that part of the London road called Newbury Street. Elcot was called St. Margaret's district from the later 16th century.[94] Most of the 81 people in the barton of Marlborough assessed for the poll tax of 1377 may have lived in those areas.[95] Smallholdings survived in the south-east angle of the parish in the 17th century.[96] Newbury Street was still so called in the later 17th century but afterwards, as London Road, was considered part of St. Margaret's district.[97]

ST. MARGARET'S took its name from the Gilbertine priory which stood beside the Marlborough-Salisbury road. Of the inns along the London-Bath road the Wheatsheaf stood at Forest Hill, then partly in Preshute, in the 18th century and earlier 19th, and the Roebuck, mentioned from the earlier 18th century, at its junction with Elcot Lane.[98] The George, from which part of the London-Bath road took its name in 1752 or earlier, may have been an inn in the earlier 17th century and was so in 1713. A Roman Catholic church marked its site in 1981.[99]

[78] V.C.H. Wilts. iv. 263; W.R.O. 9/2/366, ff. 14v. sqq.
[79] Blenheim Mun., map of St. Margaret's, 1752; V.C.H. Wilts. iv. 270; O.S. Map 1/2,500, Wilts. XXIX. 9 (1900 edn.).
[80] V.C.H. Wilts. iv. 257, 271.
[81] Andrews and Dury, Map (W.R.S. viii), pl. 12; W.R.O. 9/2/65; 9/2/69; ibid. Manton inclosure award.
[82] Andrews and Dury, Map (W.R.S. viii), pl. 12.
[83] Chandler, Hist. Marlborough, 74.
[84] V.C.H. Wilts. iv. 287-8.
[85] Ibid. 289-90.
[86] Ibid. 292-3; Chandler, Hist. Marlborough, 74.
[87] Chandler, op. cit. 75.
[88] Inf. from P.R. Dept., British Rail, W.R.
[89] V.C.H. Wilts. iv. 296, 301, 306, 310.
[90] P.R.O., E 179/197/165; E 179/198/257; E 179/198/276; E 179/198/334; E 179/199/369; Taxation Lists (W.R.S. x), 101-4.
[91] Except where stated, population figures are from V.C.H. Wilts. iv. 355.
[92] Ibid. 320-1, 324; v. 364-5.
[93] Census, 1961, 1971.
[94] V.C.H. Wilts. iv. 396, 419; P.R.O., E 179/239/193 IIA; E 179/198/276.   [95] V.C.H. Wilts. iv. 306.
[96] Alnwick Castle Mun., X.II.11, box 6, survey of Hertford lands, 1634- , pp. 341, 367; W.R.O. 9/2/371.
[97] Above.
[98] Chandler, Hist. Marlborough, 59, 71; Blenheim Mun., map of St. Margaret's, 1752; W.R.O., reg. alehousekeepers' recognizances, 1822-7; P.R.O., IR 29/38/188; IR 30/38/188.
[99] W.A.M. xxx. 110-11; Alnwick Castle Mun., X.II.11, box 6, survey of Hertford lands, 1634- , p. 343; Blenheim Mun., Wilts. deeds, articles, Hawes and Fettiplace, 1713; below, Marlborough, Rom. Catholicism. The George is depicted in Chandler, Hist. Marlborough, at pp. 52-3.

The Red Cow, which stood beside the old road over Granham Hill in 1773, was burnt down c. 1838.[1] The only building in St. Margaret's older than the 19th century is a range of 17th-century timber-framed cottages at the junction of George Lane and Salisbury Road.

In the late 19th century and earlier 20th Marlborough expanded commercially and residentially into St. Margaret's and much of the housing which fronts London Road and Salisbury Road is of those dates. Marlborough police station was opened in George Lane in 1898 and in 1900 sewage works in Elcot Lane.[2] Savernake Hospital was opened in 1872 south of London Road at Forest Hill.[3] Council houses were built in Isbury Road and Cherry Orchard from c. 1920.[4] St. Margaret's mead east of Low Level station was bought by the borough in 1945 and a council estate built on it c. 1950.[5] Priorsfield east of Salisbury Road was developed as a private estate in the 1970s. North of Elcot Lane and north-west and east of some earlier private houses interspersed with light industrial development dating mostly from the mid 20th century, Stonebridge Close, Barrow Close, and Willow Close contain private houses of the 1960s. Barnfield between Elcot Lane and London Road was first built upon in the 1920s. The estate was further expanded after the Second World War.

North of the London–Bath road Barton Farm was the only large private house in Elcot tithing west of Marlborough. It was extensively renovated, if not rebuilt, c. 1722 and extended southwards in the early 19th century by the addition of an entrance hall with principal rooms on either side.[6] The house, reroofed and altered in the 20th century for Marlborough College, was the college estate office in 1981. Near the house stood an aisled barn, built in the 17th century, extensively repaired c. 1722, and burnt down in 1976.[7] Westward expansion of Marlborough was blocked by Marlborough Castle and successive houses which later occupied its site. The second house, used as an inn called the Castle in the later 18th century and early 19th, was converted to a school, later Marlborough College, in 1843.[8] The buildings erected north of the house to accommodate the school straddle the former Preshute–Marlborough boundary. A court built in the style of c. 1700 to the north-west by Edward Blore, college architect 1844–9, had a dining hall and boarding house on the south-west side and another boarding house on the south-east.[9] The dining hall was replaced in 1961–2 by another, Norwood Hall, designed by David Roberts. The south-eastern range was replaced, but its style perpetuated and

elaborated, by the Bradleian building constructed in 1871–3 by G. E. Street and by the Museum Block of 1882–3. That, which partly incorporated the stables of the old house, was perhaps designed by Street but completed by his son A. E. Street and partner A. W. Blomfield. The chapel in 13th-century style which Blore erected in the western angle of the court was replaced in 1883–6 by another designed by Bodley & Garner and built of stone in 14th-century style. The northern angle was filled in 1893–9 by the North Block built in 16th-century style by Bodley & Garner. The Master's Lodge built south-east of the old house by Blore was enlarged in the 1860s by William White, who also erected minor school buildings in 1858 and 1863.

The school sick house built by White north of the London–Bath road stood in Marlborough, and the first substantial college buildings to be put up in Preshute on the north side of that road were two boarding houses, Cotton and Littlefield, designed by G. E. Street and built of cast concrete in 1870–2 by Charles Drake, a pioneer of that material. In the early 20th century the college expanded northwards into Marlborough where, on the north side of the London–Bath road, a gymnasium was built in 1908 by C. E. Ponting and Field House, linked to North Block on the south side by an enclosed footbridge, by Sir Aston Webb in 1910–11; the gymnasium incorporated windows from the Marlborough bridewell which had previously occupied the site.

Of the buildings designed between the First and Second World Wars by the college architect, W. G. Newton, the Memorial Hall of 1921–5 and Science Building of shuttered concrete begun in 1933 were west of the Mount and the Leaf Block of 1936 east of it.

The Marlborough union workhouse, designed by W. Cooper, became a children's convalescent home after 1929 and was still so used in 1981.[10] An isolation hospital built to the north-west by Marlborough rural district council in 1890 had merged with it by 1970.[11] North-west of the workhouse 2 a. of land bought in 1853 were consecrated in 1855 as a burial ground for Preshute and the two Marlborough parishes. A mortuary chapel built there in 1859 was consecrated in 1860.[12]

There was a village of MANTON in the early 14th century and in 1377 it had 28 poll-tax payers.[13] Several inhabitants seem to have been prosperous in the later 16th century.[14] In 1841, when 290 people lived there, it was, apart from St. Margaret's, the most populous settlement in Preshute.[15] There was apparently no settlement

[1] Andrews and Dury, Map (W.R.S. viii), pl. 12; Chandler, op. cit. 71.
[2] C. Hughes, Marlborough: the Story of a Small and Anct. Boro. (Swindon, priv. print. [1953]), 91–2.
[3] V.C.H. Wilts. v. 342–3.
[4] Except where stated, inf. about housing developments from Co. Planning Officer, Co. Hall, Trowbridge.
[5] Hughes, Marlborough, 95.
[6] Alnwick Castle Mun., X.II.11, box 23, survey of Barton Farm, 1722; acct. of repairs, 1722–6.
[7] Ibid. X.II.11, box 6, survey of Hertford lands, 1634– , p. 355; Pevsner, Wilts. (2nd edn.), 341 n.; Chandler,

Hist. Marlborough, underline to illustration at pp. 52–3.
[8] Below, manors.
[9] The description of the coll. bldgs. is based on Pevsner, Wilts. (2nd edn.), 338–41; Marlborough Coll. Guide (1979).
[10] Inf. on bldg.; V.C.H. Wilts. v. 345.
[11] A. R. Stedman, Marlborough and the Upper Kennet Country (Marlborough, priv. print. 1960), 321; O.S. Map 1/2,500, SU 1869–1969 (1970 edn.).
[12] W.R.O. 9/2/277; ibid. bishop, consecrations, bdle. 5, no. 35; bdle. 7, no. 26.
[13] V.C.H. Wilts. iv. 301, 310.
[14] Taxation Lists (W.R.S. x), 103.
[15] V.C.H. Wilts. iv. 355.

near Preshute church other than a farmhouse which was enlarged in the later 19th century as a boarding house for Marlborough College and called Preshute House. The church was linked to the London–Bath road by two lanes which in 1773 apparently forded the Kennet but by 1817 were carried over it by bridges.[16] The village lies west of the church along the lane, called High Street in Manton, linking the riverside settlements south of the Kennet. Several 19th-century houses, of which those at the south-western end stand above the street on a chalk embankment, are of red brick with lower courses of sarsen. From the small green at the eastern end of the street Bridge Street crosses the Kennet, by a bridge which existed in 1773, to link Manton with the London–Bath road. Manton Drove, in 1773 called Manton Lane,[17] runs south from the western end of the street to join the Marlborough–Pewsey road.

On the south side of the green the Old Post Office, formerly a farmhouse, was built of sarsen rubble in the later 16th century or the earlier 17th. It has been cased in brick but retains a thatched roof. Manton Weir, which stands south of the London–Bath road west of its junction with Bridge Street, was built as a farmhouse in the later 17th century. It was altered and cased in brick in the mid 18th century when a low kitchen wing was added on the east. It was called Braithwaite's Farm c. 1792.[18] In the later 19th century the kitchen wing was raised to two storeys and small additions were made to the north side of the main block. Manton Grange stands east of the village set back across meadows on the south side of Preshute Lane. It is a square red-brick farmhouse of c. 1800 which was enlarged, altered, and refitted, probably for the Maurice family, c. 1900.[19] A private housing estate called Manton Hollow was constructed north of the London–Bath road in the 1950s and another called West Manton west of High Street in the 1960s.[20]

Of the inns which stood along the London–Bath road, the Plough was on the south side in 1773. The Swan, on the north side, was called Lord Bruce's Arms c. 1792, the Lord's Arms in 1845, and as the Marquess of Ailesbury was still an inn in the early 20th century.[21] In the village the Oddfellows Arms at the north-west corner of the green was opened in 1878 and the Up the Garden Path on the south side of High Street in 1972.[22]

There was no settlement in Manton tithing north of the London–Bath road until racehorse stables were built on Manton Down in the later 19th century.[23] Manton House, intended for the trainer, occupies the south side of the red-brick stable block of two storeys round a courtyard. It was being altered and refitted in 1979. Near the stables are several late 19th-century cottages, an early 20th-century stable block, a hostel constructed in 1921 for stable lads, and a modern house. A landscaped garden incorporating a chain of small lakes was created in the later 1970s. The farmstead of Manton House, built in the 1970s on the downs south-east of the stables, includes extensive covered yards.[24]

The contribution made by CLATFORD to the tax of 1334, although small compared with other villages near Marlborough, was only a little less than that of its easterly neighbour Manton.[25] In 1377 there were 30 poll-tax payers, two more than at Manton.[26] In 1773 the village was closely grouped north of the lane running west from Marlborough. North-west of it Clatford Mill stood alone on the south side of the London–Bath road.[27] As the etymology of Clatford suggests, the Kennet was forded there. It seems to have remained so in 1773 but by 1817 a bridge carried the lane which linked the village with the London–Bath road across it.[28] There were 122 inhabitants in 1801, no more than 90 in 1841.[29] All that remained of the village in 1981 was Clatford Farm and a few cottages south-west of it.

The tithings of LANGDON WICK and TEMPLE ROCKLEY were never sufficiently populous for their inhabitants to be enumerated or assessed for taxation separately. In 1981 each contained a 19th-century farmstead.

MARLBOROUGH CASTLE. A castle at Marlborough is suggested by the imprisonment there of Ethelric, bishop of Selsey, in 1070.[30] It may have been built when William I early in his reign transferred a mint and a moneyer to Marlborough from Great Bedwyn.[31] Its site was the prehistoric earthwork, later called the Mount, easily defensible where the Kennet valley narrows between the chalk masses of the Marlborough Downs.[32]

Although Henry I spent Easter at Marlborough in 1110,[33] the first definite evidence of a castle there is from 1138.[34] The anarchy which followed Stephen's usurpation in 1135 caused the castle, on an east–west route loyal to the Empress Maud, to be strengthened. Many preliminary skirmishes in Maud's campaign occurred there and in 1138 the castle was fortified by John FitzGilbert, the marshal, a supporter of

[16] *Andrews and Dury, Map* (W.R.S. viii), pl. 12; O.S. Map 1″, sheet 14 (1817 edn.).
[17] *Andrews and Dury, Map* (W.R.S. viii), pl. 12.
[18] W.R.O., Manton inclosure award.
[19] The arms of Maurice appear over the E. entrance front.
[20] Inf. from Co. Planning Officer.
[21] *Andrews and Dury, Map* (W.R.S. viii), pl. 12; W.R.O., Manton inclosure award; P.R.O., IR 29/38/188; IR 30/38/188; *Kelly's Dir. Wilts.* (1903).
[22] Chandler, *Hist. Marlborough*, 70-1.
[23] O.S. Map 1″, sheet 34 (1828 edn.); P.R.O., IR 29/38/188; IR 30/38/188.
[24] Inf. from Mr. J. V. Bloomfield, Manton Ho.
[25] *V.C.H. Wilts.* iv. 301.
[26] Ibid. 310.
[27] *Andrews and Dury, Map* (W.R.S. viii), pl. 12.
[28] Ibid.; *P.N. Wilts.* (E.P.N.S.), 308; O.S. Map 1″, sheet 14 (1817 edn.).
[29] *V.C.H. Wilts.* iv. 355.
[30] *Chron. Rog. de Houedene* (Rolls Ser.), i. 124.
[31] *Numismatic Chron.* 4th ser. ii. 24-5; *Feud. Aids*, v. 205.
[32] The castle and its site are discussed by H. C. Brentnall in *W.A.M.* xlviii. 133-43; *Woodward's Notes* (W.R.S. xiii), 11.
[33] *A.-S. Chron.* ed. D. Whitelock, 181 and n.
[34] *Ann. Mon.* (Rolls Ser.), ii. 51.

the empress, and held for her against King Stephen in 1139.[35] He still held the 'very strong castle' in 1140 when he repelled the mercenary, Robert FitzHubert, who that year had captured Devizes Castle.[36] Despite harassment from Stephen's son Eustace in 1149, he held the castle for Maud until her son succeeded as Henry II in 1154, and continued to do so until 1158.[37] In 1189 Richard I gave the castle to his brother John on John's marriage with Isabel of Gloucester.[38] During John's rebellion of 1193–4 the castle was besieged and captured for the king by the regent Hubert Walter, archbishop of Canterbury.[39] Richard I committed Marlborough in 1194 to Hugh de Neville who remained keeper under John.[40]

Devizes Castle may have been more important than Marlborough to the rival factions during Stephen's reign because it was then stronger and more sophisticated. That it was not so during the civil war of 1214 and during the French invasion of 1216 was due to extensive building works undertaken by John at Marlborough between 1209 and 1211 to strengthen it, not only as a residence, but also as a provincial treasury. By 1207 it had become part of a network of such treasuries and much money and plate were kept therein.[41]

After John's death Hugh de Neville defected to the baronial party and in 1216 surrendered the castle, which had been heavily fortified in 1215, to Louis of France.[42] Louis installed Robert de Dreux as keeper but in 1217 William Marshal recaptured the castle for Henry III.[43] Its keeping was then entrusted to William's father, William Marshal, earl of Pembroke, son of John Fitz-Gilbert, and regent of England. William succeeded his father as keeper in 1219 but was deprived of the castle in 1221 for fortifying it in 1220 without royal permission.[44]

A constable is first referred to by that name in 1203.[45] It is unlikely, however, that he was other than the keeper or castellan, and the terms constable and keeper were used interchangeably throughout the 13th century.[46] The lesser officers upon whom the daily administration of the castle devolved in the later 14th century included a deputy constable, a porter, and a bailiff.[47]

Henry III spent Easter 1220 at Marlborough which for the next fifty years was favoured as a residence by him and his family.[48] He extended and strengthened the castle as a fortress and improved it as a dwelling.[49] Henry's sister Isabel was there in 1230, 1231, and 1233. Queen Eleanor was there in 1256 and the castle was assigned to her as dower in 1262.[50]

The growth of baronial opposition to Henry III after 1258 made the appointment of trust-worthy men to keep strategically placed castles of first importance. Thus in 1261 Robert Walerand, one of the king's closest advisers, was appointed keeper for a five-year term.[51] His tenure was interrupted by the intrusion in 1262, probably at the insistence of Simon de Montfort, of Roger de Clifford (d. c. 1286) then an adherent of the baronial party who, however, returned to his allegiance the following year. Walerand was reinstated by the king in 1263.[52] After the battle of Lewes in 1264 all castles in royal hands were surrendered to the adherents of Simon de Mont-fort. Marlborough, however, was soon retaken for the king by Roger de Clifford and a group of marcher lords.[53] Henry III spent some days at Marlborough in 1265 recovering after the battle of Evesham. The parliament he summoned to meet him there in 1267, which probably assembled in the great hall of the castle, enacted the statute of Marlborough.[54]

In 1194 or earlier the borough of Marlborough, the barton farm, Selkley hundred, and Savernake forest, to which, however, separate wardens were appointed, belonged to the castle.[55] Such resources possibly rendered the creation of serjeanties for the garrisoning of the castle unnecessary. The castellans held the castle at farm from the late 12th century or earlier and had to maintain it in peacetime and to support a garrison there in time of war.[56] In the mid 13th century the king allowed £26 13s. 4d. for the maintenance of the castle in peacetime.[57] At other times more was allowed to munition the garrison and in 1264, at the time of de Montfort's insurrection, 4 knights with barded horses, 4 serjeants-at-arms with barded horses, 12 serjeants with unbarded horses, and 54 footmen were maintained for about ten weeks within the castle.[58] It continued to be munitioned at times of crisis, as in 1322 and 1360, until it fell into decay after 1380.[59]

[35] Ann. Mon. (Rolls Ser.), ii. 51; A. L. Poole, From Domesday Book to Magna Carta (1955), 138.
[36] Gesta Stephani, ed. K. R. Potter, 70–1.
[37] Ibid. 144–5; Pipe R. 1156–8 (Rec. Com.), 57, 77, 116.
[38] Mat. Paris, Hist. Angl. (Rolls Ser.), ii. 5.
[39] Ann. Mon. (Rolls Ser.), i. 191; iv. 46–7; Mem. R. 1199 (Pipe R. Soc. N.S. xxi), p. lxxiv.
[40] Pipe R. 1194 (P.R.S. N.S. v), 10; Pipe R. 17 John (P.R.S. N.S. xxxvii), 59; D.N.B.
[41] Hist. King's Works, ed. H. M. Colvin, ii. 735; J. E. A. Jolliffe, 'The Chamber and the Castle Treasures under King John', Studies presented to F. M. Powicke, ed. R. W. Hunt and others, 117–42; Mem. R. 1208 (Pipe R. Soc. N.S. xxxi), 119, 120 and nn.; Rot. Litt. Pat. (Rec. Com.), 81, 84, 88, 106, 128, 147.
[42] Mem. R. 1208 (Pipe R. Soc. N.S. xxxi), 130, 134, 139; Rot. Litt. Claus. (Rec. Com.), i. 186, 226; Rot. Litt. Pat. (Rec. Com.), 136–7; D.N.B.; Hist. des Ducs de Normandie, ed. F. Michel, 175–6.
[43] Michel, op. cit. 176; Walter of Coventry (Rolls Ser.), ii. 236; Complete Peerage, x. 365 and n., 366.
[44] Rot. Litt. Claus. (Rec. Com.), i. 521; Complete Peerage, x. 358 sqq., App. G, 95; Letters of Hen. III (Rolls Ser.), i.

100–1; Ann. Mon. (Rolls Ser.), iii. 68.
[45] Rot. Litt. Pat. (Rec. Com.), 24.
[46] e.g. Rot. Litt. Claus. ii. 53; Close R. 1253–4, 17; 1264–8, 5; Cal. Lib. 1251–60, 223, 243.
[47] P.R.O., E 364/5/7, m. Gd.; Cal. Fine R. 1369–77, 68; 1377–83, 200; Cal. Inq. Misc. v, p. 167; Cal. Pat. 1377–81, 544; 1381–5, 520; 1391–6, 309.
[48] Mat. Paris, Hist. Angl. (Rolls Ser.), ii. 240.
[49] Hist. King's Works, ii. 735; below.
[50] Close R. 1227–31, 455, 507, 533; Cal. Lib. 1226–40, 224; 1251–60, 273, 313, 345; Cal. Pat. 1266–72, 358, 737.
[51] Cal. Pat. 1258–66, 144; Cal. Lib. 1260–7, 25.
[52] Cal. Pat. 1258–66, 266; D.N.B.; Complete Peerage, iii. 290.
[53] Ann. Mon. (Rolls Ser.), iii. 234; D.N.B. s.v. Rog. de Clifford.
[54] Hist. King's Works, ii. 737; Red Bk. Exch. (Rolls Ser.), i, p. cxxiii.
[55] Pipe R. 1194 (P.R.S. N.S. v), 10; V.C.H. Wilts. iv. 420–1.
[56] Pipe R. 1194 (P.R.S. N.S. v), 10.
[57] Rot. Hund. (Rec. Com.), ii (1), 235.
[58] Cal. Inq. Misc. i, pp. 109–10.
[59] Cal. Close, 1318–23, 437; V.C.H. Wilts. v. 21 n.; below.

After the death of Henry III the castle declined as a fortress because it lost favour as a residence. It continued to be used by Queen Eleanor, who spent three weeks there in 1274.[60] After her death in 1291 the accommodation within the castle, called the 'king's houses', was assigned during pleasure to Isabel (d. 1296), relict of Ingram de Fiennes who had been a knight in Henry III's household.[61] In 1295 the constable lodged Welsh hostages at the castle and was allowed 4d. daily to maintain them, probably in honourable confinement.[62] Joan (d. 1307), daughter of Edward I, who had married clandestinely Sir Ralph de Monthermer, was in 1297 allowed to retire to Marlborough where a daughter was born to her.[63] Beatrice, wife of Aymer de Valence, was also allowed to live there that year while her husband was with the king in Flanders.[64] In 1299 the castle was assigned in dower to Margaret, queen of Edward I.[65] Hugh le Despenser, later earl of Winchester, was appointed constable in 1308 and the queen's steward was ordered to deliver the castle to him. Later in 1308, however, the castle was restored to the queen.[66] In 1318 it was assigned to Isabel, queen of Edward II, but occupied by the elder Despenser in May 1321.[67] The castle was plundered by Despenser's political opponents that summer and surrendered by him on his downfall in September.[68] With the queen's agreement, the keeping of the castle was then committed to Sir Oliver de Ingham, who munitioned it.[69] The munitions were removed in 1322 before Despenser's properties and offices were restored to him. Marlborough was forfeited on his execution in 1326.[70] The castle was among the queen's estates sequestrated in 1324.[71] In 1325 the king's houses within the castle were repaired and assigned to Roger de Monthermer, Lord Monthermer, to whom the care of the king's daughters was entrusted. The charge was renewed to his relict Isabel, Despenser's daughter, in 1325.[72] Marlborough Castle was restored to Queen Isabel in 1327 but she was again deprived in 1330.[73] In the same year it was assigned to Philippa, queen of Edward III.[74] After French raiders burnt Winchelsea (Suss.) in 1360 the sheriff of Wiltshire arranged for the castle to be garrisoned.[75] Thereafter the castle

was never put into a defensive state or visited by the queens who held it in dower. It fell into decay in the late 14th century and c. 1400 was possibly derelict and uninhabited.[76] The later ownership of the site, granted in reversion by Henry IV in 1403, is treated below.[77]

A chapel within the castle precincts, perhaps the chapel of St. Nicholas mentioned in 1241, existed in 1227.[78] Before 1232 the rector of Preshute gave it to a chaplain whom he constituted perpetual vicar and endowed with the obventions and oblations of the castle and a yearly stipend of 40s.[79] The living was variously referred to as a chapelry, free chapelry, or perpetual chantry and its incumbent as chaplain or vicar.[80] In 1265 Henry III allotted 50s. yearly to the prior of St. Margaret's for the maintenance of a canon from the house to celebrate daily therein.[81]

The rectors presented chaplains until the appropriation of Preshute rectory took effect in 1329.[82] Although, when his portion was allotted in 1330, the vicar was enjoined to continue payment of the 40s. stipend, no provision for the presentation of chaplains to serve the castle chapel then appears to have been made.[83] The bishop collated in the period 1334–1417.[84] In the early 15th century the lords of the castle were considered to have lost the right to present.[85] In 1402 the king appointed a warden of the chapel who still held office in 1412.[86] The chapel was last expressly mentioned in 1417.[87]

The chapel stood within the inner bailey.[88] Henry III repaired it, enlarged it by adding a chancel and belfry with two bells, and embellished it between 1227 and 1265.[89] It was again repaired in 1300.[90] During Despenser's first occupation of the castle, marauders plundered it and removed vestments and a gold chalice.[91]

A chapel dedicated to St. Leonard, mentioned c. 1230, may have been in the king's tower. In 1246 Henry III endowed a chaplain with 50s. yearly to celebrate there daily for the soul of Eleanor of Brittany.[92] The site of the queen's chapel, mentioned in 1241, is unknown.[93] In 1246 Henry III endowed a chaplain from St. Thomas's hospital, Marlborough, with 50s. yearly to celebrate daily therein for the soul of his mother

[60] H. Johnstone, 'Wardrobe and Household of Hen. son of Edw. I', *Bull. John Rylands Libr.* vii. 405–6.
[61] Ibid. 410 n.; *Cal. Pat.* 1281–92, 446; *Cal. Inq. p.m.* iv, p. 358.
[62] *Cal. Close,* 1288–96, 430–1.
[63] *W.N. & Q.* iv. 531; *D.N.B.; Complete Peerage,* ix. 140–2; *Cal. Close,* 1313–18, 257.
[64] *Cal. Close,* 1296–1302, 58; *Complete Peerage,* x. 382 and n., 386–7.
[65] *Cal. Pat.* 1292–1301, 451 sqq.
[66] Ibid. 1307–13, 51, 91.
[67] Ibid. 1317–21, 115–16, 132, 202, 578.
[68] Ibid. 1321–4, 166, 168; *Cal. Close,* 1318–23, 544; *Complete Peerage,* iv. 264.
[69] *Cal. Pat.* 1321–4, 40; *Cal. Close,* 1318–23, 437; *D.N.B.* s.v. Oliver de Ingham.
[70] *Cal. Close,* 1318–23, 437; *Complete Peerage,* iv. 265–6.
[71] M. McKisack, *Fourteenth Cent.* 81.
[72] *Cal. Close,* 1323–7, 252; *Cal. Pat.* 1324–7, 88, 157, 243; *Complete Peerage,* ix. 140–2.
[73] McKisack, op. cit. 97, 102.
[74] *Cal. Pat.* 1330–4, 55.
[75] *V.C.H. Wilts.* v. 21 n.; *Cal. Close,* 1360–4, 9.
[76] *Cal. Pat.* 1367–70, 48; *Cal. Inq. Misc.* v, p. 167.
[77] Below, manors.

[78] *Cal. Lib.* 1226–40, 18; 1240–5, 64.
[79] D. & C. Sar. Mun., press I, box 8, no. 2.
[80] Phillipps, *Wilts. Inst.* (index in *W.A.M.* xxviii. 225); *Reg. Hallum* (Cant. & York Soc.), p. 205; D. & C. Sar. Mun., press IV, box C 3/mixed/16; *Reg. Martival* (Cant. & York Soc.), ii. 635, 640.
[81] *Cal. Lib.* 1260–7, 180; *Close R.* 1264–8, 11, 13.
[82] D. & C. Sar. Mun., press IV, box C 3/mixed/16; Phillipps, *Wilts. Inst.* i. 10, 20–1.
[83] *Reg. Martival* (Cant. & York Soc.), ii. 640.
[84] Phillipps, *Wilts. Inst.* (index in *W.A.M.* xxviii. 225).
[85] *Reg. Ghent* (Cant. & York Soc.), ii. 768 n.
[86] *Cal. Pat.* 1401–5, 107; *Reg. Hallum* (Cant. & York Soc.), p. 205.   [87] Phillipps, *Wilts. Inst.* i. 106.
[88] See H. C. Brentnall's conjectural plan of the castle in *W.A.M.* xlviii, at pp. 140–1.
[89] *Cal. Lib.* 1226–40, 18, 123, 129, 136, 176; 1245–51, 122–3, 362; 1251–60, 161; 1260–7, 183; *Close R.* 1227–31, 164; 1247–51, 464–5; 1251–3, 126; 1264–8, 71; *Mem. R.* 1230–1 (Pipe R. Soc. n.s. xi), 94. For a detailed acct. of the works see *Hist. King's Works,* ii. 734–7.
[90] *Cal. Close,* 1296–1302, 341.
[91] Ibid. 1318–23, 544.
[92] *Hist. King's Works,* ii. 736 and n.; *Cal. Lib.* 1245–51, 71.
[93] *Cal. Lib.* 1240–5, 64.

Isabel of Angoulême.[94] The stipend was paid to the hospital and still claimed by its warden in 1378.[95]

The imprisonment of Bishop Ethelric in 1070 may have been no more than honourable confinement,[96] but in 1140 the freebooter Robert FitzHubert and his followers were placed in a 'narrow dungeon'.[97] The gaol was so called in 1194.[98] In 1205 it was called the king's prison and was thereafter referred to by either name.[99] The gaol was used chiefly for the detention of suspect felons.[1] In 1309–10, however, Templars, probably from Temple Rockley since they included Walter of Rockley, were in the custody of the constable of Marlborough.[2] During the 13th century and earlier 14th the gaol was delivered several times.[3] It is unlikely that it was used as a common gaol after the early 15th century although listed among such in the early 16th.[4]

BUILDINGS. Springs rising near the site of the castle on the Mount provided a domestic water supply and water for the moat. The castle which may have been been built shortly after the Conquest was called 'strong' in the early 12th century.[5] The decay of the castle in the 15th century and later buildings on its site have made its plan difficult to determine despite much documentary evidence.

The defences were extended southwards from the castle mound over the area afterwards called the base-court or bailey of the castle.[6] There living quarters, the king's houses, and a chapel were built. Henry II constructed a chamber for himself in the later 1170s.[7] There were new works and repairs during Richard I's reign, such as those made to the king's houses by Ellis the engineer in 1197.[8] John repaired the castle wall, added a palisade and drawbridge, constructed a ring wall round the motte, and built a barbican in front of the keep to strengthen it as a repository for treasure.[9] An exchange of lands between John and the burgesses of Marlborough was possibly to extend the castle precincts into the borough, thereby providing an outer bailey to separate the castle and town.[10]

Henry III began new work on the castle in 1224 and during the next two years a two-storeyed tower was built behind the king's chamber, then apparently leaded, and a brattice put up behind the queen's bedchamber.[11] In the 1230s improvements to the great hall, such as partial

wainscoting and decoration at the 'king's end' and the insertion of louvers and windows, and the decoration of the king's bedchamber, were carried out and the construction of a tower, possibly that on the motte, completed.[12] The fortifications, in particular those of the royal apartments, and the apartments themselves, were thoroughly repaired during 1238–9 under the supervision of Hugh Blowe, the king's master mason at Marlborough.[13] Another new tower was also constructed in 1238.[14] In 1241–2 a tower, perhaps that in the curtain wall behind the king's chamber, was repaired because its foundations were faulty. During that period, too, the towers behind the hall and over the great gate were roofed with lead and a new almonry and larder were built. A new first-floor chamber for the queen and a penthouse on the west side of the great hall were built in 1244–5. In 1250 a new round tower, which had been begun in 1241, was completed and fitted with a kitchen, a new barbican was built, several chambers were enlarged and improved, and part of the castle wall was crenellated.[15] Thereafter only a few small additions and alterations were made to the castle, the last in 1270 when Henry III built a chamber for his household knights.[16]

The castle seems afterwards to have received the minimum of maintenance. It was repaired in 1354,[17] and Edward III and his queen visited it briefly in the summer of 1358.[18] Further work was carried out in 1359 and 1360.[19] By 1367, however, the castle fabric had deteriorated to such an extent that an inquiry into its dilapidated state was ordered.[20] The attempts made to remedy defects in the 1370s were probably ineffective since Nicholas Hall, rector of St. Peter's, Marlborough, and apparently responsible for works at the castle in 1371–2, was afterwards accused of misappropriating materials supplied for the purpose.[21] A commission reported in 1391 that a complete rebuilding was needed to restore the castle.[22] It was thereafter allowed to decay. The site was recognizable as that of a castle in the mid 16th century when the ruins of the keep were still visible.[23]

MANORS AND OTHER ESTATES. The reversion of the site of the castle was granted in 1403 by Henry IV to his son Humphrey, duke of Gloucester, in possession by 1415.[24] On

[94] Cal. Lib. 1245–51, 78; Cal. Pat. 1377–81, 67.
[95] Cal. Close, 1377–81, 57.
[96] Chron. Rog. de Houedene (Rolls Ser.), i. 124.
[97] Gesta Stephani, ed. Potter, 70–1.
[98] Cur. Reg. R. 1194–5 (Pipe R. Soc. xiv), 88.
[99] Rot. Litt. Pat. (Rec. Com.), 54; Rot. Litt. Claus. (Rec. Com.), ii. 96; Close R. 1259–61, 334; Cal. Pat. 1317–21, 182; 1405–8, 410.
[1] Rot. Litt. Claus. (Rec. Com.), i. 416; Cal. Lib. 1240–5, 164; Cal. Close, 1288–96, 356; Cal. Pat. 1381–5, 520.
[2] Cal. Close, 1307–13, 177, 187.
[3] R. B. Pugh, Imprisonment in Medieval Eng. 84 and n., 268; Cal. Pat. 1317–21, 182.
[4] Cal. Pat. 1405–8, 410; Pugh, op. cit. 84.
[5] Gesta Stephani, ed. Potter, 70.
[6] Cal. Inq. Misc. v, p. 167. A conjectural plan is in W.A.M. xlviii, at pp. 140–1. The bldgs. are described in Hist. King's Works, ii. 734–8.
[7] Pipe R. 1176 (P.R.S. xxv), 188.

[8] Ibid. 1194 (P.R.S. N.S. v), 175, 211–12; 1197 (P.R.S. N.S. viii), 216.
[9] Ibid. 1203 (P.R.S. N.S. xvi), 161; 1211 (P.R.S. N.S. xxviii), 83; Rot. Litt. Claus. (Rec. Com.), i. 52; Rot. Lib. (Rec. Com.), 115, 137.
[10] Rot. Hund. (Rec. Com.), ii (1), 263; W.A.M. xlviii. 138–9.
[11] Rot. Litt. Claus. (Rec. Com.), i. 604, 650; Hist. King's Works, ii. 735.
[12] Hist. King's Works, ii. 736.
[13] Collectanea (W.R.S. xii), 9, 29–48.
[14] Cal. Lib. 1226–40, 350.
[15] Hist. King's Works, ii. 736–7.
[16] Cal. Lib. 1267–72, p. 139.
[17] Cal. Pat. 1354–8, 106.
[18] D.N.B. s.v. Philippa.
[19] Cal. Pat. 1358–61, 303; Cal. Close, 1360–4, 6.
[20] Cal. Pat. 1367–70, 48.
[21] Cal. Inq. Misc. v, p. 167.
[22] Ibid.; Cal. Pat. 1388–92, 272.
[23] Leland, Itin. ed. Toulmin Smith, iv. 130.
[24] Cal. Pat. 1401–5, 320; 1413–16, 338.

Humphrey's death in 1447 the site was granted to Margaret, queen of Henry VI, but was presumably forfeited on her attainder in 1461.[25] It was formally resumed by Act of 1464 and granted in 1465, to be held from 1464, to Elizabeth, queen of Edward IV, whose estates were sequestrated in 1483-4. The estate was restored to her in 1485 but she was finally deprived in 1487 when her daughter Elizabeth (d. 1503), queen of Henry VII, received a grant of it for life.[26] The site was granted to Catherine of Aragon the day before her marriage to Henry VIII in 1509 and passed to each of his wives in turn.[27] In 1547 Edward VI granted its reversion on the death of the last, Catherine Parr (d. 1548), to Edward Seymour, duke of Somerset.[28] Somerset was deprived of it in 1549 but it was restored to him in 1550.[29] The castle site was forfeited on the duke's execution and attainder in 1552 but was restored to his son Edward, later earl of Hertford, in 1553.[30] On Hertford's death in 1621 the site passed to his grandson William Seymour, created marquess of Hertford in 1640 and restored as duke of Somerset in 1660.[31]

William in 1621 conveyed the site to his brother Sir Francis. It then comprised some 30 a. in Preshute and included the castle 'hill and motte' and Bailey's close on which Sir Francis had built a house.[32] Francis, then Baron Seymour of Trowbridge, was succeeded by his son Charles in 1664. The house and lands passed successively to Charles's sons Francis, Baron Seymour and from 1675 duke of Somerset (d. 1678), and Charles, duke of Somerset (d. 1748). The property was settled in 1715 on the marriage of Charles's son Algernon, earl of Hertford and from 1748 duke of Somerset (d. 1750). From Algernon the property descended to his half-sisters Frances, afterwards wife of John Manners, marquess of Granby, and Charlotte, wife of Heneage Finch, earl of Aylesford, and his nephew Sir Charles Wyndham, Bt., afterwards earl of Egremont, as tenants in common. In 1779 the property was allotted to Frances's son, Charles Manners, marquess of Granby, who in the same year became duke of Rutland and sold it to Thomas Brudenell-Bruce, earl of Ailesbury.[33]

The manor of *MARLBOROUGH*, or *BARTON*, consisted of a large demesne farm

west, north, and south of the castle.[34] In 1262 it was assigned with Marlborough Castle as dower to Eleanor, queen of Henry III, and passed with the castle until the death of Queen Philippa in 1369.[35] The Crown afterwards leased the manor to farmers and used the revenues chiefly to provide pensions for royal kinsfolk and servants.[36] In 1403 Henry IV granted the farm he received from the manor and the reversion of the estate itself to his son Humphrey, duke of Gloucester, in possession by 1415.[37] The land afterwards descended with the site of the castle to William, duke of Somerset (d. 1660),[38] who retained the manor when he granted the castle site to his brother. The duke was succeeded by his grandson William Seymour, upon whose death in 1671 the manor passed to his sister Elizabeth, afterwards the wife of Thomas Bruce, earl of Ailesbury from 1685.[39] It passed with the Ailesbury title to Thomas Brudenell-Bruce, earl of Ailesbury, who in 1779 acquired the castle estate.[40]

Thus reunited the site of the castle and the manor descended with the Ailesbury title until 1871 when the castle site, on which the buildings of Marlborough College stood, was sold to the college governors,[41] who bought the 1,042-a. Barton estate from George, marquess of Ailesbury, in 1930.[42] The land was sold to F. G. Barker in 1968 and in 1981 belonged to Mr. J. V. Bloomfield. The college retained Barton Farm.[43]

No trace remains of the house built by Sir Francis Seymour before 1621. It probably stood east of the old castle moat. The 'great rambling building' was set amid formal gardens which extended over the remainder of the outer bailey and incorporated the inner bailey, with moat and castle mound, as their principal feature. The gardens were probably created for Seymour, who occupied the house.[44] The mound, renamed the Mount before 1668 and possibly when it became the focus of the new garden, was ascended by a spiral walk flanked by low hedges.[45] The gardens were carefully maintained by Seymour's son Charles and grandson Francis.[46] In 1668 a water tower on the summit of the Mount supplied the house with water. A banqueting house and arbour on the Mount were mentioned in 1669.[47]

[25] *Complete Peerage*, v. 736; Rymer, *Foedera* (1737-45 edn.), v (i), 170; *Rot. Parl.* v. 479.
[26] *Rot. Parl.* v. 515; vi. 263, 288, 386; *Cal. Pat.* 1461-7, 430; 1485-94, 75-7.
[27] *L. & P. Hen. VIII*, i (1), pp. 48-9; vii, pp. 145-7; xv, p. 52; xvi, pp. 240-1; xviii (1), p. 198; xix (1), pp. 82-3.
[28] *Cal. Pat.* 1547-8, 124-5.
[29] Ibid. 1549-51, 430, 432; *Complete Peerage*, xii (1), 63 and n.
[30] *Complete Peerage*, xii (1), 63-6; P.R.O., E 328/117.
[31] *Wilts. Inq. p.m.* 1625-49 (Index Libr.), 27-8, 30-1; Burke, *Peerage* (1959), 2098-9.
[32] Alnwick Castle Mun., X.II.11, box 17, deed, Hertford to Seymour.
[33] *V.C.H. Wilts.* vii. 129-30; Somerset Estate Act, 19 Geo. III, c. 46 (Priv. Act); *Complete Peerage*, xi. 267-70; W.R.O. 9/19/249.
[34] The designation 'of Marlborough', used in 1250 and throughout the Middle Ages, was replaced by that 'of Barton' in the 16th cent.: *Cal. Lib.* 1245-51, 276; *Cal. Pat.* 1494-1509, 365; *Wilts. Inq. p.m.* 1625-49 (Index Libr.), 27.
[35] Above, Marlborough Castle.
[36] *Cal. Pat.* 1377-81, 450; 1385-9, 18; 1399-1401, 473.

[37] Ibid. 1401-5, 320; 1413-16, 338.
[38] Above.
[39] Burke, *Peerage* (1959), 2098-9; *Complete Peerage*, i. 59-61.
[40] *Complete Peerage*, i. 61-3; above.
[41] *Complete Peerage*, i. 64-7; *Marlborough Coll. Guide* (1979), 41.
[42] Burke, *Peerage* (1959), 29; deed, Ailesbury to Marlborough Coll. *penes* the bursar, Marlborough Coll.
[43] Deed, Marlborough Coll. to Barker, *penes* the bursar, Marlborough Coll.; local inf.
[44] *Journeys of Celia Fiennes*, ed. Morris, 330. The documentary evidence for the gardens and for the hos. on the castle site is surveyed by P. E. C. H[ayman] and E. G. H. Kempson, 'Early Hist. of Hos. built on Site of Marlborough Castle', *Rep. Marlborough Coll. Natural Hist. Soc.* xcix. 34 sqq.
[45] *Woodward's Notes* (W.R.S. xiii), 11; *Journeys of Celia Fiennes*, 331. It is probably the 17th-cent. garden which is depicted on a map of 1706: W.S.R.O., PHA 3565.
[46] *Rep. Marlborough Coll. Natural Hist. Soc.* xcix. 41 sqq.
[47] *Woodward's Notes* (W.R.S. xiii), 11; *Rep. Marlborough Coll. Natural Hist. Soc.* xcix. 41.

The banqueting house was ruinous in the early 18th century.[48] The old house was visited by Charles I twice in 1644,[49] by James II in 1686, and by Mary of Modena in 1687. William III in 1690 and Queen Anne in 1702 and 1703 presumably stayed in the new house.[50]

The main house, called Marlborough House in 1683, was rebuilt over 30-40 years by Charles, duke of Somerset (d. 1748).[51] In 1684 he commissioned John Deane of Reading to design a new house.[52] The old house was apparently demolished and work begun on the new one in 1688.[53] Work greatly accelerated in the later 1690s. Two identical double-pile blocks linked by a hall range were planned. The north-east wing had been built by 1706. Before 1706 small formal gardens were laid out north-east and south-east of the house, a wilderness planted south of the Mount in the inner bailey, a 'green walk' constructed south of the moat, the south-eastern arm of the moat straightened to form an ornamental canal with a raised walk on the east bank, and a summer house built at its southern end above the place where the canal cascaded into the Kennet.[54]

The eastward diversion of the London–Bath road c. 1705 was to make room for domestic offices to be built in Marlborough round a square courtyard north-east of the house.[55] The house was apparently completed between 1715 and 1723 by Algernon, earl of Hertford.[56] It had a south-east front of fifteen bays with a high basement, two storeys, and attics. The north-west front was of thirteen bays: the central three were deeply recessed and approached through a long porch which was possibly re-used from a house at Woodlands in Mildenhall.[57] The north-east wing contained mainly bedrooms and dressing rooms and the south-west wing the main staircase and principal rooms. The house was approached from the north-west across an axially planned forecourt. Stables north-east of the forecourt may have incorporated those of the earlier house.

The house was one of the principal residences of Algernon, earl of Hertford, from 1726 or earlier.[58] His countess, Frances, improved the gardens and built a grotto at the foot of the Mount.[59] That grotto and the spiral path around the Mount were still visible in 1981. By the later 19th century all that remained of the moat was a south-westerly section called, as still in 1981, the Bathing Place.[60] After 1751 Marlborough House, renamed the Castle, became an inn.[61] It was the subject of Stanley Weyman's novel *The Castle Inn* published in 1898. In 1842 plans were drawn up by J. M. Nelson to convert it to a school.[62] It was let as such in 1843.[63] In 1845 the lease was renewed to the governors of the school, then newly constituted Marlborough College.[64] In 1981 the building survived as C House of the college. Part of the stable range north-east of it in Marlborough was incorporated in the Museum Block of the school.[65]

The revenues of Preshute *RECTORY*, arising from tithes, land, and oblations, belonged to the warden and choristers of Salisbury cathedral from 1329.[66] Parliamentary commissioners sold them to William Hitchcock in 1651 but they were afterwards restored.[67] From 1330 to the later 15th century the vicar of Preshute collected them, paid £20 to the appropriators, and kept the residue.[68] From the later 15th century the revenues were leased to lay tenants, including members of the Hitchcock family from 1495 or earlier until 1711.[69] After 1711 the estate was let in portions. The tithes of Elcot, including Barton farm, were let as one holding.[70] Leases of the small glebe farm which surrounded the church, reckoned at 60 a. in 1649 and 45 a. in 1926, and of the Manton tithes were held from 1714 to 1735 by the Nalder family, tenants of Barton farm, from 1739 by the Comptons, and from 1778 by the Clarks, whose interest passed to D. P. Maurice, tenant in 1872.[71] In 1847 the appropriators were allotted a tithe rent charge, fixed initially at £850, for Elcot and Manton.[72] The farm was sold to C. J. K. Maurice in 1926 and the rectory house and 3 a. to the governors of Marlborough College in 1929.[73]

The rectory house, mentioned in 1649, was dilapidated in 1711 and rebuilt in 1712.[74] It was rebuilt in stone c. 1840 by the tenant J. W. Clark as an Italianate villa with an imposing north entrance front and a lower south service wing.[75] It was called Preshute House when it was let to

[48] *Journeys of Celia Fiennes*, 331.
[49] *Diary of the Marches of the Royal Army* (Camd. Soc. [1st ser.], lxxiv), 3, 151.
[50] *Rep. Marlborough Coll. Natural Hist. Soc.* xcix. 38.
[51] Alnwick Castle Mun., X.II.11, box 17, evidence concerning settlement, 1715.   [52] Colvin, *Brit. Architects*, 255.
[53] W.S.R.O., PHA 204.
[54] Ibid. PHA 205-6; 1078, articles, 1699; 3565; 6347; *Journeys of Celia Fiennes*, 330-1.
[55] *Rep. Marlborough Coll. Natural Hist. Soc.* xcix. 54; W.S.R.O., PHA 3565.
[56] *Rep. Marlborough Coll. Natural Hist. Soc.* xcix. 69, 72; 19 Geo. III, c. 46 (Priv. Act); W. Stukeley, *Itinerarium Curiosum* (1724), pl. 3; see above, plates facing p. 160.
[57] *W.A.M.* xlii. 116.
[58] *Rep. Marlborough Coll. Natural Hist. Soc.* xcix. 76.
[59] Described by Stephen Duck, a protégé of the countess, in *Description of a Journey to Marlborough, Bath, Portsmouth, etc.: Poems on Several Occasions* (1764 edn.), 146-8.
[60] P.R.O., IR 29/38/188; IR 30/38/188; O.S. Map 6", Wilts. XXIX (1889 edn.).
[61] *Marlborough Coll. Guide* (1979), 21; W.R.O. 9/19/246-7.
[62] *Rep. Marlborough Coll. Natural Hist. Soc.* xcviii, plan at pp. 44-5.

[63] W.R.O. 9/19/859.   [64] Ibid. 9/19/860.
[65] Pevsner, *Wilts.* (2nd edn.), 338-9.
[66] Below, church.
[67] P.R.O., C 54/3604, no. 4; D. & C. Sar. Mun., choristers, press III, box 4, no. 20; ibid. lease bk. XXVI, pp. 177-81.
[68] Below, church.
[69] D. & C. Sar. Mun., choristers, press III, box 1, nos. 6, 9, 17-18; ibid. lease bks. I, f. 98; III, p. 50; V, f. 57v.; ibid. chap. act bk. 1696-1741, p. 71.
[70] Ibid. lease bks. X, p. 341; XI, ff. 74v., 98 v., 177v. sqq.; XII, ff. 19v., 181; XIII, f. 181.
[71] Ibid. lease bks. X, pp. 99 sqq., 367; XI, ff. 86v. sqq., 169; XII, ff. 34 sqq., 132v. sqq.; XIII, ff. 32, 168v. sqq.; XIV, f. 54; XV, ff. 62v.-63; XXVI, pp. 177-81; ibid. choristers, press III, box 4, nos. 19-20; *W.A.M.* xli. 113-14; deed, choristers of Salisbury cath. to Maurice *penes* the bursar, Marlborough Coll.
[72] P.R.O., IR 29/38/188.
[73] Deeds, choristers of Salisbury cath. to Maurice and governors of Marlborough Coll. *penes* the bursar, Marlborough Coll.
[74] *W.A.M.* xli. 113-14; D. & C. Sar. Mun., chap. act bk. 1696-1741, pp. 71, 76.
[75] P.R.O., IR 29/38/188; IR 30/38/188. The date 1841 and 'J.W.C.' appear on a garden wall.

Marlborough College as a boarding house in the later 19th century. It was still so used in 1981. To adapt it a red-brick extension, designed by William White, was added west of the service range c. 1863.[76] The house has been much altered inside and further extended in the 20th century.

The manor of ST. MARGARET'S was built up piecemeal by St. Margaret's priory. About 1235 Robert of Elcot gave the canons 2 a. within Marlborough barton.[77] Henry III leased 2 a. near the priory to the canons in 1248.[78] About 1318 John Goodhind granted 62 a. and 20s. rent within the barton.[79] In 1334 Edward III released to the prior and convent a rent of 16s. 8d. which they paid to him for lands in Newbury Street and Savernake forest.[80] Feoffees conveyed an estate which included land in Elcot tithing to the priory in 1412.[81] The manor thus formed passed to the Crown at the Dissolution.[82]

From 1539 the site of the priory was held in dower by the queens of Henry VIII,[83] but in 1544 the king granted it to Geoffrey Daniell with tenements in Marlborough and Newbury Street.[84] Geoffrey died c. 1561 and in 1604 his nephew William Daniell, M.P. for Marlborough in 1558 and 1559, died seised of the manor,[85] which passed in the direct male line to William (d. 1621), William, Geoffrey (d. 1681), M.P. for Marlborough in 1660 and 1661,[86] and William Daniell (d.s.p. 1698), M.P. for Marlborough 1695–8. The last William's sister Rachel (d. 1708) married Thomas Fettiplace. Thomas held the manor until his death in 1710 when it passed to his son Thomas, who sold it in 1715 to Francis Hawes, a director of the South Sea Company.[87] After the South Sea Bubble burst in 1720 Hawes's property was confiscated by parliamentary trustees who sold St. Margaret's in 1733 to the trustees of John Churchill, duke of Marlborough (d. 1722).[88] The manor descended like that of East Overton in Overton to George Spencer, duke of Marlborough (d. 1817), whose trustees sold it in 1820 to Charles Brudenell-Bruce, earl, later marquess, of Ailesbury, the owner in 1847.[89] A small part of the manor was possibly acquired in 1885 by R. W. Merriman and belonged to him in 1898.[90] George, marquess

of Ailesbury, offered the remainder, 70 a., for sale in lots in 1929–30.[91]

The manor house, called St. Margaret's Farm or the Old Monastery, stood at the junction of the Marlborough–Salisbury road and Isbury Road until demolished c. 1930. It was of stone rubble and flint, with stone dressings and roofed with stone tiles, five bays wide with an extension.[92] The lower courses of a priory building and fragments of the house occupied by the Daniells, including the date 1680 on a south wall, are said to have been part of the house in the early 20th century when some medieval woodwork apparently survived in it.[93] Robert Cecil, earl of Salisbury, may have died there in 1612.[94]

By 1231 St. Thomas's hospital, a house for lepers, had been established on a site later called Spittle field lying east of Marlborough between London Road and the Kennet.[95] The chief duty of the brethren there was to pray for the soul of Isabel of Angoulême.[96] Its revenues were apparently of little value in 1393 when the king granted the reversion of the hospital, then held for life by a royal clerk, John Were (d. 1397), to the prior and convent of St. Margaret.[97] Its site and lands, reckoned in 1403 at 23 a., were merged with the priory lands.[98]

In 1066 Wigot held Manton. By 1086 the estate had passed to Miles Crispin.[99] The overlordship of the estate thereafter descended with the honor of Wallingford (Berks., later Oxon.).[1] Moieties of the estate are last expressly mentioned as members of the honor in 1335 and 1428.[2]

Sir Sampson Foliot held ½ knight's fee at Manton of the honor of Wallingford in 1242–3.[3] The mesne lordship probably descended like that of Draycot Foliat to Alice de Lisle who was lord in 1335.[4]

Hugh of Dover held MANTON of Sir Sampson in 1242–3.[5] The estate passed to Nicholas Barfleur (d. by 1295) whose son Nicholas[6] in 1300 conveyed land at Manton to Richard of Manton.[7] What was probably the same estate was held in 1412 by Thomas Russell.[8] The land may afterwards have passed to Robert Russell, who held it for ¼ knight's fee,[9] and later to John Russell. It was acquired by William Collingbourne in 1476.[10] Collingbourne forfeited it in 1485 for

[76] D. & C. Sar. Mun., chap. act bk. 1852–64, p. 253.
[77] Rot. Hund. (Rec. Com.), ii (1), 263.
[78] V.C.H. Wilts. iii. 317.
[79] Cal. Pat. 1317–21, 190.
[80] Ibid. 1330–4, 522.
[81] Ibid. 1408–13, 450.
[82] Valor Eccl. (Rec. Com.), ii. 148, where the manor is described as in 'Marlborough and Elcombe', probably in error for 'Marlborough and Elcot'.
[83] L. & P. Hen. VIII, xiv (2), p. 154; xvi, p. 716; xviii (1), p. 447.
[84] W.R.O. 9/2/130; P.R.O., E 318/Box 9/346, rott. 1, 5.
[85] Wilts. Pedigrees (Harl. Soc. cv, cvi), 42, where Wm. is wrongly said to have died in 1621; P.R.O., PROB 11/44 (P.C.C. 4 Loftes, will of Geof. Daniell); ibid. C 142/289, no. 70; Hist. Parl., Commons, 1509–58, ii. 12. The following descent corrects and amplifies that in V.C.H. Wilts. vii. 98–9.
[86] P.R.O., C 60/448, no. 13; W.R.O. 9/2/137–8; 9/2/140; TS. biog. of Geof. Daniell, M.P., penes Hist. of Parl. Trust.
[87] Coll. Topog. et Gen. v. 348–9, 349 n.; W.R.O. 9/2/141; 9/2/147–8; 9/2/151.
[88] W.R.O. 9/2/153.
[89] Ibid.; 9/2/159; V.C.H. Wilts. xi. 188; P.R.O., IR 29/38/188; IR 30/38/188.
[90] W.A.M. xxx. 104–5; xxxiv. 265.
[91] W.R.O. 9, sale cats.
[92] Blenheim Mun., E/P/85; W.A.M. xxxiv. 264–5; Chandler, Hist. Marlborough, pl. at pp. 52–3; W.A.S. Libr., sale cat. v, no. 6.
[93] W.A.M. xxxiv. 263–5.
[94] A. Cecil, Life of Rob. Cecil, 342 and n.
[95] V.C.H. Wilts. iii. 342; W.A.M. lx. 130.
[96] Cal. Pat. 1232–47, 485; Cal. Close, 1296–1302, 469.
[97] Cal. Pat. 1385–9, 476; 1391–6, 320; Cal. Inq. Misc. vii, p. 123.
[98] Cal. Inq. Misc. vii, p. 123; P.R.O., SC 6/1055/17–19.
[99] V.C.H. Wilts. ii, pp. 146–7.
[1] Ibid. p. 111; V.C.H. Berks. iii. 523 sqq.; Bk. of Fees, ii. 748.
[2] Wilts. Inq. p.m. 1327–77 (Index Libr.), 113–14; Feud. Aids, v. 269.
[3] Bk. of Fees, ii. 748.
[4] Wilts. Inq. p.m. 1327–77 (Index Libr.), 113–14; V.C.H. Wilts. ix. 44–5.
[5] Bk. of Fees, ii. 748.
[6] Wilts. Inq. p.m. 1242–1326 (Index Libr.), 205–6.
[7] Feet of F. 1272–1327 (W.R.S. i), p. 45.
[8] Feud. Aids, vi. 537.
[9] Ibid. v. 269.
[10] Cal. Close, 1476–85, p. 15.

supporting Henry Tudor and was attainted and executed. In that year Richard III granted it to his chaplain Edmund Chaddington, possibly as a trustee.[11] Collingbourne's lands were afterwards restored to his heirs and Manton was allotted to his daughter Jane or Joan who married James Lowther.[12] Joan and James were in possession by 1520.[13] On Joan's death in 1541 the estate passed to James Chaddington.[14] Chaddington sold it in 1547 to William Button, who in the same year sold it to Edward Seymour, earl of Hertford and later duke of Somerset.[15]

The estate was forfeited to the Crown in 1549–50 and after Somerset's execution and attainder in 1552.[16] In 1564 it was granted to Thomas Chaddington.[17] William Chaddington and his wife Bridget in 1571 conveyed the estate to Thomas Michelborne (d. 1582).[18] Although Thomas devised it to a younger son Edward it was held by Thomas's eldest son Laurence at his death in 1611.[19] Laurence was succeeded by his brother Thomas.[20] What was possibly the same estate was sold by Thomas Bennett to William, earl of Hertford, in 1633.[21] It descended with the manor of Barton to the earls and marquesses of Ailesbury, owners in the earlier 20th century.[22]

In 1320 John Goodhind held the remainder of Manton manor, then reckoned at 60 a. In 1336 he granted the estate, then 106 a. held for ¼ knight's fee, and 50s. rent to the prior and convent of St. Margaret in Preshute. That house held the estate until the Dissolution.[23] From 1539 the estate was held in dower by the queens of Henry VIII.[24] In 1547 its reversion on the death of the last, Catherine Parr, was granted to Edward, duke of Somerset,[25] who, except briefly in 1549–50, held the whole manor until 1552. In 1553 what had been the St. Margaret's estate was granted to William Herbert, earl of Pembroke, who sold the estate in 1561 to William Daniell (d. 1604).[26] In 1618 William Bristowe, his wife Catherine, Anthony Bristowe, and Edward Thurman sold it to William Young,[27] who c. 1633 sold it in parcels.[28] Part, called Manton farm, was bought by John Hewlett, on whose death c. 1666 it passed to his son and namesake. From the younger John (d. c. 1679) Manton farm passed to a kinswoman Judith Garlick, whose descendant Edward Garlick sold it to Thomas Bruce-Brudenell

(afterwards Brudenell-Bruce), Lord Bruce and from 1776 earl of Ailesbury, in 1774. Thomas, earl of Ailesbury, bought another small estate in Manton in 1780 and his son Charles, marquess of Ailesbury, bought others there in 1828 and 1832.[29] Some downland, however, was apparently sold to Alexander Taylor c. 1869.[30] Another farm, also originally part of the manor and owned in 1792 by the trustees of John Braithwaite and in 1847 by Thomas Baskerville Mynors Baskerville (d. 1864), was bought from Thomas's son W. T. Mynors Baskerville by George, marquess of Ailesbury, in 1872.[31] The reunited estate, apportioned between Manton Weir farm, 488 a., and Elm Tree farm, 93 a., was offered for sale by George, marquess of Ailesbury, in 1929.[32] The downland acquired by Taylor was afterwards bought by Joseph Watson (created Baron Manton, d. 1922), chairman of the Olympia Agricultural Co. Ltd. Watson's trustees sold the estate in 1927 to Tattersalls Ltd., bloodstock auctioneers, who sold it in 1947 to George Todd, the owner in 1973. Mr. J. V. Bloomfield owned most of the land in Manton held by the marquesses of Ailesbury including the downland in 1974 and 1981.[33]

There were two small estates at Flexborough in Manton in the late 12th century. An estate formerly Ralph de Babban's was granted by John, while count of Mortain, to Robert the Frenchman, who held it in 1202 and 1214.[34] A Robert of Flexborough held the land in 1230.[35] Possibly the same land was held in 1275 by Picot of Flexborough and, like the second Flexborough estate, may afterwards have belonged to St. Margaret's priory.[36]

John, when count of Mortain, granted the second estate to William Arblaster, to whom Richard I apparently confirmed it. In 1236 Henry III, with the consent of William's son Thomas, granted it to the priory of St. Margaret.[37] It was possibly the small estate which comprised land in Flexborough field in the 16th century.[38] In 1553 the land was part of the Manton estate granted to the earl of Pembroke.[39]

In 1535 the hospital of St. John at Marlborough possessed a small estate at Manton which passed with other hospital lands in 1550 to the mayor and burgesses of Marlborough for the

[11] Cal. Pat. 1476–85, 542; A. B. Emden, Biog. Reg. Univ. Oxf. to 1500, i. 382–3; V.C.H. Wilts. xi. 242.
[12] P.R.O., STAC 2/8/242–3.
[13] Ibid. CP 25(2)/46/318/12 Hen. VIII Mich.
[14] Ibid. C 142/64, no. 86.
[15] Ibid. CP 25(2)/46/324/38 Hen. VIII Hil.; ibid. E 326/12138.
[16] Complete Peerage, xii (1), 59 sqq.
[17] P.R.O., E 318/Box 43/2307.
[18] Ibid. CP 25(2)/239/13 Eliz. I East.; ibid. C 142/200, no. 47.
[19] Ibid. C 142/200, no. 47; C 142/680, no. 28; ibid. PROB 11/65 (P.C.C. 24 Rowe).
[20] Ibid. C 142/680, no. 28; W.R.O. 9/2/362.
[21] W.R.O. 9/2/15.
[22] Ibid. 106, map, 1906.
[23] Feet of F. 1272–1327 (W.R.S. i), p. 104; Wilts. Inq. p.m. 1327–77 (Index Libr.), 113–14; Cal. Pat. 1334–8, 241; Valor Eccl. (Rec. Com.), ii. 148; P.R.O., SC 6/Hen. VIII/3985, rot. 65 and d.
[24] L. & P. Hen. VIII, xv, p. 8; xvi, pp. 240–1; xix (1), pp. 82–3.

[25] Cal. Pat. 1547–8, 125, 131–3.
[26] P.R.O., E 318/Box 33/1861; ibid. CP 25(2)/239/3 Eliz. I East.
[27] Ibid. CP 25(2)/371/15 Jas. I Hil.
[28] W.R.O. 9/2/30.
[29] Ibid. 9, sched. of deeds, 1870, pp. 261–3, 266–7.
[30] Ibid. 9, deed, Ailesbury to Taylor, 1869.
[31] Ibid. Manton inclosure award; ibid. 9/2/272; 9/2/275; P.R.O., IR 29/38/188; IR 30/38/188; Burke, Land. Gent. (1952), 125.
[32] W.R.O. 9, sale cat.
[33] Brit. Racehorse, xxv, no. 4 (Sept. 1973), 456, 459; inf. from Mr. J. V. Bloomfield, Manton Ho.
[34] Mem. R. 1199 (Pipe R. Soc. n.s. xxi), 14; Pipe R. 1202 (P.R.S. n.s. xv), 124; 1214 (P.R.S. n.s. xxxv), 44.
[35] Pipe R. 1230 (P.R.S. n.s. iv), 3.
[36] Rot. Hund. (Rec. Com.), ii (1), 262; P.R.O., E 315/400, f. 364.
[37] Ex. e Rot. Fin. (Rec. Com.), i. 299–300.
[38] P.R.O., E 315/400, f. 364. In 1535 the estate was wrongly identified as Clatford manor: Valor Eccl. (Rec. Com.), ii. 148.
[39] P.R.O., E 318/Box 33/1861.

endowment of a free grammar school within the borough.[40] A farm of 78 a. at Manton still formed part of that endowment in 1883.[41] Some 30 a. were sold to C. Smith in 1926, 40 a. to W. E. Free & Sons Ltd. in 1928, and 8 a. to A. Pocock in 1938.[42]

The estate called *CLATFORD* manor in 1328[43] was held in 1066 by Alwin. By 1086 it had passed to Ralph Mortimer.[44] The overlordship of the estate descended in the Mortimer family and is last expressly mentioned in 1368 when Edmund Mortimer, earl of March (d. 1381), was lord.[45]

Ralph's son Hugh, probably in the earlier 12th century, gave Clatford to the abbey of St. Victor en Caux (Seine Maritime). The cell established at Clatford, to which priors were appointed, was called the priory either of Clatford or of Hullavington but is unlikely ever to have been more than a farmhouse inhabited by a few monks who oversaw the estate and served a chapel.[46] From 1338, on the outbreak of war with France, to 1360 and again after 1369 the estate was frequently taken into the king's hands and administered by keepers, usually the priors of Clatford themselves, appointed by the Crown.[47] When the alien priories were finally suppressed in 1414 the manor was assigned in dower to Queen Joan (d. 1437), relict of Henry IV.[48] In 1439 the Crown assigned Clatford to Humphrey, duke of Gloucester, for life[49] and in 1441 granted the reversion to Eton College (Bucks.), to which Humphrey surrendered it in 1443.[50]

In 1547 the college exchanged Clatford with the Crown for other property and the same year it was granted to Edward, duke of Somerset.[51] The manor was forfeited to the Crown on Somerset's execution and attainder in 1552.[52] William Herbert, earl of Pembroke, received a grant of Clatford in 1553[53] and in 1562 sold it to Thomas Goddard (d. *c.* 1598), who devised it to his wife Winifred for life.[54] Clatford passed to Thomas's son Richard (d. 1668) and afterwards to Richard's daughter-in-law Joan Goddard for life.[55] On Joan's death the manor passed, between 1685 and 1689, to her nephew George FitzJames (d. 1693). George was succeeded by his relict Ann, from 1699 the wife of Edmund Percival.[56] Ann's kinswoman Hester Kent, from 1716 wife of John Chetwynd, later Viscount Chetwynd, held the

reversion which Chetwynd bought before 1728. After Ann Percival's death he sold Clatford to Charles Spencer, duke of Marlborough, in 1756.[57]

Clatford manor, 673 a. in 1906, descended like the manor of East Overton to Sir Henry Bruce Meux, Bt. (d. 1900), and passed like other Meux estates to Alexander Taylor and afterwards to the Olympia Agricultural Co. Ltd.[58] In 1923 that company sold Clatford farm, except its downland, to J. B. Wroth whose son Mr. J. T. Wroth succeeded him in 1965. Mr. Wroth sold the farm in 1978 to Mr. and Mrs. G. J. Goodwin, owners in 1981.[59] The downland became part of the Manton estate owned by the Olympia Agricultural Co. Ltd. and passed with it to Mr. J. V. Bloomfield, owner in 1981.

Clatford Farm, called Clatford Hall in the early 20th century,[60] faces north across the Kennet valley. Its central range was apparently built in the earlier 17th century, perhaps following an older plan, by the Goddards who in the later 17th century may have added the eastern cross wing and formed the walled forecourt with ornamental gatepiers north of the house.[61] A western cross wing of unknown date was rebuilt in the 18th century and early in the 19th the northern entrance front was partly refaced in ashlar. The house was being extensively altered in 1979.

The estate which became the manor of *LANGDON WICK* originated in land within the barton of Marlborough which the king granted to Stanley abbey at fee farm in 1194.[62] The great tithes were acquired by the abbey in 1250 for a pension of 20s. and thereafter passed with the manor.[63]

Stanley abbey was dissolved in 1536 and in that year the manor was granted to Edward, Viscount Beauchamp (later earl of Hertford and duke of Somerset). The estate, like the site of Marlborough Castle, was forfeited to the Crown in 1549, restored to Somerset in 1550, and again forfeited by him in 1552. It was apparently restored to Somerset's son Sir Edward Seymour, later earl of Hertford (d. 1621), in 1553.[64] On Hertford's death the manor passed to his grandson Francis, Baron Seymour, and descended like the site of Marlborough Castle until 1779 when, called Langdon and Wick, it was allotted to

[40] *Valor Eccl.* (Rec. Com.), ii. 147; below, Marlborough, estates.
[41] W.R.O., Marlborough Grammar Sch. min. bk. 1.
[42] Ibid. Marlborough Grammar Sch. min. bk. 2, p. 408; A. R. Stedman, *Hist. Marlborough Grammar Sch.* (Devizes, priv. print. [1946]), 104.
[43] *Cal. Chart. R.* 1327-41, 67.
[44] *V.C.H. Wilts.* ii, p. 152.
[45] *Complete Peerage*, viii. 445-8; ix. 267 sqq.; *Cal. Close, 1364-8,* 419.
[46] *V.C.H. Wilts.* iii. 393-4.
[47] e.g. *Cal. Close, 1337-9,* 398; *1354-8,* 578; *Cal. Pat. 1358-61,* 560; *Cal. Fine R. 1368-77,* 14, 25, 405; *1377-83,* 71; *1391-9,* 134, 161, 199; *1399-1405,* 10.
[48] *Cal. Pat. 1413-16,* 165; *Feud. Aids,* v. 270.
[49] *Cal. Pat. 1436-41,* 304.
[50] *Rot. Parl.* v. 48; *Cal. Close, 1441-7,* 163.
[51] P.R.O., E 318/Box 28/1601; *Cal. Pat. 1547-8,* 121-2.
[52] *Complete Peerage*, xii (1), 61-3.
[53] *Cal. Pat. 1547-53,* 169-70.
[54] Ibid. *1560-3,* 397; P.R.O., CP 25(2)/239/4 Eliz. I Trin.; ibid. PROB 11/91 (P.C.C. 34 Lewyn).
[55] W.R.O. 753, f. 2; *Wilts. Pedigrees* (Harl. Soc. cv, cvi), 69; P.R.O., PROB 11/327 (P.C.C. 65 Hene, will of Ric. Goddard); Blenheim Mun., Wilts. deeds, deed, Goddard to Goddard, 1655.
[56] Blenheim Mun., Wilts. deeds, marriage settlement of Geo. FitzJames; will of Geo. FitzJames.
[57] Ibid. Wilts. deeds, marriage settlements of 1699, 1716, 1728; demise of jointure, 1717; *V.C.H. Wilts.* xi. 189; P.R.O., CP 25(2)/1235/29 Geo. II East.
[58] *V.C.H. Wilts.* xi. 188-9; W.R.O. 106.
[59] Inf. from Mr. J. T. Wroth, Westfield, Clatford; Mrs. A. Goodwin, Clatford Farm.
[60] W.R.O. 106.
[61] The suggestion in *V.C.H. Wilts.* iii. 394 that the ho. incorporates remains of monastic bldgs. appears unfounded.
[62] *Pipe R.* 1194 (P.R.S. n.s. v), 200.
[63] D. & C. Sar. Mun., press I, box 8, no. 13; P.R.O., IR 29/38/163.
[64] *Valor Eccl.* (Rec. Com.), ii. 114-15; *V.C.H. Wilts.* iii. 274; *L. & P. Hen. VIII,* x, p. 526; *Complete Peerage,* xii (1), 59 sqq.; *Cal. Pat. 1549-51,* 430, 432; P.R.O., E 328/117.

Charles William Wyndham, son of Charles Wyndham, earl of Egremont. C. W. Wyndham (d. 1828) was succeeded in turn by his brothers Percy Charles Wyndham (d. 1833) and George, earl of Egremont (d. 1837), and nephew George, earl of Egremont, who in 1844 sold the estate to Joseph Neeld.[65] On Neeld's death in 1856 Wick Down farm passed to his brother John, later a baronet, who held it in 1860.[66] The farm later, like Clatford manor, became part of the Meux estate until sold to George Cowing in 1906. From 1911 it passed like Rockley manor.[67]

Azor held an estate at Rockley in 1066. In 1086 it was held by Edward of Salisbury and reckoned as 1 hide.[68] From Edward the land, afterwards the manor of *TEMPLE ROCKLEY*, passed successively to his son Walter and grandson Patrick, earl of Salisbury.[69] The overlordship was not mentioned again.

In 1155-6 John FitzGilbert, husband of Patrick's sister Sibyl, held the estate. By 1159 John had conveyed it to the Templars,[70] who held it until the suppression of their order in 1308.[71] In 1312 the estate passed with other Temple lands to the knights of St. John of Jerusalem in England, the Hospitallers, who held it until the Dissolution.[72]

The manor was granted to Sir Edward Baynton and his wife Isabel in 1541.[73] After her husband's death in 1544,[74] Isabel, who married secondly Sir James Stumpe and thirdly Thomas Stafford, held it until her own death in 1573.[75] She was succeeded by her son Henry Baynton who sold it to the tenant Thomas Hutchins in 1595.[76] On Hutchins's death in 1607 the manor passed to Thomas Baskerville.[77] From Thomas Baskerville (d. 1621) the estate, variously called Temple Down, Temple Rockley, or Temple farm, passed like Winterbourne Bassett manor in the direct male line to Richard Baskerville, who by will proved 1739 devised it to his grandson Thomas Baskerville (d. 1817). Thomas's cousin and successor Thomas Baskerville Mynors, who in 1818 adopted the surname Baskerville,[78] was the owner in 1846 and 1860.[79] The estate was apparently acquired by George Cowing in the earlier 20th century and merged with his lands at Langdon Wick and Rockley.[80]

The tithes arising from Rockley were possibly granted to Amesbury abbey by John FitzGilbert and were confirmed to Amesbury priory when it was refounded in 1177.[81] They passed with the manor of Rabson in Winterbourne Bassett to Henry Edward Fox, Baron Holland, who was allotted a rent charge when the tithes were commuted in 1846.[82]

ECONOMIC HISTORY. THE BARTON. In the 12th century the lands which surrounded Marlborough Castle were called the barton.[83] They included the demesne, meadows beside the Kennet and downland north and south of it, customary holdings at Elcot and Newbury Street, and St. Margaret's priory and its lands.

Until the later 14th century the demesne land of the castle estate was managed directly for the Crown or the keepers or lessees of the castle. Among those employed in 1230 were a hayward, a swineherd, a granger, a shepherd for lambs, 5 carters, 7 ploughmen, and 2 dairymaids.[84] Sheep-and-corn husbandry prevailed and in 1196 and in 1279 over a thousand sheep were kept.[85] In the mid 13th century the hundred of Selkley was accustomed to supply 15 plough-teams for the land on which wheat was sown, 15 to plough for barley, and 15 to plough for oats. The hundred also found 50 men to hoop barrels, 17 to mow, 50 to reap, 17 carts to carry hay and another 17 to carry corn.[86] The men of the abbot of Glastonbury at Winterbourne Monkton were freed from their customary services in 1235.[87] Men at Rockley apparently subtracted theirs in 1252.[88] In 1285 free tenants of the barton manor had to do daywork at haymaking and harvest. Customary tenants then each held ½ yardland, presumably in the open fields of Elcot tithing south of the Kennet, and worked for the lord for 3 days each week in winter and for 5 each week in summer.[89] There were 25 customary tenants at Elcot and Newbury Street in 1466.[90] Demesne meadows and pastures had been leased in parcels for £46 a year by 1455. In 1473 certain other demesne lands were leased as a farm, later called Barton farm.[91] Successive leases were held by farmers until the later 16th century but Sir Thomas Wroughton and Sir George Wroughton, lessees from 1578 or earlier to 1634, sublet. From 1634 to 1722 leases belonged to the Seymours of Marlborough House who also sublet, but thereafter the land was again leased to farmers. The farm, worked from Barton Farm, was over 1,000

[65] Above; 19 Geo. III, c. 46 (Priv. Act); *Complete Peerage*, v. 35; G. F. Russell Barker and A. H. Stenning, *Rec. of Old Westminsters*, ii. 1030; W.R.O. 415/272, sched. of estates.
[66] Foster, *Baronetage* (1882), 459; W.R.O. 415/272, sched. of estates.
[67] W.A.S. Libr., sale cat. xvii, no. 26; above, Ogbourne St. Andrew, manors.
[68] *V.C.H. Wilts.* ii, p. 138.
[69] Ibid. p. 107; *L. & P. Hen. VIII*, xvi, p. 278.
[70] *Complete Peerage*, x, App. G. 95; *Sandford Cart.* (Oxon. Rec. Soc. xxii), ii, p. 179 and n.
[71] *V.C.H. Wilts.* iii. 328.
[72] P.R.O., SC 6/Hen. VIII/3996.
[73] *L. & P. Hen. VIII*, xvi, p. 278.
[74] P.R.O., E 150/982, no. 6.
[75] Ibid. C 142/167, no. 122; *Wilts. Pedigrees* (Harl. Soc. cv, cvi), 7.
[76] P.R.O., C 142/167, no. 122; ibid. E 159/378, rot. 213; ibid. C 2/Eliz. I/H 5/8; ibid. CP 25(2)/242/37 Eliz. I Hil.
[77] Ibid. C 142/297, no. 161.

[78] Below, Winterbourne Bassett, manors; Burke, *Commoners* (1833-8), i. 92-3.
[79] P.R.O., IR 29/38/163; IR 30/38/163; W.R.O. 9/2/272.
[80] W.A.S. Libr., sale cat. xvii, no. 26.
[81] *Cal. Chart. R.* 1257-1300, 158.
[82] Below, Winterbourne Bassett, manors; P.R.O., IR 29/38/163.
[83] *Pipe R.* 1199 (P.R.S. n.s. x), 178.
[84] Ibid. 1230 (P.R.S. n.s. iv), 1 sqq.
[85] *Chanc. R.* 1196 (P.R.S. n.s. vii), 33; P.R.O., SC 6/1055/12, rott. 37 sqq.
[86] *Rot. Hund.* (Rec. Com.), ii (1), 234.
[87] *Glastonbury Cart.* iii (Som. Rec. Soc. lxiv), pp. ccxxiv, 673, where the men are said to have been exempted from castle-guard and other services. The words used in the deed are 'de arruris et aliis operacionibus'.
[88] *Rot. Hund.* (Rec. Com.), ii (1), 234.
[89] *Cal. Inq. Misc.* i, p. 386.
[90] P.R.O., SC 6/1094/1.
[91] Ibid. SC 6/1055/19; SC 6/1094/2; ibid. DL 29/724/11800.

a. in the 18th and 19th centuries.[92] Its meadows were watered from the mid 17th century or earlier to the early 20th century.[93] In 1847 the largest areas of arable lay north-west of Barton Farm in Thorn field, 93 a., King's field, 82 a., and Stars field, 54 a., and the most extensive pastures were north of them on Barton Down, 305 a., and Rough Down, 50 a. Barton Copse, 10 a., was then the only woodland within the farm, timber having been supplied to the owners of the estate from Savernake forest since the Middle Ages.[94] The right to train racehorses on Barton Down was leased to Alexander Taylor in 1869 and gallops there have since been used by the trainers based at Manton House. Barton farm, part of the Manton estate of the marquesses of Ailesbury in 1929, was a mixed farm c. 1930.[95] Still part of that estate and in hand in 1981, it was then used for cereal production and the rearing of stock for beef.[96]

In 1535 the estate of St. Margaret's priory included land near the priory and a few properties in Marlborough and Newbury Street which were worth a total of £4. Its demesne lands of 80 a., scattered throughout the open fields of Elcot tithing, were in hand at the Dissolution and worth £1 12s.[97] Meadow lands, and pasture rights for sheep, possibly on a sheep common on the downs south of the Kennet, were then part of the estate.[98] St. Margaret's farm, 282 a. in 1820, had been largely dispersed by 1847 when it comprised only 86 a.[99]

Free, leasehold, and customary tenancies within the barton manor and St. Margaret's manor remained at St. Margaret's and Newbury Street in the 17th century and in the 18th. Each comprised small parcels of inclosed arable land, some meadows, and shares in Marlborough Common and the sheep common south of the Kennet.[1] The narrow strip of land at the south end of the parish perhaps represents a corridor to Clench Common in Milton Lilbourne where the barton tenants, and possibly those of St. Margaret's, Clatford, and Manton, may at some time have shared the pasture with other communities. There were 10 freeholders, 17 leaseholders, and 6 copyholders within the barton manor in 1638.[2] In 1768 there were 14 freeholders, 9 leaseholders, one the tenant of Elcot mill and the others of no more than a few acres each in Baymead, and 7

copyholders who each held small amounts of land.[3] In 1759 the tenants of George Spencer, duke of Marlborough, at St. Margaret's comprised, besides the occupier of St. Margaret's farm, 13 leaseholders and 6 copyholders.[4] By the mid 19th century the tenantry land, including the common south of the Kennet, had been apportioned among a few small farms all of less than 100 a.[5] What remained in 1929 was apportioned among two 30-a. smallholdings and some allotments.[6] In 1981 Marlborough Common was still open.

By 1204 a large fishpond had been made on the demesne land of the castle estate in the Og valley north-east of Marlborough. An earthen dam, sometimes called a bay, was raised across the Og to make a long narrow pond which extended north to Bay Bridge.[7] The dam could still be seen in 1981. The pond was stocked with bream in the 13th century when there were also pike and eels in it. Pike and bream were supplied as gifts and to royal residences including Windsor and Clarendon for food and breeding.[8] A quarter of the fish needed for Edward I's stay of five days at the castle in December 1302 was supplied from the pond.[9] In 1239 a new dam was built and the pond was raised and enclosed by a hedge.[10] The dam was raised in 1250 and in 1301 the sluices, which had been broken by floods, were repaired.[11] The pond was called Baylake in 1466 and, called Baywater, was part of Barton farm in the 17th century.[12] It had been drained by the earlier 19th century and most of its site, 15 a., became pasture.[13]

The reach of the Kennet between Manton village and Preshute church was divided into two fisheries which were part of the barton manor. Manton Water, the westerly one, and Stars mead, the easterly one, were apparently leased separately in the Middle Ages. Both were leased with Barton farm from the early 16th century and since the 17th have provided trout fishing.[14]

There was a large warren on Marlborough Common. In 1232 hares from it were sent to Reading for the king's use.[15] The constable of the castle in 1269 impounded twelve greyhounds taken into it illegally. Some sixty men with crossbows and other weapons and shielding themselves with doors and windows taken from houses near the castle gates rescued the dogs.[16] In

[92] Ibid. REQ 2/77/49; IR 29/38/188; IR 30/38/188; Cal. Pat. 1494–1509, 365; L. & P. Hen. VIII, xvii, p. 105; W.R.O. 9/2/4–5; 9/2/308; 9/2/341; Alnwick Castle Mun., X.II.11, box 6, survey of Hertford lands, 1634–, p. 341; X.II.11, box 23, deeds, Wroughton to Seymour, 1634; Hertford to Seymour, 1655; Seymour to Cripps, 1668; X.II.11, box 17, deeds, Hertford to Seymour, 1635; Somerset to Seymour, 1672; Ailesbury to Seymour, 1693; X.II.11, box 21, deed, Somerset to Neate, 1722.

[93] Rep. Marlborough Coll. Natural Hist. Soc. xcviii. 20, 23.

[94] P.R.O., IR 29/38/188; IR 30/38/188; Close R. 1268–72, 166, 329; Cal. Close, 1296–1302, 341; Cal. Fine R. 1369–77, 68.

[95] W.R.O. 9/2/349; 9, sale cat. 1929; [1st] Land Util. Surv. Map, sheet 112.

[96] Inf. from Mr. J. V. Bloomfield, Manton Ho.

[97] Valor Eccl. (Rec. Com.), ii. 148; Cal. Pat. 1547–53, 116.

[98] P.R.O., E 318/Box 20/1072, rot. C 9; W.R.O., TS. cal. of Ailesbury deeds, comp. E. S. Scroggs, ii, no. 2673; Blenheim Mun., E/P/85, f. 41.

[99] W.R.O. 9/2/159; P.R.O., IR 29/38/188; IR 30/38/188.

[1] Alnwick Castle Mun., X.II.11, box 6, survey of Hert-

ford lands, 1634–, pp. 341, 367; W.R.O. 9/2/371; 9/2/378; ibid. TS. cal. of Ailesbury deeds, comp. Scroggs, ii, no. 2673; Blenheim Mun., E/P/6, pp. 39–40.

[2] Alnwick Castle Mun., X.II.11, box 6, survey of Hertford lands, 1634–, pp. 339 sqq.

[3] W.R.O. 9/2/378.

[4] Blenheim Mun., E/P/6, pp. 39–40.

[5] P.R.O., IR 29/38/188; IR 30/38/188.

[6] W.R.O. 9, sale cat.

[7] Rot. Lib. (Rec. Com.), 83–4, 88.

[8] Ibid.; Close R. 1247–51, 152, 383; 1251–3, 51, 299, 301, 339; Cal. Lib. 1251–60, 346, 393.

[9] W.A.M. liv. 360.   [10] Cal. Lib. 1226–40, 415.

[11] Ibid. 1245–51, 294; Cal. Close, 1296–1302, 510.

[12] P.R.O., SC 6/1094/1; Alnwick Castle Mun., X.II.11, box 6, survey of Hertford lands, 1634–, p. 355.

[13] P.R.O., IR 29/38/188; IR 30/38/188.

[14] Ibid. SC 6/1055/19; Cal. Pat. 1494–1509, 365; W.R.O. 9/2/4–5; V.C.H. Wilts. iv. 365–6.

[15] Close R. 1231–4, 44.

[16] Sel. Cases of Procedure without Writ (Selden Soc. lx), pp. clxx, 47.

the later 15th century, when it was said to lie within Savernake forest, the warren was possibly for rabbits.[17] It was apparently discontinued in the later 16th century,[18] but a smaller rabbit warren on Marlborough Common was part of Barton farm in 1574[19] and in 1635.[20] Accounts of Port field and Marlborough Common are included in the history of Marlborough.[21]

A. W. Gale (d. 1969), who in 1922 began to breed bees for sale and later to sell beekeeping equipment, occupied premises in High Street, Marlborough, given up after 1939, and in London Road. He founded a subsidiary company, Honeybee Farmers Ltd., wound up after 1963, to distribute honey in jars. A. W. Gale (Bees) Ltd. in 1982 employed six men to tend a thousand hives at its bee farm in London Road.[22] Marlborough Ceramic Tiles was established at Barnfield in 1936. The firm opened a factory in Elcot Lane in 1955, to which employees from Barnfield were transferred in 1973, and where 22 people were employed in 1981.[23] The agricultural engineering firm of T. Pope Ltd. at Granham Hill was acquired by T. H. White Ltd. in 1946. Renamed T. H. White, Marlborough, Ltd. in 1965, the firm moved in 1978 to a factory in London Road where there were 32 employees in 1981.[24] The small factory established in Elcot Lane by Garrard & Co. during the Second World War to produce precision instruments employed 140 workers in 1960 but closed in 1964.[25] Pelham Puppets Ltd., begun in Marlborough in 1947, in 1981 occupied the site in London Road used in the later 19th century as a tannery by the Marlborough firm of C. May & Sons, and employed 100 people to make string puppets.[26] Avco Engineering Ltd., established in Elcot Lane in 1966, employed 120 people in general and precision engineering in 1981.[27]

Several mills along the Kennet, described in the early 18th century as 'a good river that turns many mills', served Marlborough Castle and its neighbourhood.[28] None is expressly mentioned until the late 12th century.

To distinguish how many mills were near Marlborough in the 13th century is difficult. The mills of Marlborough for which Hugh de Neville, keeper of Marlborough Castle, rendered account of £5 6s. 8d. in 1195 were perhaps those fitted with two new stones brought from Southampton in 1224.[29] In 1227 a mill beneath the castle was 'new'.[30] That was possibly the later Castle Mill, which stood south-east of the castle and outside its precincts. What was presumably another mill was to be 'built anew' in the king's garden in 1237.[31] That was possibly one of the two new fulling mills in the parish in 1251.[32] The mill in the king's garden is not expressly mentioned thereafter, although it may still have been in use c. 1356.[33] Castle Mill was still referred to as the 'new mill' in the later 13th century.[34] It had acquired the name Castle Mill by 1377.[35] The mill descended as part of Barton farm and remained within it in the 19th century. It was disused in 1929 or earlier.[36] Castle Mill was sublet or leased separately from 1279 or earlier until the mid 18th century. Thereafter it was leased with Barton farm.[37] Besides grinding corn, the mill perhaps also housed fulling machinery in 1613 when a newly built dyehouse stood nearby.[38] The castle mills, which restricted the supply of water to mills downstream in the mid 13th century, were themselves impeded c. 1356 by the reflux of water from Town or Port Mill.[39] The site of the garden mill may have been marked by the summer house in the garden of Marlborough House.[40] That of Castle Mill by Treacle Bolly was visible in 1981.

In 1215 King John conveyed a fulling mill, to be identified as that at Elcot, to Reynold Basset and William of Rowden.[41] Basset died c. 1224 and in 1225 the constable of Marlborough Castle was ordered to deliver his moiety to a namesake.[42] William of Rowden died c. 1235 leaving a daughter and heir married to Geoffrey Seymour.[43] The second Reynold Basset may also have died about then. His daughter and heir Isabel was a minor in 1238. The king had resumed the mill by 1237 in exchange for a pension paid to the heirs of Basset and Rowden.[44] The building de novo of a fulling mill 'under the mill of Elcot', ordered by the king in 1237, may represent the reconstruction or replacement of Elcot mill.[45] Elcot mill or mills passed with Castle Mill as part of the Barton estate until the 19th century.[46] It and the small farm attached to it were sold with

[17] Cal. Fine R. 1461–71, 15.
[18] W.R.O. 9, marquess of Hertford and mayor and burgesses of Marlborough, case concerning warren, 1721.
[19] Alnwick Castle Mun., X.II.11, box 17, copy survey of Barton farm.
[20] Ibid. X.II.11, box 17, deed, Hertford to Seymour.
[21] Below, Marlborough, agriculture.
[22] Inf. from Mr. A. C. Newman, A. W. Gale (Bees) Ltd.; Kelly's Dir. Wilts. (1927 and later edns.).
[23] Inf. from Mrs. K. M. Coote, Marlborough Ceramic Tiles.
[24] Inf. from Mr. D. I. Howells, T. H. White, Marlborough, Ltd.
[25] V.C.H. Wilts. iv. 203–4; Stedman, Marlborough, 364; Fletcher's Marlborough Dir. (1962–3); inf. from Mr. D. J. Carless, T. H. White, Marlborough, Ltd.
[26] Inf. from L. Ross, Pelham Puppets Ltd.; Kelly's Dir. Wilts. (1867, 1875); O.S. Map 6″, Wilts. XXIX (1889 edn.).
[27] Inf. from Mr. D. W. Pickston, Avco Engineering Ltd.
[28] Journeys of Celia Fiennes, ed. Morris, 330.
[29] Pipe R. 1195 (P.R.S. n.s. vi), 150–1; Rot. Litt. Claus. (Rec. Com.), i. 604; Cal. Lib. 1226–40, 18.
[30] Cal. Lib. 1226–40, 17.
[31] Ibid. 278.

[32] Close R. 1247–51, 415. The difficulty of identifying the mills is discussed in Collectanea (W.R.S. xii), 4–8.
[33] Cal. Pat. 1358–61, 292–3.
[34] P.R.O., SC 6/1055/12.
[35] Cal. Inq. Misc. iii, p. 393.
[36] Cal. Pat. 1547–8, 125; P.R.O., IR 29/38/188; IR 30/38/188; W.R.O. 9, sale cat. 1929.
[37] e.g. P.R.O., SC 6/1055/12; ibid. IR 29/38/188; IR 30/38/188; Alnwick Castle Mun., X.II.11, box 17, sched. of writings concerning Wilts. estates, deed, Seymour to Pearce, 1654; W.R.O. 9/2/314.
[38] Alnwick Castle Mun., X.II.11, box 4, deed, Scott to Johnson.
[39] Below; Cal. Pat. 1358–61, 292–3.
[40] Suggested by H. C. Brentnall: Collectanea (W.R.S. xii), 6 n.
[41] Rot. Chart. (Rec. Com.), 218.
[42] Ex. e Rot. Fin. (Rec. Com.), i. 118; Rot. Litt. Claus. (Rec. Com.), ii. 23.
[43] Ex. e Rot. Fin. (Rec. Com.), i. 284; Cal. Pat. 1232–47, 222.
[44] Cal. Pat. 1232–47, 222.
[45] Cal. Lib. 1226–40, 278.
[46] Above.

other parts of the Savernake estate to the Crown Commissioners in 1950. The house was afterwards sold as a private dwelling; the land was still Crown property in 1982.[47]

In 1273 the fulling mills 'without Marlborough', perhaps that at Elcot and that in the king's garden, were leased together. It is possible that the mill at Elcot then, as in the 16th century, incorporated a grist mill and a fulling mill within the same building.[48] Members of the Westbury family were tenants throughout the 17th century.[49] The buildings still included a fulling mill in 1757, but apparently not in 1794 when the grist mill was leased to Samuel Cook, a Trowbridge clothier.[50] Cook was expected by the lessor, Thomas, earl of Ailesbury, to provide work for the industrious poor, but not to install spinning machinery in the mill without the consent of the lessor and of the burgesses of Marlborough. He had built a new cloth mill by 1796.[51] John Brinsden became tenant in 1799 when the property comprised a grist mill, a clothing mill, and a mill house.[52] Brinsden remained tenant in 1847 when a farm of 61 a. was attached to the mills.[53]

The mills stood on the Kennet 800 m. southeast of its confluence with the Og. In 1956 they ground corn and generated electricity.[54] The 18th-century mill house stood alone in 1981.

The mill later called Town or Port Mill, beside the Kennet and approached from Marlborough high street by way of Angel Yard, was, like Castle Mill and Elcot mill, part of the royal demesne. It was granted to Robert Barfleur by John, count of Mortain, between 1189 and 1193. It was regranted by John, then king, to Robert's son Nicholas in 1204.[55] Nicholas was disseised of it by William Marshal, earl of Pembroke, keeper of Marlborough Castle 1217–19.[56] Marshal's son William was ordered to restore the mill to Nicholas in 1219.[57] Nicholas, however, had not regained possession by 1221, when the younger William's successor as keeper of the castle was in turn ordered to reinstate him.[58]

In the early 13th century there may have been two mills, as there were in 1295, since Robert Barfleur's relict Maud paid for confirmations to her of a 'mill of Marlborough' in both 1210 and 1211.[59] She apparently held a mill in 1216 and still in 1225.[60]

In 1300 Nicholas son of Nicholas Barfleur received the king's permission to enfeoff William of Harden in the two mills.[61] William in turn was licensed in 1317 to convey them to St. Margaret's priory for masses.[62] The canons acquired the mills in 1319.[63] There was possibly no more than a single mill in the 16th century.[64] Port Mill descended with the manor of St. Margaret's until 1799 when George, duke of Marlborough, sold the mill to William Plank.[65] It was owned by William White in 1847.[66] J. and E. Dell were the owners in 1907 and 1923.[67] The mill was apparently rebuilt in the 19th century and ground corn until c. 1922. The upper storey was removed in the 1950s[68] but the lower storey still stood in 1981.

In 1236 the king granted to the prior and canons of St. Margaret's the right to hold a fair near their house on 19 and 20 July each year.[69] That right was sold as part of St. Margaret's manor after the Dissolution and the owners of the manor continued to take the profits and tolls of the fair,[70] worth £1 in 1759, £2 in 1763.[71] The fair, held in Newbury Street, had become limited to 20 July by the mid 16th century.[72] After 1752 the fair was held on 31 July. It was still held in 1763 but had apparently ceased by 1817.[73]

MANTON. In 1066 Manton was assessed for geld at 3 hides. Then and in 1086 the estate was worth £3. There was land for 3 ploughteams in 1086. The 1 demesne hide supported 2 serfs and 1 team. On the remaining 2 hides 5 villeins and 5 bordars shared 2 teams. Meadows covered 4 a. and pasture land 40 a.[74]

A farmstead on Manton Down in the 12th century had been abandoned by 1300.[75] In the Middle Ages the land of Manton was apportioned among the manor of Manton, two freeholds at Flexborough, and customary holdings attached to the barton estate. The manor was divided into moieties c. 1300[76] but it is not clear whether the division affected demesne or customary land. There were twelve customary tenants in Manton of the barton estate in 1466.[77] One of the freeholds remained a small farm in the early 17th century.[78] The barton estate land was then partly in a leasehold of 95 a., held by members of the Chapman or Hitchcock family in the later 16th century and earlier 17th, and partly in copyholds of 46 a. and 26 a. The copyholds

[47] Inf. from Crown Estate Com., Bracknell, Berks.; Mr. G. Young, Stitchcombe Cottage, Mildenhall.
[48] P.R.O., E 159/47; ibid. SC 6/1055/12, rott. 26–7; W.R.O. 9/2/366, f. 4v.
[49] Alnwick Castle Mun., X.II.11, box 6, survey of Hertford lands, 1634– , p. 357; W.R.O. 9/2/371, p. 19; 9/2/296.
[50] W.R.O. 9/2/336; 9/2/378.
[51] Ibid. 9/2/337; ibid. TS. cal. of Ailesbury deeds, comp. Scroggs, ii, no. 2620.
[52] Ibid. 9/2/340.
[53] P.R.O., IR 29/38/188; IR 30/38/188.
[54] Collectanea (W.R.S. xii), 6 n.
[55] Cartae Antiquae (Pipe R. Soc. n.s. xvii), p. 125; P.R.O., IR 29/38/188; IR 30/38/188.
[56] Rot. Litt. Claus. (Rec. Com.), i. 466; above, Marlborough Castle.
[57] Rot. Litt. Claus. (Rec. Com.), i. 407.
[58] Ibid. 466.
[59] Pipe R. 1210 (P.R.S. n.s. xxvi), 78; 1211 (P.R.S. n.s. xxviii), 165; Cal. Inq. p.m. iii, pp. 154–5.
[60] Pipe R. 17 John (P.R.S. n.s. xxxvii), 59; Rot. Litt. Claus. (Rec. Com.), ii. 53.
[61] Cal. Pat. 1292–1301, 502.
[62] Ibid. 1317–21, 59.
[63] Feet of F. 1272–1327 (W.R.S. i), p. 102.
[64] P.R.O., E 318/Box 20/1072.
[65] W.R.O. 9/2/140; 9/2/153; Blenheim Mun., Wilts. deeds, Marlborough to Plank.
[66] P.R.O., IR 29/38/188; IR 30/38/188.
[67] Kelly's Dir. Wilts.
[68] The mill is shown intact on a photograph of c. 1950: Chandler, Hist. Marlborough, pl. at pp. 52–3.
[69] Cal. Chart. R. 1226–57, 219.
[70] P.R.O., E 318/Box 20/1072, rot. C 9.
[71] Blenheim Mun., E/P/6, p. 39; E/P/10, p. 65.
[72] P.R.O., E 318/Box 20/1072, rot. C 9.
[73] Blenheim Mun., case concerning waste of St. Margaret's manor, 1763; ibid. E/P/85.
[74] V.C.H. Wilts. ii, pp. 146–7.
[75] W.A.M. liii. 328–31.
[76] Above, manors.
[77] P.R.O., SC 6/1094/1.
[78] Ibid. C 2/Eliz. I/D 9/59.

were held in 1638 by Edward Mortimer and presumably formed Mortimer's farm leased with Barton farm in 1780.[79] In the 17th century there were several other small farms.[80] One of the moieties of Manton manor contained a Manton farm in 1633.[81]

Pasture rights in a meadow were unsuccessfully claimed by men of the barton c. 1246.[82] Common husbandry was practised in Manton. Barrow and Upper fields were north of the meadow land by the Kennet and South, West, and Flexborough, later Laxbury, fields were south of it. Common pasture was in Manton breach and meadows by the Kennet were held in common.[83] In the earlier 18th century some of the open fields were inclosed by agreement.[84] Others remained uninclosed. In 1792 390 a. on either side of the London–Bath road, mostly arable but including meadows and pastures, were either inclosed or reallotted. Of that, 171 a. were allotted to Thomas, earl of Ailesbury, 103 a. to the trustees of John Braithwaite, and the remaining 116 a. were divided among several smallholdings. The earl of Ailesbury and Braithwaite's trustees were also allotted watercourses in Manton marsh to water their meadows. Inclosure was accompanied by the amalgamation, rearrangement, and consolidation of most of the smaller farms. A farm of 282 a. and another of 182 a. worked from Manton Grange seem to have been formed in that way. In 1847 there were four large farms and two smaller, one of 83 a. attached to Manton mill and the other of 79 a.[85]

Woodland of 40 a. was attached to the Manton estate in 1086.[86] The township and its surrounding lands were considered to lie within Savernake forest and were still part of it in the 14th century. Tenants at Manton were deprived of their pasture rights there in 1332.[87] In 1847 the only woodland in Manton was in downland plantations of 8 a. and 6 a. north of the Kennet.[88]

Most land in the tithing was reunited in single ownership in the later 19th century. Two of the larger farms formed after parliamentary inclosure were owned by Charles, marquess of Ailesbury, in 1847 and George, marquess of Ailesbury, bought a third in 1872. In 1895 or earlier and still in 1929 the enlarged estate was divided between Manton Weir farm, 492 a., and Manton (in 1929 Elm Tree) farm, 93 a.[89] Alexander Taylor (d. 1894), who had bought land in the north part of Manton c. 1869, built up a large racehorse training establishment at Manton House surrounded by level downland gallops. He and his son Alexander (d. 1943) trained many winners of classic flat races. After the son's retirement in 1927 training at Manton was carried on under Tattersalls' ownership by Joseph Lawson. George Todd trained horses, some of which he owned, at Manton from 1947 to 1973.[90] In 1981 the Manton estate, reunited in single ownership, extended over some 2,200 a. of Preshute parish, of which 100 a. were for training and the rest for mixed farming which included the maintenance of large flocks of sheep and the rearing of stock for beef.[91]

There was a mill at Manton in 1249 when it was acquired by the prior of St. Margaret's, who retained it until the Dissolution.[92] It was sold in 1553 to William, earl of Pembroke, and apparently passed with his Manton estate to William Young who in 1632 conveyed the mill to Richard Stephens and Robert Webb, perhaps a trustee or mortgagee.[93] In 1668, when the property comprised two water mills, William son of Richard Stephens sold his interest to Thomas Webb, son of Robert Webb.[94] Both mills descended in the Webb family and in 1751 Mary Webb, relict of a Thomas Webb, sold them to Prince Sutton, whose son James sold them, with a farm of 83 a., in 1800 to William White, a baker and maltster of Marlborough.[95] White occupied the mills in 1815 and in 1835 the trustees of his will conveyed them and the farm to George White, the owner in 1847.[96] Trustees under his will in 1870 conveyed the estate to S. B. White, who immediately sold it to George, marquess of Ailesbury,[97] whose successor and namesake offered it for sale in 1929.[98]

Manton mill ceased to work in 1933.[99] It and its 19th-century red-brick mill house stand on the Kennet west of the lane linking Manton with the London–Bath road. The mill, also of red brick and perhaps of the 18th or early 19th century, incorporates some older walling. An undershot wheel of the 19th century survived in the south range in 1981.

CLATFORD. The 5-hide estate which became Clatford manor was worth £5 in 1066 and 1086. In 1086 there were 3 ploughteams and 1 serf on the 3-hide demesne. A villein and 7 bordars had 1 team. There were 5 a. of meadow and, presumably on the downs north of the Kennet, pasture ½ league long and 3 furlongs broad.[1]

In 1337 the demesne farm supported 12 oxen, 8 cows, 157 ewes, and 122 lambs; 15 or more cheeses were produced, and 20 a. were sown with

[79] W.R.O. 9/2/366, f. 19v.; 9/2/72; 9/2/370; Alnwick Castle Mun., X.II.11, box 6, survey of Hertford lands, 1634– , pp. 351, 359 sqq.

[80] W.R.O. 9/2/371, p. 2 (at end of vol.).

[81] Ibid. 9/2/30.

[82] Wilts. Inq. p.m. 1242–1326 (Index Libr.), 69–70.

[83] Alnwick Castle Mun., X.II.11, box 6, survey of Hertford lands, 1634– , pp. 359 sqq.; W.R.O. 9/2/366; ibid. Manton inclosure award.

[84] W.R.O. 9/2/17.

[85] Ibid. Manton inclosure award; P.R.O., IR 29/38/188; IR 30/38/188.

[86] V.C.H. Wilts. ii, pp. 146–7.

[87] Ibid. iv. 419, 422–3.

[88] P.R.O., IR 29/38/188; IR 30/38/188.

[89] Ibid. IR 29/38/188; W.R.O. 9, sched. of deeds, 1870, pp. 605–6; estate accts. 1895, pp. 9, 17; sale cat. 1929.

[90] Brit. Racehorse, xxv, no. 4 (Sept. 1973), pp. 454 sqq.; V.C.H. Wilts. iv. 382; see above, plate facing p. 145.

[91] Inf. from Mr. Bloomfield.

[92] P.R.O., CP 25(1)/251/15, no. 5; ibid. SC 6/Hen. VIII/3985, rot. 65d.

[93] Ibid. E 318/Box 33/1861; above, manors; W.R.O. 9/2/11.

[94] W.R.O. 9/2/103.

[95] Ibid. 9/2/106; 9/2/112; 9/2/115; 212B/2589; V.C.H. Wilts. x. 115.

[96] W.R.O. 9/2/116–17; P.R.O., IR 29/38/188; IR 30/38/188.

[97] W.R.O. 9/2/118–20.

[98] Ibid. 9, sale cat.

[99] Inf. from Mr. E. G. H. Kempson, Sun Cottage, Hyde Lane.

[1] V.C.H. Wilts. ii, p. 152.

wheat, 20 a. with barley, and 20 a. with oats. The hay crop was worth £1.[2] The demesne was leased from 1400 or earlier, from 1450 to 1532 to members of the Chapman or Hitchcock family.[3] Seven copyholds mentioned in 1443, of which four comprised a total of 9 yardlands, each included small areas of meadow and pasture in common for 80 sheep to a yardland.[4] The Goddards, owners of the manor in the later 16th century and the 17th, managed the demesne directly and may have lived at Clatford. The demesne arable was reckoned at 270 a. in 1700. In that year a common pasture was described as lately inclosed.[5] It is likely that much tenantry land was taken to enlarge Clatford farm both before and in the 18th century. Small copyholds survived in the later 18th century but had been extinguished by the earlier 19th when vestiges of the open fields remained north of the London–Bath road in East field and on both sides of that road in West field.[6]

From the mid 18th century to 1923 Clatford farm was leased and since 1923 has been occupied by the owners.[7] In 1840 it occupied the whole tithing and was a predominantly arable farm of 701 a. including water meadows beside the Kennet and 163 a. of downland in the north part of the tithing.[8] Clatford was a mixed farm c. 1930 and in 1979 when it comprised 624 a.[9] Clatford Down was leased as gallops in 1906[10] and in 1981 was still used for training racehorses stabled at Manton.

In 1086 the woodland at Clatford was ½ league square.[11] The woods, in the south part of the tithing, were considered part of Savernake forest until put out in 1330.[12] In the later 18th century and the earlier 19th they were considered part of West Woods, most of which was in Overton.[13] In 1840 the Clatford woods were Foxbury, 47 a., Short Oaks, 7 a., Bottom, 28 a., and Ashen, 12 a., coppices.[14] Bottom coppice had been grubbed up by 1906.[15]

In 1086 there was a mill on Ralph Mortimer's estate.[16] It descended with Clatford manor until the 20th century and was leased separately in the 18th century but from the earlier 19th as part of Clatford farm. It was last expressly mentioned in 1906.[17] In 1416 the farmer of Clatford priory was accused of allowing the water mill with its bridge

and flood gates to fall down.[18] The overgrown mill race in 1981 marked the site of the mill north-west of Clatford.

LANGDON WICK. The downland called Langdon Wick or Wick Down was probably cultivated from the later Bronze Age. There is evidence of enclosures of that date and of a later field system on Preshute Down.[19] It was acquired by Stanley abbey in 1194 for sheep rearing, with which the medieval enclosure near Wick Down Farm may have been connected.[20] As Wick Down farm the land was leased for £240 yearly in the earlier 18th century.[21] The 743-a. farm, worked from Wick Down Farm, was in 1840 still given over to sheep-and-corn husbandry and then supported a flock of 600 sheep.[22] In 1981 it was part of the farm worked by Mereacre Ltd. from Temple Farm in Ogbourne St. Andrew.[23]

TEMPLE ROCKLEY. In 1066 and in 1086 the estate at Temple Rockley was worth £2 and was assessed at 1 hide. The demesne contained enough land to support 1 ploughteam. The rest of the estate supported 1 villein and 3 bordars with 1 ploughteam. There were 20 a. of pasture.[24]

The demesne comprised 1 carucate in 1185: eight tenants held 5 a. each and a ninth a croft. The eight had to perform boonwork with two men in the autumn, and to reap and to mow. Wives of tenants had to wash, shear, and milk the sheep.[25] Then and later in the Middle Ages the manor was administered from the preceptory of Sandford (Oxon.).[26] It was part of an estate which included land in Ogbourne St. Andrew and in Lockeridge in Overton.[27]

In 1338 there was a chief messuage, 320 a. of arable, a several pasture for 21 large animals, pasture for 900 sheep, and 6 a. of meadow.[28] No customary tenant was mentioned then or later.

The farm was leased to William Collingbourne before 1485.[29] In 1519 it was leased to Guthlac Overton, still farmer in 1540.[30] Three Thomas Goddards were lessees in turn in the mid 16th century and farmers may be traced until the 19th century.[31] The 400-a. downland farm was mostly devoted to sheep, although c. 1736 an under-tenant built a brick kiln and drying house there.[32]

[2] Eton Coll. Mun. 4/18.
[3] P.R.O., SC 6/1062/25, m. 3; Eton Coll. Mun. 4/213; ibid. rent rolls, C 21, E 18; audit bks. 1506–29, ff. 30, 52, 96, 120, 140, 166, 184, 208, 232, 258, 290, 322, 346, 370, 390, 410, 428; 1529–45, ff. 2, 22.
[4] Eton Coll. Mun., ct. roll, 16 Mar. 1443.
[5] P.R.O., E 126/17, f. 160v.
[6] Ibid. IR 29/38/77; IR 30/38/77; Blenheim Mun., E/P/6, p. 41; E/P/10, p. 67; E/P/85, ff. 18 sqq.
[7] Blenheim Mun., E/P/6, p. 41; E/P/33, p. 25; E/P/85, f. 18v. sqq.; E/P/90; W.R.O. 106; inf. from Mr. J. T. Wroth, Westfield, Clatford; Mrs. A. Goodwin, Clatford Farm.
[8] P.R.O., IR 29/38/77; IR 30/38/77.
[9] [1st] Land Util. Surv. Map, sheet 112; inf. from Mrs. Goodwin.   [10] W.R.O. 106.
[11] V.C.H. Wilts. ii, p. 152.
[12] Ibid. iv. 419; W.A.M. xlix. 432.
[13] V.C.H. Wilts. xi. 198; Blenheim Mun., E/P/85, ff. 22v.–23; E/P/90.
[14] P.R.O., IR 29/38/77; IR 30/38/77.
[15] W.R.O. 106.
[16] V.C.H. Wilts. ii, p. 152.
[17] Eton Coll. Mun. 4/18; Blenheim Mun., E/P/6, p. 41;

E/P/10, p. 66; E/P/85, ff. 18v. sqq.; P.R.O., IR 29/38/77; IR 30/38/77; W.R.O. 106.
[18] Cal. Inq. Misc. vii, p. 300.
[19] V.C.H. Wilts. i (1), 268, 276–7; i (2), 399.
[20] Ibid. i (1), 268; iii. 270.
[21] Alnwick Castle Mun., X.II.11, box 6, Axford's acct. 1721; audit bk. 1693–1740; box 17, partics. of Preshute estates, 1726.
[22] W.R.O. 374/128, sale cat.
[23] Above, Ogbourne St. Andrew, econ. hist.
[24] V.C.H. Wilts. ii, p. 138.
[25] Rec. Templars in Eng. ed. B. A. Lees, pp. 53, 56–7.
[26] V.C.H. Wilts. x. 62.
[27] Knights Hospitallers in Eng. (Camd. Soc. [1st ser.], lxv), 187, 240, where the estate is said, wrongly, to be entirely in Ogbourne St. Andrew; V.C.H. Wilts. xi. 196.
[28] Knights Hospitallers in Eng. 187.
[29] Cal. Pat. 1476–85, 510.
[30] P.R.O., SC 6/Hen. VIII/3996.
[31] Ibid. C 2/Eliz. I/H 5/8; C 3/72/19; ibid. IR 29/38/163; IR 30/38/163.
[32] Ibid. E 134/15 Geo. II Hil./2; Extents for Debts (W.R.S. xxviii), p. 79; W.A.M. xli. 114.

The farm was worked in 1846 from the farm-house called Temple Farm in 1960, Top Temple in 1981.[33] It was part of a more extensive mixed farm worked by Mereacre Ltd. from Temple Farm in Ogbourne St. Andrew in 1981.[34]

LOCAL GOVERNMENT. The honor of Marlborough and the hundred of the barton in the 13th century[35] presumably included the tithings of Elcot and Langdon Wick, the king's tithing of Manton, and possibly the tithing of Temple Rockley. In 1275 of the two tithings in Manton one, called the king's tithing, was made up of barton tenants in Manton who owed suit at the barton courts.[36] The honor of Marlborough was administered by the constable of the castle.[37] Some jurisdiction was delegated to John Bailey, tenant of the barton farm from 1503 to 1518. Bailey was also entitled to perquisites of court, presumably from the views of frankpledge and manorial courts held for the barton from the 15th century or earlier.[38] No record of the medieval courts of the honor and hundred is known to survive.

The franchises granted with the castle and barton estate to Edward, duke of Somerset, in 1547 were those enjoyed by grantees of the estate in the Middle Ages.[39] Although also lords of Selkley hundred, Somerset and his successors as owners of the barton estate apparently never exercised their franchisal jurisdiction through the hundred courts, except perhaps occasionally for Elcot tithing in the later 18th century and in the 19th.[40] Records of courts baron for the barton manor are extant for 1732–41 and 1760–1817. The courts, at which little was done except to collect quitrents, were held each summer until c. 1762 and thereafter each autumn.[41]

Direct royal jurisdiction over estates in the parish granted to religious houses was relinquished by Henry III. Between 1216 and 1272 the abbot of Stanley, lord of Langdon Wick, withdrew his men from the barton court.[42] In 1229 the king granted the prior of St. Margaret's the right to take within the barton the toll paid by the barton tenants for brewing and selling ale.[43] That privilege was exchanged in 1344.[44] It was probably with royal permission that c. 1245 the prior withdrew the suit of his tenants from the barton court, thereby creating a tithing which possibly did not survive the Dissolution.[45]

The second tithing in Manton comprised the tenants of the honor of Wallingford there who until c. 1259 attended the courts of Selkley hundred.[46] The tithing may thereafter, as in the earlier 16th century, have been represented by its

tithingman at the views of frankpledge held at Ogbourne St. George for the honor of Wallingford.[47] Records of manorial courts for Manton manor survive for 1611–13. The courts, held each spring, were concerned with matters such as illegal undertenancies, repair of tenements, and the building of cottages on the waste. In 1611 two supervisors of the commons were elected.[48]

Between 1173 and 1182 Henry III granted to the monks of St. Victor, who held the manor of Clatford, liberties throughout their English lands including quittance from suit of shire and hundred and from tolls imposed in royal boroughs, ports, markets, and castles. Although those liberties were confirmed in 1328 the priors of Clatford, especially during the war with France, may never have fully used them.[49] At the later 14th-century courts, held once or twice yearly, the usual manorial business, such as admittances to copyholds, fugitive serfs, ruinous tenements, and the taking of the lord's wood and illegal fishing in his waters, was presented. Repairs to Broad and Blanchard's bridges were often ordered.[50] Courts from 1443 to 1446 and from 1450 to 1453 were apparently held twice yearly. Although called views of frankpledge with courts, the business transacted was limited to matters such as those mentioned above.[51] Manor courts were held in the earlier 18th century.[52]

In 1834 the parish had a cottage at Manton for the use of paupers. It was then occupied by two poor families but was later sold.[53] The parish became part of Marlborough poor-law union in 1835.[54]

CHURCH. It is likely that the church which was held in 1086 with a hide of land in Marlborough, perhaps by gift of the king, by William Beaufay, bishop of East Anglia (d. 1091), was Preshute church,[55] which is known to have been standing in the 12th century. Bishop Beaufay gave or devised to Osmund, bishop of Salisbury, 'the churches of Marlborough', among which Preshute church was probably included although it was not expressly said to be so until 1223. In 1091 Bishop Osmund endowed the newly constituted cathedral chapter at Salisbury with those churches.[56] Their revenues, and later those of Blewbury (Berks., later Oxon.), were used to endow the prebend of Blewbury and Marlborough.[57] The prebend was dissolved between 1142 and 1184 by Jocelin de Bohun, bishop of Salisbury, who used its endowments to augment the common fund of Salisbury chapter.[58] By the early 13th century, however, it had been recon-

[33] P.R.O., IR 29/38/163; IR 30/38/163.
[34] Local inf.; above, Ogbourne St. Andrew, econ. hist.
[35] Pat. R. 1216–25, 426; Gaol Delivery 1275–1306 (W.R.S. xxxiii), p. 40; Plac. de Quo Warr. (Rec. Com.), 800.
[36] Rot. Hund. (Rec. Com.), ii (1), 263.
[37] Pat. R. 1216–25, 426.
[38] Cal. Pat. 1494–1509, 365; P.R.O., E 210/10508; ibid. DL 29/724/11801.
[39] Cal. Pat. 1547–8, 133.
[40] W.R.O. 192/12A–M; 9, Selkley hund. ct. bk. 1734–1861; above, p. 66.
[41] W.R.O. 9/2/363–4.
[42] Rot. Hund. (Rec. Com.), ii (1), 263.
[43] Close R. 1227–31, 190.
[44] Cal. Pat. 1348–50, 443.
[45] Rot. Hund. (Rec. Com.), ii (1), 263.
[46] Ibid.
[47] P.R.O., SC 2/212/14; SC 2/212/18–21; SC 2/212/23–4.
[48] W.R.O. 9/2/362.
[49] Cal. Chart. R. 1327–41, 67–8.
[50] Eton Coll. Mun., ct. roll, 1381–90.
[51] Ibid. ct. roll, 1443–6; rent roll A 67; ibid. 4/213.
[52] W.R.O. 62/7.
[53] Endowed Char. Wilts. (N. Div.), 840–1.
[54] Poor Law Com. 2nd Rep. 559.
[55] V.C.H. Wilts. ii, pp. 34, 119 and n.
[56] Reg. St. Osmund (Rolls Ser.), i. 199; Sar. Chart. and Doc. (Rolls Ser.), 123–4; below.
[57] V.C.H. Berks. iii. 282, 290.
[58] Reg. St. Osmund (Rolls Ser.), i. 216.

stituted and its original endowments restored. The advowson of the prebend was then held by members of the Sandford family.[59] In 1223 the bishop challenged the right of Hugh Sandford, to whom the advowson had passed in 1222, to present prebendaries.[60] The outcome of the dispute was that Sandford remained patron but that the churches of Preshute and Marlborough were taken from the prebend and assigned to the bishop, in whose peculiar jurisdiction they thenceforth remained.[61]

The bishops of Salisbury collated rectors to Preshute for the rest of the 13th century.[62] In 1322 the bishop appropriated the church to the use of the cathedral choristers, their warden, and their schoolmaster, the appropriation to take effect on the death or resignation of the rector. The bishop reserved the right to ordain a vicarage and to nominate a vicar whom the warden would present to him for institution.[63] Although the warden and choristers were admitted as appropriate rectors in 1323, and a vicarage was ordained and a vicar nominated by the bishop in 1324, the choristers' acquisition of the church's revenues was deferred when the rector, deprived of an alternative preferment by the provision of a papal nominee, was licensed by the bishop to return to Preshute in 1324.[64] Despite attempts to find an alternative benefice for the rector,[65] the warden and choristers did not finally gain possession until his death in 1329.[66] Since then, at the nomination of the bishop, they have presented vicars.[67] The only known exception occurred in 1579 when the archdeacon of Salisbury presented.[68] In 1976 the vicarage was united with the united benefice of Marlborough, St. Mary the Virgin with St. Peter and St. Paul, and a team ministry was established.[69]

In 1291 Preshute church was valued at £20, and in 1330 at £27.[70] The vicarage was worth £8 in 1535.[71] It was augmented in 1560 by £13 6s. 8d. yearly from the choristers.[72] In 1634 the oblations, stole fees, and the tithes of Clatford were allotted to the vicar,[73] and in 1662 the choristers gave an additional £25.[74] From 1829 to 1831 the vicar received an average yearly income of £186.[75]

From 1223 to 1330 the rectors of Preshute were entitled to all tithes from the entire parish with two exceptions. By the later 12th century the tithes of Temple Rockley manor had been granted to Amesbury abbey and the abbot of Stanley claimed by papal privilege to be exempt from payment of small tithes from his manor of Langdon Wick. In 1250 the rector agreed with the abbot to receive 20s. yearly in place of the great tithes of Langdon Wick.[76] The rector established his right in 1252 to tithes from the land east of Marlborough which became 'new land' of the borough. He was, however, to pay 40s. yearly to the then vicar of St. Mary's, Marlborough, during that vicar's incumbency, and assumed the vicar of St. Mary's duty to pay to the deans of Salisbury, after the death of the incumbent dean, 20s. a year for a candle to burn in the choir of the cathedral.[77] The rector paid the pension in 1291.[78] Its payment became the responsibility of the vicar in 1330,[79] but is not afterwards recorded.

When the vicarage of Preshute was endowed in 1330 the vicars became responsible for collecting the tithes and doing the other rectorial duties. They paid £20 yearly from those revenues to the choristers.[80] By the later 15th century, however, the choristers had let the rectory at farm for £20 yearly to lay tenants, who possibly paid a yearly sum to the vicars,[81] as they were enjoined to do in the early 17th century.[82] By 1677 the vicar's tithes from the demesne lands of Clatford manor had been commuted for 20s. and 1 a. of wheat. Those from the tenantry lands were paid in kind in 1677 but, following difficulty in collecting them c. 1700, the vicars leased them to the owners of Clatford manor at rents varying from £60 to £80.[83] In 1840 they were valued at £179 and commuted.[84]

Since no glebe was apparently attached to either of the Marlborough churches, it is possible that the rectors of Preshute had the hide mentioned in 1086. It may have become the glebe farm of 60 a. held by the choristers.[85] A close allotted to the vicar in 1330 was probably the vicar's close mentioned in the 17th and 18th centuries.[86] The vicar had 1 a. of glebe in Manton in the 19th century.[87] It was presumably the land sold in 1937.[88]

The rectory house was assigned to the vicar in 1330.[89] In 1560 the vicar was given buildings newly erected in the churchyard.[90] They may have included a vicarage house, presumably that

[59] V.C.H. Berks. iii. 290.
[60] Hugh was not the prebendary, as stated in Fasti Eccl. Sar. ed. W. H. Jones, ii. 367, but patron: V.C.H. Berks. iii. 290; Sar. Chart. and Doc. (Rolls Ser.), 123–4.
[61] Sar. Chart. and Doc. (Rolls Ser.), 123–4, 126.
[62] D. & C. Sar. Mun., press I, box 8, no. 2; Phillipps, Wilts. Inst. i. 11.
[63] Reg. Martival (Cant. & York Soc.), ii. 412 sqq.
[64] Ibid. i. 296, 297 n.; ii. 416 sqq.
[65] Ibid. i. 352–3; Le Neve, Fasti, 1300–1541, Salisbury, 13.
[66] D. & C. Sar. Mun., press IV, box E 2/Preshute/2; box E 2/Preshute/5.
[67] Reg. Martival (Cant. & York Soc.), i. 404; Phillipps, Wilts. Inst. (index in W.A.M. xxviii. 227); Crockford (1896 and later edns.).
[68] Phillipps, Wilts. Inst. i. 229.
[69] Lond. Gaz. 22 Jan. 1976, p. 1020.
[70] Tax. Eccl. (Rec. Com.), 189; Reg. Martival (Cant. & York Soc.), ii. 632.
[71] Valor Eccl. (Rec. Com.), ii. 150.
[72] W.A.M. xlviii. 209–10.
[73] W.R.O., bishop, glebe terrier, 1783.

[74] D. & C. Sar. Mun., lease bk. V, f. 57v.
[75] Rep. Com. Eccl. Revenues, 844–5.
[76] D. & C. Sar. Mun., press I, box 8, no. 13; above, manors.
[77] Sar. Chart. and Doc. (Rolls Ser.), 320–1.
[78] Tax. Eccl. (Rec. Com.), 189.
[79] Reg. Martival (Cant. & York Soc.), ii. 640.
[80] Ibid. 639 sqq.
[81] D. & C. Sar. Mun., choristers, press III, box 1, no. 6; P.R.O., E 126/14, f. 289.
[82] D. & C. Sar. Mun., lease bk. III, p. 50.
[83] W.R.O., bishop, glebe terrier, 1677; Blenheim Mun., Wilts. deeds, deed, Clavering to Percival, 1729; exrs. of Percival to Chetwynd, 1747; Chetwynd to Marlborough, 1756; Henchman to Marlborough, 1787.
[84] P.R.O., IR 29/38/77.
[85] Above, manors.
[86] Reg. Martival (Cant. & York Soc.), ii. 640; W.R.O., bishop, glebe terriers, 1608, 1677, 1783.
[87] Return of Glebe, H.C. 307, p. 166 (1887), lxiv.
[88] Ch. Com., copy deeds, ccccliii, no. 45644.
[89] Reg. Martival (Cant. & York Soc.), ii. 640.
[90] W.A.M. xlviii. 209–10.

burnt down *c.* 1606.[91] The house reputedly stood in the south-east part of the churchyard.[92] Where the 17th-century incumbents lived is unknown. From the earlier 18th to the earlier 19th century, while the vicarage was held in plurality with the rectory of St. Peter, Marlborough, the vicars lived at Marlborough.[93] There was still no house in Preshute for the vicar in 1829.[94] The vicar lived in a rented house on the north side of the London-Bath road in 1850.[95] The house was bought as a glebe house in 1926 and sold in 1976, when it was replaced by a new vicarage house at West Manton.[96]

A daughter church of St. Martin was built between 1252 and 1254 by the inhabitants of the 'new land' east of Marlborough, and the area which it served was transferred to St. Mary's parish, Marlborough, *c.* 1548.[97]

A recluse called Eve who lived at Preshute, perhaps in a cell attached to the church, in 1215 received 1*d.* daily from the king for life.[98] In 1250 Roger Green, rector of Preshute, who was also a canon of Salisbury, was licensed to hold a third benefice.[99] The royalist sympathies of Aylmer Lynch caused his ejection from the vicarage in 1647. He was replaced by the vicar of St. Mary's, Marlborough, Thomas Miles, who, despite his puritan leanings, was formally instituted in 1662.[1] It is likely that the vicarage house mentioned above was not rebuilt after *c.* 1606 because 17th-century incumbents held other richer benefices on which they lived. Miles himself possibly lived at Poole Keynes (now Glos.) after he became rector there in 1662.[2] Henry Thorpe, vicar 1711-23, was also a canon of Salisbury where he possibly lived.[3] Joseph Soley, vicar 1723-6, was also a canon of Winchester.[4] From 1726 to 1829, except for the period 1795-1808, the vicarage was held in plurality with the rectory of St. Peter's, Marlborough.[5] Thomas Meyler, vicar 1773-86, remarked that one of his livings provided bread and cheese and the other a place to eat and sleep. Both he and Joseph Edwards, vicar 1795-1808, were also masters of Marlborough Grammar School.[6] Curates usually assisted the vicars from the 17th century and included John Collinson, 1779-80, author of *The History and Antiquities of the County of Somerset* published in 1791.[7]

In 1783 services with sermons were held once on Sundays, alternately in the morning and afternoon, and on Christmas day and Good Friday. The Sacrament was administered to twelve communicants on Christmas and Easter days, Whit Sunday, and Michaelmas day.[8] On Census Sunday 1851 the morning service was attended by 208 people and that held in the afternoon by 304.[9] The vicar complained in 1864 of the difficulty of exercising his ministry in a large scattered parish. He stressed the need for chapels of ease at St. Margaret's and at Rockley in Ogbourne St. Andrew where one was built in 1872. Services with sermons were held at Preshute twice on Sundays in 1864 and on Christmas day, Good Friday, Ascension day, on Wednesday and Friday evenings during Lent with sermons at the Wednesday services, and on saints' days if congregations presented themselves. No more than 20 people attended except on Sundays, Christmas day, and Good Friday, when the average congregation was 200. Holy Communion was celebrated on Christmas and Easter days, on the first Sunday in each month, and in alternate years on Whit and Trinity Sundays. An average of 26 people communicated at the great festivals and 18 at other times.[10]

The church of *ST. GEORGE*, so dedicated by 1232,[11] comprises a chancel with north vestry, nave with south aisle and south porch, and west tower.[12] Except for the tower, which is of ashlar, it is built of flint with stone dressings.

The chancel arch of a 12th-century church survived at Preshute until 1854.[13] That church was enlarged by the addition of a west tower and south aisle which was approached through an arcade of four bays. In the 14th century the south aisle, but not the piers, and the chancel were probably rebuilt and the south doorway reset. The tower was rebuilt in the 15th century. At the same time a new window and rood stair were added at the east end of the north wall of the nave. The nave roof was reconstructed to a lower pitch in the later 15th or earlier 16th century. In 1726 Algernon, earl of Hertford, put up a west gallery to serve as a family pew.[14] It was reserved for guests staying at the Castle inn in 1783. There was then a gallery in the south-east corner of the nave.[15] In 1854 the church, except the tower, tower arch, and piers, was rebuilt to designs by T. H. Wyatt.[16] In that rebuilding the outline of the medieval church was preserved.

Of the fittings of the old church little remains. Part of a square 12th-century font is built into the porch. Its successor is a large elaborately turned

[91] The ho. was reputedly burnt down before Apr. 1607, the date at which the earliest extant par. reg. was said to begin: W.R.O., bishop, glebe terrier, 1783. That reg. begins in Apr. 1606: ibid. 1298/1. [92] *W.A.M.* xli. 135.
[93] *Vis. Queries, 1783* (W.R.S. xxvii), pp. 181-2; below, Marlborough, churches.
[94] *Rep. Com. Eccl. Revenues*, 844-5.
[95] D. & C. Sar. Mun., chap. act bk. 1834-51, p. 242.
[96] W.R.O. 1298/27; Ch. Com. file CB 14389; inf. from Ch. Com. [97] Below, Marlborough, churches.
[98] *V.C.H. Wilts.* iii. 152.
[99] *Cal. Papal Reg.* i. 265.
[1] *Walker Revised*, ed. A. G. Matthews, 376-7; Phillipps, *Wilts. Inst.* ii. 25; P.R.O., E 134/36 Chas. II Mich./4; below, Marlborough, churches.
[2] Phillipps, *Wilts. Inst.* ii. 25. He was buried at Poole in 1683: *Coll. Topog. et Gen.* v. 349.
[3] Phillipps, *Wilts. Inst.* ii. 51, 58; *Alum. Oxon. 1500-1714*, iv. 1482.

[4] Phillipps, *Wilts. Inst.* ii. 58, 60; *Alum. Oxon. 1500-1714*, iv. 1388.
[5] *Alum. Oxon. 1500-1714*, i. 286; Phillipps, *Wilts. Inst.* (index in *W.A.M.* xxviii. 225, 227); *Rep. Com. Eccl. Revenues*, 842-5.
[6] Phillipps, *Wilts. Inst.* ii. 86, 98, 106; *Alum. Cantab. to 1751*, iii. 181; *V.C.H. Wilts.* v. 359; *Vis. Queries, 1783* (W.R.S. xxvii), p. 11.
[7] *Preshute Ch. Guide* (1974), 21 sqq.; *D.N.B.*
[8] *Vis. Queries, 1783* (W.R.S. xxvii), pp. 180-2.
[9] P.R.O., HO 129/255/1/11/30.
[10] W.R.O., bishop, vis. queries, 1864.
[11] D. & C. Sar. Mun., press I, box 8, no. 2.
[12] There are SE. and NW. views in 1803 by J. Buckler in W.A.S. Libr., vol. iv. 13. For the SE. see plate facing p. 144.
[13] *W.A.M.* xlii. 282; *Preshute Ch. Guide* (1974), pl. III.
[14] *Rep. Marlborough Coll. Natural Hist. Soc.* xcix. 76.
[15] W.R.O., bishop, glebe terrier.
[16] Ibid. bishop, pet. for faculties, bdle. 5, no. 6.

and polished 13th-century font of black Tournai marble, which was in the church *c.* 1600 and may have been brought from St. Nicholas's chapel in Marlborough Castle after 1417.[17] Before the mid 19th century the east wall of the chancel was apparently lined with a panelled dado and the nave fitted with high panelled box pews.[18]

The parish cottage which housed paupers in 1834 had been assigned, with 5 a. in Manton, for church repairs, for which £50 yielded by its sale was invested. In 1981 the income was £6.[19]

The parish kept a chalice weighing 11 oz. in 1553 when plate weighing 3 oz. was taken by the royal commissioners.[20] In 1783 there were a small silver cup and flagon and a pewter flagon and plate.[21] The church still possessed the pewter in 1891 and two chalices and two patens, all hallmarked 1830.[22] Another silver chalice was given in 1918.[23]

There were three bells in the church in 1553. A new ring of five bells was cast in 1710 by Robert and William Cor. The fourth bell was recast by James Wells of Aldbourne in 1809 and the entire peal by Gillett & Johnston of Croydon (Surr.) in 1925. A new treble was added in 1938.[24]

A new register was begun in the spring of 1606 after the old was burnt. Registrations of baptisms, marriages, and burials are complete.[25]

NONCONFORMITY. James White, tenant of the Castle inn, was a recusant in 1778 and later.[26] There was dissent in the St. Margaret's area in 1667 and three dissenters were recorded in the parish in 1674 and another three in 1679.[27] In the later 18th century the nearness of Marlborough with its flourishing chapels presumably discouraged chapel building in the normally favourable conditions of a large parish with scattered settlements, attracting those inclined to dissent to the borough.[28]

William Sanger of Salisbury, a noted evangelist, certified premises at Manton for Primitive Methodists in 1817.[29] That building was replaced by another, built *c.* 1860 and closed *c.* 1920, which stood at Manton Corner in the burial ground opened there by the Marlborough Friends in 1658.[30] In 1818 John Gosling, another Primitive Methodist, registered a field of 3 a. in Preshute. The land was probably in St.

Margaret's where Sanger registered a chapel belonging to Gosling in 1825.[31]

Independents certified chapels in Preshute in 1826, 1827, and 1829.[32] In 1864 there were reckoned to be a hundred dissenters in Preshute consisting of Primitive Methodists and of Wesleyans, who met in a cottage.[33]

EDUCATION. In 1833 the parishioners of Preshute were considered illiterate. The vicar's attempts that year to start a school possibly resulted in the opening of one in High Street in Manton where the school stood in 1981.[34] The school may have been rebuilt in 1845 and in 1858 was attended by 20-30 children.[35] Some 20-30 infants were taught in a cottage and the children of the St. Margaret's area were taught in a small room, inadequate for its purpose, in a large 'forlorn-looking' building in 1858. Some children, however, were then and later sent to the schools in Marlborough.[36] In 1864 both the Manton and St. Margaret's schools were attended by an average of between 30 and 40 children.[37] The education provided was thought defective because the mistresses were uncertificated and because scattered settlement in a large parish discouraged attendance.[38] The National school at St. Margaret's, so called in 1867, ceased between 1867 and 1871. In 1871 a school, perhaps that at Manton, was attended by 20 boys and 21 girls. Two private schools were attended by 27 boys and 30 girls, and an adventure school by 25 boys.[39]

In 1894 Manton school was enlarged, and in 1906, when it was the only school in Preshute Without parish, it was attended by an average of 75 pupils and belonged to the churchwardens and overseers of Preshute.[40] Average attendance was over 100 in 1908-9 and 1911-12.[41] In 1981 65 children were taught by one part-time and three full-time teachers.[42]

Marlborough College, so called from 1845, was opened in the former Castle inn in 1843. Since its story is of national rather than of local importance, it has been treated elsewhere.[43]

In 1844 J. G. George ran a boys' boarding school in St. Margaret's but no more is known of it.[44] The Misses Smith had a private school for girls at Mayfield Villa, 40 London Road, in 1865

[17] Camden, *Brit.* (1695), 98.
[18] *Preshute Ch. Guide* (1974), pl. III.
[19] Above, local govt.; *Endowed Char. Wilts.* (N. Div.), 840-1; inf. from the vicar, the Revd. B. Hopkinson.
[20] Nightingale, *Wilts. Plate*, 160.
[21] W.R.O., bishop, glebe terrier.
[22] Nightingale, *Wilts. Plate*, 160.
[23] Inf. from Mr. Hopkinson.
[24] Walters, *Wilts. Bells*, 159-60; *Preshute Ch. Guide* (1974), 6.
[25] W.R.O., bishop, glebe terrier, 1783; ibid. 1298/1-7; 1298/13-14; marriages are printed in *Wilts. Par. Reg. (Mar.)*, ed. W. P. W. Phillimore and J. Sadler, iv. 1-65, and extracts of all registrations in *Coll. Topog. et Gen.* v. 346 sqq.
[26] J. A. Williams, *Catholic Recusancy in Wilts.* (Cath. Rec. Soc.), pp. 248, 259; *Vis. Queries, 1783* (W.R.S. xxvii), p. 181; Chandler, *Hist. Marlborough*, 25.
[27] W.R.O., bishop, chwdns.' pres. 1667, 1674; bishop (peculiar), chwdns.' pres. 1679.
[28] *Vis. Queries, 1783* (W.R.S. xxvii), p. 181.
[29] W.R.O., return of regns.; ibid. bishop, return of cert. places; *V.C.H. Wilts.* vi. 160.

[30] W.R.O. 854/31; ibid. bishop, vis. queries, 1864; O.S. Map 6″, Wilts. XXIX (1889 edn.); inf. from the Revd. G. D. Gordon, the Manse, St. David's Way, Herd Street, Marlborough; below, Marlborough, prot. nonconf.
[31] W.R.O., return of regns.; P.R.O., RG 31/4.
[32] W.R.O., bishop, return of cert. places.
[33] Ibid. bishop, vis. queries.
[34] *Educ. Enquiry Abstract*, 1045; *Return of Non-Provided Schs.* 37 and n.
[35] *Kelly's Dir. Wilts.* (1903); *Acct. of Wilts. Schs.* 37.
[36] *Acct. of Wilts. Schs.* 37; below, Marlborough, educ.
[37] W.R.O., bishop, vis. queries.
[38] *2nd Rep. Employment of Children and Women in Agric.* 1867 [4202], H.C. (1868-9), xiii, p. 251.
[39] *Kelly's Dir. Wilts.* (1867); *Returns relating to Elem. Educ.* 422-3.
[40] *Kelly's Dir. Wilts.* (1903); *Return of Non-Provided Schs.* 37 and n.
[41] *Bd. of Educ.*, *List 21* (H.M.S.O.).
[42] Inf. from the vicar, the Revd. B. Hopkinson.
[43] Above, manors; *V.C.H. Wilts.* v. 364-6.
[44] Pigot, *Nat. Com. Dir.* (1844), 23.

or earlier.[45] That school was owned and run by Misses E. M. and R. Hugill from 1897 or earlier until 1921. In that year and until 1945 Mayfield, still owned by the Hugills, was used as a girls' boarding house by Marlborough Grammar School.[46] Miss R. Hugill sold it in 1945 to Mrs. L. Wynburne who ran Mayfield College as a preparatory school for boys and girls. Older pupils were admitted in the later 1960s and the school closed in 1968.[47]

CHARITIES FOR THE POOR. John Colman (d. 1619) of Dinton gave £13 6s. 8d. to apprentice poor children of Preshute. The capital had apparently been spent by 1786 and in 1905 the charity was deemed lost.[48]

By deed of 1888 H. B. Turner invested £55 for blankets to be lent to poor parishioners. The charity, called the Caroline Charlotte and Stephana Maria Turner charity, was administered in 1905, when there were 20 pairs of blankets in stock, as the donor had directed.[49] Its income in 1980 was £5.37.[50]

In 1938 Ethel Mary Dominy devised a house, formerly a mission hall called Salem, on the south side of High Street in Manton for use by an old person. A scheme of 1951 empowered the trustees to charge 5s. rent weekly.[51] The income from the Dominy charity was combined with that from the Turner charity in 1962 and in 1980 the total was used to help old people in Manton.[52]

WINTERBOURNE BASSETT

WINTERBOURNE BASSETT, 10 km. north-west of Marlborough, is the most northerly of three rectangular parishes, Winterbourne Monkton, Berwick Bassett, and Winterbourne Bassett, which lie across the valley of the upper Kennet.[53] From east to west it measures 5 km. and from north to south, at its widest point, 2 km. By c. 970 its eastern limit had been established at Hackpen Hill and it extended westwards to Stanmore on the high ground above the escarpment at Clyffe Pypard.[54] The straight northern boundary with Broad Hinton may also have been set early. The name Winterbourne was derived from the small streams at the head of the Kennet and was shared by neighbouring settlements. By the 13th century the suffix Bassett had been adopted from the lords of the manor. The parish then probably included Rabson and Richardson, south of Winterbourne Bassett. Rabson was known as Winterbourne in 1086 and as North Winterbourne, to distinguish it from Winterbourne Monkton, further south, in the 12th century. The names Rabson, derived from ownership by the abbess of Amesbury, and North Winterbourne were both used until the 16th century.[55] In the 17th century lands and tithes from Stanmore, formerly a detached but tithable part of Beckhampton chapelry in Avebury, passed to the lord of Winterbourne Bassett manor and the rector of Winterbourne Bassett respectively, and a portion of Stanmore thus became part of the parish; the remainder was absorbed into Clyffe Pypard parish.[56] The southern boundary of the modern parish of 886

ha. (2,190 a.) was defined by an exchange of lands between Richardson and Berwick Bassett in 1782.[57] In the 19th century the lands of Winterbourne Bassett township, some 1,070 a., occupied the northern half of the parish. Richardson, c. 460 a., including 150 a. at Stanmore, lay in the south-west corner and Rabson, c. 540 a., including lands formerly part of Richardson, in the south-east corner.[58]

From Winterbourne Bassett village near the centre of the parish the head stream of the Kennet flows south. It is fed by several tributaries, which sometimes disappear underground. One rises near the boundary north of the village, a second enters the parish 500 m. further east, a third follows a winding course from the western boundary south of Stanmore Copse. Only the valley south of the village lies below 168 m. Much of the land in the parish is flat but Hackpen Hill and the downland east of it reach heights above 259 m. and north-east of Stanmore Copse the land rises more gently to 198 m. Chalk outcrops over the whole parish; on the ridge of Hackpen Hill it is covered by clay-with-flints.[59]

Little evidence of prehistoric settlement survives. There are earthworks on the western slopes of Hackpen Hill and south of Stanmore Copse and barrows near Winterbourne Bassett village. The remains of a Neolithic monument of concentric stone circles, the outer ring of which was 65 m. in diameter, stand 1 km. west of the village.[60]

In historic times the flat, well drained lands of

[45] *Harrod's Dir. Wilts.* (1865).
[46] *Lucy's Marlborough Dir.* (1897); A. R. Stedman, *Marlborough*, 342; *Kelly's Dir. Wilts.* (1927 and later edns.); inf. from Mrs. Wynburne, no. 4 the Green, Marlborough.
[47] Inf. from Mrs. Wynburne; *Fletcher's Marlborough Dir.* (1962–3); *Schs. of Eng.* (1968 edn.).
[48] *Endowed Char. Wilts.* (N. Div.), 839, 841.
[49] Ibid. 841–2.
[50] Inf. from the vicar, the Revd. B. Hopkinson.
[51] Char. Com. file.
[52] Inf. from Mr. Hopkinson.
[53] This article was written in 1980. Maps used include O.S. Maps 1/50,000, sheet 173 (1974 edn.); 1/25,000, SU 07 (1959

edn.), SU 17 (1960 edn.); 6″, Wilts. XXII (1888 and later edns.).
[54] *Early Chart. E. Eng.* ed. C. R. Hart, pp. 253–4; *Arch. Jnl.* lxxvii. 24–5.
[55] *V.C.H. Wilts.* ii, pp. 124, 131, 145; *P.N. Wilts.* (E.P.N.S.), 309; *Tax. Eccl.* (Rec. Com.), 189.
[56] P.R.O., E 134/11 & 12 Wm. III Hil./8; *V.C.H. Wilts.* ix. 32; above, Avebury, introduction, church; below.
[57] B.L. Maps, 'Survey of lands in Winterbourne etc. belonging to Hen. Fox, 1760'; W.R.O. 488/7; *Census*, 1971.
[58] W.R.O., tithe award; below, econ. hist.
[59] Geol. Surv. Map 1″, drift, sheet 266 (1964 edn.).
[60] *V.C.H. Wilts.* i (1), 125, 200, 259, 271; i (2), 332.

the parish have been used chiefly for arable farming. Pasture was mainly restricted to Hackpen Hill and to the rising ground in the north-west corner of the parish. Lands between and beside the streams provided extensive meadows.[61] There were woods at Rabson in the 16th century but small plantations established near Richardson House and at Stanmore in or before the 18th century accounted for most of the woodland in 1980.[62]

There were three north–south routes through the parish in the 18th century, the Ridge Way on the crest of Hackpen Hill, the Swindon–Avebury road, then known as Harepath Way, and a road from Broad Hinton to Yatesbury. The Swindon–Avebury road, 2 km. west of Hackpen Hill, was turnpiked in 1767 and became the major route. The Ridge Way and the road from Broad Hinton to Yatesbury, which ran 600 m. west of Winterbourne Bassett village, were tracks in 1980. Then, as in the 18th century, the only road leading west from the Swindon–Avebury road ran through the village to Clyffe Pypard. East of the Swindon–Avebury road Lambourn way and Marlborough way led east across the downs in 1760.[63] Only Marlborough way, the more southerly, was visible as a track in 1980.

The parish was among the less prosperous and populous of Selkley hundred in the 14th century.[64] In the 16th century, however, tax assessments of Winterbourne Bassett were little lower than the average.[65] The population of the parish fell from 218 in 1801 to 203 in 1811 but had increased very rapidly to 291 by 1821. As men left to work in the Swindon railway yards and farm labourers were replaced by machinery numbers fell to reach 249 in 1861. The population had risen to 271 in 1891 but had declined, with occasional fluctuations, to 156 by 1971.[66]

The medieval settlements of Winterbourne Bassett, Rabson, and Richardson did not differ greatly in size or prosperity but Winterbourne Bassett was the most substantial. It was assessed for taxation at 13s. 4d. in 1334 and in 1377 had 35 poll-tax payers.[67] In the mid 16th century its taxation assessment was considerably higher than those for the other townships.[68] The older buildings of the village stand beside the road to Clyffe Pypard between the two south flowing streams. From the road a drive leads south to the church, the Manor and its farmstead, and the Old Rectory. North of the road are brick and sarsen cottages of the 17th century and later and the White Horse inn, established opposite the

Manor in or before 1757 and rebuilt after a fire in 1913.[69] In the mid 18th century farmhouses attached to copyholds and small freeholds stood east of the Manor and the eastern stream.[70] Settlement spread beyond the western stream in the late 18th century and the early 19th.[71] Cottages and a school were built north of the road in the older part of the village in the 19th century. Buildings at the west end of the village were demolished in the late 19th century and a terrace of brick cottages was built further west. A former nonconformist chapel also stands beyond the western stream. By the late 19th century some houses east of the Manor had been demolished[72] and in the 20th century council houses were built there.

Rabson was the smallest settlement in the parish in the Middle Ages and had 21 poll-tax payers in 1377.[73] In 1545 the tax assessment was similar to that for Richardson but there was only one contributor from Rabson, which may then have been no more than a single farmstead.[74] It was so in the 18th century when, as in the 20th century, Rabson Manor, 500 m. south of Winterbourne Bassett, was reached by a lane from the Swindon–Avebury road.[75]

There were 31 poll-tax payers at Richardson in 1377 and in 1545 two inhabitants were assessed for taxation.[76] The manor house stood 400 m. south-west of Rabson. In the late 17th century a second farmstead was built 1.25 km. further west, near the road from Broad Hinton to Yatesbury. In the 18th century a lane linked the large manor house directly with the Swindon–Avebury road.[77] In the 19th century there was a pair of cottages on that site which was reached only from Rabson. Of greater importance then, as in 1980, was the second farmstead, Whyr Farm.[78]

MANORS AND OTHER ESTATES. Between 967 and 975 King Edgar granted to his thegn Edric an estate at Winterbourne,[79] probably that at Winterbourne Bassett held in 1066 by two thegns and in 1086 by Humphrey Lisle.[80] Reynold de Dunstanville, husband of Adelize Lisle, a daughter and heir of Humphrey Lisle, held lands at Winterbourne Bassett in or before 1121.[81] The Dunstanvilles' estates formed the nucleus of the barony of Castle Combe, and the manor of *WINTERBOURNE BASSETT* was held of the barony until the 16th century or later.[82] In the 1240s Reynold de Mohun held the manor as intermediate lord.[83]

[61] Wilton Ho. Mun., survey, 1550s; *Survey of Lands of Wm., First Earl of Pembroke*, ed. C. R. Straton (Roxburghe Club, 1909), i. 264–9; B.L. Maps, 'Winterbourne, 1760'.

[62] P.R.O., E 318/Box 3/98; B.L. Maps, 'Winterbourne, 1760'.

[63] B.L. Maps, 'Winterbourne, 1760'; *Andrews and Dury, Map* (W.R.S. viii), pl. 14; *V.C.H. Wilts.* iv. 268.

[64] *V.C.H. Wilts.* iv. 301, 310.

[65] *Taxation Lists* (W.R.S. x), 22, 101–4.

[66] *V.C.H. Wilts.* iv. 361; W.R.O. 1506/25; *Census*, 1961, 1971. [67] *V.C.H. Wilts.* iv. 301, 310.

[68] *Taxation Lists* (W.R.S. x), 22.

[69] W.R.O., reg. alehousekeepers' recognizances, 1756–8; F. S. Thacker, *Kennet Country*, 360.

[70] B.L. Maps, 'Winterbourne, 1760'.

[71] *Andrews and Dury, Map* (W.R.S. viii), pl. 14; W.R.O., tithe award.

[72] O.S. Map 6″, Wilts. XXII (1888 edn.), XXII. NE. (1901 edn.). [73] *V.C.H. Wilts.* iv. 310.

[74] *Taxation Lists* (W.R.S. x), 22.

[75] B.L. Maps, 'Winterbourne, 1760'; *Andrews and Dury, Map* (W.R.S. viii), pl. 14.

[76] *V.C.H. Wilts.* iv. 310; *Taxation Lists* (W.R.S. x), 22.

[77] P.R.O., E 134/6 Anne Mich./10; B.L. Maps, 'Winterbourne, 1760'; *Andrews and Dury, Map* (W.R.S. viii), pl. 14.

[78] W.R.O., tithe award; ibid. 1506/25.

[79] *Early Chart. E. Eng.* ed. Hart, pp. 253–4.

[80] *V.C.H. Wilts.* ii, p. 145.

[81] *Cal. Doc. France*, ed. Round, p. 509; *V.C.H. Wilts.* ii, p. 110; below, church. Reynold is called Rob. in *V.C.H. Wilts.* xi. 242.

[82] *Bk. of Fees*, ii. 749; *W.A.M.* ii. 271.

[83] *Bk. of Fees*, ii. 749; *Civil Pleas, 1249* (W.R.S. xxvi), pp. 66–7.

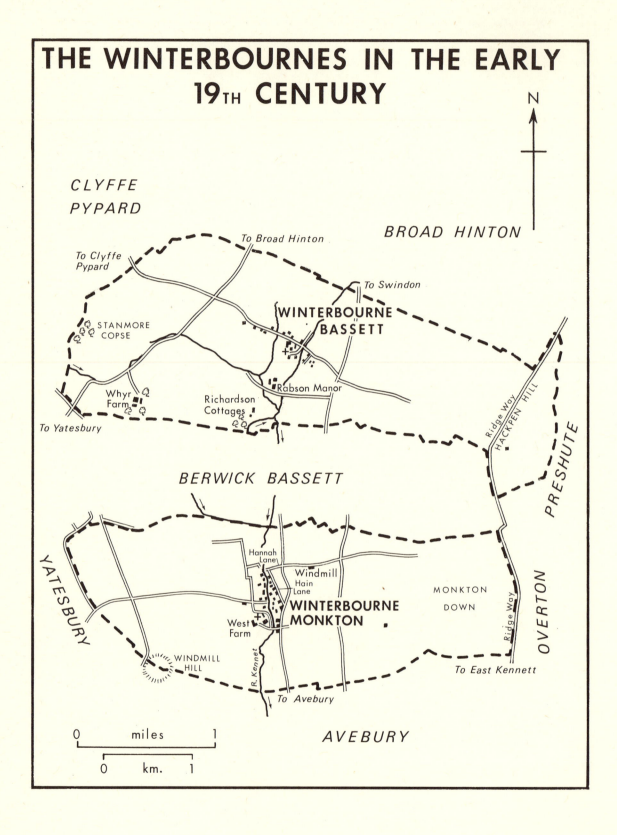

THE WINTERBOURNES IN THE EARLY 19TH CENTURY

N

CLYFFE PYPARD

BROAD HINTON

To Broad Hinton

To Clyffe Pypard

To Swindon

WINTERBOURNE BASSETT

STANMORE COPSE

Rabson Manor

RIDGE WAY

HACKPEN HILL

PRESHUTE

Whyr Farm

Richardson Cottages

To Yatesbury

BERWICK BASSETT

Hannah Lane

YATESBURY

Windmill
Hain Lane

MONKTON DOWN

WINTERBOURNE MONKTON

West Farm

RIDGE WAY

OVERTON

WINDMILL HILL

R. Kennet

To East Kennett

To Avebury

AVEBURY

0   miles   1

0   km.   1

Walter de Dunstanville, great-grandson of Reynold (fl. *c.* 1121), granted the manor to his nephew Alan Basset in 1194. The grant was confirmed in 1199.[84] Alan's son Gilbert inherited the manor *c.* 1232. Gilbert's estates were confiscated for his rebellion against Henry III but were restored in 1234. He died in 1241[85] and was succeeded by his brothers Fulk, dean of York and later bishop of London (d. 1259), and Philip (d. 1271).[86] The manor passed to Philip's daughter Aline, relict of Sir Hugh le Despenser and wife of Roger Bigod, earl of Norfolk. On her death in 1281 it was inherited by her son Sir Hugh le Despenser,[87] later earl of Winchester. Despenser was deprived of his estates in 1321 but Winterbourne Bassett was restored to him in or before 1325. The manor again passed to the Crown at his execution in 1326[88] and in 1327 was granted to Queen Isabel, Edward III's mother, for life.[89] The grant was revoked after her defeat in 1330 but was renewed in 1331.[90] Queen Isabel died in 1358 and in 1359 the manor was granted to Queen Philippa (d. 1369).[91] It reverted to the Crown and in 1377 Edward III granted it to his son Edmund of Langley, earl of Cambridge (created duke of York in 1385).[92] Edmund was succeeded in 1402 by his son Edward, duke of York,[93] who mortgaged the manor in 1415 to raise money for the foundation of Fotheringhay college (Northants.).[94] After his death at Agincourt in that year Edward's estate was held in trust for his nephew Richard Plantagenet, duke of York.[95] Winterbourne Bassett was presumably confiscated with the rest of the York estates when Richard (d. 1460) was defeated by the Lancastrians and afterwards recovered by his son Edward IV. In 1461 the king granted the manor for life to his mother Cecily, duchess of York.[96] In 1492 a further life interest was granted in reversion to Elizabeth, the queen consort, who retained that interest when the York lands were resumed by the Crown on Cecily's death in 1495.[97] The manor was granted as part of the jointure of queens consort to Catherine of Aragon in 1509, Jane Seymour in 1536, Anne of Cleves in 1540, Catherine Howard in 1541, and Catherine Parr in 1544.[98] In 1553 it was acquired by William Herbert, earl of Pembroke (d. 1570), in an exchange with the Crown. It passed with the earldom to William's son Henry (d. 1601) and

grandson William Herbert.[99] That William sold the manor to Thomas Baskerville in 1614.[1] Thomas was succeeded in 1621 by his son Francis (d. before 1685), grandson Thomas Baskerville (fl. 1707), and great-grandson Richard Baskerville.[2] By will proved 1739 Richard devised the manor to Thomas, son of his daughter Meliora and her husband and distant cousin Thomas Baskerville of Aberedw (Radnors., later Powys).[3] In 1754 the younger Thomas sold it to Henry Fox (created Baron Holland in 1763, d. 1774).[4] The manor descended with the Holland title until the death of Henry Edward Fox, Baron Holland, in 1859.[5] Lord Holland's relict Mary, Baroness Holland (d. 1889), devised it to his nephew L. W. H. Powys, who took the name Fox-Powys in 1890.[6] On his death in 1893 the manor passed to Fox-Powys's nephew John Powys, Baron Lilford, who sold it to James Horton *c.* 1906. Horton (d. 1926) was succeeded by his son John[7] who sold the estate as Manor and Whyr farms to the Gaunts Estate Company in 1938.[8] After 1951 the farms were bought by Hosier Estates and in 1964 they were sold to Mrs. D. King.[9] In 1970 Whyr farm was sold separately to Mr. M. R. Young. Mrs. King and Mr. Young owned Manor and Whyr farms respectively in 1980.[10]

In the 1550s the manor house included a hall and a parlour with chimneys.[11] Silver and coin valued at £1,000 were stolen from the house in 1557.[12] In the 18th century the house was rebuilt in brick with an east front and a north wing projecting at the back. A long back range was added south of the wing in the 19th century. The interior was altered then and *c.* 1970.

An estate at Winterbourne held by Amesbury abbey in 1066 and 1086 became the manor of *RABSON* or *NORTH WINTERBOURNE*.[13] The manor was among the endowments of Amesbury priory, refounded from the older house in 1177,[14] and passed to the Crown at the Dissolution. In 1539 it was granted to Robert Seymour for life. The reversion of the manor was granted to John Barwick and sold by him in 1544 to Edward Seymour, earl of Hertford and later duke of Somerset, probably a kinsman of Robert Seymour. It was forfeited on Somerset's attainder in 1552.[15] In 1562 the manor was granted to John Ayliffe.[16] In 1572 Ayliffe (d.

[84] *W.A.M.* ii. 137–8; *Itin. Ric. I* (Pipe R. Soc. N.S. xiii), 99; *Cat. Anct. D.* iii, A 4825.
[85] *V.C.H. Wilts.* ix. 190; x. 163.   [86] *D.N.B.*
[87] *Cal. Inq. p.m.* ii, p. 228; *Wilts. Inq. p.m. 1242–1326* (Index Libr.), 133–4.
[88] *Complete Peerage*, iv. 262–6; *Cal. Chart. R. 1300–26*, 477; P.R.O., E 142/33, rot. 8.
[89] *Cal. Pat. 1327–30*, 67.   [90] Ibid. *1330–4*, 195.
[91] *Wilts. Inq. p.m. 1327–77* (Index Libr.), 250–1; *Cal. Pat. 1358–61*, 238; *Cal. Inq. p.m.* xii, pp. 416–17.
[92] *Cal. Pat. 1374–7*, 474–5.
[93] P.R.O., C 137/32, no. 36; *Complete Peerage*, xii (2), 897–9.
[94] *Cal. Pat. 1413–16*, 349–50.
[95] *Complete Peerage*, xii (2), 899; *Feud. Aids*, v. 269.
[96] *Complete Peerage*, xii (2), 908; *Cal. Pat. 1461–7*, 131.
[97] *Rot. Parl.* vi. 459–64; *Cal. Pat. 1485–94*, 369–70.
[98] *L. & P. Hen. VIII*, i, pp. 21–2; xv, p. 52; xvi, p. 24; xix (1), pp. 82–3.
[99] *Cal. Pat. 1553*, 177–8; P.R.O., C 142/154, no. 79; C 142/264, no. 181.

[1] P.R.O., CP 25(2)/370/11 Jas. I East.
[2] Burke, *Commoners* (1833–8), i. 92–3; P.R.O., E 134/6 Anne Mich./10.
[3] P.R.O., E 134/15 Geo. II Hil./2.
[4] Dors. R.O., D 124, box 181, deed of sale, Baskerville to Fox.
[5] *Complete Peerage*, vi. 543–5; *Kelly's Dir. Wilts.* (1848 and later edns.).
[6] *Complete Peerage*, vi. 545.
[7] Burke, *Peerage* (1907), 1031; *W.A.M.* xliii. 355.
[8] W.R.O. 1008/31.
[9] Ibid.; inf. from Mrs. R. Horton, Winterbourne Bassett Manor.
[10] Wilts. Cuttings, xxiii. 335; inf. from Mrs. Horton.
[11] Wilton Ho. Mun., survey, 1550s.
[12] *Cal. Pat. 1555–7*, 465.
[13] *V.C.H. Wilts.* ii, pp. 132, 199–200.
[14] Ibid. iii. 244; *Rot. Chart.* (Rec. Com.), 13.
[15] P.R.O., E 328/99; *L. & P. Hen. VIII*, xix (1), p. 382; *Complete Peerage*, xii (1), 63.
[16] *Cal. Pat. 1560–3*, 239–40.

1581) settled it on his wife Susan for life with remainder to his younger son George (fl. 1602).[17] George was succeeded by John Ayliffe (d. 1631), probably his son.[18] The manor passed to John's son Sir George (d. c. 1647) and grandson John Ayliffe. That John's son John was executed in 1685, perhaps before his father's death, and the manor passed to his brother George (d. 1712) and George's daughter Judith. She devised it to her cousin Susanna, wife of Thomas Horner,[19] who in 1744 settled it on herself for life with remainder to Henry Fox, later Baron Holland, brother of her son-in-law Stephen Fox, Baron Ilchester. After Susanna's death in 1758 the manor descended with that of Winterbourne Bassett.[20] Rabson was sold by Hosier Estates c. 1965 to Mr. W. K. Horton, the owner in 1980.[21] Rabson Manor is a substantial L-shaped house of sarsen, built in the early 17th century and heightened and extended in the 18th and 19th centuries. It retains some original fittings and part of a late 17th-century staircase.

In 1242-3 ¼ knight's fee in Richardson was held of the honor of Hereford.[22] The overlordship of *RICHARDSON* manor descended with the earldom of Hereford until the death of Humphrey de Bohun, earl of Hereford and Essex, in 1383.[23] On the division of Humphrey's estates it was allotted to his daughter Mary, wife of Henry of Lancaster, earl of Derby, later Henry IV.[24] William Quintin held Richardson of the honor in 1242-3[25] and Reynold of Lavington, in his wife's right, in 1275.[26] In 1368 William Houghton and Thomas Torand, probably acting as feoffees, granted Richardson to William Wroughton (d. 1392) and his wife Isabel (fl. c. 1402).[27] It passed in the Wroughton family with Hinton Wase manor in Broad Hinton to William Wroughton (d. 1559).[28] In 1604 Thomas Hutchins (d. 1607) settled the manor on himself for life with reversion to Thomas Baskerville, and from 1614 Richardson descended with Winterbourne Bassett manor.[29] There was a substantial house set in formal gardens at Richardson in the mid 18th century.[30] Since the mid 19th century, however, the site has been occupied by cottages.[31]

Walter Marshal, earl of Pembroke, held ½ knight's fee in Richardson in 1242-3.[32] The overlordship passed with the marshalcy to Roger Bigod, earl of Norfolk, who held it in 1275.[33] No later reference to a marshal as overlord has been found but the fee was probably that held in 1316 by William Mauduit as mesne lord and later by Ralph Mauduit.[34] Rents and services from Richardson, perhaps derived from that lordship, were settled on John Clyffe in 1395[35] and in 1399 on Sir John Roches (d. 1400) and his wife William (d. 1410).[36] They passed with the Rocheses' other property in Winterbourne Bassett to their daughter Elizabeth, wife of Sir Walter Beauchamp (d. 1430).[37]

In 1387 Simon Best held lands at 'Fippesdene' in Winterbourne Bassett. John Lypiatt held them for life in 1394[38] and in 1399 the reversion was granted by feoffees to Sir John Roches and his wife William.[39] The lands were inherited by the Rocheses' daughter Elizabeth (fl. 1430), wife of Sir Walter Beauchamp, who was succeeded by her son Sir William Beauchamp (d. 1457).[40] They passed in turn to Sir William's relict Elizabeth, Lady St. Amand (d. 1491), and son Sir Richard Beauchamp, Lord St. Amand (d. 1508).[41] In 1534 the estate of a messuage and 1 yardland was held by Edward Baynton who sold it to John Goddard of Upham in Aldbourne in 1557.[42] In that year it passed to John's son Thomas (d. 1598).[43] Another John Goddard held lands in Winterbourne Bassett, probably the same estate, at his death in 1635. He was succeeded by his grandson Edward Goddard[44] and Edward or a descendant of the same name sold the lands to Caleb Bailey c. 1708.[45] Later they presumably became part of Winterbourne Bassett manor.

Before 1242 an estate was held in demesne by Roger Baril, who sold land in Richardson, perhaps part of it, to Stanley abbey. The remainder of Baril's land passed in turn to Theobald of Winterbourne and his son Richard Theobald.[46] Richard or his son of the same name held it in 1242-3.[47]

In or before the 13th century Stanley abbey received 1 yardland from Theobald of Winterbourne, 4 a. from Richard Theobald the elder, and 1½ a. from Richard Theobald the younger, all of which was evidently held of the earldom of Pembroke.[48] From Nicholas Wase the abbey received small parcels of land in Richardson, probably part of 1 yardland conveyed to him by

[17] P.R.O., C 142/191, no. 112; *Extents for Debts* (W.R.S. xxviii), p. 125.
[18] *Wilts. Inq. p.m.* 1625-49 (Index Libr.), 175.
[19] *Abstr. of P.C.C. Year Bk.* 1645-7, ed. J. and G. F. Matthews, 176; *W.A.M.* xxi. 201; *D.N.B.* s.v. Ayloffe.
[20] Dors. R.O., D 124, box 247, deposition in suit Fox v. Ayliffe; above.
[21] Inf. from Mr. W. K. Horton, Rabson Manor.
[22] *Bk. of Fees*, ii. 749.
[23] *Complete Peerage*, vi. 459-77; *Wilts. Inq. p.m.* 1327-77 (Index Libr.), 371-2.
[24] *Cal. Close*, 1381-5, 514.
[25] *Bk. of Fees*, ii. 749.
[26] *Rot. Hund.* (Rec. Com.), ii (1), 269.
[27] *Feet of F.* 1327-77 (W.R.S. xxix), p. 133; P.R.O., C 136/78, no. 4; *Feud. Aids*, vi. 632.
[28] Above, Broad Hinton, manors.
[29] P.R.O., C 142/297, no. 16; Aubrey, *Topog. Coll.* ed. Jackson, 344.
[30] B.L. Maps, 'Winterbourne, 1760'.
[31] W.R.O. 1506/25.
[32] *Bk. of Fees*, ii. 749; *Complete Peerage*, x. 374-5.

[33] *Complete Peerage*, ix. 593-6; *Rot. Hund.* (Rec. Com.), ii (1), 269.
[34] *Feud. Aids*, v. 206, 269.
[35] P.R.O., CP 25(1)/256/57, no. 24.
[36] *Cal. Close*, 1396-9, 500; P.R.O., C 137/23, no. 40.
[37] P.R.O., C 137/84, no. 78; *Cal. Close*, 1409-13, 138; below.
[38] *Hist. MSS. Com.* 55, *Var. Coll.* iv, pp. 117-18.
[39] *Cal. Close*, 1396-9, 500.
[40] Ibid. 1409-13, 138; P.R.O., C 139/49, no. 36; *Complete Peerage*, xi. 301-2.
[41] *Cal. Inq. p.m. Hen. VII*, i, p. 313; *Cal. Close*, 1485-1500, pp. 161-2; *Complete Peerage*, xi. 302.
[42] P.R.O., SC 6/Hen. VIII/3776, rot. 7d.; W.R.O. 488/2.
[43] *First Pembroke Survey*, ed. Straton, i. 265; above, Aldbourne, manors.
[44] *Wilts. Inq. p.m.* 1625-49 (Index Libr.), 203.
[45] W.R.O. 488/4.
[46] *W.A.M.* xv. 274-6; *Rot. Hund.* (Rec. Com.), ii (1), 234.
[47] *Cat. Anct. D.* iv, A 9377; *Bk. of Fees*, ii. 749.
[48] *W.A.M.* xv. 275; *Cat. Anct. D.* iv, A 9246, A 9377.

William Long,[49] and from Reynold of Lavington and his wife Emme 1 a. by exchange.[50] In 1227 William the clerk of Berwick and his son John of Berwick gave 24 a. and 5 a. respectively to the abbey.[51] In the same year Edmund of Rockley and his wife Scholace granted ⅓ knight's fee in Richardson to the hospital of St. Bartholomew in Bristol.[52] The hospital granted its holdings in Richardson to Stanley abbey, apparently in return for a rent.[53] The Crown conveyed the estates of the abbey to Edward Seymour, Viscount Beauchamp (later earl of Hertford and duke of Somerset), in 1536 and presumably recovered them on his attainder in 1552.[54] In 1562 Cuthbert Vaughan and his wife Elizabeth were licensed to alienate the greater part of the former abbey's holdings to Thomas Hutchins. The lands were later part of Hutchins's manor of Richardson.[55]

In 1066 Stanmore was held by Bruning and in 1086 by Ansfrid as a tenant of Gilbert of Breteuil.[56] The portion of Stanmore which became part of the parish of Winterbourne Bassett passed with Gilbert's manor of Beckhampton in Avebury to the Stourton family and was held by John Stourton, Lord Stourton, at his death in 1462.[57] Thomas Hutchins (d. 1607) held lands in Stanmore, probably those formerly held by Stourton, which were afterwards absorbed into Winterbourne Bassett manor.[58]

Other lands in Stanmore were part of the endowment of the chapel of Beckhampton and passed to the Crown at its dissolution. In 1561 they were granted to Thomas Browne.[59] In the mid 17th century, and perhaps earlier, they were held with Winterbourne Bassett manor.[60]

ECONOMIC HISTORY. In the late 10th century the lands of Winterbourne Bassett were described as '5 hides of land in individual holding to the west of the village and 5 hides in common occupation to the east of the village'. The boundary of the lands west of the village was then fixed but that east of the village is not recorded. It is not clear whether the division, presumably marked by the stream, was between the several holdings and the open fields, both used only by the inhabitants of Winterbourne Bassett, or between the lands of the township and the pasture shared by that and neighbouring townships.[61] In the later Middle Ages the lands of Winterbourne Bassett manor were probably worked with those of other estates in the parish, except at Stanmore which had its own fields.[62] In the 16th century the lord and

tenants of that manor had holdings in severalty in the recently inclosed west field; there remained three open fields north and east of the village. There was common pasture at the eastern end of the parish on Hackpen Hill and Winterbourne Down, west of the hill. The lord or farmer and tenants of Winterbourne Bassett manor had summer pasture for cattle on Hackpen Hill; in winter it was grazed by the lord's sheep. Another pasture, called 'inlander', was reserved for the lord's sheep until Hocktide and then grazed in common as long as the grass was sufficient. Both lord or farmer and tenants had pasture for cattle in summer and winter in 'west leaze'.[63] By the mid 18th century Hackpen Hill and Winterbourne Down had been inclosed.[64] Open-field farming ended with the absorption of almost all the lands of the parish into a few large farms in the early 19th century.[65]

The estate which became Winterbourne Bassett manor was rated as 10 hides in 1066. In 1086 there was land for 6 ploughteams. In demesne were 4 hides and 10 a. with 3 teams and 8 serfs; 4 villeins and 8 bordars had 3 teams. There were 14 a. of meadow and 20 a. of pasture. The estate was valued at £10 in 1066 and 1086.[66] Rabson was a smaller estate on which geld was paid for 3 hides in 1066. Its value increased from £4 in 1066 to £5 in 1086 when it was rated as 6 hides. The demesne of 3 hides with 3 teams was then proportionately larger than that of Winterbourne Bassett although there were only 2 serfs. There were, however, more tenants: 5 villeins and 10 bordars held 1 team. There were 3 a. of meadow and pasture ½ league long and ½ league broad.[67]

In 1331 and 1338 Winterbourne Bassett manor was leased to Gilbert of Berwick, as it may have been earlier to Edward of Berwick Bassett.[68] The manor was leased for terms of years from the mid 14th century to the 16th.[69] In 1281 the demesne of the manor extended to 260 a. of arable, 8 a. of meadow, and pasture for 300 sheep. Rents totalling 46s. were received from customary tenants.[70] In the late 15th century the demesne was assessed at 16 yardlands, of which 10 yardlands were known as courtlands.[71] The size of the demesne farm increased as customary holdings were brought in hand. There were 300 a. of demesne arable in the open fields, 100 a. of several arable, mostly in the west field, and pasture for 500 sheep c. 1560.[72]

Other farms in the parish were smaller. The demesne of Richardson manor was said to consist of 6 yardlands in 1392.[73] Rabson manor was

[49] W.A.M. xv. 276; Cat. Anct. D. v, A 11410.
[50] W.A.M. xv. 276; Cat. Anct. D. v, A 12128.
[51] P.R.O., CP 25(1)/250/7, nos. 78, 96.
[52] Ibid. CP 25(1)/250/5, no. 4.
[53] W.A.M. xv. 275; Aubrey, Topog. Coll. ed. Jackson, 30.
[54] L. & P. Hen. VIII, x, p. 526; Complete Peerage, s.v. Somerset.
[55] Cal. Pat. 1560–3, 400; above.
[56] V.C.H. Wilts. ii, p. 147.
[57] Above, Avebury, manors; P.R.O., C 140/8, no. 18.
[58] P.R.O., C 142/297, no. 161; ibid. E 134/11 & 12 Wm. III Hil./8.   [59] Cal. Pat. 1560–3, 202.
[60] P.R.O., E 134/11 & 12 Wm. III Hil./8.
[61] Early Chart. E. Eng. ed. Hart, pp. 253–4; V.C.H. Wilts. ii, pp. 12–13.
[62] P.R.O., E 301/58, f. 77; E 134/11 & 12 Wm. III Hil./8.

[63] Wilton Ho. Mun., survey, 1550s; First Pembroke Survey, ed. Straton, i. 264–9.
[64] B.L. Maps, 'Winterbourne, 1760'.
[65] Below.
[66] V.C.H. Wilts. ii, p. 145.
[67] Ibid. p. 131.
[68] Hist. MSS. Com. 55, Var. Coll. iv, p. 126; Abbrev. Rot. Orig. (Rec. Com.), ii. 40; Cal. Pat. 1338–40, 447.
[69] e.g. Cal. Fine R. 1364–77, 30–1; P.R.O., SC 6/Hen. VIII/3755, rott. 8d.–9.
[70] Wilts. Inq. p.m. 1242–1326 (Index Libr.), 133–4.
[71] P.R.O., SC 6/1115/1, rot. 8; SC 6/Hen. VII/878, rott. 11d.–12.
[72] Wilton Ho. Mun., survey, 1550s; First Pembroke Survey, ed. Straton, i. 267–9.
[73] P.R.O., C 136/78, no. 4.

leased with portions of tithes outside the parish in the mid 16th century.[74] There were two free tenants of Winterbourne Bassett manor in the 15th and 16th centuries; their holdings were of 20 a. with pasture for 40 sheep and of 80 a. with pasture for 80 sheep in 1564. The number of customary tenants of the manor fell from thirteen in 1450 to three in 1564, and the average size of their holdings doubled from 1 to 2 yardlands.[75]

In the mid 17th century there were three principal farms in the parish, derived from the demesne farms of the three manors, Winterbourne or Winterbourne Down, Rabson, and Richardson. Richardson was divided into Upper and Lower Richardson farms c. 1685.[76] Rabson and the Richardson farms were inclosed farms in the mid 18th century but most of the arable land of Winterbourne farm was still commonable in the 1740s. Some 60 a. of down, recently ploughed, were, however, several. By 1760 much of the farm had been consolidated and there was a large inclosed arable holding north of the village. A further 250 a. north of the village remained open and was worked by the holders of the farm and of eight small copyhold and freehold estates, including the rectorial glebe.[77] Those holdings, except the glebe, had been absorbed into Winterbourne farm by the early 19th century. The glebe lands were exchanged for a consolidated holding in 1823 and in 1844 the whole parish was held in severalty.[78]

Winterbourne farm was worked by tenants in the 18th and 19th centuries.[79] It was chiefly arable and the area of pasture was further reduced when downland was ploughed in the early 18th century. That and restrictions on the folding of sheep on the open fields were then said to have reduced the value of the farm.[80] In the early 19th century the tenant, H. H. Budd, adopted advanced farming methods, including the planting of root crops, and his use of agricultural machinery made him a target of protest during the disturbances of the 1830s.[81] In 1844 Winterbourne farm contained 1,071 a. in the eastern and northern parts of the parish. Only 94 a. were pasture but there were 120 a. of meadow land.[82] In the 1930s wheat was the principal crop, although the land was difficult to drain, and pigs were kept on Hackpen Hill.[83] In 1980 the farm was of 1,186 a., including 710 a. of arable, 360 a. of grass, and 99 a. of rough grazing, and there was a dairy herd of 120 cows.[84]

The lands of Rabson farm were mostly grouped around Rabson Manor in the mid 18th century. Rabson down, 30 a. west of Hackpen Hill, was a detached part of the farm.[85] Part of Lower Richardson farm was worked with Rabson farm c. 1780 and had been absorbed into it by 1844. Rabson farm then included 322 a. of arable, 94 a. of pasture, and 122 a. of meadow.[86] The farm was worked by tenants in the 18th century and the 19th and by members of the Horton family as owners or tenants from 1880.[87] In 1980 it was of 560 a., chiefly arable land.[88]

The lands of Lower Richardson farm lay in the west part of the parish in parcels along the southern boundary.[89] The farm was in hand in the late 17th century but was worked by tenants in the 1760s and 1770s. Its lands were divided between Rabson and Whyr farms after 1780.[90] Upper Richardson farm, known as Whyr farm from the mid 18th century, was at the west end of the parish and included a larger area of pasture than the other farms; c. 1700 there was a flock of 600 sheep. A farmstead had then recently been built and the farm included 110 a. of arable and 36 a. of meadow land, formerly part of Stanmore, and a further 120 a. of arable land, some of which was newly broken.[91] In 1844 Whyr farm, 464 a., included 237 a. of arable south of the road to Clyffe Pypard and 75 a. of meadow. Then, as in the 17th and 18th centuries, it was worked by tenants.[92] Whyr was a dairy farm in the 1920s. In 1966, when it comprised c. 480 a., it was converted from corn and stock to a wholly arable farm.[93]

A mill, valued at 12s. a year, was part of Winterbourne Bassett manor in 1281.[94]

LOCAL GOVERNMENT. Although tithingmen from Winterbourne Bassett and Richardson attended hundred courts from the 15th century until the 19th,[95] separate views of frankpledge were held for Winterbourne Bassett in the mid 16th century. There is no evidence that Rabson was a tithing nor is a tithingman from Rabson or Richardson known to have attended the views for Winterbourne Bassett. The views were held with manor courts and presentments were made by a tithingman. Business before the courts included tenurial matters and the regulation of common pastures.[96] Nothing is known of manorial courts for Rabson or Richardson.

In the early 19th century the lord of Winterbourne Bassett manor made leases of farms conditional upon agreement to pay a labour rate.

[74] P.R.O., SC 6/Hen. VIII/3986, rot. 8; Cal. Pat. 1560-3, 239-40.
[75] P.R.O., SC 6/1115/1, rot. 8; First Pembroke Survey, ed. Straton, i. 264-5, 268-9.
[76] P.R.O., E 134/11 & 12 Wm. III Hil./8; E 134/14 Geo. II Trin./6.
[77] Ibid. E 134/14 Geo. II Trin./6; B.L. Maps, 'Winterbourne, 1760'.
[78] W.R.O., land tax; tithe award; ibid. 1506/25.
[79] Ibid. land tax; P.R.O., E 134/14 Geo. II Trin./6; Dors. R.O., D 124, box 181, rental, 1772-3; Kelly's Dir. Wilts. (1848 and later edns.).
[80] P.R.O., E 134/14 Geo. II Trin./6.
[81] Wilts. Tracts, xxiv, no. 13.
[82] W.R.O., tithe award.
[83] Wilts. Cuttings, xviii. 4.
[84] Inf. from Mr. R. Horton, Winterbourne Bassett Manor. [85] B.L. Maps, 'Winterbourne, 1760'.
[86] W.R.O., land tax; tithe award.
[87] Ibid. land tax; Kelly's Dir. Wilts. (1848 and later edns.); inf. from Mrs. R. Horton, Winterbourne Bassett Manor.
[88] Inf. from Mr. W. K. Horton, Rabson Manor.
[89] B.L. Maps, 'Winterbourne, 1760'.
[90] P.R.O., E 134/11 & 12 Wm. III Hil./8; Dors. R.O., D 124, box 181, rental, 1772-3; W.R.O., land tax.
[91] B.L. Maps, 'Winterbourne, 1760'; P.R.O., E 134/11 & 12 Wm. III Hil./8; E 134/6 Anne Mich./10.
[92] W.R.O., tithe award; land tax; P.R.O., E 134/6 Anne Mich./10.
[93] Wilts. Cuttings, xviii. 4; W.R.O. 1008/31; inf. from Mr. M. R. Young, Whyr Farm.
[94] Wilts. Inq. p.m. 1242-1326 (Index Libr.), 133.
[95] P.R.O., DL 30/127/1908; W.R.O. 192/12A-K; 9, Selkley hund. ct. bk. 1734-1861.
[96] P.R.O., SC 2/209/69, rot. 6; B.L. Add. Ch. 24440, rot. 6d.

It is not clear whether the rate was a minimum wage or a tax related to the number of labourers employed but it was said to reduce the level of the poor rate.[97] In the 1830s, however, the average annual expenditure on the poor was £150, little lower than that in neighbouring parishes of similar size. In 1835 Winterbourne Bassett became part of Marlborough poor-law union.[98]

CHURCH. In or before 1121 Reynold de Dunstanville gave Winterbourne Bassett church to Lewes priory.[99] The church was not appropriated, and from the 13th century until the Dissolution the rector of Winterbourne Bassett paid an annual pension of 30s. to the priory.[1] In 1538 the pension was granted to Thomas Cromwell, later earl of Essex. It presumably reverted to the Crown on his attainder in 1539 and no further record of it has been found.[2] The priory held the advowson until the Dissolution. In the early 13th century the prior presented candidates nominated by Alan Basset. The patronage was exercised by the bishop of Salisbury in 1322 and, by lapse, in 1449. John de Warenne, earl of Surrey, presented in the 1340s possibly by virtue of a grant from the prior.[3] As a result of grants made shortly before the Dissolution, there were various claimants to the patronage in the mid 16th century. In 1531 the advowson was granted for a single turn to Sir John Gage and Sir Edward Baynton, who sold it c. 1544 to Robert Ward. Ward sold the same turn to John Thimble and to John Taylor. Thimble's right was acknowledged as valid[4] but there is no record of a presentation by him. Sir William Wroughton was said to hold the advowson in the 1550s.[5] After the Dissolution the Crown granted the patronage to William Herbert, earl of Pembroke, in 1553.[6] Rights of next presentation granted by earls of Pembroke were conveyed by the grantees to Charles Wotton and Robert Holloway who presented in 1572 and 1608 respectively.[7] The advowson was sold in 1682[8] and in 1696 Richard Glass presented.[9] His kinsman, the Revd. Richard Glass, then rector of Winterbourne Bassett, sold the advowson to Magdalen College, Oxford, in 1714.[10] The college was sole patron of the united benefice of Winterbourne Bassett with Berwick Bassett,

established in 1929,[11] and held the presentation at alternate turns after 1951, when Winterbourne Bassett was held in plurality with Broad Hinton.[12] The living became part of the Upper Kennet team ministry in 1975.[13]

From the 13th century the rector's income was well above the average for the deanery of Avebury. The living was valued at £10 in 1291 and at £18 9s. in 1535.[14] In the 1830s the rector received £634 a year.[15] Tithes from the whole parish were paid to the rector in the 16th century.[16] In the late 17th century he also received half the tithes of Stanmore, except those from 20 a. of arable and meadow, formerly part of the glebe of Beckhampton chapel, in return for rights of baptism, marriage, and burial in Winterbourne Bassett church.[17] The tithes were replaced by a rent charge of £688 in 1844.[18] The glebe consisted of 24 a. and pasture for 60 sheep in 1564.[19] In 1662 there were also 13 a. of several pasture in the west field.[20] Some 30 a. of glebe were sold in 1915 and another 20 a. later.[21] In 1671 there was a rectory house of four bays.[22] In the 1830s the house was of two storeys, each of two rooms, and a kitchen and scullery. Although described as unfit for residence, it was occupied by the curate.[23] A new house was built in 1850 and sold in 1951.[24]

The valuable living attracted pluralist incumbents, including Fulk Basset, rector from c.1214 to c. 1239, who was nominated to the living by his father.[25] Of his successors one was licensed as a non-resident in 1396, another as a pluralist in 1471.[26] In the mid 16th century and the mid 17th, following periods of disruption, the furnishings, ornaments, and service of the church were inadequate; quarterly sermons were omitted in the 1550s and in 1662 communion was not celebrated properly because the minister was sick and the people 'backward'.[27] Pre-Reformation traditions apparently died hard in the parish; in the early 17th century the clerk still invoked St. Catherine, patron saint of the parish.[28] From 1726 until the mid 19th century the rectors, most of them former fellows of Magdalen College, were pluralists who appointed curates to serve the parish.[29] Members of the Goddard family, who were also vicars and curates of Clyffe Pypard, were curates of Winterbourne Bassett between 1783 and 1842.[30] In 1783 morning and afternoon services

[97] Poor Law Com. 1st Rep. app. A, p. 6.
[98] Poor Law Com. 2nd Rep. 559.
[99] Cal. Doc. France, ed. Round, p. 509; Anct. Chart. (Pipe R. Soc. x), p. 11.
[1] Lewes Cart. Supplt. Wilts. portion (Suss. Rec. Soc. xl), pp. 27–8; Valor Eccl. (Rec. Com.), i. 329.
[2] L. & P. Hen. VIII, xiii (2), pp. 138–9; D.N.B.
[3] Lewes Cart. Supplt. Wilts. portion (Suss. Rec. Soc. xl), pp. 4–5, 27–8; Phillipps, Wilts. Inst. (index in W.A.M. xxviii. 234).
[4] P.R.O., C 3/181/41.
[5] Wilton Ho. Mun., survey, 1550s.
[6] Cal. Pat. 1553, 177–8.
[7] Phillipps, Wilts. Inst. i. 226; ii. 5.
[8] P.R.O., CP 43/398, rot. 38.
[9] Phillipps, Wilts. Inst. ii. 44.
[10] P.R.O., CP 25(2)/1077/1 Geo. I Trin.
[11] Lond. Gaz. 7 May 1929, pp. 3114–17.
[12] W.R.O. 1506/15.
[13] Lond. Gaz. 21 Mar. 1975, p. 2845; above, Avebury, church.
[14] Tax. Eccl. (Rec. Com.), 189; Valor Eccl. (Rec. Com.), ii. 130.
[15] Rep. Com. Eccl. Revenues, 854–5.
[16] Valor Eccl. (Rec. Com.), ii. 130.
[17] P.R.O., E 134/11 & 12 Wm. III Hil./8.
[18] W.R.O., tithe award.
[19] First Pembroke Survey, ed. Straton, i. 264.
[20] W.R.O., bishop, glebe terrier.
[21] W.A.S. Libr., sale cat. xxvi, no. 38; inf. from the Revd. B. A. Tigwell, Broad Hinton Vicarage.
[22] W.R.O., bishop, glebe terrier.
[23] F. Goddard, Reminiscences (reprinted from Wilts. Gaz. 7 June 1928 and later edns.), 13; Rep. Com. Eccl. Revenues, 854–5.
[24] W.R.O. 1506/25; inf. from Mr. Tigwell.
[25] Lewes Cart. Supplt. Wilts. portion (Suss. Rec. Soc. xl), pp. 4–5.
[26] W.R.O., bishop, reg. Mitford, f. 115; Cal. Papal Reg. xii. 800.
[27] W.R.O., bishop, detecta bk. 1550–3; bishop, chwdns.' pres. 1662.
[28] J. Aubrey, Remains of Gentilisme and Judaisme, ed. J. Britton (Folk-Lore Soc. 1881), 28–9.
[29] Alum. Oxon. 1500–1714, ii. 478; Alum. Oxon. 1715–1886, ii. 588, 686; iv. 1347, 1551; Rep. Com. Eccl. Revenues, 854–5.
[30] Goddard, Reminiscences, 13–14.

on Sundays alternated with those at Clyffe Pypard. Communion was celebrated at the three principal festivals.[31] Morning and afternoon services were held each Sunday in the mid 19th century; 65 people attended in the morning and 72 in the afternoon on Census Sunday in 1851.[32] Additional services at festivals and in Lent and more frequent celebrations of communion were introduced in the 1860s and c. 1900 services were held daily.[33]

The church was dedicated to St. Catherine in the 16th century but was known as St. Peter's in 1848.[34] Since 1904 it has been dedicated to *ST. KATHERINE AND ST. PETER*.[35] Much of the building is of coursed sarsen rubble with freestone dressings. It has a chancel, a nave with north transeptal chapel, north aisle, and south porch, and a west tower. The earliest features are an early 13th-century font and a late 13th-century effigy slab in the north chapel. The chancel and the nave with its aisle and chapel were apparently rebuilt in the mid 14th century although the nave may follow an older plan. In the late 15th century the tower was added, new windows were made in the north aisle, and the south-west corner of the nave, including a window and the south doorway, was rebuilt. Another window on the south side of the nave is of the 16th century. The south porch was added in 1611.[36] Most of the fittings in the nave, including the pews, pulpit, and font cover, are of the 17th century. The chancel roof, which was lowered at that time, was raised again at a restoration of 1857. New roofs were then built over the nave, aisle, and transept.[37]

In 1553 plate weighing 2½ oz. was confiscated and a chalice of 6 oz. left in the parish.[38] There was no communion cup or flagon in 1662.[39] A large late 17th-century chalice and a paten of 1695 were held by the parish in 1980.[40] There were three bells in 1553. Two new bells were cast in 1583 and another in 1609. One of the bells of 1583 and late 19th-century replacements for the other two bells still hung in the church in 1980.[41]

Registers of baptisms begin in 1681 but are incomplete before 1722. Registers of burials begin in 1724 and of marriages in 1727.[42]

NONCONFORMITY. A house was licensed for dissenters' meetings in 1824.[43] In 1864 Primitive Methodists met in a cottage; many members of the congregation also attended the parish church.[44] There were two services each Sunday and one during the week in the 1880s.[45] A small brick chapel, built c. 1903,[46] fell into disuse in the 1950s and was sold in 1960.[47]

EDUCATION. Although there was a small day school in the parish in 1818, the poor were said to desire more adequate means of education.[48] There was no school in 1833[49] but c. 1835 a cottage on the south side of the village street was converted for use as a school attached to the Church of England.[50] In 1858 there were 28 pupils and some older children attended Broad Hinton school.[51] A new school was built north of the village street in 1875.[52] Average attendance fell from 45 in 1914 to 36 in 1927[53] although in the 1920s the pupils included some children from Berwick Bassett.[54] The school was closed in 1966.[55]

CHARITIES FOR THE POOR. None known.

WINTERBOURNE MONKTON

WINTERBOURNE MONKTON, 761 ha. (1,879 a.), lies in the upper Kennet valley north of Avebury.[56] The eastern head stream of the Kennet flows through the parish from north to south and by 869 had given the name Winterbourne to lands there.[57] In the early 13th century the village was distinguished from Winterbourne Bassett and North Winterbourne by the suffix Monkton, referring to the estate there of Glastonbury abbey.[58] Like those to the north of it Winterbourne Monkton is a long narrow parish, the eastern boundary of which is marked by the

31 *Vis. Queries, 1783* (W.R.S. xxvii), p. 236.
32 P.R.O., HO 129/255/1/4/7.
33 W.R.O., bishop, vis. queries, 1864; D. Primrose, *Mod. Boeotia* (1904), 56-65, 171.
34 Aubrey, *Remains*, ed. Britton, 28-9; *Kelly's Dir. Wilts.* (1848).
35 W.R.O. 1526/25.
36 Date stone in church.
37 Wilts. Cuttings, xvi. 379.
38 *W.A.M.* xii. 364.
39 W.R.O., bishop, chwdns.' pres.
40 Nightingale, *Wilts. Plate*, 144; inf. from Mr. Tigwell.
41 Walters, *Wilts. Bells*, 235; inf. from Mr. Tigwell.
42 W.R.O. 1506/1-2; transcripts for 1607-9, 1619-23, 1632-5, 1666-79, 1710-11, 1720-2, and 1725-6 are ibid. bishop.
43 Ibid. return of regns.
44 Ibid. bishop, vis. queries.
45 Ibid. 1506/25.
46 Primrose, *Mod. Boeotia*, 32.
47 Inf. from Mr. R. Horton, Winterbourne Bassett Manor.
48 *Educ. of Poor Digest*, 1041.
49 *Educ. Enquiry Abstract*, 1052.
50 P.R.O., ED 7/131, no. 321; W.R.O., tithe award.
51 W.R.O. 1506/25; *Acct. of Wilts. Schs.* 50.
52 P.R.O., ED 7/131, no. 321; O.S. Map 6", Wilts. XXII (1888 edn.).
53 *Bd. of Educ.*, *List 21* (H.M.S.O.).
54 P.R.O., ED 21/42435.
55 Inf. from the Revd. B. A. Tigwell, Broad Hinton Vicarage.
56 This article was written in 1980. Maps used include O.S. Maps 1", sheet 34 (1828 edn.); 1/50,000, sheet 173 (1974 edn.); 1/25,000, SU 07 (1959 edn.), SU 17 (1960 edn.); 6", Wilts. XXVIII (1889 and later edns.).
57 Finberg, *Early Wessex Chart.* pp. 75-6.
58 *Interdict Doc.* (Pipe R. Soc. N.S. xxxiv), 18; below, manor.

The north doorway of the chancel of St. Mary's church in 1810

Russley Park *c.* 1758

BISHOPSTONE

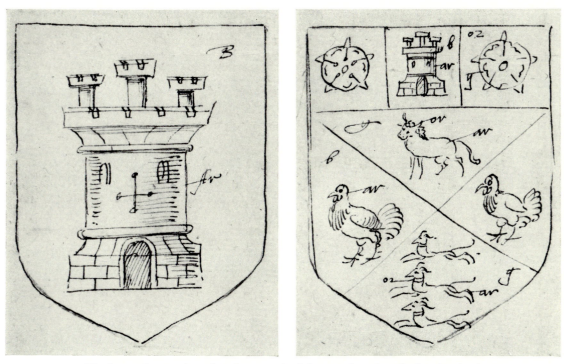

The borough arms in 1565: those on the left were then described as 'ancient'.

MARLBOROUGH

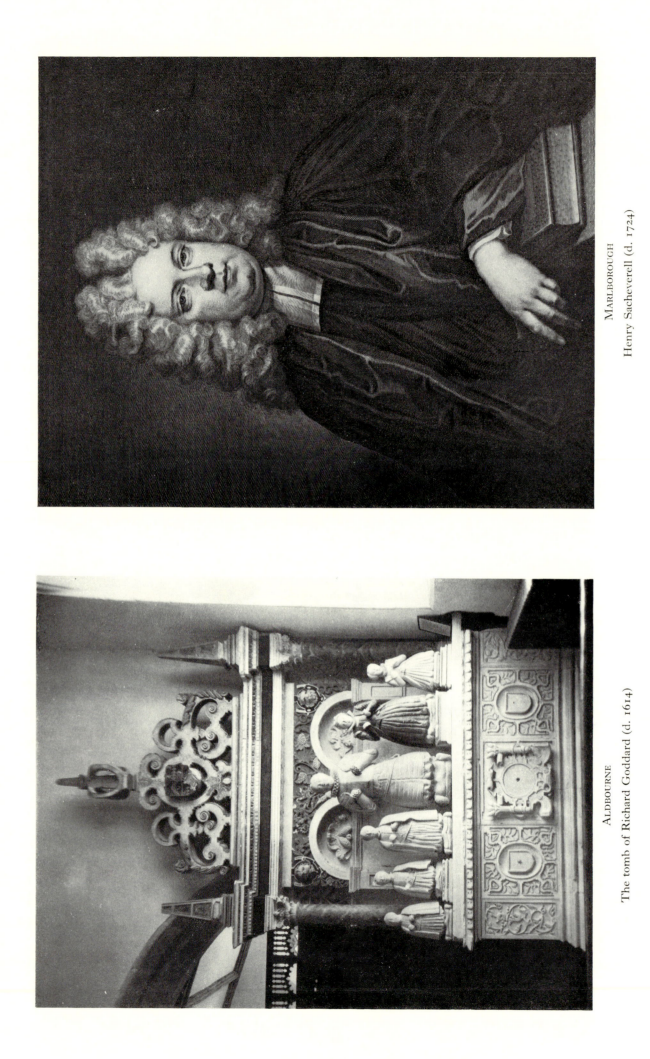

MARLBOROUGH
Henry Sacheverell (d. 1724)

ALDBOURNE
The tomb of Richard Goddard (d. 1614)

Ridge Way on Hackpen Hill. It extends 5 km. westwards and at its widest point near the stream measures nearly 2 km. from north to south. The steep slopes of Hackpen Hill, known as Monkton Down, rise to 254 m. in the south-east corner of the parish and have a scattering of sarsen stones. Below 183 m. there is a more gentle incline to the Kennet, west of which the land is almost flat. Another small stream, perhaps man-made, rises in Berwick Bassett and flows east by the northern boundary for 500 m. to the head stream. Near the western boundary the land rises gradually to 176 m. and Windmill Hill in the south-west corner of the parish is above 183 m. Chalk outcrops over the whole parish and there are deposits of gravel and alluvium near the head stream. An east–west tongue of gravel extends into the southern part of the parish towards the lower slopes of Hackpen Hill.[59]

Evidence of prehistoric activity in the parish is most abundant on Windmill Hill, the site of a Neolithic causewayed camp, and on Monkton Down, where barrows and artefacts of early Iron-Age and Roman origin have been found.[60] The site of Mill Barrow, a long barrow excavated in the 18th century, is thought to be 400 m. north-west of the church. Near that site are the Shelving Stones, sarsen slabs beneath which skeletons of the early and middle Bronze Age have been found.[61]

The flat or gently sloping ground east and west of the Kennet head stream provided the arable lands of the parish and there was pasture on Hackpen Hill and Windmill Hill.[62] In the 12th and 13th centuries Winterbourne Monkton apparently lay within the boundary of Savernake forest.[63] There is, however, no evidence that the parish was then well wooded and in the 18th century, as in the 20th, it was almost treeless: what trees there were stood near the village.[64]

The Ridge Way runs along Hackpen Hill on the eastern boundary of the parish. A path west of the head stream which linked Avebury, Winterbourne Monkton, Berwick Bassett, Winterbourne Bassett, and Broad Hinton churches in 1980 may mark another old route but it was apparently not used as a road north and south of Winterbourne Monkton village in the late 18th century. Then, as in the 20th century, the principal route through the parish was a north–south road east of the head stream. It was turnpiked in 1767 as part of the Swindon–Devizes road.[65] A parallel track 750 m. east of the road was still visible in 1980. Few roads ran east–west in the late 18th century. One, which passed through Winterbourne Monkton village to Yatesbury, was a path in 1980; others which crossed Hackpen Hill had been cut short by the late 19th century.[66]

In the 14th century Winterbourne Monkton was one of the smaller settlements in Selkley hundred; there were 69 poll-tax payers in 1377.[67] It was one of the poorer communities in the hundred in the 14th and 16th centuries.[68] The population increased in the early 19th century from 177 in 1801 to 263 in 1831. Numbers fluctuated during the rest of the century and had fallen to 182 by 1901. The total had risen again to 215 by 1911 but had fallen to 162 by 1931. There were 189 inhabitants in 1951,[69] 166 in 1971.[70]

Winterbourne Monkton village stands near the centre of the parish west of the Swindon–Devizes road, straddling the head stream. The buildings are scattered along two lanes leading west from the road. The southern lane crosses the stream by Low Bridge to the church. In the 18th century it then turned north for 500 m. and east to recross the stream and, as Hannah's Lane, rejoin the Swindon–Devizes road. North of the church and west of the stream the lane had become a footpath by 1980. The second lane, known in the early 19th century as Hain Lane, leaves the road 100 m. north of the junction with the lane to the church and runs north-west to join Hannah's Lane a little east of the stream. In the 18th century there were a few houses on the west side of the Swindon–Devizes road.[71] Middle Farm, built north of the junction with the southern lane c. 1720,[72] is of sarsen with freestone dressings and has a symmetrical east front. There are cottages of the 18th and 19th centuries north of that farmhouse. Most of the buildings, however, stood beside the southern lane east of the church, on the west bank of the stream, and along Hain Lane.[73] Manor Farm, east of the church, is a red-brick building with a symmetrical south front of the mid 18th century, which has been extended and altered since 1967. Most of the 18th-century cottages beside Hain Lane have sarsen walling and some are thatched. The Post Office, at the northern end of the lane, bears the date 1743. In the late 18th century and the 19th the settlement east of the stream grew while that west of it declined. By 1889 many buildings west of the stream had disappeared and the church and Manor Farm then formed an isolated group.[74] Most 19th-century building took place beside Hain Lane. Of that date are the former Parsonage Farm and the school, which stand west of the lane near its junction with the road, and the New Inn, open in 1889,[75] south of the Post Office. Bungalows opposite the Post Office and council houses at the northern end of the lane were built in the 20th century and in the 1970s cottages near the junction of Hain and Hannah's Lanes were demolished.[76] East Farm was built on the southern boundary east of the road in the mid 19th

[59] Geol. Surv. Map 1″, drift, sheet 266 (1964 edn.).
[60] V.C.H. Wilts. i (1), 125–6, 146, 200, 212, 220–1, 224.
[61] Ibid. 125–6, 146; W.A.M. iv. 343; xlii. 54.
[62] W.R.O. 39/8; B.L. Eg. MS. 3321, ff. 252–255v.; below, econ. hist.
[63] V.C.H. Wilts. iv. 417–18.   [64] W.R.O. 39/8.
[65] Andrews and Dury, Map (W.R.S. viii), pls. 11, 14; V.C.H. Wilts. iv. 268.
[66] Andrews and Dury, Map (W.R.S. viii), pls. 11, 14; O.S. Map 6″, Wilts. XXVIII (1889 edn.).

[67] V.C.H. Wilts. iv. 310.
[68] Ibid. 301; Taxation Lists (W.R.S. x), 23, 102.
[69] V.C.H. Wilts. iv. 361.
[70] Census, 1971.
[71] P.R.O., C 54/9626, map; Andrews and Dury, Map (W.R.S. viii), pls. 11, 14.
[72] Date stone on ho.
[73] Andrews and Dury, Map (W.R.S. viii), pls. 11, 14.
[74] O.S. Map 6″, Wilts. XXVIII (1889 edn.).
[75] Ibid.
[76] Inf. from Mr. F. Wallis, Manor Farm.

century.[77] Further north and 300 m. east of the road is Windmill House, a 19th-century house on the site of a windmill.[78]

MANOR AND OTHER ESTATES. In 869 King Ethelred gave 25 *cassati* at Winterbourne to his ealdorman Wulfere who later granted all or part of the estate to Glastonbury abbey. Although other lands received by Wulfere from the king were confiscated after his desertion of King Alfred, that grant apparently took effect and in 1086 the abbot held 25 hides at Winterbourne Monkton.[79] An estate of 9 *mansiones* in Winterbourne, perhaps part of Wulfere's, was granted by King Athelstan to Elfleda, perhaps wife of Edward the Elder, in 928 and by her to the monks of Glastonbury.[80] In 1330 the abbot of Glastonbury was granted free warren in his demesne at Winterbourne Monkton.[81] At the Dissolution *WINTERBOURNE MONKTON* manor reverted to the Crown and in 1542 it was granted to Edward Seymour, earl of Hertford (created duke of Somerset in 1547).[82] In 1545 Hertford sold the manor to Sir Edward Darell (d. 1549),[83] whose son William sold it in 1577 to Sir James Harvey (d. 1583).[84] It passed to Harvey's son Sir Sebastian (d. 1621) and granddaughter Mary Harvey, wife of John Popham. In 1636 Popham was succeeded by his brother Alexander (d. 1669).[85] The manor passed in the Popham family with that of Littlecote in Ramsbury[86] to F. W. Leyborne-Popham who sold it *c.* 1899 to Holland Franklyn. It was bought *c.* 1910 by N. R. R. Young[87] who sold it as four farms in 1917. West farm was then bought by H. J. Horton[88] and *c.* 1920 by W. Tucker who sold it *c.* 1939 to a Dr. Carr. After Carr's death it was bought by members of the Grunenberg family and in 1967, as Manor farm, by Mr. F. Wallis, the owner in 1980.[89] East farm was bought in 1917 by a Mr. Smith of Newport (I.W.) and sold *c.* 1920 to Frederick Heath.[90] In 1948 Heath sold it to C. B. Cooper (d. 1979), whose relict Mrs. M. F. Cooper was owner in 1980.[91] Middle farm was bought in 1917 by H. Greader and *c.* 1935 by F. G. Troup.[92] In 1963 R. T. Vaughan sold some 200 a., which became part of East farm, to C. B.

Cooper and the remainder of Middle farm, *c.* 350 a., to Mr. R. J. and Mrs. M. Longstreet, the owners of the farm in 1980.[93] Parsonage farm was bought in 1917 by Frederick Smyth.[94] It passed through various hands and in the 1960s part was sold to Mr. and Mrs. R. J. Longstreet and part to Mr. L. W. J. Chalk.[95]

Before 1066 Orgar held 3½ hides of Glastonbury abbey. Gilbert Gibard held them in 1084 and 1086[96] and Hugh de Polstead in 1189.[97] Hugh granted the estate to Geoffrey de Maizey in 1195.[98] Geoffrey was succeeded by Robert de Maizey (fl. *c.* 1235) and Grace de Maizey (fl. 1242–3).[99] In 1261 the estate belonged to Gregory de la Mare[1] and a Gregory de la Mare held it in 1319.[2] Part of the estate passed to Gilbert of Berwick whose lands were forfeited to the Crown for rebellion in 1326.[3] From Gilbert's holding were probably derived lands granted by John Lovel, Lord Lovel (d. 1408), to the priory of St. Margaret near Marlborough in or before 1399.[4] At the Dissolution those lands passed to the Crown and they were granted as dower to Anne of Cleves in 1540 and to Catherine Howard in 1541.[5] In 1553 William Herbert, earl of Pembroke, acquired them by exchange with the Crown;[6] their later descent has not been traced.

Another part of the estate of Gregory de la Mare (fl. 1319) was held by William Dunershe in 1428[7] and passed to the Dismars family. Nicholas Dismars was succeeded by his son John who in 1518 held 2 yardlands in Winterbourne Monkton.[8] John's son Christopher inherited that estate *c.* 1527 and sold it to his sister Agnes (fl. 1539) who devised it to her son Robert Sloper (d. before 1564).[9] The estate passed to Robert's son John (fl. 1584)[10] and descended in the Sloper family to Walter Sloper (fl. 1675)[11] who sold it to Joseph Houlton. By will proved 1716 Houlton devised it to Elizabeth Houlton, perhaps his daughter.[12] The estate was probably that held in the late 18th century by members of the Brown family. John Brown (fl. 1815) was succeeded *c.* 1850 by his son Henry.[13] The lands were absorbed into Winterbourne Monkton manor soon afterwards.[14]

Winterbourne Monkton rectory was appropriated by Cirencester abbey before 1229[15] and the abbey's rights there were confirmed in

[77] W.R.O. 1295/4.
[78] Below, econ. hist.
[79] *Glastonbury Cart.* iii (Som. Rec. Soc. lxiv), 671; *Adami de Domerham Historia*, ed. T. Hearne (Oxf. 1727), 69; *V.C.H. Wilts.* ii, pp. 6–7, 124.
[80] Finberg, *Early Wessex Chart.* p. 81.
[81] *Cal. Chart. R.* 1327–41, 169.
[82] *L. & P. Hen. VIII*, xvii, p. 322.
[83] Ibid. xx (1), p. 427; P.R.O., C 142/92, no. 11.
[84] P.R.O., CP 25(2)/240/20 Eliz. I Hil.; ibid. C 142/205, no. 190.
[85] Ibid. C 142/390, no. 143; *D.N.B.* s.v. Francis Popham; *Wilts. Inq. p.m. 1625–49* (Index Libr.), 250–3.
[86] Above, Ramsbury, manors.
[87] *Kelly's Dir. Wilts.* (1899, 1911).
[88] W.A.S. Libr., sale cat. x, no. 3.
[89] *Kelly's Dir. Wilts.* (1920); inf. from Mr. F. Wallis, Manor Farm.
[90] W.A.S. Libr., sale cat. x, no. 3; *Kelly's Dir. Wilts.* (1920).
[91] Inf. from Mr. M. R. Cooper, East Farm.
[92] W.A.S. Libr., sale cat. x, no. 3; *Kelly's Dir. Wilts.* (1931, 1935).
[93] Inf. from Mrs. M. Longstreet, Middle Farm.
[94] W.A.S. Libr., sale cat. x, no. 3.

[95] Inf. from Mrs. Longstreet.
[96] *V.C.H. Wilts.* ii, pp. 124, 199.
[97] *Liber Henrici de Soliaco*, ed. J. A. Jackson (Roxburghe Club, 1882), 123.
[98] P.R.O., CP 25(1)/250/1, no. 8.
[99] *Rentalia Abbatum Glastoniae* (Som. Rec. Soc. v), 64; *Bk. of Fees*, ii. 749.
[1] *Rentalia* (Som. Rec. Soc. v), 232.
[2] *Feet of F. 1272–1327* (W.R.S. i), p. 103.
[3] P.R.O., SC 6/1148/19A.
[4] *Cal. Pat.* 1396–9, 560; *Feud. Aids*, v. 269.
[5] *L. & P. Hen. VIII*, xv, p. 8; xvi, p. 716.
[6] *Cal. Pat.* 1553, 177–8.
[7] *Feud. Aids*, v. 269.
[8] P.R.O., SC 6/Hen. VIII/3177, rot. 4.
[9] Ibid. REQ 2/18/164.
[10] Ibid. C 3/116/15; *Sess. Mins.* (W.R.S. iv), 95.
[11] Herts. R.O. 27240.
[12] *W.N. & Q.* vi. 212.
[13] W.R.O., land tax; P.R.O., C 54/9626; *Kelly's Dir. Wilts.* (1848, 1855).
[14] *Kelly's Dir. Wilts.* (1875); W.A.S. Libr., sale cat. x, no. 3.
[15] *Cirencester Cart.* ed. C. D. Ross and M. Devine, ii, pp. 431–2.

1337.[16] The rectory estate, consisting only of tithes, was probably granted by the Crown with that of Avebury to Maria Dunche in 1604 and sold by her grandson William Dunche to John Popham in 1633. Popham held the rectory estate at his death in 1636[17] and thereafter it passed with Winterbourne Monkton manor. At inclosure in 1815 the tithes were replaced by an allotment of land.[18]

A free chapel at Winterbourne Monkton was endowed with the tithes of the demesne farm of the manor. The tithes passed to the Crown at the Dissolution and in 1574 Simon Sloper bought the reversion of the freehold.[19] He was succeeded c. 1587 by another Simon Sloper, probably his son. In 1625 that Simon settled the estate on his son William (fl. 1650).[20] It was held in 1675 by Thomas Sloper[21] and in 1713 was conveyed by Frances, relict of John Curle, to her daughter Sarah and Sarah's husband Robert Mellior.[22] In 1734 Sarah, then a widow, conveyed her life estate to Robert's sisters and coheirs, Elizabeth, wife of Robert Banbury, and Grace, wife of Benjamin Kirby.[23] John Hitchcock held the estate in 1781[24] and in 1815 Charles Hitchcock was allotted 150 a. in place of the tithes.[25] The land was held in 1848 by William Hitchcock (d. c. 1854)[26] and in 1875 by the Revd. Freeman Wilson.[27] Wilson was succeeded by his son A. W. F. Wilson c. 1910.[28] The land was sold to N. R. R. Young, the owner of Winterbourne Monkton manor, before 1917.[29]

ECONOMIC HISTORY. The husbandry practised at Winterbourne Monkton in the Middle Ages was of the sheep-and-corn type usual on the Wiltshire downs and in the upland manors of Glastonbury abbey.[30] Arable farming, however, was more important than pastoral. In the 11th century there were 100 a. of pasture on an estate rated as 25 hides and the proportion of pasture to arable remained unusually low.[31]

The estate which became Winterbourne Monkton manor was assessed at 25 *cassati* in 869[32] and at 25 hides in 1066.

In the 11th and 12th centuries the estate comprised the manorial demesne, which occupied an unusually large proportion of the whole estate, a freehold farm, and the land held by customary tenants. There were 10 hides in demesne with 4 ploughteams and 7 serfs in 1086; the freehold farm was assessed at 3½ hides then

and at 4 hides in 1194. In 1086 17 villeins and 8 bordars had 7 teams,[33] and in 1189 there were 12 yardlanders, 5 ½-yardlanders, and 10 cottagers holding c. 5 a. each.[34] The value of the manor, £12 in 1066, had risen to £20 by 1086.[35]

In the 13th and 14th centuries the two open fields of Winterbourne Monkton lay east and west of the Kennet.[36] New land, probably on the edge of the downs, was brought under the plough in the 13th century.[37] There was pasture on Windmill Hill, which probably included the lord's several pasture of 'Berghdown', and on Monkton Down. Part of the down was common grazing for cattle in summer and feeding for the lord's sheep in winter.[38]

The demesne of the manor, as of most manors held by Glastonbury abbey, was kept in hand at least until the 14th century and probably until the late 15th. In the early 14th century there were 426 a. of demesne arable, probably including sown and fallow land. In 1333–4 the sown area was 287 a., larger than on most of the abbey's Wiltshire manors.[39] There was said to be pasture for 500 sheep in 1189.[40] The flock was of only 300 c. 1235 but in the early 14th century there were some 400 sheep.[41] The main burden of services in the manor was borne by the cottagers. They worked for the lord on 3 days each week from Michaelmas to 1 August and daily during harvest. The yardlanders performed three boonworks of ploughing and services of mowing, shearing, and weeding. In the late 12th century they were required to reap ½ a. each day during harvest; in the 14th century they were obliged to reap for 2 days and to cut another 2 a. in 2 days.[42]

The husbandry of Winterbourne Monkton was integrated with that of other estates of Glastonbury abbey. Grain was exchanged with other manors; 102 qr. of grain were sent to Glastonbury in 1333–4 and smaller amounts were supplied to Badbury in Chiseldon, Mells (Som.), and Ashbury (Berks., later Oxon.). In the 14th century the flocks of Badbury, Ashbury, and Winterbourne Monkton were managed together.[43] Carrying services, mainly to Glastonbury abbey and its estates, were required of customary tenants. Cottagers were obliged to drive beasts to Badbury and Christian Malford and once a year to Glastonbury. Yardlanders owed carrying services to Glastonbury and Bristol as well as to local markets.[44]

In the 16th century c. 1,000 a. were worked in three open fields, South, East, and West. South

[16] Ibid. iii, p. 1059.
[17] Above, Avebury, manors; *Wilts. Inq. p.m.* 1625–49 (Index Libr.), 251–2.
[18] P.R.O., C 54/9626.
[19] Below, church; W.R.O. 650/4–6.
[20] *W.N. & Q.* viii. 467; W.R.O. 650/7; 650/9.
[21] Herts. R.O. 27240.
[22] W.R.O. 650/13.
[23] Ibid. 650/15.
[24] Ibid. land tax.
[25] P.R.O., C 54/9626.
[26] *Kelly's Dir. Wilts.* (1848); *Endowed Char. Wilts.* (N. Div.), 1023.   [27] *Kelly's Dir. Wilts.*
[28] W.R.O. 1569/3; *Alum. Oxon. 1715–1886*, iv. 1581–2.
[29] Wilts. Cuttings, xiv. 110.
[30] I. J. E. Keil, 'Estates of Glastonbury Abbey in the Later Middle Ages' (Bristol Univ. Ph.D. thesis, 1964), 79–82.
[31] *V.C.H. Wilts.* ii, p. 124; below.

[32] Finberg, *Early Wessex Chart.* pp. 75–6.
[33] *V.C.H. Wilts.* ii, p. 124; *Cur. Reg. R.* 1194–5 (Pipe R. Soc. xiv), 118.
[34] *Liber Henrici*, ed. Jackson, 123–4.
[35] *V.C.H. Wilts.* ii, p. 124.
[36] *Rentalia* (Som. Rec. Soc. v), 61–3; B.L. Eg. MS. 3321, f. 251v.   [37] *Cirencester Cart.* iii, p. 1055.
[38] W.R.O. 192/52; B.L. Eg. MS. 3321, f. 252; Harl. MS. 3961, f. 88v.
[39] B.L. Eg. MS. 3321, f. 252; Keil, 'Glastonbury Estates', 88, 99, 102.
[40] *Liber Henrici*, ed. Jackson, 124.
[41] *Interdict Doc.* (Pipe R. Soc. N.S. xxxiv), 29; B.L. Eg. MS. 3321, f. 254.
[42] B.L. Eg. MS. 3321, ff. 253–4; *Liber Henrici*, ed. Jackson, 123–4; *Rentalia* (Som. Rec. Soc. v), 61–3.
[43] Keil, 'Glastonbury Estates', 88, 99, 127–9.
[44] *Rentalia* (Som. Rec. Soc. v), 62–3.

field was the smallest and was occupied only by copyhold tenants. Inclosures of meadow and pasture had been made[45] and in 1675 some 40 a. of pasture on Hackpen Hill and 60 a. on Windmill Hill were held in severalty.[46] By 1774 the south part of Hackpen Hill was several pasture and there were two large blocks of inclosed arable south-west and east of the village.[47] Common husbandry was ended by an award of 1815 under an Act of 1813. Allotments were then made of 965 a.[48]

From the early 16th century or earlier the demesne farm was worked by lessees. Members of the Dismars and Sloper families held leases for terms of years for much of the 16th century.[49] The area of the demesne farm, over 600 a. c. 1540, changed little before the 19th century.[50] In the 16th century there were some 300 a. of arable and in 1774 the farm included 360 a. of arable and 131 a. of pasture which were held in severalty.[51] The holders of ten copyhold farms had 600 a. of commonable arable in the 16th century.[52] The area of common arable had decreased to 470 a. by 1675 when there were twelve copyholders. In 1774 there were only six copyholders, three of whom held more than 100 a. each.[53] Former copyhold land was probably absorbed into the freehold farm, later Brown's, during the 17th and 18th centuries, and in the early 19th century most of the land of the parish was divided between that farm and the manor farm. By the inclosure award of 1815 the rectorial tithes and those from the demesne farm were replaced by allotments of land. Thereafter there were three principal farms in the parish, Manor farm, Parsonage, 150 a., and Brown's, which included 218 a. allotted at inclosure.[54] Manor farm, into which Brown's was absorbed c. 1850, was divided into West, later Manor, East, and Middle farms in 1861.[55] West farm measured 650 a. in 1880, East 478 a. of which c. 150 a. were in Avebury, and Middle 530 a.[56] In the early 20th century the lands of those farms and of Parsonage farm were evenly divided between arable and pasture.[57] In the 1920s and 1930s much of the arable land was converted to pasture for dairying but mixed farming again became usual in the 1940s. In 1980 Manor farm, 760 a., and Middle farm, 350 a., were principally arable but East, 640 a., was an arable and dairy farm.[58]

A windmill built west of the village for the abbot of Glastonbury c. 1265[59] was let in the early 14th century.[60] A new windmill was built in the early 16th century.[61] In the 1530s and 1540s the tenant of the demesne farm also held the mill.[62] A windmill stood 500 m. north-east of the village in 1815 but was disused in 1889.[63] In 1980 only the stones of its base remained beside Windmill House.

LOCAL GOVERNMENT. Use of a tumbrel and a gallows were claimed in Winterbourne Monkton in the 13th century.[64] The abbot of Glastonbury was granted return of writs in all his lands in 1280, and in 1327 the return of summonses to the exchequer and of all royal precepts and mandates was added.[65] From the early 14th century the abbot also enjoyed the right to hold pleas de vetito namio in Winterbourne Monkton.[66] Court rolls for the manor survive for various dates from the mid 13th century to the 15th[67] and for 1561-2.[68] From the early 13th century courts known as halimotes were held at Hocktide and halimotes and tourns at Michaelmas.[69] Presentments were made at both halimotes and tourns from the early 14th century by the tithingman. Offences presented included breaches of the assize of bread and of ale, of manorial custom, and of the peace. The courts also dealt with the conveyance and tenure of customary estates and suits between tenants.[70] Some pleas were referred to the abbot's bailiff, presumably to be heard at his court of North Damerham.[71] In the mid 16th century presentments were made by the homage, and the use of common pasture was regulated by the court.[72]

Average expenditure on the poor of the parish was £144 a year in the early 1830s. Winterbourne Monkton became part of Marlborough poor-law union in 1835.[73]

CHURCH. Before 1229 the church of Winterbourne Monkton was appropriated by Cirencester abbey and a vicarage ordained.[74] The appropriation was confirmed in 1335.[75] In the 13th and 14th centuries the church was described as a chapel annexed to Avebury church which had also been appropriated by the abbey,[76] but no record has been found of the dependence of Winterbourne Monkton church on Avebury. In 1431 the abbot of Cirencester petitioned unsuccessfully for the union of the vicarages of the

[45] W.R.O. 192/52; B.L. Harl. MS. 3961, ff. 89-96v.
[46] Herts. R.O. 27240.   [47] W.R.O. 39/8.
[48] P.R.O., C 54/9626.
[49] Ibid. SC 6/Hen. VIII/3177, rot. 4; ibid. C 3/116/15; W.R.O. 192/52; B.L. Harl. MS. 3961, f. 87v.
[50] W.R.O. 192/52; P.R.O., C 54/9626.
[51] W.R.O. 192/52; 39/8.
[52] Ibid. 192/52; B.L. Harl. MS. 3961, ff. 89-96v.
[53] Herts. R.O. 27240; W.R.O. 39/8.
[54] P.R.O., C 54/9626.
[55] Kelly's Dir. Wilts. (1848 and later edns.); W.R.O. 1295/4.
[56] W.R.O. 1650, Popham Mun., rental.
[57] W.A.S. Libr., sale cat. x, no. 3.
[58] Inf. from Mr. M. R. Cooper, East Farm; Mrs. M. Longstreet, Middle Farm; Mr. F. Wallis, Manor Farm.
[59] Adami de Domerham, ed. Hearne, 535-6; Glastonbury Cart. iii (Som. Rec. Soc. lxiv), 672.
[60] B.L. Eg. MS. 3321, ff. 254-255v.

[61] Ibid. Harl. MS. 3961, f. 9v.
[62] Ibid. Add. MS. 17451, f. 110; W.R.O. 192/52.
[63] W.A.M. xlii. 62; O.S. Map 1″, sheet 34 (1828 edn.); 6″, Wilts. XXVIII (1889 edn.).
[64] Rot. Hund. (Rec. Com.), ii (1), 270.
[65] Cal. Chart. R. 1327-41, 260.
[66] B.L. Eg. MS. 3321, f. 251.
[67] Ct. rolls for Glastonbury abbey estates, 1259-1535, are among Longleat Mun.; most are for various manors and some include Winterbourne Monkton.
[68] P.R.O., SC 2/209/71.
[69] e.g. Longleat Mun. 10654, 10773.
[70] Ibid. 10658, 10661, 11225.
[71] Ibid. 10773; Keil, 'Glastonbury Estates', 45.
[72] P.R.O., SC 2/209/71.
[73] Poor Law Com. 2nd Rep. 559.
[74] Cirencester Cart. ii, pp. 431-2.
[75] Ibid. iii, p. 1059.
[76] Ibid. pp. 1054-5, 1059; above, Avebury, church.

two churches.[77] In 1658 the parishes of Winterbourne Monkton and Berwick Bassett were united,[78] but they were separated at the Restoration. The vicarages of Winterbourne Monkton and Avebury were united from 1747 to 1864. Winterbourne Monkton was in 1865 again united with Berwick Bassett[79] until 1929 when the united benefice of Avebury with Winterbourne Monkton was formed.[80] That benefice was served in plurality with Berwick Bassett from 1952 until the livings and parishes were united in 1970. In 1975 Winterbourne Monkton became part of the Upper Kennet team ministry.[81]

The abbot of Cirencester presented to Winterbourne Monkton in 1361 and the patronage was held and exercised by the abbey until the Dissolution. The advowson then passed to the Crown but in 1561 and 1583 lessees of the rectory estate presented to the vicarage, presumably by grants of the next presentation. From 1626 the Crown exercised the patronage.[82] The advowson was conveyed to the bishop of Salisbury in 1864.[83]

Medieval incumbents complained repeatedly of the inadequate endowment of the vicarage. After one such complaint Cirencester abbey was required in 1229 to augment the vicar's income.[84] Another augmentation was agreed in the mid 13th century but did not take effect. In 1268, when the abbey was again ordered to increase the endowment, the vicarage was valued at 70s. a year.[85] The poverty of the living was cited as an argument in favour of its union with Avebury in the 15th century.[86] In 1535 the clear value of the living was said to be £5. It is not clear whether that figure included the pension of 40s. a year paid by Cirencester abbey.[87] The pension continued to be paid by holders of the rectory estate and was £10 a year in 1815.[88] Although the endowment of Winterbourne Monkton vicarage was augmented before 1815, the combined benefice of Avebury with Winterbourne Monkton was one of the poorer Wiltshire livings c. 1830 when the whole annual income was £178.[89] In 1865 the income of Winterbourne Monkton vicarage was retained by the vicar of Avebury and that of the united benefice of Berwick Bassett with Winterbourne Monkton was drawn from the endowment of Berwick Bassett, augmented by the Ecclesiastical Commissioners.[90]

Before 1229 Winterbourne Monkton vicarage was endowed with certain small tithes and all offerings.[91] The hay tithes of Winterbourne Monkton and 1 qr. of corn and 1 qr. of oats, due annually from Cirencester abbey's lands in Avebury, were then added.[92] An additional payment to the vicar of 3 qr. of wheat and 2 qr. of barley from the abbey's Avebury lands and of all tithes from a piece of land called 'old land' was agreed in 1268.[93] All the allowances of grain were replaced c. 1630 by a yearly pension of £8.[94] At least two further augmentations of the vicarage were made but in neither case is the date or donor recorded. In the 1670s the incumbent received hay, wool, lamb, and lesser tithes from all but the demesne of Winterbourne Monkton manor, and corn tithes from a few acres in the parish.[95] In 1815 grain tithes from 100 a. and other tithes from all but the 640 a. of the demesne were paid to the vicar.[96]

The vicarial glebe was 1 yardland and a messuage before 1229.[97] In 1671 the vicar held 25 a. of arable, 5 a. of meadow, and pasture for 30 sheep.[98] At inclosure in 1815 those lands, the vicar's tithes, and perhaps the pensions due to him were replaced by an allotment of 61 a. Parishioners whose lands were insufficient for them to contribute to that allotment were to pay small lump sums of money.[99] A glebe house mentioned in 1678[1] may have been the 'ruinous' cottage on Winterbourne Monkton glebe demolished in 1852.[2]

In 1291 a portion of tithes provided another ecclesiastical living in Winterbourne Monkton.[3] In the late 15th century or earlier the living was attached to a chapel which had been built ⅓ mile from the church.[4] The abbot of Glastonbury presented to the living, except in 1395 when the patronage was exercised by the bishop.[5] In 1536 the abbot granted the advowson of 'Monkton', probably Winterbourne Monkton chapel, to Thomas Cromwell, later earl of Essex, apparently at Cromwell's request. It is not clear whether the grant, presumably of a single turn, was to Cromwell, the chief minister, or to the Crown; neither presented before the dissolution of the chapel in 1547.[6] The chaplain received tithes valued at £4 a year from the demesne of Winterbourne Monkton manor in 1535.[7] No cure of souls was attached to the living although in the late 16th century the endowment was said to have been for the provision of a priest.[8] Nothing remains of the chapel.

The poverty of the vicarage may explain the neglect of quarterly sermons in the 1580s and the non-residence of the vicar in 1636 when a curate was licensed to serve the parish.[9] New fittings in

[77] W.R.O., bishop, reg. Nevill, f. 47.
[78] Cal. S.P. Dom. 1658–9, 220.
[79] Vis. Queries, 1783 (W.R.S. xxvii), p. 26; inf. from Dioc. Registrar, Minster Chambers, Castle St., Salisbury.
[80] Lond. Gaz. 10 May 1929, pp. 3114–17.
[81] Above, Avebury, church.
[82] Phillipps, Wilts. Inst. (index in W.A.M. xxviii. 234).
[83] Inf. from Dioc. Registrar.
[84] Cirencester Cart. ii, pp. 431–2.
[85] Ibid. iii, pp. 1055–7.
[86] W.R.O., bishop, reg. Nevill, f. 47.
[87] Valor Eccl. (Rec. Com.), ii. 131, 466.
[88] P.R.O., C 54/9626.
[89] Rep. Com. Eccl. Revenues, 822; below.
[90] W.R.O. 1569/10; Lond. Gaz. 10 Oct. 1865, p. 4775.
[91] Cirencester Cart. iii, pp. 1054–5.
[92] Ibid. ii, pp. 431–2.
[93] Ibid. iii, pp. 1056–7.
[94] W.R.O., bishop, glebe terriers, 1671, 1678.

[95] Ibid. bishop, glebe terriers; Tax. Eccl. (Rec. Com.), 189; Valor Eccl. (Rec. Com.), ii. 466.
[96] P.R.O., C 54/9626.
[97] Cirencester Cart. iii, pp. 1054–5.
[98] W.R.O., bishop, glebe terrier.
[99] P.R.O., C 54/9626.
[1] W.R.O., bishop, glebe terrier.
[2] Ibid. bishop, pet. for faculties, bdle. 4, no. 5.
[3] Tax. Eccl. (Rec. Com.), 189.
[4] Cal. Papal Reg. xiii (1), 272; W.A.M. xii. 376.
[5] Phillipps, Wilts. Inst. i. 7, 9, 25, 31, 81, 114, 150, 153, 161, 181, 188, 193, 200.
[6] Orig. Letters, ed. H. Ellis, 3rd ser. ii. 348; W.A.M. xii. 376.
[7] Valor Eccl. (Rec. Com.), ii. 131; P.R.O., C 1/1117/45.
[8] Cal. Papal Reg. xiii (1), 272; Cal. Pat. 1572–5, p. 223; W.A.M. xii. 376.
[9] W.R.O., bishop, detecta bk. 1584; Subscription Bk. (W.R.S. xxxii), p. 71.

the church in the early 17th century included an altar rail in keeping with the requirements of the Laudian authorities. A little later William London, who in 1647 marched with the clubmen against the parliamentary forces, may have been vicar; his presentation in 1645 may not, however, have taken effect.[10] Other 17th-century incumbents were Thomas Bannings, who took the parish's surplice with him on moving to another living c. 1660, and his successor Francis Hubert, who was ejected in 1662.[11] Perhaps as a result of Hubert's influence the altar rail was removed and had not been replaced by 1674.[12] From 1747 to 1865 the parish was served from Avebury.[13] A service with a sermon was held at Winterbourne Monkton on alternate Sundays and communion was celebrated four times a year in the late 18th century. Church attendance was poor and absentees excused themselves on grounds considered trivial by the vicar, such as the lack of respectable clothing.[14] In 1864 services were held every Sunday and the average congregation numbered 65 people.[15] In 1865 augmentation of the united benefice of Berwick Bassett with Winterbourne Monkton was made conditional upon the employment of a curate at Winterbourne Monkton.[16] That condition was replaced in 1875 by the stipulation that two services be held there each Sunday.[17]

The dedication of the church of *ST. MARY MAGDALENE* has not been traced before the mid 18th century.[18] The church is built of coursed sarsen rubble and has a chancel with north vestry, a nave with south porch, and a timber-framed and boarded tower rising from the west end of the nave. The bowl of the font is of the late 12th century but the earliest part of the building is the 13th-century chancel. The nave was completely rebuilt in the 14th century. Beside the chancel arch there are cusped niches and a small piscina to serve an altar. In the 15th century the east window and the nave roof were renewed and the porch was added. The tower, the date of which is not known, is supported on the west side by the nave wall. On the east side there are two heavy cylindrical wooden posts which rise from the floor of the nave. The church was refitted in the 17th century. A communion table of 1678 and an early 17th-century pulpit survive and there were formerly pews and a communion rail of similar date to the pulpit. In the 18th century a gallery was built at the west

end of the nave. It was removed before 1878 when the church was restored.[19]

In 1553 some church plate was confiscated but a chalice was left.[20] A late 16th-century chalice, an almsdish of 1683, and a chalice and paten of 1723, all given in 1844, remained in the parish in 1980.[21] There were three bells in 1553. New bells were cast in 1617, 1641, and 1663.[22] The three 17th-century bells hung in the church in 1980.[23] The parish registers begin in 1656 but are incomplete between 1674 and 1719.[24]

NONCONFORMITY. Francis Hubert, the vicar of Winterbourne Monkton ejected in 1662, was later imprisoned presumably for nonconformist activities.[25] In 1669 another ejected minister, John Baker of Chiseldon, lived in the parish and preached in the surrounding area. A conventicle of two or three hundred 'anabaptists, quakers, and presbyterians' met at the house where Baker lodged.[26] Support for dissent within the parish did not last; no dissenter was recorded in 1676 or 1783.[27] A house was registered for nonconformist meetings in 1821.[28] Dissenting teaching was said to retain some influence in 1864 but there was no regular meeting.[29]

EDUCATION. In 1783 the vicar suggested to the bishop that poor children from Winterbourne Monkton should attend the school at Avebury.[30] There was still no school at Winterbourne Monkton in 1818 although the poor were said to desire education for their children.[31] A stone schoolroom and teacher's house were built in 1847 and the school was affiliated to the National Society.[32] By will proved 1854 William Hitchcock gave £360 to be invested for the school. It was thereafter known as Hitchcock's school and in 1905 received £9 a year from the investment.[33] There were eighteen pupils in 1871. The average attendance had risen to 40 by 1906[34] and in 1907 an additional classroom was built.[35] In 1919 there were only 27 pupils but the number rose to c. 45 in the 1930s.[36] The school was closed in 1971 and thereafter children from Winterbourne Monkton attended schools in Avebury and Broad Hinton.[37]

CHARITIES FOR THE POOR. None known.

[10] Below; *Walker Revised*, ed. A. G. Matthews, 376; *W.A.M.* xxxiv. 169.
[11] W.R.O., bishop, chwdns.' pres. 1662; *Calamy Revised*, ed. A. G. Matthews, 280-1.
[12] W.R.O., bishop, chwdns.' pres. 1674.
[13] Above; above, Avebury, church.
[14] *Vis. Queries, 1783* (W.R.S. xxvii), pp. 26, 238-9.
[15] W.R.O., bishop, vis. queries.
[16] *Lond. Gaz.* 5 Oct. 1865, pp. 4775-6.
[17] Ibid. 21 May 1875, p. 2736.
[18] J. Ecton, *Thesaurus* (1763), 400.
[19] *W.A.M.* xxxvii. 453; W.R.O., bishop, pet. for faculties, bdle. 25, no. 7.   [20] *W.A.M.* xii. 364.
[21] Nightingale, *Wilts. Plate*, 144-5; inf. from the Revd. B. A. Tigwell, Broad Hinton Vicarage.
[22] Walters, *Wilts. Bells*, 238.
[23] Inf. from Mr. Tigwell.
[24] W.R.O. 1295/1-8. Transcripts exist for 1605-9, 1621-4, 1636, 1653-79: ibid. bishop.

[25] *Calamy Revised*, ed. Matthews, 280-1; *W.N. & Q.* viii. 154.
[26] G. L. Turner, *Orig. Rec.* i. 108.
[27] *W.N. & Q.* iii. 536; *Vis. Queries, 1783* (W.R.S. xxvii), p. 238.
[28] W.R.O., certs. dissenters' meeting hos.
[29] Ibid. bishop, vis. queries.
[30] *Vis. Queries, 1783* (W.R.S. xxvii), p. 238.
[31] *Educ. of Poor Digest*, 1041.
[32] *Endowed Char. Wilts.* (N. Div.), 1023; *Acct. of Wilts. Schs.* 5.
[33] *Endowed Char. Wilts.* (N. Div.), 1023; P.R.O., ED 21/18619.
[34] *Returns relating to Elem. Educ.* 422; *Return of Non-Provided Schs.* 837.
[35] P.R.O., ED 21/18619.
[36] *Bd. of Educ.*, *List 21* (H.M.S.O.).
[37] Inf. from the Revd. B. A. Tigwell, Broad Hinton Vicarage.

THE BOROUGH OF MARLBOROUGH

THE BOROUGH,[1] first referred to in 1086 when it paid a third of its revenues to the Crown,[2] was founded on a royal estate which extended from the Kennet north and south over downland. In the 11th century both borough and estate were called Marlborough ('barrow of Maerla'), perhaps from the prehistoric earthwork which formed the motte of Marlborough Castle.[3] The church recorded at Marlborough in 1086 may have been Preshute church. Preshute parish extended over the rest of the royal estate including Marlborough Castle, and largely (until the 16th century, entirely) enclosed the borough.[4] Marlborough College was opened in 1843 in a house, later an inn, built in Preshute on the castle site from 1688.[5]

The borough lay on a south-west and north-east axis.[6] In the 19th century and earlier it was bounded south-east by the Kennet, south-west by Marlborough Castle, and north-west partly by Back Lane, which followed the line of part of the town ditch mentioned in the 16th century,[7] and Cross, earlier Dark, Lane. On the north-east Marlborough was until the 16th century separated from Preshute by a boundary perhaps marked by Blowhorn Street and Stonebridge Lane where, on the west side of the lane near the junction with the road called St. Martin's, the borough bank is visible.[8] East of that boundary 'new land' belonged to Marlborough before 1252.[9] It remained in Preshute parish as the chapelry of St. Martin until c. 1548[10] when its transfer to Marlborough extended the borough to the river Og. Marlborough Common, given by King John to the borough for pasture,[11] and Port field, acquired by the burgesses in the Middle Ages as arable land, remained in Preshute[12] until 1934,[13] but both are treated as part of Marlborough in this article.

The borough comprised 198 a. (80 ha.), divided on the line of Kingsbury Street between St. Mary's parish, 117 a. (47 ha.), on the east and St. Peter's, 81 a. (33 ha.), on the west.[14] Land around Preshute church, other land south-west and the St. Margaret's district south-east of Marlborough, and the western edge of Marlborough Common, were added to the borough in 1901 as the civil parish of Preshute Within, 400 a. (162 ha.).[15] In 1925 Preshute Within merged with the civil parishes of St. Mary and St. Peter to form the civil parish of Marlborough. The addition of 46 a. (19 ha.) from Mildenhall, 32 a. (13 ha.) from North Savernake (both pieces being part of the areas transferred to those parishes from Preshute in 1901), and a further 824 a. (333 ha.) from Preshute in 1934[16] gave Marlborough an area of 605 ha. (1,496 a.).[17]

Settlement in the borough has been on the clay-with-flints deposits north of High Street and St. Martin's, at c. 150 m., and, at c. 137 m., on the gravel and alluvium of the Kennet and Og south of those streets. The line marked by High Street and St. Martin's is that of the only chalk outcrop in the borough.[18]

A Romano-British burial and pottery near Tin Pit and coins found elsewhere in Marlborough attest Roman activity.[19] The Old Bowling Green at the north-west end of Kingsbury Street is an embanked rectangular enclosure of medieval or later date.[20] The London–Bath road ran through Marlborough but from c. 1706 until c. 1752 it was diverted south of the borough, and re-entered it across Castle Bridge, mentioned in the 16th century and earlier.[21] In 1726 the section from Speenhamland (Berks.) to Marlborough and in 1743 the section from Marlborough to Beckhampton in Avebury were turnpiked.[22] The road began to decline as a coach route in 1840 when the G.W.R. opened a railway line from London to

---

[1] This article was written over the period 1981–2. Thanks are rendered to Mr. E. G. H. Kempson, Sun Cottage, Hyde Lane, for extensive help.
[2] V.C.H. Wilts. ii, pp. 19, 115.
[3] W.A.M. liii. 295; P.N. Wilts. (E.P.N.S.), 297–8; above, Preshute, manors.
[4] Above, Preshute, introduction, church.
[5] Above, Preshute, manors.
[6] Maps used include O.S. Maps 1″, sheets 14 (1817 edn.), 34 (1828 edn.), 157 (1968 edn.); 1/50,000, sheets 173 (1974 edn.), 174 (1974 edn.); 1/25,000, SU 16 (1961 edn.), SU 17 (1960 edn.), SU 26 (1961 edn.); 6″, Wilts. XXIX (1889 edn.); 1/10,000, SU 16 NE. (1961 edn.), SU 17 SE. (1960 edn.), SU 26 SW. (1961 edn.); 1/2,500, Wilts. XXIX. 9 (1900 edn.), SU 1868–1968, SU 1869–1969, SU 2068–2168, SU 2069–2169 (1970 edn.). See plate facing p. 209.
[7] W.A.M. xxxviii. 38; Alnwick Castle Mun., X.II.11, box 14, deed, Lawrence to Yorke, 1637; J. E. Chandler, Hist. Marlborough (priv. print. 1977), 13.

[8] The bank could be seen in 1980 in the garden of Little Thatch, Stonebridge Lane. H. C. Brentnall suggested that the boundary continued on the line of Blowhorn Street south of St. Martin's: W.A.M. liii. 294, 300.
[9] Sar. Chart. and Doc. (Rolls Ser.), 320–1.
[10] P.R.O., C 3/189/78.
[11] Rot. Hund. (Rec. Com.), ii (1), 263.
[12] P.R.O., IR 29/38/188; IR 30/38/188.
[13] Below.
[14] P.R.O., IR 30/38/190; IR 30/38/191; O.S. Map 6″, Wilts. XXIX (1889 edn.).
[15] Census, 1901.
[16] Ibid. 1931.
[17] Ibid. 1971.
[18] Geol. Surv. Map 1″, drift, sheet 266 (1964 edn.).
[19] Chandler, Hist. Marlborough, 3.
[20] V.C.H. Wilts. i (1), 267.
[21] W.S.R.O., PHA 3565; W.R.O., G 22/1/205/2, f. 13v.; Blenheim Mun., map of St. Margaret's, 1752.
[22] V.C.H. Wilts. iv. 258; L.J. xxii. 664; xxvi. 241.

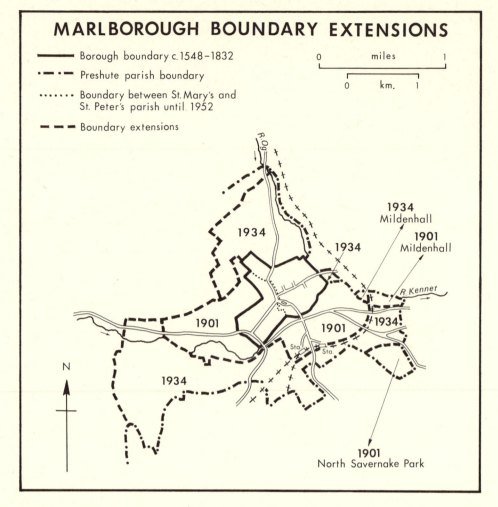

MARLBOROUGH BOUNDARY EXTENSIONS

——— Borough boundary c. 1548–1832

·—·—· Preshute parish boundary

········· Boundary between St. Mary's and St. Peter's parish until 1952

– – – Boundary extensions

0   miles   1

0   km.   1

R. Og.

1934

1934

1934

1934 Mildenhall

1901 Mildenhall

R. Kennet

1901

1901

1934

Sta.   Sta.

N

1934

1901 North Savernake Park

Swindon.[23] Although much traffic was diverted to the London and south Wales motorway opened 12 km. north of Marlborough in 1971,[24] the road was still a main east–west route in 1982. Castle Bridge, renamed Cow Bridge in the 19th century,[25] but also called the Pewsey Road bridge and Duck's Bridge in the 20th,[26] was rebuilt as a concrete beam bridge to designs by F. S. Cutler in 1925.[27] A road which ran north from Marlborough to join the Roman road from Mildenhall to Cirencester possibly followed the line of Barn Street, the Green, and Herd Street from London Road. The Kennet was forded where it left Marlborough:[28] a bridge, called Culbridge c. 1300 and Cow Bridge in the 16th century and 1752, had been built there by 1300.[29] In 1773 the main road from Swindon ran by way of the Old Eagle in Ogbourne St. Andrew and through the borough as Kingsbury Street and the Parade to join the Andover and Salisbury road at the south end of Barn Street.[30] The road was turnpiked in 1762.[31] The Parade was replaced as the main

thoroughfare in 1800 by New Road, so called in 1838 and earlier.[32] Another road from Swindon through Ogbourne St. George, which entered Marlborough as Port Hill, was turnpiked in 1819[33] and became the main road to Swindon. Cow Bridge, the name of which was transferred to Castle Bridge in the 19th century,[34] was resited when the Salisbury road in Preshute was diverted eastwards in 1821[35] and was called London Road bridge in 1982. A road from Hungerford (Berks.) through the Kennet valley by Ramsbury and Mildenhall entered Marlborough along St. Martin's. In 1675 that road was used by some travellers and coaches rather than the London–Bath road.[36] Among the smaller bridges which linked Marlborough with Preshute was New Bridge, so called in the 16th century and 1825 but called Stonebridges in 1826,[37] at the south end of Stonebridge (formerly Newbridge) Lane.[38] The railways which served Marlborough from 1864 and 1881 to 1964 lay outside the borough.[39]

Marlborough was the fifth most highly taxed

[23] V.C.H. Wilts. ix. 105.
[24] Rep. Co. Surveyor, 1971–2 (Wilts. co. council), 3.
[25] W.A.M. lxx–lxxi, 100.
[26] Chandler, Hist. Marlborough, 15.
[27] Tablet on bridge.   [28] W.A.M. lxx–lxxi, 100.
[29] P.N. Wilts. (E.P.N.S.), 299; Chandler, Hist. Marlborough, 15; Blenheim Mun., map of St. Margaret's, 1752.
[30] Andrews and Dury, Map (W.R.S. viii), pl. 12.
[31] V.C.H. Wilts. iv. 262; L.J. xxx. 205.

[32] W.R.O., G 22/1/259, bdle. 31, deed, 1800; ibid. 871/36.
[33] V.C.H. Wilts. iv. 263.
[34] Above.
[35] V.C.H. Wilts. iv. 270.
[36] Leland, Itin. ed. Toulmin Smith, iv. 130; J. Ogilby, Brit. (1675), p. 20.
[37] W.R.O., G 22/1/205/2, f. 20; G 22/1/110, pp. 17, 27.
[38] Blenheim Mun., map of St. Margaret's, 1752.
[39] Above, Preshute, introduction.

borough in the county in 1334.[40] Its 462 poll-tax payers constituted the fifth largest fiscal unit in Wiltshire in 1377.[41] Surnames of the members of small Irish and French communities at Marlborough in 1440 indicate their activity in the tanning, gloving, and cloth industries.[42] In 1545 and 1576 there were 47 and 70 people assessed for taxation.[43] From then until the end of the 17th century, when it lost ground to Devizes, Marlborough may have maintained a position in the county second only to Salisbury.[44] In 1801 Marlborough had 2,367 inhabitants,[45] and was clearly more populous than Westbury, probably Calne, and possibly Chippenham.[46] That number was nearly evenly apportioned between the two Marlborough parishes. The population grew until 1871 when of the 3,660 inhabitants 2,004 lived in St. Mary's and 1,656, including 229 Marlborough College pupils, in St. Peter's.[47] Numbers declined to 3,046 in 1901. The addition of Preshute Within to the borough increased Marlborough's population, which had reached 4,401 by 1911: 1,289 lived in Preshute Within, 1,677 in St. Mary's parish, and 1,435 in St. Peter's. The population declined from 1911 to 1931 when the particularly low total of 3,492 was attributed to the temporary absence of Marlborough College pupils.[48] The addition of more land from Preshute and Mildenhall in 1934 increased the population. In 1951 the enlarged borough had 4,557 inhabitants, 6,108 in 1971.[49] Numbers had declined to 5,771 by 1981 when Marlborough was the eleventh largest town in Wiltshire.[50]

General eyres were held at Marlborough in the 13th century,[51] and in 1280 the transfer of the county court thither from Wilton was considered.[52] Forest eyres were often held at Marlborough in the 14th and 15th centuries.[53] County quarter sessions were held there in 1383 or earlier, in 1660 and later at Michaelmas,[54] until abolished by Act of 1971.[55]

The town supported the parliamentary cause during the Civil War. It was captured on 5 December 1642 by royalist forces from Oxford and houses and property were destroyed.[56] Charles I in 1644 quartered his troops on the downs north of the town.[57] Marlborough was reoccupied by parliamentary forces in 1645.[58]

Marlborough gave its name to a suffragan see established in 1534.[59] A bishop suffragan of Marlborough was appointed in 1537 to assist the

bishop of Salisbury,[60] but the title afterwards lapsed. It was revived in 1888 when a bishop suffragan of Marlborough was appointed to assist the bishop of London but lapsed in 1919.[61]

Walter Map, who stayed at Marlborough Castle with Henry II in 1182, commenting on Marlborough's lack of sophistication, told a story that whoever drank from a particular spring there would thereafter speak bad, or 'Marlborough', French.[62] The same rusticity perhaps produced 'Marlborough-handed' as a local adjective meaning left-handed or clumsy.[63]

Cardinal Wolsey was ordained priest in St. Peter's church in 1498.[64] Henry Sacheverell was born at Marlborough in 1674,[65] the son of Joshua Sacheverell, rector of St. Peter's church.[66] The writer and dramatist John Hughes (d. 1720) was born in 1677 in Marlborough where his grandfather William Hughes, who had been ejected from St. Mary's vicarage in 1662, remained as a dissenting minister and schoolmaster.[67] Sir Michael Foster (d. 1763), born in the town in 1689 and educated at the grammar school, became a judge of King's Bench.[68] Walter Harte (d. 1774), a writer on miscellaneous subjects, may have been born in Marlborough and certainly attended the grammar school. Three of the Merriman family, all born in Marlborough, became medical men of note in London, Samuel (1731-1818) and his nephews Samuel (1771-1852) and John (1774-1839).[69] Thomas Hancock (d. 1865), founder of the British indiarubber industry, and his brother Walter (d. 1852), pioneer of steam locomotives, were born in Marlborough.[70]

The town lies where two main routes cross, the London–Bath road forming High Street and at one time St. Martin's, and the Salisbury–Swindon road formerly taking two possible routes, one along the Parade and Kingsbury Street, the other along Barn Street and Herd Street. The crossing of the Kennet by the Salisbury–Swindon road was shared by an alternative route from London which by the late 17th century had taken some, and by the 18th all, of the traffic from St. Martin's.[71] It is unknown whether the rectilinear settlement marked by Kingsbury Street and Herd Street is earlier or later than the linear settlement along High Street. High Street, mentioned in 1289,[72] follows the line of the chalk outcrop, has a breadth of

[40] V.C.H. Wilts. iv. 296.
[41] Ibid. 306, 312.
[42] P.R.O., E 179/196/100.
[43] Taxation Lists (W.R.S. x), 25, 91-3.
[44] V.C.H. Wilts. x. 256.
[45] Except where stated, population figures are from ibid. iv. 353.
[46] Ibid. 343-4, 360.
[47] Ibid. 324.
[48] Ibid. 326.
[49] Census, 1971.
[50] Ibid. 1981.
[51] e.g. P.R.O., JUST 1/1011, rot. 64.
[52] Cal. Inq. Misc. i, p. 359.
[53] V.C.H. Wilts. iv. 394-5, 420.
[54] Ibid. v. 35, 177.
[55] Courts Act, 1971, c. 23.
[56] V.C.H. Wilts. v. 140, 143.
[57] Diary of Marches of Royal Army (Camd. Soc. [1st ser.], lxxiv), 3, 151.
[58] V.C.H. Wilts. v. 142.
[59] Nomination of Suffragans Act, 26 Hen. VIII, c. 14.
[60] Lamb. Palace Libr., reg. Cranmer, f. 202v.
[61] Crockford (1896, 1926).
[62] De Nugis Curialum (Camd. Soc. [1st ser.], l), 235-6; R. W. Eyton, Itin. Hen. II, 246. Evidence of a sch. at Marlborough for the teaching of French may, wrongly, have been deduced from Map's story: Encyc. Brit. (11th edn.), ii. 31.
[63] J. Wright, Eng. Dialect Dict. iv. 40.
[64] E.H.R. ix. 709.
[65] Coll. Topog. et Gen. v. 260; see above, plate facing p. 193.
[66] A. R. Stedman, Marlborough and the Upper Kennet Country (Marlborough, priv. print. 1960), 195.
[67] D.N.B.; below, churches, prot. nonconf., educ.
[68] E. Foss, Judges of Eng. viii. 285-7.
[69] D.N.B.
[70] Ibid.
[71] Ogilby, Brit. pp. 20-1, pls. 10-11; W.S.R.O., PHA 3565; Blenheim Mun., map of St. Margaret's, 1752.
[72] P.R.O., JUST 1/1011, rot. 64.

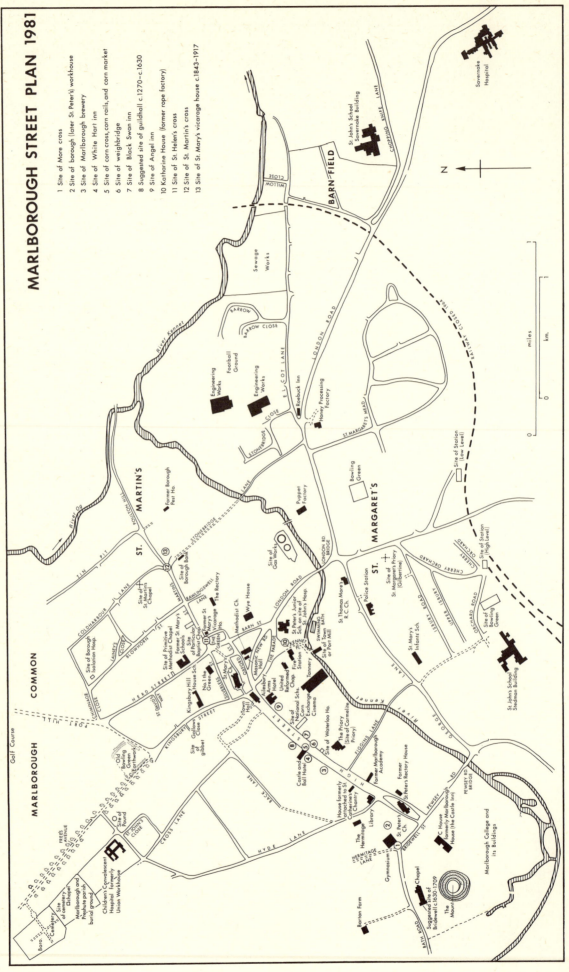

MARLBOROUGH STREET PLAN 1981

1 Site of More cross
2 Site of borough (later St. Peter's) workhouse
3 Site of Marlborough brewery
4 Site of White Hart inn
5 Site of corn cross, corn rails, and corn market
6 Site of weighbridge
7 Site of Black Swan inn
8 Suggested site of guildhall c.1270–c.1630
9 Site of Angel inn
10 Katharine House (former rope factory)
11 Site of St. Helen's cross
12 Site of St. Martin's cross
13 Site of St. Mary's vicarage house c.1843–1917

32 m.,[73] and is flanked by characteristically long and narrow burgage tenements,[74] features which suggest that it represents the borough established by 1086.[75] From the 15th century it contained many inns.[76] It may once have run the full 900 m. between the Green, where its line crosses that of Herd Street and Barn Street, and the castle, but within that length a church had been built by 1223[77] at each end on the line of the middle of the street; each church lies within a churchyard, and St. Mary's churchyard, at the east end, is enclosed by houses. The Green was mentioned in 1289, when the 'new land' north-east of it had been built on, formed a ward of the borough, and was crossed by the highway later called St. Martin's.[78] Land in Barn Street was leased for building in the later 14th century,[79] and Herd Street was mentioned in the earlier 15th.[80] North of St. Mary's church Silverless Street, called Silver Street in 1536[81] and 1540,[82] Silverless Street in 1582,[83] may have been inhabited by the Jews who lived in Marlborough in the 13th century.[84] North-east of the Green, Blowhorn (or Pylat) Street, Coldharbour (or St. Martin's) Lane, and Bay (or Tin) Pit, were mentioned in the 16th century. Kingsbury Street north-west of St. Mary's church was mentioned in the 15th century.[85] Its south-eastern continuation was called the Marsh in the 15th century, by which time it may have been built on,[86] and c. 1900,[87] the Parade in 1982. The lanes and passages between the burgage plots on the south side of High Street included Figgins Lane, called Dame Isabel's Lane in 1320[88] and Dame Isabel's or Lovell's Lane in 1652.[89] To the north Hyde Lane was named after the Hyde family who lived there in the 18th century:[90] it was called Blind Lane in the 15th[91] and 18th centuries,[92] Sun Lane briefly from c. 1900.[93] Hermitage Lane was mentioned in the 1560s.[94] The bridewell built on the east side of it in 1709 gave its name to Bridewell Street,[95] that part of the Bath road west of St. Peter's church.

There were four or more town crosses in the 16th century and six in the 17th. The high or market cross, which c. 1570 stood at the east end of High Street,[96] was rebuilt or much repaired in 1572–3.[97] It contained the market house.[98] A new town hall and market house were erected on its site c. 1630 and rebuilt in the mid 17th century, the late 18th, and early 20th.[99] The corn cross, frequently repaired in the 16th century and earlier 17th,[1] was in High Street,[2] near the Castle and Ball inn outside which the corn market may have been held.[3] St. Martin's cross may have stood c. 1565 at the junction of St. Martin's, Coldharbour Lane, and Stonebridge Lane.[4] St. Helen's cross, mentioned in 1584 and 1616,[5] may have stood at the entrance to St. Martin's north of the Green.[6] More cross, mentioned in 1625, may have stood east of Bridewell Street;[7] the site of St. Denis's cross, named in 1617,[8] is unknown.

Surviving buildings suggest that in the 17th century most of High Street, the south end of Kingsbury Street, Silverless Street, and the north and west sides of the Green were continuously built up with two-storeyed timber-framed and plastered houses of which some had attics. The area north of High Street called the Hermitage[9] had on it successive houses of that name. One of them, on the west side of Hyde Lane, was built in 1628 by John Lawrence, whose initials and the date appear on the north gable.[10] John Hyde, who became owner in 1740,[11] may have extended the house westwards and refitted it. Further alterations were made by Thomas Brudenell-Bruce, earl of Ailesbury, who bought it c. 1812.[12] It was a boarding house of Marlborough College in 1982.

The destruction caused on 28 April 1653 by a fire which began in a tannery at the western end of the south side of High Street[13] has been described as nearly total,[14] but may have been much less. Jettied houses of the mid 16th century in High Street and other jettied houses at nos. 9 and 43 Kingsbury Street,[15] nos. 6–7 and 13–15 Silverless Street, and nos. 2–3 the Green survived it, and more pre-1653 houses may have been obscured by later alterations. On the north side of High Street no. 136 (the White Horse bookshop) has moulded ceiling beams of the later 16th or earlier 17th century, and in no. 138

[73] Although High Street runs SW. and NE. it is hereafter treated as running W. and E. See plate facing p. 209.
[74] *Cal. Inq. Misc.* i, pp. 75–6; W.R.O. 9, survey of Marlborough, 1547.
[75] *V.C.H. Wilts.* ii, pp. 19, 115.
[76] Below, econ. hist.
[77] *Sar. Chart. and Doc.* (Rolls Ser.), 123–4.
[78] P.R.O., JUST 1/1011, rot. 64; see plate facing p. 208.
[79] *Bradenstoke Cart.* (W.R.S. xxxv), pp. 88–9.
[80] *P.N. Wilts.* (E.P.N.S.), 299.
[81] W.R.O., G 22/1/17, p. 52.
[82] *P.N. Wilts.* (E.P.N.S.), 299.
[83] W.R.O. 1197/21.
[84] Below, econ. hist.
[85] *P.N. Wilts.* (E.P.N.S.), 298–9.
[86] *Cat. Anct. D.* vi, C 3772.
[87] O.S. Map 1/2,500, Wilts. XXIX. 9 (1900 edn.).
[88] *Reg. Martival* (Cant. & York Soc.), ii. 272.
[89] Alnwick Castle Mun., X.II.11, box 17, draft deed, Brown to Lawrence.
[90] W.R.O. 9/19/567. It is unlikely that the name derives from Sir Nic. Hyde as suggested in *P.N. Wilts.* (E.P.N.S.), 299.
[91] P.R.O., DL 29/724/11800.
[92] W.R.O. 9/19/567.
[93] O.S. Map 1/2,500, Wilts. XXIX. 9 (1900 edn.).
[94] W.R.O., G 22/1/236, f. 12v.; *W.A.M.* xxxviii. 37.

[95] W.R.O., q. sess. order bk. 1709–37, pp. 1–2; ibid. 9/19/567, deed, Bell to Willoughby, 1738.
[96] C. Hughes, *Marlborough: the Story of a Small and Anct. Boro.* (Swindon, priv. print. [1953]), 17.
[97] W.R.O., G 22/1/205/2, ff. 3–4v.
[98] Below, mkts. and fairs.
[99] J. Waylen, *Hist. Military and Municipal of Marlborough* (1854), 125; below, local govt. (boro. govt.).
[1] *W.A.M.* iii. 112; Hughes, *Marlborough*, 46, 48.
[2] W.R.O., TS. cal. of Ailesbury deeds, comp. E. S. Scroggs, ii, no. 197.
[3] Below, mkts. and fairs.
[4] W.R.O., G 22/1/236, ff. 32–3; MS. map of Marlborough *penes* Mr. Kempson.
[5] W.R.O., G 22/1/205/2, ff. 16, 52.
[6] MS. map *penes* Mr. Kempson.
[7] W.R.O., TS. cal. of Ailesbury deeds, comp. Scroggs, ii, no. 197; ibid. G 22/1/236; ibid. 871/106.
[8] Ibid. G 22/1/205/2, f. 53.
[9] P.R.O., E 318/Box 34/1881.
[10] Waylen, *Hist. Marlborough*, 134.
[11] W.R.O. 9/19/567, deed, Willoughby to Hall and Hyde; *V.C.H. Berks.* iv. 242.
[12] W.R.O. 9/19/572–3.
[13] Waylen, *Hist. Marlborough*, 257.
[14] Stedman, *Marlborough*, 138.
[15] For no. 43 see plate facing p. 209.

(Cavendish House) similar beams and a principal chimney stack and fireplace of *c.* 1600 survive. Following the fire of 1653 a national collection was taken to enable the inhabitants to rebuild,[16] but claims to compensation from it were met only after delay.[17] The fact that John Evelyn could describe Marlborough as 'new built' in June 1654[18] suggests that recovery was by repair rather than by reconstruction. Samuel Pepys, who in 1668 stayed at the White Hart, considered Marlborough to be 'a pretty fair town for a street or two' and remarked upon the walk afforded by the penthouses in High Street.[19] Short stretches, apparently of 19th-century construction, survived in 1982 at the east end of both sides.[20] The continued use of timber and thatch caused other, less severe, fires in 1679 and 1690.[21] The ineffective bylaw of 1622 under which a penalty of £5 might be imposed on those who built thatched houses with inadequate foundations or chimney stacks[22] was reinforced in 1690 by a private Act which forbade the thatching of roofs.[23]

From the mid 18th century much of High Street was either rebuilt in brick or refronted with patterned or mathematical tiles. Characteristic of the buildings of the period were the initialled and dated lead rainwater heads, such as that of 1748 at no. 98 High Street, and the use of red brick with dark headers. The upper floors of most houses at the eastern end of the north side of High Street were given canted bays, often of two storeys, in the earlier 19th century.[24]

In the late 18th century groups and terraces of houses, usually of red brick with slated roofs, were built along St. Martin's, Kingsbury Street, Barn Street, and elsewhere, possibly on new sites.[25] Of those houses, only Kingsbury Hill House in Kingsbury Street is large: it is dated 1774. Yards surviving from earlier inns on either, but mostly on the south, side of High Street, from which they were entered by passages, were closely built up with cottages in the later 18th century. Those, and other poor houses in the town, were removed between 1925 and 1933,[26] and replaced by council houses in the Lainey's Close and St. Margaret's areas.[27] Marlborough College expanded west of High Street in the 19th century and the 20th, and most building, both council and private, has taken place in the roads running north and south of St. Martin's and in the St. Margaret's area transferred to the borough in 1901. The only substantial buildings between High Street and London Road bridge are in the Parade. Katharine House, formerly a rope

factory, is of the 16th century, Wye House, built *c.* 1800 at the south end of Barn Street, was the home of the architect C. E. Ponting from 1905,[28] and St. Peter's Junior School, formerly the grammar school, is a red-brick building of 1905.

SOCIAL AND CULTURAL ACTIVITIES. Race meetings were held intermittently on Barton Down in Preshute in the 18th century and in the 19th. The 18th-century meetings, which usually lasted two days, were social events accompanied by backsword-playing, balls, plays, public dinners, and assemblies. Assemblies held at the town hall in 1771 were attended by local nobility and gentry. Race meetings ceased *c.* 1773, were revived *c.* 1840, but had finally ceased by 1874. The course ran parallel to the Marlborough–Rockley road on Marlborough Common. A grandstand was erected in 1846 and demolished in 1876.[29]

Cricket was played at Marlborough in 1774 when Marlborough tradesmen played against Devizes tradesmen on neutral ground. A game between townsmen was played on Marlborough Common in 1787.[30] A pitch was made there *c.* 1881.[31] In the late 19th century Wiltshire County Cricket Club occasionally played matches at Marlborough.[32] Marlborough Town Football Club, formed in 1871, at first played on Marlborough Common[33] but by 1937 had acquired a ground north of Elcot Lane which was still used in 1982. Marlborough Golf Club, founded in 1888, had a course on the common west of Port Hill.[34] Play ceased there during the Second World War. The course was afterwards remade, and until 1970, when it regained its independence, the club was run by the borough council.[35] Marlborough Bowling Club, founded *c.* 1930,[36] had a green south of Orchard Road. A new green at the recreation ground in Salisbury Road had been laid out by 1970.[37] Other groups, such as gymnastic and athletic clubs in the later 19th century,[38] and hockey, rifle, tennis, and badminton clubs in the 20th,[39] have also existed.

The guild of Palmers at Ludlow (Salop.) had members at Marlborough, one of whom devised property in Kingsbury Street to it, in the later 15th century and earlier 16th.[40]

A masonic lodge which met in 1768 at the Castle inn had been dissolved by 1777. A Wiltshire Militia lodge met from 1803 to 1805, became permanent when the regimental headquarters of the Wiltshire Militia were established at Marlborough in 1818, and took the name Lodge of Loyalty. It was dissolved in 1834.

[16] *Cal. S.P. Dom.* 1652–3, 336.
[17] Stedman, *Marlborough*, 140.
[18] J. Evelyn, *Diary*, ed. E. S. de Beer, iii. 99.
[19] S. Pepys, *Diary*, ed. R. Latham and W. Matthews, ix. 241, where the White Hart is identified as the inn of that name at the corner of the Green and St. Martin's. It is more likely to have been the White Hart on the site of nos. 114–15 High Street: Chandler, *Hist. Marlborough*, 13.
[20] See plate facing p. 208.
[21] *C.J.* x. 410.
[22] Waylen, *Hist. Marlborough*, 123.
[23] *C.J.* x. 410; *L.J.* xiv. 557.
[24] See plate facing p. 208.
[25] For Barn Street see plate facing p. 209.
[26] Stedman, *Marlborough*, 328.
[27] Below, public services.

[28] Stedman, *Marlborough*, 345–6.
[29] *V.C.H. Wilts.* iv. 381.
[30] Ibid. 377–8.
[31] Stedman, *Marlborough*, 309.
[32] *V.C.H. Wilts.* iv. 378.
[33] *Lucy's Marlborough Dir.* (1879).
[34] *Gale's Marlborough Dir.* (1937).
[35] Stedman, *Marlborough*, 309–10; inf. from the Town Clerk, Council Offices.
[36] Stedman, *Marlborough*, 328.
[37] *Gale's Marlborough Dir.* (1937); O.S. Map 1/2,500, SU 1868–1968 (1970 edn.).
[38] *Lucy's Marlborough Dir.* (1879, 1897).
[39] *Gale's Marlborough Dir.* (1937); *Fletcher's Marlborough Dir.* (1962–3); *Marlborough Official Guide* (1978).
[40] *W.A.M.* lvii. 50–4.

Marlborough Lodge of Unity, renamed Lodge of Loyalty, was formed in 1875 and since 1911 or earlier has met at the Masonic Hall, Oxford Street. The Methuen Chapter of Royal Arch Masons, formed in 1883, the St. Peter and St. Paul Preceptory of Masonic Knights Templar, formed in 1962, and the Lodge of Good Fellowship, formed in 1971, also met there in 1982.[41]

The Independent Order of Good Templars had established the Hope of Marlborough Lodge by 1879. In that year the Ancient Order of Foresters met monthly, and the Independent Order of Oddfellows fortnightly, at the Royal Oak.[42] There were five friendly societies, including Foresters, Oddfellows, and Rechabites, in Marlborough in 1937.[43] The Savernake Forest and Sir William Dickson lodges of the Royal Antediluvian Order of Buffaloes met at Marlborough in 1978.[44]

There was a coffee house in the town in 1771.[45] The Marlborough Club, whose members were Tory gentlemen from Marlborough and the surrounding area, was established in 1774. It met at the Castle inn until 1842 and at the Ailesbury Arms until 1846 when it was wound up.[46] The Marlborough Reading and Mutual Improvement Society was formed in 1844.[47] It had 90 'middle class' members and a library of 800 volumes in 1849.[48] The society opened a reading room in High Street in 1854,[49] still flourished in 1903,[50] but had been wound up by 1907.[51]

A working men's hall was opened in High Street in 1866 with a reading room, smoking room, and classroom which was used each evening.[52] The hall was still used in 1903.[53] Marlborough and District Unionist Association had been formed by 1907.[54] Since 1923[55] Marlborough and District Conservative Club has had premises in High Street.

Marlborough Choral Society, founded in 1877, had c. 80 members in 1879[56] and still met in 1937[57] and 1982. A silver band flourished in the town in the late 19th century and earlier 20th.[58] An amateur dramatic and operatic society was founded in 1923.[59] The corn exchange was converted c. 1914 to a cinema,[60] which closed in 1970.[61]

Apart from Salisbury, Marlborough was the only Wiltshire town in which a newspaper was published in the later 18th century. The *Marlborough Journal* was printed weekly at no. 132 High Street, by J. Smith and E. Harold in 1771, by Harold alone in 1773, but ceased publication in 1774.[62] The *Marlborough Times*, the title of which has been extended and changed frequently, was founded in 1859 by Charles Perkins. It was printed weekly at Waterloo House in High Street.[63] Its Tory attitudes reflected those of the marquesses of Ailesbury, lords of the borough, until 1885 when the newspaper became politically neutral.[64] Publication was continued after Perkins's death in 1899 by his son H. G. Perkins.[65] The newspaper was bought from E. H. Perkins & Son Ltd. in 1962 by Woodrow Wyatt Ltd. Its printing works and offices were moved from Waterloo House, which had been demolished by 1977, to Banbury (Oxon.). In 1966 the newspaper was bought by Cirencester Newspaper Co. Ltd., publishers in 1982, and printed at Dursley (Glos.).[66] The *Marlborough and Hungerford Express*, begun by William Cane in 1860, expressed Liberal views. It was printed weekly at no. 100 High Street until 1863 when it ceased publication.[67] From 1902 to 1928 *Wiltshire Opinion*, later *Wiltshire Opinion Special*, and from 1910 to 1914 the *Andover Times and Wilts., Berks., and Hants County Paper* were published at Marlborough. The *Wiltshire Echo* was published in Marlborough from 1964 to 1966, afterwards in Trowbridge and Swindon.[68]

ESTATES. Marlborough was in the king's hands in 1086.[69] Except during the period 1189–93 when John, count of Mortain, held it with Marlborough Castle, the BOROUGH belonged to successive kings until 1273. Their authority over it was delegated to the constables who were appointed to keep the castle.[70] The borough was assigned in 1273 for life to Queen Eleanor (d. 1291), in 1299 to Queen Margaret, in 1318 to Queen Isabel, who was deprived of it in the period 1324–7, and in 1330 to Queen Philippa, on whose death in 1369 it reverted to the Crown.[71] In 1403 the reversion of the lordship on the death of Henry IV was granted to Humphrey, duke of Gloucester; from 1415 or earlier until 1621 the lordship descended with the site of Marlborough Castle, from 1621 to 1779 with Barton manor in Preshute, and from 1779 to 1929–30 with both.[72]

[41] Inf. from Mr. J. M. Hamill, Libr. and Mus. of United Grand Lodge of Eng., Freemasons' Hall, Lond.
[42] *Lucy's Marlborough Dir.* (1879).
[43] *Gale's Marlborough Dir.* (1937).
[44] *Marlborough Official Guide* (1978).
[45] *V.C.H. Wilts.* iv. 381.
[46] W.R.O. 9, list of meetings; Stedman, *Marlborough*, 250.
[47] *Harrod's Dir. Wilts.* (1865).
[48] *Rep. Sel. Cttee. on Public Libr.* H.C. 548, App. 3, p. 313 (1849), xvii.
[49] *Harrod's Dir. Wilts.* (1865).
[50] *Kelly's Dir. Wilts.* (1903).
[51] Ibid. (1907).
[52] *Lucy's Marlborough Dir.* (1879).
[53] *Kelly's Dir. Wilts.* (1903).
[54] Ibid. (1907).
[55] Ibid. (1923).
[56] *Lucy's Marlborough Dir.* (1879).
[57] *Gale's Marlborough Dir.* (1937).
[58] W.R.O., G 22/991/1–9; *Lucy's Marlborough Dir.* (1897); *Gale's Marlborough Dir.* (1937).
[59] *Gale's Marlborough Dir.* (1937).
[60] W.R.O., G 22/111/7, pp. 37, 114.
[61] Chandler, *Hist. Marlborough*, 12. The Waitrose supermarket occupied the site in 1981.
[62] *W.A.M.* xl. 129–31; Stedman, *Marlborough*, 251.
[63] *W.A.M.* xl. 133–4.
[64] Ibid. 134; below, estates.
[65] *W.A.M.* xl. 136.
[66] Inf. from Mr. G. H. Collicutt, Cirencester Newspaper Co. Ltd., Cirencester, Glos.; Chandler, *Hist. Marlborough*, 12.
[67] *W.A.M.* xl. 133, where publ. is wrongly said to have begun in 1861: cf. *Bibliog. Brit. Newspapers: Wilts.* (Libr. Assoc.), 19.
[68] *Bibliog. Brit. Newspapers: Wilts.* (Libr. Assoc.), 19.
[69] *V.C.H. Wilts.* ii, p. 115.
[70] Mat. Paris, *Hist. Angl.* (Rolls Ser.), ii. 5; *Ann. Mon.* (Rolls Ser.), iv. 46–7; above, Preshute, Marlborough Castle.
[71] *Cal. Pat.* 1272–81, 27; 1292–1301, 451–4; 1317–21, 115; 1327–30, 556; 1330–4, 55; 1367–70, 301, 452; *Cal. Close*, 1272–9, 31; M. McKisack, *Fourteenth Cent.* 81, 97, 102.
[72] Above, Preshute, manors.

In 1929–30 George, marquess of Ailesbury, sold the lordship of the borough to Marlborough borough council.[73]

The site in the Marsh given by Levenoth son of Levenoth for the hospital of St. John the Baptist, and other land in Marlborough given by John son of Elfric and by Walter Pinnock, were confirmed to the hospital by King John in 1215.[74] In 1550 the mayor and burgesses of Marlborough, who had presented masters of the hospital from 1315 or earlier, received royal permission to convert the house to a free grammar school. The school was endowed with the lands of the hospital and with those of the Jesus services in the churches of St. Mary and St. Peter.[75] Most of the hospital's lands may have been alienated before 1637. Small properties in the town were sold in 1799 and 1867.[76] In 1883 the endowments included 11 a. in Marlborough.[77] The largest remaining town properties, St. John's close south-west of Marlborough Common and a close in St. Martin's, were sold in 1907 and in 1924 respectively.[78]

In 1316 William Ramshill and John Goodhind received royal permission to convey land in Marlborough to the Carmelites, who built a priory on it.[79] Ramshill and Goodhind conveyed more land in 1321 and in 1328 Adam Long gave a messuage in Marlborough to the friars.[80] The priory was dissolved in 1538. Its property, which comprised church, cloister, chapter house, dormitory, prior's lodging, kitchen, and land,[81] was conveyed by the Crown to Robert Were or Brown in 1543.[82] Robert, M.P. for Marlborough in 1553 and many times mayor of the borough,[83] died in 1570 and was succeeded by his wife Agnes. On Agnes's death the property passed to their son Richard Were or Brown (d. 1577), to successive sons Thomas Were or Brown (d. 1599), Thomas Were or Brown (d. 1608), and Thomas Brown (d. 1625), and then to the last Thomas's brother Robert Brown.[84] By the early 17th century the estate had been augmented by numerous town properties.[85] In 1652 a Robert Brown, perhaps the Robert who succeeded in 1625, settled it on his son Robert who in 1658 sold it to Isaac Burgess.[86] In 1676 the estate belonged to another Isaac Burgess and his wife Cecily,[87] and in 1701 to Cecily and her second husband William Master. Isaac's and Cecily's heirs were their daughters Cecily, wife of James Worthington, and Anne who married Thomas Fletcher.[88] Cecily Worthington was dead by 1708 when the Fletchers owned the estate.[89]

Parts of that estate, including, after 1701, the house called the Friars in 1596 and in the early 18th century the Priory, were sold and later became part of the Savernake estate of the earls and marquesses of Ailesbury.[90] What remained Anne Fletcher's in 1751 included inns in High Street then called the Swan, the Antelope (later the Castle and Ball), the Bull, and the Half Moon.[91] They were sold in 1773 by the executors of her daughter Anne Fletcher to Thomas, Lord Bruce,[92] and added to the Savernake estate. The Savernake estate sold parts of what had once belonged to the Fletchers, such as the Castle and Ball in 1872,[93] but leased Priory House to the governors of Marlborough College in 1850.[94] It was a college boarding house from 1861 to 1967.[95] A housemaster, W. Mansell, bought it from the Savernake estate in 1876 and sold it in 1899 to another, J. P. Cummins. T. C. G. Sandford bought Priory House from Cummins in 1917 and in 1923 sold it to Marlborough College,[96] from which it was bought in 1971 by the borough council with help from Mrs. J. Clay.[97] In 1981 the house contained a day centre and flatlets for the elderly and the gardens were a public park.

The remains of the priory buildings were replaced in 1823 by Priory House built in Gothic style of flint and sarsen.[98] A west block, which matched the style of the house of 1823, was built to designs by Ernest Newton in 1926.[99]

Arnold Fathers gave 1½ burgage to Bradenstoke priory c. 1245 and also in the 13th century Eustace, parson of 'Wootton', gave to the priory three shops and a store abutting the market place beside St. Mary's churchyard.[1] In 1272 Thomas Green gave the priory 1¼ burgage and a messuage.[2] The properties, which included market stalls, were in High Street, the Green, Barn Street, and the Marsh.[3] They passed to the Crown at the Dissolution and were sold to Geoffrey Daniell in 1544.[4]

Maiden Bradley priory acquired, all in Marlborough, a burgage from John Whatley c. 1260, a

[73] W.R.O., G 22/100/11, pp. 154, 198, 200.
[74] Rot. Chart. (Rec. Com.), 205.
[75] V.C.H. Wilts. iii. 341–2; v. 359–60; Cal. Pat. 1549–51, 226.
[76] A. R. Stedman, Hist. Marlborough Grammar Sch. (Devizes, priv. print. [1946]), 104.
[77] W.R.O., Marlborough Grammar Sch. min. bk. 1.
[78] Stedman, Hist. Marlborough Grammar Sch. 104.
[79] Cal. Pat. 1313–17, 378. An acct. of the priory is in V.C.H. Wilts. iii. 333–4.
[80] Cal. Pat. 1317–21, 551; 1327–30, 333.
[81] V.C.H. Wilts. iii. 333; P.R.O., SC 6/Hen. VIII/7407, rot. 3; ibid. E 318/Box 18/910, rot. 2.
[82] L. & P. Hen. VIII, xviii (1), p. 132.
[83] Hist. Parl., Commons, 1509–58, iii. 562–3; Chandler, Hist. Marlborough, 44.
[84] W.A.M. xxxiv. 199–200; Taxation Lists (W.R.S. x), 91; P.R.O., PROB 11/52 (P.C.C. 37 Lyon, will of Rob. Were or Brown); PROB 11/59 (P.C.C. 35 Daughtry, will of Ric. Were or Brown); ibid. C 142/263, no. 2 (i); C 142/301, no. 85; C 60/434, no. 28; C 60/494, no. 31; Wilts. Inq. p.m. 1625–49 (Index Libr.), 1–2.
[85] P.R.O., C 142/301, no. 85.
[86] W.R.O. 9/19/113–14; 9/19/119.

[87] Ibid. 9/19/123.
[88] Ibid. 9/19/124; P.R.O., C 78/1342, no. 2.
[89] W.R.O. 9/19/125–7; D.N.B. where Fletcher's wife is said, wrongly, to have been the daughter of Wm. Master.
[90] W.R.O. 9/19/112; P.R.O., C 78/1342, no. 2; Alnwick Castle Mun., X.II.11, box 14, deed, Fletcher to Hertford, 1727.
[91] W.R.O. 9/19/139; Chandler, Hist. Marlborough, 12–13.
[92] W.R.O. 9/19/145; 9/19/147–8.
[93] W.A.S. Libr., sale cat. viii, no. 18.
[94] W.R.O. 9/19/864.
[95] Chandler, Hist. Marlborough, 37.
[96] Inf. from Mr. Kempson.
[97] W.R.O., G 22/111/18, gen. purposes cttee. min. 21 Oct. 1968; G 22/100/16, min. 20 Jan. 1969; G 22/100/17, min. 15 Sept. 1970; G 22/100/18, mins. 26 Jan., 20 July, 1971.
[98] Date on NE. wall.
[99] Plans penes the Bursar, Marlborough Coll.
[1] Rot. Hund. (Rec. Com.), ii (1), 261; Bradenstoke Cart. (W.R.S. xxxv), p. 90.
[2] Rot. Hund. (Rec. Com.), ii (1), 261.
[3] Bradenstoke Cart. (W.R.S. xxxv), pp. 87–9.
[4] P.R.O., E 318/Box 9/346.

tenement from John, canon of Wells (Som.), in 1274, 6*d.* rent from a tenement held by Maud Ballemund in the later 13th century, and, at an unknown date, a tenement from Thomas Romsey.[5] The properties, one or more of which was in High Street, passed to the Crown at the Dissolution and were sold to Geoffrey Daniell in 1544.[6]

In the earlier 12th century the Empress Maud gave to Reading abbey the property in Marlborough of Herbert son of Fulk, who had become a monk there. The abbey leased the messuage in 1192 on condition that monks from Reading might lodge there when visiting Marlborough.[7] Stanley abbey was given a burgage in the town *c.* 1266 and, at an unknown date, a house.[8] Bicester priory (Oxon.) had property in Marlborough in 1291.[9] None of the three houses accounted for property in Marlborough in 1535.[10]

AGRICULTURE. A pasture held by the burgesses of Marlborough in 1194 or earlier for 10*s.* paid yearly to the lord of the borough may have been east of Marlborough Castle.[11] In King John's reign the burgesses gave up that pasture in exchange for one which may be identified with Marlborough Common, sometimes called the Thorns, *c.* 80 a., which apart from its south-west corner was in Preshute. The burgesses paid 10*s.* rent for it to the lord of the borough in 1275 and in 1768.[12] Tenants of Barton farm in Preshute also had pasture rights there in 1638.[13] A small rabbit warren on the common was part of Barton farm in the later 16th century and the earlier 17th.[14] Bylaws of 1577 regulated use of the common. A burgess might keep not more than two cows or bullocks on it and was to pay 8*d.* yearly for each animal to the mayor, a day's board to the herdsman who drove the animals to pasture each morning and brought them back in the evening, and 1*d.* yearly for destruction of vermin.[15] A bull, provided until 1836 by the mayor and afterwards by the borough fund, could be hired for 8*d.* It ceased to be kept in 1904.[16] Wandering animals were taken by the herdsman, or hayward as he was apparently called in 1777, to the borough pound which was moved in 1846 from Kingsbury Street to the common.[17] Pasturage fees and the herdsman's wages were increased in the later 19th century and earlier 20th.[18] Rights of pasturage were

apparently extended to all inhabitants of Marlborough from 1836.[19] In 1908 and later the inhabitants could pasture as many cows as they wished for 1*s.* a week for each cow. Yearly income from pasturage of cows declined in the earlier 20th century and in 1919 averaged only £30. That decline led the corporation to allow sheep fairs, agricultural shows, military manoeuvres, and organized games to be held on the common although no regular use, except for race meetings in the 19th century and golf in the 20th, has been allowed.[20] Furze planted on the common in the later 17th century was grubbed up in 1831.[21] Marlborough Common was levelled and reseeded in 1958.[22] It was open in 1982 when it was used chiefly for grazing and recreation.

Arable land in Preshute east of Marlborough Common and called Port field, *c.* 80 a. or more, was acquired between 1216 and 1272 by the mayor and burgesses who paid £6 4*s.* rent yearly for it to the lord of the borough.[23] It was apportioned among the burgesses in plots of 1 a. or 2 a.[24] Its use, like that of the common, was regulated in 1577. The hedges and ditches adjoining the plots which the burgesses were enjoined to maintain in that year may indicate inclosure. For each acre held, the burgesses paid 1*d.* yearly for the destruction of vermin.[25] All the inhabitants of Marlborough could pasture cattle on the linchets of Port field after harvest, a right they may still have enjoyed in the earlier 19th century.[26] The tenant of Barton farm in Preshute had similar rights in 1574[27] and 1638.[28] Inclosures existed in 1627. In that year burgesses, who held for life, were forbidden to hold more than 2 a. each, for which they were to pay 1*s.* 4*d.* yearly and do suit at the mayor's courts.[29] They paid small entry fines, and in 1759 were allowed to hold a maximum of 6 a. each.[30] Any land not held by burgesses was sublet. In 1808 Port field comprised a south field, 36 a., and a north field, 54 a., containing 13 and 38 allotments respectively. By subletting, however, three holdings in the south and four in the north field had been created.[31] Port field was inclosed *c.* 1823[32] and in 1847 had in it allotments of 21 a. and 8 a. and fifteen smaller plots totalling 60 a.[33] In 1930 Marlborough borough council bought the freehold of Port field from George, marquess of Ailesbury.[34] Council houses were built on part of it from the 1960s. The remainder was let as allotments and pasture land in 1982.[35]

[5] *Rot. Hund.* (Rec. Com.), ii (1), 262; P.R.O., E 210/3206; E 210/3516; E 210/4588.
[6] P.R.O., E 318/Box 9/346; E 210/5138.
[7] B.L. Harl. MS. 1708, ff. 17v., 170v.
[8] *V.C.H. Wilts.* iii. 270; *Cat. Anct. D.* iv, A 9375.
[9] *Tax. Eccl.* (Rec. Com.), 192.
[10] e.g. *Valor Eccl.* (Rec. Com.), ii. 114–15, 154, 187.
[11] *Pipe R.* 1194 (P.R.S. n.s. v), 10; *W.A.M.* xlviii. 139.
[12] *Rot. Hund.* (Rec. Com.), ii (1), 263; W.R.O. 9/2/378; Waylen, *Hist. Marlborough*, 103.
[13] Alnwick Castle Mun., X.II.11, box 6, survey of Hertford lands, 1634– , p. 341.
[14] Ibid. X.II.11, box 17, copy survey of Barton farm, 1574; deed, Hertford to Seymour, 1635.
[15] Waylen, *Hist. Marlborough*, 120, 122–3.
[16] Stedman, *Marlborough*, 270.
[17] Ibid. 270–1; W.R.O., G 22/1/150.
[18] Stedman, *Marlborough*, 311.
[19] W.R.O., G 22/100/1.

[20] Stedman, *Marlborough*, 309–11.
[21] Hughes, *Marlborough*, 80.
[22] Stedman, *Marlborough*, 310.
[23] *Rot. Hund.* (Rec. Com.), ii (1), 263; Waylen, *Hist. Marlborough*, 103; P.R.O., SC 6/1055/19; W.R.O., G 22/100/11, p. 154.
[24] Waylen, *Hist. Marlborough*, 103.
[25] Ibid. 120, 122–3.
[26] Ibid. 120; *1st Rep. Com. Mun. Corp.* H.C. 116, App. I, p. 85 (1835), xxiii.
[27] Alnwick Castle Mun., X.II.11, box 17, copy survey of Barton farm.
[28] Ibid. X.II.11, box 6, survey of Hertford lands, 1634– , p. 341. [29] Waylen, *Hist. Marlborough*, 123.
[30] Ibid. 373.
[31] W.R.O., G 22/1/241.
[32] Waylen, *Hist. Marlborough*, 103.
[33] P.R.O., IR 29/38/188; IR 30/38/188.
[34] W.R.O. 9, sale cat. 1929; ibid. G 22/100/11, pp. 154, 198. [35] Inf. from the Town Clerk, Council Offices.

TRADE AND INDUSTRY. The position of Marlborough on a favoured royal estate and a main east–west route made the town a likely commercial centre in the 12th century and earlier. Although no burgess was mentioned in 1086, Marlborough had a mint in the later 11th century and was sufficiently developed commercially for the burgesses to pay £5 to the king to have a merchant guild in 1163.[36] That privilege was confirmed to the burgesses in 1204 when others, mostly modelled on those of Winchester and including a general grant of freedom from toll, were extended to them.[37] That the privileges were limited to members of the merchant guild, which comprised all the burgesses, is clear because in 1239, under the grant of 1204, only they were free of payment of tolls at Southampton.[38] In 1408 Henry IV granted to the burgesses quittance of murage, quayage, coverage, and chiminage on goods and merchandise.[39]

Henry III may have encouraged Jews to settle in the town in 1234 or earlier,[40] and in 1241 five Jewish families lived in Marlborough, possibly under the protection and jurisdiction of the constable of the castle.[41] A chirograph chest, in which records of the Jews' financial dealings were kept, was mentioned in 1268 and the chirographers who compiled the records in 1272.[42] The community was ordered to move to Devizes in 1275[43] but there were still Jews at Marlborough in 1277 and a chirograph chest in 1279.[44] They had all apparently left when in 1281 their property was granted to Christians.[45]

A thriving merchant class, in which John Goodhind, mentioned in the period 1311–43, was apparently pre-eminent, was evident in Marlborough c. 1300 or earlier.[46] It included Irishmen and men from northern France in the earlier 15th century.[47] Much of Marlborough's trade was by way of Bristol and Southampton in the Middle Ages when the town was a market centre for the surrounding countryside. In 1365 wine, iron, and steel were carted to Marlborough from Southampton.[48] In 1439–40 wine, garlic, and grindstones were conveyed to Marlborough and Marlborough merchants distributed woad and fish from Southampton to Salisbury and Broughton Gifford.[49] Seventeen journeys were made from Southampton to cart wine and herrings to Marlborough in 1443–4.[50]

Burel, coarse woollen cloth, was made in Marlborough in the 12th century or earlier. The weavers and fullers who made it were allowed to work only for the burgesses and could not become freemen unless they gave up their crafts. Fulling in nearby mills, including one at Elcot in Preshute used for fulling in 1215 or earlier and for the production of cloth until c. 1800, was presumably connected with the industry in the 13th century and later.[51] It is likely that most of the cloth was sold locally for the poor's use although in 1391 Thomas Tanner, a Marlborough merchant, exported ten cloths to Ireland.[52] Clothmaking was apparently in decline in 1379, when there were only 2 shearmen, 1 tucker, 1 dyer, and 5 weavers in Marlborough, but had recovered by the later 15th century when kerseys may have been made there.[53] Finishing processes may then have been more important than manufacture, although a 'woolman' was mentioned c. 1500.[54] Some of the woad brought from Southampton to Marlborough in the 15th century may have been for use in Marlborough and c. 1460 a dyer from Newbury (Berks.) took a lease of a house in Marlborough which was altered to incorporate a furnace and vats.[55] A weaver, a woollen draper, and a mercer were mentioned in 1674, and a clothier in 1679.[56] Then, as in the Middle Ages, the workers were poor and c. 1698 included those in the workhouse.[57] There was a weaver of broad cloths in the town in 1711, a drugget maker in 1717, and in 1797 a feltmonger, a clothier, and a worsted maker.[58] A woolhouse mentioned in 1744 was possibly no longer used as such in 1771.[59] In 1791 a shed to contain looms was erected at St. Mary's workhouse and in the 1790s a new clothing mill, intended to provide work for the industrious poor, was built to adjoin Elcot mill.[60] The venture may have had little success: in 1799 both the clothing mill and the grist mill were leased to a Marlborough baker.[61] Wool stapling was still carried on at Marlborough in 1753 and 1865.[62] Manufacture of fustians may have partly replaced that of woollens by 1800. The spinning of cotton, supplied during the first few months by a Mr. Crook and thereafter until 1773 or later by a Mr. Sheppard, was begun in St. Peter's workhouse in 1751. From 1760 to 1767 John Crook of Marlborough sent cotton to be spun in the Bristol workhouse.[63] Hand spinning of cotton continued at Marlborough until the mid 19th century.[64] An

[36] V.C.H. Wilts. ii, p. 20; Pipe R. 1163 (P.R.S. vi), 46.
[37] Rot. Chart. (Rec. Com.), 135.
[38] Cal. Chart. R. 1226–57, 244.
[39] Ibid. 1341–1417, 438.
[40] Cur. Reg. R. xv. 296; Sel. Cases of Procedure without Writ (Selden Soc. lx), p. 20.
[41] Close R. 1237–42, 355; H. G. Richardson, Eng. Jewry under Angevin Kings, 12, 155.
[42] Sel. Pleas from Exch. of Jews (Selden Soc. xv), pp. 42–3; Plea R. of Exch. of Jews, ii (Jewish Hist. Soc.), 20.
[43] Cal. Pat. 1272–81, 76; Sel. Pleas from Exch. of Jews (Selden Soc. xv), p. 85.
[44] Plea R. of Exch. of Jews, iii (Jewish Hist. Soc.), 273, 307; Richardson, Eng. Jewry, 18.
[45] Cal. Pat. 1272–81, 428–9.
[46] P.R.O., E 179/196/17; e.g. W.R.O., G 22/1/92; Cal. Close, 1343–6, 229; Cal. Inq. Misc. ii, p. 512.
[47] P.R.O., E 179/196/100.
[48] H. S. Cobb, 'Port Bk. of Southampton, 1439–40' (Lond. Univ. M.A. thesis, 1957), pp. xxx–xxxiii.
[49] Brokage Bk. of Southampton, 1439–40 (Southampton

Rec. Soc.), i. 53, 94, 141, 147, 173, 183.
[50] Brokage Bk. of Southampton, 1443–4, i (Southampton Rec. Ser. iv), pp. xxix, 74, 107, 117, 122, 132–3, 140, 183, 191.
[51] V.C.H. Wilts. iv. 117–19; above, Preshute, econ. hist. (Barton).
[52] V.C.H. Wilts. iv. 120; Overseas Trade of Bristol in Later Middle Ages (Bristol Rec. Soc. vii), 199.
[53] V.C.H. Wilts. iv. 122, 140.
[54] Cal. Pat. 1494–1509, 184.
[55] V.C.H. Wilts. iv. 140 and n.
[56] W.R.O. 212B/4698; P.R.O., E 134/26 Chas. II Mich./1.
[57] Waylen, Hist. Marlborough, 274; Endowed Char. Wilts. (N. Div.), 703.
[58] W.R.O. 1197/22; V.C.H. Wilts. iv. 179; Univ. Brit. Dir. v (1797), App. 125–6. [59] W.R.O. 212B/4732; 212B/4747.
[60] Above, Preshute, econ. hist. (Barton).
[61] W.R.O. 9/2/337; 9/2/340.
[62] Ibid. 212B/4738–9; Harrod's Dir. Wilts. (1865).
[63] W.R.O. 871/190; V.C.H. Wilts. iv. 179; Bristol Corp. of Poor, 1696–1834 (Bristol Rec. Soc. iii), 109–10, 112–13.
[64] V.C.H. Wilts. iv. 180.

The Green from the west *c.* 1837. The borough beadle is in the foreground, and R. H. Tucker, vicar of St. Mary's, stands in front of the vicarage house in the centre background.

The eastern end of High Street, flanked by penthouses. The town hall and the tower of St. Mary's church are in the centre background.

MARLBOROUGH

Barn Street from the south-east

Dormy House, no. 43 Kingsbury Street, which survived the fire of 1653

View of the borough from the west, 1960. In the foreground Marlborough College is on the left, St. Peter's church in the centre. The town hall, St. Mary's church, and the Green are in the left background.

MARLBOROUGH

attempt in the early 1790s to establish a silk manufactory, to be financed by public subscription, was apparently unsuccessful.[65]

Sheepskins, wood from Savernake forest, and water from the Kennet provided the means for tanning which flourished in the town in the 14th century. In 1379 there were ten tanners. They included the mayor, who may have traded with Northampton.[66] There were tanners in Marlborough in the earlier 17th century.[67] A decline which the industry later suffered may have been a result of the outbreak of the fire of 1653 in a tannery.[68] The trades associated with tanning at Marlborough since the Middle Ages continued. Gloves were made there in the 17th century[69] as they had been in the 15th.[70] In 1797 there were a fellmonger, a currier, and a leather cutter in the town: their trades were still carried on in the 19th century.[71] The firm of George May & Sons, in business at the Green as curriers and leather cutters in 1830 or earlier, still traded there as Charles B. May in 1907.[72] In 1830 or earlier there was a tannery in Black Swan Yard, and in the 1850s there was one in Angel Yard.[73] In 1865 tanning was again one of the principal industries in Marlborough.[74] Wingrove & Edge Ltd. established a sheepskin tannery in Angel Yard in 1937. The production of hide leather there began in 1950. The firm merged in 1963 with Whitmore's Ltd. of Edenbridge (Kent), afterwards the Whitmore Bacon Organization, which supplied wet chrome-tanned hides to Marlborough for the production of leathers of different grains and suede leathers. From 1967 no sheepskin was treated and most leather produced, of which a fifth was suede, was sold to shoe manufacturers and makers of sports equipment.[75] Some fifty people were employed in 1982.[76]

Rope making was carried on in Marlborough in 1660 or earlier.[77] There was a hemp dresser in the town in 1716, a sack maker in 1719, and a rope maker in 1738.[78] Sail cloth was made there in 1749.[79] Two Henry Shepherds manufactured sacking in 1797, when there were also two ropers in the town, and William Shepherd did so in 1830 in Kingsbury Street and in 1844 in High Street.[80] In St. Mary's parish John Palmer had, in 1844 or earlier, a factory in which in 1862 about twenty people were employed to make rope.[81] In 1865

and until 1965 James Morrison & Co. of High Street made hempen cloth, rope, and twine in a factory, in the Parade, where eleven people were employed in 1960.[82]

Pin making, sufficiently well established in Marlborough for the pin makers to have their own building in 1576, flourished in the 17th century and in the early 18th, as did the associated trade of wire drawing.[83] Clay pipes were made in the town in the earlier 17th century. The manufacture was at its height c. 1700 but had declined by c. 1750 when there was only one pipe maker.[84] Bone lace was made in the 17th century.[85] There were then, and in the 18th century, numerous clock makers, including George Hewett who was at work in the period 1769–97. In 1865 there was only one.[86]

Among the trades usual in a market town that of cheese factor may have gained wider importance in the 17th century when the 'Marlborough' cheeses of the surrounding area, made thin for quick drying, became popular in London, and London cheesemongers may have kept their own factors in the town. Despite waning demand in London c. 1680, Marlborough remained a centre for the sale of cheese and was still such in 1907.[87] There were seven cheese factors in the town in 1797 and in 1844.[88]

Marlborough's prosperity derived not only from its industries and markets but also from the many inns for travellers to and from the west of England.[89] Chief among them from 1456 or earlier to c. 1730 was the Hart, or Old Hart, on the north side of High Street.[90] The coach trade expanded in the early 18th century with the development of Bath, and to a lesser extent of Marlborough itself, as resorts. The principal inns which catered for it were, on the south side of High Street, the Angel, the Black Swan, and the Duke's Arms, in 1843 or earlier called the Ailesbury Arms, and, on the north side, the Antelope, an inn in 1745 and called in 1764 and 1982 the Castle and Ball. An inn called the Castle was opened in 1751 in Marlborough House in Preshute.[91] In 1797 coaches ran daily from the Duke's Arms and the Black Swan to London and Bath, three each way from the Castle daily, and one each way from the Castle and Ball on Mondays, Wednesdays, and Fridays. Nightly

---

[65] Hist. MSS. Com. 43, *15th Rep. VII, Ailesbury*, p. 251.
[66] *V.C.H. Wilts.* iv. 122, 234; *Cal. Pat.* 1391–6, 677.
[67] *W.A.M.* xix. 262; *Early-Stuart Tradesmen* (W.R.S. xv), p. 75.
[68] Waylen, *Hist. Marlborough*, 257, 260.
[69] *W.A.M.* xix. 262.   [70] P.R.O., E 179/196/100.
[71] *V.C.H. Wilts.* iv. 122; *Univ. Brit. Dir.* v (1797), App. 125; Pigot, *Nat. Com. Dir.* (1830), iii. 807; (1844), 24; *Harrod's Dir. Wilts.* (1865).
[72] Pigot, *Nat. Com. Dir.* (1830), iii. 807; *Kelly's Dir. Wilts.* (1907).
[73] Pigot, *Nat. Com. Dir.* (1830), iii. 807; Wilts. Cuttings, xxiii. 268.   [74] *Harrod's Dir. Wilts.* (1865).
[75] Wilts. Cuttings, xxiii. 49, 268.
[76] Inf. from Mrs. G. Pike, Wingrove & Edge Ltd.
[77] B. H. Cunnington, *Pres. of Grand Jury of Q. Sess., Leet & Law Days held at Marlborough 1706–51* (Devizes, priv. print. 1929), 58.
[78] *Wilts. Apprentices* (W.R.S. xvii), pp. 40, 65; W.R.O. 871/23, deed, 1738.
[79] *V.C.H. Wilts.* iv. 178.
[80] *Univ. Brit. Dir.* v (1797), App. 126; Pigot, *Nat. Com. Dir.* (1830), iii. 807; (1844), 24.

[81] Pigot, *Nat. Com. Dir.* (1844), 24; W.R.O. 9/19/697; 1197/6, f. 10.
[82] *Harrod's Dir. Wilts.* (1865); *Kelly's Dir. Wilts.* (1907 and later edns.); Stedman, *Marlborough*, 365; Chandler, *Hist. Marlborough*, 64 and photograph at pp. 52–3.
[83] W.R.O. 1197/21–2; *W.N. & Q.* ii. 388; *W.A.M.* xlv. 130; Cunnington, *Pres. Grand Jury Q. Sess. 1706–51*, 58–9; *Wilts. Apprentices* (W.R.S. xvii), pp. 70, 108.
[84] D. R. Atkinson, 'Clay Tobacco Pipes and Pipemakers of Marlborough', *W.A.M.* lx. 85–94; *V.C.H. Wilts.* iv. 244.
[85] *V.C.H. Wilts.* iv. 180.
[86] *W.A.M.* xlviii. 313–17; *Univ. Brit. Dir.* v (1797), App. 125; *Harrod's Dir. Wilts.* (1865).
[87] Aubrey, *Nat. Hist. Wilts.* ed. Britton, 105, 115; *Kelly's Dir. Wilts.* (1907); below, mkts. and fairs.
[88] *Univ. Brit. Dir.* v (1797), App. 125–6; Pigot, *Nat. Com. Dir.* (1844), 23.
[89] Listed, with dates and sites, by Chandler, *Hist. Marlborough*, 68–72.
[90] Hughes, *Marlborough*, 15; inf. from Mr. E. G. H. Kempson, Sun Cottage, Hyde Lane.
[91] Chandler, *Hist. Marlborough*, 68–9; above, Preshute, manors.

mail coaches ran to London and daily ones to Exeter. Daily post coaches ran to London and Bristol. There was still a daily service in 1833 from the principal inns to London, Bath, Bristol, Cheltenham, Frome (Som.), and Reading. The G.W.R. line from London to Bristol was opened in 1840–1, however, and in 1844 only three coaches a day ran to London and one to Bath and Bristol. Coaches occasionally ran to Southampton. Of the two coach makers in High Street in 1797 one, Thomas Forty, was still in business in 1830. There were then two other coach makers in High Street, of whom one, Joseph Eden, still traded as Eden & Son in 1865.[92]

The town's emergence as a resort, encouraged by the lords of the borough resident nearby, with race meetings during which various entertainments were held,[93] may have contributed indirectly to its commercial and industrial decline. It was described in 1764 as having few manufactures and in 1831–2, some eight years before the opening of the G.W.R. line, as 'a respectable country place' with no trade.[94]

There was a private bank, Thomas Hancock & Co., in business at Marlborough in 1797 or earlier.[95] Other early bankers were King, Gosling, & Tanner in High Street and Ward, Brown, Merriman, & Halcomb in Silverless Street in 1830.[96] The Silverless Street bank, as Ward & Co., was still in business in 1865.[97] The North Wilts. Banking Co. had a branch in High Street from 1844 or earlier to 1865 or later and the Wilts. and Dorset Banking Co. Ltd. had a branch there from 1844 or earlier until between 1907 and 1923. The branch of the Capital & Counties Bank in High Street in 1907 had been acquired by Lloyds Bank Ltd. by 1923.[98]

In 1833 Stephen Brown had a brewery in High Street which by 1843 had passed to Dixon & Co.[99] There were breweries in the Marsh and Kingsbury Street in 1838.[1] Brewing was one of the chief trades of Marlborough in 1865 when S. B. & H. P. Dixon and Reed & Co. each had a brewery in High Street.[2] In 1899 Reed & Co.'s brewery was called the Anchor brewery and was owned then and in 1903 by G. & T. Spencer's Brewery Ltd.[3] Dixon's brewery at no. 109 High Street had been leased to A. M. Adams by 1897 and in 1917, when it was called the Marlborough brewery, belonged to Usher's Wiltshire Brewery Ltd.[4] No brewing took place in the town in 1923.[5]

Agricultural machinery was made in High Street in 1844.[6] In 1870 T. Pope started an

agricultural engineering business which in the earlier 19th century was at Chantry Works, no. 99 High Street, and was continued by J. A. Pope. In 1946 Thomas Pope sold the business, which was then carried on in High Street and in works at Granham Hill, to T. H. White Ltd. of Devizes. Its name was changed from T. Pope Ltd. to T. H. White, Marlborough, Ltd. The High Street premises, then a retail shop, were closed in 1966 but engineering continued at Granham Hill.[7] A. E. Farr Ltd., civil engineers, came to Marlborough in 1939 and occupied Wye House as an office until 1941.[8]

Although some employment was provided by Marlborough College, the local schools and hospitals, Wingrove & Edge Ltd., and a few small engineering and light industrial factories in London Road and Elcot Lane,[9] most people worked outside the town in 1982.

MARKETS AND FAIRS. In 1204 King John granted Wednesday and Saturday markets to the burgesses of Marlborough.[10] The prosperity of the markets may have been increased in 1240 when, in an exchange with the king, the bishop of Salisbury gave up his right to a weekly market at Ramsbury.[11] By 1255, however, tenants of the bishop, of the dean and chapter of Salisbury, and of several other lords had ceased to pay tolls at Marlborough markets, a loss reckoned at £10. A weekly market which had been held at Swindon from c. 1260 was considered in 1275 to have damaged that at Marlborough by £2 a year.[12] The burgesses exercised the same rights, including freedom from pavage, pontage, passage, pedage, peage, pesage, stallage, and lastage, as the burgesses of Oxford and Winchester enjoyed in their markets.[13] When the borough was incorporated in 1576 those rights were confirmed, the mayor became ex officio clerk of the market, and the mayor and burgesses were empowered to regulate the markets by passing bylaws, which they did in 1577.[14] In 1625, in return for the lord of the borough's confirmation of their right to take the market tolls, the burgesses agreed to pay pickage and stallage to him.[15] From 1626 the lords of the borough leased the profits of pickage and stallage to the burgesses.[16] The burgesses leased the market tolls.[17] When Marlborough corporation was dissolved in 1835 the right to take the tolls seems to have passed from the burgesses[18] to the lord of the borough, who

[92] Univ. Brit. Dir. v (1797), App. 124–5; Pigot, Nat. Com. Dir. (1830), iii. 806–7; (1844), 23–4; Harrod's Dir. Wilts. (1865); V.C.H. Wilts. iv. 282.
[93] V.C.H. Wilts. iv. 381; above, introduction (social and cultural activities).
[94] Eng. Illustrated (1764), ii. 331; Rep. Boundary Com. iii (i), H.C. 141, p. 111 (1831–2), xl.
[95] Univ. Brit. Dir. v (1797), App. 125.
[96] Pigot, Nat. Com. Dir. (1830), iii. 806.
[97] Harrod's Dir. Wilts. (1865).
[98] Ibid.; Pigot, Nat. Com. Dir. (1844), 23; Kelly's Dir. Wilts. (1907, 1923).   [99] W.R.O. 871/106.
[1] Ibid. 871/36.
[2] Harrod's Dir. Wilts. (1865).
[3] W.A.S. Libr., sale cat. vii, no. 47; Kelly's Dir. Wilts. (1903).
[4] Lucy's Marlborough Dir. (1897); W.R.O. 871/88, f. 71 and v.; W.A.S. Libr., sale cat. xii, no. 35.
[5] Kelly's Dir. Wilts. (1923).

[6] Pigot, Nat. Com. Dir. (1844), 23.
[7] V.C.H. Wilts. iv. 195; Kelly's Dir. Wilts. (1907 and later edns.); inf. from Mr. D. I. Howells, T. H. White, Marlborough, Ltd.; above, Preshute, econ. hist. (Barton).
[8] V.C.H. Wilts. viii. 171; Stedman, Marlborough, 345–6.
[9] Above, Preshute, econ. hist. (Barton).
[10] Rot. Chart. (Rec. Com.), 135.
[11] Cal. Chart. R. 1226–57, 252; above, Ramsbury, econ. hist. (mkt. and fairs).
[12] Rot. Hund. (Rec. Com.), ii (1), 234–5, 261.
[13] Rot. Chart. (Rec. Com.), 135.
[14] Waylen, Hist. Marlborough, 116, 119.
[15] W.R.O., TS. cal. of Ailesbury deeds, comp. Scroggs, ii, no. 197.
[16] Alnwick Castle Mun., X.II.11, box 6, survey of lands of earl of Hertford, 1634– , p. 353; W.R.O. 9/19/758, f. 5.
[17] e.g. W.A.M. iii. 110–11; W.R.O., G 22/1/108.
[18] 1st Rep. Com. Mun. Corp. H.C. 116, App. I, p. 85 (1835), xxiii.

afterwards leased them.[19] The borough council bought them from George, marquess of Ailesbury, in 1929-30.[20] In 1836 a committee to regulate market affairs was appointed by the borough council.[21]

The market place, in High Street in 1289 or earlier, was at the east end of the street between the high or market cross, called the cross house in the later 16th century, and the corn cross near the Castle and Ball inn. The high cross, which was probably a timber building on piers set in a stone base, contained the market house.[22] In the early 17th century the cheese and butter market was held under it and later under the town hall which occupied the site from c. 1630.[23] Fish and salt beef were also sold there in the early 19th century.[24] After the town hall replaced the high cross the wool market was held in it.[25] The bakers also had their stalls in it until 1634 when, apparently because of lack of space, they were expelled.[26] A Wednesday market place, where there was another market house, was mentioned in 1625 and may also have been in High Street.[27] Always apparently less important, the Wednesday market occasionally lapsed. None was held in the later 17th century, when the Saturday market was an important cheese market attended by factors of London cheesemongers, in 1797, or in the later 19th century and earlier 20th.[28] Meat was sold in shambles in High Street called Butcher or Close Row in the later 16th century or earlier and in the 17th.[29] In the early 19th century, however, white meat and bacon could also be sold under the town hall.[30] The shambles, rebuilt c. 1573 and c. 1654, were shaded by trees in 1750 or earlier. They were demolished, and the trees felled, in 1812.[31] From 1838 meat was sold at the east end of the south side of High Street.[32] In the earlier 19th century the market for eggs, poultry, and fruit was at the east end of the penthouse on the north side of High Street. It was moved in 1838 to a building on the south side which also housed the National schools. Toys, confectionery, and fruit were sold in front of the town hall c. 1800 and at the north-east corner of High Street in 1838 and later. After 1838 farm implements, cattle, and horses were sold at the east end of High Street and pigs and sheep outside the National schools.[33] The corn market was held outside the Castle and Ball round the corn rails, the site of the corn cross, until 1864 when George, marquess of Ailesbury, built a corn exchange on the site of the National schools. Business had ceased there before 1900. The corn rails were removed in 1929.[34] In 1981 small general markets were held at the east end of High Street on Wednesdays and Saturdays.

A weighing beam, which by Act of 1429 the borough had to maintain and which in 1576 was housed in the high cross, and scales were held by the bailiffs of Marlborough.[35] The beam like the market house was leased.[36] The weighbridge and the house containing it, which stood on the south side of High Street opposite the Castle and Ball, were rebuilt in 1853-4 and removed in 1925.[37]

In 1204 the king granted to the burgesses of Marlborough an eight-day fair to begin on the eve of the Assumption (14 August).[38] It was presumably held in St. Mary's parish, possibly on the Green. After 1752 the fair was held on 22 August and in 1929, when it was described as agricultural, on 23 August.[39] In 1931 and until the 1960s Marlborough fair, sheep fair, or great sheep fair, was held on Marlborough Common on 22 August.[40]

Henry III in 1229 granted that a four-day fair to begin on the eve of St. Martin (10 November) might be held on the 'new land' of Marlborough.[41] It was held on the Green in the later 18th century.[42] From 1752 the fair was held on 22 November and in 1888 and in 1929, when it was held on Marlborough Common for agricultural purposes, on 23 November.[43] It was still held in 1938,[44] but lapsed in the 1960s.[45]

In 1246 Henry III granted that a four-day fair, to begin on the eve of St. Peter and St. Paul (28 June), might be held around St. Peter's churchyard.[46] In the same year the king suppressed a wake held at the same time in Little Wittenham (Berks., later Oxon.) because it detracted from St. Peter's fair.[47] It was chiefly a horse fair in the early 18th century.[48] From 1752 it was held on 10 July,[49] in 1809 and 1865 on 11 July.[50] It was held in 1875 but had lapsed by 1879.[51]

[19] *Harrod's Dir. Wilts.* (1865); *Kelly's Dir. Wilts.* (1923); *Rep. Com. Market Rights and Tolls* [C. 6268], pp. 536-8, H.C. (1890-1), xl.   [20] W.R.O., G 22/100/11, pp. 154, 198.
[21] Stedman, *Marlborough*, 268.
[22] P.R.O., JUST 1/1011, rot. 64; Hughes, *Marlborough*, 45; *Bradenstoke Cart.* (W.R.S. xxxv), p. 90; W.R.O., TS. cal. of Ailesbury deeds, comp. Scroggs, ii, no. 197.
[23] Hughes, *Marlborough*, 51; *Rep. Com. Market Rights and Tolls* (1890-1), 536-8.   [24] Stedman, *Marlborough*, 216.
[25] Hughes, *Marlborough*, 51.
[26] W.R.O., G 22/1/195.
[27] Ibid. TS. cal. of Ailesbury deeds, comp. Scroggs, ii, no. 197.
[28] Aubrey, *Nat. Hist. Wilts.* ed. Britton, 105, 115; *Univ. Brit. Dir.* v (1797), App. 123; *Kelly's Dir. Wilts.* (1855 and later edns.); *Harrod's Dir. Wilts.* (1865); *Rep. Com. Market Rights and Tolls* (1890-1), 536-8; *Gale's Marlborough Dir.* (1937).   [29] W.R.O. 9/19/112; 9/19/758.
[30] Stedman, *Marlborough*, 215.
[31] W.R.O., G 22/1/205/2, ff. 5, 106; Hughes, *Marlborough*, 61, 75-6, 79.
[32] W.R.O., G 22/1/202, declaration, 1838.
[33] Ibid.; Stedman, *Marlborough*, 216, 268.
[34] Hughes, *Marlborough*, 45, 79, 92-3; Chandler, *Hist. Marlborough*, 12. The Waitrose supermarket occupied the site of the corn exchange in 1981.

[35] W.R.O., G 22/1/20, p. 180; 8 Hen. VI, c. 5; *W.A.M.* iii. 112 and nn.
[36] W.R.O., G 22/1/205/2, f. 115v.; G 22/100/1; G 22/100/10, p. 163.
[37] Ibid. G 22/100/2; inf. from Mr. E. G. H. Kempson, Sun Cottage, Hyde Lane.
[38] *Rot. Chart.* (Rec. Com.), 135.
[39] *Rep. Com. Market Rights and Tolls* [C. 5550], p. 214, H.C. (1888), liii; *Rep. Markets and Fairs in Eng. and Wales*, pt. 4 (H.M.S.O. 1929), 209.
[40] W.R.O., G 22/155/1; inf. from the Town Clerk, Council Offices.   [41] *Cal. Chart. R.* 1226-57, 91.
[42] W.R.O. 9, survey of Marlborough, 1770, p. 25.
[43] *Rep. Com. Market Rights and Tolls* (1888), 214; *Rep. Markets and Fairs in Eng. and Wales*, pt. 4 (H.M.S.O. 1929), 209; W.R.O., G 22/100/11, p. 154.
[44] W.R.O., G 22/111/12, p. 122.
[45] Inf. from the Town Clerk.
[46] *Cal. Chart. R.* 1226-57, 291.
[47] *Camb. Hist. Jnl.* ii. 209.
[48] W.R.O., TS. cal. of Ailesbury deeds, comp. Scroggs, i, no. 19.
[49] *Rep. Com. Market Rights and Tolls* (1888), 214.
[50] W.R.O., G 22/1/34; *Harrod's Dir. Wilts.* (1865).
[51] *Kelly's Dir. Wilts.* (1875); *Lucy's Marlborough Dir.* (1879).

Hiring or mop fairs were held in the early 19th century. In 1888 and in 1982, when they were for pleasure, Little Mop and Big Mop fairs were held in High Street on the Saturday before and the Saturday after old Michaelmas day (10 October).[52]

LOCAL GOVERNMENT. BOROUGH GOVERN-MENT. Before 1204 Marlborough was presumably governed by the king through the keeper of the castle. A guild merchant received royal approval in 1163 and confirmation in 1204.[53] King John also in 1204 granted liberties to the burgesses modelled on those of Winchester and, to a lesser extent, on those of Oxford. The privileges consisted of exemption from suit of shire and hundred and from attendance at forest courts except to answer for breaches of forest law, of the right to hold their houses in chief, and of soc and sac, toll and team, infangthief and outfangthief, trial of pleas by the law of Winchester and not by combat, cessation of customs unjustly levied in war, the recovery of debts by their own bailiff, immunity from distraint except for debtors and their pledges, freedom from pleading in pleas of land outside the borough, and, within it, trial of those pleas by the law of Winchester.[54] The burgesses were not exempt from Crown pleas, however, and attended eyres.[55] The right to hold a borough court and view of frankpledge was implicit in the grant.[56] From 1224 the burgesses farmed the borough for £50 yearly.[57]

The charter of 1204, frequently inspected and confirmed,[58] formed the basis of borough government until 1576. In that year Marlborough was incorporated by charter as the free borough of the mayor and burgesses. The burgesses were confirmed in the privileges granted to them in 1204. They were allowed to pass bylaws, a right which they first exercised in 1577. They were allowed to have a commission of the peace, comprising three justices of the peace, and a gaol. The justices were required, however, to send those indicted at borough quarter sessions for treason, murder, or felony to the county gaol. The power of the mayor was greatly extended: thenceforth he was *ex officio* escheator, coroner, clerk of the market, and, with powers more limited than those of the county justices, a justice of the peace empowered to act with the two burgesses who had preceded him as mayor and whom he nominated fellow justices.[59] The charter of 1576, under which the borough was governed until 1835, was twice abrogated. In 1642 it was withdrawn by Marl-

borough's royalist captors. A new charter, granted by Cromwell in 1657, increased the corporation's officers to mayor, recorder, town clerk, 8 aldermen, 5 justices of the peace, 7 'assistants', 2 high constables, 5 constables, 2 bailiffs, and 2 serjeants at mace, but was annulled at the Restoration when the charter of 1576 was confirmed.[60] That charter was again withdrawn at the end of Charles II's reign and was replaced in 1688 by another which allowed the Crown to pack the corporation, consisting of a mayor, 13 aldermen, 24 burgesses or common councillors, and a common clerk, with royal nominees. It was annulled shortly afterwards by proclamation.[61]

Wards existed within the borough in 1268.[62] New land ward, although it remained part of Elcot tithing, was a ward in 1289[63] but was later merged with Green ward. In 1547, and until 1835 when they were abolished, there were five wards, Bailey, High or High Street, Kingsbury, Green, and Marsh.[64] The alderman, later constable, of each ward had to summon its inhabitants to borough courts, at which he presented nuisances and breaches of the peace and of bylaws. He also saw that watch was kept and precautions against fire taken.[65] With his fellow constables he kept the peace at fairs in the later 18th century and earlier 19th.[66]

Few records survive to show how the borough was governed in the Middle Ages.[67] The governing body was the guild merchant and comprised all the burgesses, who had a common seal in the 13th century. The burgesses may have been entrepreneurs rather than artificers and the guild oligarchical.[68] By the 16th century new burgesses were elected at the morrow, or morning, speech courts held in early autumn and on admittance made money payments to the mayor rather than the supposedly traditional gifts, depicted on the borough arms, of a bull, capon, and hounds.[69] By 1514 the guild had been replaced as the governing body by a small number of burgesses chosen from it to form a common council. Councillors were chosen by the mayor and existing council at the morrow speech courts at which all borough officials were elected.[70] A bylaw of 1577 confirmed that method. From 1577 to 1835 the common council made bylaws with the agreement of the other burgesses, approved leases of borough lands, and each year nominated three men from whom all the burgesses elected a mayor. A bylaw of 1622 empowered the councillors to elect borough constables and chamberlains. In 1833, however, the mayor appointed the constables. From 1633 until 1835 the mayor and

[52] Hughes, *Marlborough*, 80; *Rep. Com. Market Rights and Tolls* (1888), 214.
[53] *Pipe R.* 1163 (P.R.S. vi), 46; P.R.O., C 52/23, no. 5.
[54] P.R.O., C 52/23, no. 5.
[55] e.g. *Crown Pleas, 1249* (W.R.S. xvi), p. 229; P.R.O., JUST 1/998A, rot. 37.
[56] P.R.O., C 52/23, no. 5.
[57] Ibid. E 372/67-8; e.g. E 372/79.
[58] e.g. ibid. C 53/21, m. 11; ibid. E 159/338, Recorda Hil. rot. 55; *Cal. Pat.* 1422-9, 285-6.
[59] P.R.O., C 66/1139, m. 3; the bylaws, with later enactments, are printed in Waylen, *Hist. Marlborough*, 117-25.
[60] *Cal. S.P. Dom.* 1656-7, 208, 307; P.R.O., AO 3/411; Waylen, *Hist. Marlborough*, 275, 330-1.
[61] *V.C.H. Wilts.* v. 164; P.R.O., C 66/3321, no. 1; Waylen, *Hist. Marlborough*, 341-3.
[62] P.R.O., JUST 1/998A, rot. 37.
[63] Ibid. JUST 1/1011, rot. 64.
[64] W.R.O. 9, survey of Marlborough, 1547; ibid. G 22/1/110.
[65] Waylen, *Hist. Marlborough*, 108, 122, 124-5.
[66] W.R.O., G 22/1/31; G 22/1/34.
[67] The boro. rec. in W.R.O. are described to 1835 in *Boro. Rec.* (W.R.S. v), pp. 35-62, and from 1835 in a TS. list in W.R.O.
[68] *V.C.H. Wilts.* iv. 118; *Cal. Chart. R.* 1226-57, 244; J. Tait, *Medieval Eng. Boro.* 230; below.
[69] Waylen, *Hist. Marlborough*, 113; Camden, *Brit.* (1695), 98.
[70] W.R.O., G 22/1/13, p. 1.

common council approved, and from 1652 nominated, new burgesses.[71] The number of burgesses declined from 60–80, of whom a third were common councillors, in the 16th century,[72] to 32, of whom a quarter were councillors, in 1713.[73] Besides the mayor and justices, there were 11 burgesses, 8 of whom were councillors and 3 'undignified' in 1772, and in 1809 there were 6 burgesses, all councillors.[74]

There seems to have been no serious conflict over the exercise of the liberties granted in 1204 between the burgesses and the grantees of the borough whose lordship was considered to include return of writs, gallows, and other liberties in the 13th century and later.[75] In 1625 William, earl of Hertford, in return for their acknowledging him as lord of the borough and permitting him to nominate one of the borough bailiffs from among the burgesses each year, confirmed the burgesses' economic privileges and right to exercise leet jurisdiction in the borough.[76] In the period 1676–1734 the new lords of Marlborough, the Bruces, displaced the Whig interest of the old lords, the Seymours, in parliamentary elections at Marlborough by ensuring that burgesses, to whom voting was restricted, returned Tory candidates. Success was achieved by admitting to the corporation only men acceptable to the Bruces and by reducing it after 1734 to a small oligarchy.[77] In that way the corporation became subservient to the lord of the borough. By the later 18th century most corporation members were common councillors, with whom, in the first instance, the making of decisions rested. In the later 18th century, early 19th, and still in 1833, the Ailesburys' steward was the corporation's leading member and ensured that only men acceptable to Lord Ailesbury were nominated as burgesses.[78]

Although the king's court, the later town court or court of civil pleas, to which the 1204 charter entitled the burgesses and which the new borough council was allowed to retain in 1835,[79] was mentioned in 1473,[80] no record of it survives before 1641 or after 1847. It was a court of record usually held weekly but sometimes less frequently: in the 19th century it was held every three weeks in the town hall on Wednesdays. There, before the mayor as chairman, civil pleas such as those of debt, and claims for damages, were heard and determined. Pleas more properly the concern of the borough quarter sessions, such as trespass on the case, trespass and assault, assault and battery,

entry, and entry and assault were also dealt with, presumably because they involved claims for damages. The town clerk acted as registrar, and the serjeants at mace as bailiffs of the court serving process.[81] Although most of its functions passed to the county court established by Act of 1846 the king's court was not formally abolished until 1974.[82]

The right to be exempt from the sheriff's tourn and to take other liberties was implied in the charter of 1204.[83] The mayor's court, first recorded in 1501, seems in the earlier 16th century to have fulfilled some of the functions of a court leet. It was attended by all the inhabitants and held, usually every three weeks, on Fridays, and at it the ward aldermen presented minor breaches of the peace. The administrative business of the borough was conducted from 1501 and earlier at courts of morrow speech which were held, generally each quarter, on Fridays. There bylaws were passed, leases of borough property were enrolled, and transfers of such property were proclaimed. At the autumn court the mayor and borough officials were elected and the common council chosen.[84] The mayor's and the morrow speech courts were held together once in 1537.[85] They were separate in 1553–4[86] but had merged by 1614 under the title of the court of morrow speech with the mayor's court[87] and were held, under various similar titles, every three weeks on a Friday until the earlier 19th century.[88]

Pie powder courts, records of which are extant only for the earlier 16th century, were held on Wednesdays and Saturdays to deal with market offences such as debts and infringements of the assize of bread.[89] Biannual views of frankpledge, of which no record survives before 1514 or after 1554, were also held. Presentments of matters such as the fouling of gutters and thoroughfares, buildings in need of repair, and malicious wounding were made to a jury by the ward aldermen.[90] The view was, perhaps exceptionally, held with a court of pie powder in 1514.[91]

Although the newly incorporated borough was granted a commission of the peace in 1576,[92] no record of a distinct borough court of quarter sessions survives before the 18th century. In the later 17th century and early 18th justice business, such as larceny, the removal of paupers from the town, trespass, assault, and ejectment, was dealt with at the king's court and at the court of the mayor with the morrow speech court. Quarter sessions business was distinguished in the first

[71] Waylen, *Hist. Marlborough*, 118, 123–4; *1st Rep. Com. Mun. Corp.* App. I, 83–4.
[72] *Boro. Rec.* (W.R.S. v), p. 37.
[73] W.R.O., G 22/1/28, pp. 1–3.
[74] Ibid. G 22/1/31; G 22/1/34.
[75] *Rot. Hund.* (Rec. Com.), ii (1), 261; e.g. *Cal. Close*, 1318–23, 149.
[76] W.R.O., TS. cal. of Ailesbury deeds, comp. Scroggs, ii, no. 197.
[77] Below, parl. rep.
[78] W.R.O., G 22/1/30–1; *1st Rep. Com. Mun. Corp.* App. I, 84–5.
[79] P.R.O., C 52/23, no. 5; Mun. Corp. Act, 5 & 6 Wm. IV, c. 76.
[80] *Cal. Close*, 1468–76, 298.
[81] W.R.O., G 22/1/154; G 22/1/156; G 22/1/159; G 22/1/163; G 22/1/165; G 22/1/169; G 22/1/172; G 22/144/1; *Return*

of Cts. of Rec. H.C. 619, pp. 164–5 (1840), xli; Mun. Corp. Act, 5 & 6 Wm. IV, c. 76.
[82] Co. Cts. Act, 9 & 10 Vic. c. 95; Local Govt. Act, 1972, c. 70.   [83] P.R.O., C 52/23, no. 5.
[84] W.R.O., G 22/1/12–13; G 22/1/17; G 22/1/19.
[85] Ibid. G 22/1/17, p. 60.
[86] Ibid. G 22/1/19.
[87] Ibid. G 22/1/20.
[88] e.g. ibid. G 22/1/25; G 22/1/28; G 22/1/30. The extant rec. are listed in *Boro. Rec.* (W.R.S. v), pp. 40–1. No evidence has been found to support the statement, made ibid. p. 36, that the mayor's ct. heard civil pleas.
[89] e.g. W.R.O., G 22/1/12–13; G 22/1/17; G 22/1/19, pp. 1–20.
[90] Ibid. G 22/1/13; G 22/1/17; G 22/1/19.
[91] Ibid. G 22/1/13, pp. 4–8.
[92] P.R.O., C 66/1139, m. 3.

court in 1705 and in the second court in 1715, and a separate borough court of quarter sessions may date from that period.[93] In the 18th century, too, the sessions held at Easter and Michaelmas drew to themselves the leet business formerly done in the mayor's court and later in the court of the mayor with the court of morrow speech and matters dealt with in the 16th-century views of frankpledge and courts of pie powder. In 1772, and probably earlier, the title of the Easter and Michaelmas sessions was general quarter sessions of the peace, leet, and law day. The two strands of jurisdiction exercised at them are illustrated by the attendance of and presentments by the overseers of the two Marlborough parishes, who were appointed by the justices on the churchwardens' nominations, and the ward constables or their deputies who were appointed at the Michaelmas sessions. From the 18th century cases including bastardy, grand and petty larceny, and assault were presented to the three borough justices by a grand jury.[94] Felonies were tried, without authority, until 1824,[95] and in the later 16th century and earlier 17th the corporation had a gibbet west of Kingsbury Street on the site of Gallows Close.[96]

From 1576 the mayor was *ex officio* clerk of the market.[97] No record of a market court survives before 1785. In that year, and until 1836, minutes of the mayor's court otherwise called the court of the clerk of the market show the mayor, as clerk of the market and a justice, sitting every six weeks with another borough justice to regulate market affairs, and to receive presentments by a jury sworn each autumn of matters such as the sale of butter in short measure and the use of short weights.[98]

In the 16th century and later the income of the borough derived from rents and entry fines of Port field, payments for pasturage on Marlborough Common, rents from houses and inns in Marlborough, some of them former chantry property bought from the Crown in 1550, the profits of a weighing engine, and tolls which were leased in 1626 and later. The total income of £633 in 1832 included £484 from the properties, £99 from the land, £20 from the tolls, and £30 from the weighing engine.[99] Marlborough was exempt from the county rate,[1] and from 1775 borough rates were imposed on the two Marlborough parishes at borough quarter sessions by

the borough justices. Although the jurisdiction of the borough justices was assumed by the county justices in 1835, the borough continued to be exempt from the county rate but apparently contributed from the borough fund to the costs of committing prisoners from Marlborough to the county gaols, and, on the orders of the county justices and of the justices of assize, paid the expenses of prosecutions of offences committed in the borough. In 1848, however, the borough was judged liable to contribute to the county rate.[2]

Borough bailiffs were in office in 1223.[3] They were in charge of the borough weights[4] and acted as officers of the borough courts. A coroner, an officer the burgesses claimed to have had from 1204, was in office in 1249 and there were two in 1289 and later.[5] There were ward aldermen in 1268,[6] a mayor in 1273,[7] and two underbailiffs and a constable in 1462.[8] All the officers were elected in early autumn at the morrow speech court, later the courts of morrow speech with the mayor's court,[9] but coroners, although the office was elective, seem to have served for longer periods.[10] Borough officials, except the ward aldermen called constables from 1649, continued to be elected at those courts in the earlier 19th century.[11] In the later 18th century the ward constables, who then appeared at borough quarter sessions by deputy, were elected at the Michaelmas sessions, leet, and law days.[12] Two chamberlains in 1572 and one in 1593 and 1833, apparently appointed by the corporation rather than elected, were in charge of borough finances.[13] A borough treasurer, perhaps the chamberlain, was mentioned in 1824.[14] A town clerk, who also acted as recorder and clerk of the peace, was in office in 1579.[15] The two constables mentioned in 1641 were called high constables in the later 17th century to distinguish them from the ward constables. The two serjeants at mace mentioned from the 16th century may have performed functions similar to those of the medieval underbailiffs.[16] A beadle was mentioned in 1833.[17]

A guildhall, which may have stood on the north side of High Street at its east end, was mentioned in 1270.[18] The building or its successor was repaired in 1575 and 1583.[19] In the 17th century and earlier 19th the borough courts and quarter sessions were held there.[20] That building,

[93] Stedman, *Marlborough*, 220-2.
[94] Ibid. 222-3; W.R.O., G 22/1/108-10. Presentments of the grand jury, 1707-53, in ibid. G 22/1/111/1 were transcribed and published by Cunnington, *Pres. Grand Jury Q. Sess. 1706-51*. Those and other q. sess. rec. are listed in *Boro. Rec.* (W.R.S. v), pp. 46-50.
[95] *1st Rep. Com. Mun. Corp.* App. I, 85.
[96] Hughes, *Marlborough*, 47, 52.
[97] P.R.O., C 66/1139, m. 3.
[98] W.R.O., G 22/1/188/1-3. The rec. are listed in *Boro. Rec.* (W.R.S. v), pp. 52-3.
[99] *1st Rep. Com. Mun. Corp.* App. I, 85-6; above, agric., mkts. and fairs; below, churches.
[1] *Rep. Boundary Com.* ii, H.C. 238 (1837), xxvii.
[2] J. L. Adolphus and T. F. Ellis, *Law Reports, Queen's Bench, Mich., Hil., East. 1847-8* (N.S. xi), pp. 758-68.
[3] *Rot. Litt. Claus.* (Rec. Com.), i. 565.
[4] Above, mkts. and fairs.
[5] *Crown Pleas, 1249* (W.R.S. xvi), p. 229; P.R.O., JUST 1/1005, rot. 158; JUST 1/1011, rot. 64; *Cal. Close, 1422-9*, 286.

[6] P.R.O., JUST 1/998A, rot. 37.
[7] *Cal. Close, 1272-9*, 63; named mayors are recorded from 1311: W.R.O. 212B/4684. A list is printed in Chandler, *Hist. Marlborough*, 43-8.
[8] *Cal. Close, 1461-8*, 137.
[9] Waylen, *Hist. Marlborough*, 124-5; e.g. W.R.O., G 22/1/13, p. 1; G 22/1/20, pp. 5-6; G 22/1/25, pp. 1-2; G 22/1/31.
[10] *Cal. Close, 1413-19*, 153; 1422-9, 286; 1441-7, 264.
[11] W.R.O., G 22/1/34.
[12] Ibid. G 22/1/109.
[13] Ibid. G 22/1/205/2, f. 3; *Boro. Rec.* (W.R.S. v), p. 37; *1st Rep. Com. Mun. Corp.* App. I, 83-4.
[14] W.R.O., G 22/1/110, p. 3.
[15] Ibid. G 22/1/205/2, f. 11v.
[16] Ibid. 1804/2; ibid. G 22/1/154, f. 1; G 22/1/25, p. 2.
[17] *1st Rep. Com. Mun. Corp.* App. I, 83.
[18] The site of nos. 119-20 High Street is suggested: Chandler, *Hist. Marlborough*, 13, 73.
[19] W.R.O., G 22/1/205/2, ff. 7, 14v.
[20] e.g. ibid. G 22/1/20, f. 5; G 22/1/34; G 22/1/110, p. 180; G 22/1/154, f. 2; G 22/1/172; G 22/1/188/1, p. 13.

apparently inadequate for county quarter sessions for which temporary buildings were provided, was replaced *c.* 1630 by a new guildhall or town hall, incorporating a market house, built at the east end of High Street on the site of the market or high cross.[21] That town hall, burned down in 1653, was rebuilt on the same site in 1654–5.[22] It was rebuilt by John Hammond in 1792–3, altered and repaired to provide better accommodation for county sessions in 1867, and rebuilt again in 1901–2 to designs in a late 17th-century style by C. E. Ponting.[23]

The right of the burgesses to have a prison was implicit in the terms of the 1204 charter. One was mentioned in 1281, in 1561 when the mayor committed a felon to it, and in 1575 when it was repaired.[24] A gaol was expressly granted to the corporation in 1576.[25] It was beneath the guildhall in 1625.[26] Extra and temporary accommodation may have been provided for prisoners at county sessions in the earlier 17th century.[27] Prisons or blindhouses were incorporated in the town halls of *c.* 1630, 1654–5, and 1792–3.[28] In the late 19th century the prison accommodated prisoners awaiting trial at county quarter sessions; the lower part had gone out of use by 1867, but the upper part was used until the new town hall was built in 1901–2.[29] The doorway of the 18th-century blindhouse was built into the town hall of 1901–2, which incorporated cells.[30]

In 1575 or earlier the borough maintained an almshouse next to the grammar school.[31] A workhouse, which possibly stood west of Marlborough, was built by the corporation *c.* 1631.[32] That building was demolished *c.* 1709 and replaced by another on the west side of Hyde Lane.[33] In 1725 the corporation conveyed the almshouse to St. Mary's parish to house its paupers and the workhouse to St. Peter's for the same purpose.[34]

The borough contributed towards a bridewell in Preshute in 1624.[35] Another, built partly at the expense of the county and partly at that of the borough in 1630–1,[36] stood on the south side of the London–Bath road in Preshute,[37] possibly on the site of Marlborough College chapel. The corporation contributed to the cost of repairs and to the master's salary. In 1648 the county justices

expressly allowed the borough justices to send people there.[38] The bridewell was rebuilt within the borough on the east side of Hermitage Lane in 1709.[39] In 1781 it was wrongly described as in Preshute.[40] That building was repaired and enlarged in 1723[41] and rebuilt in 1787.[42] In 1825 and later it was used mainly for confining prisoners before trial.[43] Agricultural rioters were detained there in 1830.[44] There was no debtor, only criminals, in its 15 cells, 12 for men and 3 for women, in 1836. A chaplain was employed and a surgeon visited thrice weekly. The placing of chains on the doors 'to afford somewhat of the appearance of a prison' was suggested in 1842.[45] The number of prisoners confined there during 1843 was 312.[46] It ceased to be a prison in 1854 and from then until 1898 was a police station.[47] The building was afterwards acquired by Marlborough College, and a gymnasium, which incorporated windows from the bridewell, and a college boarding house were built on the site.[48]

In 1835 the oligarchical corporation which had been controlled by the earls and marquesses of Ailesbury was replaced by a town council styled the mayor and burgesses of the borough and town of Marlborough. Any male householder who had lived in Marlborough for three or more years and had occupied property upon which poor rates were levied, and who himself had not received parish relief, could be enrolled as a burgess. The council comprised a mayor, 4 aldermen, of whom 2 went out of office every third year, and 12 councillors of whom a third went out of office each year. The burgesses elected councillors each year. The councillors elected from their number a mayor each year and aldermen every third year.[49] The council was bound to hold quarterly meetings but usually met, on adjournments, every three weeks, possibly in imitation of the former three weeks court. The borough officers, appointed by the council, were a town clerk, 2 serjeants at mace and bailiffs, a beadle who was also town crier, billet master, and borough policeman, and a treasurer. Committees were appointed to oversee watching and market affairs[50] and to deal with business arising from the legislation of the later 19th century and earlier 20th.[51] The borough lost its coroner and its commission of the peace in

[21] Ibid. G 22/1/20, p. 180; Waylen, *Hist. Marlborough*, 125, 133–4.

[22] Waylen, *Hist. Marlborough*, 257; W.R.O., G 22/1/205/2, ff. 104v.–105, 109.

[23] Stedman, *Marlborough*, 253–4, 306; Pevsner, *Wilts.* (2nd edn.), 334. See above, plate facing p. 208.

[24] P.R.O., JUST 1/1005, rot. 158; *Cal. Pat.* 1560–3, 39; Chandler, *Hist. Marlborough*, 44; W.R.O., G 22/1/205/2, f. 7.

[25] P.R.O., C 66/1139, m. 3.

[26] W.R.O., TS. cal. of Ailesbury deeds, comp. Scroggs, ii, no. 197.

[27] Ibid. G 22/1/205/2, f. 74v.

[28] *Cal. S.P. Dom.* 1666–7, 488; Waylen, *Hist. Marlborough*, 125.

[29] Stedman, *Marlborough*, 307; Hughes, *Marlborough*, 88.

[30] *Kelly's Dir. Wilts.* (1907).

[31] W.R.O., G 22/1/205/2, ff. 7, 74v.

[32] *Acts of P.C.* 1630–1, p. 329.

[33] Alnwick Castle Mun., X.II.11, box 14, deed, 27 Feb. 1709.

[34] *Endowed Char. Wilts.* (N. Div.), 704; below.

[35] W.R.O., G 22/1/205/2, f. 61.

[36] Ibid. q. sess. order bk. 1709–37, pp. 1–2; Alnwick Castle Mun., X.II.11, box 17, charge of bldg. bridewell, 1631.

[37] W.S.R.O., PHA 3565.

[38] W.R.O., q. sess. order bk. 1642–54, 11 Apr. 1648.

[39] Ibid. 1709–37, pp. 1–2; ibid. 9/19/567, deed, Bell to Willoughby, 1738.

[40] *Coroners' Bills* (W.R.S. xxxvi), p. 77.

[41] W.R.O., q. sess. order bk. 1709–37, p. 301.

[42] Ibid. 871/191; 9/19/346–7.

[43] *V.C.H. Wilts.* v. 188.

[44] P.R.O., HO 40/25; HO 52/11.

[45] *2nd Rep. Prisons Inspectors, S. and W. District* [89], pp. 14–16, H.C. (1837), xxxii; *7th Rep.* [421], p. 153, H.C. (1842), xxi.

[46] *V.C.H. Wilts.* v. 240 n.

[47] Waylen, *Hist. Marlborough*, 462, 560; Hughes, *Marlborough*, 91.

[48] Pevsner, *Wilts.* (2nd edn.), 340; inf. from Mr. E. G. H. Kempson, Sun Cottage, Hyde Lane; above, introduction.

[49] *Mun. Corp. Act*, 5 & 6 Wm. IV, c. 76.

[50] W.R.O., G 22/100/1.

[51] Ibid. G 22/111/1–18.

1835.[52] The county coroner acted in the borough from 1835 and continued to do so after the council in 1851 obtained a new commission of the peace which entitled it to restore the office of borough coroner.[53] In 1860 Marlborough became part of the North Wiltshire Coroner's District.[54] Borough sessions were held from 1851 until 1951 when, under the Justices of the Peace Act, 1949, Marlborough became the meeting place of a county petty sessional division.[55] Petty sessions were still held in the town hall in 1982.[56]

A sanitary inspector was appointed in 1855. The town council in 1859 agreed to adopt the Local Government Act of 1858 which enabled it to act as a sanitary authority. It did not, however, begin to function as a local board of health until 1866. The town clerk became clerk to the board, and a surveyor, a treasurer, a collector, and an inspector of nuisances were appointed.[57] Under the Public Health Act, 1872, the borough constituted itself an urban sanitary authority[58] and appointed a medical officer of health. That part-time officer was replaced in 1915 by a full-time one for Marlborough and the rural districts of Amesbury, Marlborough, Pewsey, and Ramsbury. The council acquired no. 1 the Green as offices in 1936.[59] It administered the municipal borough until 1974. In that year Marlborough ceased to be a borough, became a parish with town status, and was included in Kennet district. The borough council became the parish or town council and its nominated chairman the town mayor.[60]

ARMS, SEALS, AND INSIGNIA. The medieval borough arms were tricked in 1565 as azure, a castle triple-towered argent. That charge was incorporated in the elaborate coat confirmed to the borough in the same year and still used with minor variations in 1982; the coat was then tricked as per saltire gules and azure, in chief a bull passant argent armed or, in fesse two capons argent, in base three greyhounds courant in pale argent collared or, and on a chief or, upon a pale azure between two roses gules, a tower triple-towered argent.[61] A tower on a helm was adopted as a crest in 1714.[62] The helm was replaced by a mound, and two greyhounds adopted as supporters, in 1836.[63] The motto 'Ubi nunc sapientis

ossa Merlini?', of which there is no record before 1854, alludes to the medieval tradition that Marlborough was the burying place of Merlin, and is adapted from a line of Boethius.[64] Those arms, with an amended legend, were transferred to the new town council in 1974.[65]

The matrix of the earliest common seal of the borough was cast in the 13th century. The first known impression is of 1354. It is round, 5.3 cm. in diameter, and shows a triple-towered castle embattled and masoned, with long round-headed windows and a round-headed doorway with a hinged door closed: legend, lombardic, [S]IG [IL]L[UM COMMUNE DE M]ARLEBERG[E].[66] The queen granted the mayor and burgesses the use of a common seal in 1576,[67] but, if a new matrix was made,[68] it was a replica of the old because impressions did not change.[69] In 1714 a round silver matrix 5 cm. in diameter, bearing within a carved border the date 1714 and, flanked by ornamental mantling and surmounted by a tower on a helm, the arms confirmed in 1565, was given by Charles Bruce, Lord Bruce, whose arms appear on the handle: legend, humanistic, SIGILLUM MAIORIS & BURGENSIUM BURGI & VILLAE DE MARLEBERG.[70] Old and new seals were both used until 1727 when the destruction of the old one was ordered.[71] A brass matrix of the old seal was found at Stone (Staffs.) in the 1930s.[72] The matrix of 1714, on which the engraver omitted to represent the tower in chief on a pale, survives but was replaced in 1836 by another of silver, 5.3 cm. in diameter, bearing the borough arms, the date 1836, a mound surmounted by a tower as a crest, and two greyhounds as supporters: legend, humanistic, THE SEAL OF THE MAYOR ALDERMEN AND BURGESSES OF THE BOROUGH OF MARLBOROUGH. The last word is on a scroll beneath the supporters.[73] In 1974 a new seal, bearing that date and the town arms, was adopted.[74]

The mayor's seal was made anew in 1590.[75] A new mayoral seal, a smaller version of the common seal of 1714, was given, probably in 1714, by Charles, Lord Bruce: legend, humanistic, SIGILLUM MAIORIS BURGI DE MARLEBERG.[76] It survived in 1982.

The borough had maces in the 16th century.[77] Two maces, bought in 1601, were altered in

[52] Mun. Corp. Act, 5 & 6 Wm. IV, c. 76; W.R.O., G 22/1/110, pp. 184–5.
[53] Mun. Corp. Act, 5 & 6 Wm. IV, c. 76; W.R.O., G 22/100/2; e.g. ibid. q. sess. bills and vouchers, coroner's bills of W. B. Whitmarsh, 1841, 1858.
[54] Lond. Gaz. 30 Oct. 1860, p. 3897.
[55] W.R.O., G 22/111/15, town hall cttee. 17 Sept. 1951.
[56] Inf. from the Town Clerk, Council Offices.
[57] W.R.O., G 22/1/2.
[58] V.C.H. Wilts. iv. 316.
[59] Stedman, Marlborough, 305.
[60] Local Govt. Act, 1972, c. 70; Local Govt. in Eng. and Wales (H.M.S.O. 1974), 96, 157–8, 168.
[61] B.L. Harl. MS. 888, f. 11; see plate facing p. 192. The Coll. of Arms records 'three white greyhounds with red collars and gold rings': C. W. Scott-Giles, Civic Heraldry, 386.
[62] It appears on the boro. seal of 1714: below.
[63] W.R.O., G 22/100/1.
[64] 'Ubi nunc fidelis ossa Fabricii manent': Boethius, Theological Tractates [and] Consolation of Philosophy, ed. H. F. Stewart and E. K. Rand, p. 218; A. Neckham, De Laudibus Divinae Sapientiae (Rolls Ser.), 461. The motto first appears,

so far as is known, on the title page of Waylen, Hist. Marlborough, and the suggestion by H. C. Brentnall, W.A.M. xlviii. 142, that it was devised by an 'Elizabethan king of arms' appears unfounded.
[65] W.R.O., G 22/100/20.
[66] B.L. Cat. of Seals, ii, no. 5177; P.R.O., E 42/187.
[67] P.R.O., C 66/1139, m. 3.
[68] W.R.O., G 22/1/205/2, f. 9.
[69] Examples occur in 1657, 1695, and 1708: Alnwick Castle Mun., X.II.11, box 21, deed, 1657; P.R.O., C 219/81; C 219/105.
[70] B.L. Cat. of Seals, ii, no. 5181; Ll. Jewitt and W. St. J. Hope, Corp. Plate and Insignia, ii. 426. Impressions occur in 1734 and 1763: W.R.O. 9/19/805; 9/19/830.
[71] Waylen, Hist. Marlborough, 373.
[72] Trans. N. Staffs. Field Club, lxviii. 165–6.
[73] W.R.O., G 22/100/1; Jewitt and Hope, Corp. Plate and Insignia, ii. 427.
[74] Inf. from the Town Clerk.
[75] W.R.O., G 22/1/205/2, f. 21v.
[76] B.L. Cat. of Seals, ii, no. 5182; Jewitt and Hope, Corp. Plate and Insignia, ii. 427.
[77] W.R.O. 1804/2; ibid. G 22/1/205/2, f. 9v.

London in 1607.[78] They were altered, or new ones made, in London by Tobias Coleman in 1652. The silver gilt maces, each 1.04 m. long, were converted from Commonwealth to royal maces in 1660.[79] A mayoral chain was bought by subscription authorized in 1896.[80] The town council also possessed a mayor's day chain, a mayoress's chain, and a deputy mayor's badge of office in 1982.[81]

Mayoral plate, perhaps that mentioned in 1492–3,[82] was sold c. 1550.[83] A pewter dining service, bought for the borough in 1615,[84] was destroyed in 1653.[85] A new set was bought in 1664 and added to in 1667, 1675, and 1676.[86] Four plates, engraved with a stylized tower,[87] survived in 1982.[88]

PARISH GOVERNMENT. In the 18th century and presumably earlier, parish government was controlled by the borough. The parish surveyors and overseers, who until 1835 were nominated by the churchwardens and appointed by the borough justices at the Easter general quarter sessions, acted in matters concerning both roads and the poor in accordance with decisions taken and orders made at borough sessions, which they attended.[89] In 1716, for example, the St. Peter's overseers were ordered to contribute £2 weekly for the relief of the St. Mary's poor,[90] and rates imposed on St. Peter's parish were invariably double those levied in St. Mary's. Both parishes also contributed to the borough constables' bills and to other borough expenses.[91] After borough quarter sessions ceased in 1835, parish officers were elected at vestry meetings.[92]

St. Mary's may have had a workhouse near the churchyard in 1698.[93] In 1725 the borough conveyed its almshouse in the Parade to St. Mary's parish for a workhouse.[94] It was out of repair in 1788 and its inmates were neglected.[95] A proposal to have one workhouse for the two parishes was rejected in 1790 and St. Mary's workhouse was repaired and enlarged in that year.[96] It had 43 inmates in 1834[97] and was closed when St. Mary's parish became part of Marlborough union in 1835.[98] The building had been sold by 1860.[99] Expenditure on the poor increased after the adverse report on conditions in the workhouse in 1788.[1] Poor rates rose from £216 levied in 1782 to £745 in 1800 but decreased to £537 in 1824.[2] They rose from £586 in

1830 to £661 in 1834.[3] A shed for looms was erected at the workhouse in 1791 and a contractor appointed to employ the inmates in clothmaking. In the same year St. Mary's vestry resolved to inoculate the poor and in 1796 to deny outdoor relief to any pauper who kept a dog.[4]

The borough workhouse in Hyde Lane was conveyed to St. Peter's parish in 1725.[5] The master agreed with the trustees and parish officers in 1728 to keep the workhouse inmates for 1s. 8d. each weekly, 'pudding and butter excepted'.[6] From 1751 to 1773 contractors were found to employ the inmates in cotton spinning. In 1757 there were 17 adults, 9 girls, and 5 boys so employed.[7] Major repairs to the workhouse were made in 1792.[8] When St. Peter's parish was included in Marlborough poor-law union in 1835[9] the building was used as a union workhouse until a new one was built in 1837 on Marlborough Common in Preshute.[10] The workhouse in Hyde Lane was sold in that year.[11] Poor rates levied in St. Peter's in the period 1745–55 averaged £16 a month and in the years 1755–80 averaged £36–£38 monthly. In the later 18th century and earlier 19th there were usually four overseers.[12] As in St. Mary's parish, increased expenditure may have been encouraged by the report in 1788 on the dilapidated state of the workhouse and on its sick and dirty inmates.[13] Outdoor relief, however, remained low: £4 was spent in 1790–1, £6 in 1803. It seems that inoculation of the poor agreed upon in 1794 may have been resisted because in 1803 paupers who refused to be inoculated or to have their children inoculated were denied relief.[14] Rates totalled £548 in 1830, inexplicably only £396 in 1832, and £663 in 1834.[15] A paid assistant overseer was appointed in 1834.[16]

PUBLIC SERVICES. The borough was policed by constables, high constables from 1776 or earlier, who helped the mayor to keep the peace. In each ward a petty constable, formerly called ward alderman, arranged for the watch to be kept and for precautions against fire to be taken. In the 18th century and earlier 19th the petty constables also kept order at fairs. Offences committed in the wards were reported by the petty constables at the courts of the mayor or three weeks' court with the court of morrow speech and at the

[78] Ibid. G 22/1/205/2, f. 40v.
[79] Jewitt and Hope, *Corp. Plate and Insignia*, ii. 426, where the maces are described.
[80] Stedman, *Marlborough*, 315.
[81] Inf. from the Town Clerk.
[82] *W.A.M.* lxx–lxxi, 100.
[83] Hist. MSS. Com. 3, *4th Rep., Mostyn*, p. 351.
[84] W.R.O., G 22/1/205/2, f. 50v.
[85] Stedman, *Marlborough*, 139.
[86] Ibid. 157.
[87] Hughes, *Marlborough*, 8, where they are described as 'Elizabethan'.
[88] Inf. from the Town Clerk.
[89] e.g. W.R.O., G 22/1/108–10; G 22/1/111/1.
[90] Ibid. G 22/1/108, f. 8.
[91] e.g. ibid. G 22/1/109 (12 Apr. 1790); G 22/1/110, pp. 2–3 (11 Aug. 1824), p. 13 (11 Apr. 1825).
[92] Ibid. 871/106; 1197/14; above.
[93] W.R.O., bishop, glebe terrier.
[94] *Endowed Char. Wilts.* (N. Div.), 704.
[95] Wilts. Cuttings, xiii. 229.

[96] W.R.O. 871/66; 871/181.
[97] *Endowed Char. Wilts.* (N. Div.), 704.
[98] *Poor Law Com. 2nd Rep.* 559.
[99] *Endowed Char. Wilts.* (N. Div.), 739.
[1] Wilts. Cuttings, xiii. 229; W.R.O. 871/66.
[2] W.R.O. 871/68.
[3] *Poor Rate Returns, 1830–4*, H.C. 444, p. 214 (1835), xlvii.
[4] W.R.O. 871/66.
[5] Above.
[6] W.R.O. 871/192.
[7] Ibid. 871/190; above, trade and ind.
[8] W.R.O. 871/181.
[9] *Poor Law Com. 2nd Rep.* 559.
[10] Inf. on bldg.; W.R.O. 871/106.
[11] Notes *penes* Mr. Kempson.
[12] W.R.O. 871/137–40.
[13] Wilts. Cuttings, xiii. 229.
[14] W.R.O. 871/181.
[15] *Poor Rate Returns, 1830–4*, 214.
[16] W.R.O. 871/10.

borough quarter sessions held at Easter and Michaelmas.[17] The constables were supported by special rates.[18] An association for the prosecution of felons was founded in 1774 and still flourished in 1834.[19] A public subscription was raised in 1805 to enable watch to be kept in the borough from 29 September to 25 March. Inhabitants subscribing 5s. or more could provide deputies but those subscribing less were to serve in person. A committee was to choose two men who were to be paid to watch each night and to appoint a third to supervise them.[20] In 1836 the new borough council established a watch committee and appointed the borough beadle as policeman.[21] Watchmen were discontinued in 1850 when the county police force provided two constables, partly maintained at the borough's expense. A police station was opened in St. Margaret's, then in Preshute.[22] The old bridewell became the police station in 1854.[23] The borough police became part of the county force in 1875. A new police station was built in George Lane in Preshute in 1898.[24]

In the early 18th century the petty constables were responsible for maintaining fire-fighting equipment and for taking precautions against fire.[25] Before 1747, however, the borough appointed a separate manager of its two fire engines. The manager's salary and the upkeep of the engines were paid for by subscription.[26] From 1836, however, both were paid for from the borough fund.[27] In 1848 the engines were housed behind the National schools south of High Street.[28] After fire destroyed part of High Street in 1879 the old engines were replaced, new equipment bought, and a paid fire brigade formed. A motor engine was bought in 1926 and housed in London Road. By the Act of 1947 control of the borough fire brigade, which had been part of a national fire service during the Second World War, passed to the county council. A new fire station was opened in the Parade in 1952.[29]

The town was being lighted at corporation expense by oil lamps in the 1690s,[30] a practice which probably continued until the 19th century. A private gas company, formed c. 1822, erected works on corporation land,[31] east of London Road and north of the Kennet.[32] Gas lighting had been installed in part of the town hall by 1829[33] and in High Street by 1831.[34] In 1846 the supply

was extended, partly at the expense of the borough fund and partly by donations, to the remainder of the town by Marlborough Gas Co.[35] By 1907 gas lighting had been extended to the area taken into the borough in 1901.[36] The works were acquired by Swindon United Gas Co. in 1935 and closed in 1945. Thereafter gas was supplied from Swindon. The Swindon Gas Co. merged in the South Western Gas Board in 1949. One of the town's gas holders ceased to be used in 1961 but the other stored North Sea gas in 1982.[37]

Unsuccessful administrative attempts to light the borough by electricity were made in 1904 and 1913.[38] Herbert Leaf's gift of electric lighting to Marlborough College in 1923 was made on the condition that the town should also benefit. In that year mains were laid and an electricity committee of the town council was formed: it oversaw the installation of electric light in the town hall in 1924 and in the remainder of the town in 1926.[39] The borough had acquired its own electricity station in Pewsey Road by 1937.[40] The town scheme was nationalized by the Act of 1947,[41] and was vested in the Southern Electricity Board in 1948.[42]

The borough maintained a pest house in 1608.[43] Various *ad hoc* measures, such as the provision of accommodation for, and the isolation and nursing of, the infected poor, and the burial of the dead, were taken by the corporation during outbreaks of plague in Marlborough during the 17th century.[44] A bylaw of 1636 provided for the appointment of three men, whose wages of 6d. a day were paid for by a tax on householders, to patrol the town daily during such outbreaks and to allow entry only to strangers who could prove that they came from uninfected areas.[45]

Marlborough had a branch of the health of towns association in 1847.[46] Although in 1848 tenants of corporation property were enjoined to attend to their cesspits,[47] little was done to improve water supply, sewage disposal, or the care of fever patients until a local board of health was established in 1866.[48] A pest house, called the Rest House in 1977, which stood alone in a lane running south from Poulton Hill,[49] was closed when an isolation hospital, mainly of cast iron, was built in Blowhorn Street in 1871.[50] The iron hospital was let[51] except when needed, as in 1874.[52] It was demolished c. 1928.[53] In 1891 the

[17] Waylen, *Hist. Marlborough*, 108, 118, 122, 124-5; W.R.O., G 22/1/109; e.g. G 22/1/12; G 22/1/19, pp. 31-2; G 22/1/20, p. 5; G 22/1/30, pp. 2, 67; G 22/1/31, 6 Nov. 1772, 8 Nov. 1782; G 22/1/34, 23 June 1809, 5 Nov. 1824.
[18] e.g. W.R.O., G 22/1/109; G 22/1/110, p. 13.
[19] Ibid. G 22/1/297.
[20] Ibid. 871/80.
[21] Ibid. G 22/100/1, pp. 6, 14.
[22] Ibid. G 22/100/2.   [23] *V.C.H. Wilts.* v. 239.
[24] Hughes, *Marlborough*, 89, 91.
[25] Stedman, *Marlborough*, 225.
[26] W.R.O., G 22/1/296.
[27] Ibid. G 22/100/1, p. 17.
[28] Hughes, *Marlborough*, 86.
[29] Stedman, *Marlborough*, 313-14.
[30] Hughes, *Marlborough*, 67.
[31] Inf. from Mr. H. Nabb, Marketing Services Manager, S.W. Gas, Keynsham, Bristol.
[32] P.R.O., IR 30/38/190.
[33] Hughes, *Marlborough*, 80.
[34] Lewis, *Topog. Dict. Eng.* (1831), iii. 257.

[35] W.R.O., G 22/100/1.
[36] Stedman, *Marlborough*, 318.
[37] Inf. from Mr. Nabb.
[38] W.R.O., q. sess. deposited plans, electricity, nos. 9, 11; Stedman, *Marlborough*, 318-19.
[39] Stedman, *Marlborough*, 319.
[40] *Gale's Marlborough Dir.* (1937).
[41] Electricity Act, 1947, 10 & 11 Geo. VI, c. 54.
[42] Inf. from Mr. J. A. Wedgwood, Chairman, Southern Electricity, Maidenhead, Berks.
[43] W.R.O., G 22/1/205/2, f. 42v.
[44] Stedman, *Marlborough*, 131.
[45] *V.C.H. Wilts.* v. 320.
[46] Ibid. 325.   [47] Hughes, *Marlborough*, 86.
[48] W.R.O., G 22/111/1, p. 141; G 22/112/1.
[49] O.S. Map 1/2,500, Wilts. XXIX. 9 (1900 edn.); Chandler, *Hist. Marlborough*, 63.
[50] W.R.O., G 22/111/1, p. 189.
[51] Ibid. G 22/111/1, p. 216; G 22/111/4, pp. 379-80.
[52] Ibid. G 22/111/2, p. 37.
[53] Ibid. G 22/100/11, p. 115.

corporation undertook to provide a public water supply. Waterworks, which comprised an engine house, pumping machinery, and a reservoir, had been constructed on Postern Hill in Preshute and main supply pipes had been laid by 1896. Another reservoir was provided and additional machinery installed on Postern Hill in 1915. A tank for storing water built on Marlborough Common in 1941[54] was demolished in 1970.[55] The main outlet for the town sewage was the Kennet in 1864. Attempts in 1894 to enlarge the borough were unsuccessful because its disposal system was inadequate. Although sewerage works were opened in Elcot Lane, then in Preshute, in 1900,[56] the system did not function fully until the 1920s.[57] Sewers were afterwards extended to remaining parts of Preshute transferred to Marlborough in 1934.[58]

A bylaw of 1577 required householders to clear their frontages on fair and market days and on Saturday nights.[59] Breaches of it were the concern of the views and courts leet until the earlier 19th century.[60] It was suggested in 1866 that a general rate be levied for watering the streets.[61] That was done in 1885 and earlier by the town's water cart.[62]

Houses in Marlborough were numbered c. 1874.[63] The town council built houses for letting in Chiminage Close in 1912 and 1923, in Lainey's Close in 1921, 1926, and 1928, and in Coldharbour Lane in 1921.[64] Council houses were also built at St. Margaret's from c. 1920 to c. 1950,[65] and on part of Port field from the 1960s.[66]

A swimming pool south of Kennet Place, built after the First World War by the town improvement committee, was taken over by the corporation in 1937 and still used in 1982.[67] A cemetery for the borough was opened in 1924[68] on Marlborough Common in Preshute north-west of the burial ground provided for Preshute and the Marlborough parishes in 1855.[69]

A branch of the county library was opened in no. 1 the Green in 1936 or 1937.[70] It was moved in 1964 to the buildings in High Street vacated by St. Peter's school.[71] Marlborough, which stood on a main 17th-century postal route, had a postmaster, and presumably a post office, in 1610 or earlier.[72] A post office on the south side of High Street was burned down in 1879[73] and replaced by another on the north. In 1909 a new post office was built at no. 101 High Street.[74]

PARLIAMENTARY REPRESENTATION.
Marlborough was represented at the parliament of 1275[75] and returned two burgesses in 1295 and later.[76] The borough was frequently represented during the period 1392–1420, presumably because it was the most important town in north-east Wiltshire at the time.[77] In the 14th century, and perhaps earlier, the queen's bailiff in the county, who was her deputy at Marlborough, returned names of elected members.[78] After 1405 the burgesses sent the names of those elected to the county court to be returned in the county indenture.[79] Marlborough was generally accounted a Crown borough until c. 1500.[80] Most members were prominent townsmen who often held not only borough but county office. John Bird (d. 1445), a resident burgess who represented Marlborough in 1402, 1413–15, 1426, 1429, 1435, and 1437, also acted as county tax collector and escheator and, from 1405 and earlier to 1433 and later, as steward of Queen Joan's Wiltshire lands.[81]

The influence of the Seymour family gradually replaced that of the Crown during the earlier 16th century and became firmly established after the reversion of the borough lordship was granted to Edward Seymour, duke of Somerset, in 1547.[82] Most members were still resident townsmen such as Robert Were or Brown (d. 1570), M.P. in 1553,[83] and William Daniell (d. 1604), M.P. in 1558 and 1559. Daniell's patron was possibly William Herbert, earl of Pembroke, whose influence displaced that of the Seymours in the 1550s during the minority of Edward Seymour, later earl of Hertford.[84] The borough seems to have paid its members in the 16th century,[85] and in the earlier 17th when a member received £2 and incidental expenses for a parliament.[86]

The franchise in the 17th century and later was restricted to the burgesses.[87] Under a new system of representation imposed briefly during the Interregnum, Marlborough was allowed only one member and, with Devizes and Salisbury, was one of only three Wiltshire towns summoned to parliament in 1654.[88] In the 17th century and earlier 18th the polls, in which each burgess had two votes, were held in the town hall at special sessions of the morrow speech courts.[89]

After 1676 the Whig interest of the Seymours was challenged by the Tory interest of Thomas

[54] Stedman, *Marlborough*, 321–2.
[55] Wilts. Cuttings, xxiii. 311.
[56] Hughes, *Marlborough*, 87, 91–2.
[57] Stedman, *Marlborough*, 324–5.
[58] Hughes, *Marlborough*, 94.
[59] Waylen, *Hist. Marlborough*, 119.
[60] e.g. W.R.O., G 22/1/13, pp. 4–8; G 22/1/17, p. 48; G 22/1/110, pp. 4–9.
[61] Ibid. G 22/111/1, p. 11.
[62] Hughes, *Marlborough*, 90.
[63] Ibid. 89.
[64] Stedman, *Marlborough*, 327–8.
[65] Above, Preshute, introduction.
[66] Inf. from the Town Clerk, Council Offices.
[67] Stedman, *Marlborough*, 315.
[68] Chandler, *Hist. Marlborough*, 74.
[69] Above, Preshute, introduction.
[70] Gale's *Marlborough Dir.* (1937); Fletcher's *Marlborough Dir.* (1962–3).
[71] Inf. from the Director, Libr. and Mus. Service, Co. Hall, Trowbridge; below, educ.

[72] Ogilby, *Brit.* p. 19; Stedman, *Marlborough*, 296.
[73] Hughes, *Marlborough*, 90; Chandler, *Hist. Marlborough*, 12.
[74] Chandler, *Hist. Marlborough*, 13–14.
[75] *V.C.H. Wilts.* v. 72.
[76] *Names of Members Returned*, H.C. 69, pp. 6 sqq. (1878), lxii.
[77] *V.C.H. Wilts.* v. 73–4.
[78] TS. article on boro. 1386–1421 *penes* Hist. of Parl. Trust.
[79] 7 Hen. IV, c. 15; T. Carew, *Rights of Elections*, i. 385.
[80] *Hist. Parl., Reg.* 1439–1500, 711.
[81] TS. biog. *penes* Hist. of Parl. Trust.
[82] *Cal. Pat.* 1547–8, 124; *Hist. Parl., Commons*, 1558–1603, i. 275.   [83] *Hist. Parl., Commons*, 1509–58, iii. 562–3.
[84] Ibid. i. 228; ii. 12; *Complete Peerage*, vi. 505.
[85] *Hist. Parl., Commons*, 1509–58, i. 229.
[86] Stedman, *Marlborough*, 125.
[87] Ibid. 125–6; *1st Rep. Com. Mun. Corp.* App. I, 84.
[88] *V.C.H. Wilts.* v. 150.
[89] Stedman, *Marlborough*, 214.

Bruce, from 1685 earl of Ailesbury.[90] The efforts of the rival parties to control the corporation resulted in attempts, in 1679 and later, to extend the franchise to all householders[91] and in the period 1711–14 led to the election of rival mayors, who in 1715 supported rival parliamentary candidates.[92] The electorate in 1705 was 'very mercenary and resolved to serve the highest bidder . . . being now grown as corrupt as any other borough'.[93] In 1712 Charles, duke of Somerset, offered £50 to any who would desert the Bruce interest.[94] The restriction of votes to the burgesses was confirmed in 1717[95] and 1830.[96] The electorate numbered 77 in 1623.[97] The 40 burgesses recorded in 1704 had been reduced to 21 in 1734.[98] Bruce and Seymour interests shared the representation from 1722, when Algernon Seymour, earl of Hertford, was returned, until 1734, when the return of two Bruce candidates was secured. Thereafter Marlborough was a pocket borough of the Bruces.[99] Sir John Hynde Cotton, Bt., the Jacobite leader, was one of the borough members from 1741 until his death in 1752 and was succeeded by his son and namesake, who sat for the borough during the period 1752–61.[1] The constituency was managed for Thomas Bruce, Lord Bruce, from 1776 earl of Ailesbury, by his agent Charles Bill who was a member of the corporation and served as mayor. In 1771 the corporation agreed to nominate new burgesses only with Lord Bruce's consent.[2] An unsuccessful attempt to widen the franchise was made in the later 18th century and earlier 19th by the Marlborough independent and constitutional association.[3]

In 1832 Preshute parish was added to the parliamentary borough,[4] which in 1833 had 230 registered voters. At that time, however, the steward of Charles, marquess of Ailesbury, was a leading member of the corporation and Lord Ailesbury could still be sure that the members chosen were his nominees.[5] The borough lost one member in 1867 when the franchise was again widened.[6] Its allegiance was Tory[7] until 1885 when it lost its remaining member and was merged in the Devizes division of the county.[8]

CHURCHES. The churches which William Beaufay, bishop of East Anglia (d. 1091), gave or devised to Osmund, bishop of Salisbury,

possibly included those of St. Mary and St. Peter in Marlborough. Bishop Osmund endowed Salisbury cathedral chapter with the churches in 1091 and their histories were the same as that of Preshute church until 1223.[9] In that year the bishop of Salisbury detached both St. Mary's and St. Peter's from the prebend of Blewbury (Berks., later Oxon.) and Marlborough and included them within his peculiar jurisdiction.[10] In the 19th century St. Mary's served the borough east of Kingsbury Street and St. Peter's the borough west of it.[11]

In 1238 the bishop ordained a vicarage in St. Mary's church, which as architectural evidence shows existed in the 12th century, and assigned the advowson of it to the dean of Salisbury.[12] Thereafter the deans, or their proctors as in 1334 and 1376, presented vicars until the early 19th century. The bishop collated in 1563, presumably because the deanery was vacant, and for unknown reasons in 1583 and 1663. In 1608 John Sharpe presented under grant of a turn from, inexplicably, Salisbury chapter.[13] By Act of 1840 the advowson was transferred to the bishop.[14] In 1917 the bishop, also patron of St. Peter's church, presented the same man to both benefices which were held in plurality until united in 1924 as the rectory of Marlborough, St. Peter and St. Paul with St. Mary the Virgin.[15] The title was altered in 1952 to the united benefice of Marlborough, St. Mary the Virgin with St. Peter and St. Paul. The parishes were united in 1952 and St. Mary's became the parish church.[16] The united benefice was united with Preshute vicarage in 1976 and a team ministry established.[17]

In 1238 the revenues of St. Mary's, mainly tithes, were assigned to the vicars, who until 1252 paid £1 yearly to Salisbury chapter to maintain a candle in the cathedral choir.[18] The vicarage was worth £6 13s. 4d. in 1255 and £10 9s. 4d. in 1535.[19] The poverty of the living is suggested by several augmentations of it. Parishioners subscribed to augment the income of £13 6s. 8d. in 1674.[20] In 1733 the Revd. Benjamin D'Aranda and Leonard Twells, vicar 1722–37, gave, to augment the vicarage, £200 which was matched by £200 from Queen Anne's Bounty.[21] Edward Cressett (d. 1693) bequeathed £80 for the vicars but by 1783 the capital had been lost.[22] A bequest

[90] Hist. Parl., Commons, 1715–54, i. 349; Complete Peerage, i. 59.
[91] Stedman, Marlborough, 158–60.
[92] Hist. Parl., Commons, 1715–54, i. 349.
[93] Hist. MSS. Com. 43, 15th Rep. VII, Ailesbury, p. 190.
[94] V.C.H. Wilts. v. 213.
[95] 1st Rep. Com. Mun. Corp. App. I, 84.
[96] Lond. Gaz. 3 Dec. 1830, p. 2540.
[97] Stedman, Marlborough, 125.
[98] 1st Rep. Com. Mun. Corp. App. I, 84.
[99] Hist. Parl., Commons, 1715–54, i. 349.
[1] Ibid. 584–6.
[2] Ibid. 1754–90, i. 418; Complete Peerage, i. 63.
[3] V.C.H. Wilts. v. 214.
[4] Reform Act, 2 Wm. IV, c. 45, s. 7; 2 & 3 Wm. IV, c. 64, s. 35 and sched. O. 38.
[5] 1st Rep. Com. Mun. Corp. App. I, 84–5.
[6] V.C.H. Wilts. v. 310.
[7] Ibid. 308.
[8] Redistribution of Seats Act, 48 & 49 Vic. c. 23.

[9] Reg. St. Osmund (Rolls Ser.), i. 199; above, Preshute, church.
[10] Sar. Chart. and Doc. (Rolls Ser.), 123–4; Reg. St. Osmund (Rolls Ser.), i. 327–8.
[11] P.R.O., IR 30/38/190–1.
[12] Sar. Chart. and Doc. (Rolls Ser.), 244–5.
[13] Phillipps, Wilts. Inst. (index in W.A.M. xxviii. 225).
[14] 3 & 4 Vic. c. 113, s. 41.
[15] Crockford (1926), where the benefices are wrongly said to have been united in 1925; Lond. Gaz. 28 Mar. 1924, pp. 2600–1. [16] Lond. Gaz. 5 Sept. 1952, pp. 4708–9.
[17] Ibid. 22 Jan. 1976, p. 1020.
[18] Sar. Chart. and Doc. (Rolls Ser.), 244–5; W.R.O., bishop, glebe terriers, 1698, ?1783.
[19] Rot. Hund. (Rec. Com.), ii (1), 235; Valor Eccl. (Rec. Com.), ii. 150.
[20] P.R.O., E 134/26 Chas. II Mich./1.
[21] C. Hodgson, Queen Anne's Bounty (1826 edn.), 157, 417; D.N.B.; Alum. Oxon. 1500–1714, i. 372.
[22] P.R.O., PROB 11/414 (P.C.C. 76 Coker); W.R.O., bishop, glebe terrier, ?1783.

of £200 from Sarah Franklin and a parliamentary grant of £300 in 1811 and another parliamentary grant made in 1812 were used partly to buy 12 a. in Liddington, sold in 1919.[23] Charles Francis, rector of Collingbourne Ducis and of Mildenhall and four times mayor of Marlborough, by will proved 1821 gave £100 which produced £3 3s. 8d. in 1905 but by 1982 had merged with other endowments of the benefice.[24] From 1829 to 1831 the benefice had an average income of £100.[25] In 1839 £350 by subscription and £100 from a Mrs. Pyncombe's trustees were given.[26] The tithes were valued at £25 15s. in 1843 and commuted.[27]

The vicar had a house on the Green in 1380.[28] A later vicarage house was apparently no. 8 the Green,[29] which is a 17th-century timber-framed building. It was uninhabitable in 1698[30] and 1812,[31] and was sold c. 1838.[32] A new house at the junction of St. Martin's and Stonebridge Lane had been built by 1843.[33] From 1917 the incumbent lived in St. Peter's Rectory which became the Rectory of the united benefice in 1924. St. Mary's Vicarage was sold in 1927.[34]

Between 1252 and 1254 the inhabitants of the 'new land' east of Marlborough built a church dedicated to St. Martin and from 1254 gave the rector of Preshute 40s. a year to find a chaplain to serve it.[35] The church was either enlarged or repaired in 1270 when the king allowed the inhabitants to take six oaks from Savernake forest for work then in progress.[36] From 1330 the vicar of Preshute received the pension and paid the chaplain's stipend.[37] The church was later endowed with land and nine tenements.[38] In 1499, when it was worth £4 a year, the church was served, contrary to canon law, by a friar.[39] St. Martin's was called a parish in the earlier 16th century because it had its own church, was separated by Marlborough from its mother church, and was separately assessed for taxation.[40] It was transferred from Preshute to St. Mary's parish, Marlborough, c. 1548.[41] The church had ceased to be used as such by 1567;[42] it stood in Coldharbour Lane.[43]

In 1258 Eustace Blowe granted land in Marlborough to Idony of Mildenhall who was to pay 6s. to St. Mary's for masses of the Blessed Virgin Mary.[44] The chantry so founded was perhaps that which John Kingswood, a canon of St. Mary's priory, Studley (Warws.), was allowed to serve by papal dispensation in 1466.[45] Its endowments were perhaps the lands reputed in 1579 to have belonged to a chantry of St. Mary in Marlborough.[46] Thomas Poulton, bishop of Worcester, by will proved 1433 gave money for masses to be said for five years at the lady altar.[47]

By will proved 1502 Robert Hutchins or Forster gave £1 from his lands in Marlborough, one of the Ogbournes, Elcot, and Bourton (Berks., later Oxon.), which he devised to Henry Pengryve, for an obit in St. Mary's church.[48] Pengryve by will proved 1518 charged those lands with £9 yearly, of which £6 was for a priest to pray for him, Hutchins or Forster, and their friends, and £1 6s. 8d. was for his obit.[49] At its dissolution the chantry, worth £10 3s. 4d. yearly, was served by an old priest who had no other living.[50] By deed of 1503 an unknown donor conveyed property in Marlborough to endow a chantry in St. Mary's. Its property was worth £8 8s. 2d. in 1548.[51]

In 1527 William Serle endowed a Jesus service in St. Mary's with property in the Green ward and in Kingsbury Street, which, worth £1 5s. 4d. in 1548, was sold with other chantry property in Marlborough to the mayor and burgesses in 1550.[52] Rents from some of those properties were afterwards used to maintain St. Mary's church. Income from the Church Estate, then no. 5 the Green and a cottage in Herd Street, was so used in 1905.[53] The estate was sold at an unknown date and the capital invested. In 1982 the income of St. Mary's Church Estates charity was still used for church maintenance.[54]

The chantry priests apparently acted as assistant curates in the earlier 16th century.[55] Curates frequently assisted the vicars thereafter.[56] Thomas Miles, vicar 1643–9, was also vicar of Preshute 1647–9.[57] William Hughes (d. 1688), ejected from the vicarage in 1662, remained in Marlborough as a dissenting minister.[58] Leonard Twells, vicar 1722–37, wrote theological works.[59] In 1783 services with sermons, omitted when the Sacrament was administered, were held

[23] Hodgson, *Queen Anne's Bounty* (1826 edn.), 208, 417; Ch. Com. files NB 34/220c; NB 34/221.
[24] *Endowed Char. Wilts.* (N. Div.), 737; *V.C.H. Wilts.* xi. 114; Chandler, *Hist. Marlborough*, 46; above, Mildenhall, church; inf. from the Revd. W. Down, the Rectory, Rawlingswell Lane.
[25] *Rep. Com. Eccl. Revenues*, 840.
[26] Hodgson, *Queen Anne's Bounty* (1845 edn.), p. ccxxvi.
[27] P.R.O., IR 29/38/190.
[28] *Bradenstoke Cart.* (W.R.S. xxxv), p. 89.
[29] *W.A.M.* li. 201 n.
[30] W.R.O., bishop, glebe terrier, 1698.
[31] *W.A.M.* xli. 134.
[32] Ch. Com. file 15928.
[33] P.R.O., IR 29/38/190; IR 30/38/190.
[34] Ch. Com. file 10786; ibid. copy deeds, ccccxv, no. 41823.
[35] *Sar. Chart. and Doc.* (Rolls Ser.), 320–2.
[36] *Close R.* 1268–72, 224.
[37] *Reg. Martival* (Cant. & York Soc.), ii. 640.
[38] P.R.O., E 310/26/153, f. 7.
[39] *W.A.M.* xxxvi. 547.
[40] e.g. *L. & P. Hen. VIII*, iii (2), p. 1490; P.R.O., C 3/189/78.
[41] P.R.O., C 3/189/78.
[42] Ibid. E 310/26/153, f. 7.

[43] Waylen, *Hist. Marlborough*, 494–5; O.S. Map 6″, SU 16 NE. (1961 edn.).
[44] *Cat. Anct. D.* iii, D 332.
[45] *Cal. Papal Reg.* xii. 510, where Kingswood is described as of 'Stanley in Arden'. He was clearly from Studley: D. Knowles and R. N. Hadcock, *Medieval Religious Hos.* 175.
[46] P.R.O., E 178/2414.
[47] *W.A.M.* xxvi. 58.
[48] P.R.O., PROB 11/13 (P.C.C. 11 Blamyr).
[49] Ibid. PROB 11/19 (P.C.C. 8 Ayloffe).
[50] Ibid. E 301/58, no. 54.
[51] Ibid. E 301/58, no. 49.
[52] Ibid. E 301/58, no. 52; E 318/Box 34/1881; *W.A.M.* xxxvi. 572.
[53] *Endowed Char. Wilts.* (N. Div.), 713–14, 736.
[54] Inf. from Mr. Down.
[55] P.R.O., E 301/58, unnumbered entry after no. 49.
[56] e.g. ibid. C 1/1118/30; *Vis. Queries, 1783* (W.R.S. xxvii), pp. 152–3; W.R.O., bishop, vis. queries, 1864; *Clergy List* (1866 and later edns.); *Crockford* (1896 and later edns.); *Lond. Gaz.* 28 Mar. 1924, pp. 2600–1.
[57] Phillipps, *Wilts. Inst.* ii. 21; *Calamy Revised*, ed. A. G. Matthews, 282–3.
[58] *Calamy Revised*, ed. Matthews, 282–3; below, prot. noncof.
[59] *D.N.B.*

on Sunday mornings and afternoons. Other services were held on Monday and Wednesday mornings and on Saturday evenings. Holy Communion was celebrated on Christmas and Easter days, Whit and Trinity Sundays, and the first Sunday in the month. There were usually between 20 and 30 communicants but 60 at Easter.[60] In 1851 an average of 650 had attended morning services and 450 evening ones over the past year. Services held every third Sunday afternoon had congregations averaging 400 people.[61] Morning and evening services were held on Sundays and great festivals in 1864. Extra Lent and Advent services were held. Prayers, attended by about ten people, were said on Friday mornings and, attended by about fifty, on saints' days. Holy Communion was celebrated on the same days as it had been in 1783. Of the 250 communicants in the parish, an average of 60 received the Sacrament at great festivals and 40 at other times.[62]

By will proved 1678 William White, rector of Pusey and of Appleton (both Berks.), gave £5 yearly to the vicars on condition that they catechized at evening prayer.[63] The money was still received in 1905 and in 1982.[64] White also bequeathed his extensive library to the mayor and burgesses of Marlborough in trust for the vicars of St. Mary's.[65] A room to house it was incorporated in the west gallery of the church built c. 1707. The books, catalogued by Christopher Wordsworth, rector of St. Peter's, in 1903, were deposited in 1944 at Marlborough College where they remained in 1981.[66]

The church of *ST. MARY*, so dedicated by 1223,[67] is built of ashlar and rubble, with ashlar dressings, and comprises a chancel with north chapel, a nave with south aisle and south porch, and a west tower.[68] During the 15th century and early 16th the aisles of the 12th-century church were rebuilt and extended to six bays, of which the easternmost formed chapels flanking the chancel, and a crenellated west tower, in which the west door of the 12th-century church was reset, was built. Partial rebuilding after the fire of 1653 included the shortening of the chancel,[69] the erection of Tuscan columns supporting semicircular arches to replace the south arcade dividing nave and south aisle, the merging of the nave and the north aisle, and the heightening of the north wall of the church. West, south, and north galleries were put up in the early 18th century

and four square three-light windows inserted in the north wall at clerestory level. The galleries were dismantled and the windows blocked in the 19th century.[70] In 1873 a new chancel was built to designs by G. E. Street and a 15th-century window reset as an east window.[71] The south porch was added and a new nave ceiling inserted in the 19th century. The church was thoroughly restored in the period 1955–7.[72] A Roman stone relief of the goddess Fortuna is set in the west nave wall.[73] A clock with chimes was in the church in the 18th century. It was replaced in 1888.[74]

Thomas Poulton, bishop of Worcester 1426–33, bequeathed a silver chalice and other plate. In 1553 the king's commissioners took 17 oz. of plate and left the same amount for the parish. St. Mary's in 1982 possessed two silver chalices hallmarked 1657 and 1846, two patens, one hallmarked 1690 and the other given in the later 19th century, a flagon hallmarked 1843,[75] and additional plate given in 1967.[76]

There were five bells in 1553 and in the earlier 20th century a ring of six: (i) 1699, Robert Cor, recast by Taylor, 1922; (ii) 1653, William and Thomas Purdue, recast by Taylor, 1922; (iii) 1769, Robert Wells; (iv) 1653, William and Thomas Purdue; (v) 1724, Robert Cor; (vi) 1669, William and Roger Purdue.[77] In 1969 new treble and second bells, cast from the discarded peal of St. Peter's, were added to make a peal of eight.[78]

Registrations of baptisms, marriages, and burials survive from 1602. Entries of baptisms are missing for the years 1716–20 and 1736–9, those of marriages for 1716–37, and those of burials for 1716–39.[79]

After 1223 the bishop collated to the rectory of St. Peter's until it was united in 1924 with the vicarage of St. Mary's. Exceptions occurred in 1246 and 1388 when the king presented *sede vacante*, in 1556 when Sir Edward Baynton presented by grant of a turn, and in 1579 when for an unknown reason the queen presented.[80] When the parishes of St. Mary's and St. Peter's were united in 1952 St. Peter's became a chapel of ease.[81] It was declared redundant in 1974.[82]

The rectory, the revenue of which came only from tithes and oblations, was valued at £5 in 1255.[83] The rector protested c. 1319 that parishioners attended the Carmelite chapel nearby

[60] *Vis. Queries, 1783* (W.R.S. xxvii), pp. 151–3.
[61] P.R.O., HO 129/255/1/9/20.
[62] W.R.O., bishop, vis. queries, 1864.
[63] P.R.O., PROB 11/357 (P.C.C. 80 Reeve).
[64] *Endowed Char. Wilts.* (N. Div.), 737; inf. from Mr. Down.　[65] P.R.O., PROB 11/357 (P.C.C. 80 Reeve).
[66] The libr. is described in *W.A.M.* li. 194–215.
[67] *Sar. Chart. and Doc.* (Rolls Ser.), 123. In the later 19th cent. and the 20th the usual dedication was to St. Mary the Virgin: e.g. *Lond. Gaz.* 9 June 1854, p. 1784; 22 Jan. 1976, p. 1020.
[68] There are NE. and SW. views in 1803 by J. Buckler in W.A.S. Libr., vol. iv. 18–19. For the church from the NE. see plate facing p. 144.
[69] The shortened E. end is depicted in 1803: Buckler, watercolour in W.A.S. Libr., vol. iv. 18.
[70] W.R.O., G 22/1/205/2, f. 184; Chandler, *Hist. Marlborough*, 22.
[71] W.R.O., bishop, pet. for faculties, bdle. 21, no. 8; Pevsner, *Wilts.* (2nd edn.), 333.

[72] Chandler, *Hist. Marlborough*, 22.
[73] *V.C.H. Wilts.* i (1), 85–6.
[74] Chandler, *Hist. Marlborough*, 23; W.R.O., bishop, glebe terrier, ?1783.
[75] *W.A.M.* xxvi. 58; Nightingale, *Wilts. Plate*, 156–7; inf. from Mr. Down.
[76] Chandler, *Hist. Marlborough*, 23.
[77] Walters, *Wilts. Bells*, 132–3, 290, 310, 314.
[78] Chandler, *Hist. Marlborough*, 23.
[79] W.R.O. 1050/1–14. Extracts are printed in *Coll. Topog. et Gen.* v. 268–72, and reg. of marriages, except those for 1751–3, in *Wilts. Par. Reg.* (Mar.), ed. W. P. W. Phillimore and J. Sadler, ii. 65–125.
[80] Phillipps, *Wilts. Inst.* (index in *W.A.M.* xxviii. 225); *Clerical Guide* (1822); *Clergy List* (1859 and later edns.); *Crockford* (1896 and later edns.); *Cal. Pat. 1232–47*, 493.
[81] *Lond. Gaz.* 5 Sept. 1952, pp. 4708–9.
[82] Ibid. 8 Oct. 1974, p. 8537.
[83] *Rot. Hund.* (Rec. Com.), ii (1), 235; W.R.O., bishop, glebe terriers, 1677, 1783.

and in 1320 the friars agreed to compensate the rector with 10s. yearly.[84] The rector still received the rent from the former priory lands in 1625.[85] The rectory was worth £12 in 1535.[86] Its poverty, like that of St. Mary's vicarage, was relieved by augmentations. Most of them were made by the benefactors who augmented St. Mary's. In 1655 £30 was given.[87] Edward Cressett by will proved 1693 gave £80 to the rectors but the capital was afterwards lost.[88] In 1783 Cressett's kinswoman Anne Liddiard gave £80 to Queen Anne's Bounty to replace it, Thomas Meyler, rector 1774–86, and Mrs. A. Hammond gave £20, and a Mrs. Pyncombe's trustees gave £100, benefactions matched by £200 from bounty funds.[89] Those sums were used in 1786 to buy 9 a. at Badbury in Chiseldon, sold in 1971.[90] In 1811 Sarah Franklin's executors gave £200 and in the same year there was a parliamentary grant of £300.[91] By will proved 1821 Charles Francis gave £200, the income from which was £6 in 1905 and 1982.[92] From 1829 to 1831 the rectory had an average yearly income of £130.[93] The tithes were valued at £16 in 1843 and commuted.[94] The Ecclesiastical Commissioners augmented the living by £76 yearly in 1844.[95]

The Rectory was in High Street. It was apparently rebuilt c. 1653 in a similar style to other buildings in the street.[96] The house was considered uninhabitable c. 1830[97] and was replaced in 1832–3 by another west of it built of grey stone to designs by Henry Harrison.[98] The incumbent of the united benefice lived there from 1924 until 1966. The house was then sold and replaced by the Rectory in Rawlingswell Lane where the rector lived in 1981.[99]

In 1446 Isabel Bird (d. 1476) was licensed to found and endow a chantry at St. Catherine's altar where a chaplain was to say masses for the soul of her husband John Bird (d. 1445), many times M.P. for Marlborough in the earlier 15th century, for Humphrey, duke of Gloucester, and for herself.[1] She endowed the chantry in 1449 with 6 tenements, 52 a. of land, and rents worth £4 in Marlborough and elsewhere.[2] In 1473 she appointed the rector of Huish as chaplain and granted the advowson to Thomas Beke and his wife Isabel.[3] The advowson was intended to pass with Huish manor but in 1479 and 1502, when the lordship of that manor was being disputed, the rectors of St. Peter's and the mayor of Marlborough presented, and the bishop collated in 1496, 1506, and 1512.[4] The chantry, which had property worth £8 in 1535, was dissolved in 1548.[5] In the earlier 20th century no. 99 High Street, in which the chaplain may have lived, still had features of the later 15th century and the earlier 16th, but many such features were destroyed c. 1923[6] and a timber-framed room on the first floor was the only one to survive in 1981.

By will proved 1433 Thomas Poulton, bishop of Worcester, gave books on condition that a chaplain say masses for his soul in St. Peter's for three years and devised a tenement in Marlborough to enable his nephew, or if he failed to do so the rector of St. Peter's, to maintain them.[7] No more is known of the masses.

Masses in St. Peter's, which an unknown donor endowed with lands in Marlborough by deed of 1504, may have been Our Lady's service mentioned c. 1548. The lands, worth £8 3s. 9d., passed to the Crown in 1548.[8]

The Jesus service, the only living of an old priest in 1548, was endowed piecemeal in the period 1519–27. Its properties in Marlborough were sold in 1550 by the Crown to the mayor and burgesses of Marlborough, who may have assigned the profits of some to maintain St. Peter's church.[9] Some of the endowments were sold before 1834 when rents from the Sun, the Marlborough Arms, and former inns in High Street and from the Bell and a former inn in Kingsbury Street were so applied. More property was sold in 1868, 1885,[10] and 1909, the proceeds were invested, and in 1981 the income of £86 was used to meet the expenses of the united benefice of Marlborough.[11]

A hermit, John Benton, possibly lived in the parish in the period 1519–21.[12] In 1523 another was given land, probably north of High Street, on which he built a hermitage which became vested in the mayor of Marlborough.[13] Of the many rectors who held other preferments, Robert Neel, rector 1388–90, was also a canon of Chichester, Ralph Hethcote, collated in 1481, was a notary public by apostolic authority and in 1484 the king's orator at the Roman *curia*, and others were canons of Salisbury.[14] In the 15th century and the earlier 16th the chantry priests

[84] *Reg. Martival* (Cant. & York Soc.), ii. 258, 271–3.
[85] *Wilts. Inq. p.m.* 1625–49 (Index Libr.), 2.
[86] *Valor Eccl.* (Rec. Com.), ii. 150.
[87] *Cal. S.P. Dom.* 1655–6, 73.
[88] P.R.O., PROB 11/414 (P.C.C. 76 Coker); W.R.O., bishop, glebe terrier, 1783.
[89] Hodgson, *Queen Anne's Bounty* (1845 edn.), pp. clxxiv, cccxxxvi; W.R.O., bishop, glebe terrier, 1783.
[90] Ch. Com. file F 3177; K 6967; inf. from Ch. Com., Lond.
[91] Hodgson, *Queen Anne's Bounty* (1845 edn.), pp. clxxxv, cccxxxvi.
[92] *Endowed Char. Wilts.* (N. Div.), 731; inf. from Mr. Down. [93] *Rep. Com. Eccl. Revenues*, 842–3.
[94] P.R.O., IR 29/38/191.
[95] *Lond. Gaz.* 3 May 1844, p. 1509.
[96] W.R.O., bishop, glebe terrier, 1783.
[97] *Rep. Com. Eccl. Revenues*, 842–3.
[98] W.R.O., bishop, pet. for faculties, bdle. 2, no. 44; Colvin, *Brit. Architects*, 393.
[99] *Lond. Gaz.* 28 Mar. 1924, pp. 2600–1; inf. from Ch. Com.

[1] *Cal. Pat.* 1441–6, 416; *V.C.H. Wilts.* x. 78; W.R.O. 9/19/712; above, parl. rep.
[2] *Cal. Pat.* 1446–52, 301; above, Ogbourne St. Andrew, manors; Ogbourne St. Geo., manors.
[3] W.R.O. 9/19/713; Phillipps, *Wilts. Inst.* i. 161, 164.
[4] Phillipps, *Wilts. Inst.* i. 167, 178, 180, 184, 190–1, 193–5; *V.C.H. Wilts.* x. 78–9.
[5] *Valor Eccl.* (Rec. Com.), ii. 150; P.R.O., E 301/58, no. 53.
[6] The ho. is described and illustrated by C. E. Ponting in *W.A.M.* xxxvi. 585–9; xlii. 349.
[7] Ibid. xxvi. 59, 71.
[8] Ibid. xxii. 329; P.R.O., E 318/Box 25/1423.
[9] *W.A.M.* xxxvi. 571–2; P.R.O., E 301/58, no. 47; E 318/Box 34/1881.
[10] *Endowed Char. Wilts.* (N. Div.), 706–13, 731–3.
[11] Inf. from Mr. Down.
[12] *L. & P. Hen. VIII*, iii (1), p. 500; iv (3), p. 2732.
[13] Notes *penes* Mr. Kempson.
[14] A. B. Emden, *Biog. Reg. Univ. Oxf. to 1500*, ii. 923, 1341; *Cal. Papal Reg.* iv. 330; Phillipps, *Wilts. Inst.* i. 208, 212; ii. 30, 40; *Fasti Eccl. Sar.* ed. W. H. Jones, ii. 403.

may have acted as assistant curates.[15] From 1726 to 1829, except in the period 1795-1808, the rectory was held in plurality with the vicarage of Preshute.[16] Erasmus Williams, rector from 1830 to 1858 and a baronet from 1843, the author of political works, held the rectory in plurality with Rushall.[17] Christopher Wordsworth, rector 1897-1911, a canon of Lincoln and master of St. Nicholas's hospital, Salisbury, wrote and edited historical and liturgical works.[18] Curates assisted him and his successors and in 1924 it was expressly stipulated that a curate should assist the incumbent of the united benefice.[19]

In 1783 services with sermons were held twice on Sundays. The morning sermon was omitted when the Sacrament, received by an average of 30 people, was administered on the last Sunday in the month. In addition Holy Communion was celebrated on Christmas and Easter days and on Whit Sunday when many more communicated. Morning prayers were said on Tuesdays, Thursdays, Fridays, and holy days. The rector complained that the strong dissenting tradition in Marlborough hampered his ministry.[20] Congregations averaging 500-600 people were reckoned in 1851 to have attended Sunday services over the past year.[21] Two Sunday services were held in 1864, and morning prayers said on Wednesdays, Fridays, and holy days were attended by 12-20 people. Advent and Lent services attended by 100-200 people were held. Two services were held on Good Friday and on certain festivals. Holy Communion was celebrated on the same occasions as in 1783. Of the 160 communicants between 80 and 109 received the Sacrament at great festivals and an average of 55 at other times.[22]

The church of *ST. PETER AND ST. PAUL*, so called from the later 16th century, was called St. Peter's in 1223 and intermittently until the later 19th century.[23] It is built of limestone ashlar and has a chancel, with north vestry and north and south chapels, and an aisled and crenellated nave with south porch and south-west tower.[24] The church had been built by 1223 within the width of High Street; because the street runs south-west and north-east[25] limiting the length of the church, the tower was built at the west end of the south aisle and the north aisle has its west wall at an oblique angle.[26] Little of that church

remains except rubble walling in the north-west corner of the present nave. The church was rebuilt from the later 15th century to the earlier 16th, nave, aisles, and tower first, and then the vaulted chancel, with north and south chapels, and the two-storeyed porch. The tower pinnacles were replaced in 1701.[27] The church was restored and the chancel refitted during 1862-3 by T. H. Wyatt, who removed the west gallery inserted in 1627, built the north vestry, reroofed the nave and raised the pitch of the chancel roof, and replaced the earlier 16th-century five-light east window with one of three lights.[28]

The church had a clock in 1575 and 1746.[29] There was an organ in 1576.[30] Another installed in 1776 attracted Preshute parishioners to services in 1783.[31] A memorial brass commemorates Robert Were or Brown (d. 1570), M.P. for the borough in 1553 and many times mayor of Marlborough. There are many wall monuments of the 17th, 18th, and 19th centuries. The church, redundant in 1974, was given over for the use of the town in 1978. It was maintained by St. Peter's and St. Paul's Trust in 1980 when it housed an information centre and was used for exhibitions and concerts.[32]

In 1553 the king's commissioners took 6 oz. of plate and left a chalice of 12 oz. St. Peter's had a silver cup with cover, a silver offertory basin, and a silver salver in 1783, which were all presumably sold when a set of parcel-gilt plate hallmarked 1842 was acquired.[33] The plate was transferred to St. Mary's church in 1974.[34]

The peal of five bells in the church in 1553 was recast in Devizes in 1579. The 'great' bell was recast, possibly by John Wallis, in 1612. A bell, or bells, may have been recast in 1698. A sanctus bell was cast in 1741, probably by Abel Rudhall. In 1783 there was a peal of six bells, of which three or more were by Rudhall. A new ring of eight was cast by T. Mears of London in 1831.[35] It was taken down in 1968, some of the metal used to cast two bells for St. Mary's, and the rest sold.[36]

Registrations of baptisms, marriages, and burials survive from 1611 and are complete.[37]

ROMAN CATHOLICISM. There were two papists, one in St. Mary's parish and the other in

[15] P.R.O., E 301/58, unnumbered entry after no. 49.
[16] Phillipps, *Wilts. Inst.* (index in *W.A.M.* xxviii. 225, 227); *Alum. Oxon. 1500-1714*, i. 286; *Rep. Com. Eccl. Revenues*, 842-3, 844-5.
[17] *Alum. Cantab. 1752-1900*, ii (6), 488; *Rep. Com. Eccl. Revenues*, 842-3. He remained rector until appointed chancellor of St. David's in 1858 and died in 1870, not until 1851 and in 1873 respectively as stated in *V.C.H. Wilts.* x. 145.
[18] *Alum. Cantab. 1752-1900*, ii (6), 579. His main works and articles are listed ibid. and in *Who Was Who*, 1929-40, 1488.
[19] Crockford (1896 and later edns.); *Clergy List* (1905 and later edns.); *Lond. Gaz.* 28 Mar. 1924, p. 2601.
[20] *Vis. Queries, 1783* (W.R.S. xxvii), pp. 153-4.
[21] P.R.O., HO 129/255/1/10/26.
[22] W.R.O., bishop, vis. queries, 1864.
[23] Ibid.; *Sar. Chart. and Doc.* (Rolls Ser.), 123; *Vis. Queries, 1783* (W.R.S. xxvii), pp. 153-4; P.R.O., E 178/2416; ibid. IR 29/38/191; Crockford (1896 and later edns.); *Lond. Gaz.* 28 Mar. 1924, pp. 2600-1.
[24] There are NE. and SW. views in 1803 by J. Buckler in

W.A.S. Libr., vol. iv. 20-1.
[25] Conventional directions are used in this description.
[26] See plate facing p. 209.   [27] *W.A.M.* xxxiv. 197.
[28] W.R.O., bishop, pet. for faculties, bdle. 11, no. 12; *W.A.M.* xxxiv. 195; Chandler, *Hist. Marlborough*, 24.
[29] W.R.O. 1197/21; *W.A.M.* xxxiv. 195.
[30] W.R.O. 1197/21.
[31] Ibid. bishop, glebe terrier, 1783; *Vis. Queries, 1783* (W.R.S. xxvii), p. 180.
[32] Ch. Com. file NB 34/220C; inf. sheet produced by St. Peter's and St. Paul's Trust.
[33] Nightingale, *Wilts. Plate*, 157-8; W.R.O., bishop, glebe terrier, 1783.
[34] Inf. from Mr. Down.
[35] Walters, *Wilts. Bells*, 134, 157-8, 249, 294, 318; W.R.O., bishop, glebe terrier, 1783.
[36] Chandler, *Hist. Marlborough*, 25.
[37] W.R.O. 1050/15-26. No registration was made in the period 1652-3. Extracts are printed in *Coll. Topog. et Gen.* v. 260-8, and marriages in *Wilts. Par. Reg. (Mar.)*, ed. Phillimore and Sadler, ii. 1-64.

St. Peter's, in 1585.[38] Two recusants lived in St. Mary's parish in 1706 and 1780.[39] The Hermitage in Hyde Lane, occupied by members of the recusant Hyde family from c. 1740 to c. 1794, was used as a local mass centre.[40] The Hydes' resident Benedictine chaplains, of whom the last, William Gregory Cowley, 1790–4, later became president-general of the English Benedictines, served it from 1753 or earlier until 1794 but acted as priests and confessors rather than as missioners.[41] Seven people were confirmed at the Hermitage in 1753 and fifteen heard mass there in 1767 and 1780.[42]

In 1937 the Missionaries of St. Francis de Sales (Fransalians) opened a chapel, which was served by a resident priest, in a house in Elcot Lane. The house ceased to be used as a chapel in 1947 when a Nissen hut on the site of the George, George Lane, was erected and used as a mass centre until replaced by a new church, dedicated to St. Thomas More, opened in 1959.[43] That was served in 1979 by two Fransalian priests who lived in the Presbytery in George Lane.[44]

PROTESTANT NONCONFORMITY.

Thomas Bailey, ejected from Mildenhall rectory in 1660, may have propagated Fifth Monarchy views at Marlborough until his death in 1663.[45] In 1676 there were 250 dissenters in Marlborough, 150 in St. Mary's parish, and 100 in St. Peter's, the largest number in any Wiltshire town.[46] In 1678 burgesses were forbidden to hold office or to be members of the council if they attended conventicles.[47] Inhabitants of Marlborough were considered a 'seditious, schismatical people' in 1681.[48]

The founder of the Independent, or Presbyterian, church in Marlborough was William Hughes (d. 1688), who was ejected from the vicarage of St. Mary's in 1662. His conventicles met first in Savernake forest and afterwards in Marlborough. He apparently resorted to open-air preaching whenever his indoor conventicles were suppressed. He was joined by Daniel Burgess (d. 1679), deprived of Collingbourne Ducis rectory in 1662.[49] Hughes's ministry was continued by Matthew Pemberton (d. 1691), William Gough, and Samuel Tomlyns (d. 1700).[50] The congregation built a meeting house in 1706[51] but afterwards met in several buildings.[52] One may have been a chapel in Herd Street leased to unspecified dissenters from 1758 or earlier to 1792.[53] That was probably the chapel outside which Rowland Hill preached in 1771.[54] Another was a chapel, certified in 1727, built in Back Lane[55] on land belonging to Thomas Hancock (d. 1788). Hancock devised the chapel to his wife with £300 so that in her lifetime £10 might be paid yearly to a minister whom she was to appoint.[56] Cornelius Winter, minister 1778–88, reorganized that chapel on Congregational principles and established a school to train young men for the ministry.[57] In 1783 there were 30 'presbyterians' in St. Mary's parish and in St. Peter's 5 or 6 'presbyterian' families who attended a chapel,[58] perhaps that in Herd Street.

In 1802 Thomas Hancock's son closed the Back Lane chapel and the congregation had no permanent home until 1817 when a chapel was built in the Marsh. A resident minister was appointed in 1823 for the congregation of 53.[59] On Census Sunday in 1851 morning service was attended by 262, afternoon service by 129, and evening service by 178 people.[60] In the later 19th century a Sunday school and lecture room were added to the chapel and a manse was built beside it.[61] The United Reformed chapel was served from Swindon in the 1970s. In 1979 the minister of the New Road Methodist church was appointed to it and united evening services were held. In 1980 all services, held on Sundays alternately in each church, were shared with the Methodists. The manse was let as flats in 1981. The church then had 30 members.[62] A register of births and baptisms, 1823–37, is extant.[63]

The Friends who met at Marlborough after George Fox spoke there in 1656 suffered imprisonment and public humiliation in the town in the years 1656–8.[64] The meeting house was built in the burial ground at Manton Corner in Preshute given by William Hitchcock in 1658.[65] Fox, who revisited Marlborough in 1673 and 1677, and William Penn, who came to the town in 1687, both spoke at Hitchcock's house in Marlborough.[66] The meeting was chiefly composed of members of the Hitchcock, Lawrence, Freeman, and Crabb families in the later 17th century.[67] A

[38] W.R.O., bishop, detecta bk. f. 37.
[39] J. A. Williams, *Catholic Recusancy in Wilts*. (Cath. Rec. Soc.), p. 233; *V.C.H. Wilts*. iii. 96.
[40] Williams, *Cath. Recusancy* (Cath. Rec. Soc.), pp. 64, 248; Burke, *Commoners* (1833–8), iv. 675–6; *V.C.H. Berks*. iv. 242; W.R.O. 9/19/567; *Downside Rev*. lxxviii. 273.
[41] *Downside Rev*. lxxviii. 271–3; *Vis. Queries, 1783* (W.R.S. xxvii), p. 153.
[42] *Downside Rev*. lxxviii. 271–2; *V.C.H. Wilts*. iii. 91, 96.
[43] *V.C.H. Wilts*. iii. 96–7; W.R.O., G 22/111/14, gen. purposes cttee. mins. 5 May, 20 Sept. 1947; Chandler, *Hist. Marlborough*, 28–9.
[44] 'Tower and Town, Marlborough' (TS. mag. of ecumenical par. of Marlborough, June, 1979), 2.
[45] *V.C.H. Wilts*. iii. 105; *Calamy Revised*, ed. Matthews, 40.
[46] *W.N. & Q*. iii. 537.
[47] Waylen, *Hist. Marlborough*, 309–10.
[48] *Cal. S.P. Dom*. 1680–1, 563.
[49] *V.C.H. Wilts*. iii. 105, 107; *Calamy Revised*, ed. Matthews, 88, 282–3.
[50] *Calamy Revised*, ed. Matthews, 230, 385–6, 488–9.

[51] J. W. Gale, *Marlborough Congregational Ch*. (Marlborough, priv. print. 1957), 10.
[52] P.R.O., RG 31/4; W.R.O., bishop, return of cert. places.
[53] W.R.O. 871/23.
[54] Waylen, *Hist. Marlborough*, 485.
[55] W.R.O., G 22/1/123.
[56] Gale, *Marlborough Congregational Ch*. 11.
[57] *V.C.H. Wilts*. iii. 125, 132–4; *W.A.M*. lxi. 66–7.
[58] *Vis. Queries, 1783* (W.R.S. xxvii), pp. 152–4.
[59] *V.C.H. Wilts*. iii. 132; Gale, *Marlborough Congregational Ch*. 4.
[60] P.R.O., HO 129/255/1/9/23.
[61] Gale, *Marlborough Congregational Ch*. 17, 19.
[62] Inf. from Mr. G. D. Gordon, the Manse, St. David's Way.
[63] P.R.O., RG 4/3329.
[64] *V.C.H. Wilts*. iii. 103–4; J. Besse, *Coll. of Sufferings of People called Quakers*, i. 293–7.
[65] W.R.O. 854/31.
[66] *Jnl. of Geo. Fox*, ed. N. Penney, ii. 263; *Short Jnl. and Itin. Jnls. of Geo. Fox*, ed. N. Penney, 262, 374.
[67] W.R.O. 854/31; *W.N. & Q*. ii. 292, 344, 428; iii. 369.

few members emigrated to Pennsylvania.[68] In 1727 Quakers certified a meeting house in High Street where they may still have met in 1772.[69] The Marlborough particular meeting was part of Charlcote monthly meeting in 1677, of the Wiltshire quarterly meeting in 1678, of the Wiltshire monthly meeting in 1775, and of the Devizes preparative meeting in 1788.[70] In 1783, although there were 30 Friends in St. Mary's parish and 4 or 5 families of Friends in St. Peter's, the meeting was in decline and by 1800 had been dissolved. Its members joined either the Calne or Devizes meetings or met in each other's houses.[71] The burial ground at Manton Corner, which had been desecrated in 1663, was still used in 1809.[72] It was owned by the Society of Friends, but no longer used, in 1907.[73]

General Baptists led by Edward Delamaine of Marlborough may have been influenced by Thomas Bailey's preaching. Anabaptists were licensed to meet in Nathaniel Bailey's house in 1672 but the meeting soon lapsed.[74] A Strict Baptist cause was begun c. 1814 by a Mr. Simons of Bristol and continued by a Mr. Weldon in 1818.[75] In 1851 on Census Sunday 50 people, designated Particular Baptists, met in the morning, and 54 in the afternoon.[76] The group registered a room in the Marsh in 1859.[77] There was no resident pastor and the cause declined c. 1864.[78] It was revived and the room reregistered in 1868.[79] That room was replaced by a chapel called Zoar on the north side of St. Martin's in 1876.[80] The chapel closed briefly in 1896 and finally in 1921.[81]

John Wesley preached at Marlborough in 1745 and 1747.[82] George Pocock, one of Wesley's Bristol friends and the chief evangelist of north-east Wiltshire, certified a Methodist chapel in Oxford Street in 1811.[83] In 1851 on Census Sunday 225 people attended morning, 50 afternoon, and 180 evening service there.[84] The chapel was extended in 1872 and rebuilt, with an entrance in New Road, in 1910.[85] By will proved 1899 David Goddard bequeathed £500 to provide a manse for the superintendent minister of the Marlborough circuit.[86] A house in London Road bought in 1905 was replaced in 1970 by one in St. David's Way. The chapel had 98 members in 1981, when the superintendent minister

also served the United Reformed church and held united services in each on alternate Sundays.[87]

Primitive Methodism was brought to Marlborough by William Sanger of Salisbury, who certified two houses in the town in 1820 and a chapel in St. Peter's parish in 1821.[88] In 1823 a minister certified a newly built Ebenezer chapel on the east side of Herd Street where in 1851 on Census Sunday 30 people attended morning, 40 afternoon, and 90 evening service.[89] The Ebenezer chapel was closed between 1923 and 1925.[90]

'Peculiar Calvinists' certified a room in Kingsbury Street in 1807.[91] The group may be identified with that which met at the Providence chapel in Kingsbury Street for which the transcript of a register of births and baptisms, 1805–37, survives.[92] On Census Sunday 1851 unspecified dissenters, 40 in the morning and 30 in the evening, met in a room in St. Mary's parish.[93]

Plymouth Brethren met in a room in Kingsbury Street in 1851, when on Census Sunday 26 people met there in the morning and 38 in the evening.[94] The sect still met in 1862.[95] It was perhaps that which registered a building at High Wall, New Road, in 1866 and met there until 1906.[96]

The Salvation Army opened fire in 1887 from a barracks in London Road and moved to New Road in 1903. New Road barracks closed in 1910.[97] Christadelphians had a hall in New Road in 1923 or earlier and met there until c. 1930.[98] In 1931 Closed Brethren registered premises in St. Margaret's where they still met in 1981.[99]

EDUCATION. In 1550 a free grammar school was founded in, and endowed with the property of, St. John's hospital in the Marsh. Its history to 1957 and that of Marlborough College in Preshute are given elsewhere.[1] The history of the grammar school from 1957 is recounted below.

A charity school, established in 1709 or earlier, acquired permanent buildings to accommodate 44 children from both Marlborough parishes, possibly in 1712.[2] It was no longer held in the later 18th century.[3] St. Mary's parish contained eight charity day schools in 1808, and in 1811 a

[68] Short Jnl. and Itin. Jnls. of Geo. Fox, ed. Penney, 374.
[69] W.R.O., G 22/1/124; Jnl. Friends' Hist. Soc. xliv. 5–6.
[70] Jnl. Friends' Hist. Soc. xliv. 5–8; V.C.H. Wilts. iii. 118.
[71] Vis. Queries, 1783 (W.R.S. xxvii), pp. 152, 154; Jnl. Friends' Hist. Soc. xliv. 8.
[72] P.R.O., IR 29/38/188; IR 30/38/188; Hist. MSS. Com. 2, 3rd Rep., Northumberland, pp. 92–3; W.N. & Q. vi. 228.
[73] Endowed Char. Wilts. (S. Div.), 936.
[74] V.C.H. Wilts. iii. 115; Calamy Revised, ed. Matthews, 40.
[75] R. W. Oliver, Strict Bapt. Chapels Eng. (Strict Bapt. Hist. Soc.), v. 15.
[76] P.R.O., HO 129/255/1/9/22.
[77] G.R.O. Worship Reg. no. 8681.
[78] Oliver, Strict Bapt. Chapels Eng. (Strict Bapt. Hist. Soc.), v. 15; W.R.O., bishop, vis. queries, 1864.
[79] G.R.O. Worship Reg. no. 18461.
[80] Ibid. no. 23129; cancellations, nos. 3129, 3131.
[81] Oliver, Strict Bapt. Chapels Eng. (Strict Bapt. Hist. Soc.), v. 15; inf. from Mr. A. W. Steele, 17 George Lane.
[82] Waylen, Hist. Marlborough, 484–5.
[83] V.C.H. Wilts. iii. 142; W.R.O., bishop, return of cert. places.

[84] P.R.O., HO 129/255/1/9/24.
[85] Chandler, Hist. Marlborough, 31; G.R.O. Worship Reg. no. 44316.   [86] Endowed Char. Wilts. (N. Div.), 739.
[87] Inf. from Mr. Gordon.
[88] P.R.O., RG 31/4; Endowed Char. Wilts. (N. Div.), 738–9.
[89] P.R.O., RG 31/4; ibid. HO 129/255/1/9/21.
[90] Kelly's Dir. Wilts. (1923); G.R.O. Worship Reg., cancellations, no. 20263.
[91] P.R.O., RG 31/4.
[92] Bodl. MS. Top. Wilts. d. 4.
[93] P.R.O., HO 129/255/1/9/25.
[94] Ibid. HO 129/255/1/10/28.
[95] W.R.O. 1197/6, f. 35.
[96] G.R.O. Worship Reg. no. 17396; cancellations, no. 15555; Lucy's Marlborough Dir. (1897).
[97] G.R.O. Worship Reg. nos. 30561, 39641; cancellations, no. 16744.
[98] Kelly's Dir. Wilts. (1923); inf. from Mr. Steele.
[99] G.R.O. Worship Reg. no. 57213; inf. from Mr. Steele.
[1] V.C.H. Wilts. v. 359–60, 364–6.
[2] [S.P.C.K.], Acct. of Char. Schs. (1709), 26; Univ. Brit. Dir. v (1797), App. 123.
[3] Vis. Queries, 1783 (W.R.S. xxvii), pp. 152, 154.

'school of industry', where girls were taught to sew and to knit and, as a reward for good behaviour, to read, was opened in the town.[4]

Thomas, earl of Ailesbury, in 1812 built a school containing two rooms on the south side of High Street where 100 girls were taught to sew and 76 boys, most of whom were expected to become shepherds, to knit stockings. Evening classes were attended by 20–30 boys.[5] In 1818 the school, which was conducted on National principles, was supported by voluntary contributions and attended by a total of 200 boys and girls from both parishes.[6] A master taught 67 boys and a mistress 95 girls in 1833.[7] Each parish provided its own schools from 1849.[8] By a Scheme of 1857 Marlborough's income from Thomas Ray's charity for clothiers[9] was shared by the schools of the two parishes. In 1913 the charity was renamed Thomas Ray's Exhibition Foundation. Thereafter the income was used for exhibitions which comprised money for maintenance allowances or tuition fees and were competed for by Marlborough children attending secondary schools and technical institutions. The charity income was less than £50 in 1975 and no money from the capital had been distributed since 1952. A Scheme of 1976 allowed its funds to be used generally for the education of those in Marlborough aged under 25 years and particularly to equip school or university leavers for a profession or trade.[10]

Schoolrooms for 64 boys taught by a master and for 60 girls taught by a mistress were opened in 1849, perhaps in the old schoolrooms, for children in St. Peter's parish. A school at the junction of High Street and Hyde Lane was in use in 1854.[11] It contained three rooms. In one of them 100 boys, of whom 43, including 30 from St. Mary's parish and 5 from Preshute, came from outside the parish, were taught by a master in 1858. In the second a mistress taught 70–80 girls, of whom 13 came from outside the parish, and in the third another mistress taught 60–70 infants.[12] An evening school was also held there from 1863 to 1886.[13] In 1873 the Department of Education allowed a maximum of 35 children from Preshute, probably from St. Margaret's where the school was closed in 1871 or earlier, to attend, but in 1873–4 more than 70 were attending and in 1874 their parents and Preshute parish were required to contribute to the upkeep of the school. Boys from the union workhouse on Marlborough Common attended in 1877. Children from Manton in Preshute were excluded in 1901 unless good reason for their attendance

could be given.[14] An average of 240 children attended from 1906 until 1918. Numbers were falling, however, and the fact that more boys than girls and infants attended suggests an attempt to make St. Peter's the boys' school and St. Mary's the girls' school before elementary education in the town was formally reorganized in 1918.[15]

Before 1848 a school in the Green was built for children from St. Mary's parish.[16] It was apparently used only by boys after a school, for which land on the east side of Herd Street was conveyed in 1849, was opened for girls and infants.[17] A master taught 70 boys at the Green in 1858 and at the Herd Street school 60 girls and 60 infants were taught by a mistress. The schools were then attended by 12 children, including 6 from St. Peter's, from outside the parish.[18] The boys still occupied the school on the Green in 1865 but by 1867 had moved to a new building in Herd Street.[19] Average attendance at the schools, where there was a consistently high proportion of girls and infants to boys in the years 1909–18, did not fall below 273 between 1906 and 1918 and was probably often higher.[20]

In 1918 St. Peter's became the boys' school for the town and St. Mary's the girls' and infants' school. Average numbers attending both schools fell in the 1920s and 1930s.[21] The Herd Street schools were reserved for infants in 1962 when the older girls were moved into the former grammar school buildings in the Parade. The boys from St. Peter's joined them, and the school in High Street was closed, in 1963. The 321 children attending St. Peter's Junior School had twelve full-time teachers in 1982. The Herd Street infants' school was closed in 1974 and a new one, St. Mary's Infants' School, was opened in George Lane, where in 1981 there were seven teachers for the 174 children.[22]

Marlborough Grammar School was rehoused in 1962 in new buildings south of the town.[23] Marlborough Secondary Modern School, opened in 1946 to serve the town and upper Kennet valley in huts on Marlborough Common,[24] moved to new buildings in Chopping Knife Lane in 1966.[25] The schools were amalgamated as St. John's Comprehensive School in 1975. The former grammar school buildings were renamed the Stedman building and those of the secondary modern school the Savernake building.[26] In 1981 there were 73 full-time teachers and 9 part-time for the 1,317 pupils on the two sites.[27]

Early private education in the town was connected with dissent. William Hughes, who led

[4] Lamb. Palace Libr., MS. 1732; Stedman, *Marlborough*, 353.
[5] *2nd Rep. Nat. Soc.* 175; Pigot, *Nat. Com. Dir.* (1830), iii. 806; Stedman, *Marlborough*, 353. The Waitrose supermarket occupied the site in 1981.
[6] *Educ. of Poor Digest*, 1036; W.R.O. 1197/31.
[7] *Educ. Enquiry Abstract*, 1042–3.
[8] W.R.O. 1197/31. [9] Below, charities.
[10] *Endowed Char. Wilts.* (N. Div.), 726–7; Char. Com. file.
[11] W.R.O. 1197/31.
[12] *Acct. of Wilts. Schs.* 33.
[13] Stedman, *Marlborough*, 356, 358.
[14] W.R.O. 1197/31; above, Preshute, educ.
[15] *Return of Non-Provided Schs.* 25; Bd. of Educ., List 21 (H.M.S.O.).

[16] W.R.O. 1197/31; *Kelly's Dir. Wilts.* (1855).
[17] W.R.O. 9/19/697; *Kelly's Dir. Wilts.* (1855).
[18] *Acct. of Wilts. Schs.* 33.
[19] *Harrod's Dir. Wilts.* (1865); *Kelly's Dir. Wilts.* (1867).
[20] *Return of Non-Provided Schs.* 25; Bd. of Educ., List 21 (H.M.S.O.).
[21] Bd. of Educ., List 21 (H.M.S.O.).
[22] Inf. from Chief Education Officer, Co. Hall, Trowbridge.
[23] Chandler, *Hist. Marlborough*, 34.
[24] Stedman, *Marlborough*, 357; *Fletcher's Marlborough Dir.* (1962–3).
[25] Inf. from Chief Education Officer.
[26] Chandler, *Hist. Marlborough*, 34, 75.
[27] Inf. from Chief Education Officer.

the Independents in Marlborough, established a boarding school which flourished until his death in 1688.[28] Cornelius Winter, minister of a Marlborough Congregational chapel 1778–88, set up a school for dissenters and admitted non-dissenting pupils.[29] Another dissenting minister, John Davis, founded Marlborough Academy in 1780. He was succeeded there in 1791 by William Gresley. The school, in Ivy House, no. 43 High Street, continued under Philip Wells, Richard Cundell, John Brown, and another until the mid 19th century.[30]

Numerous other small private schools for both boarders and day pupils, mostly girls, flourished in the later 18th century, the 19th, and the earlier 20th.[31] At a boarding school run from 1754 to 1777 successively by a Mrs. Sutton and a Mrs. Hilliker subjects taught to the girls included French, music, and dancing.[32] A girls' boarding school in High Street run by Mary Cousins and another in Kingsbury Street run by Mary Ann Anderson and later by Jemima Westall flourished in the 1830s and 1840s.[33] The school in High Street may perhaps have been the 'ladies' seminary' conducted by Mrs. M. A. Byfield in 1855 or earlier and in 1867.[34] There were two girls' schools in High Street in 1879 and in 1897 a preparatory school at no. 29 Kingsbury Street.[35] A school in High Street may have survived as Marlborough High School, so called in 1907 and perhaps the school at no. 35 High Street in 1923 and 1931.[36]

Kingsbury Hill House was opened c. 1943 by a Miss Thelwell, as a preparatory school for girls and small boys. It was bought in 1964 by Mr. W. I. Washbrook who enlarged its premises and its curriculum. In 1982 a total of 190 boys and girls between 3 and 16 years was taught in the school.[37]

CHARITIES FOR THE POOR.[38] By will dated 1615 Thomas Ray gave the yearly income from houses in Salisbury for poor clothiers of Trowbridge, Chippenham, Westbury, and Marlborough yearly in turn. The funds were afterwards mismanaged. In 1652 new trustees for each town were appointed to administer the income of £14 a year. From 1817 to 1821 the income was £25 yearly. It was shared each year by the four towns from c. 1821 to 1832, as were rent arrears of £100 collected in 1831. From 1833 the income, £33 in 1833, was again distributed intact each year to the four towns in turn.[39] In 1834, when there was no clothier in Marlborough, and possibly earlier, the mayor was the only trustee and the income was used for other purposes. The income was given to the National schools in 1857.[40]

Bequests by William Seyman in 1539 of a charge of 6s. 8d. on his house in the 'new land' to clothe the poor and by Robert Were or Brown in 1570 of charges of 20s. for the poor and 5s. for the mayor, and devises of properties in the town, the income from them to be given to the poor, made by John Birdsey in 1550, Richard Dickinson in 1553, and Thomas Vale in 1557 to the mayor and burgesses comprised the endowment of an eleemosynary charity called the Good Friday rents.[41] The mayor and chamberlain distributed £13 in small sums to poor people in 1834, by which time some of the original rents had been replaced by others from borough properties. The rents produced £2 in 1905. By will dated 1795 Sarah Franklin gave £400 for widowed housekeepers in both parishes of the borough. Her bequest became effective in 1826, John Baverstock afterwards added £100 to it, and £500 was invested in 1830. The income of £5 was distributed with the Good Friday rents in 1905 when nineteen women received 10s. doles. Christopher Willoughby in 1678 gave £200 by deed to enable the mayor and burgesses to distribute £2 yearly. The money was still being given to the poor in 1905. Willoughby's charity was united with the Franklin and Baverstock charity and the Good Friday rents in 1915 as the Marlborough united charities. By will dated 1881 C. J. King gave the yearly income from £100 to Marlborough people in the union workhouse. It was distributed after 1929 in 10s. doles to unsuccessful applicants to the united charities. In 1982 those charities produced £13 from which grants were made to poor and elderly people.

Other charities of which the corporation was trustee were Leaf's and Burchell's. Herbert Leaf (d. 1936)[42] by will gave £15,000 to Marlborough corporation for the townspeople. Several grants, and loans to the council and other local bodies and societies on terms favourable to the borrower, were made from the income. In 1978 the income was £1,520, of which £625, including a grant of £500 made to St. Peter's and St. Paul's Trust, was spent. Until 1971 between £90 and £120 was distributed in sums of £1 each 25 March. From 1971 £50 a year was put into a fund from which gifts were made at the mayor's discretion. The Florence and Walter John Burchell Charitable Trust was established by deed of 1972 to provide homes and financial help for the old people of Marlborough. In 1976 stock, land, and three houses in Manton produced an income of £1,281, of which £553 was spent on maintaining the houses.

In 1640 Anne Paine gave £300 to provide £5 yearly for both parishes of Marlborough. The £5 was divided and each parish added its share to the poor rate until c. 1827. St. Peter's afterwards

[28] V.C.H. Wilts. v. 349; Calamy Revised, ed. Matthews, 282–3; above, prot. nonconf.
[29] V.C.H. Wilts. iii. 132; above, prot. nonconf.
[30] Stedman, Marlborough, 279; Chandler, Hist. Marlborough, 12.
[31] Univ. Brit. Dir. v (1797), App. 124; Lamb. Palace Libr., MS. 1732; Educ. Enquiry Abstract, 1042–3; Kelly's Dir. Wilts. (1855 and later edns.).   [32] Stedman, Marlborough, 252.
[33] Pigot, Nat. Com. Dir. (1830), iii. 806; (1844), 23.
[34] Kelly's Dir. Wilts. (1855 and later edns.).
[35] Lucy's Marlborough Dir. (1879, 1897).

[36] Kelly's Dir. Wilts. (1907 and later edns.).
[37] Inf. from Mr. W. I. Washbrook, Kingsbury Hill Ho.
[38] Except where stated, inf. is from Endowed Char. Wilts. (N. Div.), 702–6, 724–5, 727–30, 733–4; Char. Com. files; the Revd. W. Down, the Rectory, Rawlingswell Lane.
[39] Endowed Char. Wilts. (S. Div.), 784–5.
[40] Above, educ.
[41] W.R.O., G 22/1/236. The amount of Were or Brown's bequest given in Endowed Char. Wilts. (N. Div.), 703 is incorrect: P.R.O., PROB 11/52 (P.C.C. 37 Lyon).
[42] Stedman, Marlborough, 350.

distributed in cash directly to the poor and St. Mary's added its share to the church rate. By will dated 1824 Nathaniel Merriman gave £100, the income to buy bread for unrelieved paupers of both parishes. T. S. Gundry by will proved 1858 gave the income from £100 stock, to be spent each Christmas on bread or clothing for the poor of both parishes. William Hill by will proved 1871 gave the interest on two sums of £100 to buy bread for the poor of each parish. From 1882 food, bedding, clothes, or fuel were sometimes provided instead of bread. Elizabeth Malpuss by will proved 1884 gave the interest on two similar sums to buy food, clothing, or fuel, and each parish received £3 in 1905. Harward Keen by will proved 1884 gave the interest on £50 to the poor of each parish: each received under £1 in 1905.

The bequest of T. M. Hancock (d. 1803) of £200, the interest for St. Peter's poor each New Year's day, was disbursed in 1834 with the St. Peter's share of Paine's charity. J. Goldyer in 1808 gave half the income from £334 stock for bread for St. Peter's poor at Christmas. Bread was bought in 1834. By will dated 1817 Elizabeth Harris gave to the same poor the interest on £100 for bread which in 1833 was received only by the unrelieved.

The parochial charities of Marlborough were reorganized in the 1870s, St. Peter's in 1872, St. Mary's in 1878. The incumbents and church-wardens, already trustees of most of the charities, became, in St. Peter's, trustees of Goldyer's and Hancock's, and, in each parish, of their respective shares in Paine's and Merriman's. In 1905 the funds of the nine St. Peter's charities, £26, were spent on coal, clothing, and blankets for loan, and those of the six St. Mary's charities, £13, on pensions, food, and help for the sick. In 1980 the small yearly incomes, £17 from the St. Mary's charities and £27 from those of St. Peter's, were distributed in small money gifts at Christmas to people living in the areas of the former parishes.

By will proved 1916 C. L. Brooke gave £600 for old unrelieved people. Because it was not clear for which parish the bequest was intended, two-fifths were invested for St. Peter's and three-fifths for St. Mary's. In 1980 at Christmas St. Peter's share, £8, and St. Mary's share, £12, were distributed to parishioners.

The Titcombe Benefaction, established by will of J. C. Titcombe proved 1934, comprised £100, the income for poor parishioners of St. Mary's, preferably old widows. In 1982 and earlier the income of £4 yearly was added to St. Mary's endowed charities. The income of the Emily Mary Lloyd Benevolent Fund, established by will of J. A. Lloyd proved 1935, was distributed among old women in St. Peter's parish. In 1980 the income of £12 was similarly distributed at Christmas.

INDEX

An italic page number refers to a map or illustration on that or the facing page.

The following are among the abbreviations used: adv., advowson; agric., agriculture; Alex., Alexander; Alf., Alfred; And., Andrew; Ant., Anthony; abp., archbishop; archit., architecture; Bart., Bartholomew; Benj., Benjamin; bp., bishop; Brit., British; bro., brother; cath., cathedral; Cath., Catherine; cent., century; chant., chantry; chap., chapel; char., charity; Chas., Charles; Chris., Christopher; ch., church; coll., college; ctss., countess; ct., court; cust., customary; Dan., Daniel; dau., daughter; d., died; dom., domestic; dchss., duchess; Edm., Edmund; Edw., Edward; Eliz., Elizabeth; fam., family; fl., flourished; Fras., Francis; Fred., Frederick; Geof., Geoffrey; Geo., George; Gilb., Gilbert; grddau., granddaughter; Hen., Henry; Herb., Herbert; hosp., hospital; ho., house; Humph., Humphrey; hund., hundred; inc., inclosure; ind., industry; Jas., James; Jos., Joseph; Laur., Laurence; Lawr., Lawrence; man., manor; Marg., Margaret; mkt., market; m., married; Mat., Matthew; Maur., Maurice; Mic., Michael; Nat., Nathaniel; Nic., Nicholas; nonconf., nonconformity; n, note; par., parish; parl., parliamentary; Phil., Philip; pop., population; prehist., prehistoric; prot., protestant; rly., railway; Reg., Reginald; rem., remains; rep., representation; Ric., Richard; riv., river; Rob., Robert; Rog., Roger; Rom., Roman; Sam., Samuel; sch., school; Sid., Sidney; Sim., Simon; s., son; Stan., Stanley; sta., station; Steph., Stephen; Thos., Thomas; Tim., Timothy; Vct., Viscount; Wal., Walter; w., wife; Wm., William.

Banbury (Oxon.), 205
bands (musical):
  brass and reed, 72
  silver, 72, 205
bankers and banking, 160, 210
Banks:
  Steph., 27
  fam., 26
Banning:
  J., 93
  J. S., 93
  John, 93
  John, s. of John, 93
  Mary, see Griffen
  fam., 93
Bannings:
  Rebecca, 155
  S. T., 155
  Steph., 155
  Thos., 155
  Thos., vicar of Winterbourne Monkton, 198
Baptists, 104, 118, 124, 139, 160
  General, 226
  Particular, 60, 150, 226
  Strict, 85, 104, 226
Barbost:
  Adam, 96
  Alice, w. of Adam, 96
  Geof., 96
  John, 96
  fam., 97
Barbury (in Ogbourne St. Andrew), 138, 141-2, 147, 149
  agric., 147
  Barbury Castle, 139
  cust. tenants, 147
  dom. archit., 141
  farm, 143, 147
  man., 142-3
  pop., 141
Barfleur:
  Maud, w. of Rob., 177
  Nic. (fl. 1204-21), 177
  Nic. (d. by 1295, ? same), 171, 177
  Nic., s. of Nic. (d. by 1295), 171, 177
  Rob., 177
Barford St. Martin, rector of, see Rashley
Baril, Rog., 188
Barker, F. G., 169
barn, aisled, 164
Barnes:
  John, 25
  Thos., 25
Barnett, Capt., 80
Barnfield, see Preshute
Barnstone:
  John, prebendary of Bishopstone, 6, 9-10
  Wm., 6
Barons' War (13th cent.), see Marlborough Castle
Barrett, Thos., 85
Barrington:
  Jane, see Guise
  Shute, bp. of Salisbury, 121, 123
Bartlett, Wm., see Burdett-Coutts-Bartlett-Coutts
Barwick, John, 159, 187
Baskerville:
  Anne, see Hancock
  Fras., 187
  Meliora, m. Thos. (of Aberedw), 187
  Ric., 174, 187
  Thos. (d. 1621), 174, 187-8
  Thos. (fl. 1707), 187
  Thos. (of Aberedw, fl. 18th cent.), 187
  Thos., s. of Thos. (of Aberedw), 187
  Thos. (d. 1817, another), 73, 174
  (formerly Mynors), Thos. Baskerville, 55, 73, 172, 174
  W. T. M., 73, 172
basket making, 39

Basset:
  Alan, 187, 191
  Aline, m. 1 Sir Hugh le Despenser (d. 1265), 2 Rog. Bigod, earl of Norfolk, 187
  Fulk, rector of Winterbourne Bassett, dean of York, bp. of London, 187, 191
  Gilb., 128, 187
  Isabel, 176
  Isabel (another), see Ferrers
  Phil., 65, 187
  Reynold (d. c. 1224), 176
  Reynold (fl. 1225), 176
bastardy, 214
Bath (Som., later Avon), 209-10
Bath and Wells, bp. of, see Curle
Bathe, John, 155
Batson:
  Alf. (d. 1856), 24
  Alf. (d. 1885), 24
  E., 24
  Fras. Cunninghame, 24
  Rob., 24
  Thos. (d. 1701), 24
  (formerly Davies), Thos. (d. 1759), 24
  (formerly Davies, Edm.), Thos. (d. 1770), and his w. Eliz., 24
  fam., 24-5
battle, see Kennett, East: 'Cynete'
Baverstock:
  J., 150
  John, 228
  W. E., 117
Baydon (in Ramsbury), 1, 7, 12, 15, 19, 22, 26-7, 30, 32-3, 35-6, 41-3, **52-61**, *54*, 67, 83
  adv., 53, 59
  agric., 57-9
  Bailey Hill, 58
  Baydon Furnett, 58
  Bayfield, 57
  boundaries, 52-3, 57
  chaplains, 59-60
  char., 60-1
  ch., 12, 42-3, 52-3, 55, 58-60, 76, *80*
  cts., 59
  curacy, 59
  curates, 60
  cust. tenants, 32-3, 57-8
  dom. archit., 53, 55
  farms, 32-3, 55-9
  field system, 15
  Ford, 15, 32, 34, 41, 53, 57-8
  Gore Lane, 15, 53, 55, 58
  inc., 53, 57-8
  inns, 53
  man., 53-7
  Peaks Downs (partly in Aldbourne), q.v.
  Pig's Court estate, 35, 56-7
  poor relief, 52, 59
  pop., 15, 53
  prot. nonconf., 60
  roads, 53
  Romano-Brit. settlement, 15
  schs., 53, 60-1
  Shortgrove, 13, 57-8
  tithing, 41
  vicarage, 83
  vicarage ho., 53, 59
  water tower, 53
  woodland, 13, 57-8; and see Baydon: Shortgrove
Baydon Manor (formerly Marridge Hill) estate, 26-8, 30, 36, 55-6, 73
Baynton:
  Chris., 113
  Sir Edw. (d. 1544), 37, 174, 191
  Edw. (fl. 1534-57), 188
  Sir Edw. (fl. 1556, ? another), 222
  Sir Edw. (d. 1657), 91, 93, 101, 121
  Hen., s. of Sir Edw. (d. 1544), 174
  Hen. (fl. 1691), 93-4

  Isabel, w. of Sir Edw. (d. 1544), m. 2 Sir Jas. Stumpe, 3 Thos. Stafford, 111, 174
  Mary, w. of Sir Edw. (d. 1657), 121
  Rob., 93-4, 96, 121
  fam., 93-4
beadle, *208*, 214-15
Beake (Beke):
  John, 96
  Thos., and his w. Isabel, 223
  ——, 159
Beauchamp:
  Anne, w. of Ric., Lord St. Amand, 94, 145
  Eliz., see Braybroke
  Ric., bp. of Salisbury, 37
  Ric., Lord St. Amand, 94, 145, 188
  Wm. de (d. 1269), 131
  Wm. de, earl of Warwick (d. 1298), 131
  Sir Wm. (d. 1457), 188
Beauchamp, Vct., see Seymour
Beaufay, Wm., bp. of East Anglia, 180, 220
Bec-Hellouin (Eure, France), abbey, 65, 141-2, 146, 149-50, 152, 154-8
'Bechenhalle', see Bincknoll
Beckhampton:
  Hamon of, 95
  Hilary of, 95-6
  John of, 95
  Ric. of, 95
Beckhampton (in Avebury), 62-3, 66, 86, 89-92, 96, 98, 101-2, 184
  agric., 99-100
  Beckhampton club, 91
  Beckhampton Ho., 91, 100; and see Beckhampton: inns
  boundaries, 99
  chap., 96, 102, 189
    adv., 102
    glebe, 191
  chaplain, 102; and see Warner
  common meadow, 99
  cust. tenants, 99
  dom. archit., 90-1, 95
  farms, 95-6, 99-100
  inc., 99
  inns, 91; and see Beckhampton: Beckhampton Ho.
  man., 95-6, 99-100, 102, 189
  mills, 100
  pop., 90
  prot. nonconf., 104
  sch., 104
  Silbury Hill, *48*, 63, 87, 89
  Stanmore, q.v.
  water meadows, 99
Beckhampton Estates, 95
Bedford, duke of, see John
Bedwyn, Great, 28, 165
Bedwyn, Little, 132
  Puthall Farm, 50
bee farming, 176; and see honey retailing
Beke, see Beake
bell founders, see Cor fam.; Gillett & Johnston; Knight, Hen.; Mears, T.; Mears & Stainbank; Purdue, Rog., Wm.; Rudhall, Abel, Abraham; Stares; Taylor, ——; Wallis, John; Warner & Sons; Wells, Jas., Rob. (two of the name)
bell founding, 63, 81
bell foundries, see Aldbourne
Benedictines, 45, 65, 92, 97, 102, 121-2, 134, 145, 147, 149-52, 156-8, 173-4, 180, 184, 194, 196-7, 207, 225; and see Cowley; Gilmore, Paul
Benger:
  Anne, m. Thos. Smith (d. c. 1558), 97
  Eleanor, see Sparsholt
  John, 97
  Ric., 97